AF413231

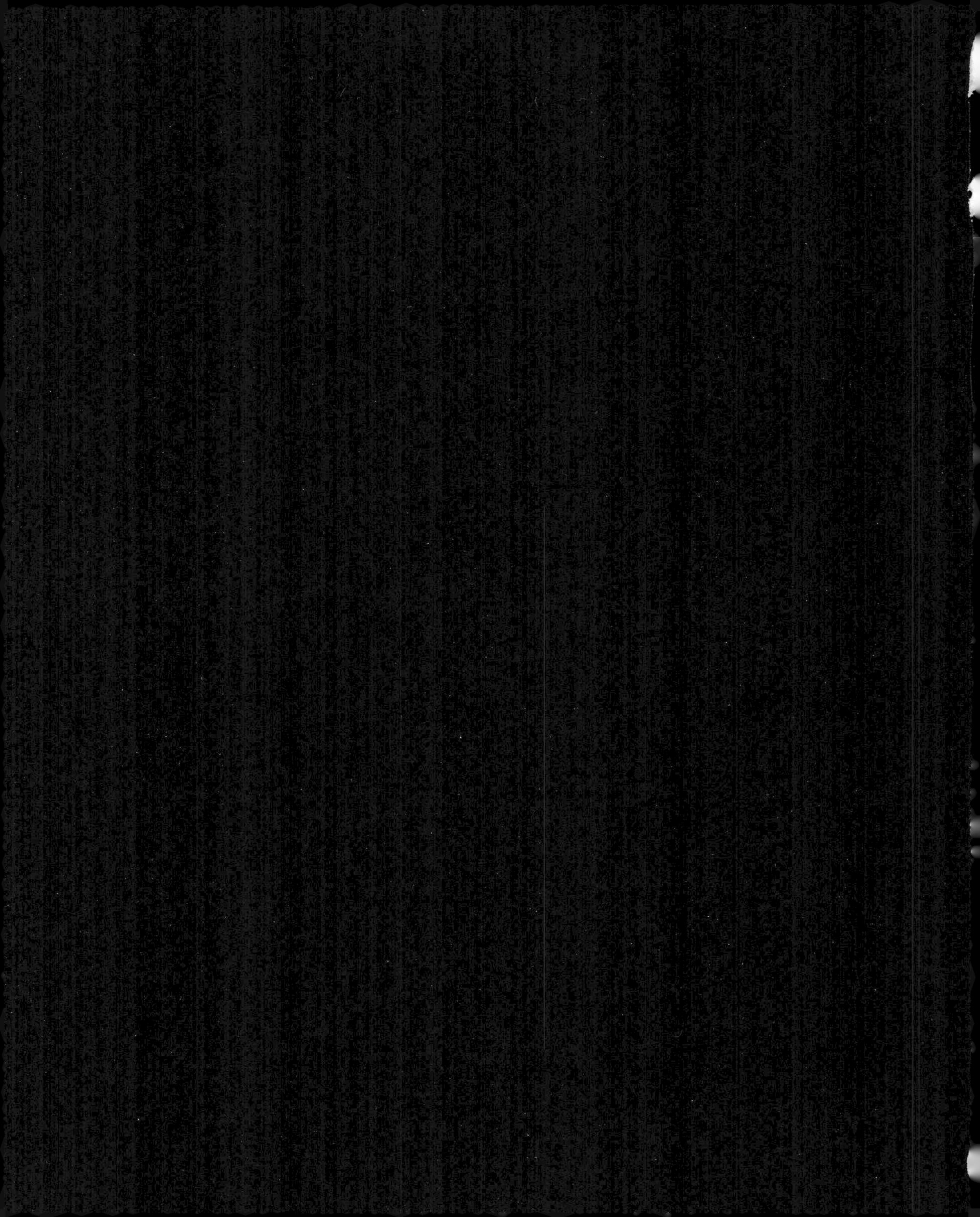

Art and Utopia
Limited Action

MACBA Museu d'Art Contemporani de Barcelona

ACTAR

Forum Barcelona 2004

The history of the project *Art and Utopia* dates back to 1998. It was first drafted by a team of researchers different from the onewhich eventually carried it out in 2002. The original team, coordinated by Catherine Zegher, included Rosalind Krauss, Benjamin Buchloh and Piet Coessens, the then director of the Palais de beaux-arts of Brussels, among others.
For various reasons, the project remained at a standstill until 2002, when Manuel J. Borja-Villel, director of MACBA, and Jean-François Chevrier resumed it together. This collaboration cristalized in the show *Art i utopia. L'acció restringida*, held at MACBA between June 3rd and Setember 12th, 2004.
The culmination of the research carried out for this exhibition and book is a new version of the show at the Musée des beaux-arts of Nantes, which will run from April 7th to June 3rd, 2005.
This book follows the concept and structure of the exhibition *Art and Utopia: Limited Action*, in which Mallarmé's poetry serves as a thread of the history of modern art in its relation with language. The images herein are ordered according to the layout and setting of the exhibition, which reviews some of the key moments In the exchanges between art and poetry in the 20th century through the late seventies. Likewise, the list of works found at the back of the book also follows the order of their display in the rooms of the MACBA.

Stéphane Mallarmé

Limited Action, 1897

Translation into English by Mary Ann Caws.

Several times a Colleague came to me, the same one, this other, to confide in me his need to act: what was he aiming at – since his approaching me announced on his part also, young as he was, the concern with creation, seemingly supreme, and success with words; I repeat, what did he mean exactly?

Unclenching your fists, breaking off with some sedentary dream, for a violent *tête-à-tête* with the idea, as when a fancy strikes one, or moving: but this generation seems not very concerned – even beyond its lack of interest in politics – with the desire for physical exertion. Except of course, with the monotony of winding along the pavement between one's shiny bones, according to the machine at present in favor, the fiction of continuous dazzling speedway.

Acting, leaving this aside, and for the one who only smokes as a beginning, meant, oh visitor I understand you, philosophically to effect motion on many, which yields in return the happy thought that you, being the cause of it, therefore exist: no one is sure of that in advance. This can be accomplished in two ways: either in a lifetime of willing and ignoring it, until the explosion – that is thinking, or in the outpourings now in reach of the prudent gasp, the daily newspapers and their whirlwind, determining in them, in one sense, some strength – which several will dispute, whatever it is – with the immunity of no result. As you like, according to disposition, plenitude, haste.

Your act is always applied to paper; for meditating without leaving any traces becomes evanescent, nor should instinct be exalted in some vehement and lost gesture that you sought.

To write –

The inkstand, crystal as a conscience, within its depths its drop of shadow relative to having something be: then take away the lamp.

You noticed, one does not write luminously on a dark field; the alphabet of stars alone, is thus indicated, sketched out or interrupted; man pursues black on white.

This pleat of somber lace which retains the infinite woven by a thousand, each according to the thread or the prolongation, its secret unknown, assembles distant interlacings where there sleeps some luxury to take account of – a ghoul, a knot, some foliage – and to present.

With the indispensable nothing of mystery, which remains, expressed little.

I do not know if the Host circumscribes perspicaciously his domain: it will please me to mark it out, and also certain conditions. The right to accomplish nothing exceptional, or lacking in vulgar bustle: anyone must pay for it by being omitted and, you might have said, by death as a person. His exploits are committed while dreaming, so as to bother no one; but still their program is displayed for those who care nothing about it.

The writer must make himself, in the text, the spiritual actor either of his sufferings, those dragons he has nurtured, or of some happiness.

Floor, lamp, clouding of clothes and melting of mirrors, real even down to the exaggerated jerking of our gauzy form around the virile stature stopped upon one foot; a Place comes forth, a stage, the public enhancement of the spectacle of Self; there, through the meditation of light, flesh, and laughter, the sacrifice of personality made by the inspirer is complete; or else in some foreign resurrection, he is finished: his word from then on, reverberating and useless, is exhaled by the orchestral chimera.

A theater hall: he celebrates himself, anonymous, in the hero.

Everything as the playing out of festivals: a people bears witness to its transfiguration into truth.

Honor.

Be on the lookout for something similar –

Will it be recognized in these suspicious buildings detached by some banal excess from the common alignment, claiming to synthesize the miscellaneous bits of the neighborhood? If some facade in the forwardlooking French taste makes an isolated apparition on some square, I salute it. Indifferent to what is uttered, in this place and that, as the flame with lowered tongues runs along the pipes.

Thus Action of the kind agreed upon, literary, does not transgress the Theater, limiting itself to a representation – the immediate disappearance of the written. Let it end; in the street, somewhere else, the mask falls; I have nothing to do with the poet: perjure your verse, it is gifted with only a feeble outer power. You preferred to feed the remainder of intrigues entrusted to the individual. Why should I make it clear for you, child, you know it just as I do, retaining no notion of it except by some quality or lack which is childhood's alone; this point, that everything, whether vehicle or investment, now offered to the ideal, is contrary to it – almost a speculation on your modesty, for your silence – or it is defective, not direct and legitimate in the sense that impulse required just now, and it is tainted. Since uneasiness was never enough, I shall certainly clarify, however many future digressions it may take, this reciprocal contamination of work and means: but first was it not good to express myself spaciously, as with a cigar in convolution whose vagueness, at the very least, traced its outline on the raw electric daylight?

A delicate being has, or so I hope, suffered –

Outside, like the cry of space, the traveler perceives the whistle's distress. "Probably," he persuades himself, "we are going through a tunnel – *the epoch* – the last long one, snaking under the city to the all-powerful train station of the virginal central palace, like a crown." The underground passage will last (how impatient you are), as long as your thoughtful preparation of the tall glass edifice wiped clean by Justice in flight.

Suicide or abstention, doing nothing, why? – Time unique in the world, since because of an event I have still to explain, there is no Present, no – a present does not exist... Lack the Crowd declares in itself, lack – of everything. Ill-informed anyone who would announce himself his own contemporary, deserting, usurping with equal impudence, when the past ceased and when a future is slow to come, or when both are mingled perplexedly to cover up the gap. Except for the first Paris editions supposed to divulge some faith in daily nothingness, inept if the malady measures its duration by a fragment, important or not, of a century.

So watch out and be there.

Poetry, consecration; trying out, lonely in its chaste crises, during the other gestation as it continues.

Publish.

The Book, where the satisfied spirit dwells, in case of misunderstanding, is obligated, by some struggle, to shake off the bulk of the moment. Not personalized, the volume, from which one is separated as the author, does not demand that any reader approach it. You should know that as such, without any human accessories, it happens all alone; made, being. The hidden meaning stirs, and lays out a choir of pages.

No more arrogant denial of the moment, even in the celebrations: it is to be noticed that some chance forbids to dreams the materials to fight with, or favors a certain attitude.

You, Friend, must not be deprived of years because you parallel the deaf drudgery of the many, the case is strange: I ask you, without judging, for lack of sudden preambles, to treat my information as a madness, I admit it, rare. However, it is already modified by this wisdom, or this understanding, if that's all it is – risking on some surrounding condition, incomplete at the very least, certain extreme conclusions about art which can explode, diamontinely, in this forever time, in the integrity of the Book – to play them, but and by a triumphant reversal, with the tacit injunction that nothing, pulsing in the unknown womb of the hour, shown in the pages as clear and evident, is to find this readily or perhaps another which this may illuminate.

Jean-François Chevrier
To "whomever...!"

Many art historians, discussing the origins of abstraction, have studied the symbolist background of modernism. Mallarmé's work seems central to this reconstitution. In the 1960's, the tendency was rather to take Mallarmé out of symbolism, showing how his thought went far past the aesthetics or the ideology of the literary and artistic movement situated in the 1880's. Already in the years around 1910, numerous participants in or observers of avant-garde art had attached Mallarméan poetics to the most advanced forms of post-Cézannian art, and cubism in particular. We cannot now reexamine the effects of that poetics upon modern art – the object of this exhibition – without taking into consideration these two moments of the interpretation called "modernist" in the 1960's and 1910. But we have also to take into account what has been omitted or marginalized from that interpretation. In order to do this, it is not sufficient to invoke Symbolism as an alternative system. We have to make an attempt to single out the exceptional "cases," the most significant ones. Odilon Redon, for example, had been almost systematically neglected by the theoreticians of modernism. Yet, Mallarmé was not only a close friend of Manet, he was also very interested indeed by the suggestive art of Redon, whose plentiful echoes can be traced during the entire twentieth century.

The effects of Mallarméan poetics cannot be reduced to the myth or the legend of a poet in search of the absolute, even if this image benefits from a long tradition invented by the nineteenth century in the flush of the first Romanticism. The effect of this poetics depends above all on its extraordinary openness, of which the modernist theory represents only a limited interpretation. Mallarmé is not the herald of the "pure poetry" celebrated by Valéry. However effective, the modernist thesis of a poetry that would have as an essential or exclusive object language itself reduces and stultifies the poetics of Mallarmé. In reality, the force of this poetics has been to reveal, after the great romantic explosion, a tension between the idea and the actuality. This tension is only partially reflected in the opposition between the ideal and the daily. The Mallarméan idea is an interpretation of the power of abstraction of language concretized in poetic writing. It is summed up in the famous saying: "I say: a flower! And besides the oblivion to which my voice relegates any shape, insofar as it is something other than the calyx, there arises musically, as the very idea and delicate, the one absent from any bouquet." But we mustn't get it wrong, Mallarmé loved flowers. The poetic flower is not only a rhetorical fact, it is a synthesis of the experience of all bouquets. Actuality itself we have to understand in the sense in which Émile Zola speaks of "actualism," referring to impressionism. It is also for Mallarmé a dimension of experience which sends us back to the misunderstanding of the subject and of its own impossibility of defining itself entirely by the conventional forms of the daily. Mallarméan actuality is a criticism of the daily and of the *présence à soi*. "Misinformed, anyone who would proclaim himself his own contemporary."

The effects of Mallarméan poetics have also had a negative result. The criticism of actualism in the name of the idea could be interpreted in the sense of a going past the present and of a utopia, but it has also appeared as a retreat of the artist into his ivory tower. The avant-gardes (all the "isms" of art since futurism) have been tempered to oppose to Mallarmé the idea of an immediate projection into the future, a sort of transfiguration, a utopian irradiation of the present. These esthetic and political utopias have often developed through an interpretation of the model of the "total work of art" (the *Gesamtkunstwerk*) Wagner put forth. Mallarmé did not believe in the Wagnerian solution. His scepticism results from his conviction that the nihilism stemming from the death of God cannot be surmounted by the reconstitution of a belief system as the foundation of a new community. This scepticism is the irreducible condition of a utopian thought which constantly reinvents rupture, against the temptation of an imaginary closure. Mallarméan poetics is thus the critical measure of avant-garde utopias. It implies a viewpoint of anthropological reconciliation (the human community ought to be able to get along without the idea of God) but each human being in his singularity multiplies "a singularity constructed on the multiplicity of internal pulsions", each individual ceaselessly experiences his own finitude and the dissatisfaction resulting from it. This individual experience is the basis "stripped of its theological foundation" of an interaction between the one and the many, the individual and the crowd. Utopia tends to resolve this interaction in an imaginary community. For Mallarmé, the community remains in the future, the artist glimpses it in the flash of poetry, the "lightning streak" which illuminates the dark depths of the virtual. The great tradition of "concrete art" in the twentieth century, whatever utopias have underlain it, depends on this possibility of actualizing a virtual richness.

The avant-garde utopias never stopped mobilizing the leftover mythologies, or, in a more ambitious mode, the perspective of a new mythology. André Breton sidelines Mallarmé, who inspired him greatly in the beginning, when he was imagining the building of a modern myth. Before surrealism, for Apollinaire and the futurists, the modern myth was summed up by the figure of an Icarus who triumphed over gravity and his destiny. The human being, that is to say, man without woman, was going finally to be able to transfigure his flesh and his finitude by projecting himself into a mechanical Eden. But Mallarmé had already reduced the polytheism of the "Gods of Yore" to a solar drama of death and resurrection. This reduction corresponds to a quest for sobriety opposed to romantic eloquence and great utopian bursts of energy. It is a dissolution of myhths, an evacuation of iconography and of the accessories of mythological representation in favor of the fundamental elements of an action limited to the scene of writing. For the attraction of myth there is substituted a table, a sheet of while paper (the model of the "empty paper" where the poem is formed and sketched out), the pen and inkwell ("with its drop, in the depths, of shadows relative to something existing"). This scene of writing is the "theatre of our mind." It's the revelation of a matricial emptiness responding to the nothingness of abolished beliefs. After the Second World War, in 1947, Artaud radicalized the Mallarméan position by refusing to participate in the esoteric exhibition organized by Breton. The person who had, in the 1930's, imagined bringing about the power of revolutionary anarchy in a "theatre of cruelty," concentrates from now on all his poetic action in what is traced and punched out. Occupied with "remaking a body," he incarnates the concrete poetry of Mallarmé in an experience of suffering like a *travail* of the flesh. This actualization of "limited action" separates itself from all the appeals to an irrational depth, formerly evoked by fascist ideologies and nazi terror. With the precise and specific violence of Artaud, Mallarméan sobriety is accomplished in the exorcism of terror.

Around Mallarméan poetics, there has been a great deal of discussion about art as a substitute for religion or the sketching out of a new communitarian link; about enigma and the occult, the value or legitimacy of "obscurity," the mysterious and the marvelous, secrecy, circles and secret societies. But modern utopias take into account the great number and individuality of the mass, thinking norms, standards, prototypes. Adapting themselves to the criteria of industrial society and to the triumph of mechanization, utopias have chosen to be constructive and productive. Marcel Duchamp was the one to transpose Mallarméan mystery into the image and the metaphoric circuits of the machine. In so doing, the creator of the *Grand Verre*, an expert in mystifications of all sorts, never stopped adjusting little anti-utopian machines, proposing an ironic version of *fin-de-siècle* eclecticism opposed by the ideologues of "Modern Style." So he has been seen as the father of post-modernism. But he is as ill-fitted to this role as is Mallarmé to that of the ancestor of modernism.

In reality, what lasts, from Mallarmé to Duchamp, but also, in a longer history, from Baudelaire to Jeff Wall passing through Marcel Broodthaers, is this anarchic freedom of art opposed to the search for a collective style. This freedom was affirmed with the great innovation of literary symbolism, the polymorphism of a literary symbolism, the polymorphism of free verse, in a break with the norms of prosodic tradition. In 1967, George Kubler, the author of *The Shape of Time* (1962) said this: "When flow and change are ignored, and when development is disregarded, style remains useful as a taxonomic convenience. But wherever the passage of time is under consideration, with its shifting identities and continuous transformations, the taxonomic notion, represented by the term style, becomes irrelevant." That explains why modern art consecrated a mysticism of formal innovation, in the idea of rhythm. Going far past the cadence of productive activity, rhythm "organic or mechanical, but also lyric and cosmic" has been celebrated as the alternative to the project of a Modern Style supposed to have the same capacity of synthesis as the great styles of the past. Unlike Modern Style, rhythm permits us to integrate the anarchic diversity of individual freedoms as well as the game of difference, beginning by sexual difference. Associating poetry to dance and music, rhythm is the condition of a space of language overflowing the spatial fixation of the object and the reification of the image. The mobility of reading set to work in *Un Coup de dés* manifests the uncertainty and variation principle that characterizes the public aspect of the modern work. Mallarmé admits that this relation participates in "communication," but he adds that the work, rather than forcing attention to itself or supposing a public made to order is addressed to "whomever"...

Art and Utopia. Limited Action

In 1897, Stéphane Mallarmé (1842-1898) published his essay, "Limited Action" (*L'action restreinte*) in *Divagations* where he describes the limits and the concentration of poetic action. At the end of the nineteenth century, after the death of Victor Hugo, the poet could no longer claim to operate directly in the political arena or even to set himself up as a moral conscience. He could talk about the world, give it a verbal equivalent, but he could not change it. His activity, however, is not contemplative. He realizes an action in a "limited", but boundless, realm which does not belong to him but which he can reevaluate and even redefine. This is the realm of language and languages; it is the scene of writing and the space of the book as a "spiritual instrument."
In an era in which progress is measured by information, the book is often related to the newspaper, but it should be differentiated from it in the same way that poetic language is differentiated from the instrumental definition of language as a means of communication and propaganda. In 1921, the Russian poet Ossip Mandelstam echoes Mallarmé when, in the context of a postrevolutionary society and culture, he writes: "Social differences and class antagonisms pale before the new division of people into friends and enemies of the word..."

This exhibition reexamines some key moments in the exchange between art and poetry in the twentieth century until the end of the 1970s. The Mallarmean poetic serves here as a thread for a history of modern art with its hold on language and its dissemination. In March 1970, Marcel Broodthaers, declared: "Mallarmé is the source of contemporary art. He unconsciously invents modern space." Broodthaers was thinking principally about the word constellation set up in *Un coup de dés* (1897). After it was belatedly published in book form in 1914, the poem effectively became the prototype for all investigations into the confluence of poetry, typography and visual art. Appollinaire's Calligrams, contemporary with cubist *papiers collés*, the Futurists' *Parole in libertà*, and the *Word as Such* of Russian poets Velimir Khlebnikov and Alexei Kruchenykh, are derived almost directly from this poem or differentiate themselves from it through a dynamic of avant-garde radicalization. This genealogical thread continues with the emergence of concrete poetry in the 1950s.

Plein air impressionism since Manet and the prismatic structure of post-Cézannean cubist painting represent two poles of the Mallarmean poetic that were already achieved in the sonnet's concentrated form (especially in *Une dentelle s'abolit*) at least ten years before *Un coup de dés*. Braque's and Picasso's cubism was often called "hermetic," as were Mallarmé's poems. Gino Severini speaks of a "divisionism of forms" and a "copenetration of planes" analogous to the task of the word in poetry. The collaboration between Juan Gris and Pierre Reverdy participates in this bipolarity of plastic writing. Parallel to this, the fantastic of Odilon Redon embodied the idea of suggestion, which defined symbolism in its opposition to impressionist optics as well as to description and literary narration. The promotion of a dream-state imagination in the twentieth century is inscribed in this tension between the optic and the symbolic. Here, collage and montage procedures used by post-cubist constructivism and surrealism, both derived from Dada, achieve historical depth. The dialogue between art and poetry – definitively condensed in Miró's *peintures-poèmes* – also opens onto other forms of visual creation such as photography and film. Rodchenko illustrates Mayakovsky's *Pro Eto* with photomontage, and the abbreviated signs of Paul Klee are akin to the disarticulations of the burlesque. Beyond that abstraction called "geometric," the emphasis on the essential constituents of painting – point, line, plane and color – participates in a speculation on the genesis of form that has much in common with poetic language. With Marcel Duchamp, a Mallarmé admirer and reader of Jules Laforgue, symbolist suggestion found its present form with mechanomorphic irony.

Nevertheless, as Duchamp's extra-pictorial activities indicate, the resonance of the Mallarmean poetic exceeds the genealogies of poetry and the visual arts. Mallarmé was also interested in music and the arts of theatre and dance while refuting the Wagnerian model of the total work of art. What is more, the speculative demand of *Un coup de dés'* author aimed to reestablish mystery in poetic experience between the vestiges of faith and the ornaments of the everyday. This distance defines the opening of modern space: from the great theatrical reformations of Edward Gordon Craig and Adolphe Appia to the "activities" of American post-modern dance, by way of the association between the biomechanical and grotesque in Meyerhold set against a symbolist backdrop.

In 1925, the collaboration between Hans Arp and El Lissitsky for *Die Kunstismen (Les ismes de l'art, The -isms of Art. 1924-1909)* witnessed a common search for synthesis in modern art at the two extremes of the European continent despite the differences in language. Similarly, the exemplariness of Sophie Taeuber's work is explained by the way it transcends the division between the fine and applied arts, establishing a new continuity between traditionally separated spaces: the studio, the domestic environment, the stage and the dance floor, at human or reduced scale. This corresponds to the most demanding formal investigations in the arts of the everyday in postrevolutionary Russia.

Mallarmé had already imagined an anthropological reconciliation of modern art, liberated from religious representation. But that anchorage was revealed to be just as precarious as the practice of poetry. Apropos of Georges Braque, Carl Einstein wrote at the beginning of the 1930s: "Art has meaning only in so far as that with it one defines and also creates a vision of the world, a myth. That is why the old optic has for a very long time no longer corresponded to psychic structure." The same author confirmed "the collapse of rationalized man" and denounced the superstitious belief in a utopia of technological progress. In the 1930s, the distressing pressure of the times brought the model of the myth back to the debates as well as to the attempts at a synthesis between rationalist utopias and a somewhat reasoned neo-primitivism, between constructivism and surrealism. Echoing the work of James Joyce, photography became the privileged medium for a poetic anthropology of the quotidian and the sacred (Evans, Sander, Hausmann, Albers, Levitt).
Immediately after the Second World War, Antonin Artaud's return to poetry – after the failure of his theatrical attempts in the 1930s – corresponds to a necessary retightening of the myth into the "limited action" of trace and *proferation*. In 1933, Artaud had defined Mallarmé's exemplariness: "A nothingness which resolved into the infinite after having passed through the finite, the concrete and the immediate; a music based on nothingness since one is struck by the sonority of syllables before understanding their meaning." With the war and the concentration camps, nothingness acquired a resonance of terror and inhumanity. Wladyslaw Strzeminski produces his collage series *To My Friends the Jews* and Rossellini

realizes the film *Germany, Year Zero*. In those European art circles centered on *art informel*, primitivism is more than ever underwritten by a desire for exorcism (Henri Michaux, Wols, Jean Fautrier). Antoni Tàpies dramatizes Miro's writing. In the United States, what Rauschenberg revives at the end of the 1940s is rather the legacy of Dada and Duchamp transmitted via John Cage, while an American painter living in France, Ellsworth Kelly, continues the trajectory of concrete art.

In the 1950s and 1960s, the augmentation of the Mallarmean corpus (with the publication of the *Correspondance* and notes on the Book) coincides with the introduction of the linguistic model in the humanities and the emergence of the artistic culture of the neo-avant-garde. Roland Barthes describes a common "structuralist activity" in literature, music and the visual arts. The impersonality extolled by Mallarmé ends in "the death of the author": a slogan-formula for conceptual art inspired by structuralism, some representative pieces of which were selected from various fields and published in *Aspen*, no. 5-6 in 1967. Inspired by information theory and the structure of serial music, Umberto Eco substitutes symbolist suggestion with "the open work," which he defines as "a field of interpretive possibilities." Yet limited action must still differentiate itself from new technological utopias in an era of economic expansion. In *La Ricotta* (1963), Pier Paolo Pasolini makes Orson Welles say: "I am a force of the past." From his retreat on Utopia Parkway in New York City, Joseph Cornell renews the poetic object and the surrealist marvelous, relating them to the symbolist imaginary.
The book, which Mallarmé calls the "total expansion of the letter," continues to be the counter-model to mass media, but it has lost its sacred dimension due to contamination: it has been vulgarized. The inclusive logic summed up by Jean-Luc Godard – "everything should be put in a film" – contrasts with the "archaic silence of the book" (Walter Benjamin) whose plastic equivalent is Tony Smith's black cube (1962). Parallel to Broodthaers and his *Peinture littéraires*, another poet-artist, Öyvind Fahlström, proposes a synthesis of the Mallarmean tradition transformed by surrealism (Roberto Matta) and popularized by pop. Detours of play and humor disrupt the confrontation between the pictorial and the conceptual. Dieter Roth's *Mundunculum* responds to Piero Manzoni's fixed *Alphabet*. With his torn posters, Raymond Hains finds proof in the street of a Matisse-Duchamp-Schwitters alliance under the sign of Mallarmé.

At the end of the 1970s René Daniels' painting, *La Muse vénale*, inspired by a poem of Baudelaire, indicates the exhaustion of the cultural alternatives proposed by the neo-avant-gardes. It likewise demonstrates a poetic gaze that knows how to detect the anachronisms of the present. "Misinformed," Mallarmé writes, "anyone who would proclaim himself his own contemporary." Artaud denounced the "lie of being". *Mettere il mondo al mondo* (Alighiero e Boetti) does not participate in the production of material goods or signs: formal invention is a symbolic activity, a concrete work within language. Drawing participates in this activity, as Philip Guston's graphic work since 1967 shows (often realized in collaboration with poets). It is likewise demonstrated by Nancy Spero's 1969 variations on the "written drawings" of Artaud and the *Image-poem* by Gunther Brus in homage to Odilon Redon. In his photographic work since 1978, Jeff Wall revisits the tradition of the painted theatre in order to interpret the conditions of speech and narration, as well as the conditions of any act of poetic expression, in the enigmatic environment of the everyday.

Selection of works

The vanished adolescent of our early years, destined to haunt the lofty or thoughtful mind with the mourning he so willingly wears – I recognise him struggling beneath the pain of appearances: because Hamlet brings to life, on stage, the unique protagonist of an intimate, mysterious tragedy, the very sight of his name exerts over me, over you as you read it, a fascination close to anguish.
[…]
Shakespeare's play is so skilfully shaped in terms of our inner theatre – prototype of all the others – that it can adjust to today's productions or ignore them with equal indifference.

Stéphane Mallarmé
"Hamlet," *La Revue indépendante,* 1886

Giorgio de Chirico

Le Printemps, 1914

[cat. 1]

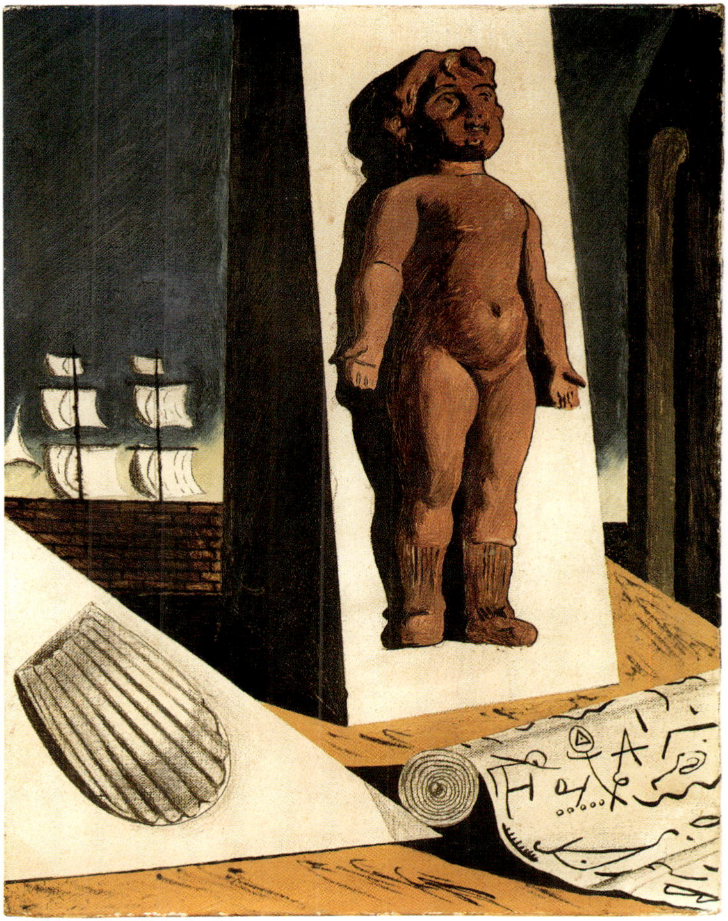

10.9.68 Wed. Duchamp/Delacroix

item : a "distant cousin" of the Debussy dreaming

queried in real life about Debussy seeing or knowing him Duchamp has spoken of his inaccessibility, "like Einstein."

consider the dream interpreting it (granting it significance beyond the enigmatical) in the light of the "OBJECT" ('l'objet') curiously observed in some kind of perspective, tradition

Delacroix – Redon – Duchamp
Redon had followed Delacroix one night out of hero worship (MELLERIO)
Duchamp openly acknowledged Redon as an influence "le royaume de l'objet" surrealism
own penchant for collecting from way back leading into preoccupation with 'l'objet'

Duchamp, Delacroix #2

note : own spontaneous outgoing admiration for Delacroix – the 3 Escholier tomes before knowing Duchamp period of cellar atelier working on the 50s Delacroix's "Journals". The Nadar reproduction on the bulletin board – the "Journal" entering into the fiber of daily life – afternoons in Flushing Main St. – snack + library pattern (the old library same site)

"Delacroix's Handkerchief" consider as a title for a crystallized vision of the random notes as an article

Joseph Cornell
Note of 9 October 1968

Joseph Cornell
Untitled (Apollinaris), 1953
[cat. 3]

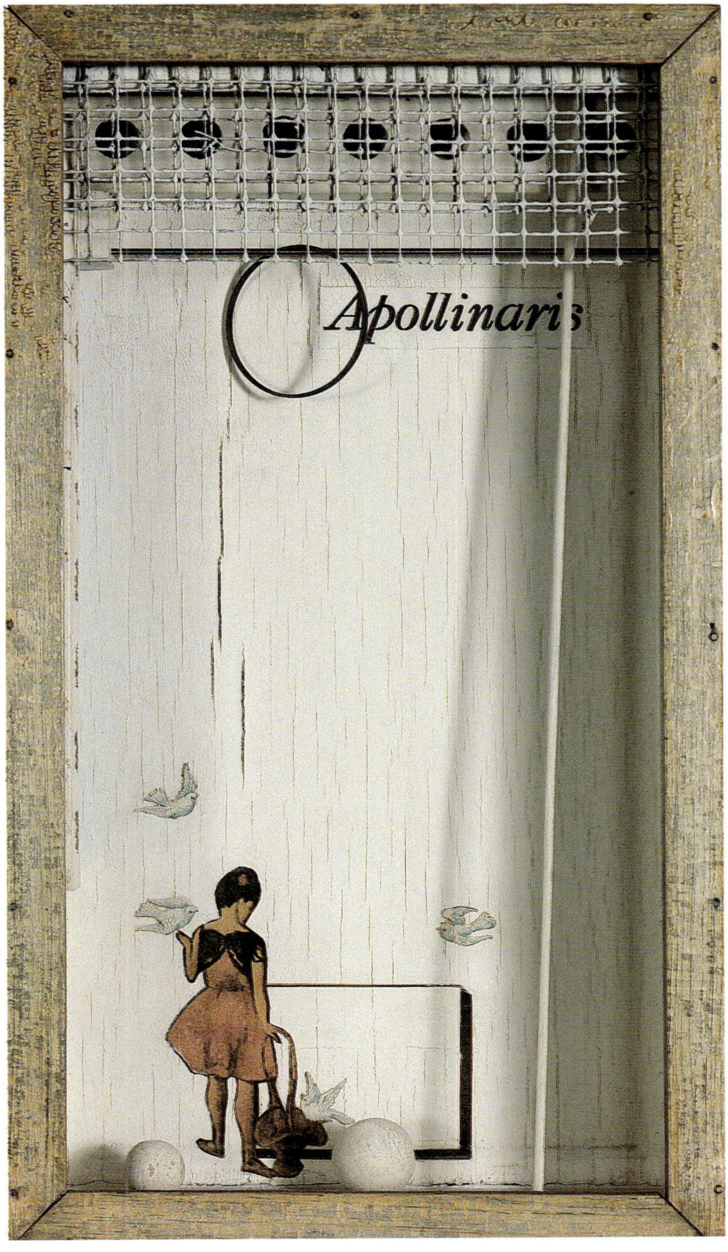

Joseph Cornell

Le Vierge, le vivace, le bel aujourd'hui..., 1970

[cat. 6]

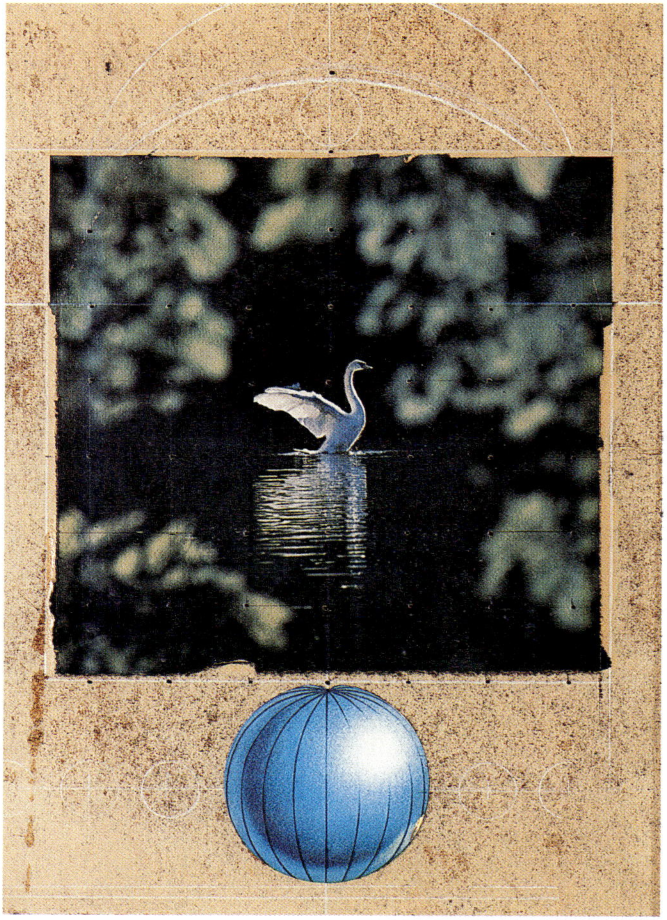

Joseph Cornell

Trade Winds Storm Warning, 1958

[cat. 4]

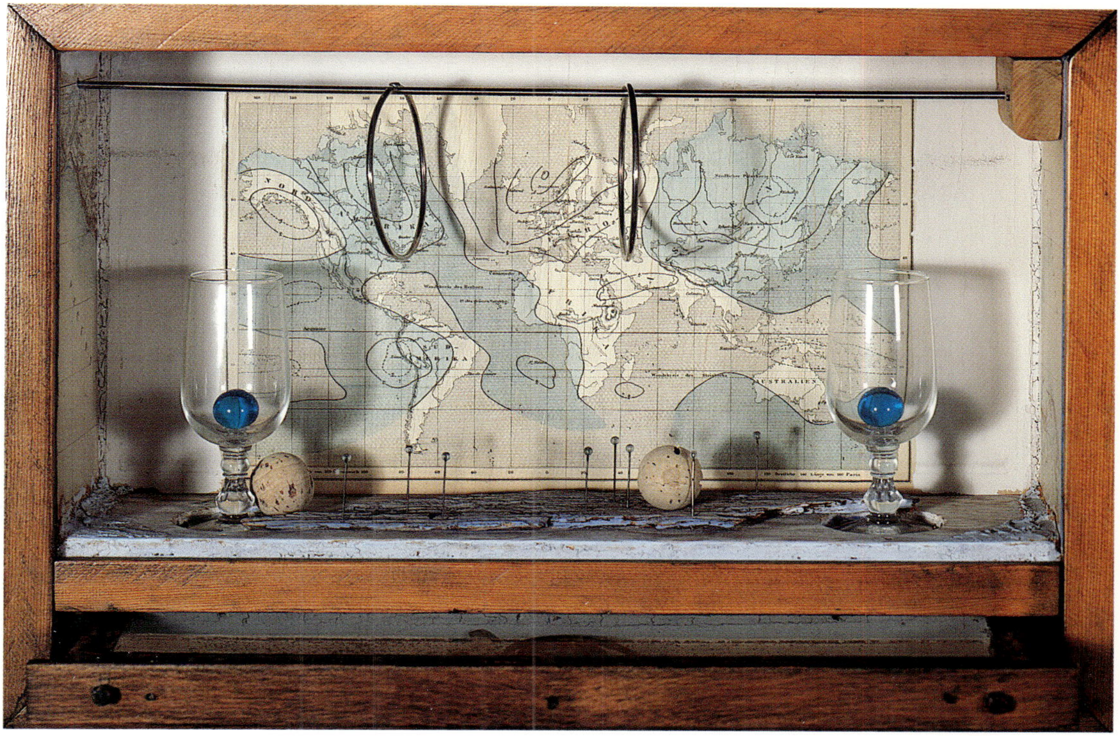

René Magritte

Le Gouffre argenté, 1926

[cat. 2]

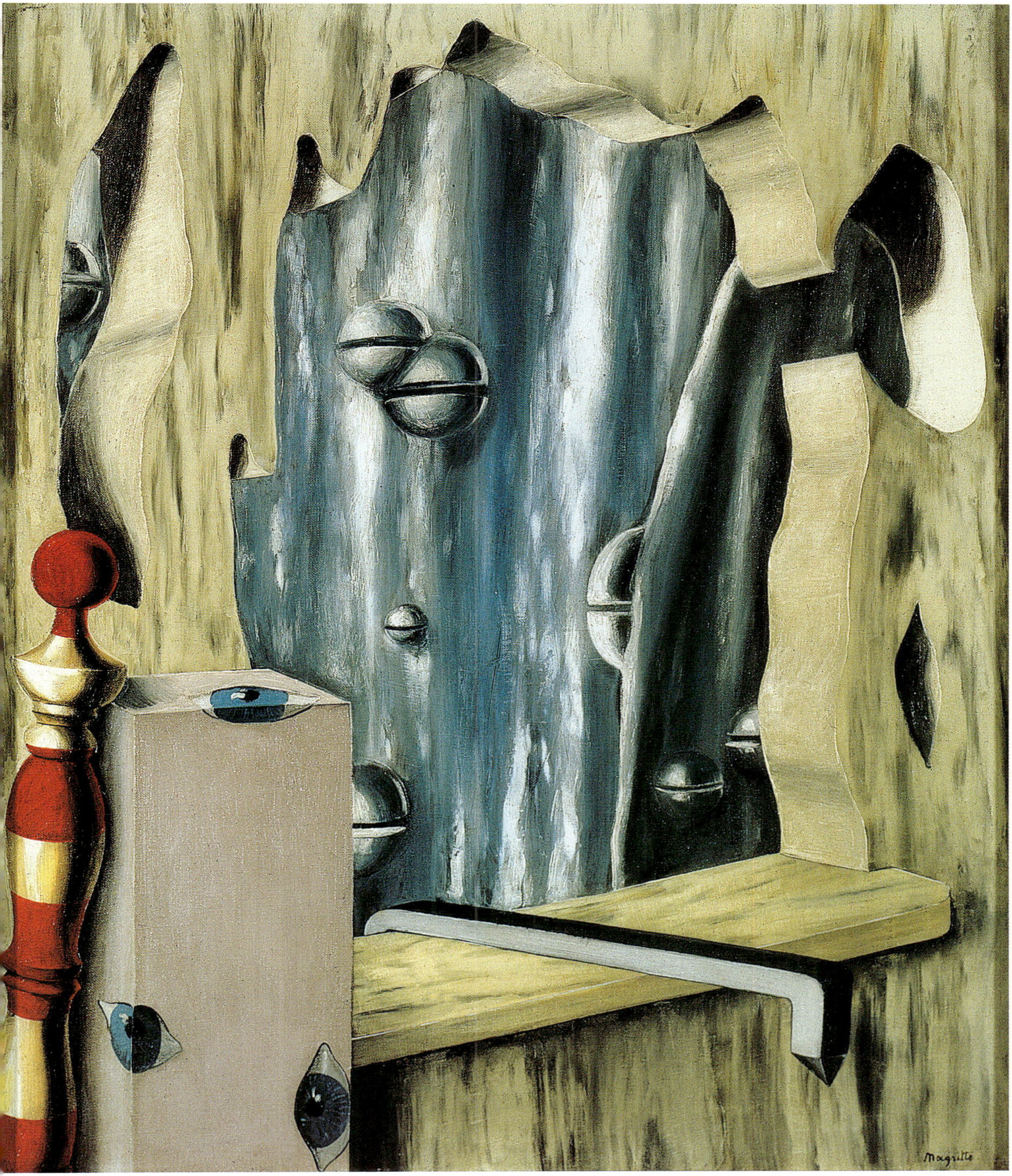
Magritte

Edward Gordon Craig
Project for a Set for Hamlet, n.d.
[cat. 8]

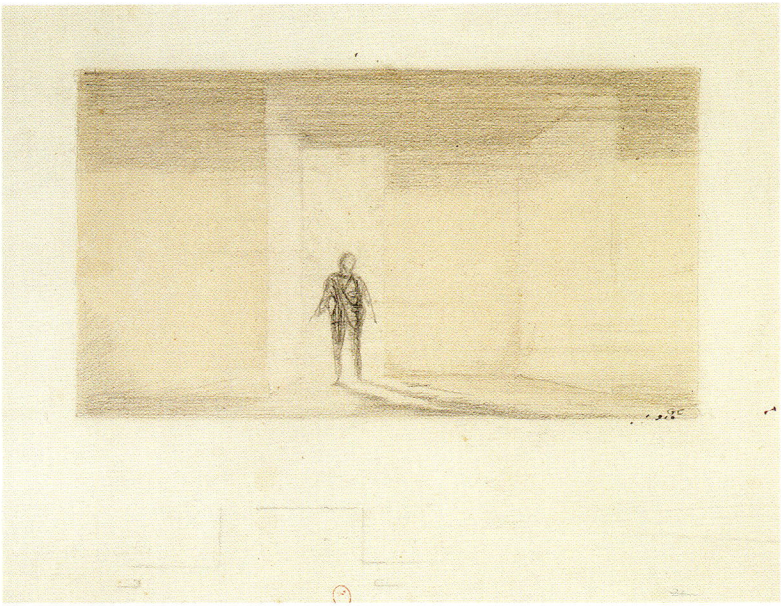

Between Hamlet and the rest of the world
I want not a single point of consonance,
not the least hope of reconciliation.

Edward Gordon Craig
On the Art of the Theatre, 1912

Edward Gordon Craig

Project for an Unused Set for Hamlet, Act III, Scene 3, n.d.

[cat. 13]

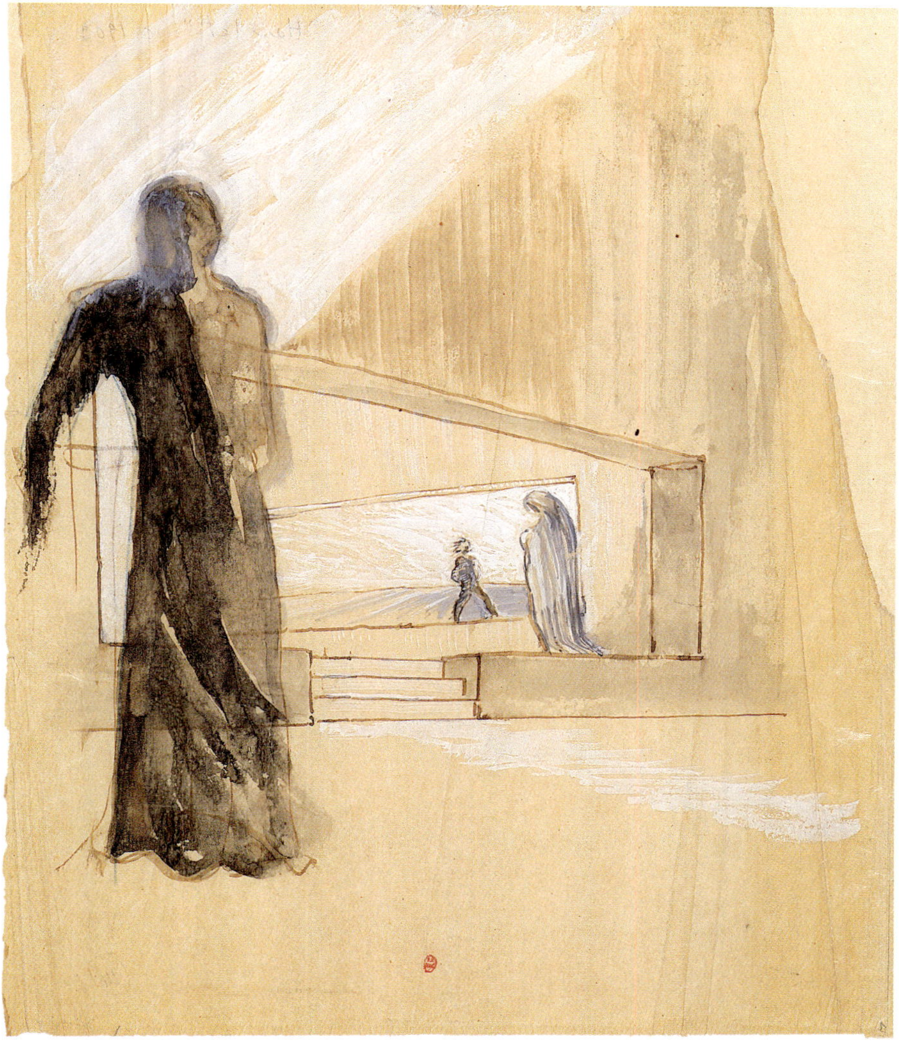

Edward Gordon Craig

Project for a Set for Hamlet, Act I, Scene 1, n.d.

[cat. 12]

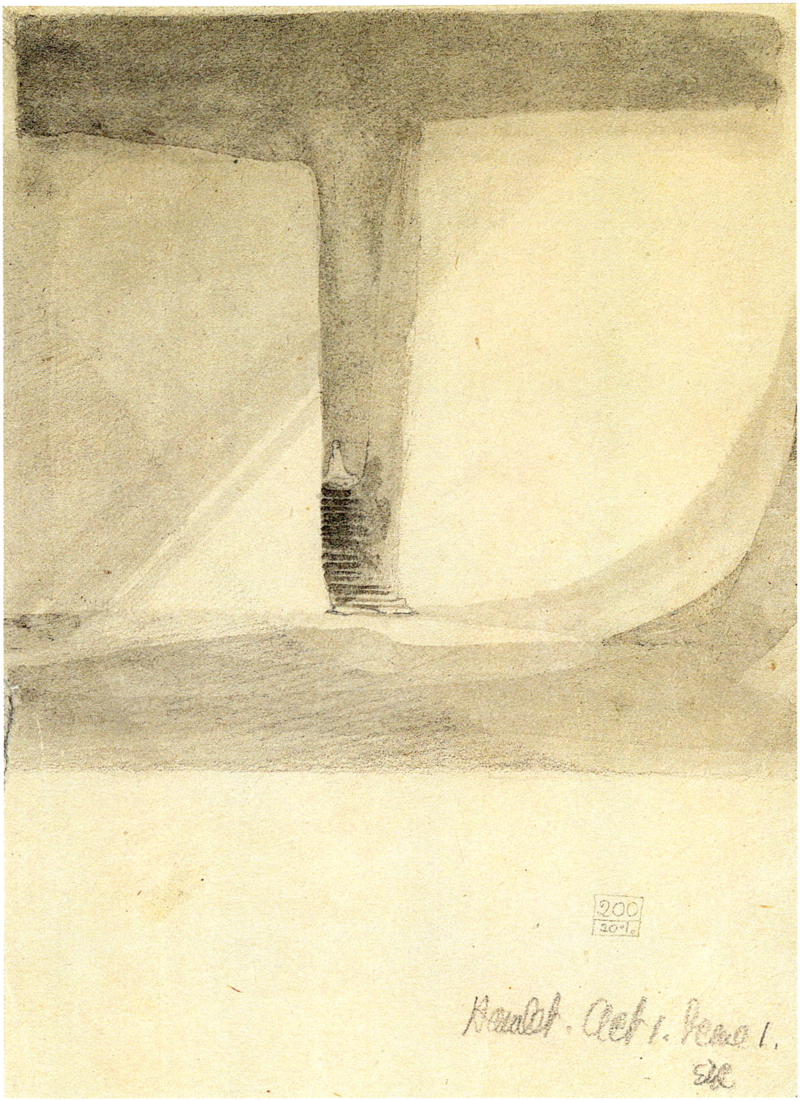

Edward Gordon Craig

Project for a Set for Hamlet, Act II, Scene 2, 1904

[cat. 14]

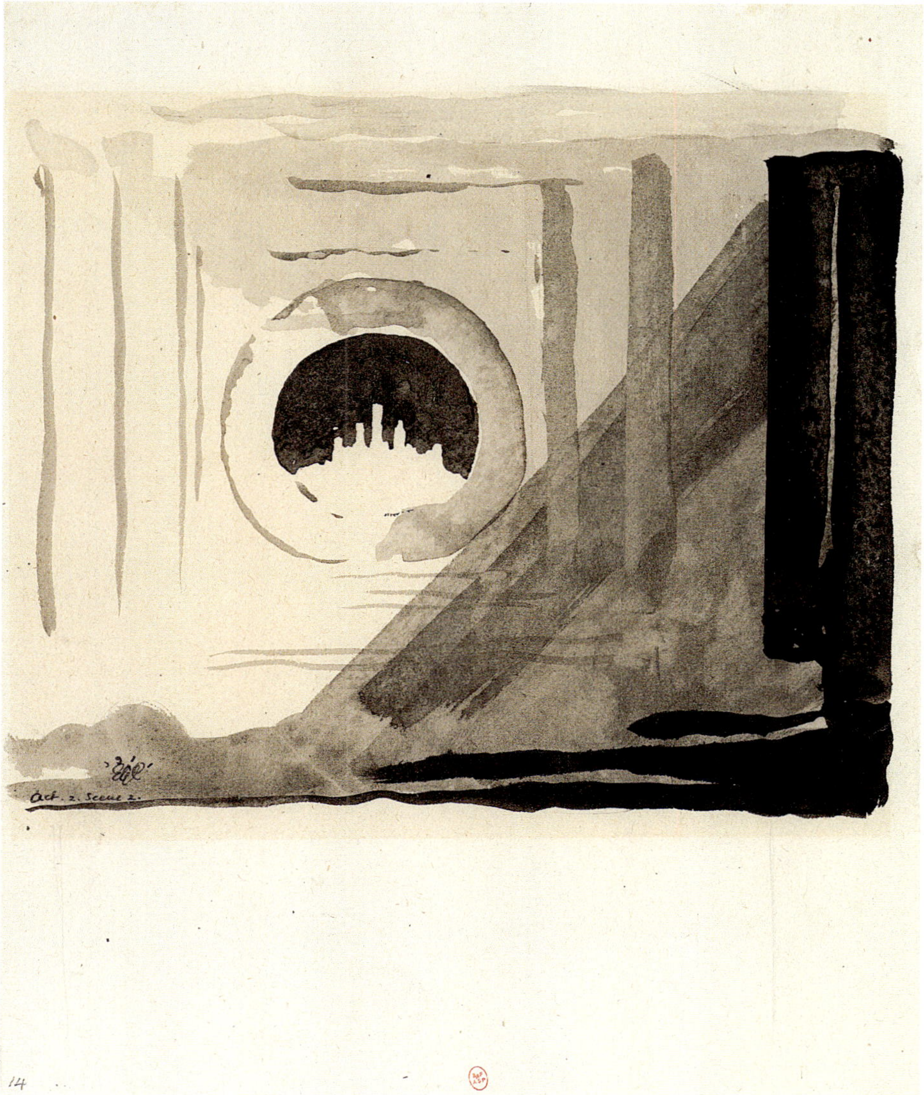

Adolphe Appia

Espace rythmique, "La ronde du soir," 1909

[cat. 18]

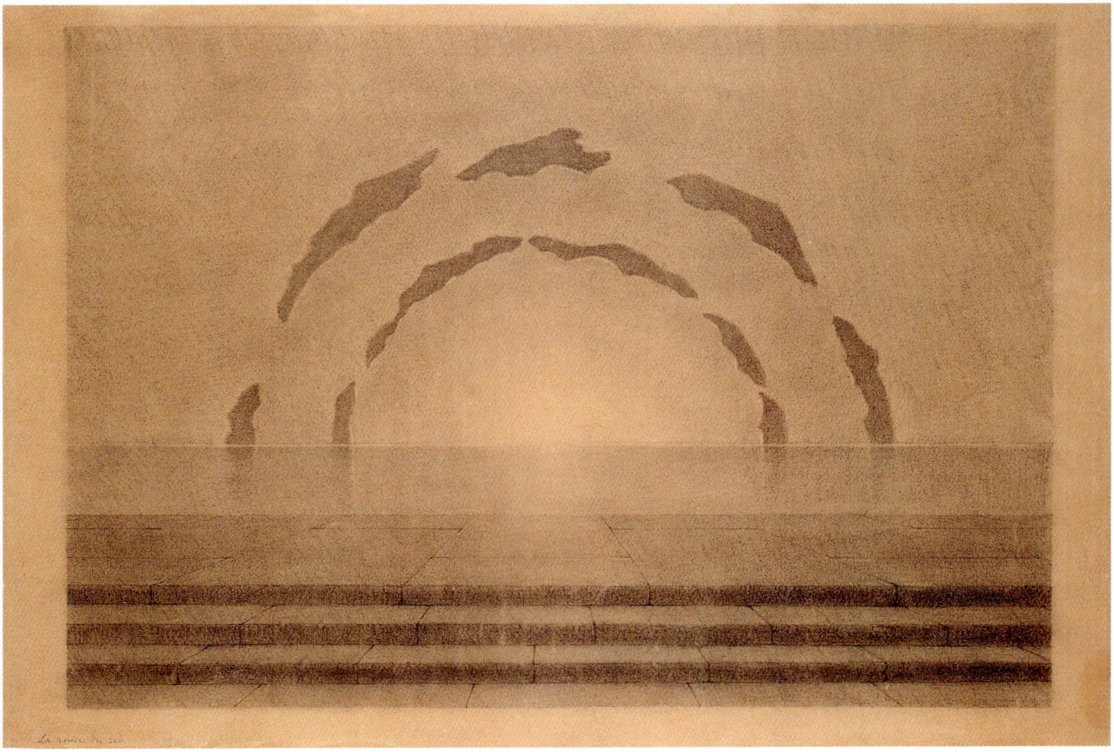

Adolphe Appia
Espace rythmique, "Cheminement," 1909
[cat. 23]

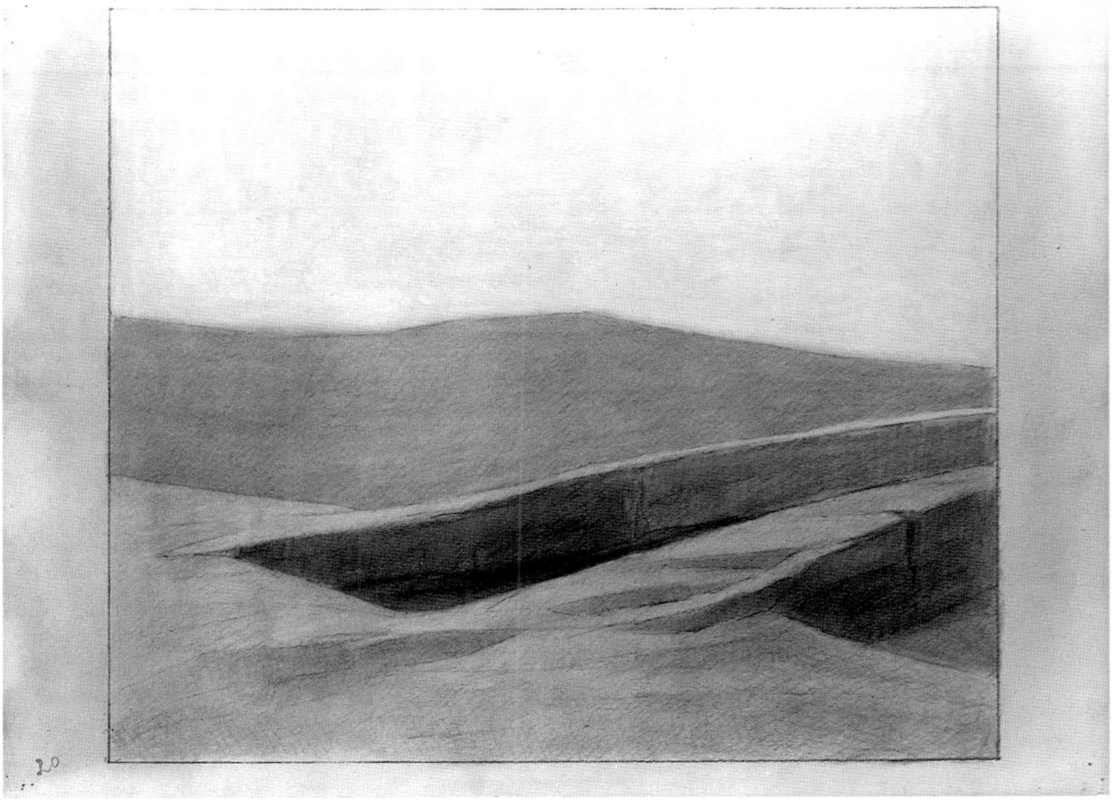

Adolphe Appia

Espace rythmique, "Les Trois piliers," 1909

[cat. 17]

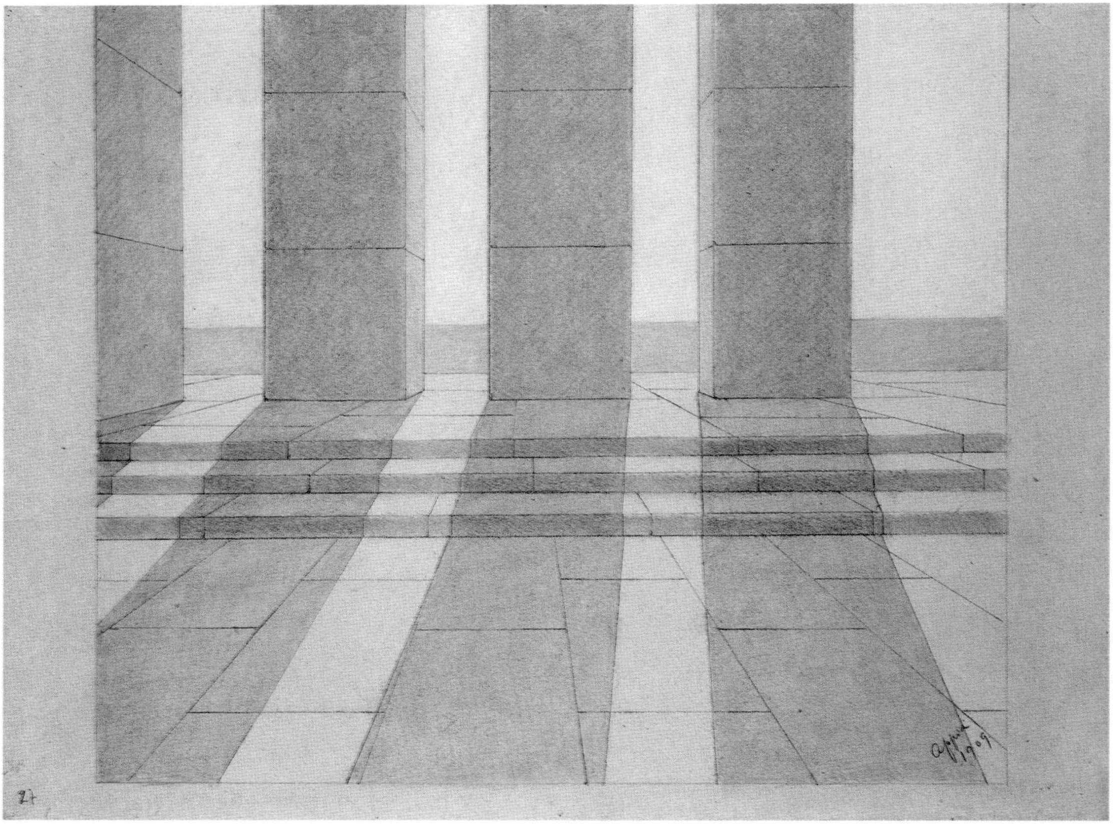

Adolphe Appia

Espace rythmique, "Les Cyprès," 1909

[cat. 20]

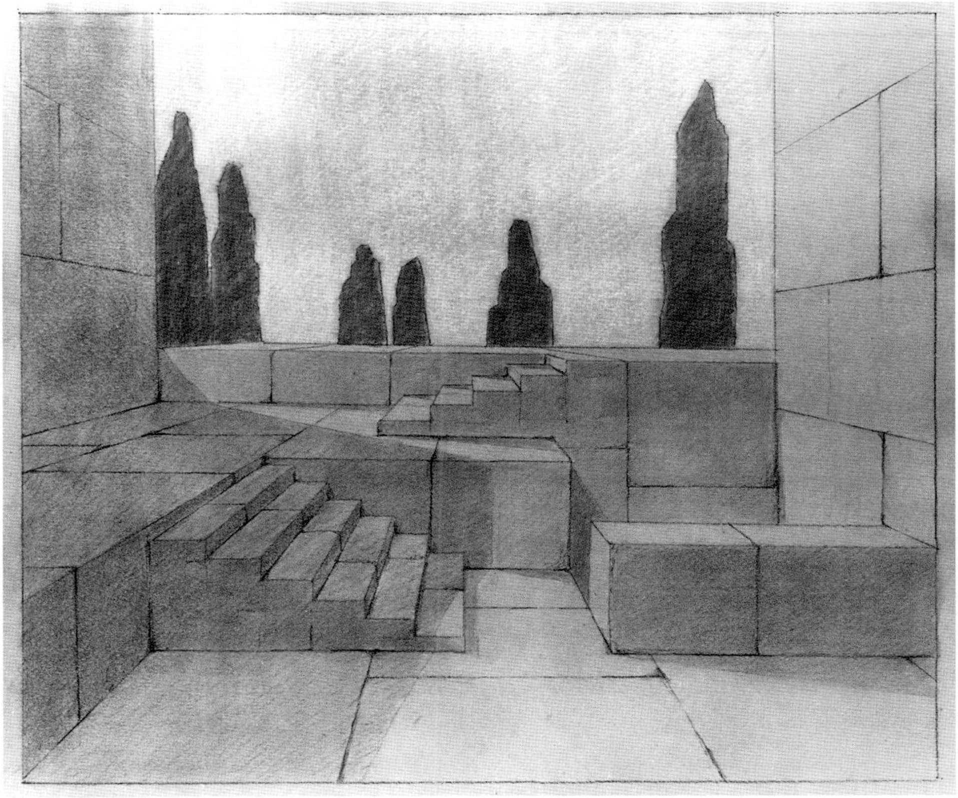

Lyonel Feininger
Tortum I, 1923-1926
[cat. 27]

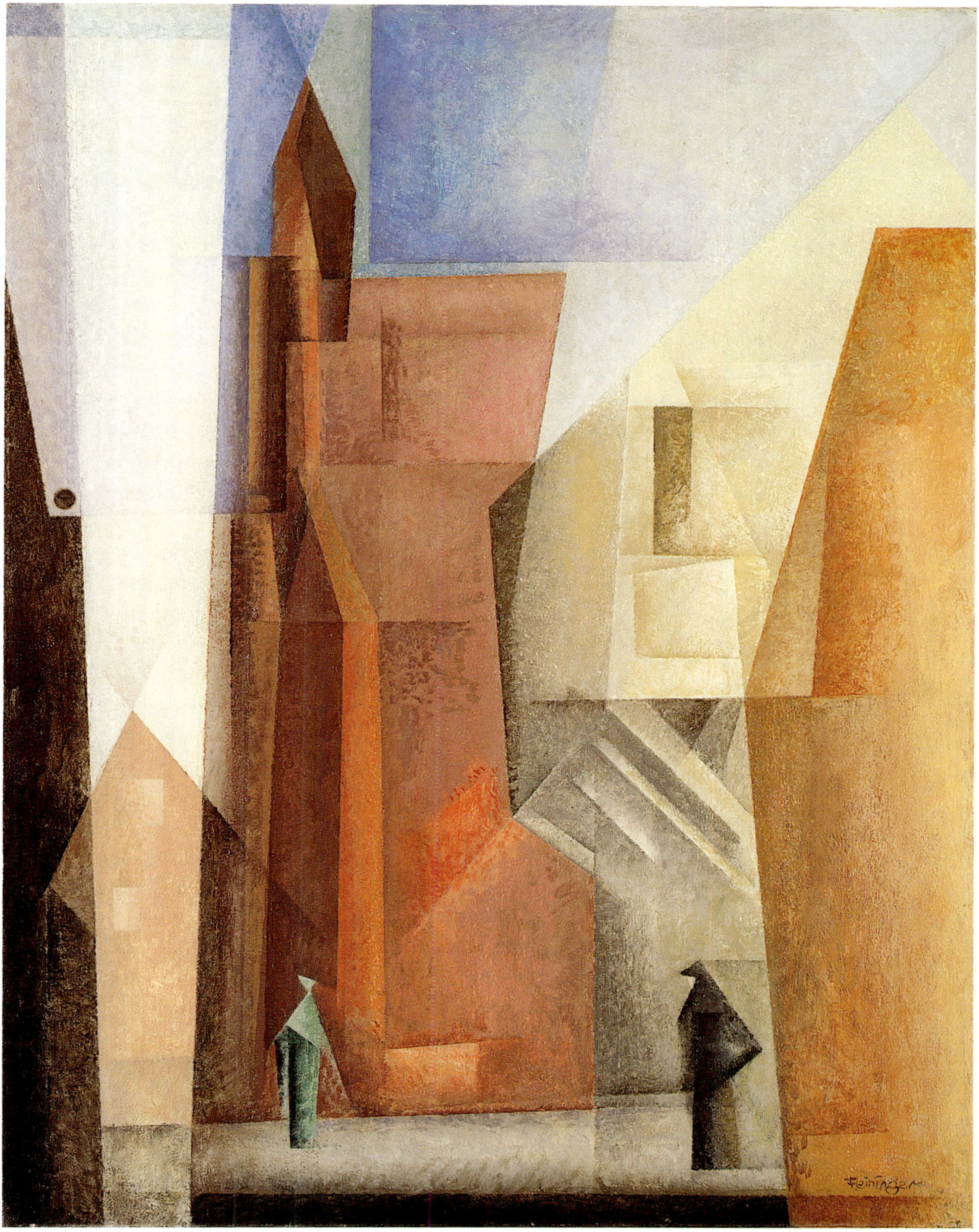

The fantastic will exist in its own right on the stage; *joie de vivre* will be discovered in the tragic as well as in the comic; the demonic will be manifested in deepest irony and the tragi-comic in the commonplace; we shall strive for "stylized improbability", for mysterious allusions, deception and transformation; we shall eradicate the sweetly sentimental from the romantic; the dissonant will sound as perfect harmony, and the commonplace of everyday life will be transcended.

Vsevolod Meyerhold
"Le Théâtre de foire," *Écrits sur le théâtre,* 1912

Vsevolod Meyerhold

Biomechcnic Exercice Le Rifle, *on the roofs of Moscow,* ca. 1934

[cat. 42]

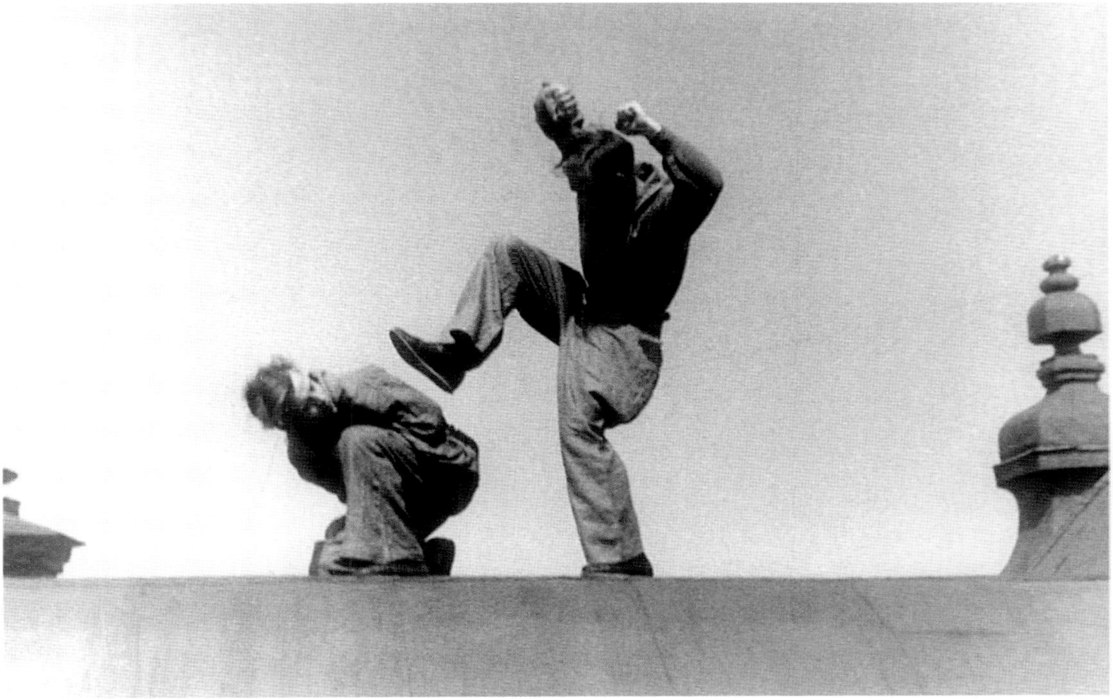

Vsevolod Meyerhold

The Rearing Earth [Zemlja dybom], according to M. Martinet, staging of the text by S. Tre'jakov. Photography of the stage for the episode 7: "A Knife in the Back of the Revolution". Ljvbov Popova's construction. TIM (Meyerhold Theatre), 1923
[cat. 26]

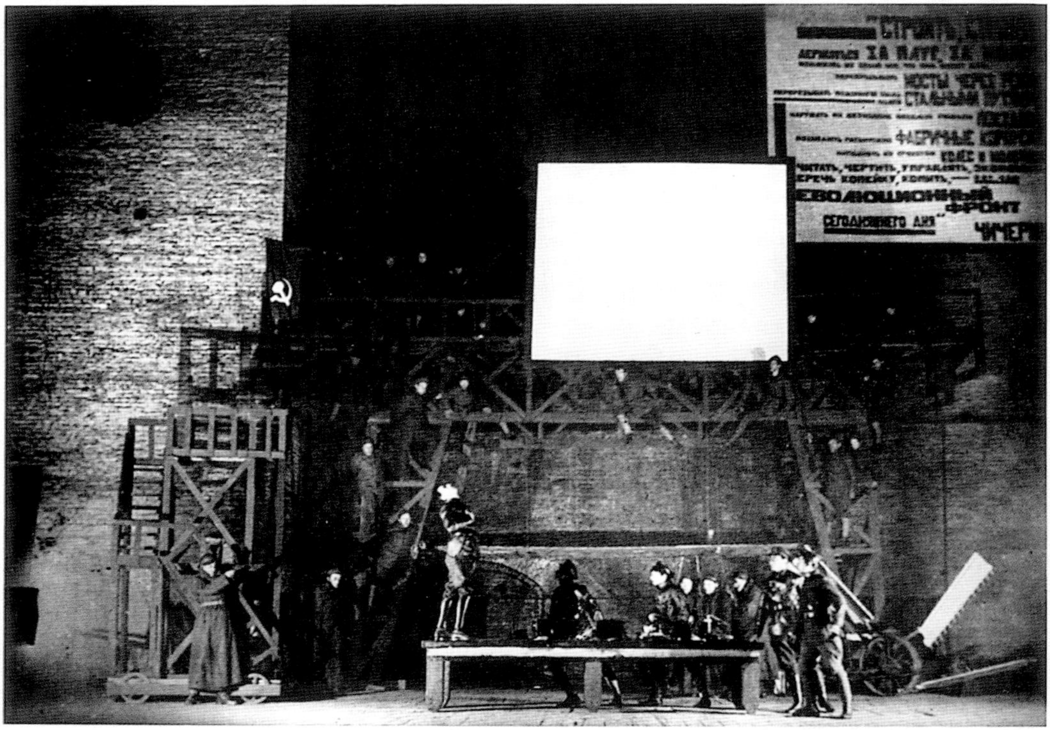

Vsevolod Meyerhold

Le Revizor, by N. Gogol. Photography of a scene of the episode 14: "A Party Is a Party". GOSTIM (Meyerhold Theatre), 1926

[cat. 25]

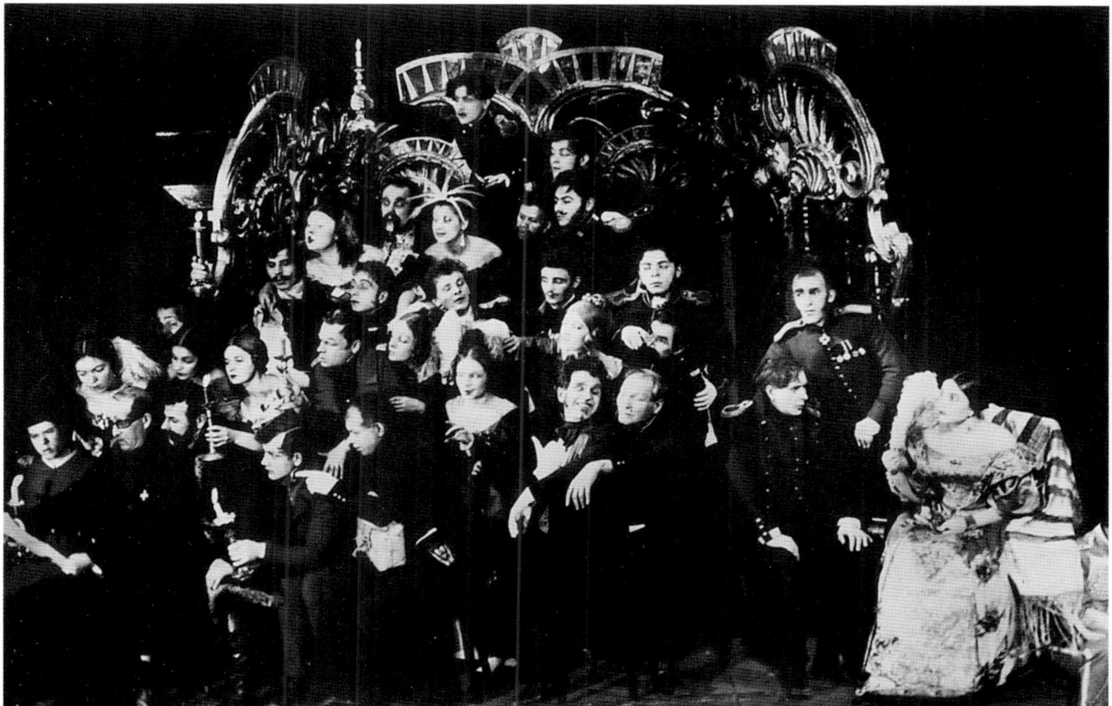

Marcel Broodthaers
Un coup de dés, 1969
[cat. 44]

Mallarmé is the source of contemporary art...
Unwittingly he invented modern space.

Marcel Broodthaers
Tractatus Logico-Catalogicus, 1970 (extract)

Un coup de dés jamais quand bien même lancé dans des circonstances éternelles du fond d'un naufrage
Soit que l'Abîme blanchi étale furieux sous une inclinaison plane désespérément d'aile la sienne retombée
par avance d'un mal à dresser le vol et couvrant les jaillissements coupant au ras les bonds très à
l'intérieur résume

L'ombre enfouie dans ~~cette~~ la profondeur
par cette voile alternative
~~[illegible]~~
~~[illegible]~~
jusqu'adapter à l'envergure
sa béante profondeur en
tant que la coque d'un
bâtiment penché de l'un
ou l'autre bord
Le Maître hors d'anciens
calculs où la manœuvre
avec l'âge oubliée surgit
jadis il

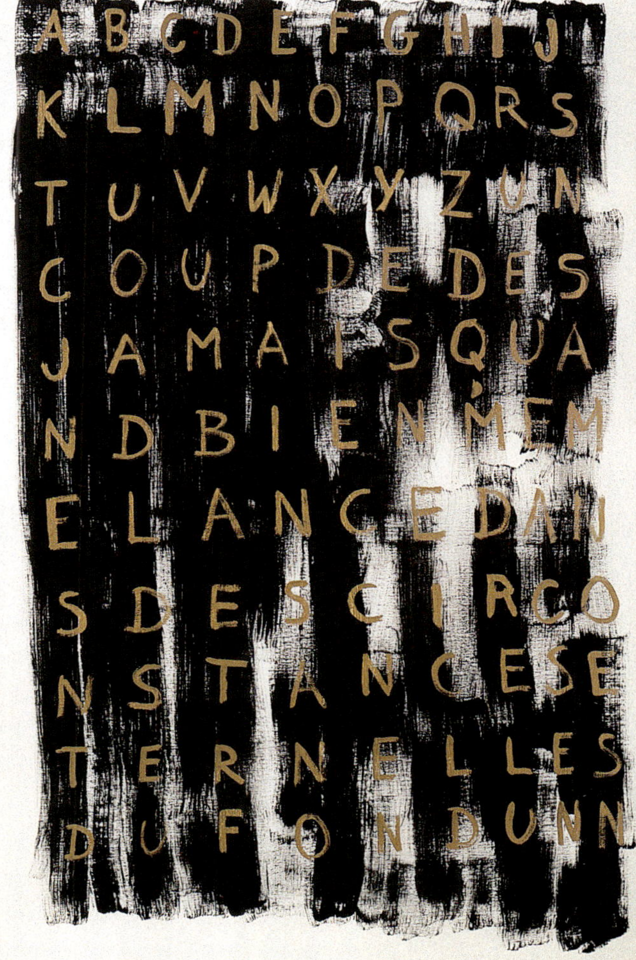

A B C D E F G H I J
K L M N O P Q R S
T U V W X Y Z U N
C O U P D E D E S
J A M A I S Q U A
N D B I E N M Ê M
E L A N C E D A N
S D E S C I R C O
N S T A N C E S E
T E R N E L L E S
D U F O N D U N N

A U F R A G E
S O I T Q U E
L A B I M E B
L A N C H I E
T A L E F U R

Marcel Broodthaers

Interior pages of *Un coup de dés jamais n'abolira le hasard,* 1969

[cat. 787]

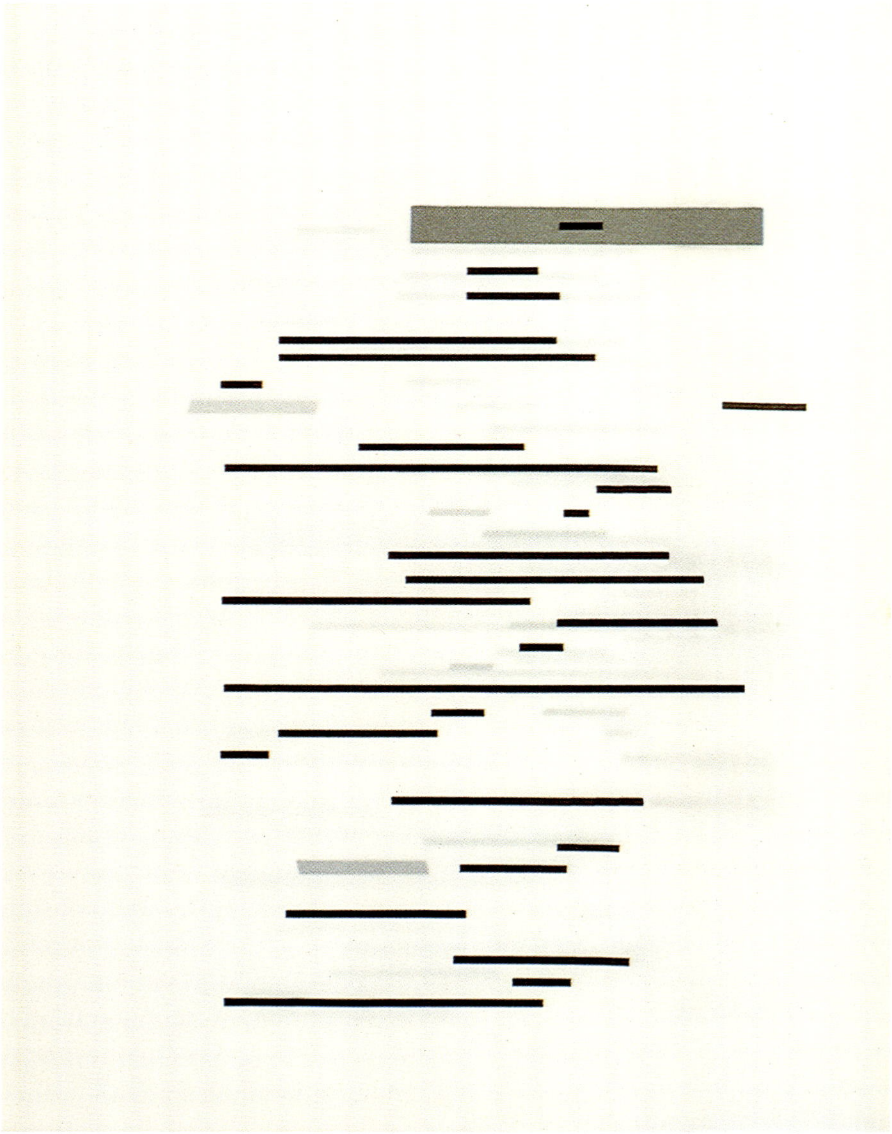

Next two double pages:

Marcel Broodthaers
Ma collection, 1971
[cat. 43]

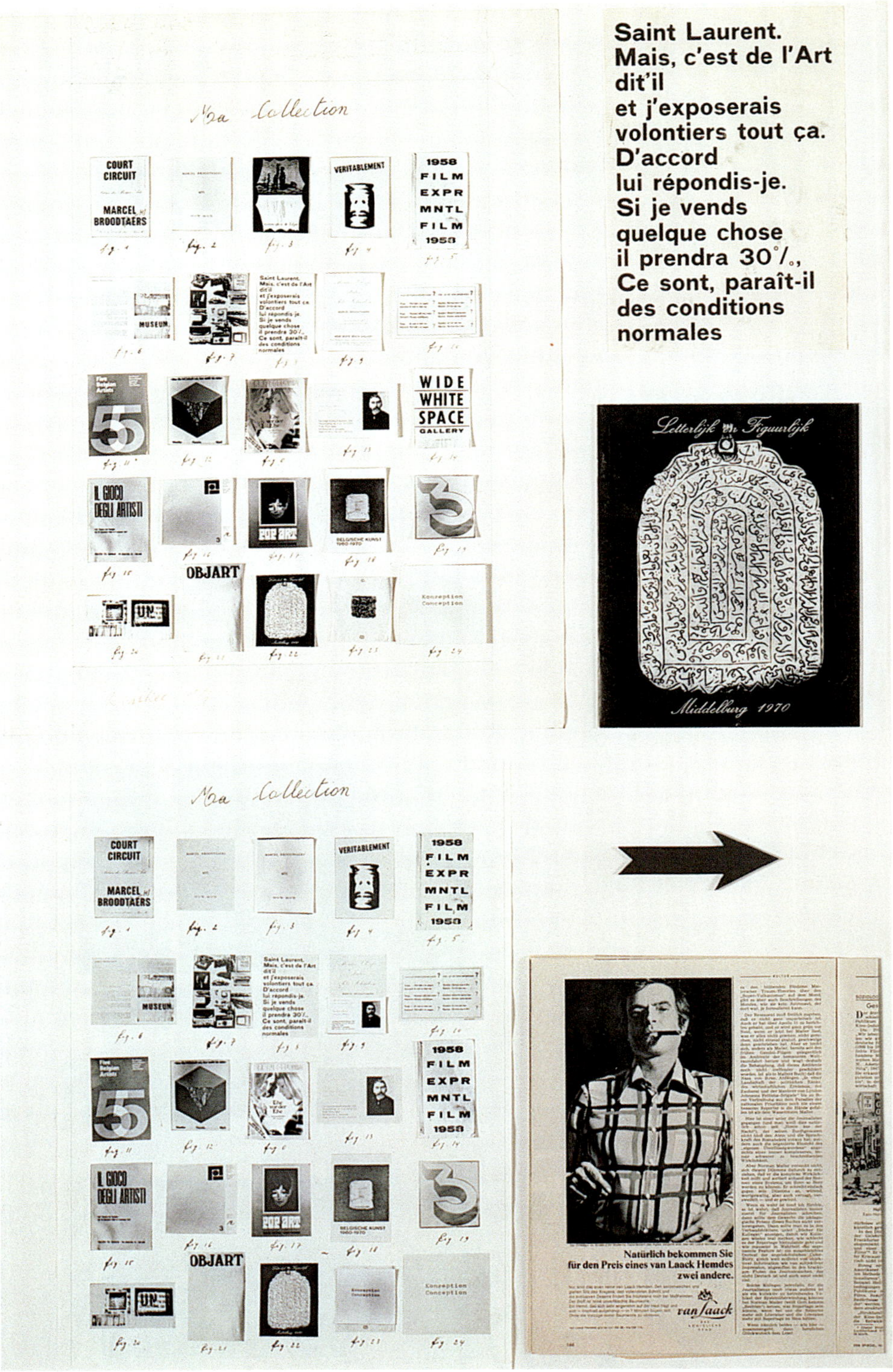
Saint Laurent.
Mais, c'est de l'Art
dit'il
et j'exposerais
volontiers tout ça.
D'accord
lui répondis-je.
Si je vends
quelque chose
il prendra 30°/。,
Ce sont, paraît-il
des conditions
normales
Ma Collection
COURT CIRCUIT
MARCEL BROODTAERS
VERITABLEMENT
1958 FILM EXPR MNTL FILM 1958
MUSEUM
WIDE WHITE SPACE GALLERY
Five Belgian Artists
IL GIOCO DEGLI ARTISTI
POP ART
BELGISCHE KUNST 1960-1970
OBJART
Konzeption Conception
Letterlijk en Figuurlijk
Middelburg 1970
Ma Collection
Natürlich bekommen Sie
für den Preis eines van Laack Hemdes
zwei andere.
van Laack

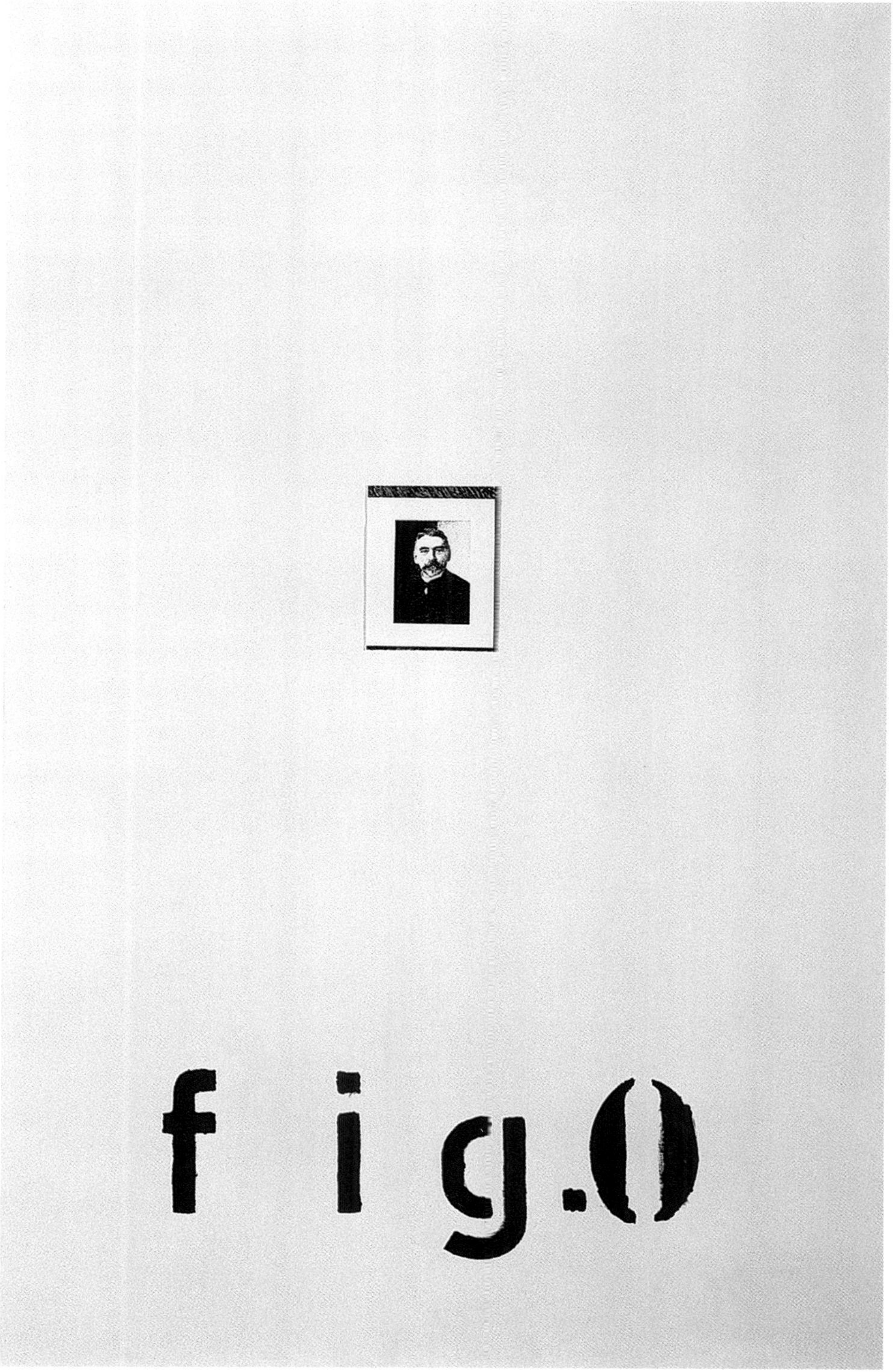
fig.0

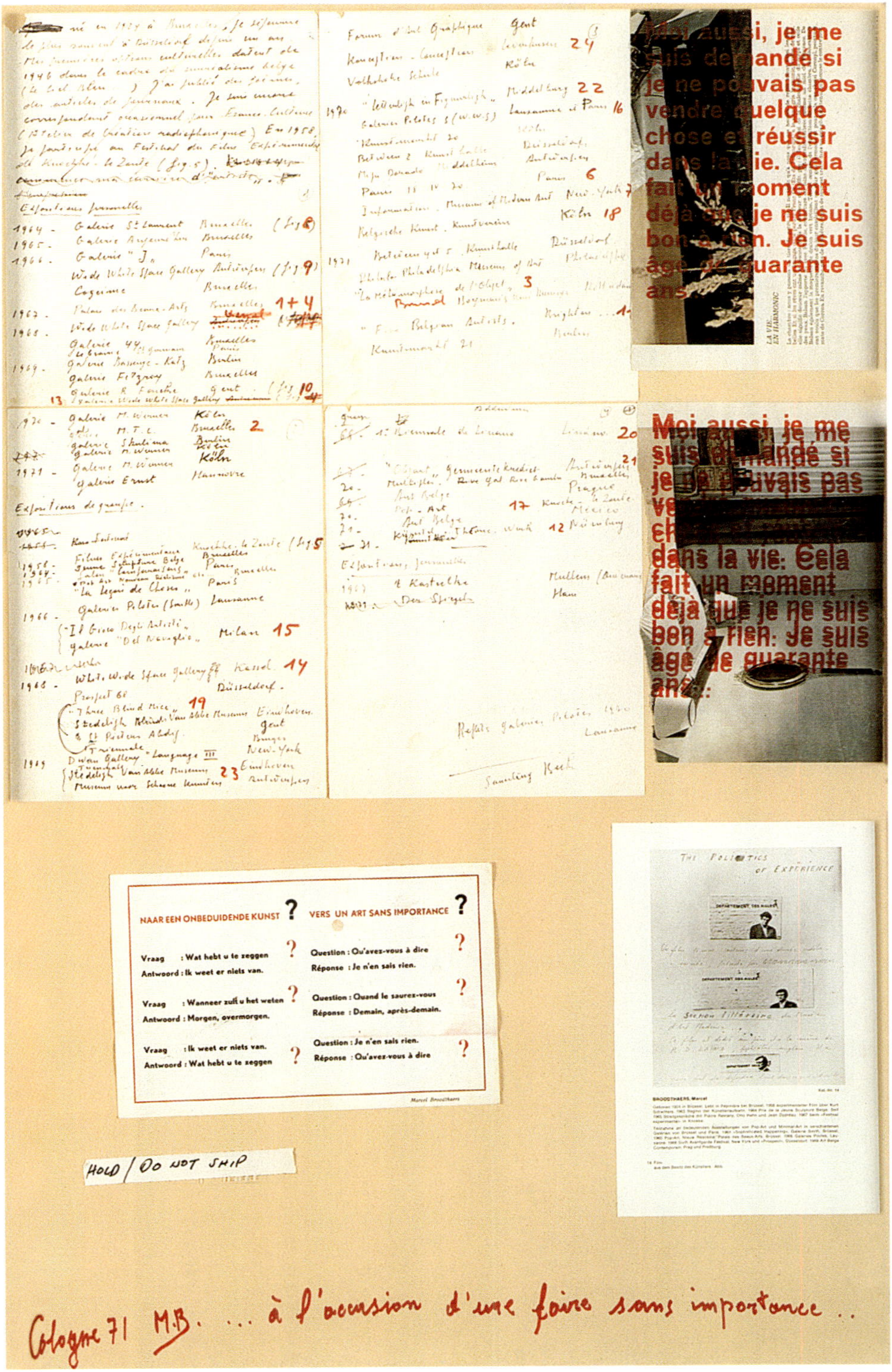
Moi aussi, je me suis demandé si je ne pouvais pas vendre quelque chose et réussir dans la vie. Cela fait un moment déjà que je ne suis bon à rien. Je suis âgé de quarante ans.
NAAR EEN ONBEDUIDENDE KUNST ?
VERS UN ART SANS IMPORTANCE ?
Vraag : Wat hebt u te zeggen ?
Antwoord : Ik weet er niets van.
Question : Qu'avez-vous à dire ?
Réponse : Je n'en sais rien.
Vraag : Wanneer zult u het weten ?
Antwoord : Morgen, overmorgen.
Question : Quand le saurez-vous ?
Réponse : Demain, après-demain.
Vraag : Ik weet er niets van.
Antwoord : Wat hebt u te zeggen ?
Question : Je n'en sais rien.
Réponse : Qu'avez-vous à dire ?
Marcel Broodthaers
THE POLITICS OF EXPERIENCE
DEPARTEMENT DES AIGLES
BROODTHAERS, Marcel
HOLD / DO NOT SHIP
Cologne 71 M.B. ... à l'occasion d'une foire sans importance ..

Robert Filliou

Trois jeux: Apollinaire, Rimbaud, Baudelaire, 1961

[cat. 59]

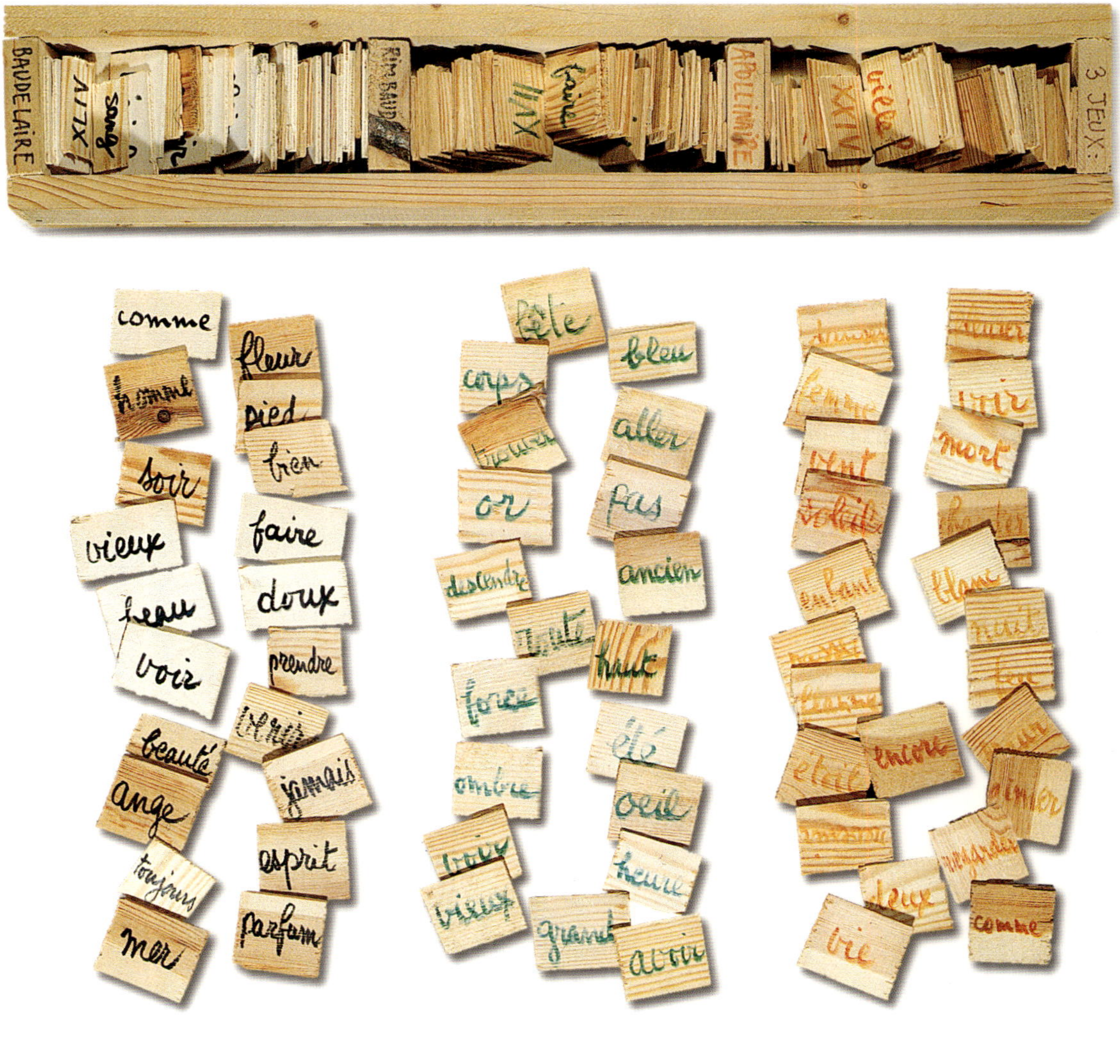
BAUDELAIRE
RIMBAUD
APOLLINAIRE
3 JEUX:
comme
fleur
pied
soir
vieux
faire
beau
doux
voir
prendre
beauté
jamais
ange
esprit
toujours
parfum
mer
bleu
corps
aller
or
pas
descendre
ancien
haut
force
été
ombre
oeil
heure
vieux
grand
avoir
femme
mort
enfant
encore
vie
comme

View of the exhibition rooms. In the centre, Jorge Oteiza, *Desocupación no cúbica del espacio*, 1958–1959 [cat. 45]; behind, from left to right, Marcel Broodthaers, *Série de neuf tableaux*, 1972 [cat. 56]; *Figures*, 1973 [cat. 57].

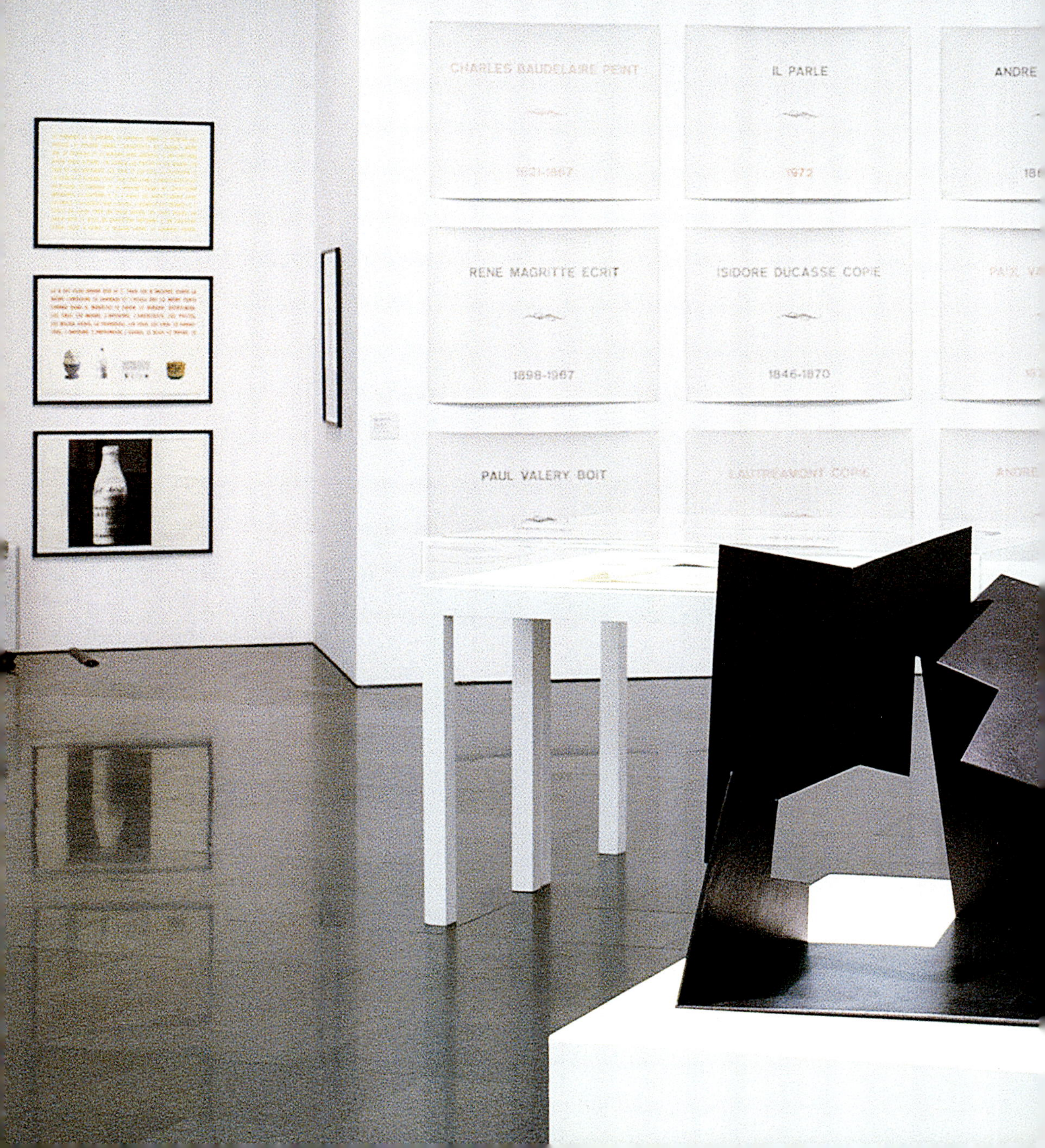

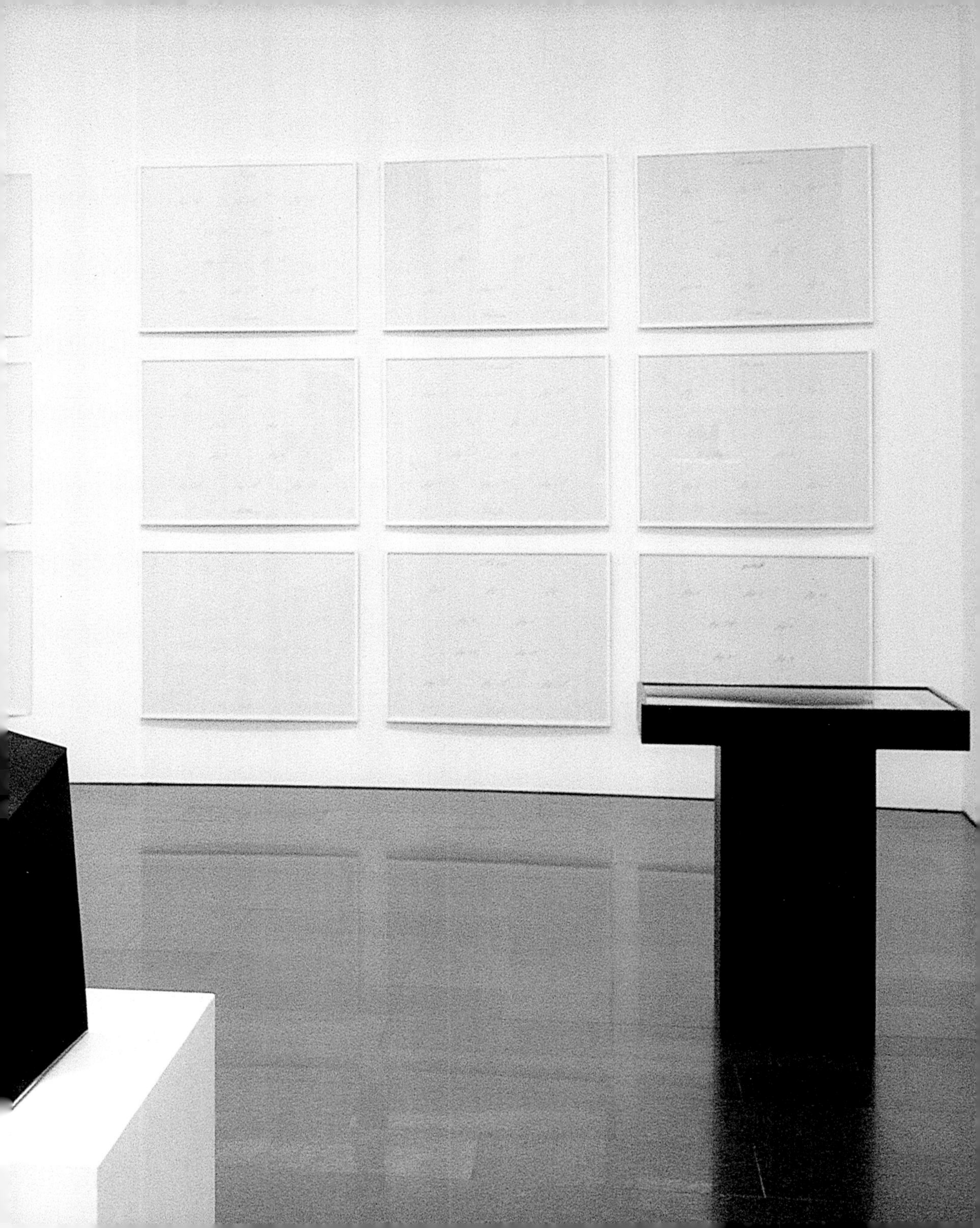

Naum Gabo
Spheric Theme: Black Variation, 1937
[cat. 46]

Next two double pages:
Stéphane Mallarmé
Poem *Un coup de dés,* 1895

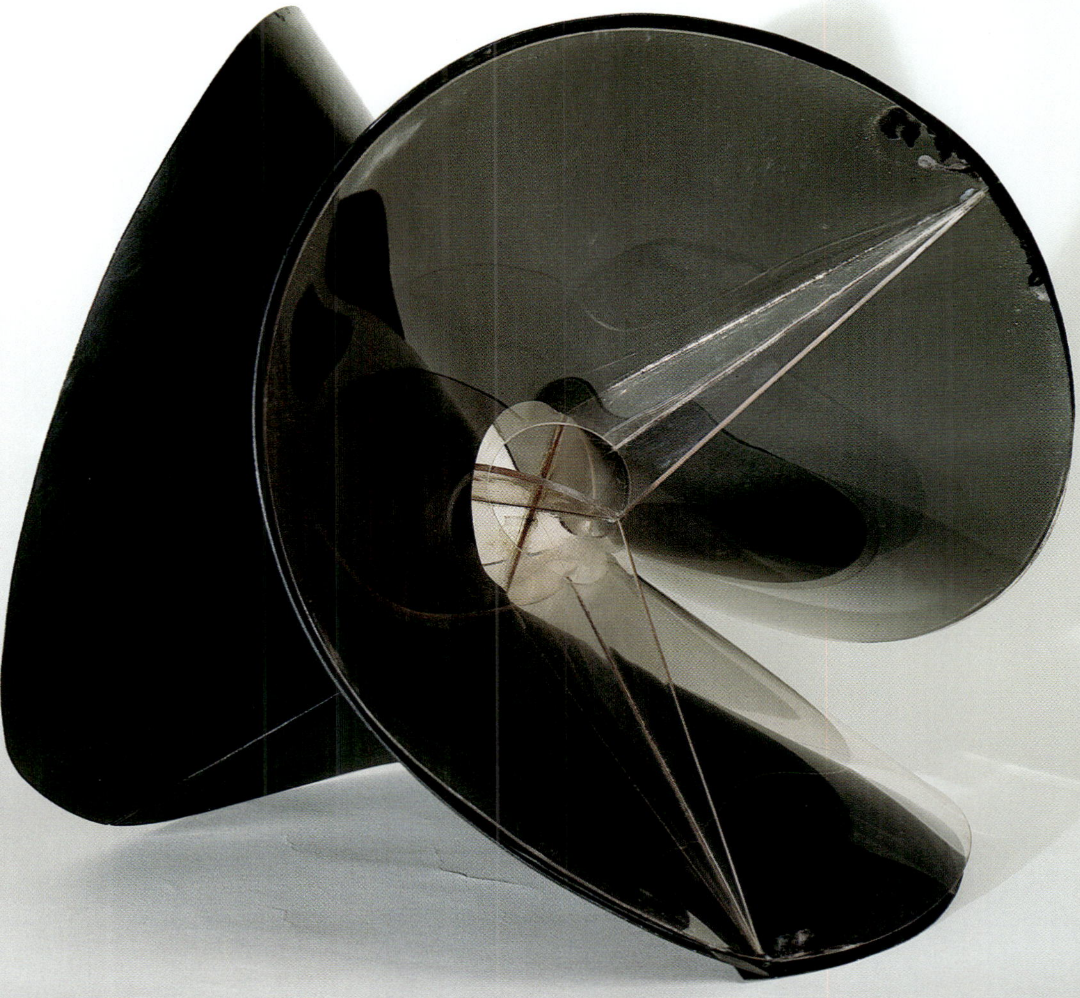

A THROW OF THE DICE

NEVER

WHEN EVEN INDEED CAST. IN CIRCUMSTANCES
OF ETERNITY

FROM THE DEPTH OF A SHIPWRECK

BE

that

the Abyss

blanched
slackwater
raging
slanted
glides despairingly even
some wing

its own

be-

forehand fallen back from incapacity to trim the flight
and covering what foams
cutting back what soars

most inwardly resumes

the shadow buried within the deep by this alternative sail

to the point of fitting
to wing-span

its yawning deep in so far forth as the shell

of a ship

listed to one or th'other board...

Odilon Redon

L'Enfant à l'arc-en-ciel, 1898. Illustration for *Un coup de dés*, poem by Stéphane Mallarmé, project of edition by Ambroise Vollard interrupted by Mallarmé's death
[cat. 49]

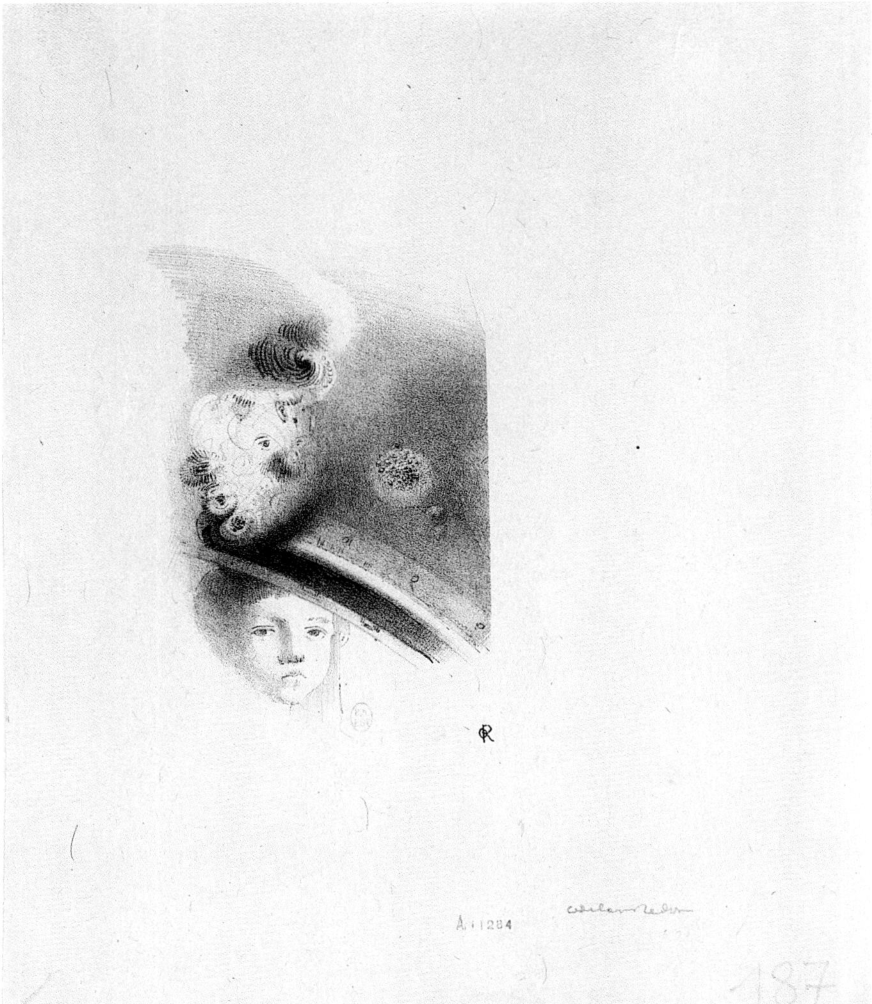

Odilon Redon

La Femme au hennin, 1898. Illustration for *Un coup de dés*, poem by Stéphane Mallarmé, project of edition by Ambroise Vollard interrupted by Mallarmé's death

[cat. 48]

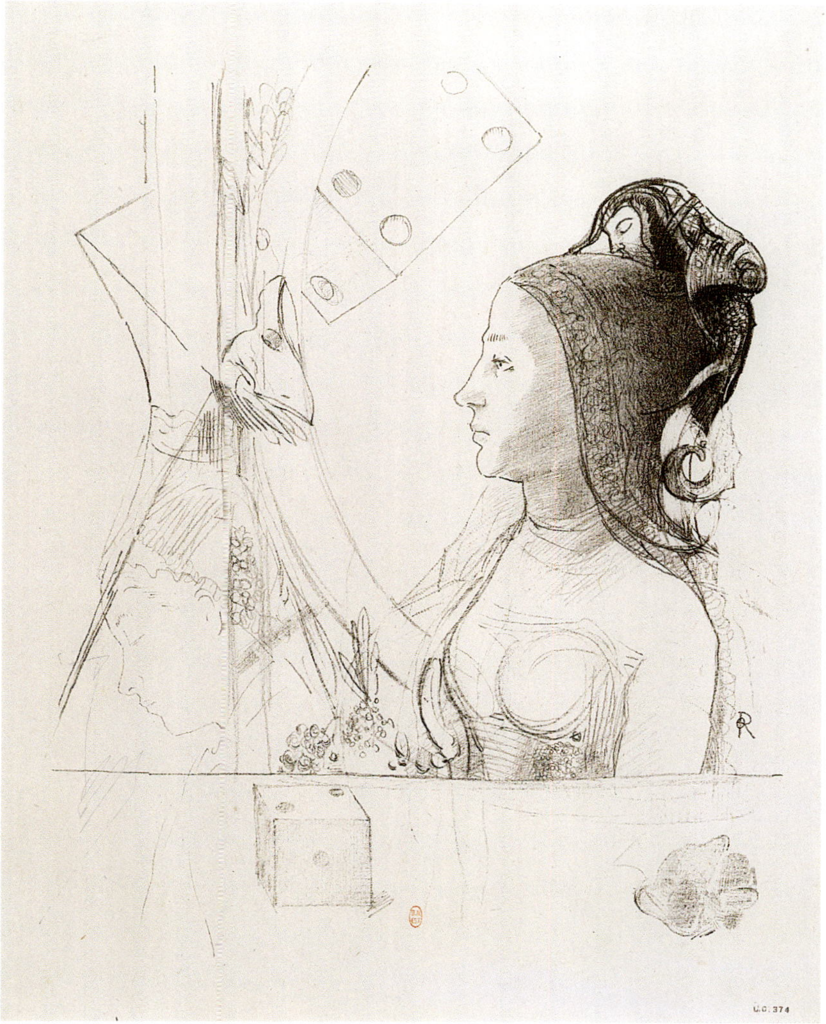

Lace passes into nothingness,
With the ultimate Gamble in doubt,
In blasphemy revealing just
Eternal absence of any bed.

This concordant enmity
Of a white garland and the same,
In flight against the pallid glass,
Hovers and does not enshroud.

But where, limned gold, the dreamers dwells,
There sleeps a mournful mandola,
Its deep lacuna source of song,

Of a kind that toward some window,
Formed by that belly or none at all,
Filial, one might have been born.

Stéphane Mallarmé
"Une dentelle s'abolit...," *La Revue indépendante,* 1887

Georges Braque
La Mandore, 1909-1910
[cat. 788]

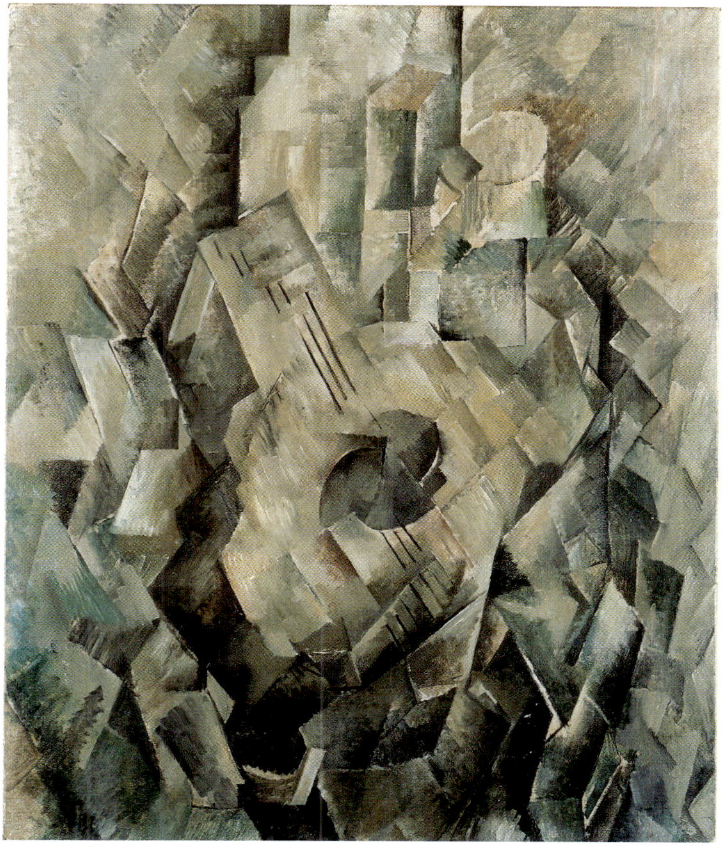

The point of departure is nothingness, a harmony in which words go further, have a meaning. When one arrives in this intellectual nothingness, this "Hollow Musical Nothingness" as Mallarmé wrote, then one is in Painting.

Georges Braque
Les Peintres vous parlent, 1964

Pablo Picasso

Mur de l'atelier du 242 bd Raspail, 1912
[cat. 148]

Bouteille, journal et verre sur une table ("Un coup de thé"), 1912
[cat. 50]

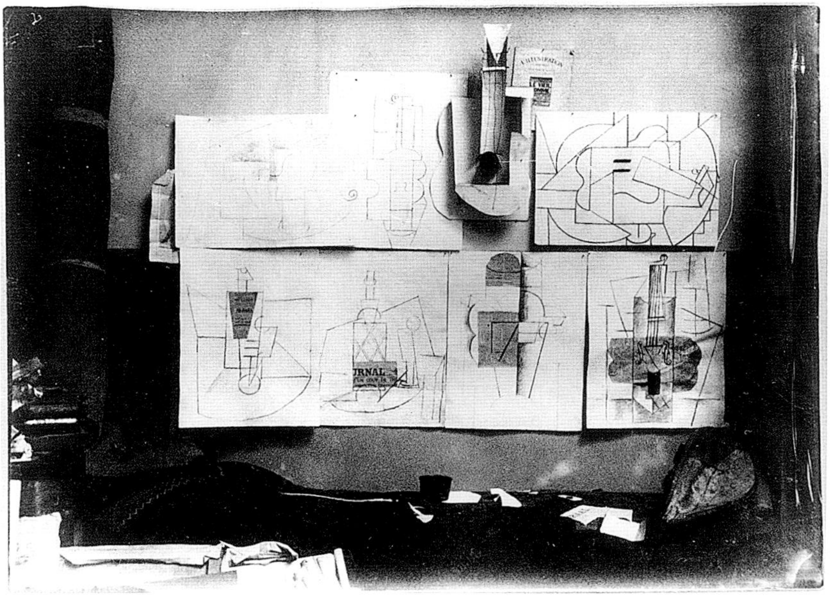

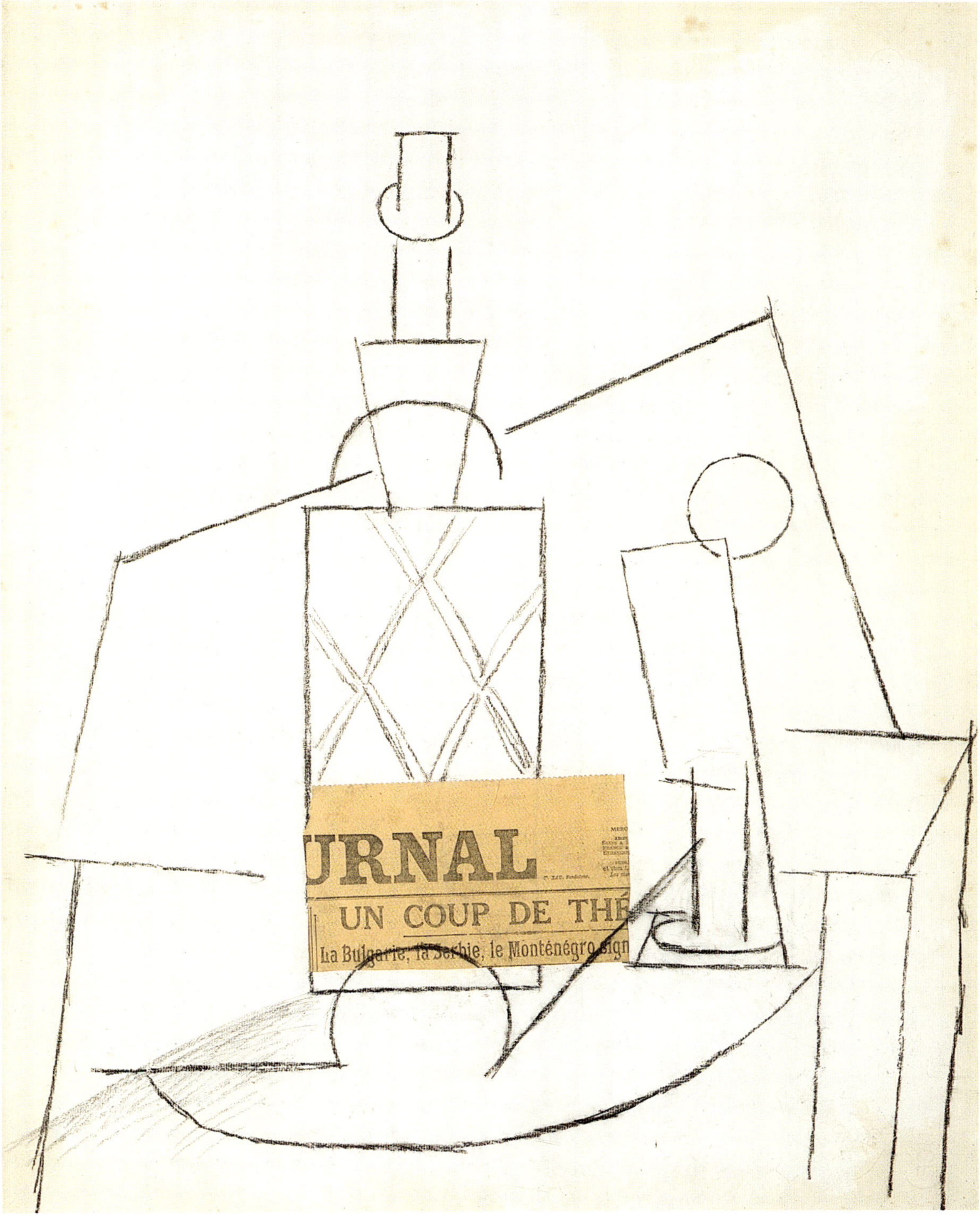
URNAL
UN COUP DE THÉ
La Bulgarie, la Serbie, le Monténégro sign

A nothingness resolving into infinity after transit through the finite, the concrete and the immediate; music founded in nothingness – we are struck by the sound of the syllables before we grasp their meaning; a music so lovely you want, deem, wish yourself fated its son, created its son, its presence signifying and symbolising the very image of creation from zero: in nothingness no sound, yet sound there is, because like nothingness and nothing the music still resounds, because everything seems born of nothing, because where there is nothing there is first of all sound, because the sound can still be born, and the music is also the image of the harmony and the numbers governing all creation.
In Mallarmé there exists an aesthetics of a transcendental poetry and of poetry itself – yet also, in an overt, willed, utterly conscious way, the idea of several concrete realities, present and presented at the same time.

Antonin Artaud
Handwritten note on the back of a page of
Heliogabalus, or the Crowned Anarchist, 1933

Ferdinand Hodler

Le Lac de Thoune et le massif du Stockhorn, 1912

[cat. 52]

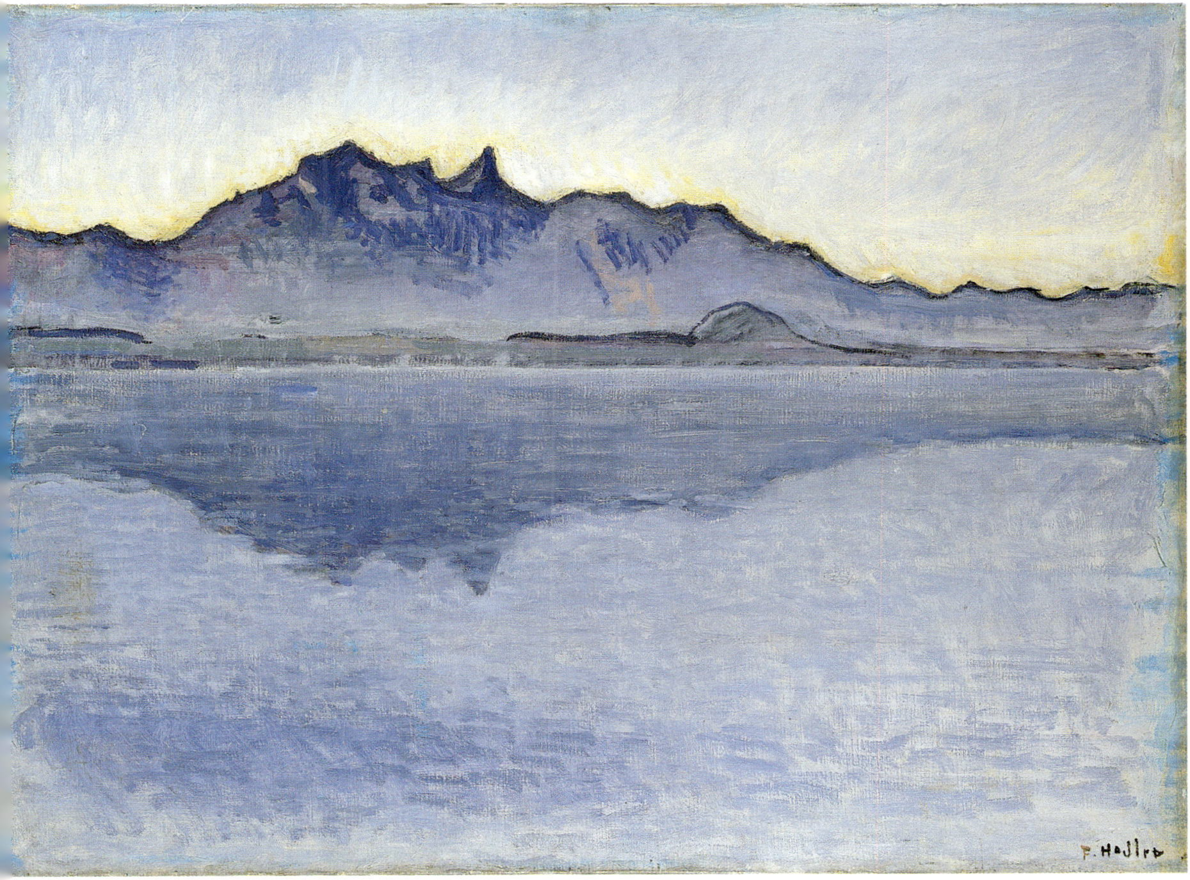

Édouard Manet

La Chaise, 1875. Illustration for *Le Corbeau. The Raven,*
poem by Edgar A. Poe, translation into French by Stéphane Mallarmé
[cat. 54]

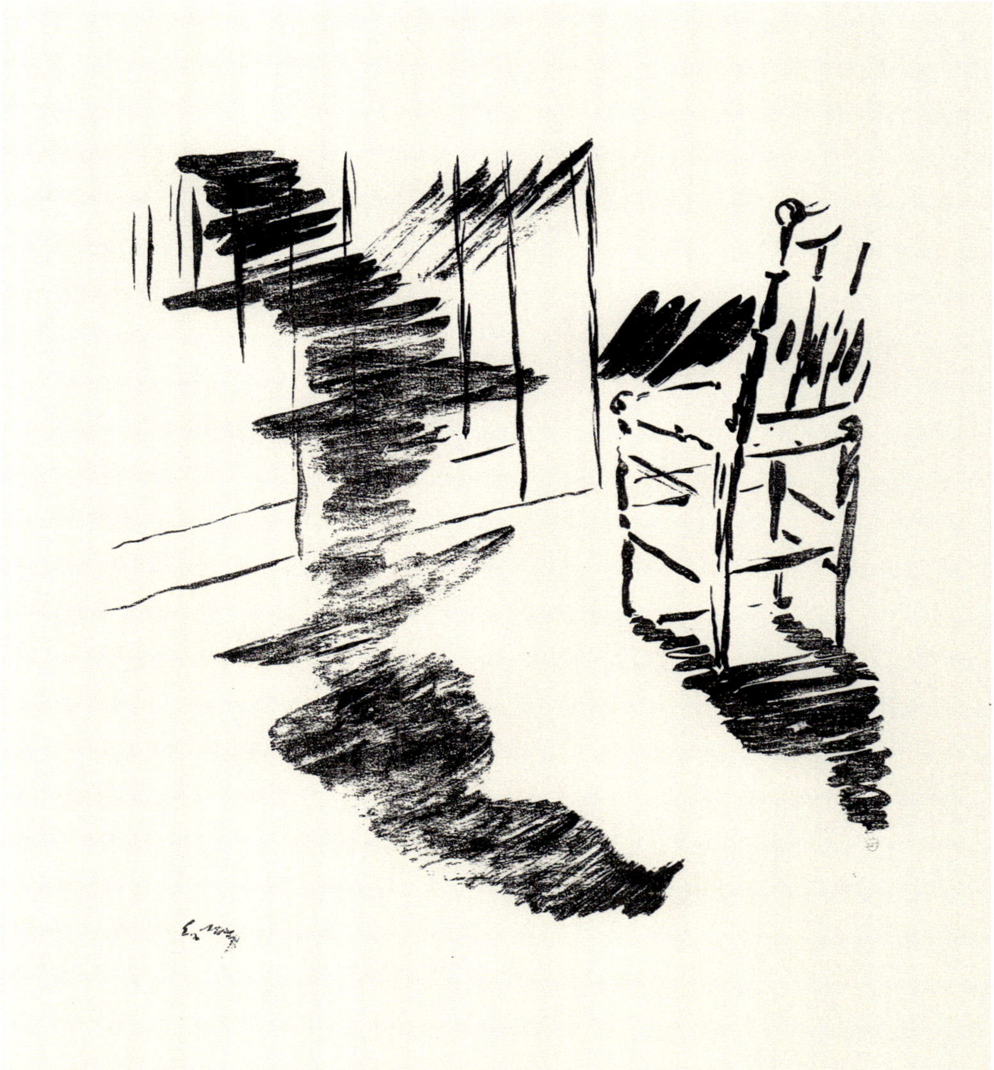

Frantisek Kupka

La Dormeuse, 1909-1910. Illustrations for *La Dormeuse,* story by Edgar A. Poe

[cat. 62]

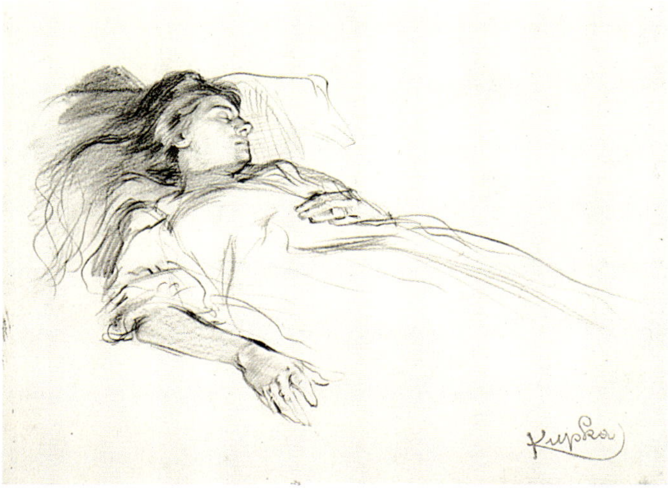

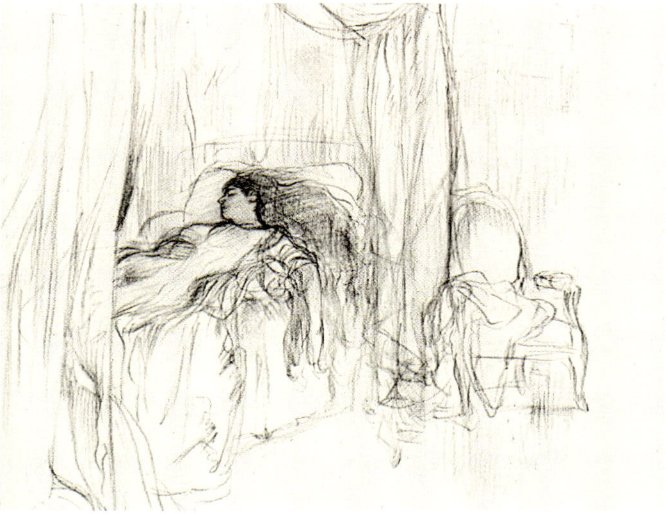

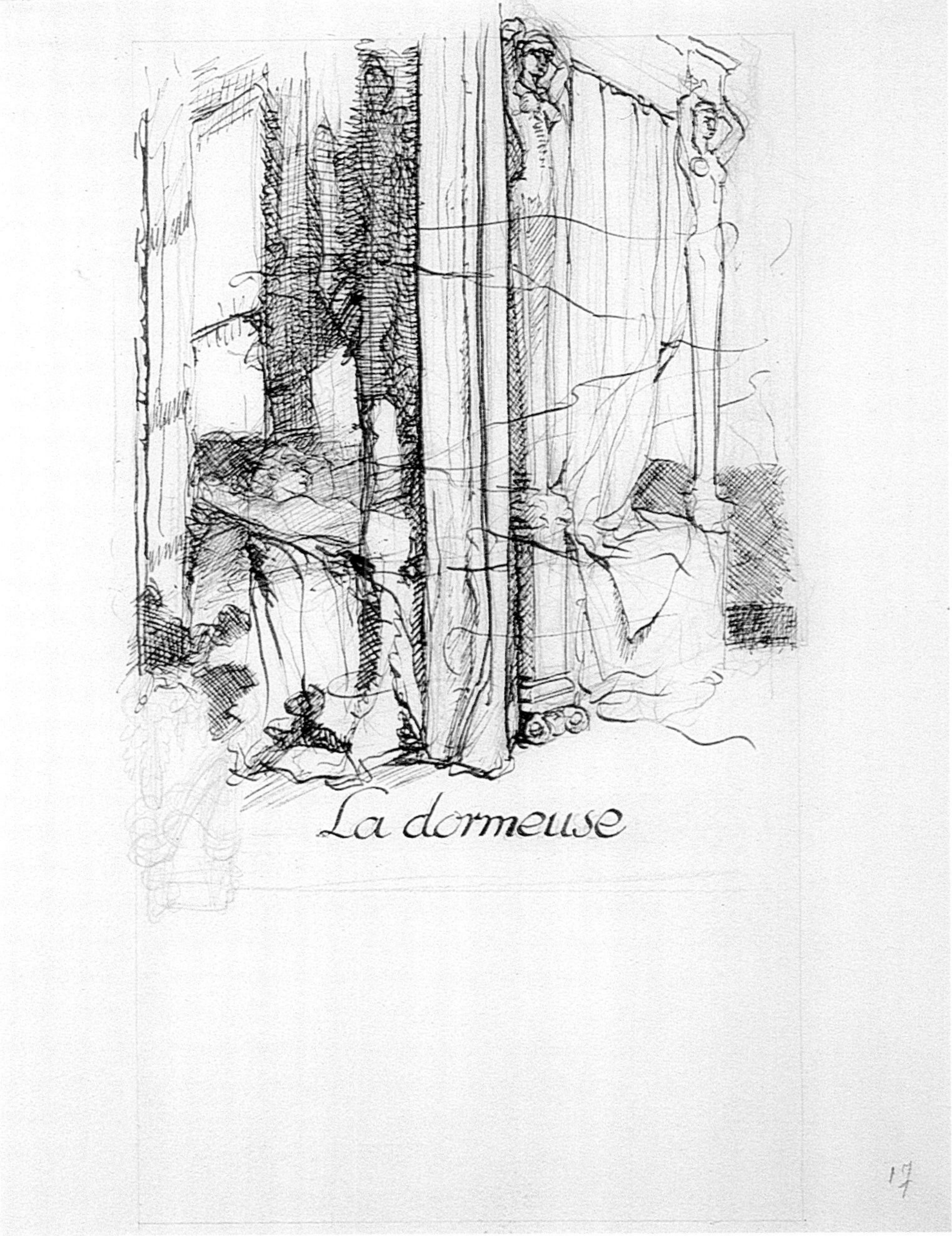
La dormeuse
17

Odilon Redon

Quadrige, n.d.

[cat. 68]

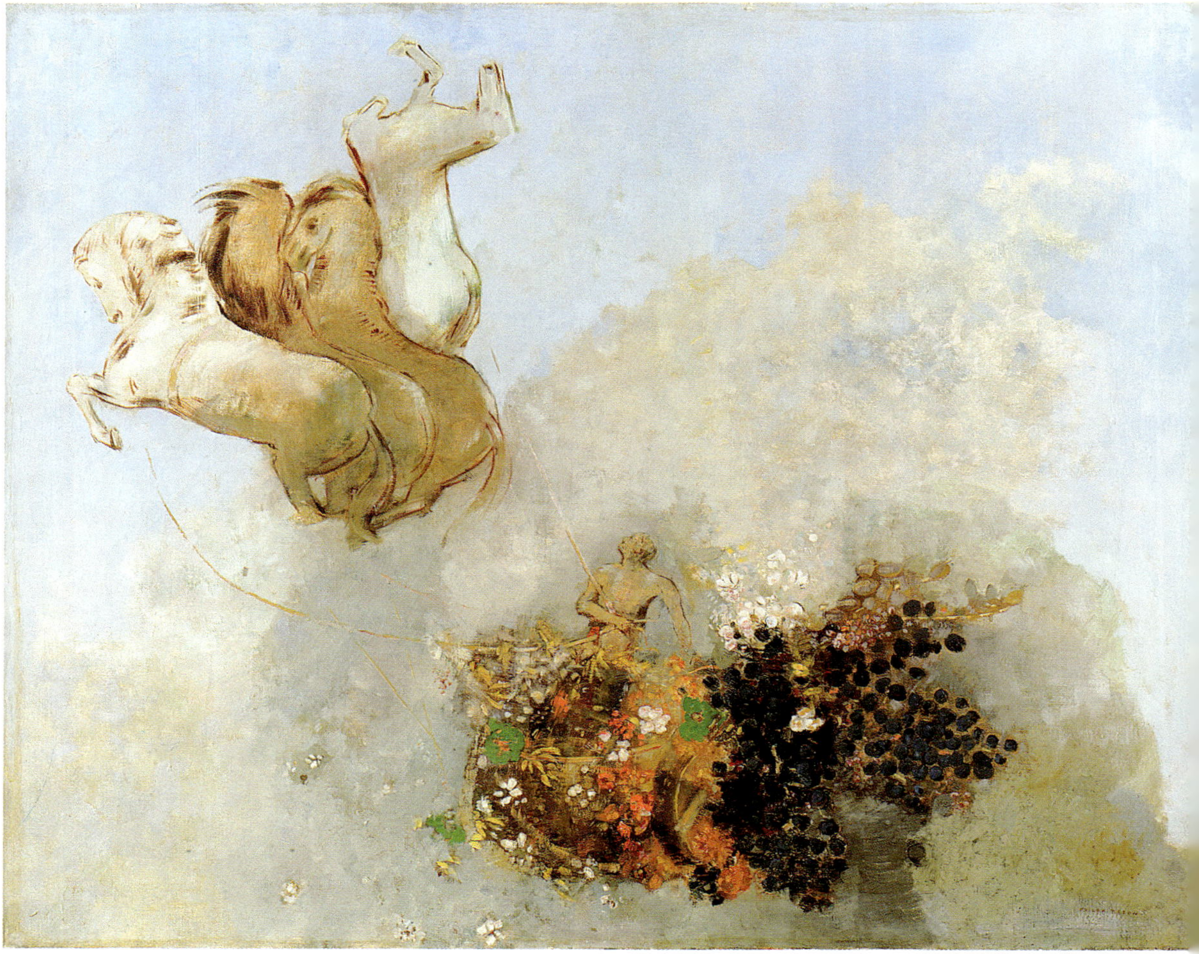

Odilon Redon

Tête d'Orphée sur la lyre, 1880

[cat. 69]

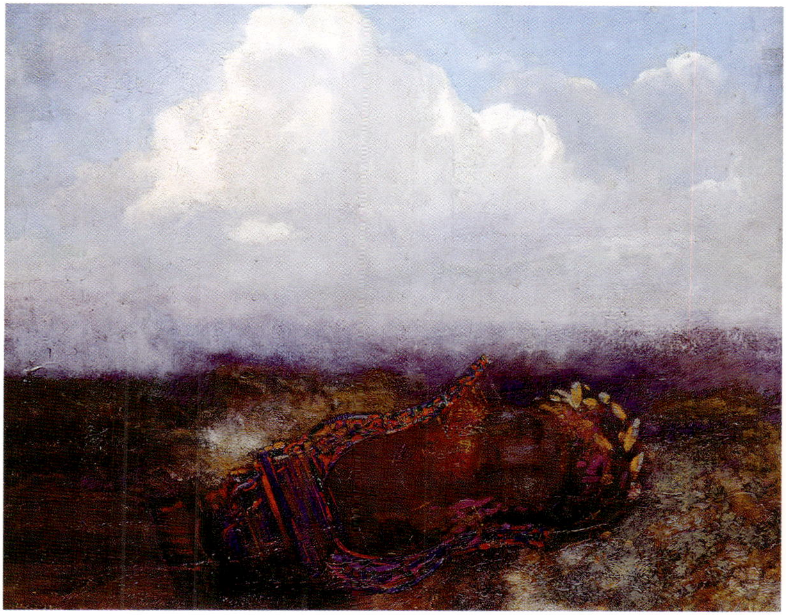

Max Ernst
Hommage à Rimbaud, 1961
[cat. 84]

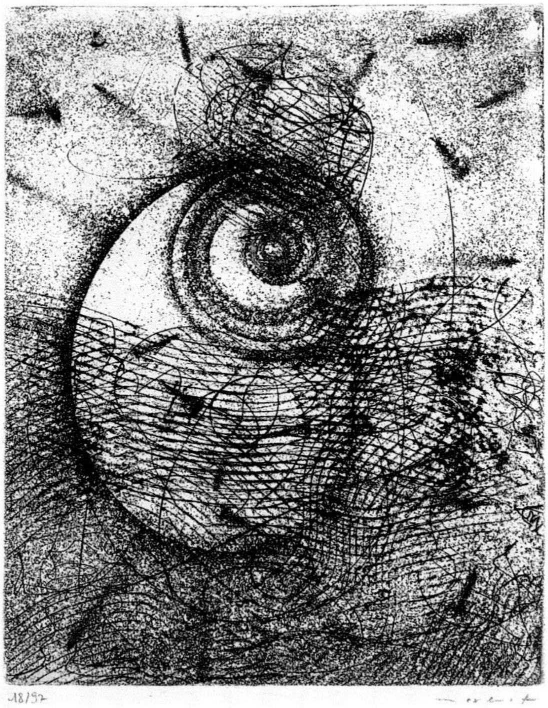

The sphere is the perfect form. The sun is the perfect star. Nothing in us is as perfect as the head, ever raised towards the sun and striving towards its form; and if not the head, the eye, the mirror of that star it so resembles.

Alfred Jarry
Les Minutes de sable mémorial, 1894

Odilon Redon
"Antoine: Quel est le but de tout cela? Le diable: Il n'y a pas de but!",
album *La Tentation de saint Antoine*, text by Gustave Flaubert, 1896
[cat. 66]

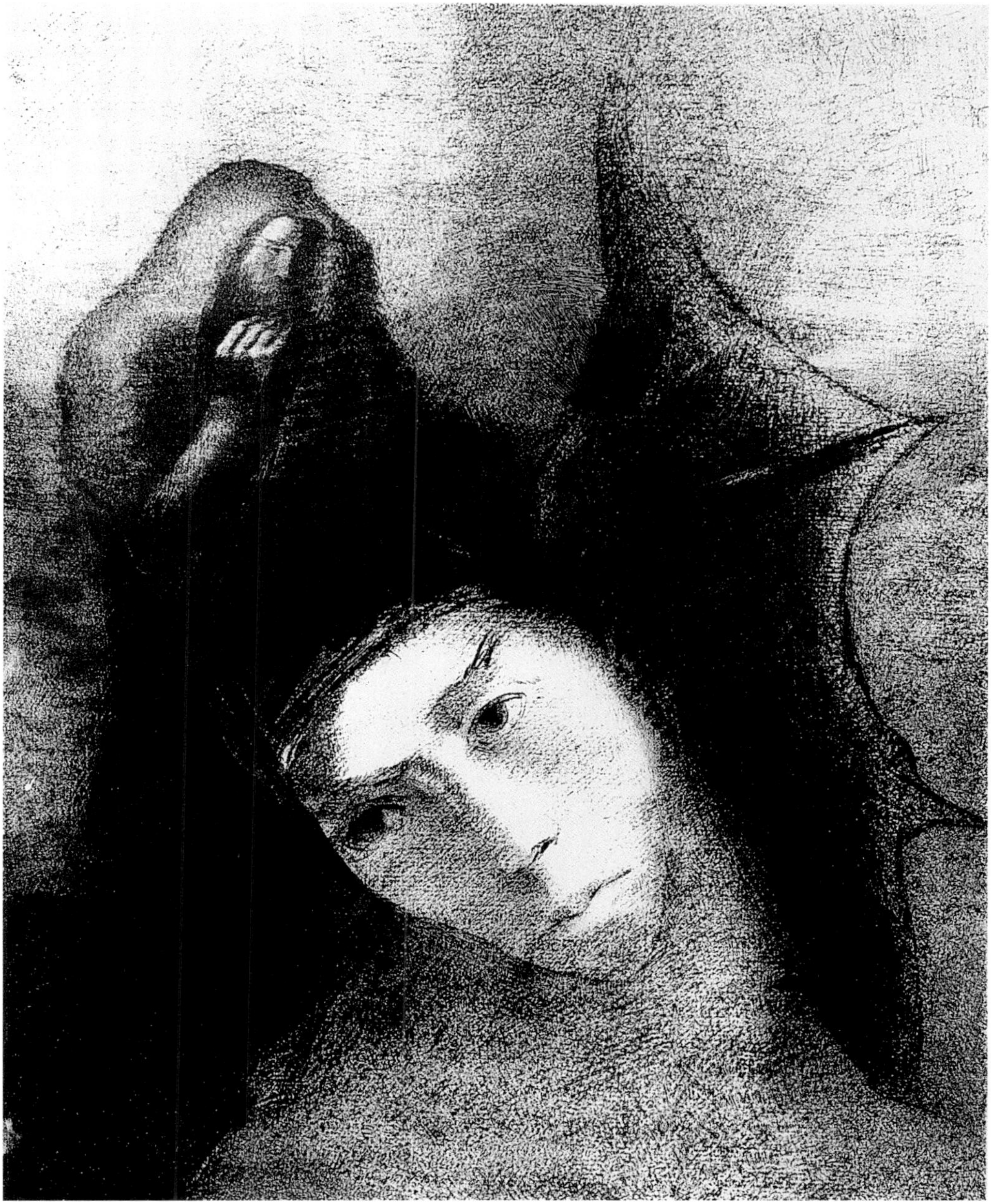

Günter Brus

Redon: die heilige Qual, Bild-Dichtung (I), 1981-1982

[cat. 70]

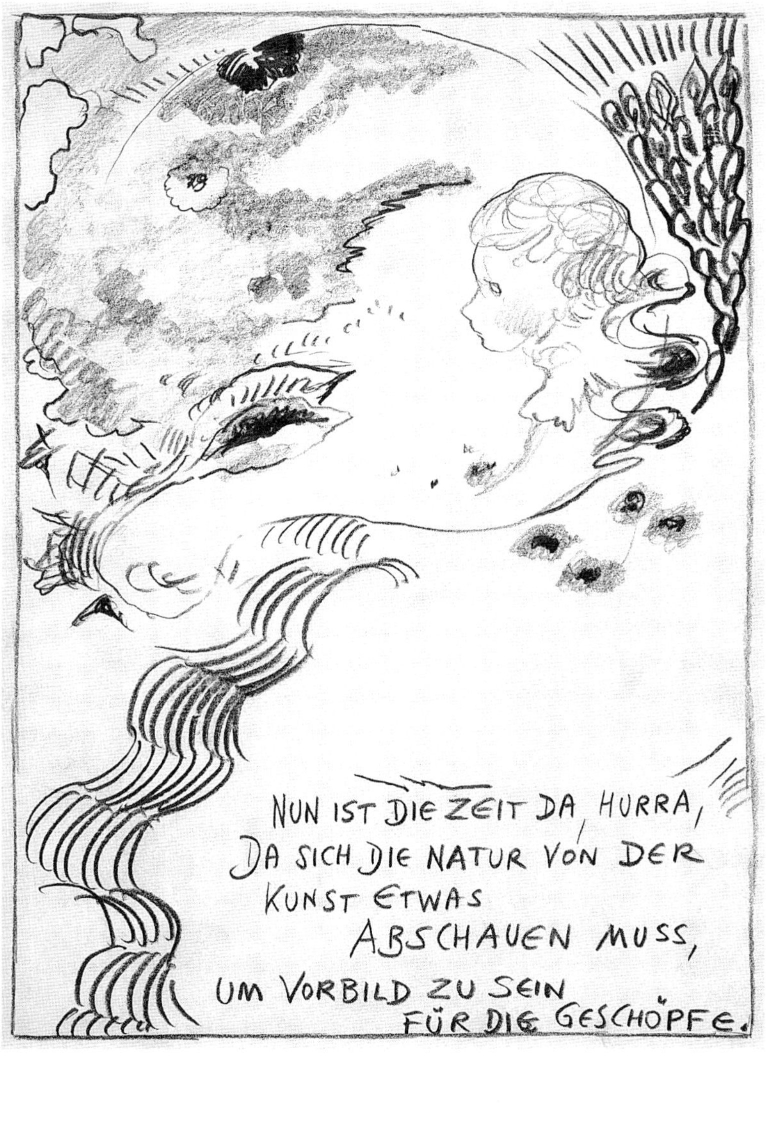

Günter Brus

Redon: die heilige Qual, Bild-Dichtung (XIII), 1981-1982

[cat. 70]

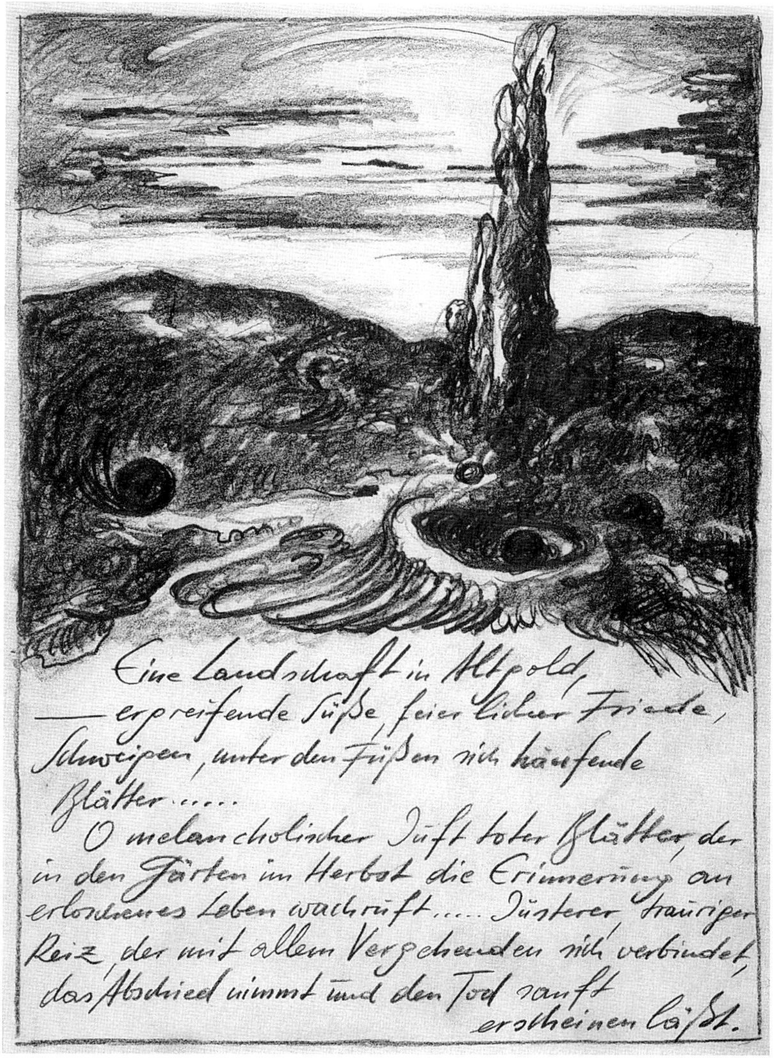

Erik Satie

Fragment of the score of *Airs à faire fuir,* 1897

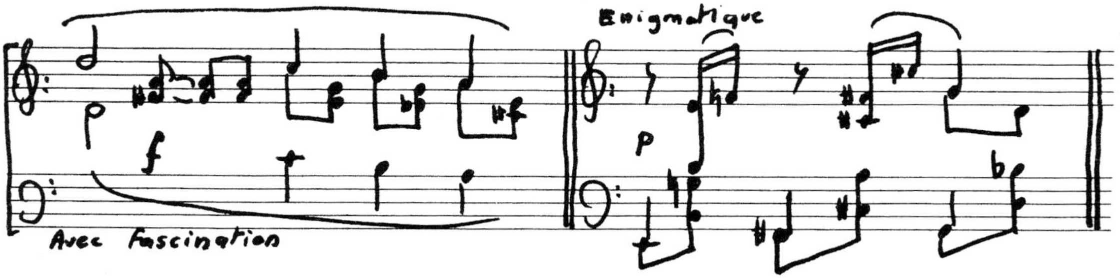

Marcel Duchamp
Étude pour Moulin à café, 1911
[cat. 108]

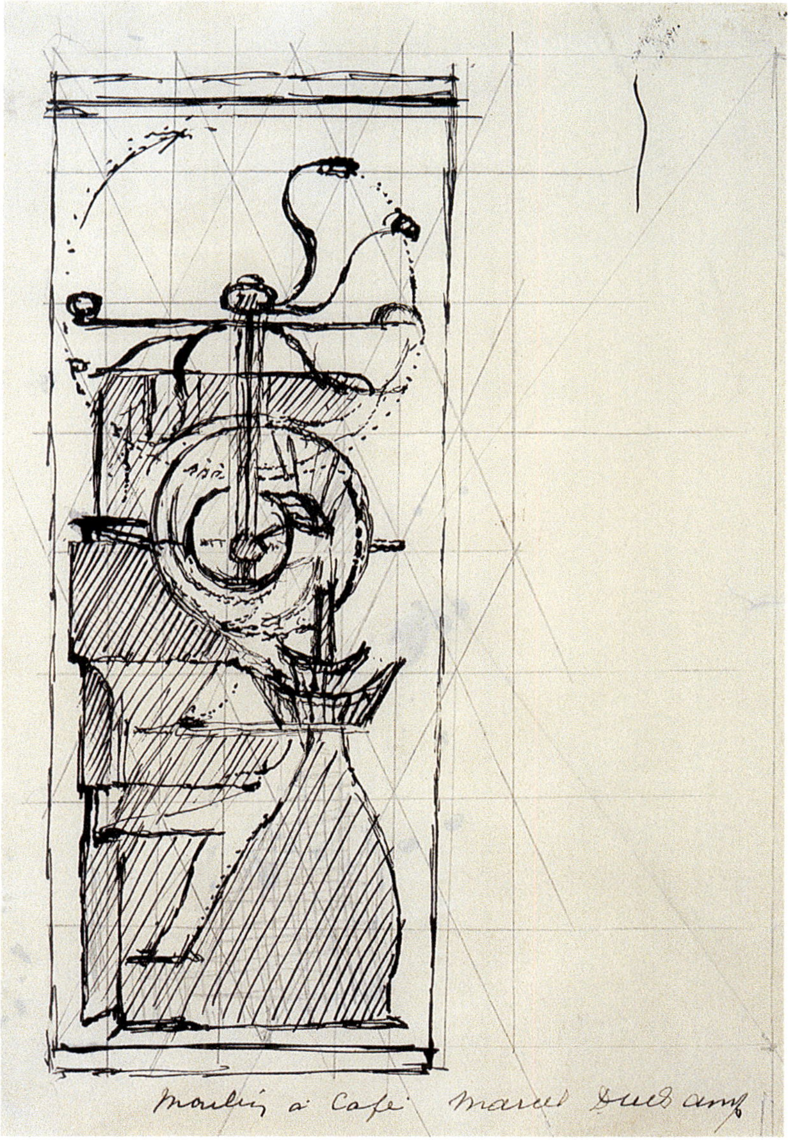

Marcel Duchamp
Obligation Monte-Carlo, 1924
[cat. 107]

Giacomo Balla
Mercurio passa davanti al sole visto dal cannocchiale, 1914
[cat. 114]

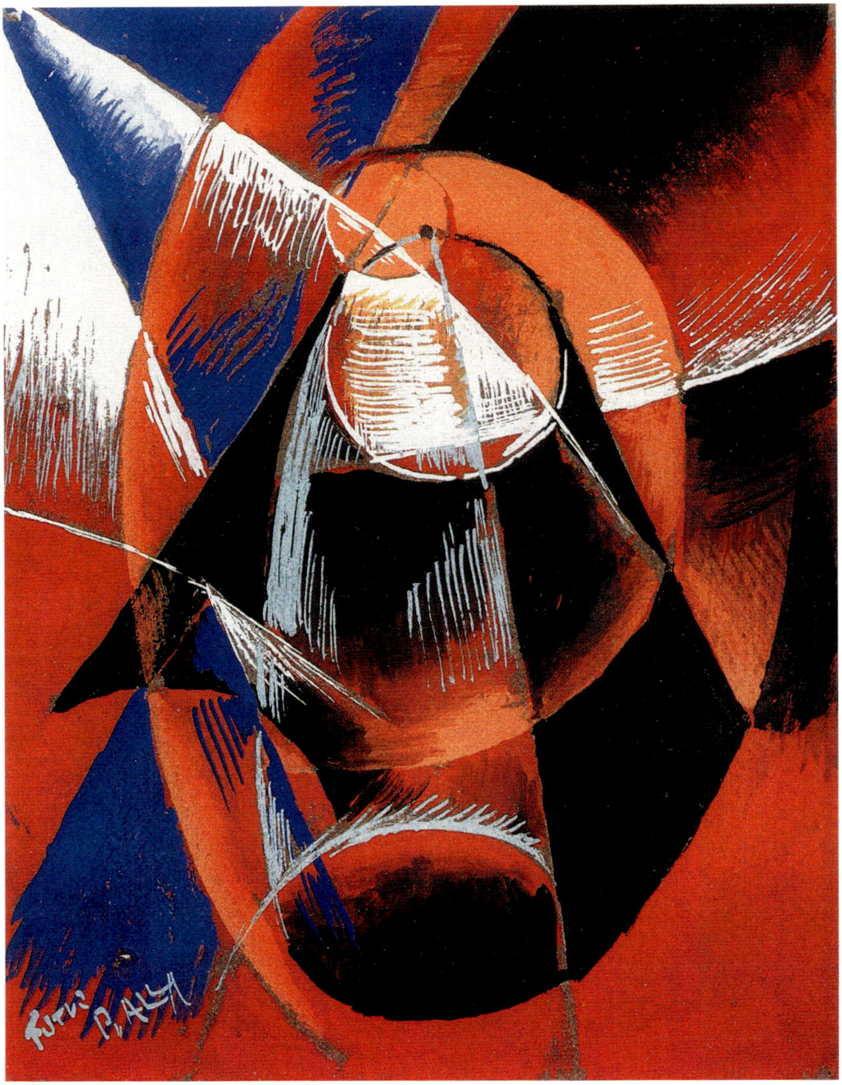

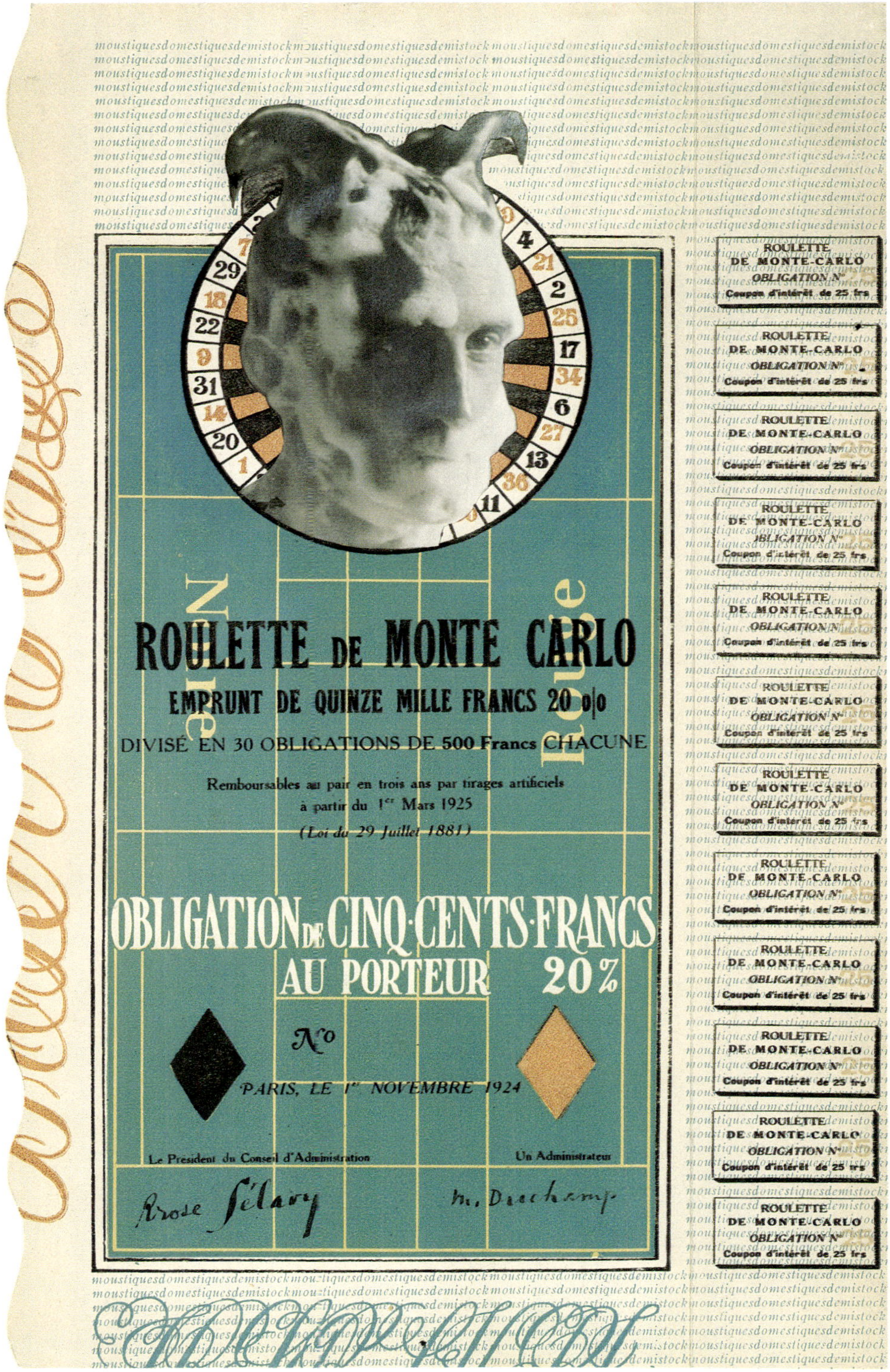
moustiquesdomestiquesdemistock
ROULETTE DE MONTE CARLO
EMPRUNT DE QUINZE MILLE FRANCS 20 o/o
DIVISÉ EN 30 OBLIGATIONS DE 500 Francs CHACUNE
Remboursables au pair en trois ans par tirages artificiels
à partir du 1er Mars 1925
(Loi du 29 Juillet 1881)
Noire
Rouge
OBLIGATION DE CINQ·CENTS·FRANCS
AU PORTEUR 20%
No
PARIS, LE 1er NOVEMBRE 1924
Le Président du Conseil d'Administration
Un Administrateur
Rrose Sélavy
M. Duchamp
ROULETTE DE MONTE-CARLO
OBLIGATION No
Coupon d'intérêt de 25 frs

Guillermo de Torre

Hélices, 1923

[cat. 219]

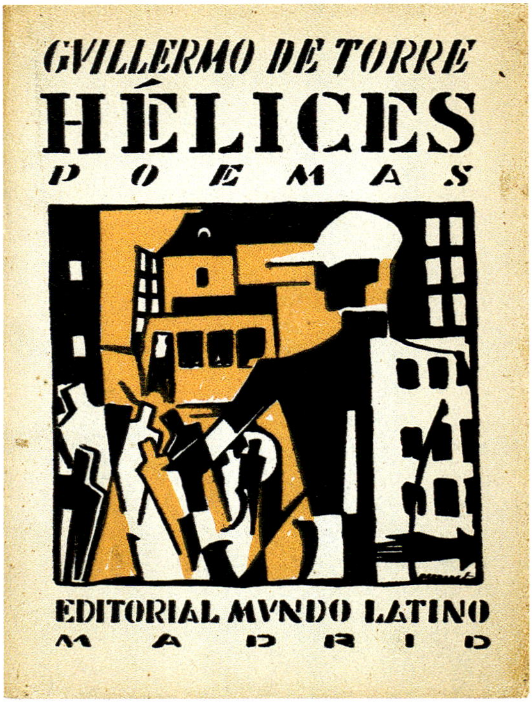

Marcel Duchamp

À Guillermo de Torre, 1927

[cat. 111]

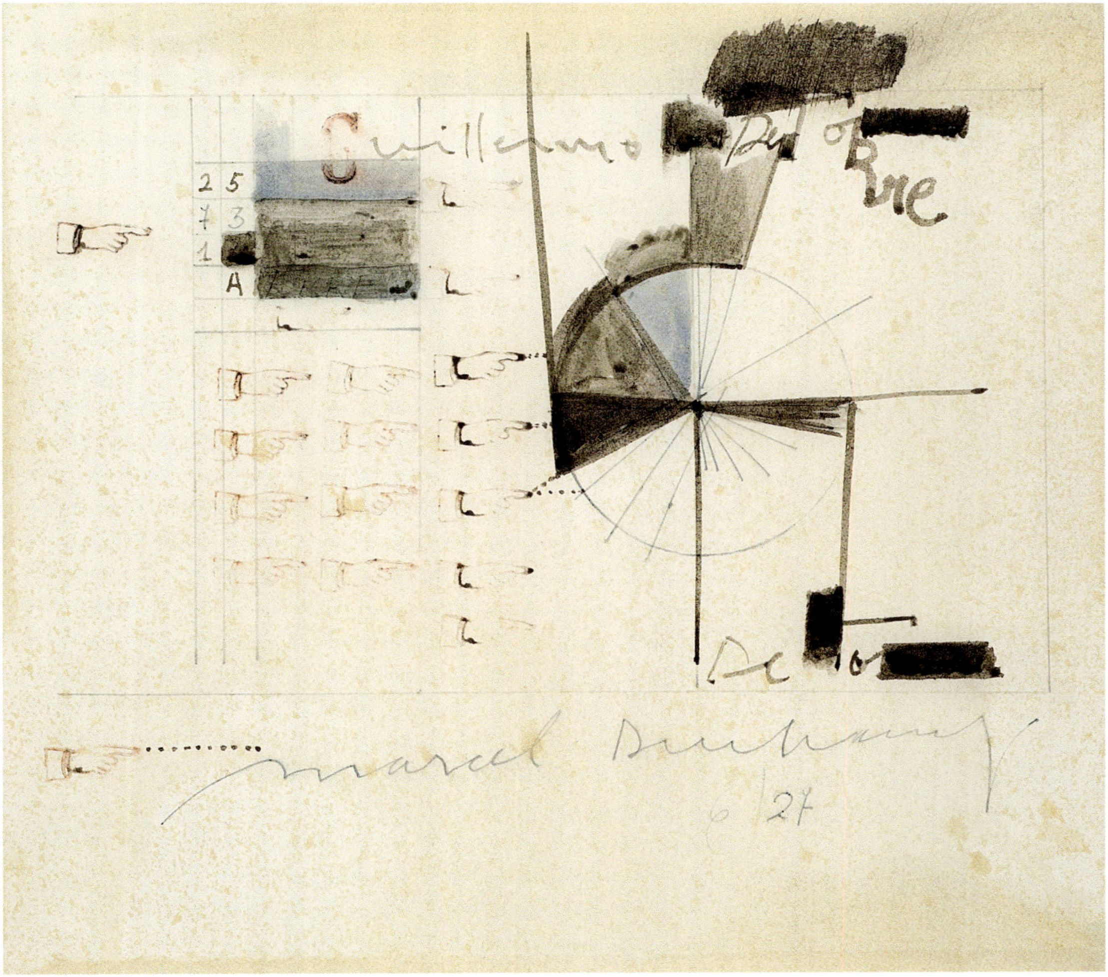

Giacomo Balla
Rumoristica plastica BALTRR, 1914
[cat. 124]

Umberto Boccioni
Dinamismo di un ciclista, 1913
[cat. 113]

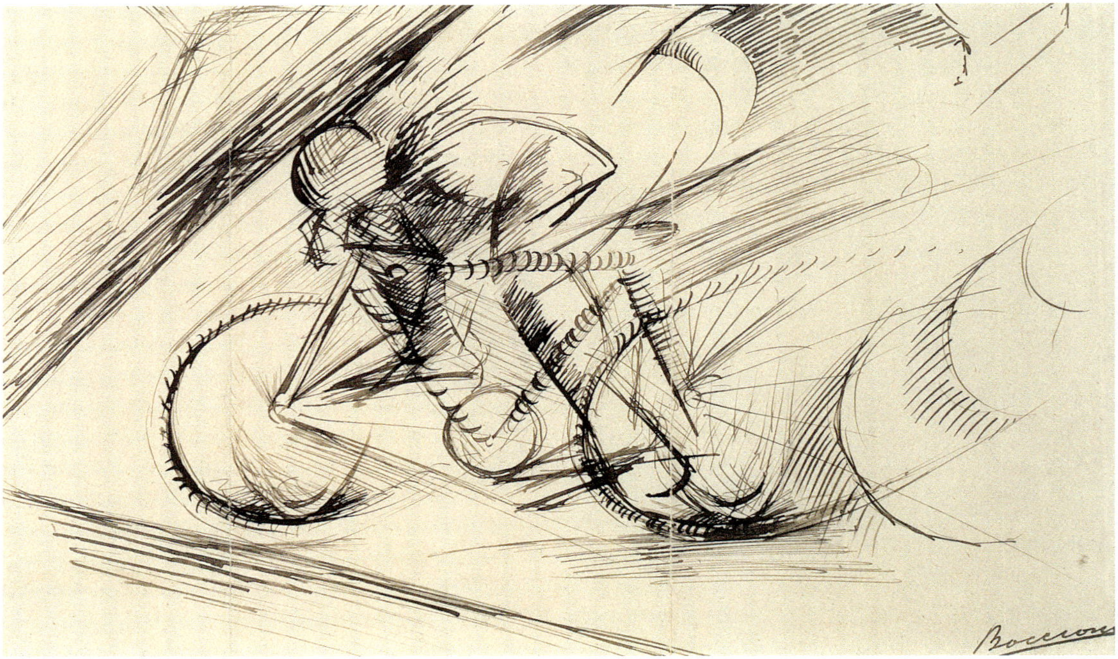

In sculpture all my convictions force me to investigate, not pure form, but *pure plastic rhythm*; not the construction of bodies, but *the construction of the action of bodies*. I do not have a pyramidal architecture (static state) as an ideal, then, but a spiral architecture (dynamism).

Umberto Boccioni
"Sculpture futuriste," *Première exposition de sculpture futuriste,* 1913

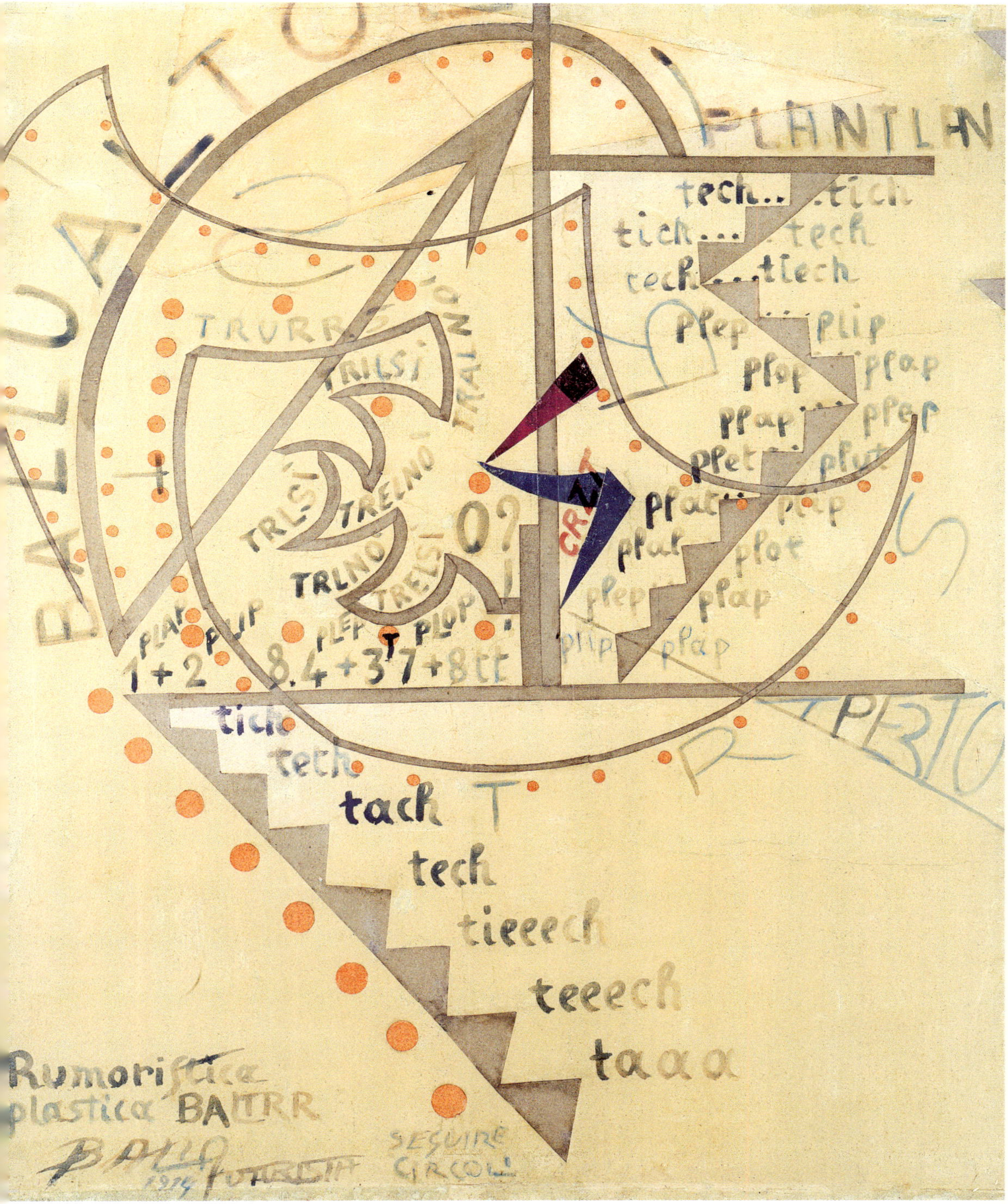
PLANTLAN
tech... tich
tich... tech
tech... tiech
plep... plip
plop... plap
TRURR
TRILSI
TRLSI
TRELNO
TRLNO
0?
plap plip plep plop
1+2
tich
tech
tach
tech
tieeech
teeech
taaa
Rumoristica plastica BALTRR
BALLA
1914
SEGUIRE CIRCOLI

Loïe Fuller. La Danse du Lys, ca. 1902
Photo: W. Isaiah Taber

Loïe Fuller dansant
Photo: Eugène Druet

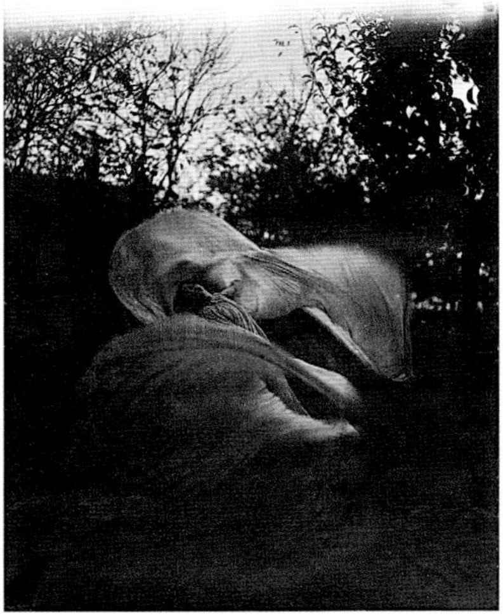

In relation to Loïe Fuller insofar as she spreads, round about, with veils attached to her person by the action of a dance, everything has been said in articles, at times in poems.
Exercise as invention, without employ, admits of an artistic rapture and at the same time an industrial accomplishment.
In the terrific bath of fabrics there swoons, radiant, cold, the dancer who illustrates many a giratory theme in which a distant, fulsome woof tautens, giant petal and butterfly, unfurling, all in a clear-cut and elementary order. Her fusion with swift nuances shedding their hydroxic fantasmagoria of twilight and of grotto, such rapidities of passions, delight, mourning, ire: to move them, prismatic, with violence or diluted, the dizziness is needed of a soul like an airing by an artifice.
That a woman may associate the flying off of vestments with the dance, potent or vast, to the point of sustaining them, infinitely, as her expansion
The lesson depends on this spiritual effect.

Stéphane Mallarmé
"Autre étude de danse. Les Fonds dans le ballet, d'après une indication récente," *National Observer,* 1893

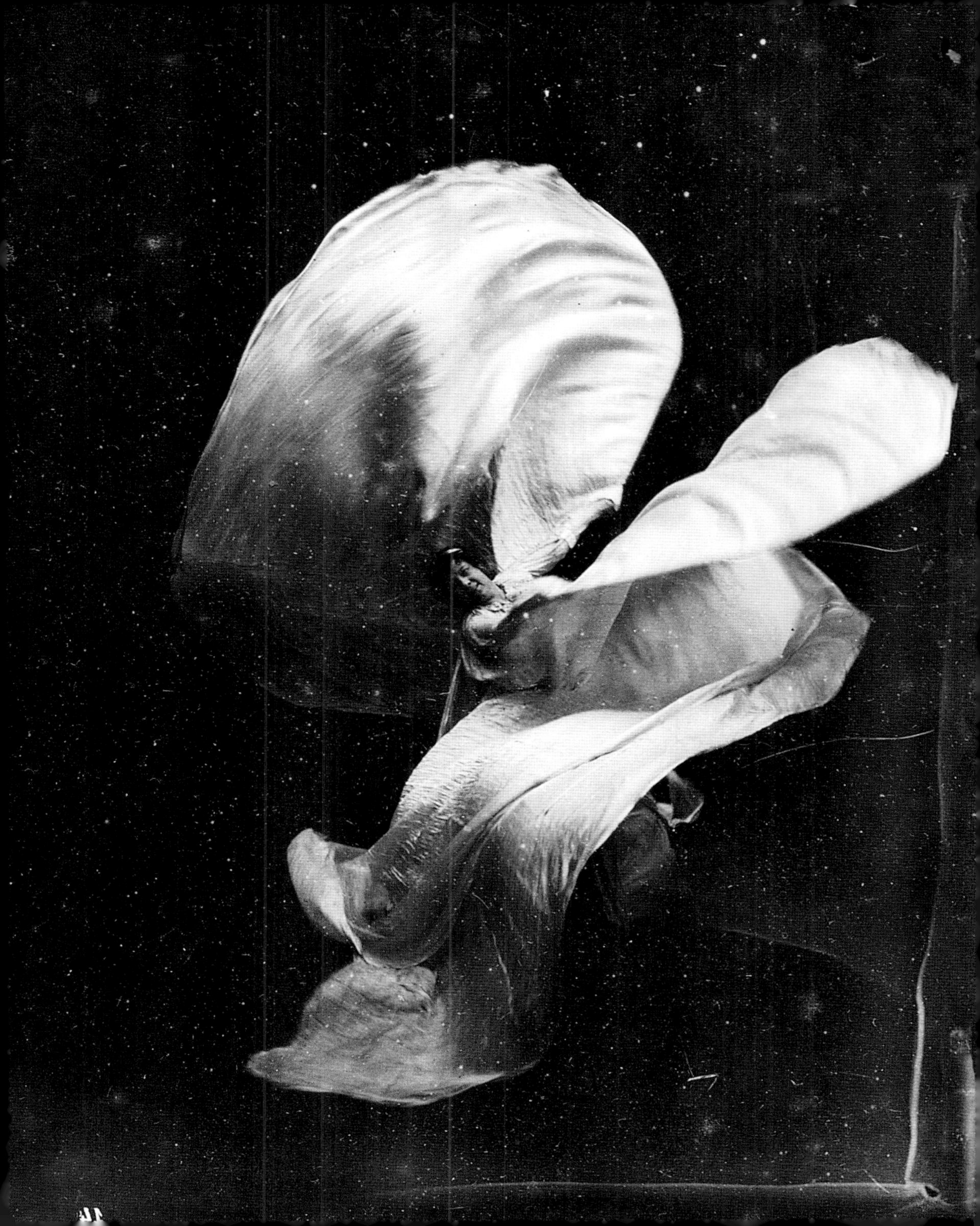

Alexandra Exter

Dynamique de couleurs, 1916-1917
[cat. 126]

Composition dynamique, 1916
[cat. 125]

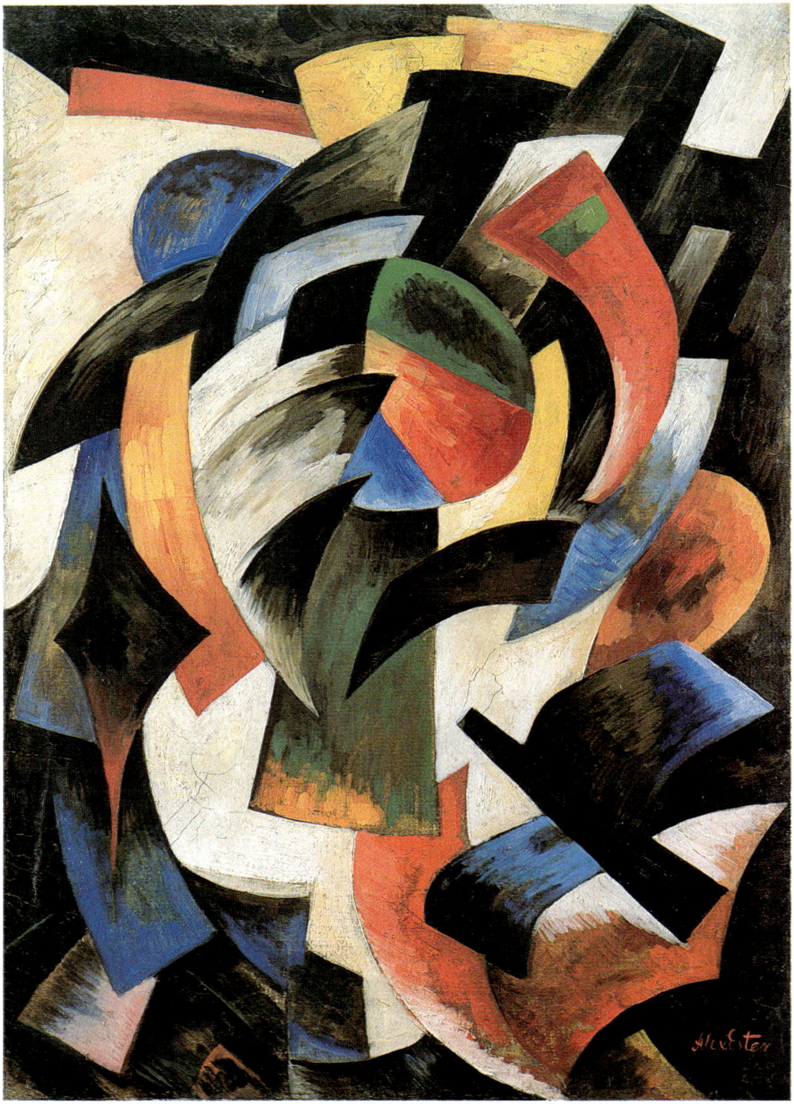

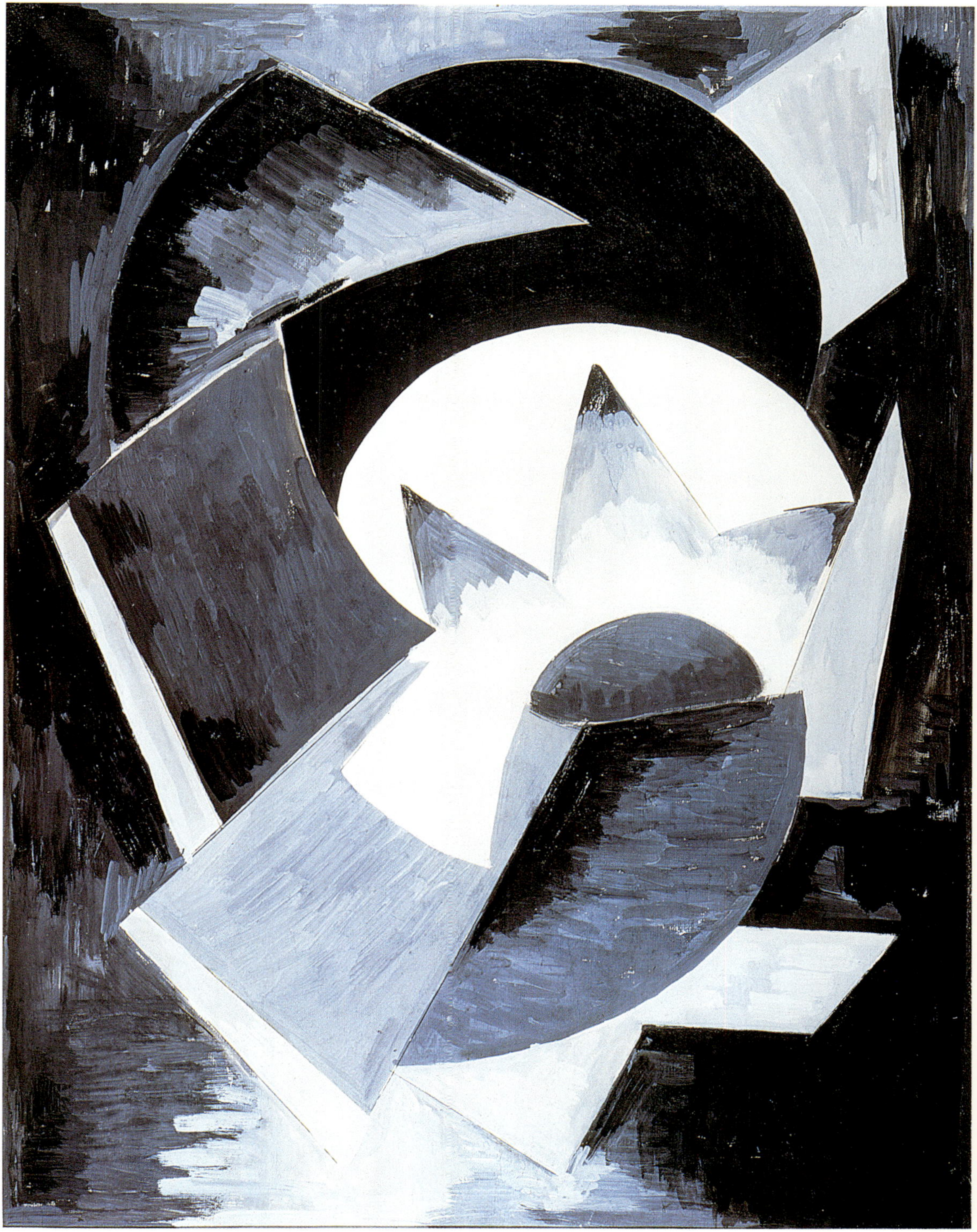

Fernand Léger
Les Trois femmes et la nature morte, 1921
[cat. 129]

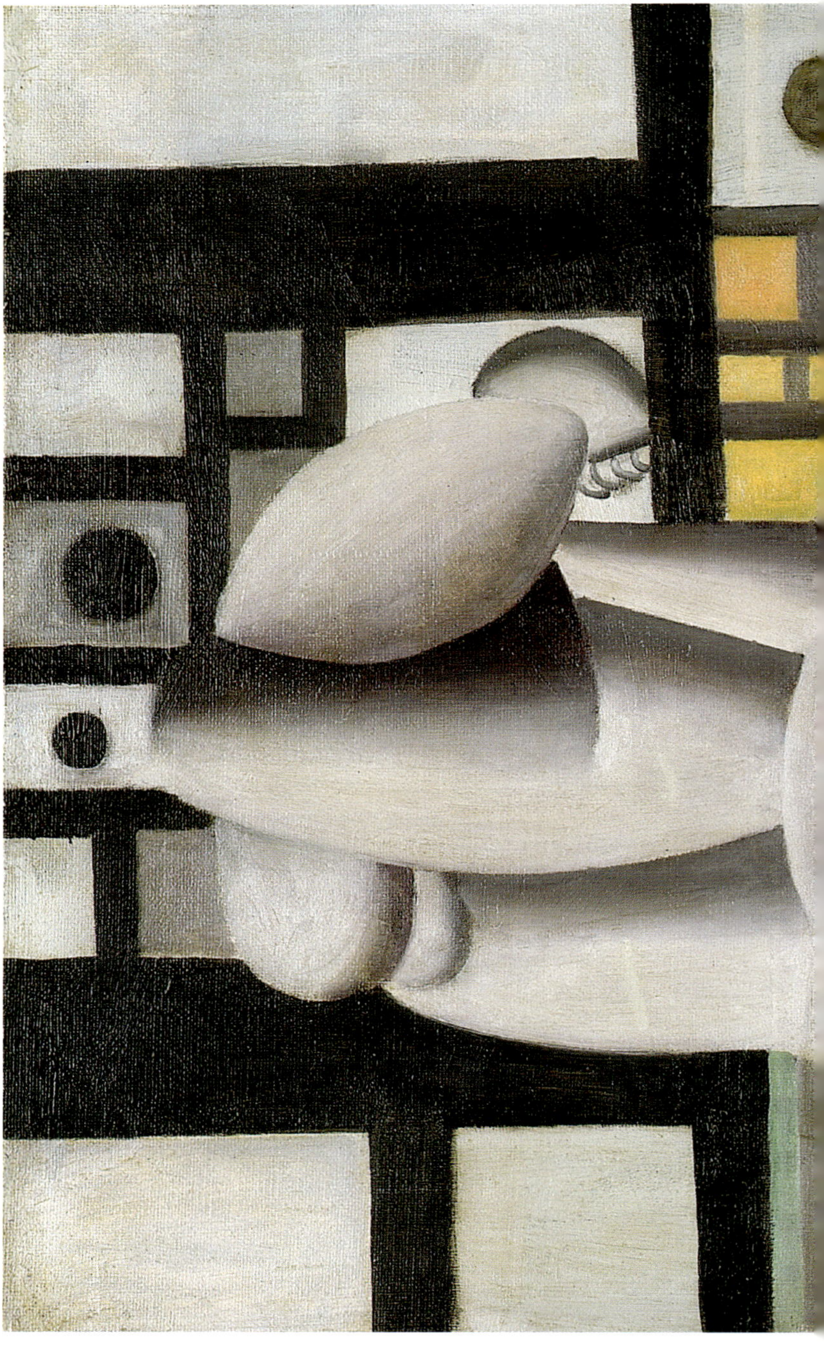

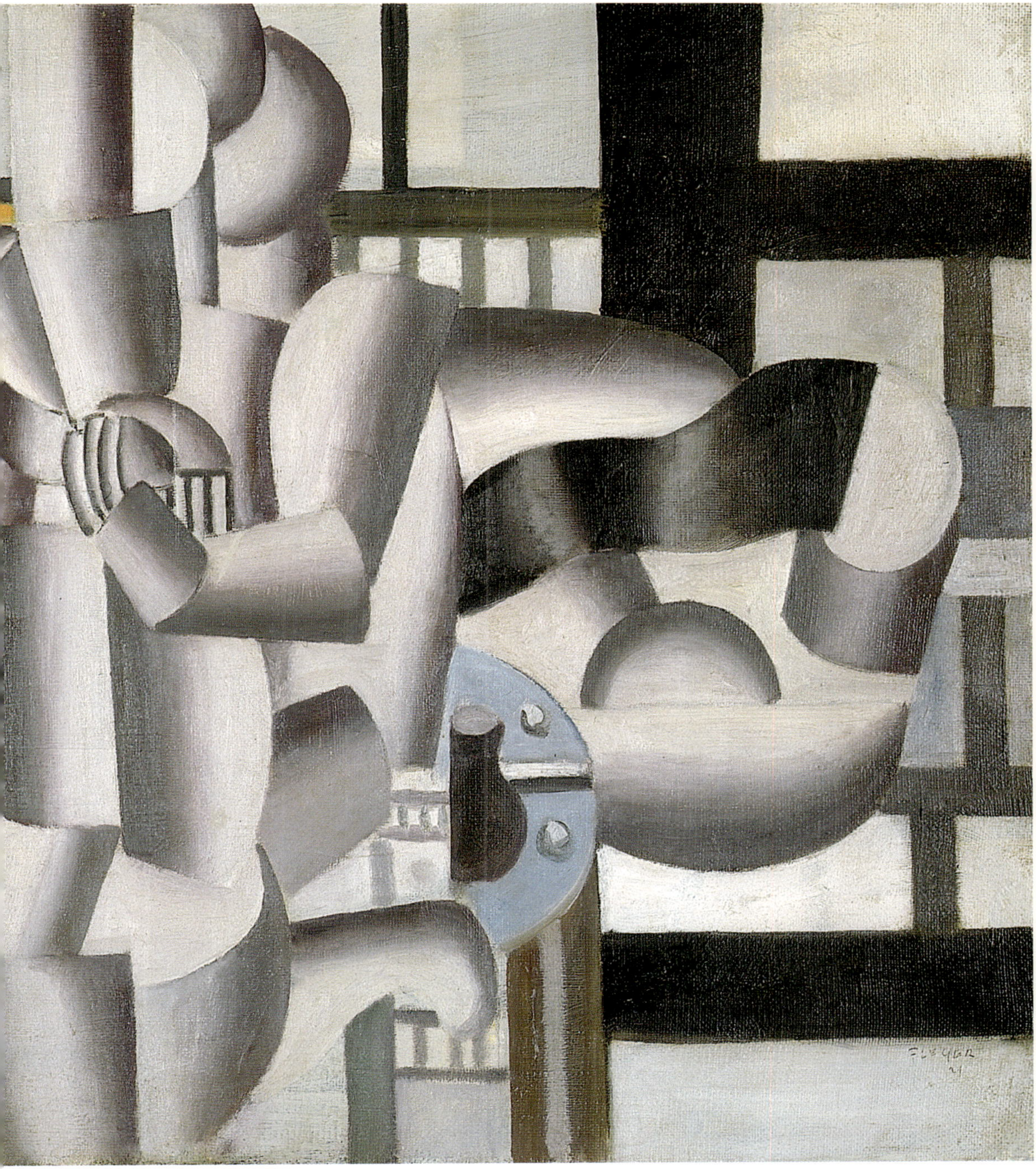

Pablo Picasso

Guillaume Apollinaire dans l'atelier de Pablo Picasso, 1910
[cat. 158]

Le Bock, 1909
[cat. 161]

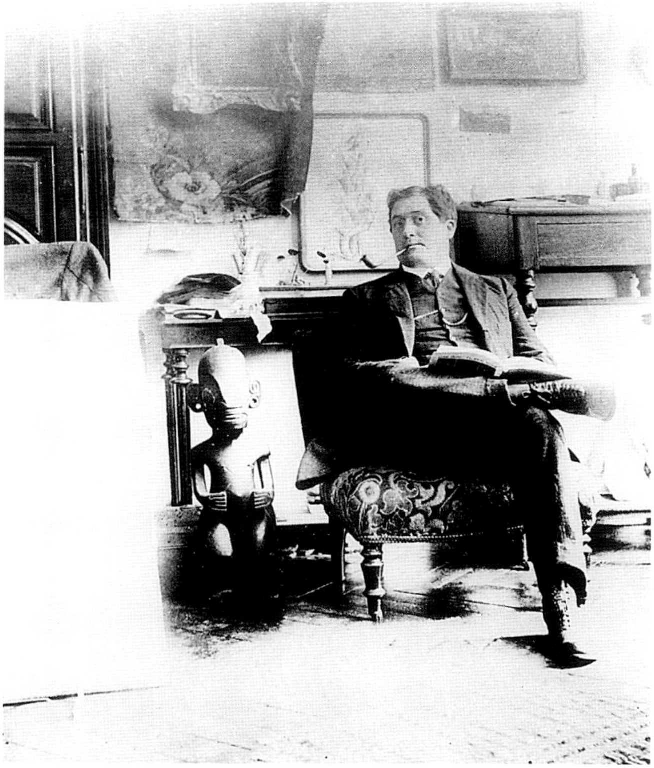

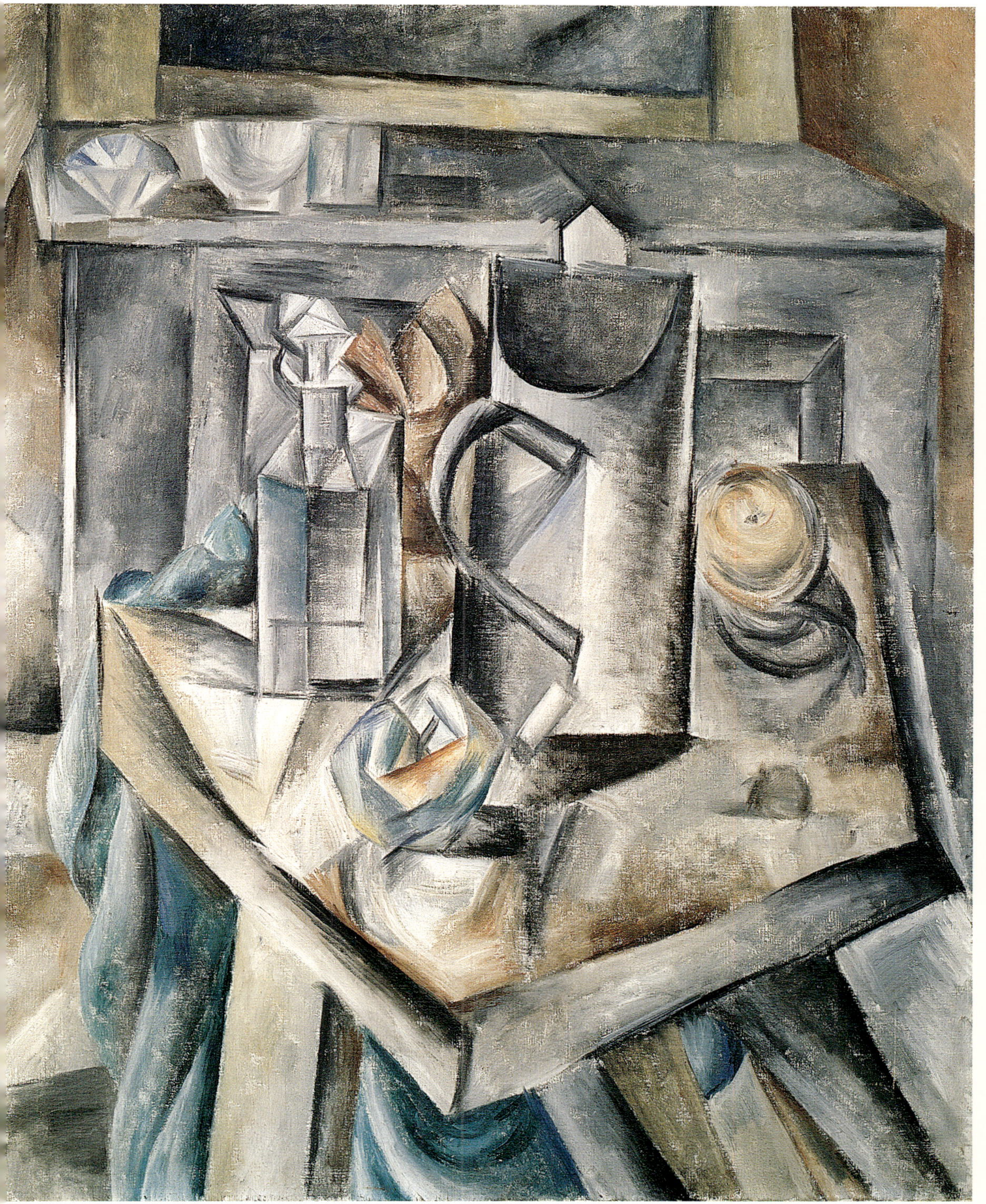

Guillaume Apollinaire

La Mandoline, l'œillet et le bambou, 1915-1917

[cat. 102]

Pablo Picasso, 1917

[cat. 103]

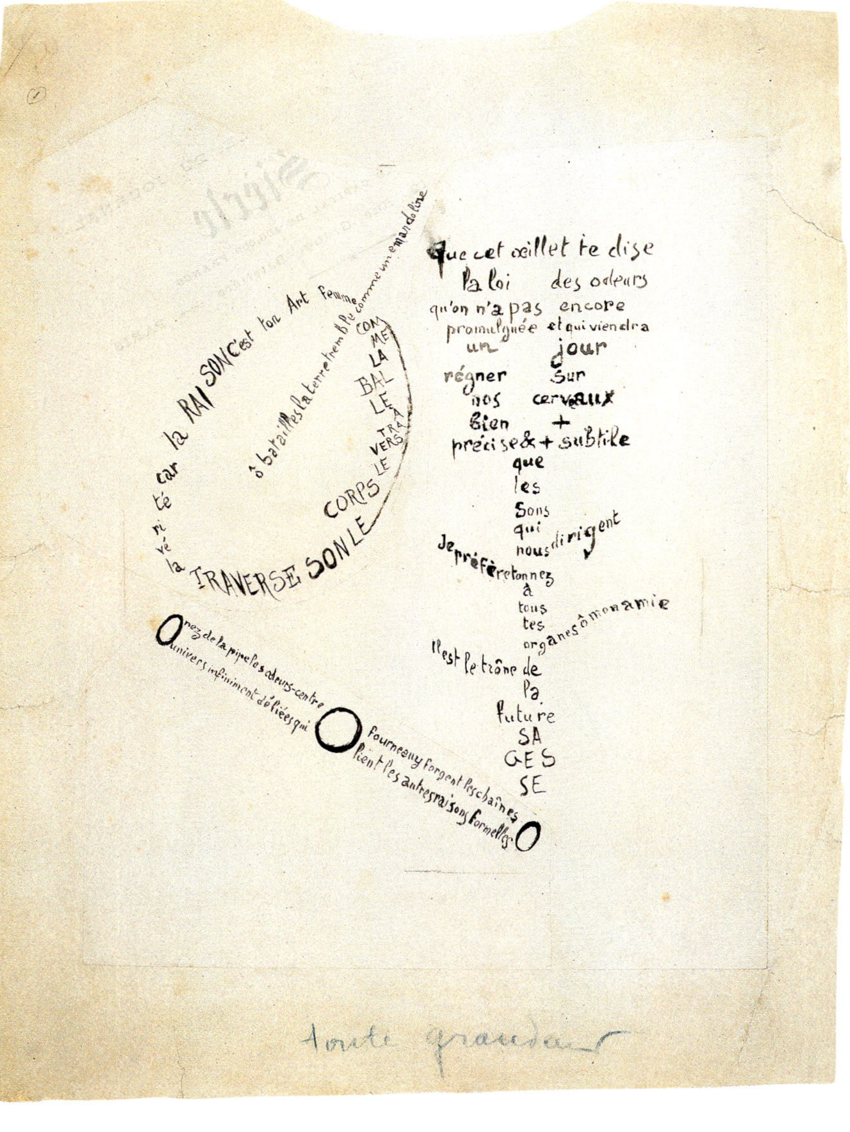

PABLO PICASSO

Voyez ce peintre il prend les choses avec leur ombre aussi et d'un coup d'œil sublimatoire
Il se déchire en accords profonds   et agréables à respirer tel l'orgue que j'aime entendre
Des Arlequines jouent dans le   rose et bleus d'un beau-ciel   Ce souvenir revit
les rêves   et les actives mains   Orient plein de glaciers   L'hiver est rigoureux
Lustres   or toile irisée or   loi des stries de feu   fond en murmurant.
Bleu   flamme légère   argent des ondes   bleues après le grand cri
Tout   en restant   elles touchent   cette sirène violon
Faons   lourdes ailes   l'incandesce   quelques brasses encore
Bourdons   femmes striées   éclat de   plongeon-diamant
Arlequins   semblables à Dieu   en variété   Aussi distingués qu'un lac
Fleurs   brillant comme deux   perles   monstres qui palpitent
Lys   cerclés d'or,   je n'étais pas seul!   fais onduler les remords
Nouveau monde très matinal   montant de l'énorme mer
L'aventure de ce vieux cheval   en Amérique
Au soir de la pêche merveilleuse   l'œil du masque
Air de petits violons au fond des   anges rangés
Dans le couchant puis au bout de   l'an des dieux
Regarde la tête géante et immense   la main verte
L'argent sera vite remplacé par   tout notre or
Morte pendue à l'hameçon... c'est   la danse bleue
L'humide voix des acrobates   des maisons
Grimace parmi les assauts du vent   qui s'assoupit
Ouis les vagues et le fracas d'une   femme bleue
Enfin la grotte à l'atmosphère dorée   par la vertu
Ce saphir veiné   il faut rire!
Rois de phosphore   sous les arbres les bottines entre des plumes bleues
La danse des   dix mouches   lui fait face quand il songe à toi
Le cadre bleu   tandis que   l'air agile s'ouvrait aussi
Au milieu des   regrets dans une vaste grotte.
Prends les araignées roses   à la nage
Regrets d'invisibles pièges   l'air
Paisible se souleva mais sur le clavier   musiques
Guitare-tempête   ô gai trémolo
O gai trémolo   ô gai trémolo
Il ne rit pas   l'artiste-peintre
Ton pauvre   étincellement pâle
L'ombre agile   d'un soir d'été qui meurt
Immense désir   et l'aube émerge des eaux si lumineuses
Je vis nos yeux   diamants enfermer le reflet du ciel vert et
J'entendis sa voix   qui dorait les forêts tandis que vous pleuriez
L'acrobate à cheval le poète à moustaches un oiseau mort et tant d'enfants sans larmes
Choses cassées des livres déchirés des couches de poussière et des aurores déferlant!

Guillaume APOLLINAIRE

Georges Braque
Le Petit éclaireur, 1913
[cat. 147]

But why, after all, should Cubism not have given us a painter who, painting perfectly insignificant things, would yet be an artist and communicate charmingness with a sort of magic, in a state of chaos and absurdity? Mallarméeism has indeed given us Mallarmé, whose lines most empty of meaning and whose most opaque poems are nevertheless expressive, through the choice of words, through a refined sense of verbal music, a certain seduction.

Anonymous
"Cubisme," *Les Marges,* 1912

Literature has stolen a march on the visual arts in expressing an aesthetic corresponding to our modern psychology.
In harmony with this idealism, which has its roots deep within the life of matter, we find the beginning of the expression of this aesthetic in Mallarmé and the Symbolist poets.
This is why we have encountered sympathy, understanding and the finest criticism in the modern poets.
For the visual oeuvre corresponding to the poetic oeuvre of Mallarmé is something we only have today.
[...]
Chosen by Mallarmé according to their complementary quality and employed in groups or separately, words constitute a technique for expressing a prismatic subdivision of the idea, a simultaneous co-penetration of images.

Gino Severini
"Symbolisme plastique, symbolisme littéraire," *Mercure de France,* 1916

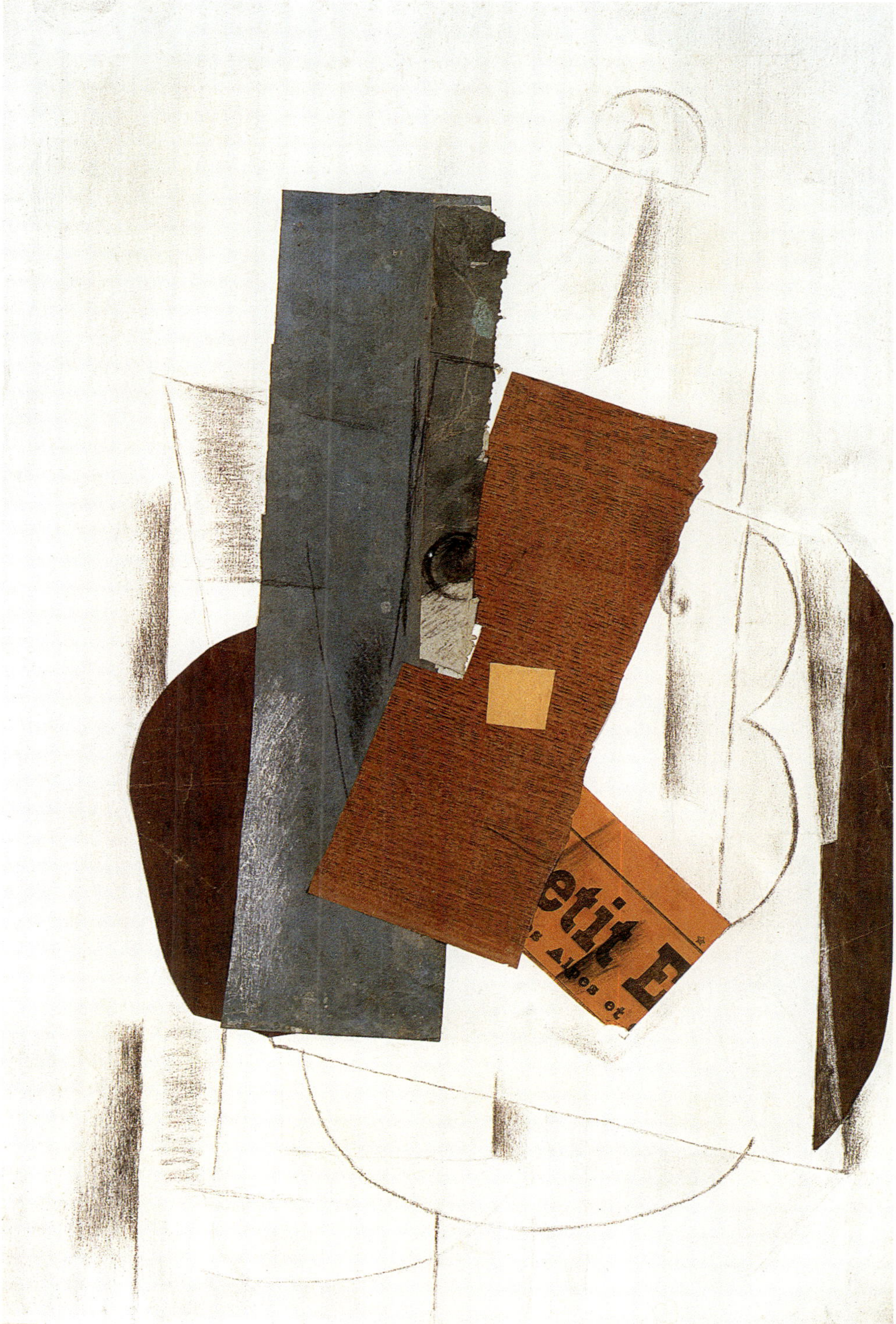
etit E

With analysis one does not build. This is the chaotic, dramatic period of Cubism. Its poetry is not abstract. There are points of contact between this pictorial period and the Poetry of a Mallarmé (Sadly sleeps a mandola in hollow musical nothingness).

Robert Delaunay
Letter to Sam Halpert, 1924

It is only after 1907 that, in my opinion, Stéphane Mallarmé's poetry has a profound effect on visual art, an effect which is combined with that of Paul Cézanne's painting. The art of our time owes much to these two men, men who barely knew of each other, who certainly never had occasion to exchange their ideas.
In Cézanne *Cubism*, which forms the basis of the art of today, encountered the example which enabled it to construct *plastic architectures*. It is the reading of Mallarmé that gave the Cubist painters the wherewithal to freely invent *signs*, in the belief that these signs would sooner or later become the objects signified for viewers.

Daniel-Henry Kahnweiler
"Mallarmé et la peinture," *Les Lettres,* 1948

A weakness of modernist painting nowadays, especially prevalent in the "constructivist" tradition, is inherent in taking over or inventing "abstract" forms insufficiently rooted in the concrete, in the world of feeling where art originates, and of which modern French poetry is an expression. Modernist painting has not evolved merely in relation to the internal structure of painting; it's not only legitimate, but necessary to include, among the documents of modern art, reference to French poetry from Baudelaire to surrealism. Cubism, for instance, could not have developed so quickly, surely, and identically for Picasso and Braque without Cézanne's surface as a model; but Kahnweiler is certainly correct in his assertion, in his remarkable book on *Juan Gris* (N.Y., 1947), that the poet Mallarmé was responsible for the atmosphere in which cubism became possible.

Robert Motherwell
"Preliminary Notice," Marcel Raymond, *From Baudelaire to Surrealism,* 1933

Pablo Picasso
Bouteille de vieux marc et journal, 1913
[cat. 157]

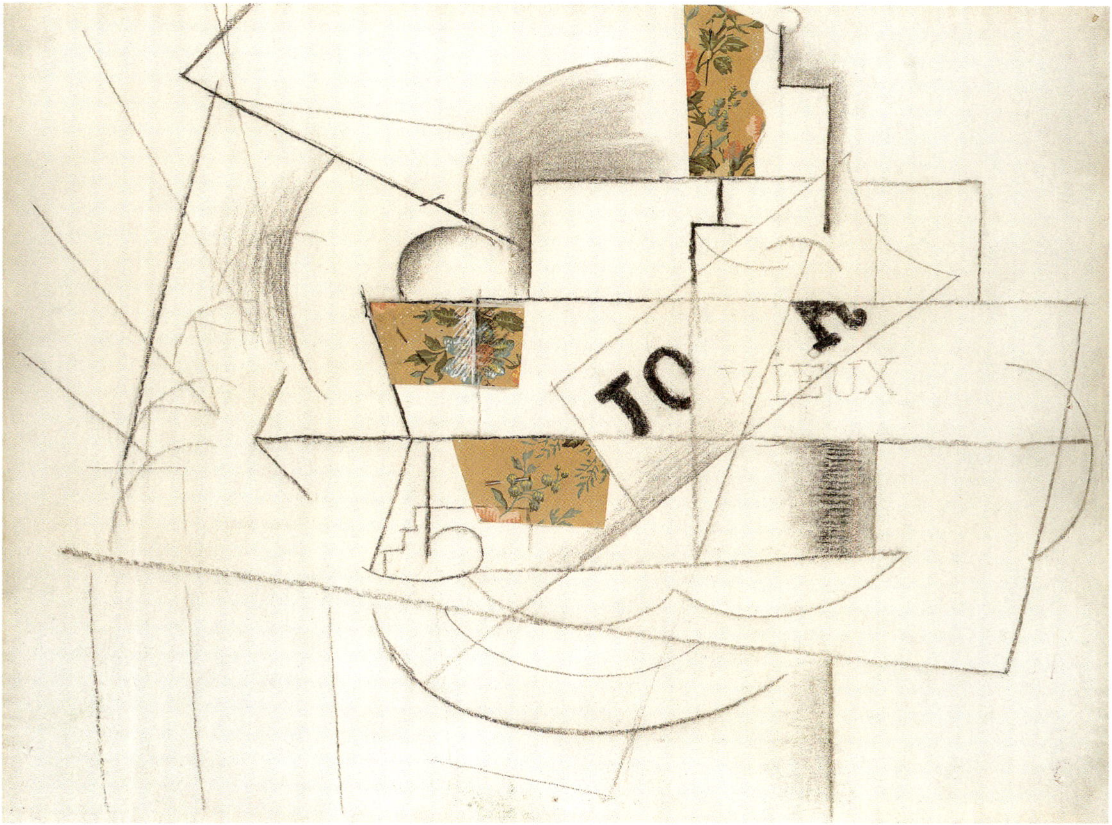

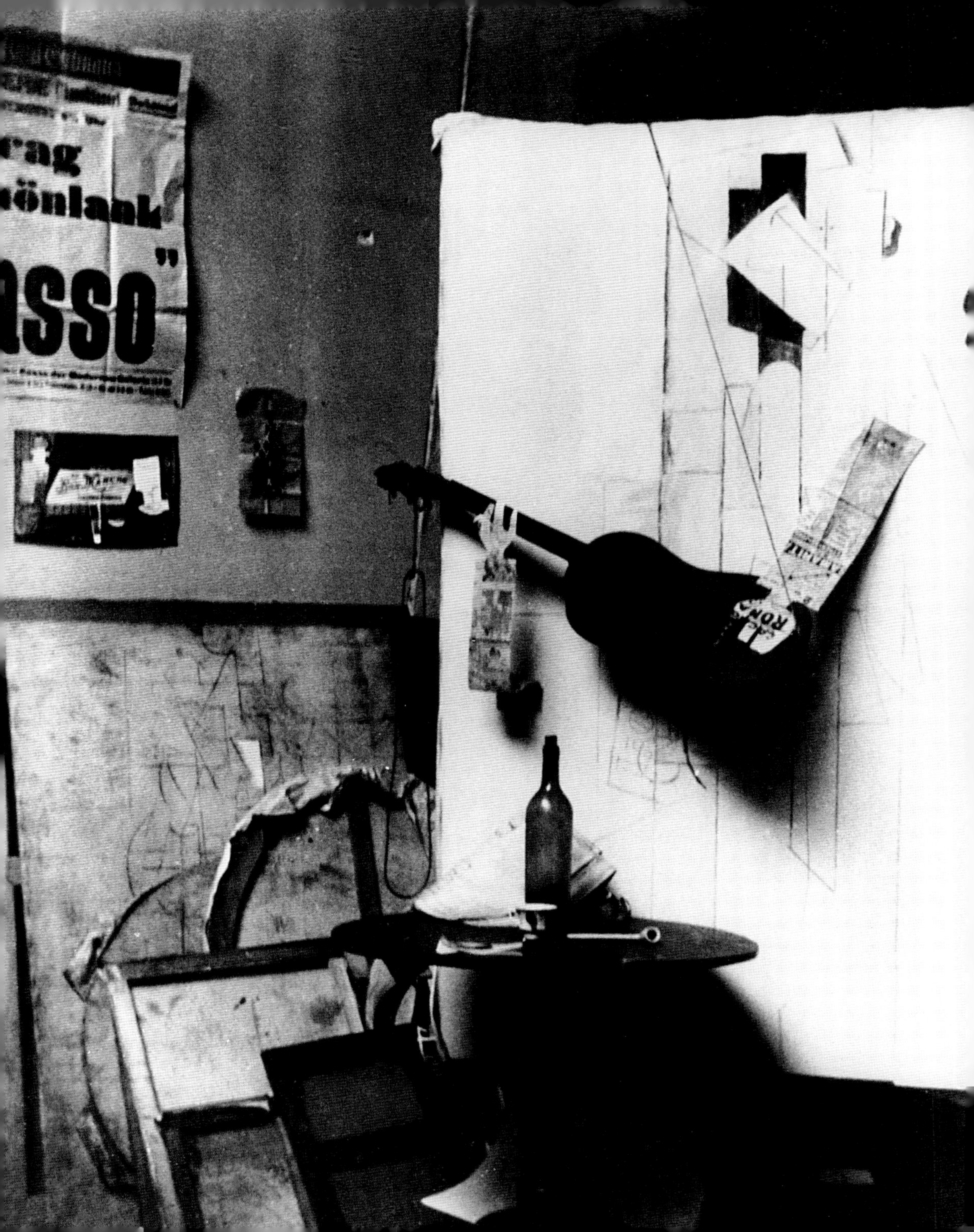
rag
önlank
ASSO

Pablo Picasso
Construction photographique au joeur de guitare, 1913
[cat. 155]

Verre et dé, 1914
[cat. 152]

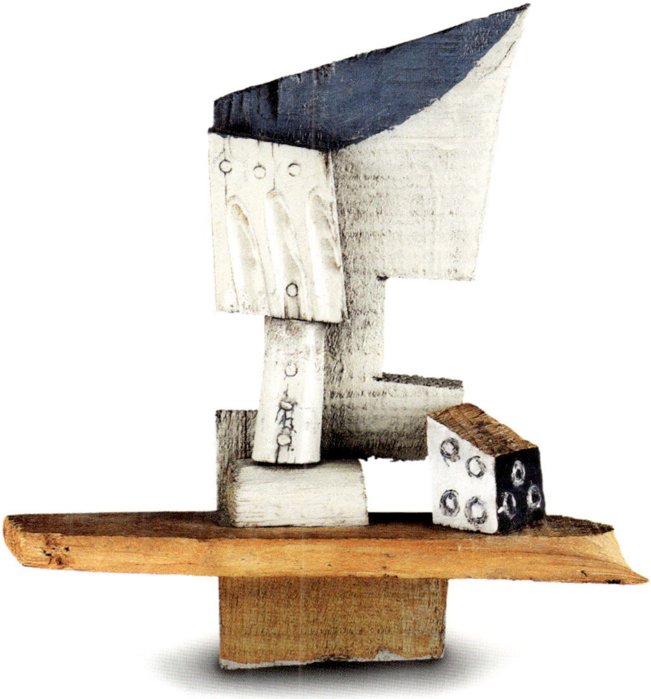

Juan Gris
Nature morte au livre (Saint Matorel), 1912–1913
[cat. 165]

For utilising an image, I would say that a performance is comparable to a game of cards. The cards are the elements making up the performance. If someone has felt moved at a performance it is because he has altered the disposition of the cards, of the elements. Without doing away with them, without changing them, he has been given them a new arrangement. He has shuffled the cards and seen them presented in a new way.

Juan Gris
"Des possibilités de la peinture," 1924 (extract of a lecture)

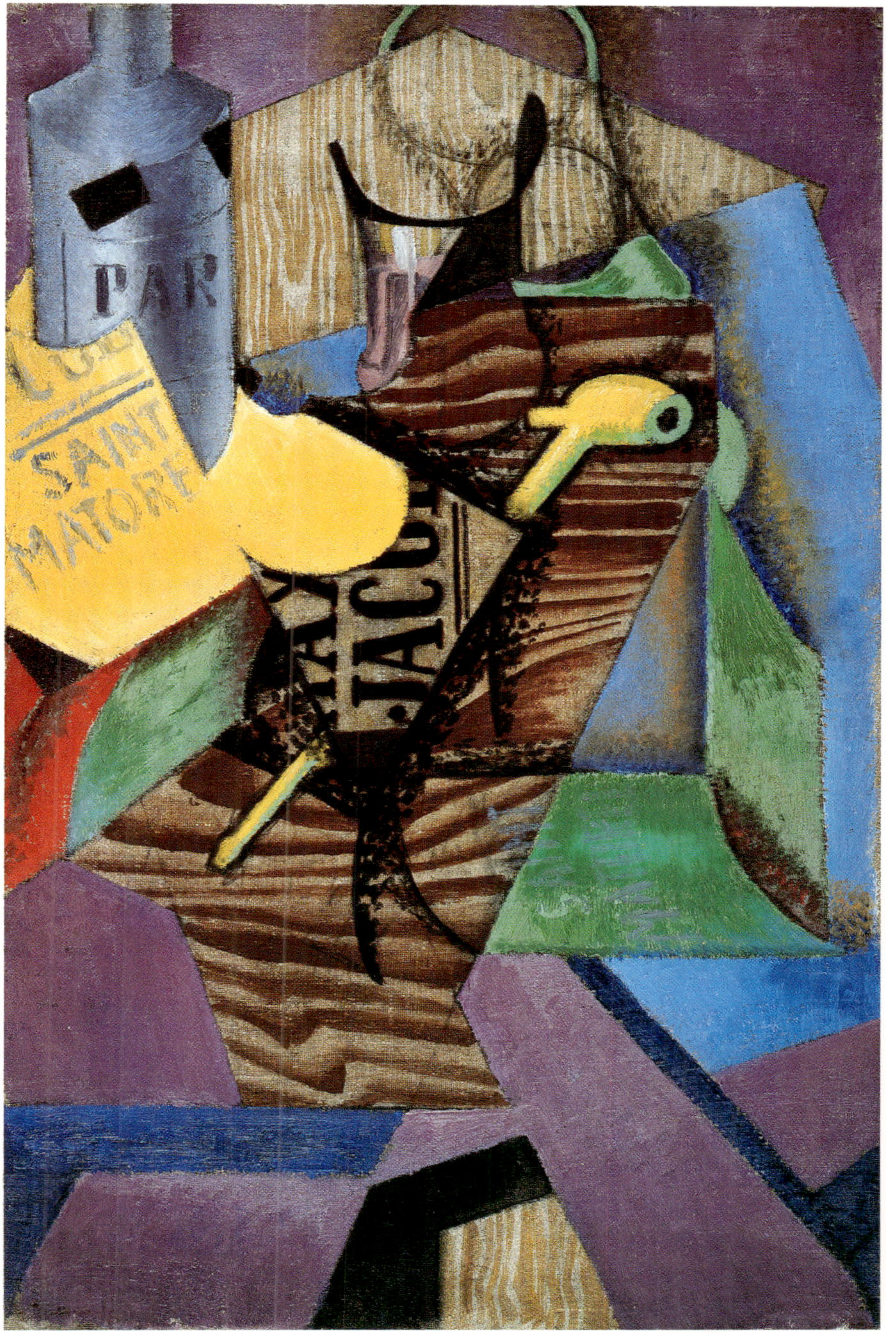
PAR
SAINT
JACO

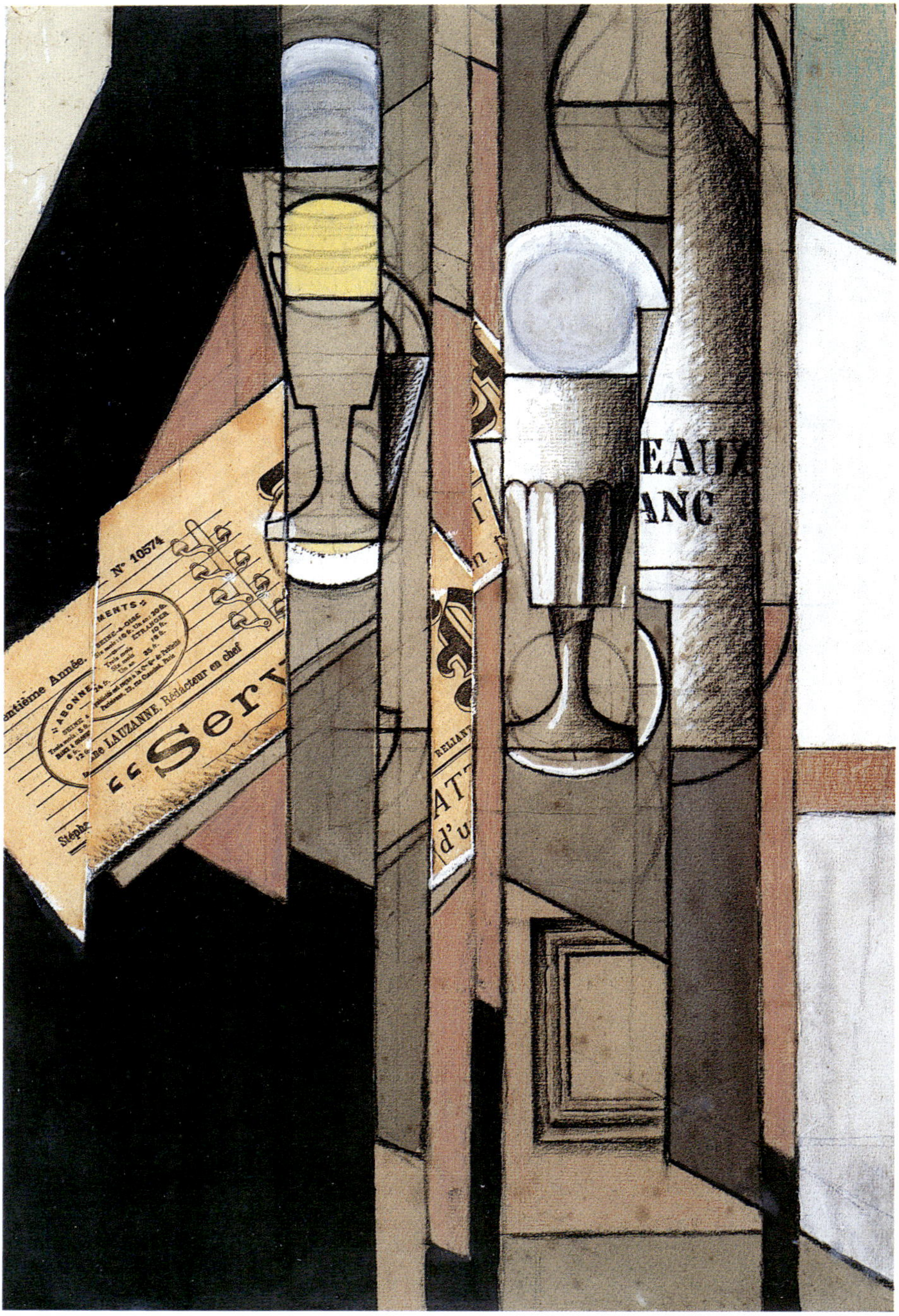
N° 10574
entième Année.
LAUZANNE, Rédacteur en chef
“Serv
EAUX
ANC

Juan Gris
Verres, journal et bouteille de vin, 1913
[cat. 164]

Fernand Léger
Étude pour La Ville, 1919
[cat. 130]

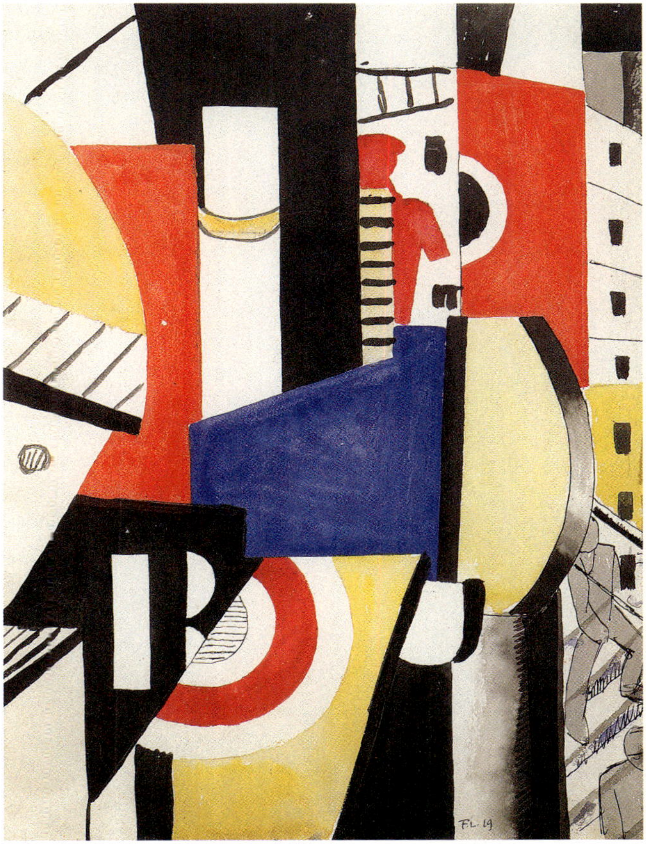

Pablo Picasso
Tête d'arlequin, 1913
[cat. 151]

Carlo Carrà
Gravitazione spaziale, 1910
[cat. 142]

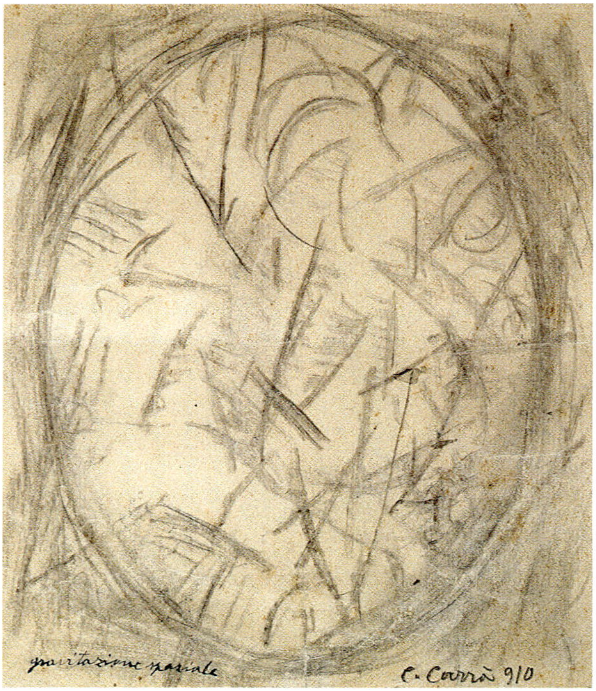

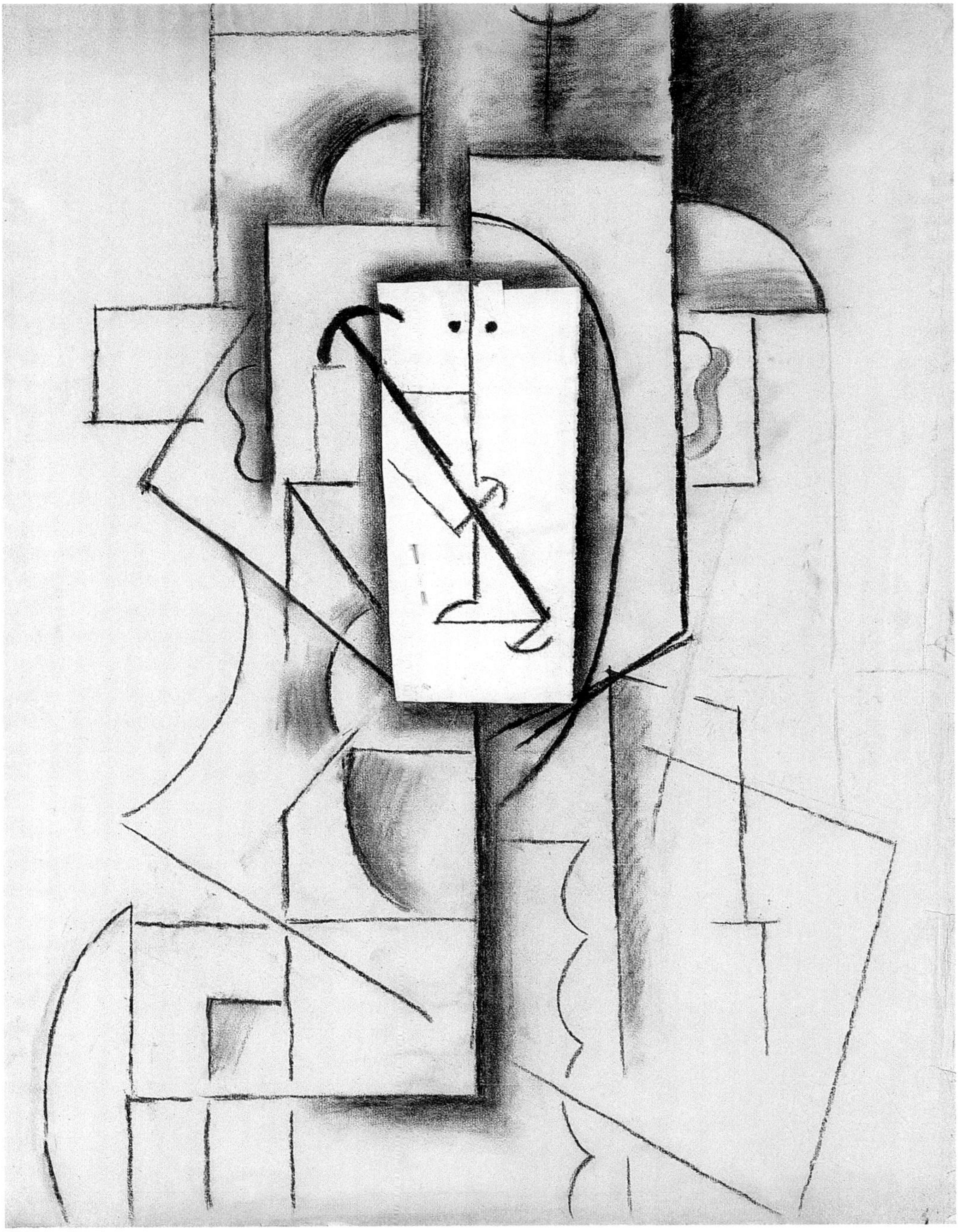

Pablo Picasso

Figure assise, 1910-1911

[cat. 154]

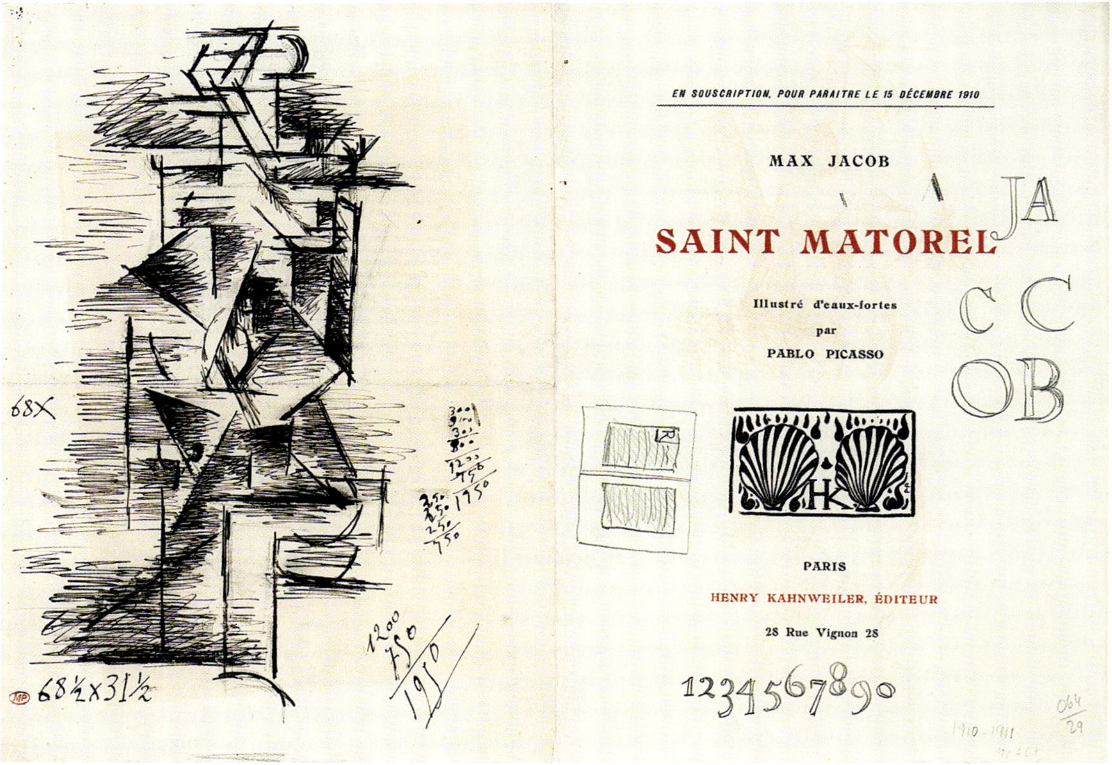

Pablo Picasso

Étude pour Mademoiselle Léonie, 1914

[cat. 153]

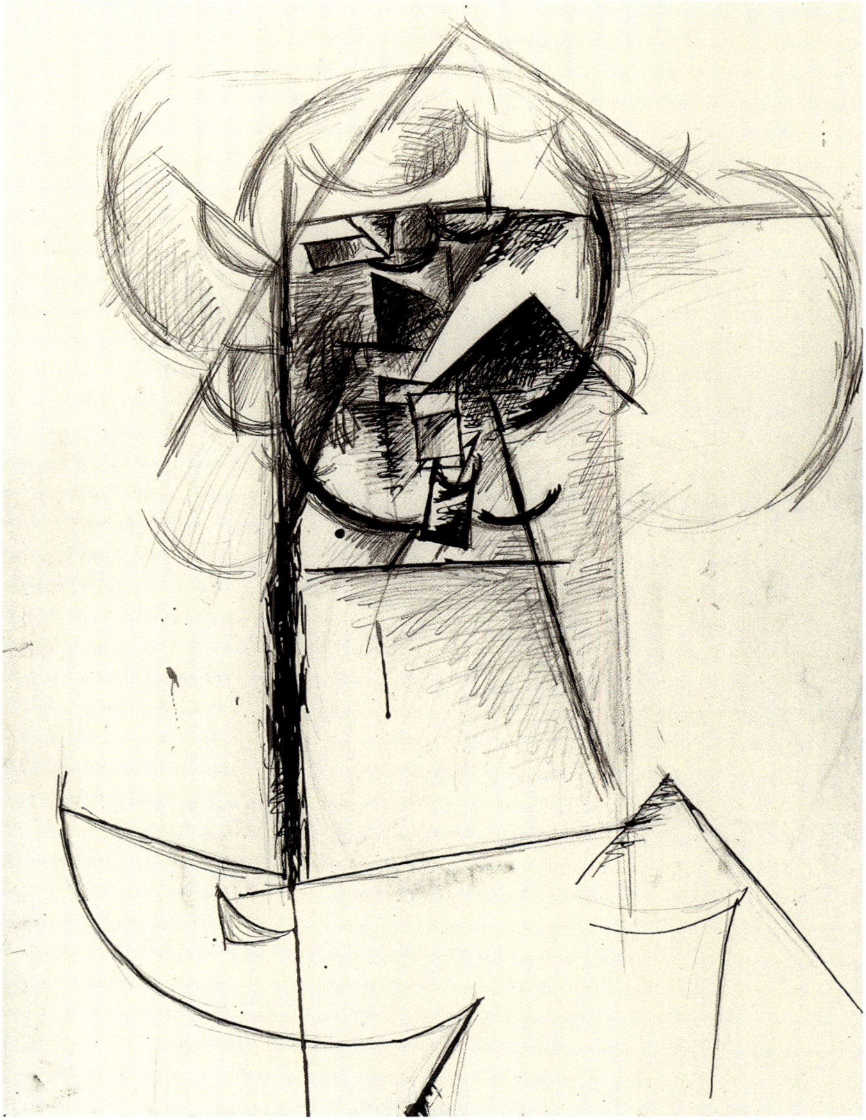

Julio González

Le Baiser, drawings, 1931-1935

[cat. 132-136]

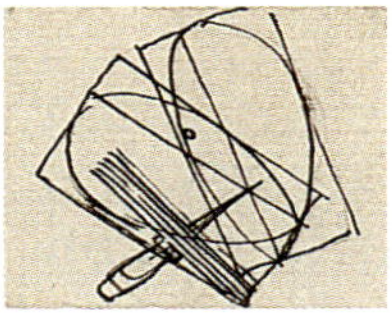

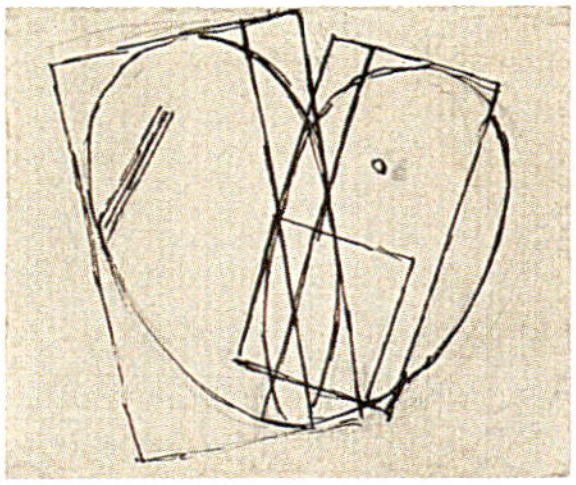

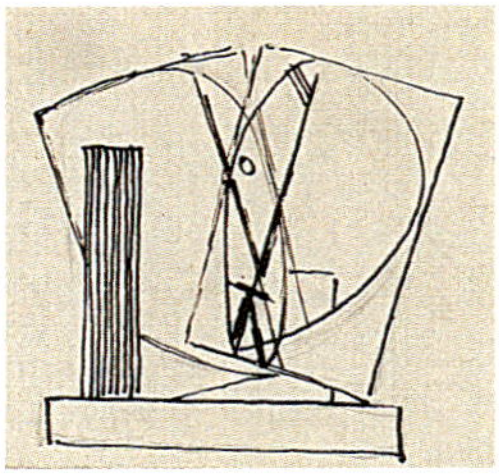

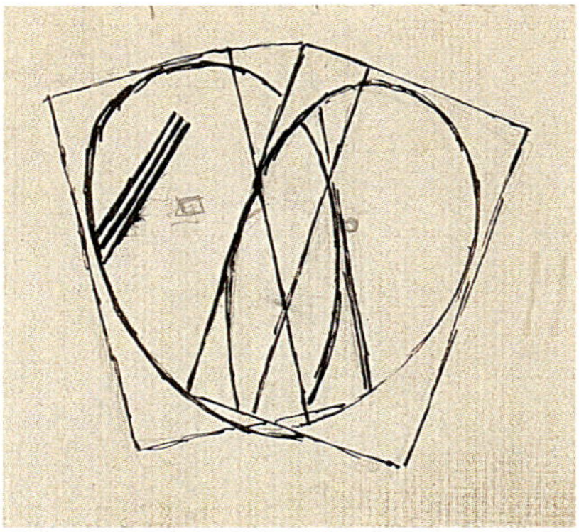

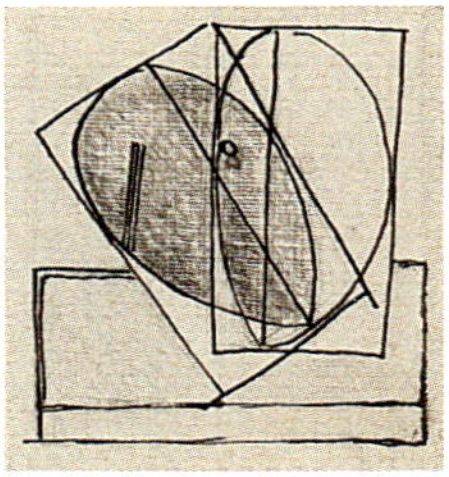

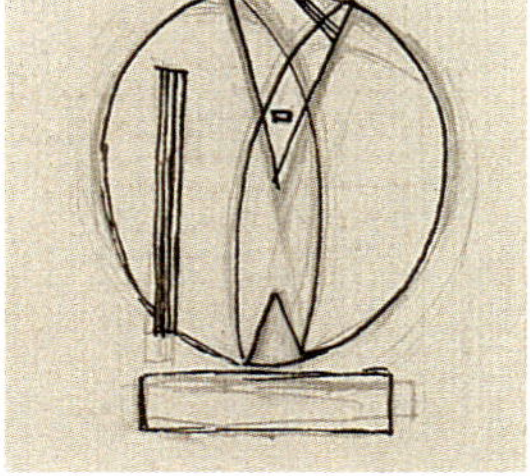

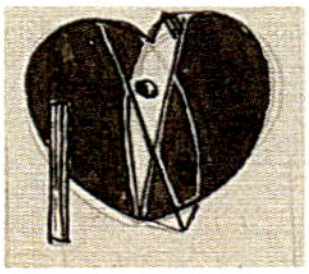

Julio González

Le Baiser I, 1930

[cat. 131]

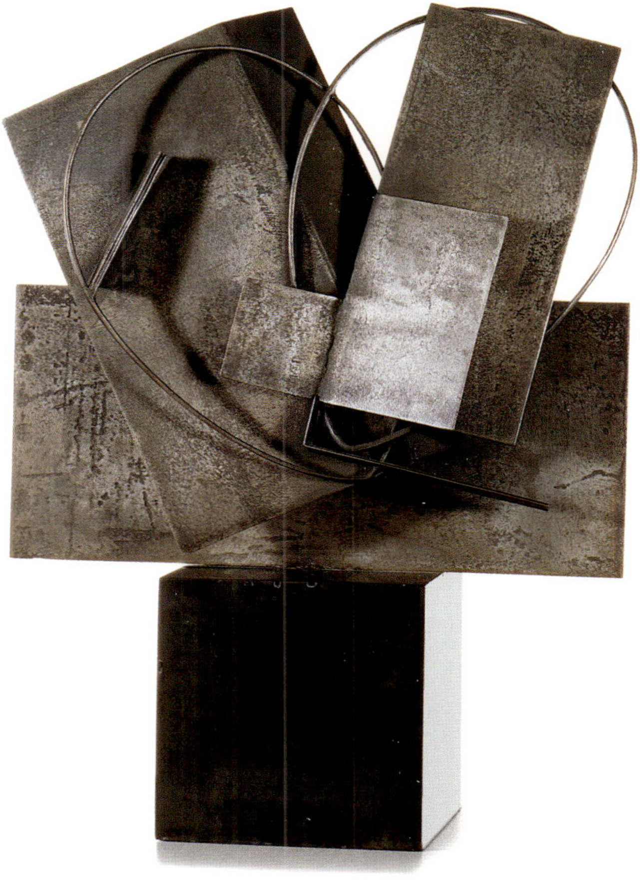

Frantisek Kupka

Étude pour Amorpha-Chromatique chaude, 1912-1914

[cat. 139]

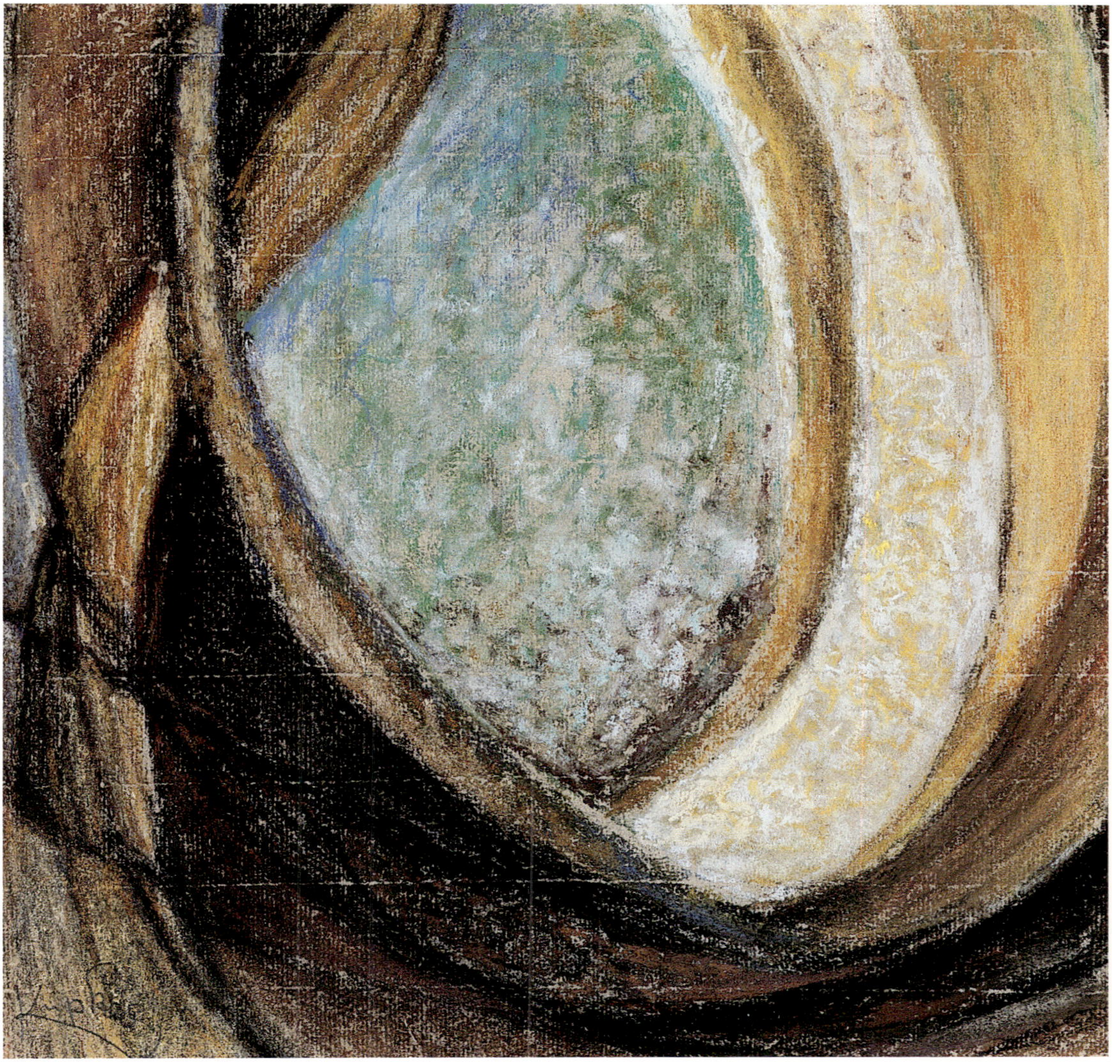

Vassily Kandinsky
Klänge, 1913
[cat. 168]

HYMNUS

Innen wiegt die blaue Woge.
Das zerrissne rote Tuch.
Rote Fetzen. Blaue Wellen.
Das verschlossne alte Buch.
Schauen schweigend in die Ferne.
Dunkles Irren in dem Wald.
Tiefer werden blaue Wellen.
Rotes Tuch versinkt nun bald.

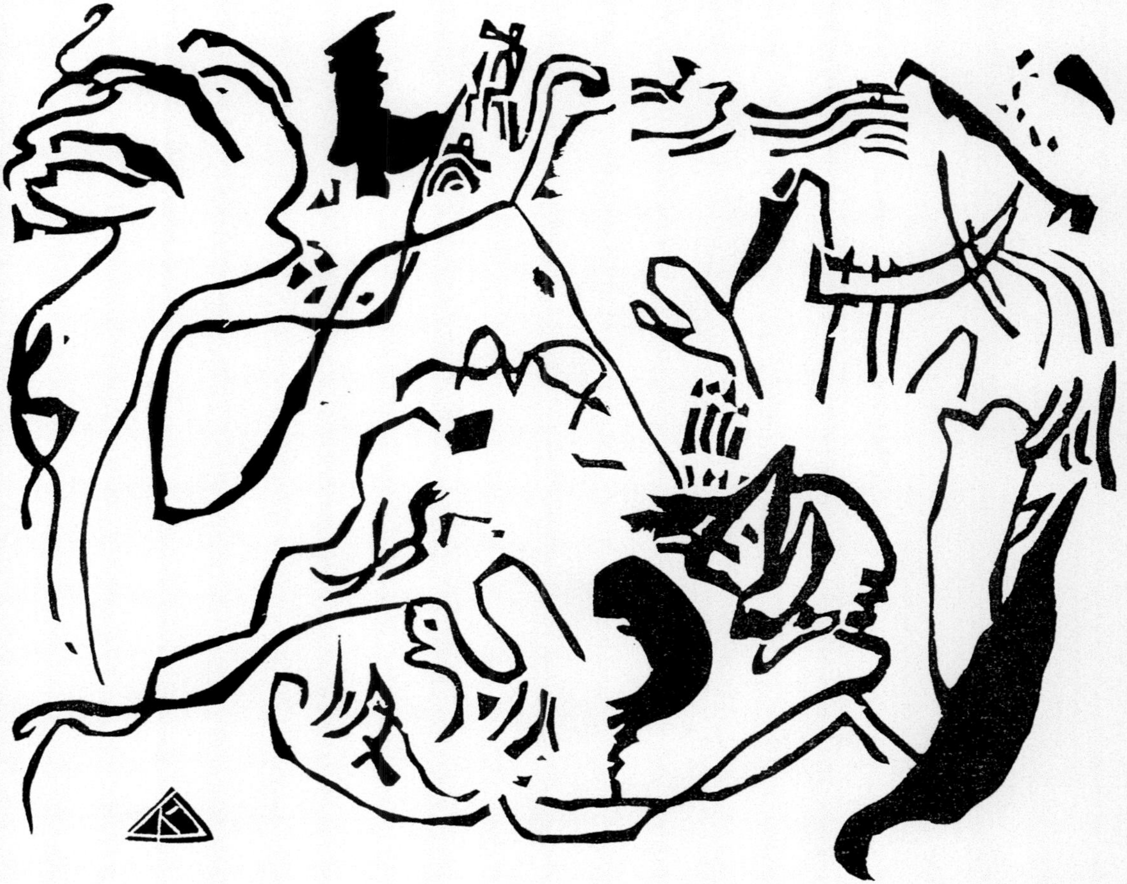

Guillaume Apollinaire

"Lettre-Océan", in the bound proof of *Et moi aussi je suis peintre,* 1914
(first version of *Calligrammes,* unpublished)
[cat. 176]

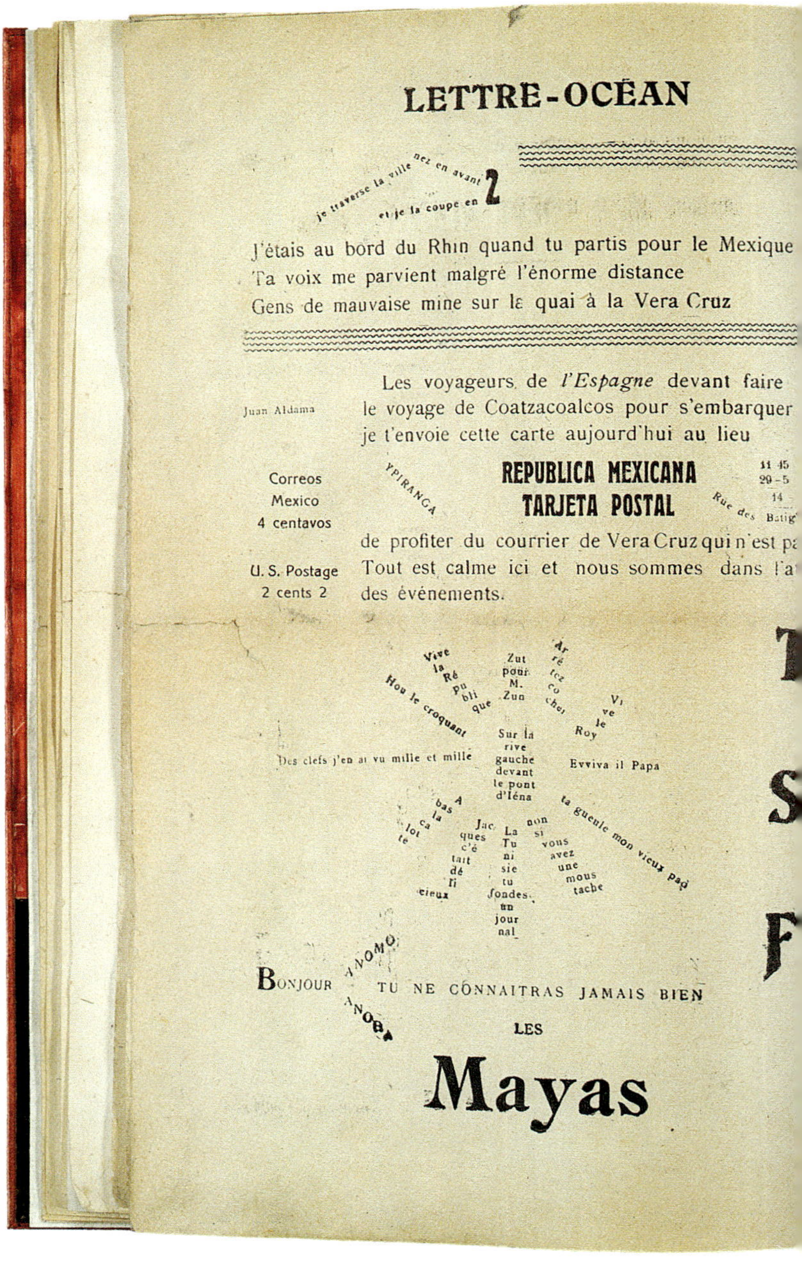

LETTRE-OCÉAN

je traverse la ville nez en avant
et je la coupe en 2

J'étais au bord du Rhin quand tu partis pour le Mexique
Ta voix me parvient malgré l'énorme distance
Gens de mauvaise mine sur la quai à la Vera Cruz

Juan Aldama

Les voyageurs de *l'Espagne* devant faire
le voyage de Coatzacoalcos pour s'embarquer
je t'envoie cette carte aujourd'hui au lieu

Correos
Mexico
4 centavos

YPIRANGA

REPUBLICA MEXICANA
TARJETA POSTAL

11 45
29 - 5
14

Rue des Batig

de profiter du courrier de Vera Cruz qui n'est pa
Tout est calme ici et nous sommes dans l'a
des événements.

U. S. Postage
2 cents 2

Vive la Ré pu bli que
Zut pour M. Zun
Ar ré tez co cher
Hou le croquant
Vi ve le Roy
Sur la rive gauche devant le pont d'Iéna
Des clefs j'en ai vu mille et mille
Evviva il Papa
A bas la ca lot te
Jac ques c'é tait dé li cieux
La Tu ni sie tu fondes un jour nal
non si vous avez une mous tache
ta gueule mon vieux pad

BONJOUR
ANOMO
ANOBA
TU NE CONNAITRAS JAMAIS BIEN
LES
Mayas

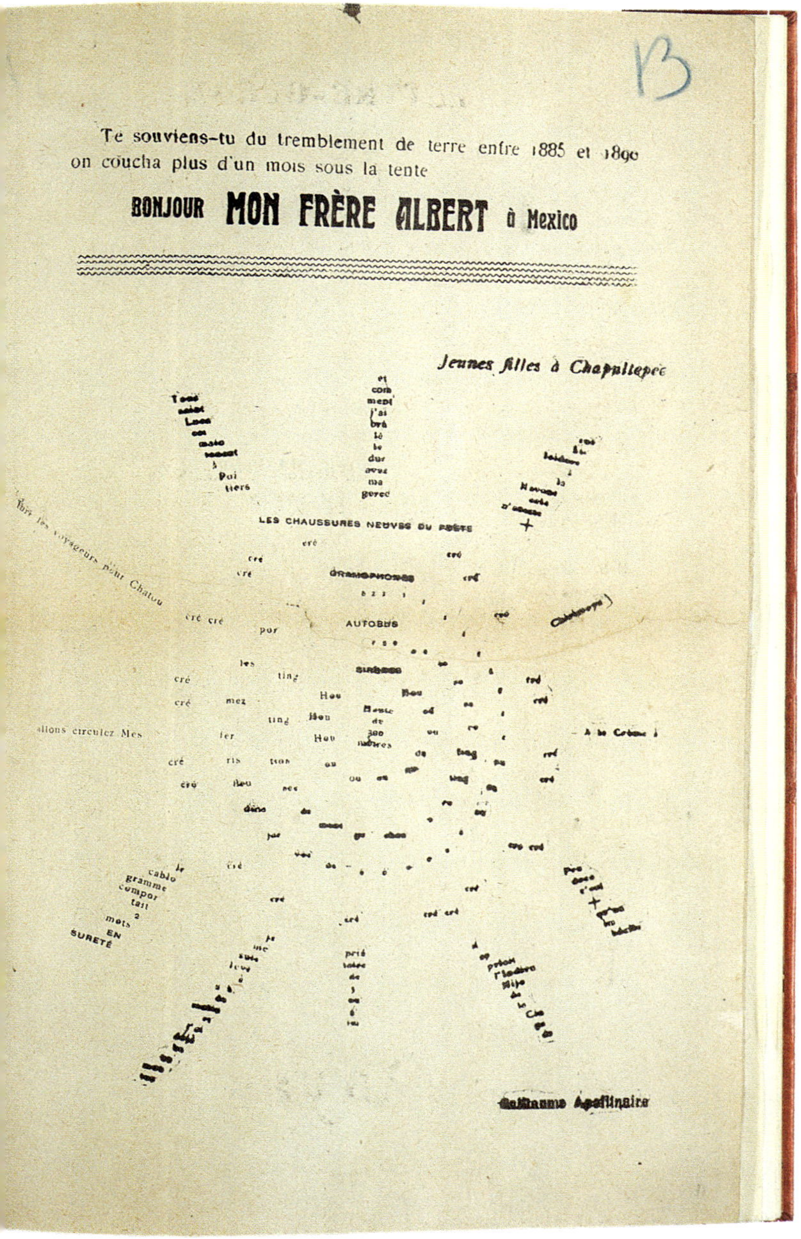

Te souviens-tu du tremblement de terre entre 1885 et 1890
on coucha plus d'un mois sous la tente

BONJOUR MON FRÈRE ALBERT à Mexico

Jeunes filles à Chapultepec

Poi
tiers

et
com
ment
j'ai
brû
lé
le
dur
avec
ma
gerec

sort les voyageurs pour Chatou

LES CHAUSSURES NEUVES DU POÈTE

cré
cré
cré
cré
cré
cré cré
por
AUTOBUS
les
cré
ting
cré
mez
Hou
Hou
ting
Hou
allons circulez Mes
fer
Hou
cré
ris
cré
Hou
À la Crème
cré
cré
cré
cré cré
cré cré
cré

le
cablo
gramme
compor
tait
2
mots
EN
SURETÉ

je
me
suis
levé
à

prié
de

à

Guillaume Apollinaire

Robert Delaunay
Fenêtres ouvertes simultanément
(1ère partie, 3ème motif), 1912
[cat. 162]

From red to green all the yellow dies
Paris Vancouver Hyères Maintenon New York
and the West Indies
The window opens like an orange
The beautiful fruit of light

Guillaume Apollinaire
"Les Fenêtres," *Calligrammes. Poèmes de la paix et de la guerre (1913–1916)*, 1918

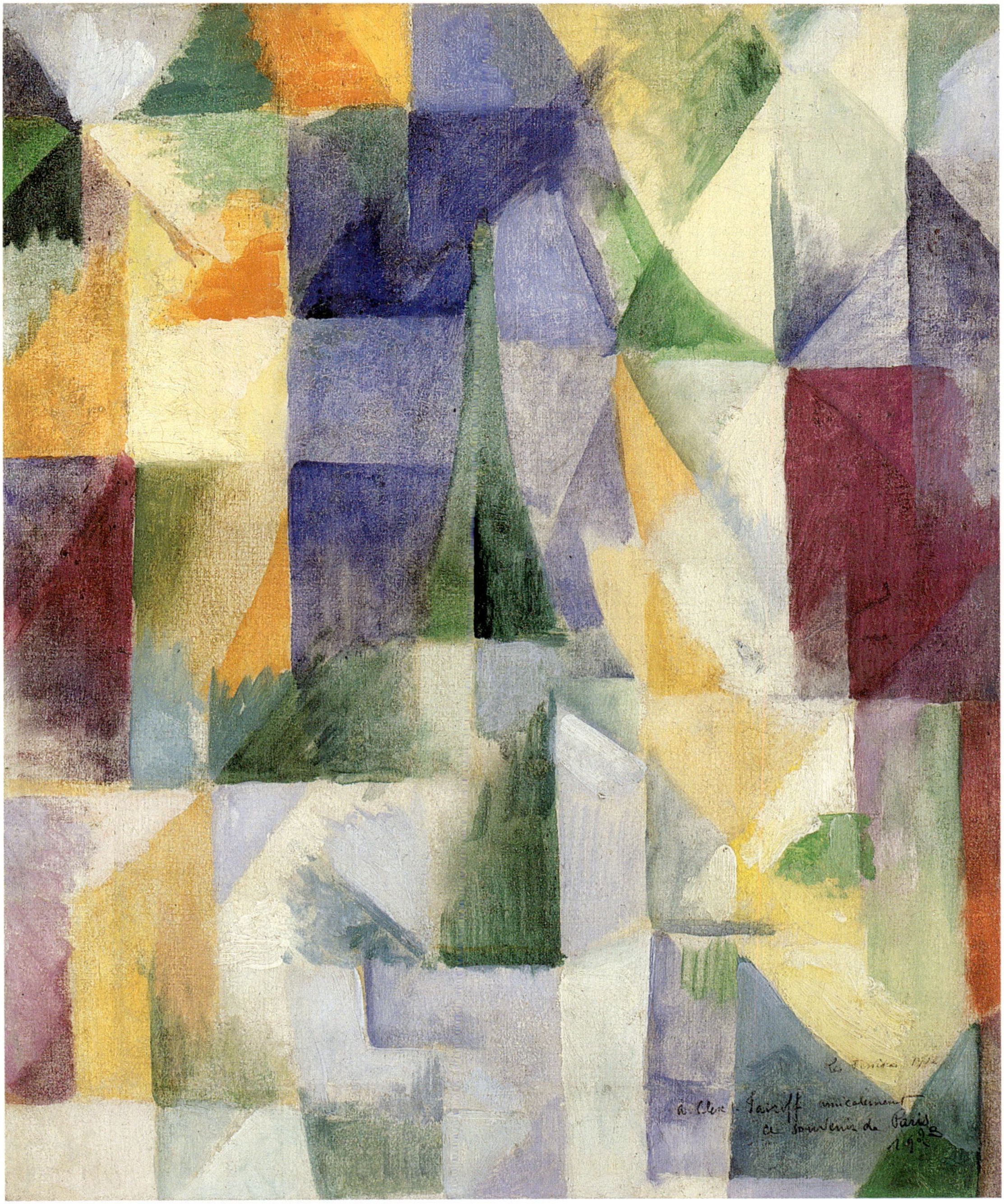

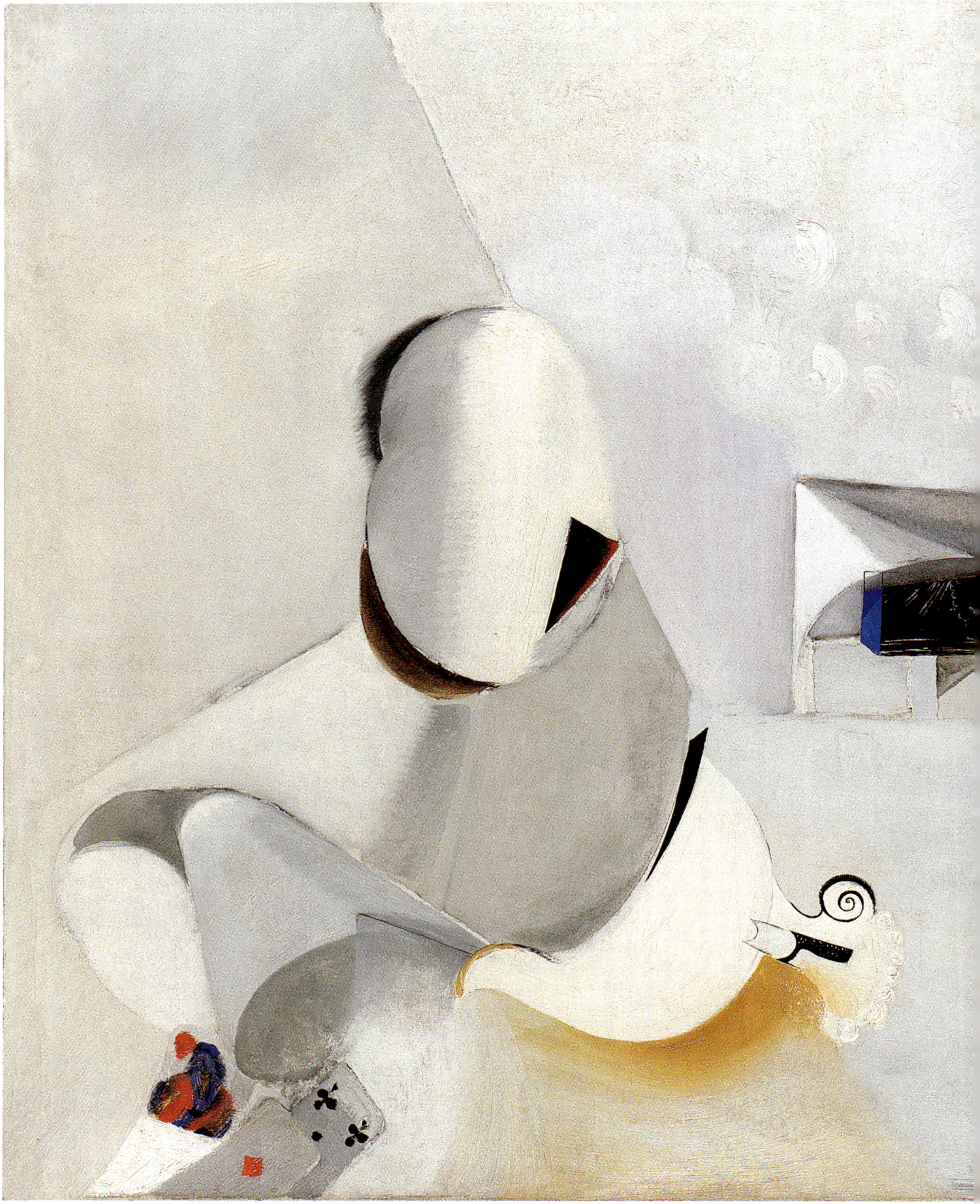

Amédée Ozenfant

Nature morte au casque, 1916

[cat. 163]

Francis Picabia
Portrait d'Apollinaire, 1918
[cat. 180]

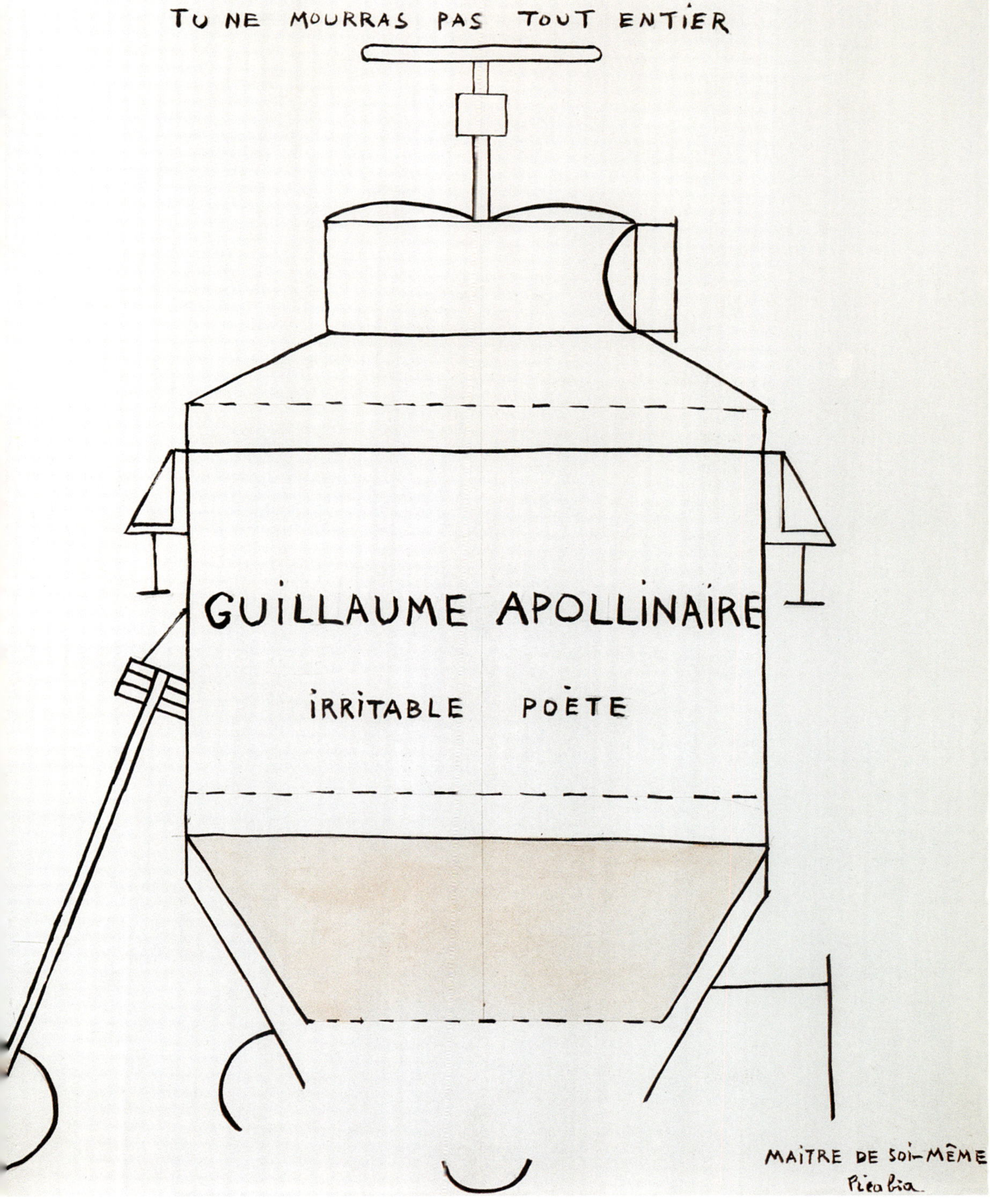
TU NE MOURRAS PAS TOUT ENTIER
GUILLAUME APOLLINAIRE
IRRITABLE POÈTE
MAITRE DE SOI-MÊME
Picabia

Man Ray

L'Impossibilité, 1917

[cat. 184]

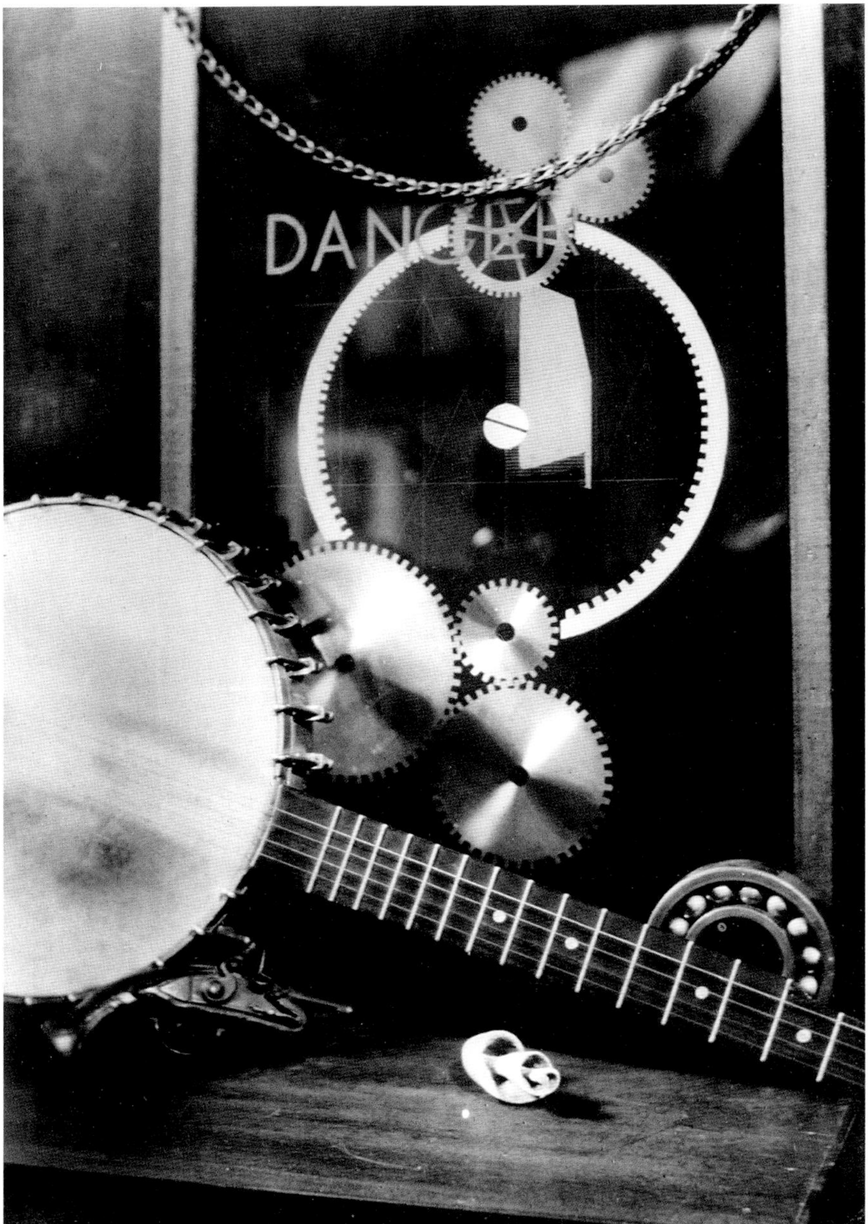

Francis Picabia

Réveil-matin, 1919

[cat. 181]

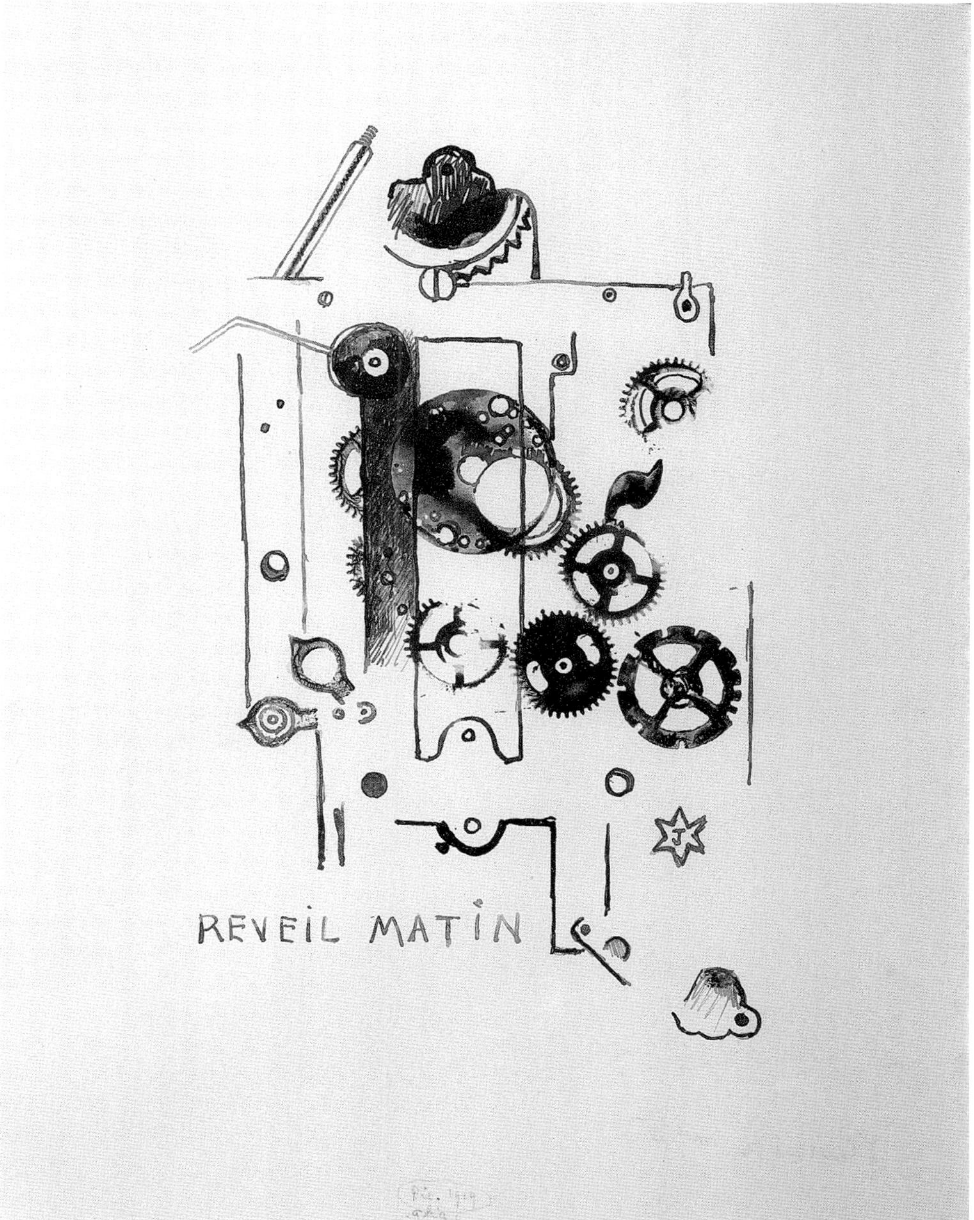

Pierre Albert-Birot

Étude finale pour La Guerre, 1916

[cat. 186]

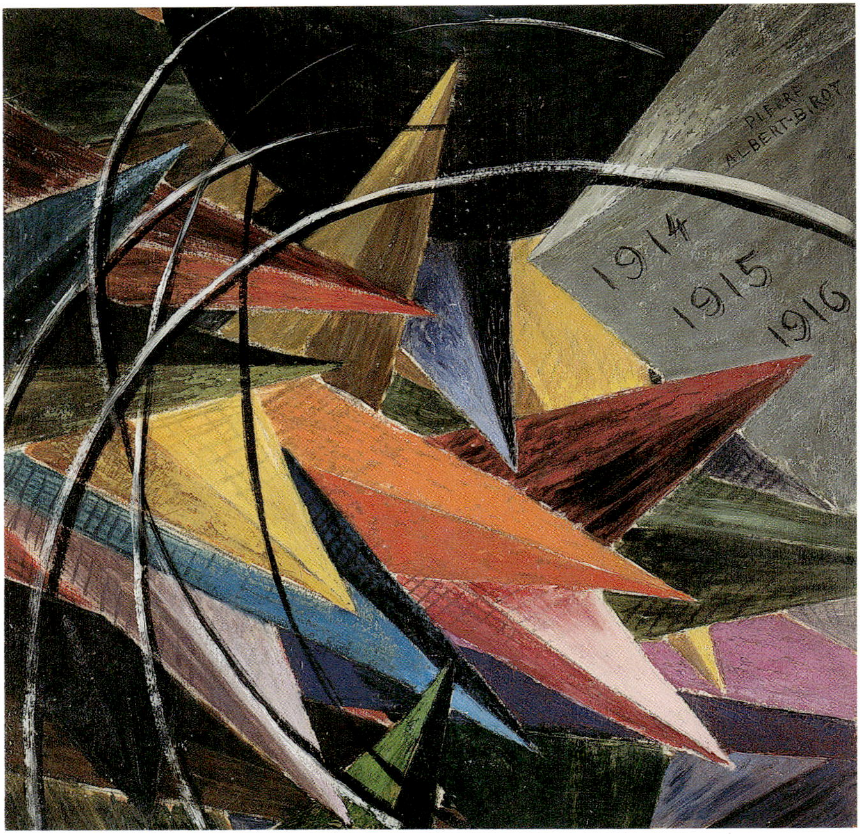

Pierre Albert-Birot

Cover of *SIC,* no. 28, April 1918

[cat. 235]

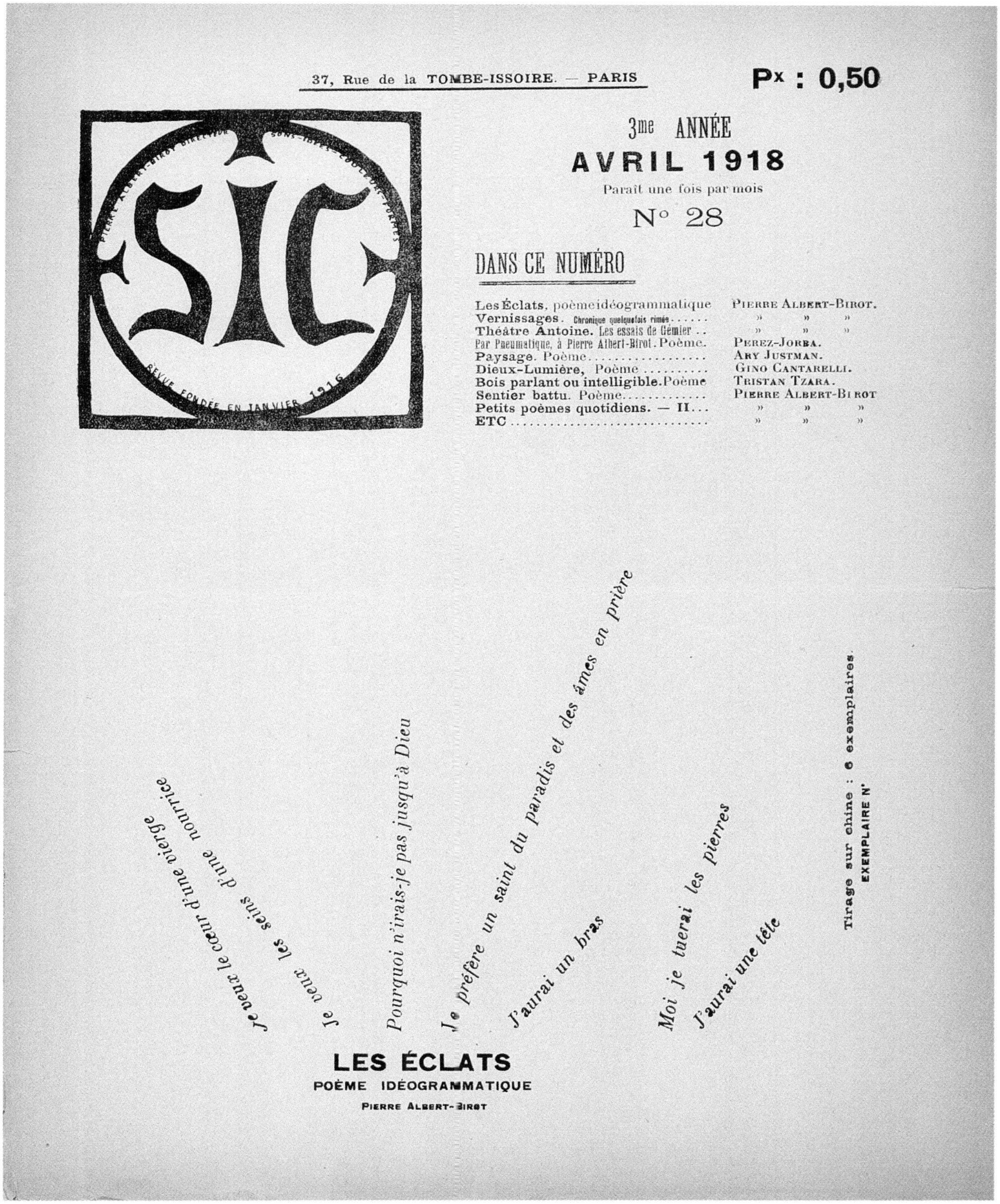

37, Rue de la TOMBE-ISSOIRE. — PARIS

Px : 0,50

SIC

3me ANNÉE

AVRIL 1918

Paraît une fois par mois

N° 28

DANS CE NUMÉRO

Les Éclats, poèmeidéogrammatique	Pierre Albert-Birot.
Vernissages. Chronique quelquefois rimés......	» » »
Théâtre Antoine. Les essais de Gémier ..	» » »
Par Pneumatique, à Pierre Albert-Birot. Poème.	Perez-Jorba.
Paysage. Poème..................	Ary Justman.
Dieux-Lumière, Poème	Gino Cantarelli.
Bois parlant ou intelligible. Poème	Tristan Tzara.
Sentier battu. Poème............	Pierre Albert-Birot
Petits poèmes quotidiens. — II...	» » »
ETC..............................	» » »

Je veux le cœur d'une vierge

Je veux les seins d'une nourrice

Pourquoi n'irais-je pas jusqu'à Dieu

Je préfère un saint du paradis et des âmes en prière

J'aurai un bras

Moi je tuerai les pierres

J'aurai une tête

LES ÉCLATS

POÈME IDÉOGRAMMATIQUE

PIERRE ALBERT-BIROT

Tirage sur chine : 6 exemplaires.

EXEMPLAIRE N°

Carlo Carrà

Rapporto di un nottambulo milanese, 1914

[cat. 195]

Gino Severini

Danza serpentina, published in *Lacerba,* July 1914

[cat. 247]

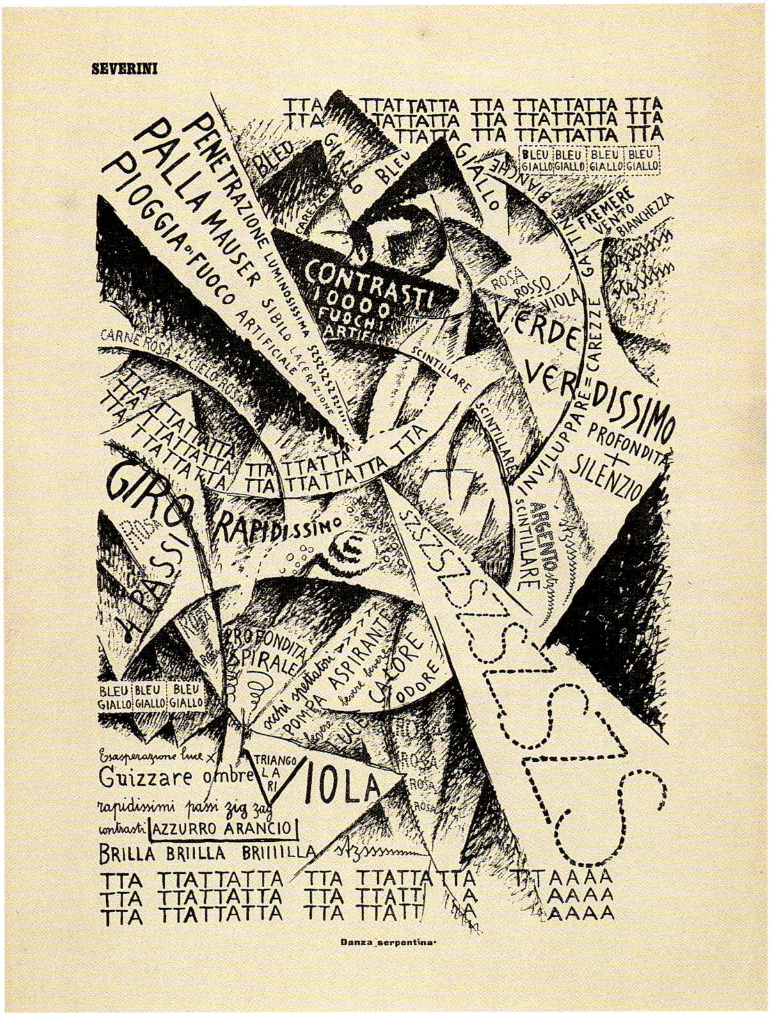

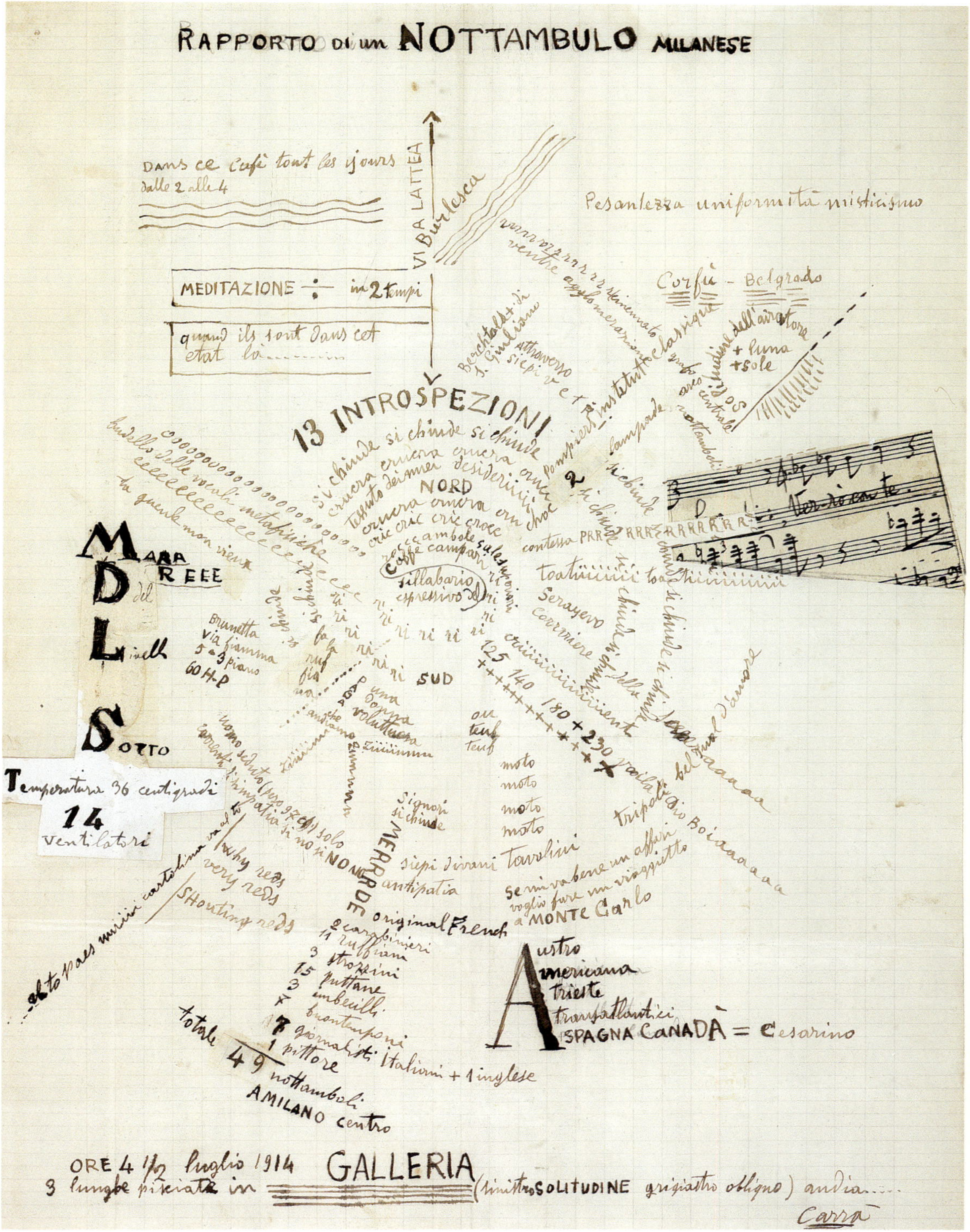

RAPPORTO DI UN NOTTAMBULO MILANESE
Dans ce café tout les jours dalle 2 alle 4
VIA LATTEA
Via Burlesca
MEDITAZIONE ÷ in 2 tempi
quand ils sont dans cet etat là.........
Pesantezza uniformità misticismo
Corfù - Belgrado
+ luna
+ sole
13 INTROSPEZIONI
NORD
Caffè Campari
Sillabario espressivo
SUD
Serayevo
Corriere
125 140 180 + 230
moto
moto
moto
moto
Signori si chiude
MERDE
siepi divani tavolini
antipatia
Se mi va bene un affare voglio fare un viaggetto a MONTE Carlo
original French
Brunetta via fiamma 5 a 3 piano 60 H.P.
Temperatura 36 centigradi
14
ventilatori
very reds
Shouting reds
Austro
Americana
Trieste
Transatlantici
SPAGNA CANADÀ = Cesarino
Italiani + 1 inglese
totale
49
nottamboli
AMILANO centro
ORE 4 1/2 luglio 1914
GALLERIA
(sinistro SOLITUDINE grigiastro obliquo) andia.....
Carrà

Francesco Cangiullo

Grande foule sur la Piazza del Popolo, 1914

[cat. 199]

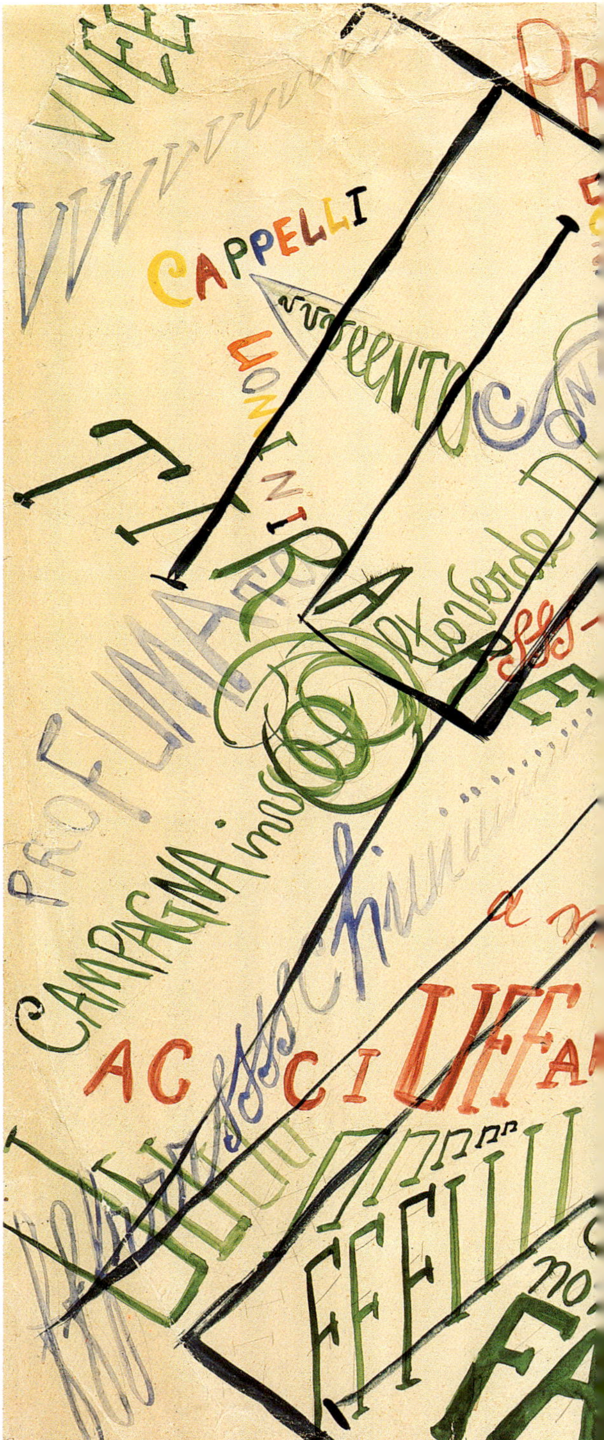

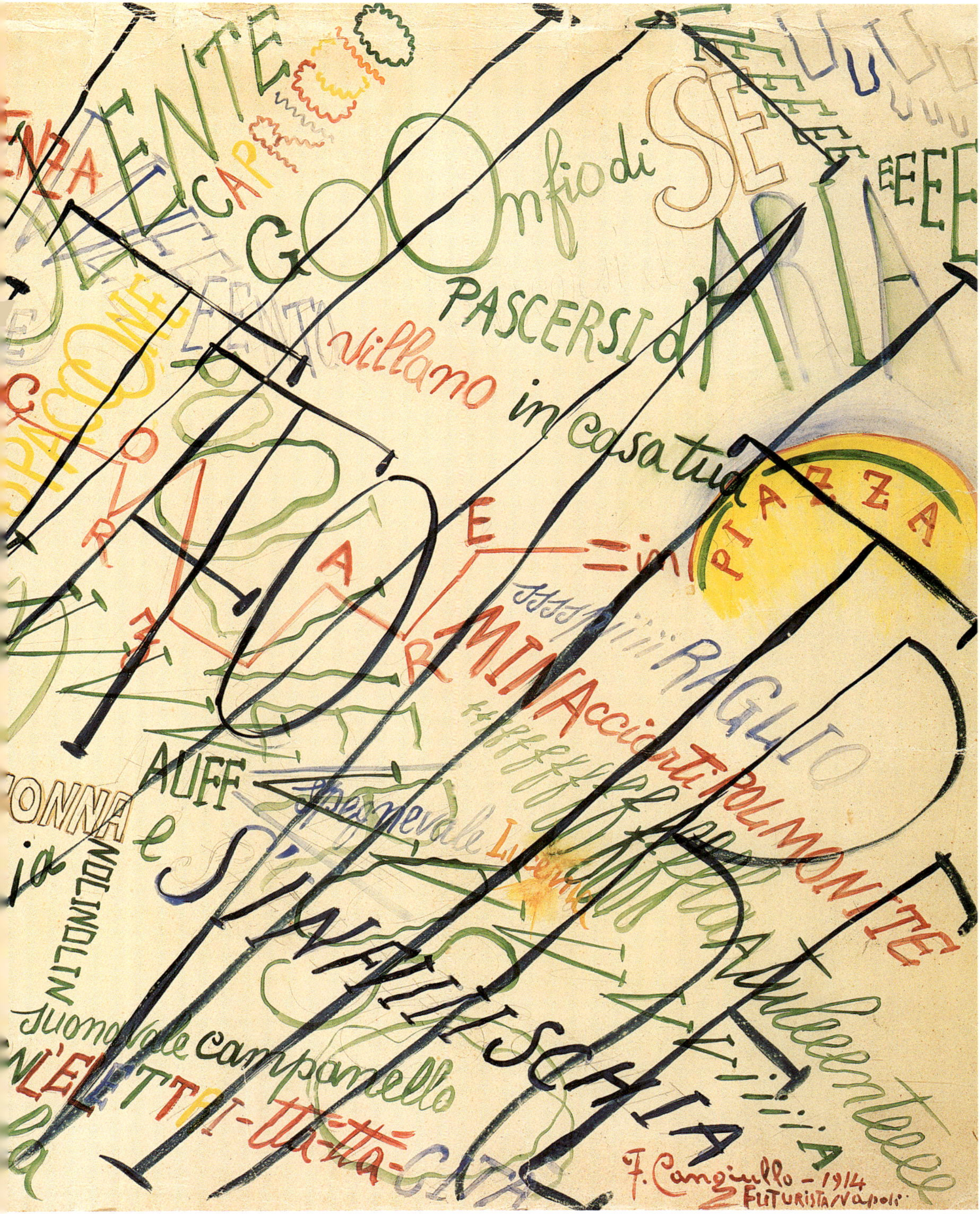
CAP
G O O O nfio di
SE
ARIA
PASCERSI d
villano in casatua
PIAZZA
MINAcciarti POLMONITE
RAGLIO
AUFF
ONNA
e
SINAFIIIISCHIA
campanello
F. Cangiullo - 1914
FUTURISTA Napoli

Francesco Cangiullo
Cover of *Piedigrotta*, 1916
[cat. 200]

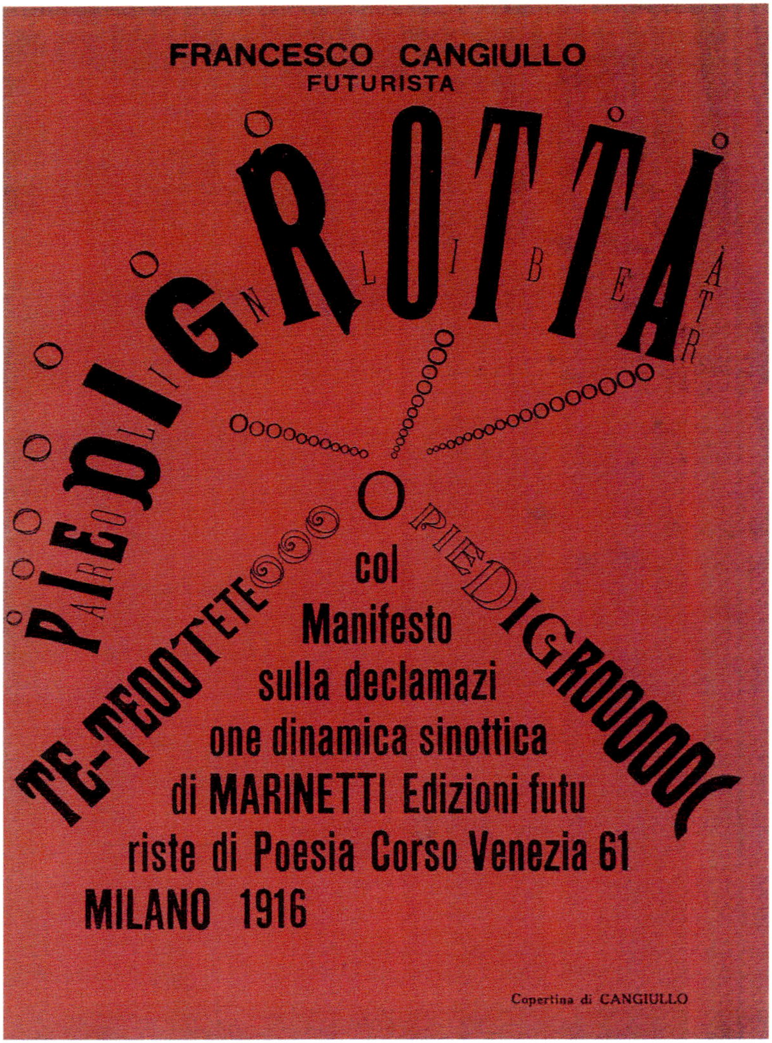

Carlo Carrà

Arrolepimento atmosferici. Scoppio di un obice, 1914

[cat. 198]

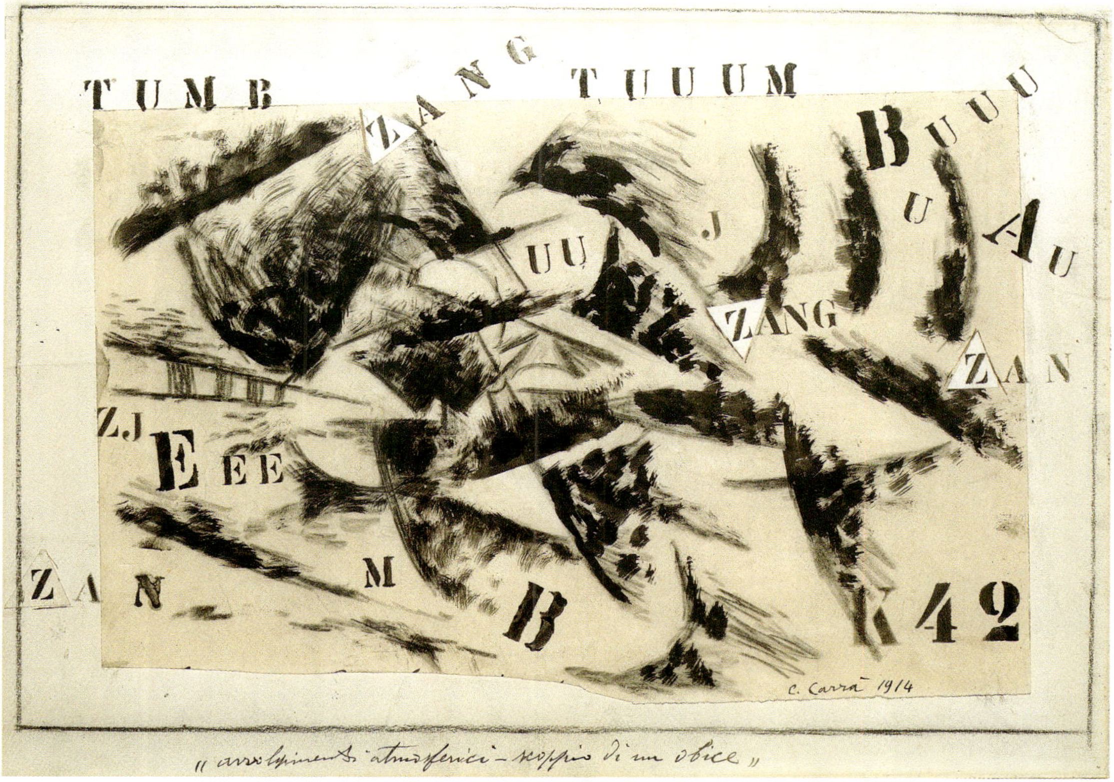

Filippo Marinetti
Futurist manifesto announcing the publication of the volume *I paroliberi futuristi* (published in 1919 under the title *Les Mots en liberté futuristes),* 1915
[cat. 236]

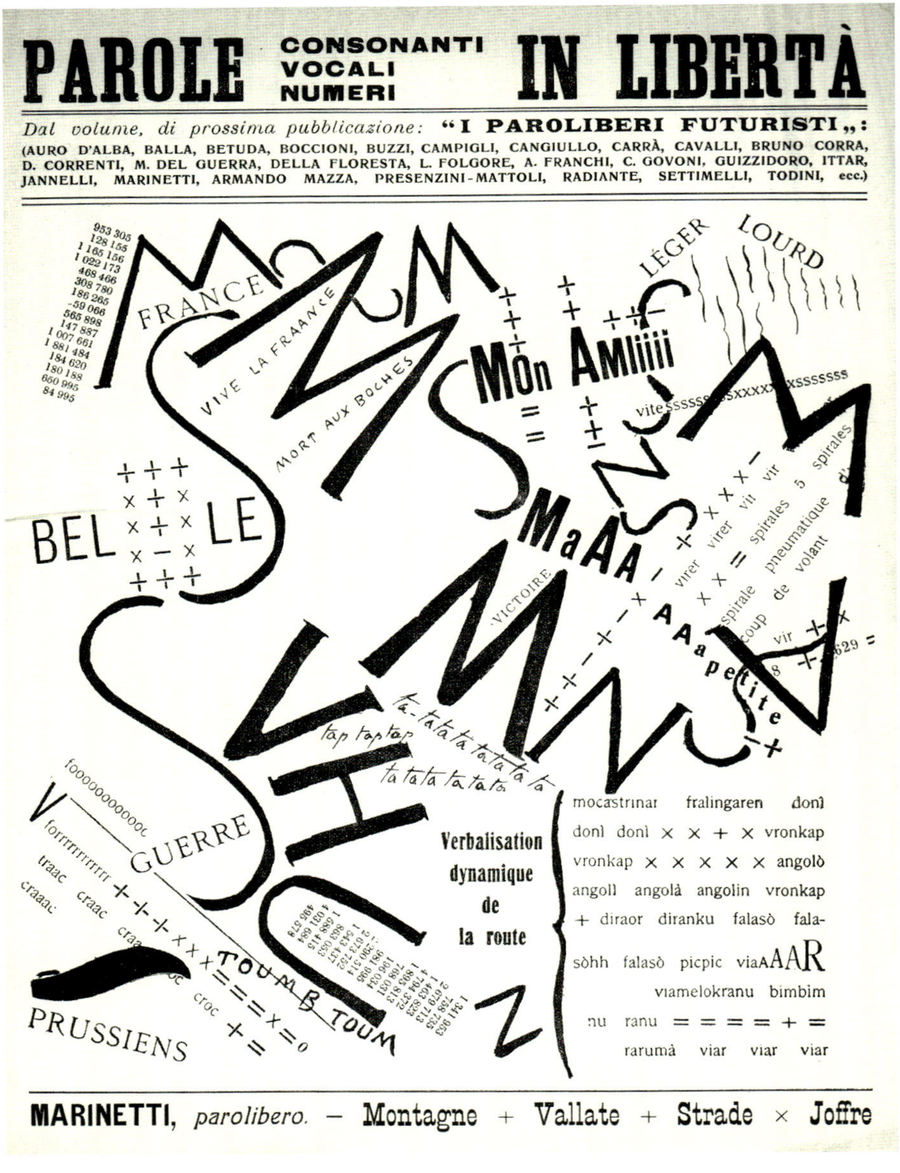

Filippo Marinetti

Proofs for *I paroliberi futuristi / Les Mots en liberté futuristes*, 1915

[cat. 192]

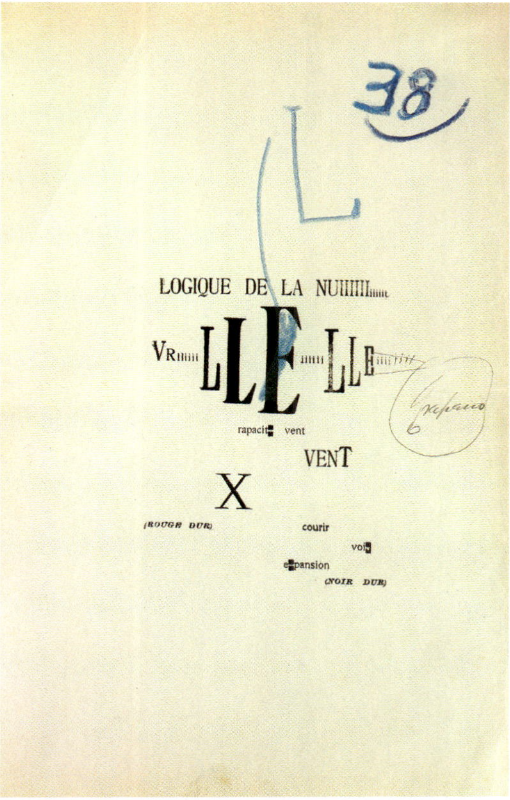

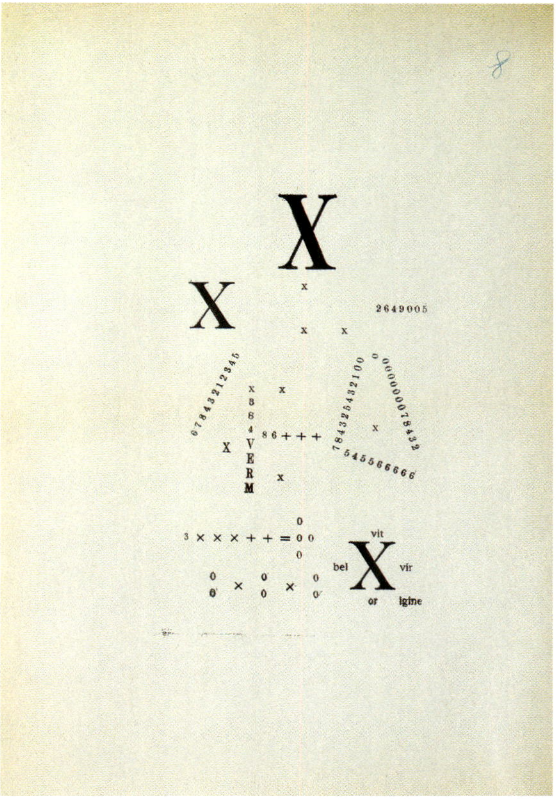

Filippo Marinetti

Cover and interior folder of *Les mots en liberté futuristes,* 1919

[cat. 191]

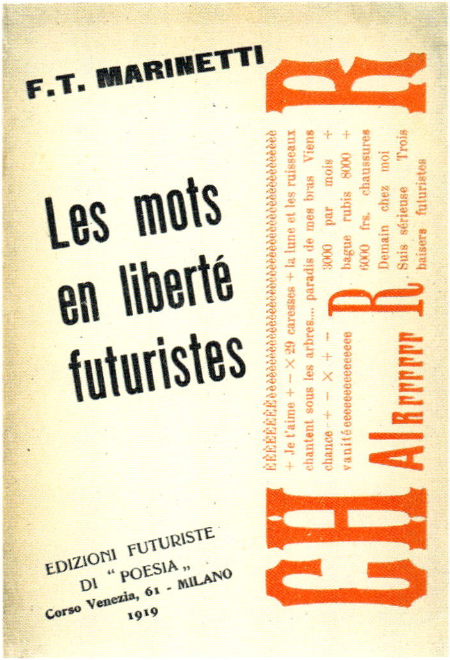

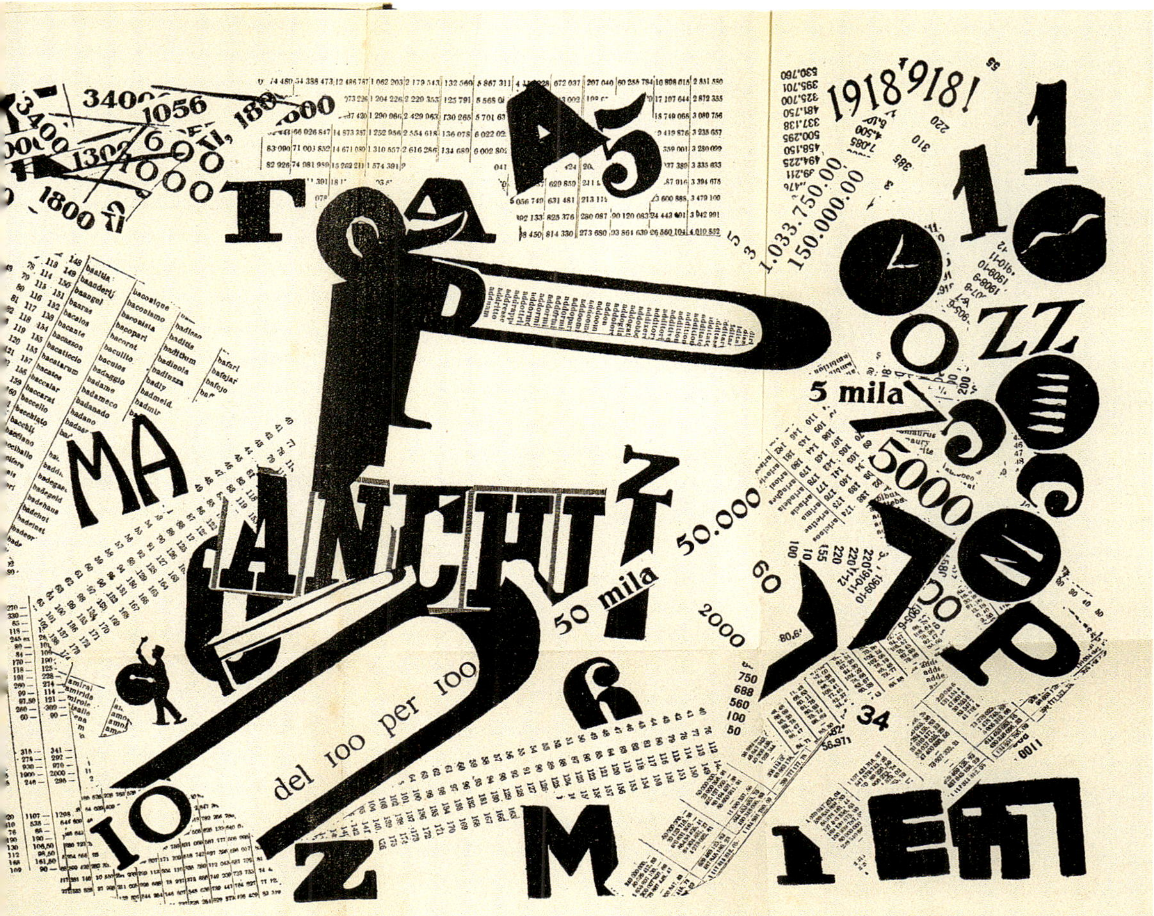
MA
5 mila
50 mila
50.000
2000
5000
del 100 per 100
1.033.750.00
150.000.00
1056
1800
34

Joan Salvat-Papasseit

L'irradiador del port i les gavines, 1921

[cat. 240]

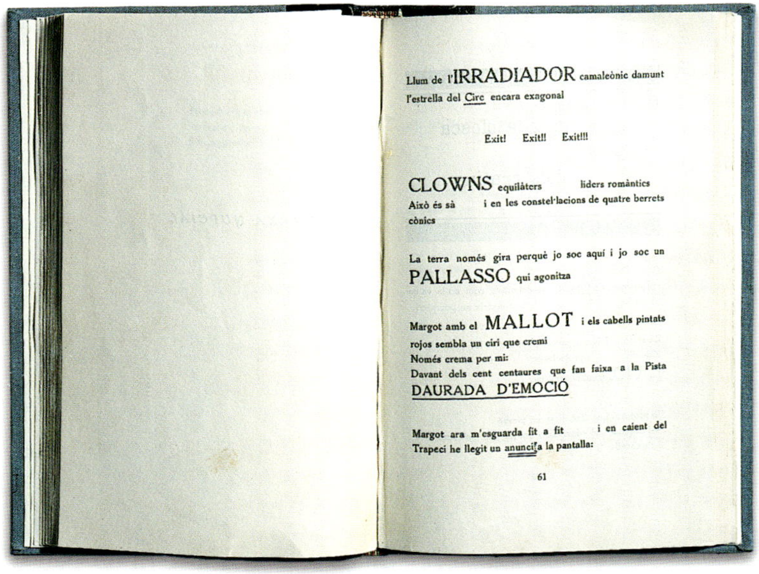

Llum de l'IRRADIADOR camaleònic damunt
l'estrella del Circ encara exagonal

Exit! Exit!! Exit!!!

CLOWNS equilàters liders romàntics
Això és sà i en les constel·lacions de quatre berrets
cònics

La terra només gira perquè jo soc aquí i jo soc un
PALLASSO qui agonitza

Margot amb el MALLOT i els cabells pintats
rojos sembla un ciri que cremi
Només crema per mi:
Davant dels cent centaures que fan faixa a la Pista
DAURADA D'EMOCIÓ

Margot ara m'esguarda fit a fit i en caient del
Trapeci he llegit un anunci a la pantalla:

61

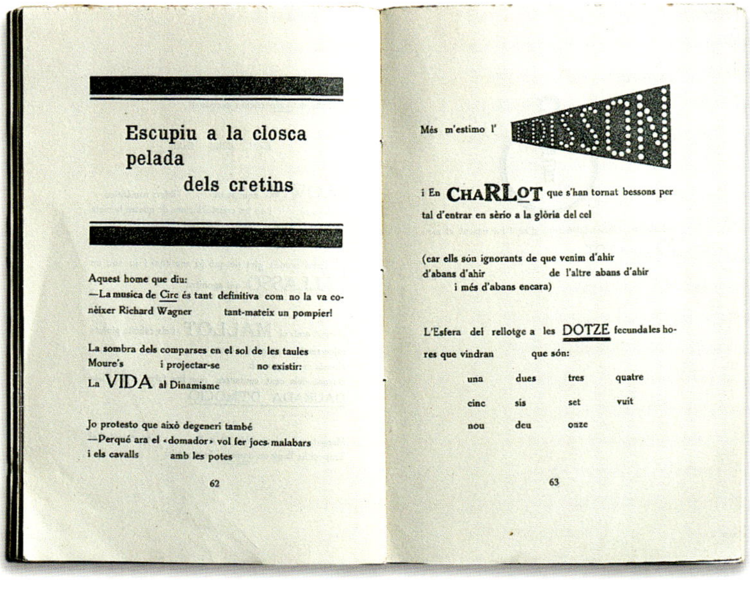

Escupiu a la closca
pelada
dels cretins

Aquest home que diu:
—La musica de Circ és tant definitiva com no la va co-
nèixer Richard Wagner tant-mateix un pompier!

La sombra dels comparses en el sol de les taules
Moure's i projectar-se no existir:
La VIDA al Dinamisme

Jo protesto que això degeneri també
—Perquè ara el «domador» vol fer jocs-malabars
i els cavalls amb les potes

62

Més m'estimo l' ADISSON

i En CHARLOT que s'han tornat bessons per
tal d'entrar en sèrio a la glòria del cel

(car ells són ignorants de que venim d'ahir
d'abans d'ahir de l'altre abans d'ahir
i més d'abans encara)

L'Esfera del rellotge a les DOTZE fecunda les ho-
res que vindran que són:

una dues tres quatre
cinc sis set vuit
nou deu onze

63

Josep Maria Junoy
Poemes & Cal·ligrames, 1920
[cat. 207]

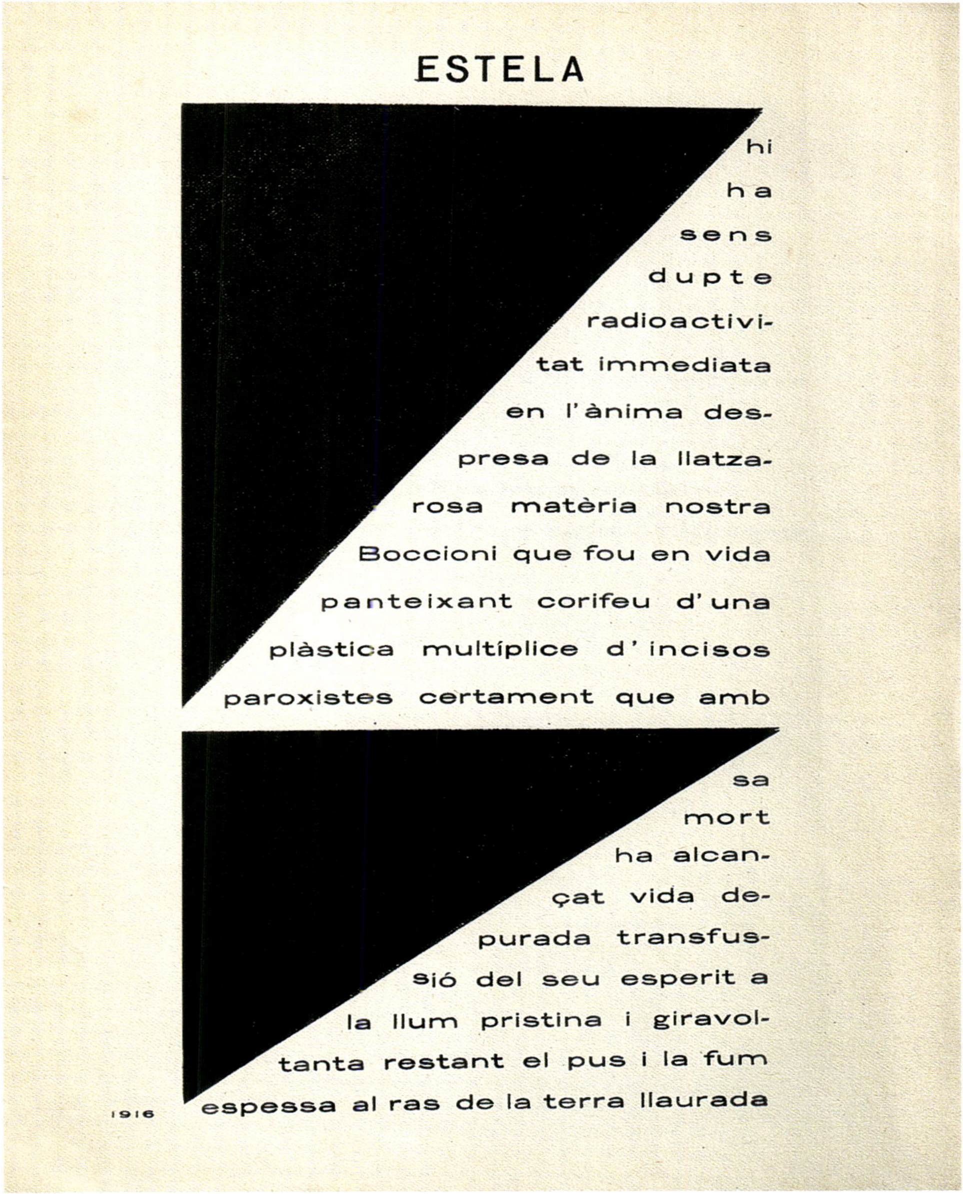

ESTELA

hi
ha
sens
dupte
radioactivi-
tat immediata
en l'ànima des-
presa de la llatza-
rosa matèria nostra
Boccioni que fou en vida
panteixant corifeu d'una
plàstica multíplice d'incisos
paroxistes certament que amb

sa
mort
ha alcan-
çat vida de-
purada transfus-
sió del seu esperit a
la llum pristina i giravol-
tanta restant el pus i la fum
espessa al ras de la terra llaurada

1916

MANIFIESTO ULTRAISTA VERTICAL

POR

GUILLERMO DE TORRE

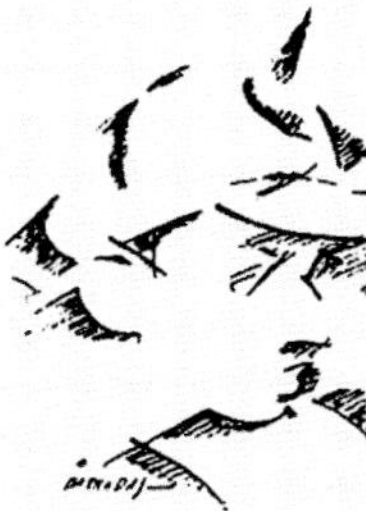

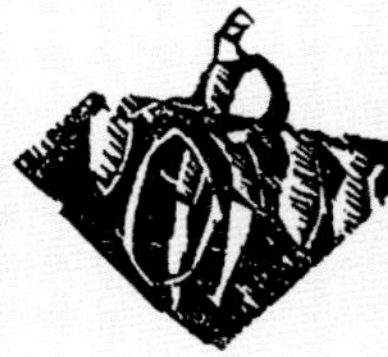

PERSPECTIVA MERIDIANA

Un Sol tentacular irradia luminosos reóforos vibrátiles a través del multiedrismo cósmico.

Dardeantes rayos térmicos que rasgan el Orto Novidimensional Estético, vivifican las fibras sensoriales e intelectivas de los Lucíferos Ultraístas.

¡Y una polarización triunfal de impulsos dinámicos hipervitalistas, acelera la hélice de nuestras inquietudes pugnaces!

ÍNDICE DE SENSACIONES, VISIONES Y CEREBRACIONES :: ::

VERTICAL: De Cenit a Nadir: Un luminoso rayo perpendicular incide las novísimas regiones estéticas: Y la rosa polipétala aflorada en la más alta cima tórrida se destríe en llamaradas sintéticas:

Dirección nórdica

Cumbre lírica

¡Palabras incendiarias!
¡Muecas burlescas!
¡Intenciones nihilistas!
¡Gestos rebeliosos!
¡ ESPASMOS HIPERESPACIALES !
Trayectorias espiralizantes en los agros zodiacales.
Introspecciones mayéuticas.
Raras cerebraciones hiperconscientes.
¡Mis miradas perforan la región del cuarto espacio!
Iluminación roëntgénica de los cerebros porvenirista.
Sístoles superatrices.
Circunvoluciones arácnidas.
Acrobacias líricas.

Descoyuntación tipográfica: Las linotipias sufren un ataque de histeria: rrrjllmodlkaanboccciitipzzevsssesifff.

Vertebración atlántica de las figuras y los paisajes fundidos en una compenetración espacial de los volúmenes flotantes

Ritmizaciones geométricas.
El séptuplo corazón de la hélice vibra al ritmo ortal.
¡Impetus ascensionales de Psiquis velivolante!
Y un arco-iris heptacorde musicaliza la armonía cnespacial.
Los ríos sangran fuego.
En el paisaje contorsionado fluye la hemorragia solar.
Dehiscencia del verticilo heptacromista.
Meridio plenisolar.

Y, ante los ojos resurrectos, un fragante PANORAMA ULTRAESPACIAL.

:: :: SÍNTESIS PANORÁMICA

APOTEOSIS DE HOY: Vibración concéntrica del momento poliédrico, al ritmo de las hélices cosmogónicas.

En el vórtice de nuestro instante ultraico, se plasma una hipervitalista apoteosis antiliteraria de las cerebraciones maquinísticas, los orgasmos aviónicos y los paroxismos líricamente centrífugos...

¿Cómo vislumbramos la síntesis afranjada de esta hora multiédrica, polirrítmica y multánime? Yuxtaposición policromática de las perspectivas intermundiales. Escuchad la polifonía intraoceánica en los auriculares telefónicos. El Hombre Vertical se despliega alado abrazando los continentes. Los vocablos truncados, se abaten velivolantes sobre las antenas radiotelegráficas. Albatros e hidroaviones logaritmizan la pizarra marina, y planean sobre los faros del oleaje astral. Los corazones aterrizan en un periscopio emergente.

Panorama multitudinario de las ciudades contorsionadas en su mecanicismo eufóricamente veloz. ¡Oh, los gestos luminosos de los carteles formados por bujías astrales en el horizonte nocturno! Y en el aire, el grito virgen de los trolleys—que dice un cantor fraterno de la profundidad sinfrónica.

Circuitos perihélicos: Viajes en la planitud pura del espacio isótropo: Anhelos antropocéntricos: Vibracionismo de los colores impolutos y de las palabras abstractas: Hay un ciclón sensual en el cráter erótico. Exaltaciones phálicas: Los sexos subvertidos deambulan insurrectos: Y las visiones léticias se transforman tras las introyecciones metafóricas.

Un friso de núbiles corzas se sumerge en el lago de su espejo lésbico. Féminas cygneas, en la ribera nostálgica, punzan su endocárdio, ablucionándose en sangre sentimental. En el museo hay un cuadro anacrónico: campesinos de égloga exprimen la ubre de un sol que transmonta vesperal. Y en el estadio: adolescentes púgiles cultivan su musculatura mental al pasear a través de un laberinto ideológico y verbalizar abstractamente.

SIMULTANEISMO NUNISTA

Los espectadores son arrollados por las calles que desfilan cinemáticas. Sinfonía motorística de las sirenas y klaxons en las avenidas arteriales. Itinerario noviespacial del paisaje al volante de un 60 HP. Hay billetes de circunvalación lunaria, tarifa especial, para los poetas delicuescentes. Anuncio: «Se ofrece un gran stock de figuras orientalistas decorativas—Schahrazadas, Salomés, Judiths—como señoritas de compañía en los paseos lésbicos de morfinómanas irredimibles.»

Pesquisas nouménicas en los laboratorios de radioactividad. Y en contraste, precipitados alquímicos en las páginas de libros noviestructurales: Ved aquí un puzzle de las arduas y dinámicas alegorías occidentalistas: Kaleidoscopio imaginativo del complexo noviespacial: Mi manifiesto traza cabriolas caprichosas en el éter abstracto, rehuyendo las citas matemáticas, y dibuja una espiral de alucinaciones sugerentes. Ritmos plurales acompasan los instintos nómadas. Y la urgencia innovadora justifica la erección vertical.

:: :: ACTITUD VERTICALISTA

Tras la bélica convulsión europea, en el panorama ideológico, artístico y literario del Occidente resurrecto, se ha iniciado una transmutación vertebral: El gran error, tendido como una noche opaca—preñada de sangre—entre los años 1914-18—, ha abortado una generación juvenil e innovadora que polariza sus nihilismos burlescos paradójicamente simultáneos a sus esfuerzos reconstructores o renacentistas. Y, en el orden ético y estético, destruye las viejas y topificadas «ideas-madres», los crasos «conceptos fundamentales», generadores de falsedades y aberraciones mortíferas—cuyo reciente ejemplo sangra aún. Allende las fronteras capturadas, al derrocar burlescamente las normas vigentes, y sentirse reciennacida ideológicamente, e ingrávida en el espacio, la nueva generación ultraísta ha ascendido a un medio día luminoso, pluralmente henchido de inéditas y sugerentes perspectivas mentales.

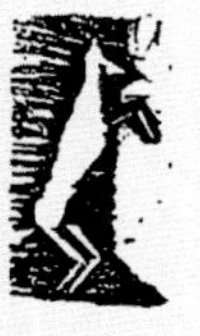

En la nueva planimetría estética, de un área ultradimensional y de una altitud hiperbórea, frutece un meridio plenisolar verticalmente simbólico. Los electrodos—aniones y cationes—del voltáico globo solar suscitan un luminoso circuito porvenirista, rompiendo el brumario caótico. Electrolisis lírica. En los búcaros aéreos, que contienen los nepenthes atmosféricos, fluye una potente endósmosis que galvaniza la caquexia petálea de las rosas astrales. Y vigoriza la musculatura de los pugilistas polémicos.

En la pleamar celeste del intenso azul esdrújulo, un apolíneo sol de Occidente irisa y refracta el aleteo tornátil de los espíritus aviónicos. Bajo la bautismal aspersión solar nuestros ojos-antorchas de lucíferos ultraístas perforan e iluminan las inéditas perspectivas verticales. Fluye un «simoun» que vaporiza atmosféricamente las bellezas ortales. ¡¡Todo, protagonistas y ambiente, recíprocamente interpenetrados, vibran ercctos en un escorzo avanzativo! En el laboratorio cerebral ultraísta, se efectúa un precipitado barroco de emociones y sensaciones verticistas. Nuestros músculos discobólicos adquieren una tensión eléctrica de infinitos watios Y se extienden, en un ademán pugnaz, hacia los horizontes dinámicos de un área cnespacial.

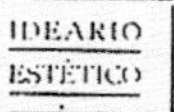

IDEARIO ESTÉTICO

Mis concepciones estéticas ultraístas están situadas, y logran su más perfecta proyección, en la planimetría noviespacial, en la región del Espacio Absoluto: En cuyos dintornos resalta sugeridoramente el enorme geométrico de la cuarta dimensión: Y se abren las perspectivas ilimitadas del Hiperespacio, donde se desarrolla la introspección espiritual y la mayéutica crítica de las novísimas direcciones estéticas.

Los apotegmas cubistas—en el sector literario—de la pura sensa-

Manifiesto vertical ultraíst (supplement of the magazine *Grecia*, no. 50, Madrid, November 1, 1920. Cartoon by Rafael Barradas, text by Guillermo de Torre)
[cat. 253]

Joaquín Torres-García
Hoy, ca. 1921
[cat. 189]

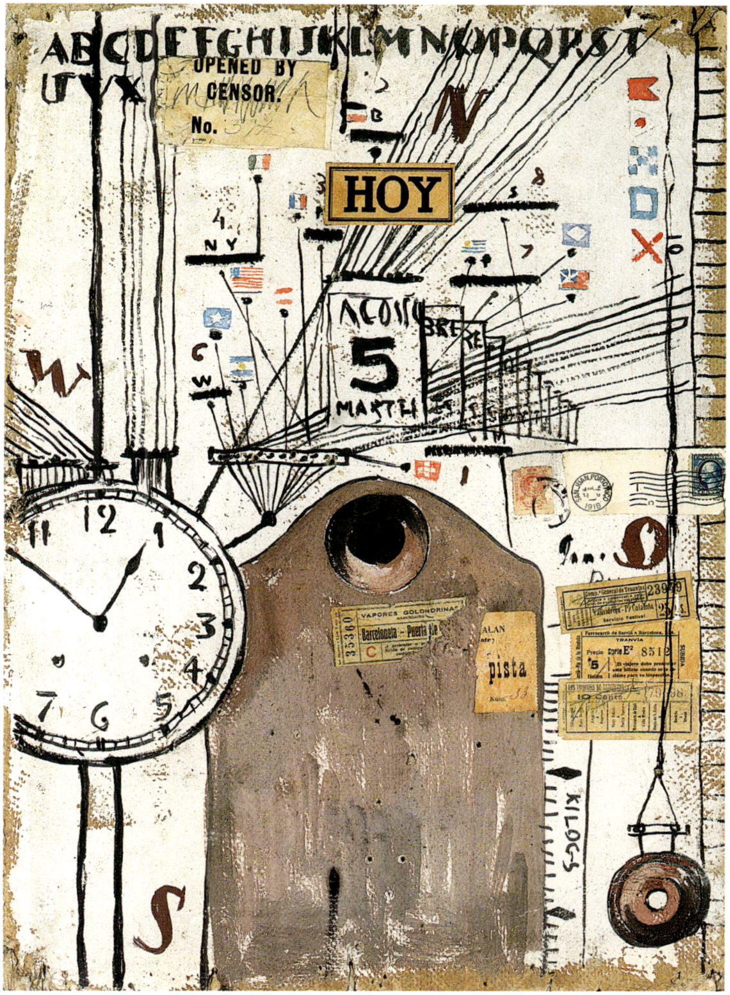

Next double page:
Raoul Hausmann
Kp'erioUM, Manifest von der Gesetzmäsigkeit des Lautes, 1919
[cat. 258]

kp' erioUM lp'er ioum

Nm' periii pERnomoum

bprEtiBerreeeRREbee
e

ONNOo gplanpouk

konmpout pERIKOUL

RREEeeEEeerrrrreeeeeA

oapAerrre EEE

mgl ed padANou

MTNOU tnoum t

Typographische Anordnung für DADAKO / Druckerei Waldowsky

manifest vOll dEr geSetz mässigkeit des lautes

r hausmann

Wenn man, die Lippen teilend, das Rauchen beginnt als dreifaches Bewegungsmoment dem ein viertes accidentielles Segment zufällt. Der Wille zur Macht des Tabaks als navy cut spottet in der Calorie der Verbrennung der geistigen Profitrate. Das Rauchen, an sich Ruhe im infantilen Verhalten des Lebens, steigert sich bei der Cigarette zum Dandyismus einer hemmungslosen Projektion des Sündenfalls. Während die Kunst die einzige gewachsene Sache des Menschen ist, stellt das Rauchen eines shag calumets die trostvolle Gewißheit von der Einzigartigkeit des Geschehens und zugleich die Absolutheit, Indifferenz des Moments dar, die unvergängliche Wiederkehr alles Schwebenden in der inneren Versenktheit des Auflösens in Rauch. Das Rauchen, betrachtet vom abstrakt-konkreten Sein, enthält die Aufhebung einer sozialen Verlorenheit in den Wohlgerüchen des bryar-holzes und einer vollendeten Form W D & H O Wills mild capstan tobacco Bristol London dessen Windungen unter dem Aufrollen des Glimmens im Ansaugen eines der Pranas oder Tattwas durch den leichten Geruch der feinen Maserung und seine Hornmundstückdichte umlagert. Das tabu einer totemmedicin in der Erlebenssectante des Westeuropäers beseitigt alle Einwände einer primitiven Ausdrucksform wie der Wirtschaftspolitik. Geboren aus der Notwendigkeit, alles Eitle einer unklaren Bildung zu überwinden, ist die Form hingebend, elegant und kurz. Die Freude des Silbers am Beschlagenwerden und um den Vierkant des calumethalses aufblätternd zur gehaltvollen Hohlheit eines doppelt gegliederten Kopfes, dessen Luftaxe sich zwischen den Zähnen des Rauchenden manifestiert als fünffache Dimension der Freiheit des Atmens und von Raum und Zeit.

Die Kunst der Besitzgier ist der Anteil einer unbegreiflichen Schöpfung, deren plastische Prismatik im Huflattich der Buche eine Beziehungsform der Rose mitteilt. Der lebendige Gedanke der Rose in Gelb ist das Eigenverkehrsproblem einer wechselnden Undulation im Aroma des Duftes der festen Spitzigkeit ihrer Dornen. Der Mensch, bedürfend eines Katalysators seiner Gehördiscrepanzen, verleiht dem Fett die Beweglichkeit des Geruchs in der Seife, als Analogie wertet er die spectrale Tricolore der zerspringenden Kugel, abgestoßen von einem Strohhalm. d■r d■s Darüb■rd■nk■ns s■in■r Entst■hung als quantitativ■ Qualität s■in■r Kat■gori■ ■ntfr■md■t bl■ibt — di■ Pn■umatiks d■s transc■nd■ntimman■nt■n S■■l■nautos sind ang■blas■n vom Elan ■in■r comprimi■rt■n Wid■rstandsfähigk■it, verwandt d■m B■nzol. Di■ ■inzigartige V■rbund■nh■it d■s subj■ctiv■n Ods mit d■m obj■ctiv■n Oscilli■r■n d■s Parfums macht d■n G■brauch d■s Eucalyptusinhalators zu ■in■r lunarisch■n Ang■l■g■nh■it d■r chaotisch■n Mundhöhl■ Was nun di■ G■s■tz■ d■s Laut■s ang■ht . . . .

R. Hausmann 1919

Paul Klee
Revolving House, 1921
[cat. 254]

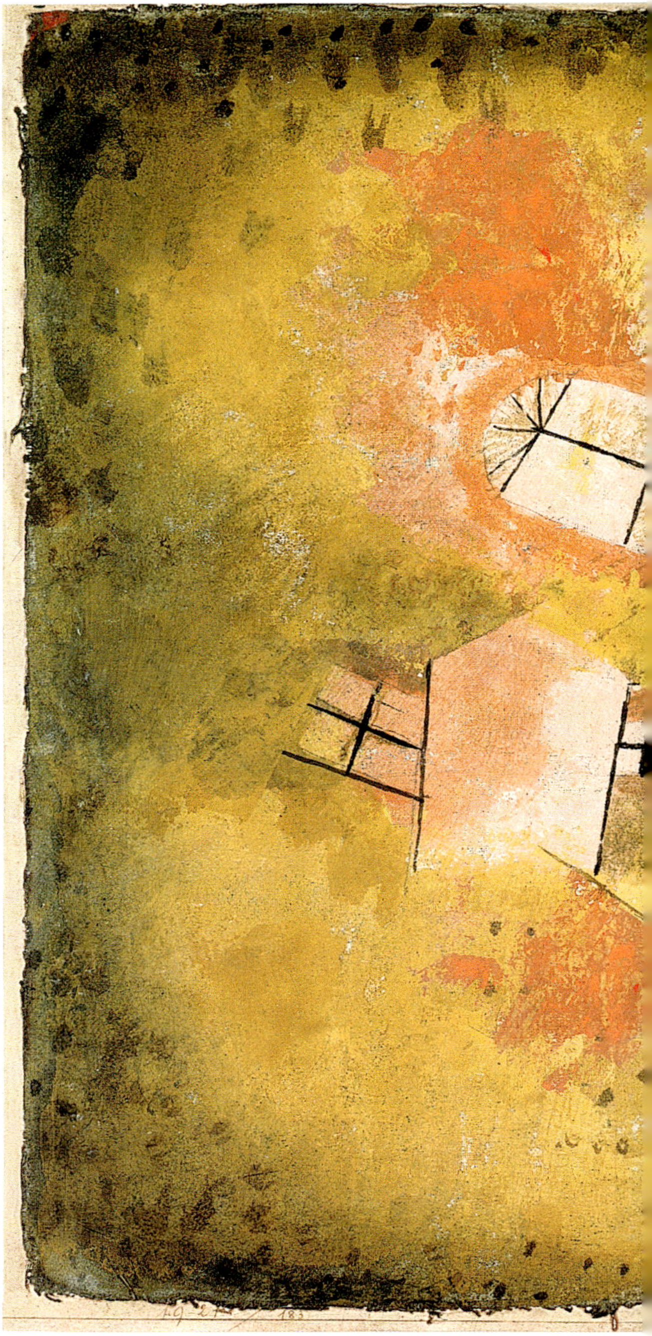

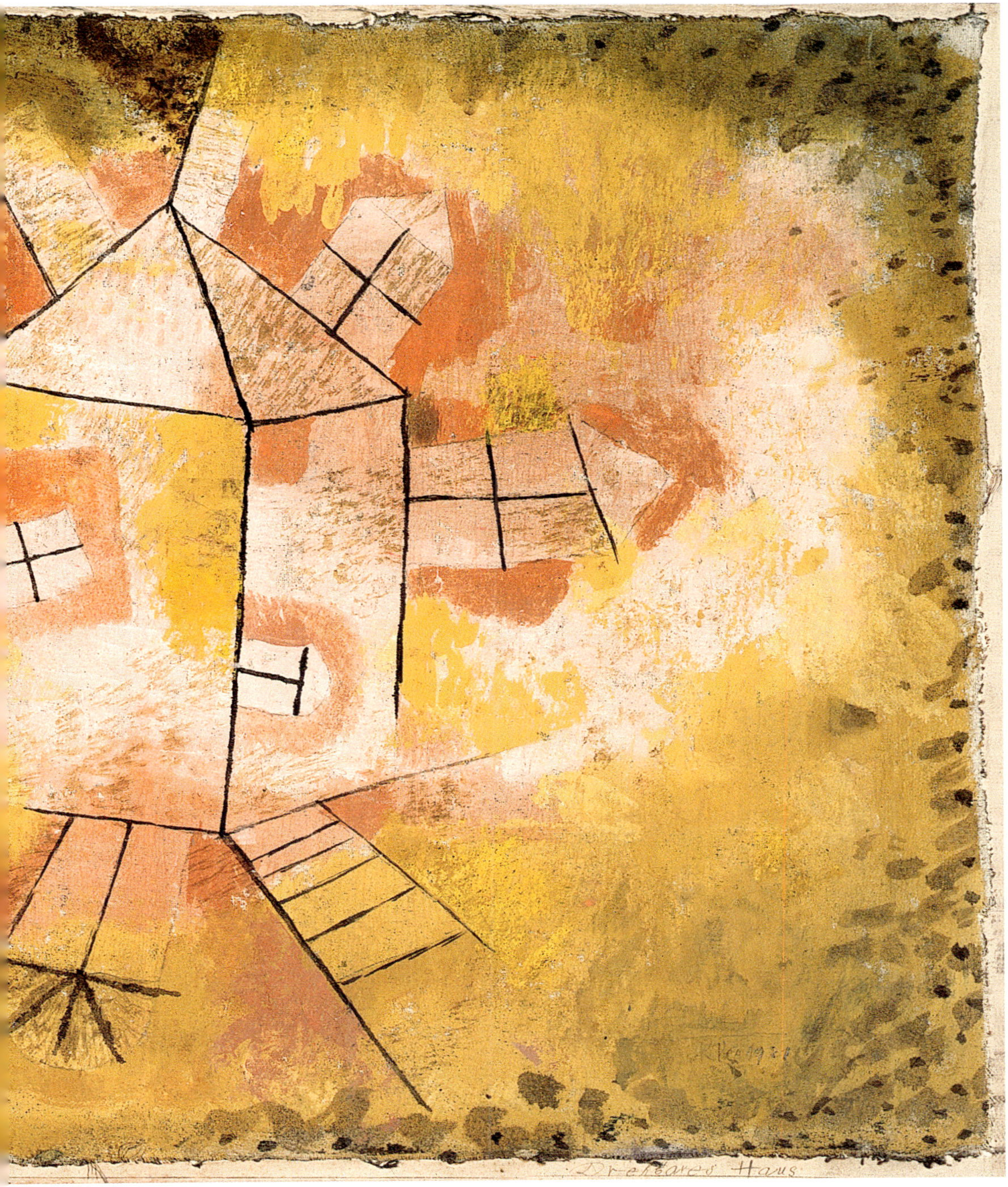

Raoul Hausmann
Grün, 1918
[cat. 257]

Disgusted by the slaughter of the World War in 1914, we dedicated ourselves to the fine arts in Zurich. While in the distance the thunder of the cannons rumbled, we sang, painted, glued, wrote with all our strength. We were looking for an elemental art which would heal people of the madness of the times and a new order which would restore the balance between heaven and hell.

Hans Arp
"Dadaland," *On My Way. Poetry and Essays, 1912-1947,* 1948

The components of poetic art are letters, syllables, words, sentences. From the reciprocal development of these components poetry is born. Sense is only important when developed in the same way as each of these factors. I utilise sense in relation to nonsense. I prefer nonsense, but this is a completely personal matter. Nonsense arouses pity in me since up until now it has only rarely been given form in art and that's why I like nonsense.

Kurt Schwitters
"Merz," *Der Ararat,* 1920

In a world free of the need to dominate out of fear, we would no longer dare to assert our tiny physical ego as the optical arbiter of spiritual realities for a world not made of physical limitations.

Raoul Hausmann
"Nous ne sommes pas des photographes," 1921

25 Mai 1918

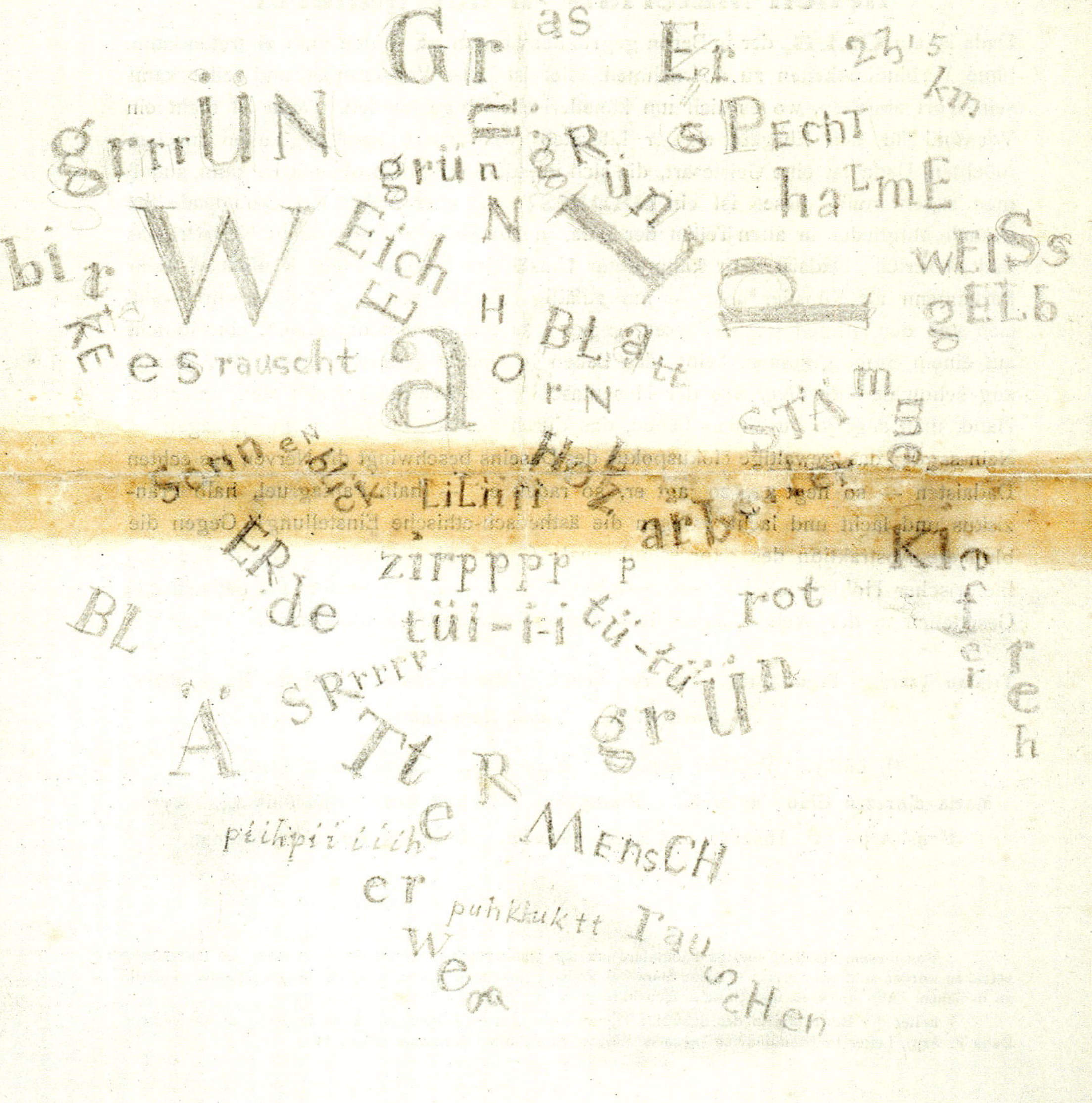

Gr äs Er
grrrÜN
grün
SPECHT
halme
WEISSs
gELb
bi rKE
es rauscht
Eich
BLatt
HOL
STAm
sonnen
LiLiLi
arbeiten
Kle
zirpppp
ERde
tüi-i-i
tü-tü
rot
BL
SRrrrr
grÜn
Ä Tter
MEnsCH
er
puhkluktt
Tauschen

l' inconnu raoul hausmann

une aile la laide promis

contient ciRcuit VIOLENCE

rEgarde calorie de Balanc

SOUTIENS dur carambole

Drolatique

sepulchure

sacrifie

cornichons astronomiques

relative epaulette

j'en fit mepriser SOUVENIR

sabotir declancher carbonnade

exister en la cloche grisverte

l'escalier d'etoile se finit

r. hausmann

mouchoir d'un pays exalte

Raoul Hausmann
L'Inconnu, 1919
[cat. 256]

Hans Arp
Dessin dada, 1916
[cat. 261]

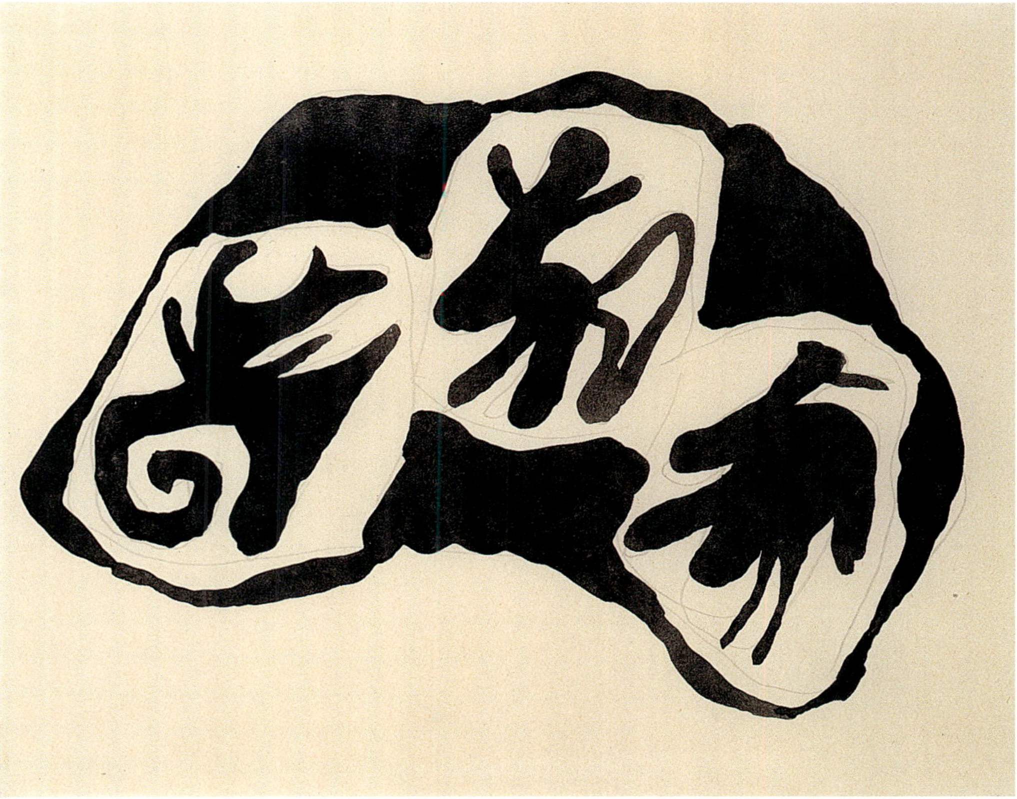

Next double page:
Tristan Tzara - Hans Arp
Vingt-cinq poèmes, 1918
[cat. 289]

aux colonies
souvenir senteur de propre phar-
macie vieille servante
cheval vert et céréales
corne crie
flûte
bagages ménageries obscures
mords scie veux-tu
horizontale voir

printemps

à h arp

placer l'enfant dans le vase au
fond de minuit
et la plaie
une rose des vents avec tes doigts
aux belles ongles
le tonnerre dans des plumes voir
une eau mauvaise coule des
membres de l'antilope

souffrir en bas avez-vous trouvé
des vaches des oiseaux?
la soif le fiel du paon dans la
cage
le roi en exil par la clarté du
puits se momifie lentement
dans le jardin de légumes
semer des sauterelles brisées
planter des cœurs de fourmis le
brouillard de sel une lampe tire
la queue sur le ciel

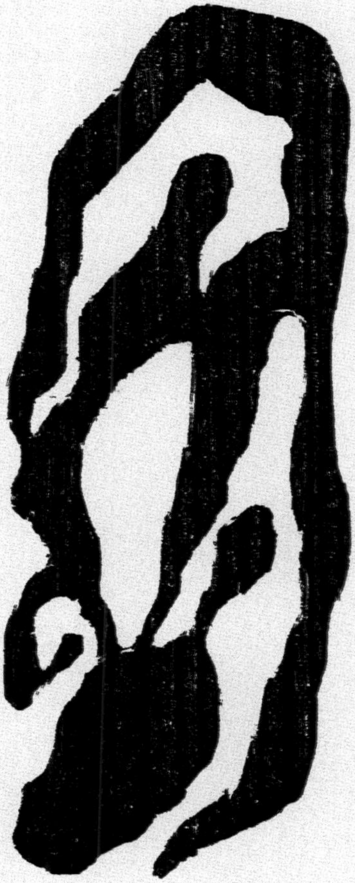

Janco has made a number of masks for the new soiree, and they are more than just clever. They are reminiscent of the Japanese or ancient Greek theater, yet they are wholly modern. They were designed to be effective from a distance; in the relatively small space of the cabaret they have a sensational effect. We were all there when Janco arrived with his masks, and everyone immediately put one on. Then something strange happened. Not only did the mask immediately call for a costume; it also demanded a quite definite, passionate gesture, bordering on madness. Although we could not have imagined it five minutes earlier, we were walking around with the most bizarre movements, festooned and draped with impossible objects, each one of us trying to outdo the other in inventiveness. The motive power of these masks was irresistibly conveyed to us. All at once we realized the significance of such a mask for mime and for the theater. The masks simply demanded that their wearers start to move in a tragic-absurd dance.
Then we looked more closely at the masks; they were made of cardboard and were painted and glued. Their varied individuality inspired us to invent dances, and for each of them I composed a short piece of music on the spot. We called one dance "Fliegenfangen" [Flycatching]. The only things suitable for this mask were clumsy, fumbling steps and some quick snatches and wild swings of the arms, accompanied by nervous, shrill music. We called the second dance "Cauchemar" [Nightmare]. The dancing figure starts from a crouching position, gets straight up, and moves forward. The mouth of the mask is wide open, the nose is broad and in the wrong place. The performer's arms, menacingly raised, are elongated by special tubes. The third dance we called "Festliche Verzweiflung" [Festive Despair]. Long, cutout, golden hands on the curved arms. The figure turns a few times to the left and to the right, then slowly turns on its axis, and finally collapses abruptly to return slowly to the first movement. What fascinates us all about the masks is that they represent not human characters and passions, but characters and passions that are larger than life. The horror of our time, the paralyzing background of events, is made visible.

Hugo Ball
Note of 24 May 1916

Sophie Taeuber dancing with Janco's mask in the Cabaret Voltaire, Zurich, 1916

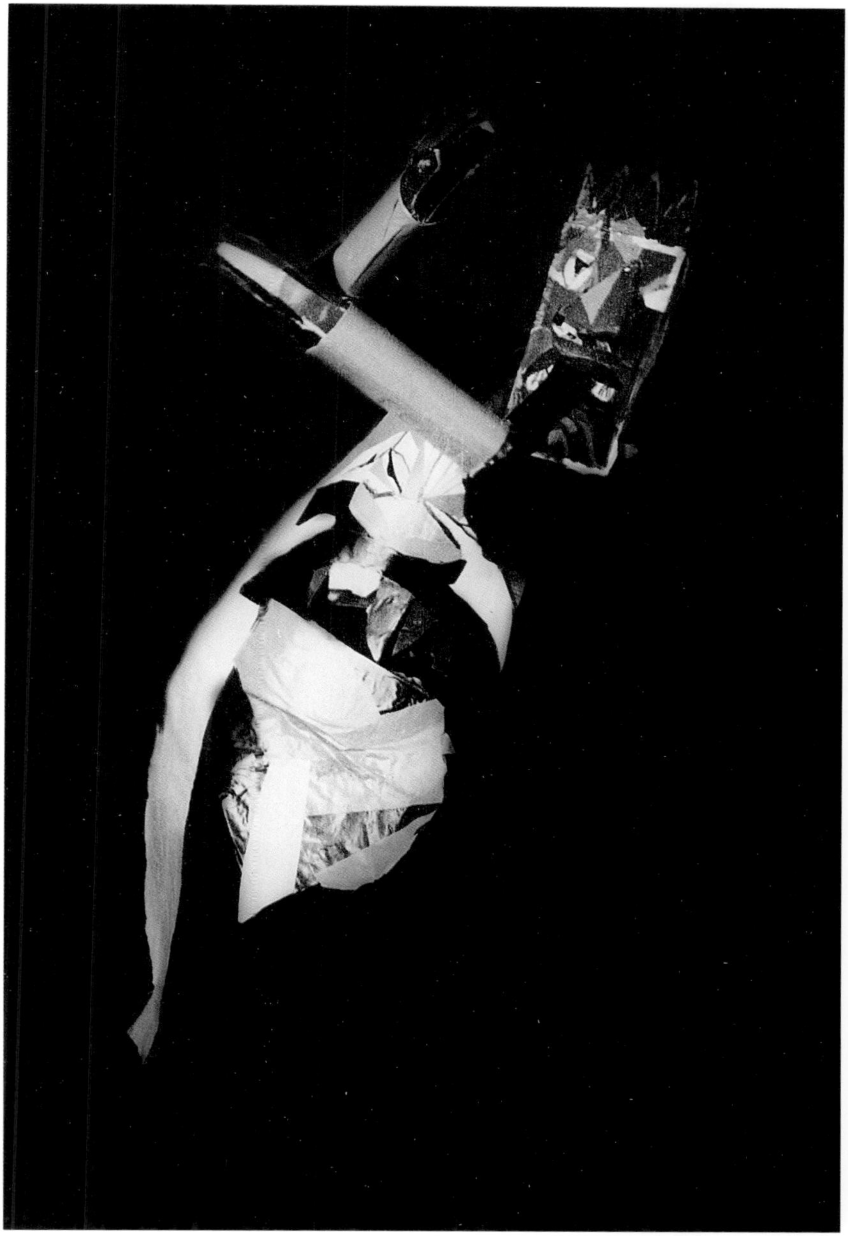

Raoul Hausmann

"fmsbw...", 1918

[cat. 789]

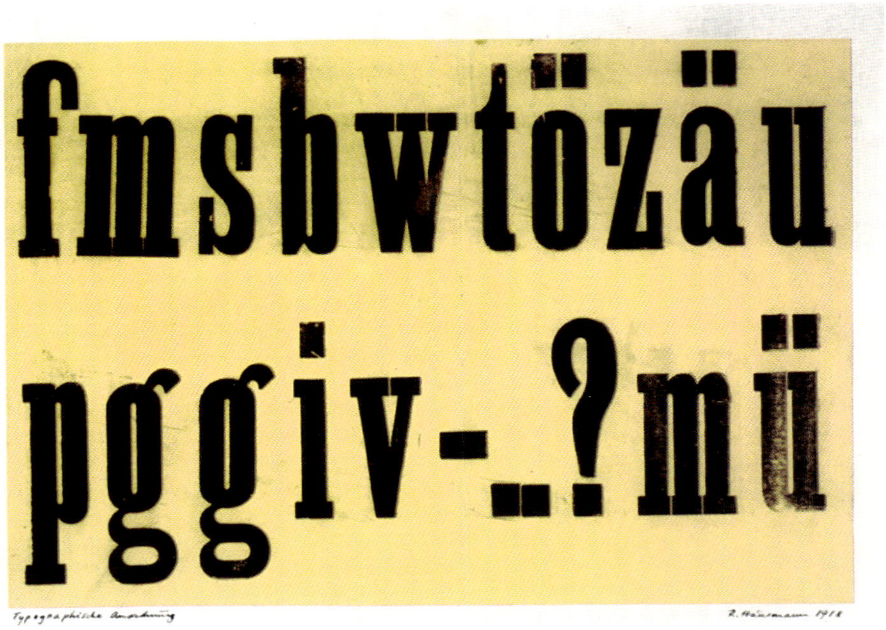

Max Ernst

Lächeln Sie nicht!, 1919

[cat. 259]

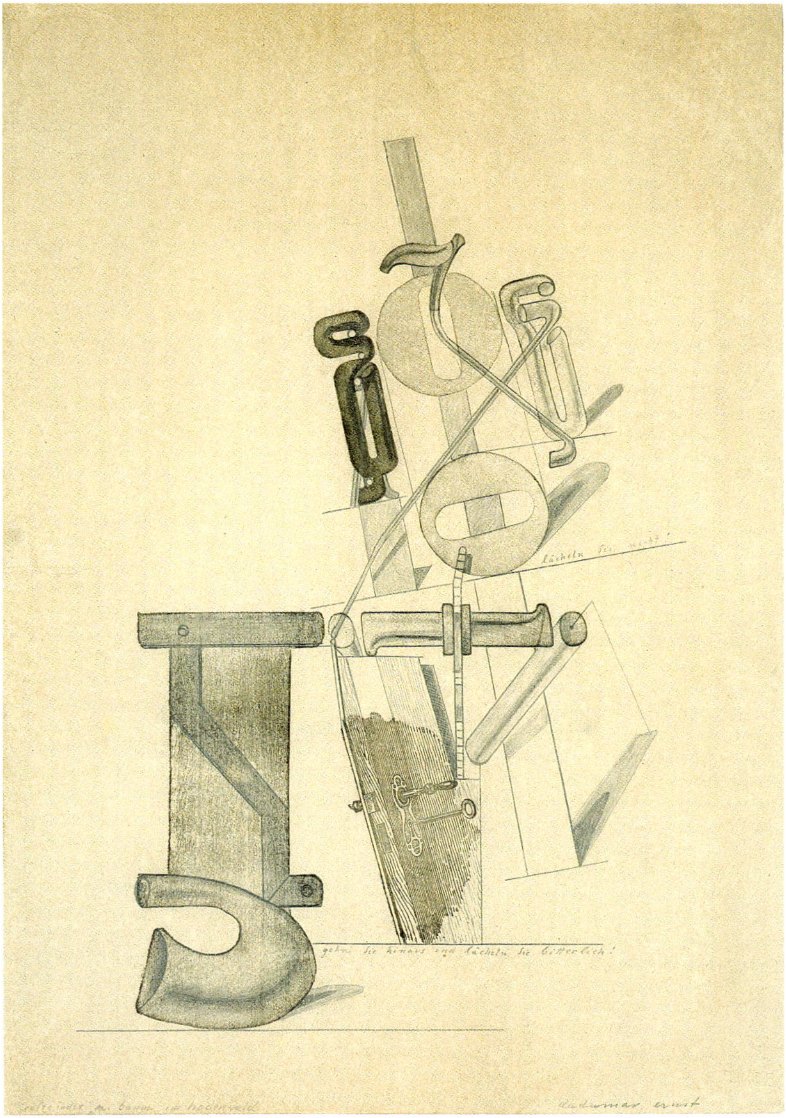

Kurt Schwitters

"Ursonate", published in *Merz*, no. 24, Hannover, 1932

[cat. 297]

einleitung:

Fümms bö wö tää zää Uu, 1
pögiff,
kwii Ee.

Oooooooooooooooooooooooooooooooo, 6

dll rrrrrr beeeee bö, (A) 5
dll rrrrrr beeeee bö fümms bö,
rrrrrr beeeee bö fümms bö wö,
beeeee bö fümms bö wö tää,
bö fümms bö wö tää zää,
fümms bö wö tää zää Uu:

erster teil:

thema 1:
Fümms bö wö tää zää Uu, 1
pögiff,
kwii Ee.

thema 2:
Dedesnn nn rrrrrr, 2
Ii Ee,
mpiff tillff too,
tillll,
Jüü Kaa? *(gesungen)*

thema 3:
Rinnzekete bee bee nnz krr müü ? 3
ziiuu ennze, ziiuu rinnzkrrmüü,

rakete bee bee. 3 a

thema 4:
Rrummpff tillff toooo? 4

überleitung:

Ziiuu ennze ziiuu nnzkrrmüü, ü 3
Ziiuu ennze ziiuu rinnzkrrmüü,

rakete bee bee? rakete bee zee. ü 3 a

durcharbeitung:

Fümms bö wö tää zää Uu, ü 1
Uu zee tee wee bee fümms.

rakete rinnzekete (B) ü3+ 3 a
rakete rinnzekete
rakete rinnzekete
rakete rinnzekete
rakete rinnzekete
rakete rinnzekete
Beeeee
bö.

Raoul Hausmann

Ventre de carrosse ou Dupont-Durand fait des poèmes, 1920

[cat. 274]

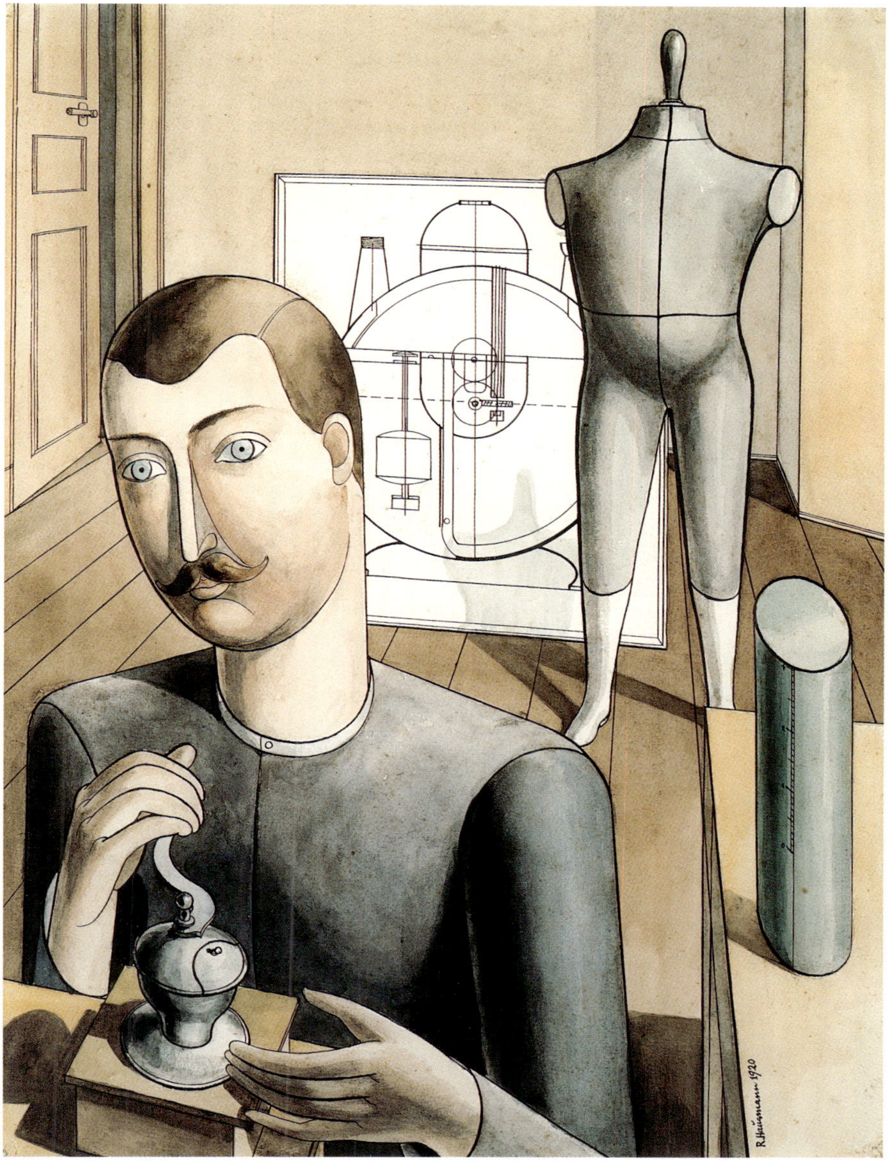

Hannah Höch

Astronomie, 1922

[cat. 276]

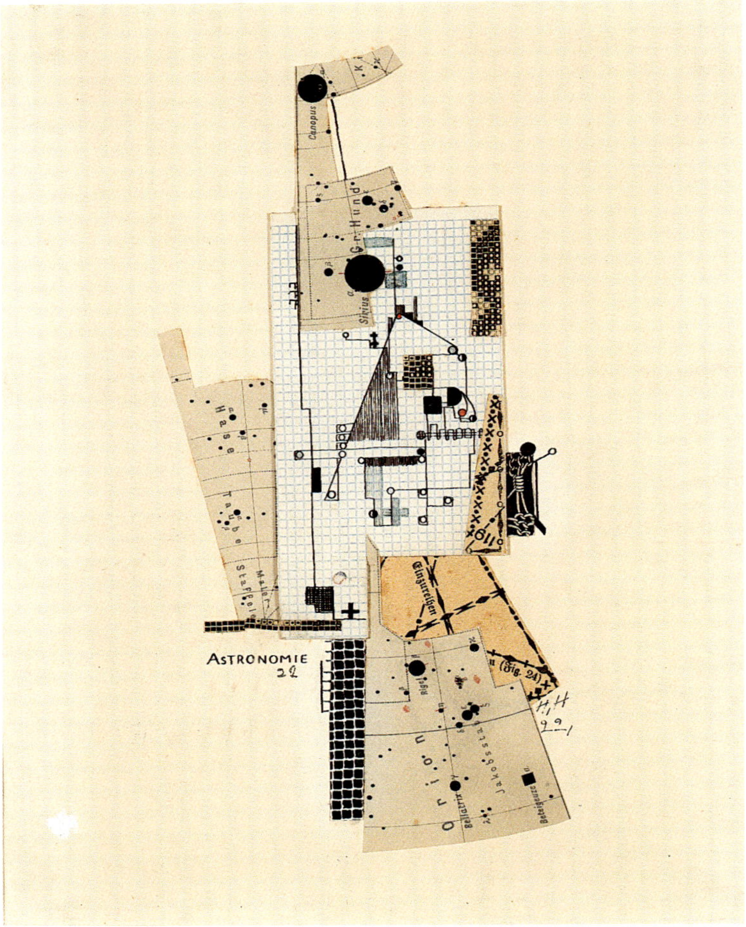

Hannah Höch
Hochfinanz, 1923
[cat. 275]

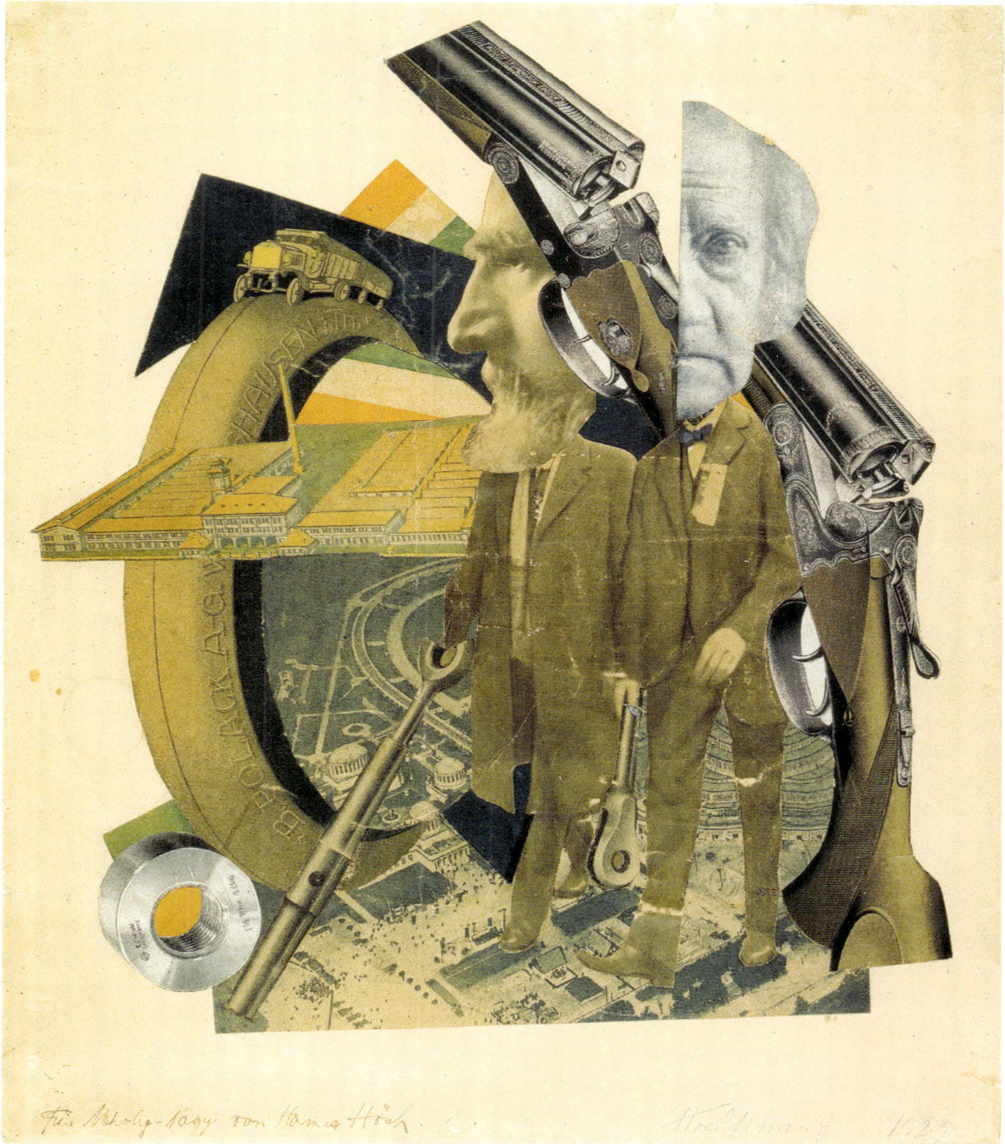

Kurt Schwitters
Herz (Mz 253), 1921
[cat. 301]

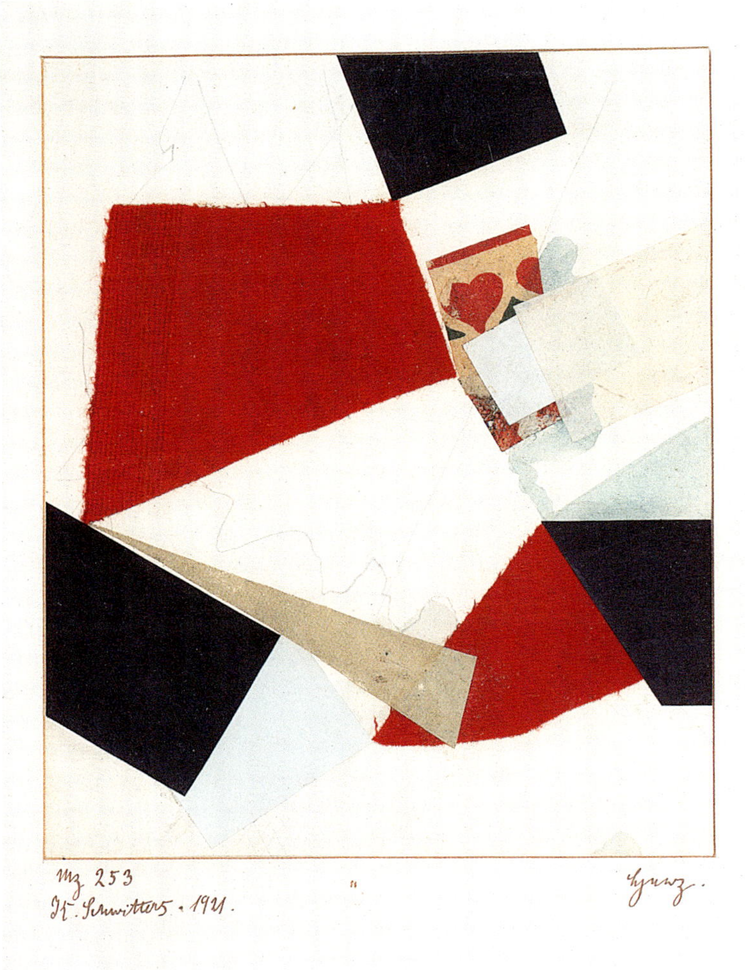

Ivan Puni
La Neige (Vitebsk), 1919
[cat. 271]

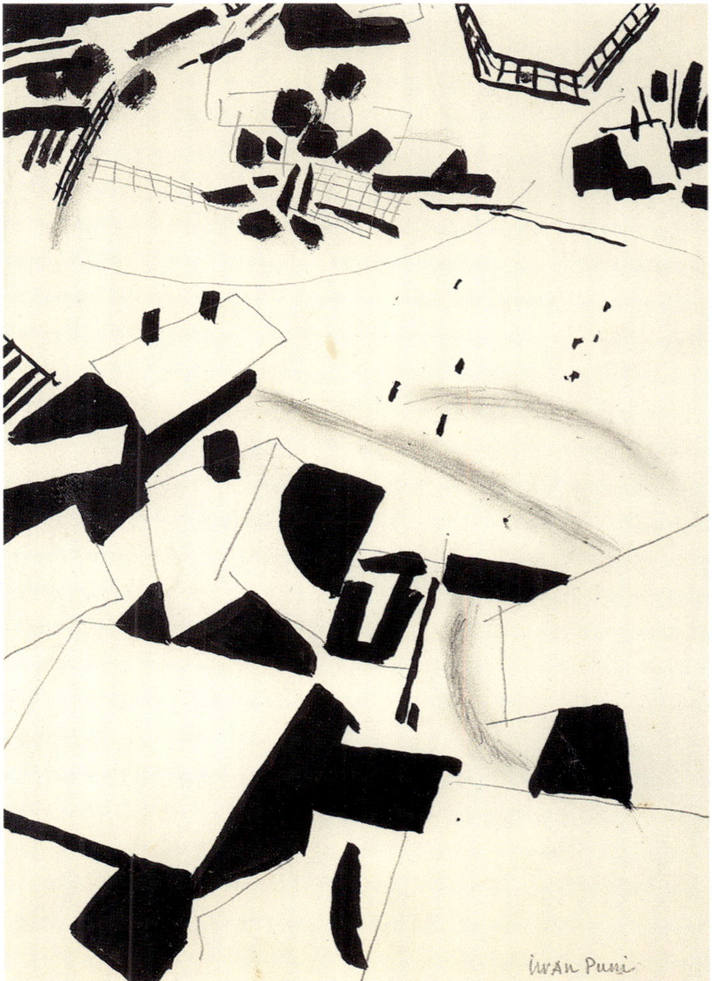

Paul Klee

Braunes Rechtw. Strebendes Dreieck, 1915

[cat. 283]

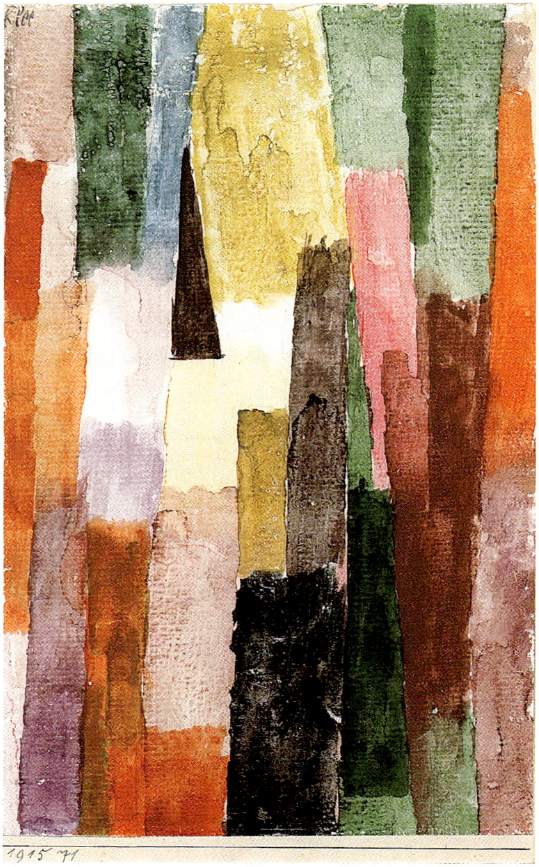

It has become common to call the succession of similar elements rhythm; not only is music called rhythmic, but quite generally the formed developments of a gesture is called "rhythmic," because of the original meaning, which is "flowing." Rhythm emphasises all formal gestures and their manifestations as bearers of vital processes above other occurrences which follow measurable rules, whether through geometric regularity, an exact sequence of formal elements, curves, etc. [...]
Because we have become used to machine-produced uniformity our response to the rhythm of life is extraordinarily low today.

Hans Prinzhorn
Bildernei der Geisterkranken, 1922

Dream. I flew home, where the beginning lies. It started with brooding and chewing of fingers. Then I smelled or tasted something. The scent freed me. I was completely freed at once and melted away like a piece of sugar in water.
My heart too was involved; it had been far too large for a long time, now it was blown up to inordinate size. But not a trace of oppression. It was borne to places where one no longer seeks voluptuousness.
If a delegation were to come to me now and bow solemnly before the artist gratefully pointing to his works, I would not be surprised much. For I was there where the beginning lies. I was with my adored Madame Monad, which means, so to speak, being fruitful.

Paul Klee
Note of January 1906

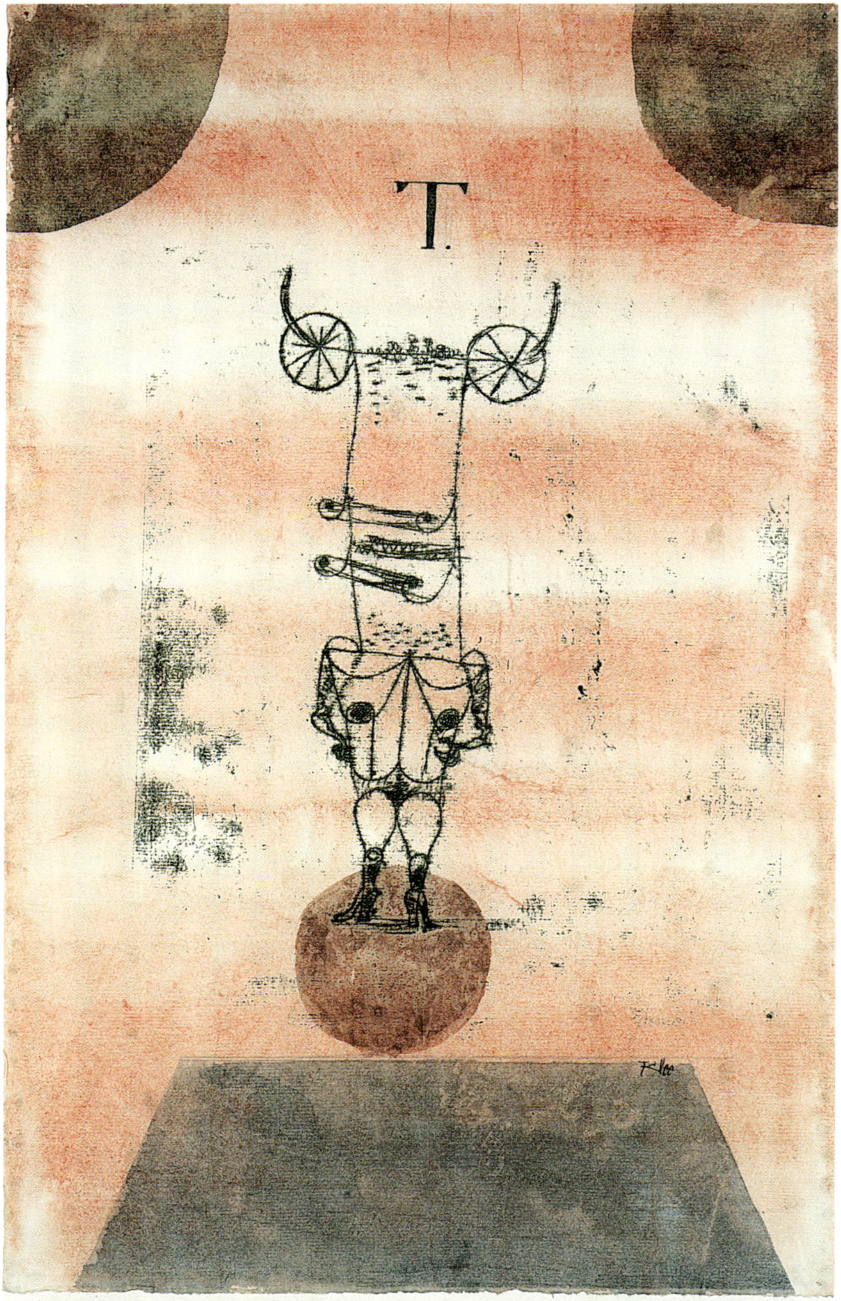
T.
Klee
1921 / 73 Weibsteufel, die Welt beherrschend.

Paul Klee

Weissteufel, die Welt beherrschend, 1921

[cat. 281]

Komödie, 1921

[cat. 282]

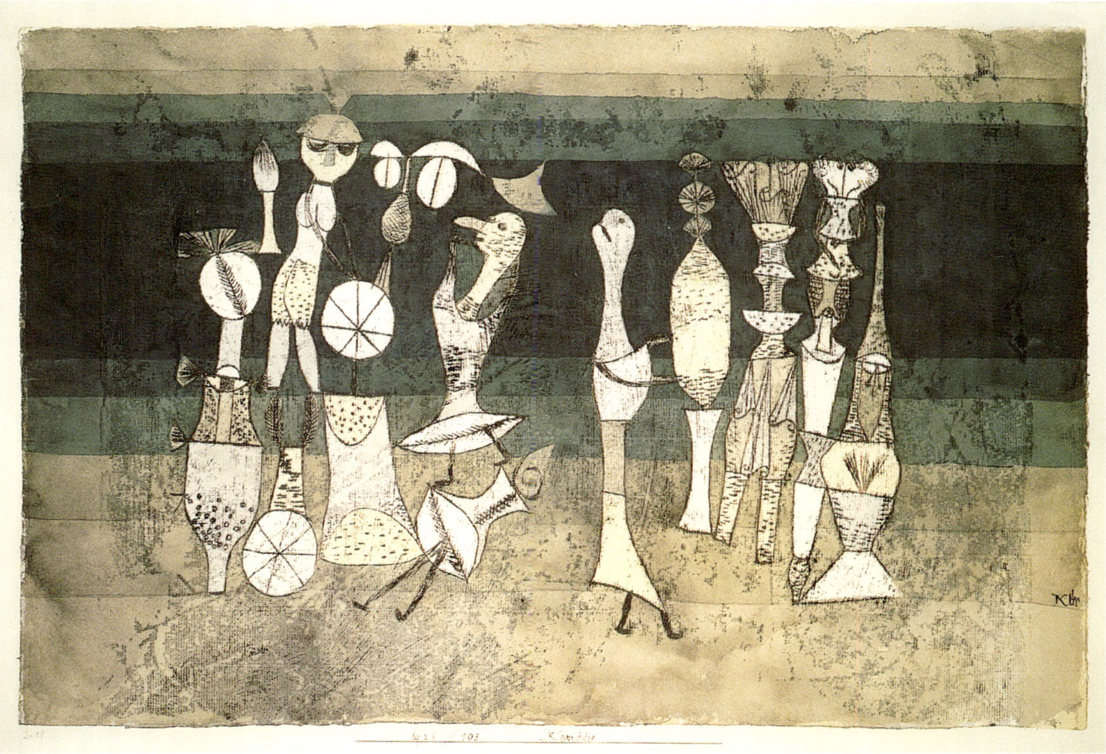

Kurt Schwitters

Aufschlag ("Tempera-Fart"), 1928

[cat. 300]

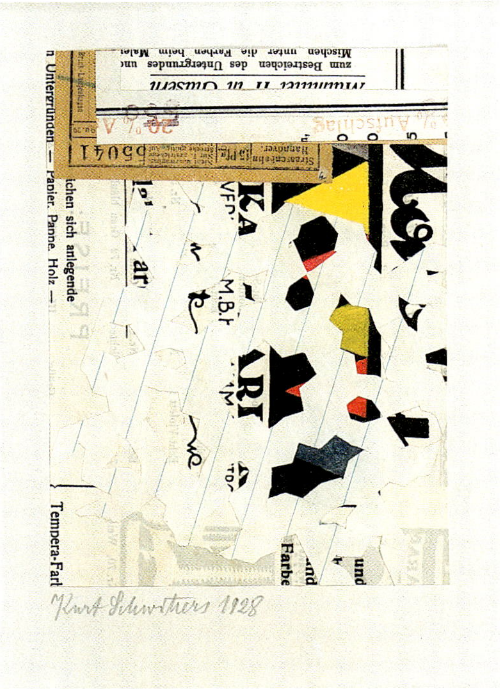

Bart van der Leck
Compositie (Bloesemtak), 1921
[cat. 299]

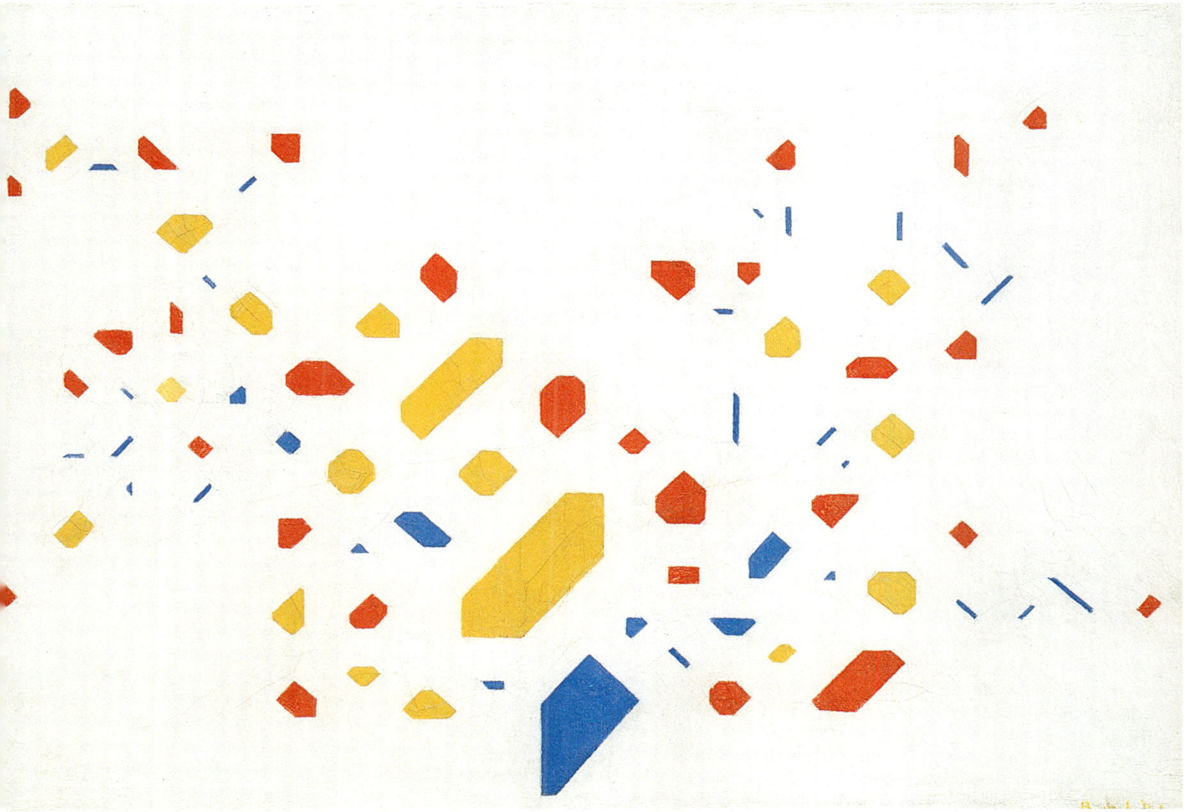

Hans Arp
Formes géométriques-biologiques, 1917
[cat. 307]

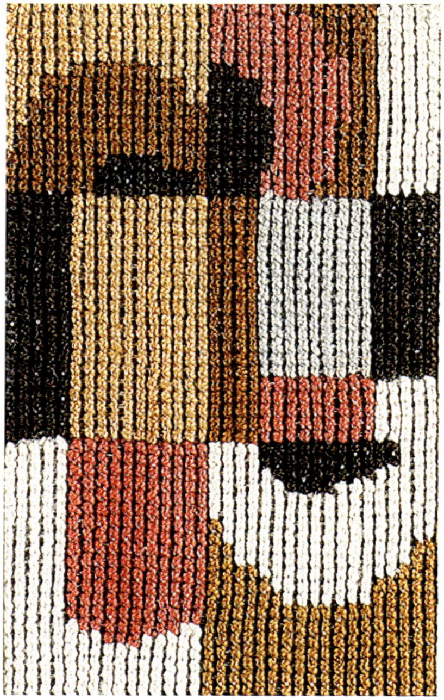

It was that same year, 1915, that I met Sophie Taeuber. The stature and purity of her works, their amazing and courageous use of rectangles, greatly influenced me. It is difficult to make the younger generation realize the importance of that discovery of the rectangle.

Hans Arp
"Collage," *Arp Collages,* 1955

Sophie Taeuber-Arp

Composition verticale-horizontale, 1916

[cat. 310]

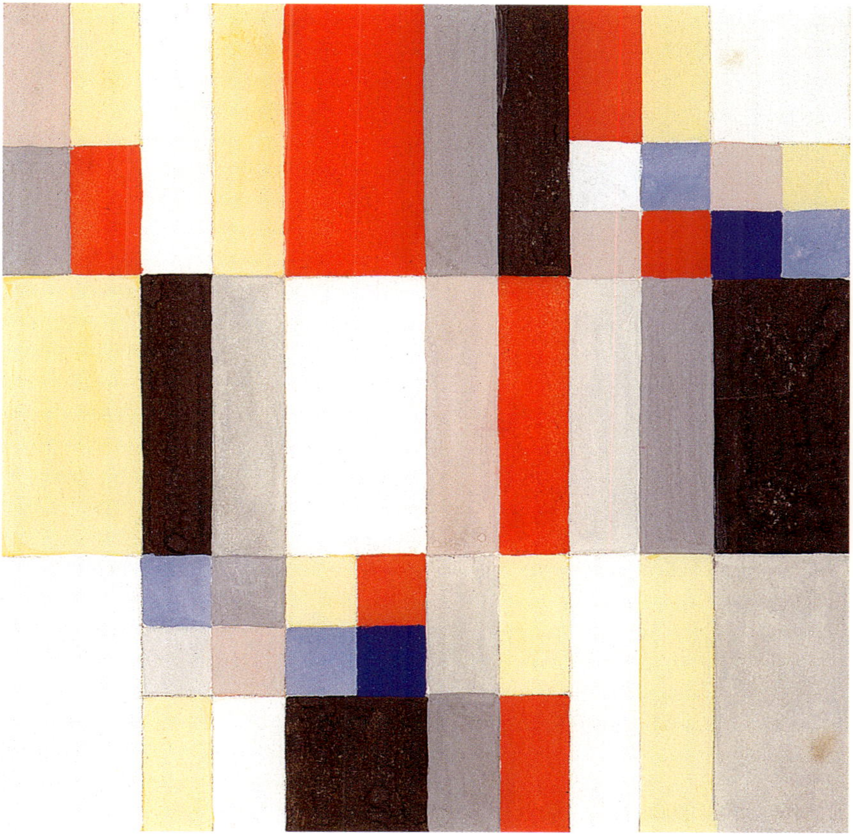

Portrait of Hans Arp, 1924

Sophie Taeuber-Arp behind her Dada head, 1920
Photo: Nic Aluf

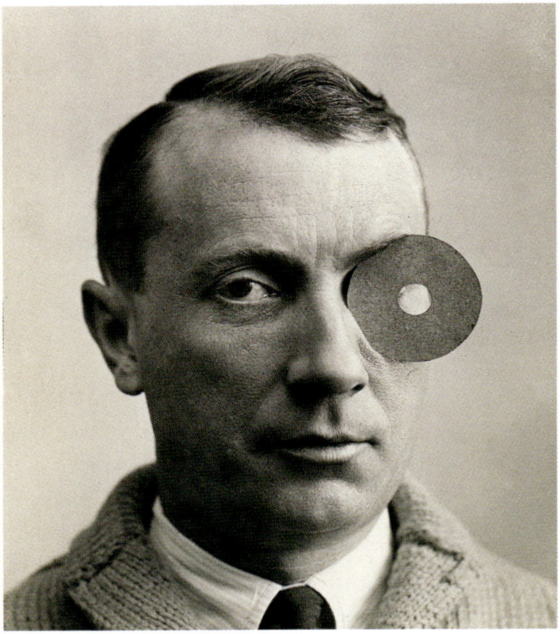

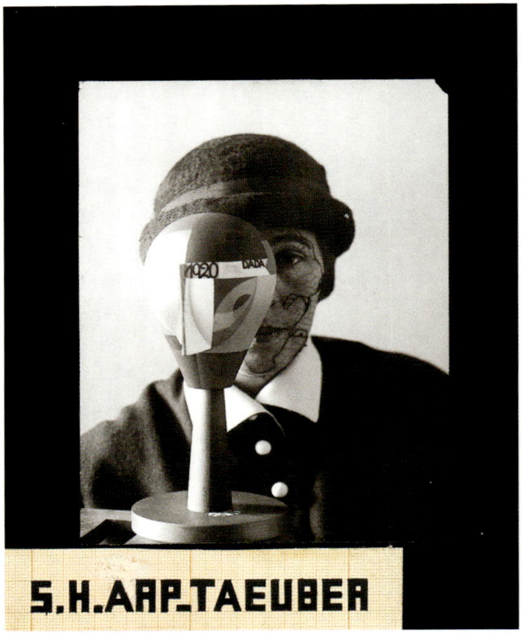

Sophie Taeuber-Arp

Composition à forme de U, 1918

[cat. 312]

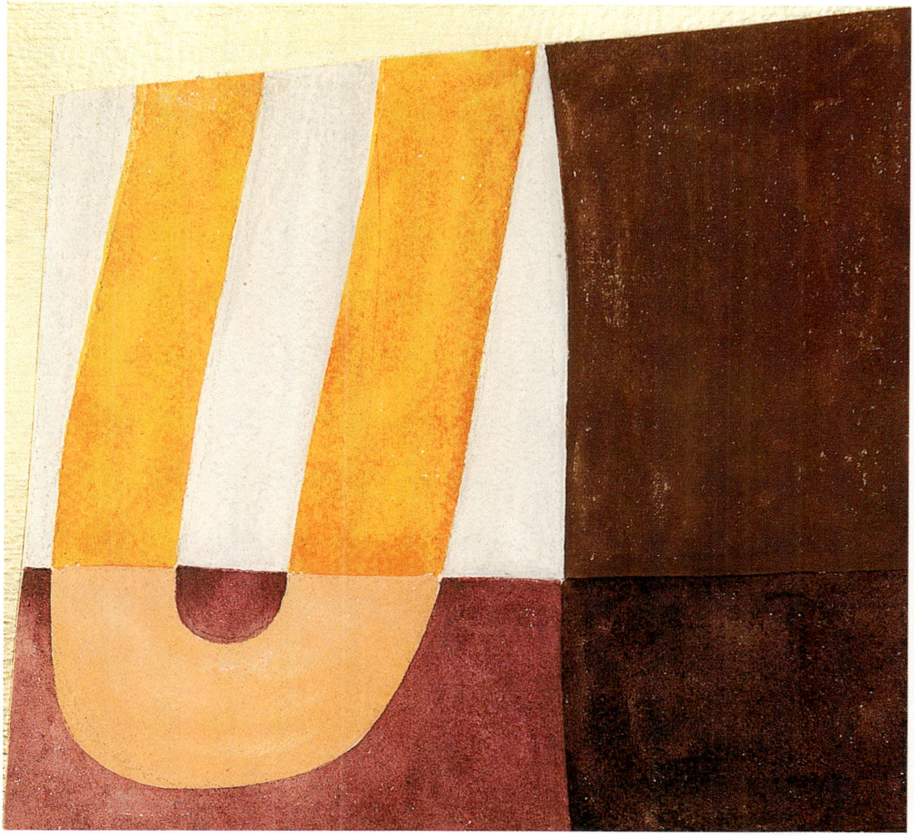

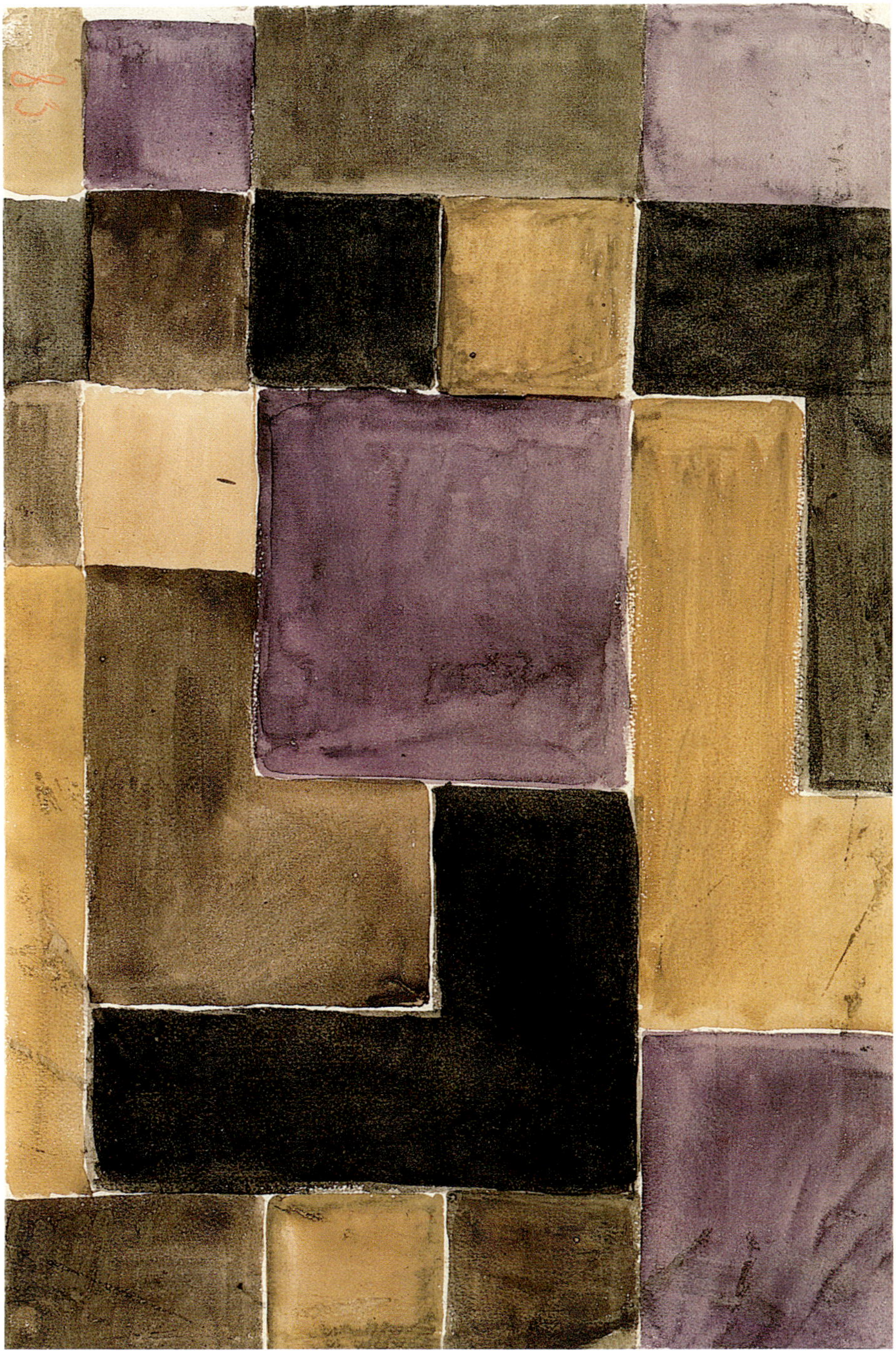

Sonia Delaunay
Composition abstraite, 1924
[cat. 304]

Sophie Taeuber-Arp
Composition verticale-horizontale à éléments d'objets, 1919
[cat. 311]

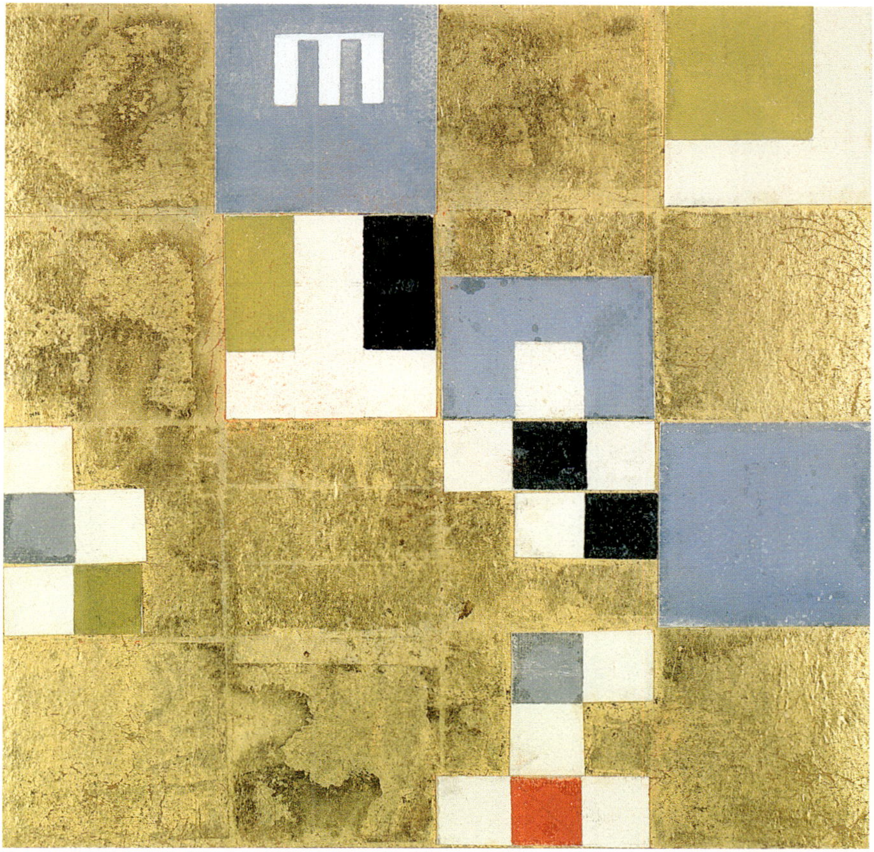

Hans Arp

Hombre, bigote y ombligo, 1928

[cat. 262]

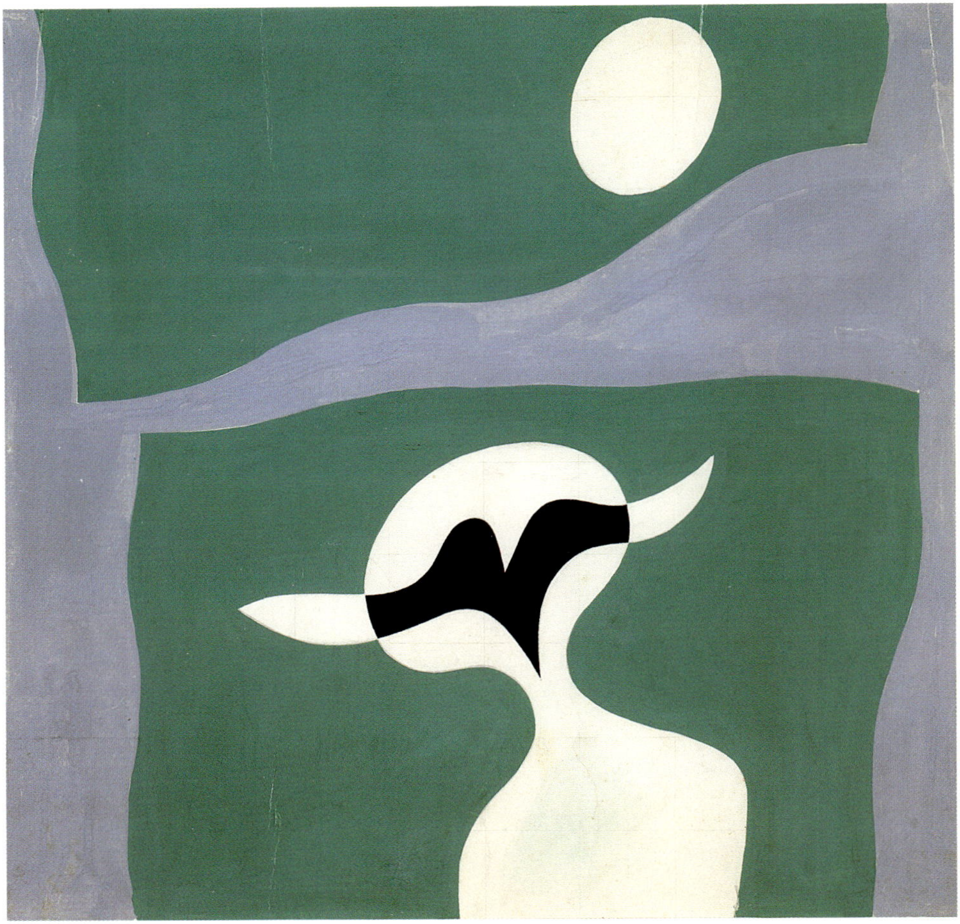

Joan Miró

Peinture-poème ("Bonheur d'aimer ma brune"), 1925

[cat. 412]

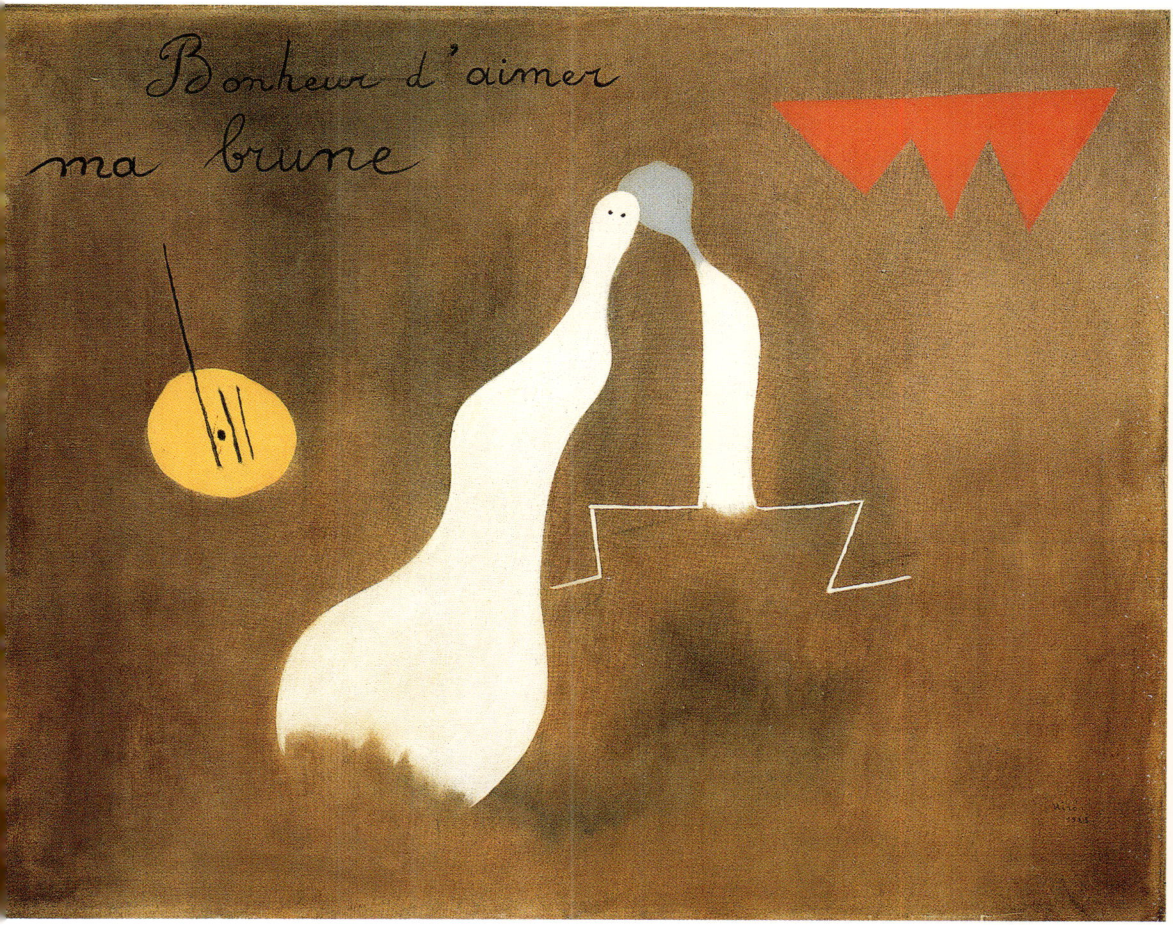

Amédée Ozenfant

Pot et pipe II, 1918

[cat. 317]

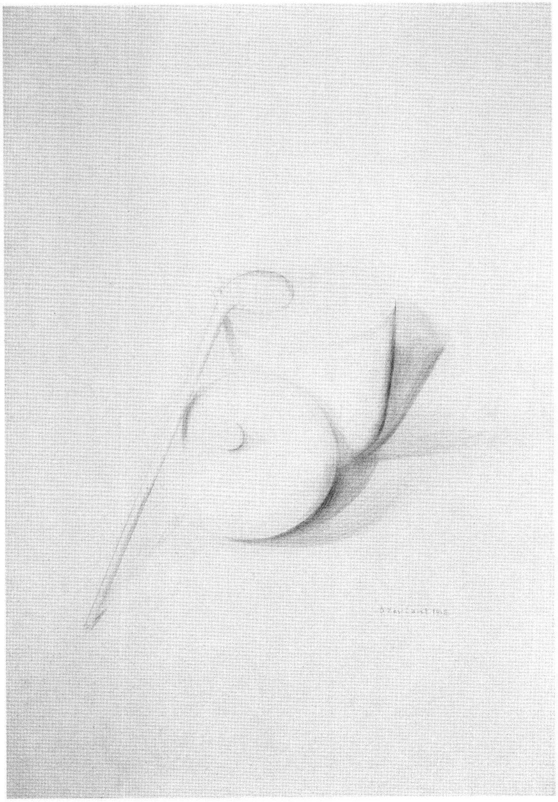

Amédée Ozenfant
Reds, Rome, 1920-1925
[cat. 318]

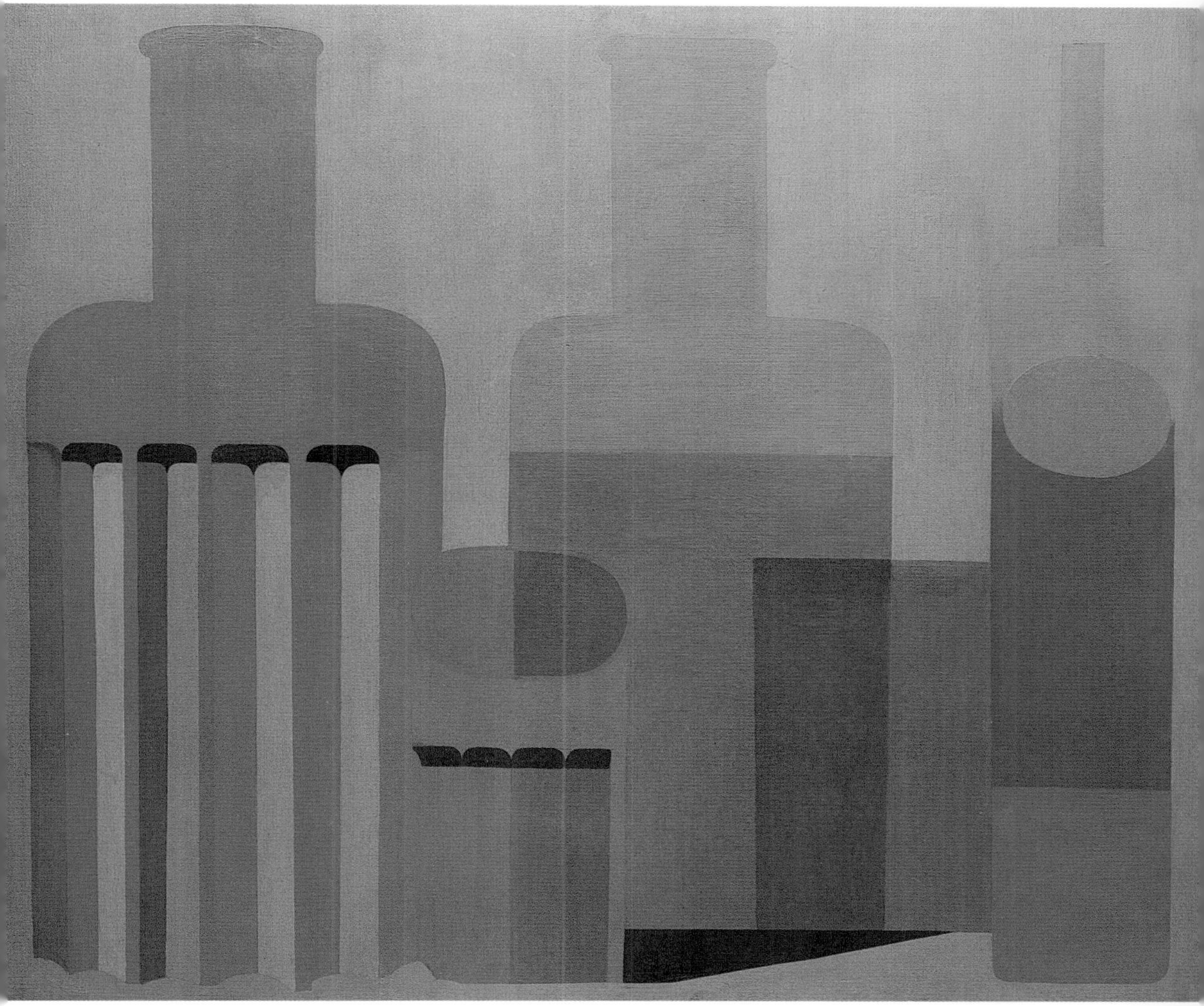

Max Ernst
Illustration for *Le Château étoilé,* text by André Breton, 1937
[cat. 346]

The human psyche in its most universal manifestation has developed such a fixation on the Gothic castle and everything that goes with it that we absolutely must establish what the equivalent is for our time. (All the evidence suggests it is not a factory.)

André Breton
"Limites non-frontières du surréalisme," *La Nouvelle Revue Française,* 1937

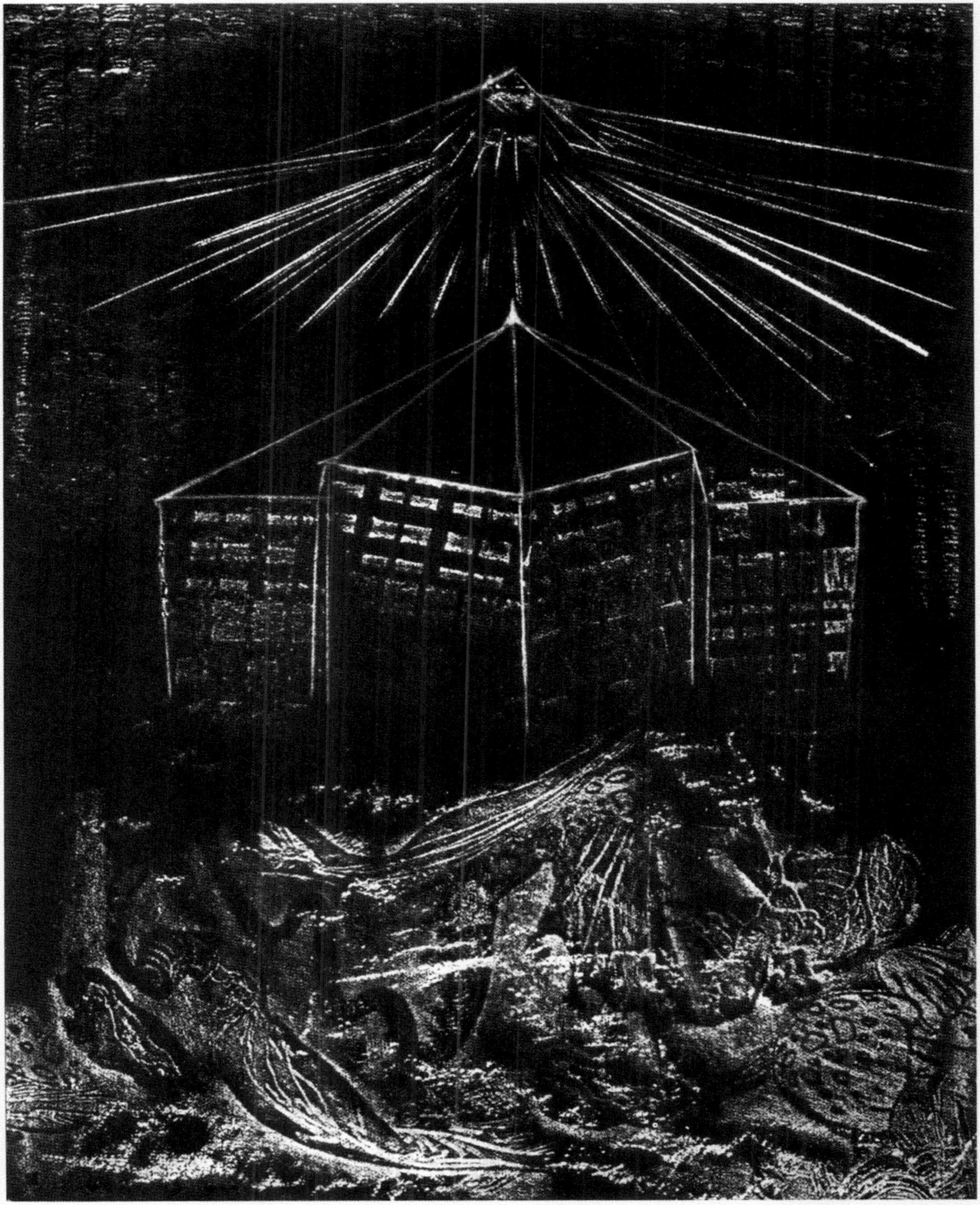

A FLANC D'ABIME, CONSTRUIT EN PIERRE PHILOSOPHALE

Max Ernst

Un autre monde, 1965

[cat. 349]

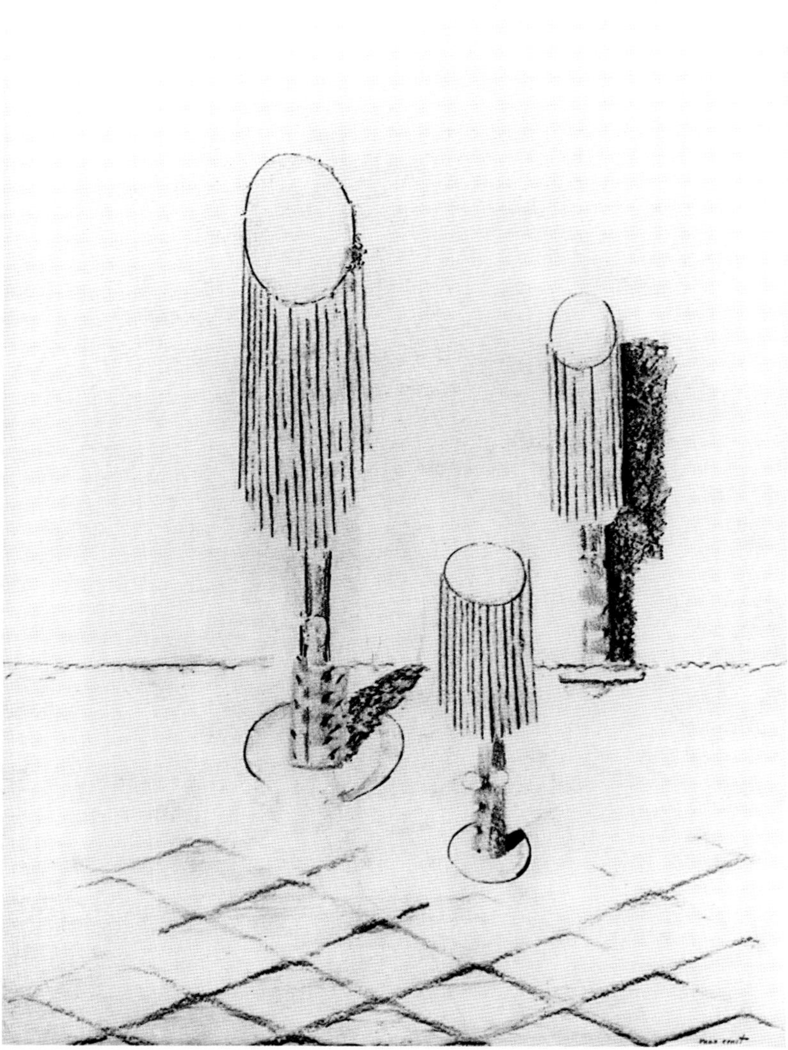

Max Ernst

Untitled (Sun over the Forest), 1927

[cat. 353]

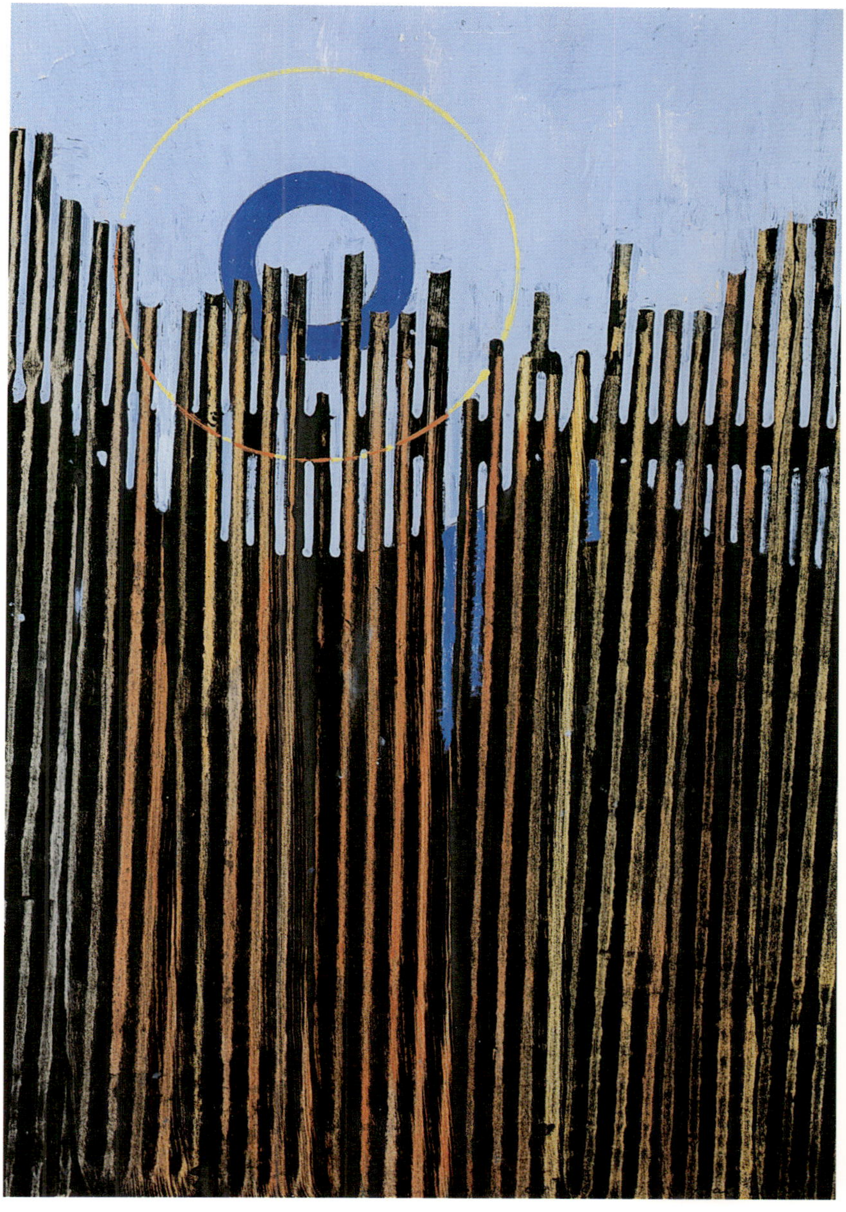

László Moholy-Nagy
Untitled, 1925-1928
[cat. 338]

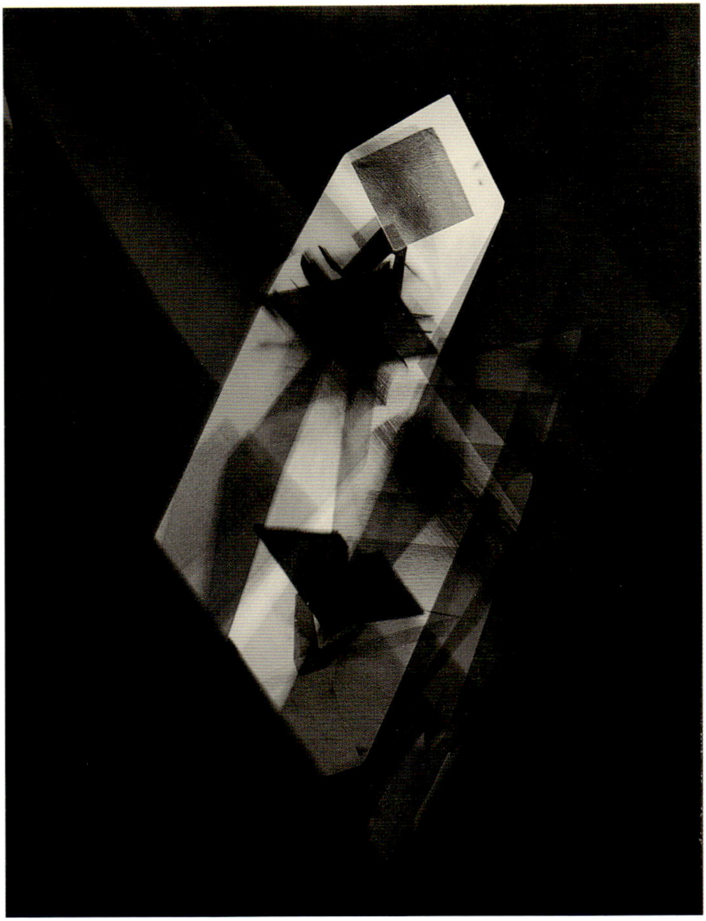

László Moholy-Nagy
Untitled, 1923-1925
[cat. 337]

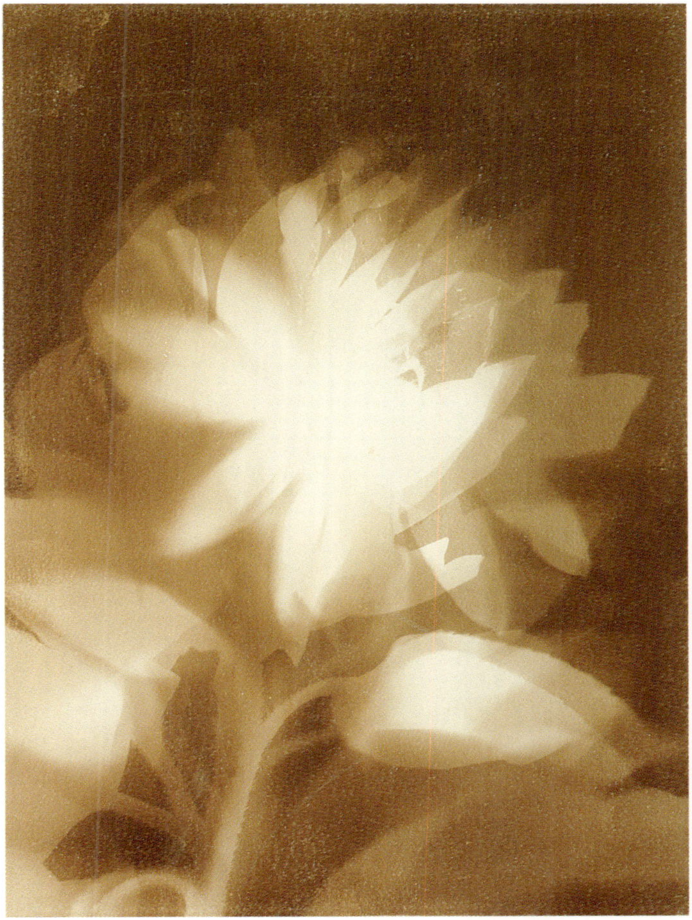

Kurt Schwitters

Ohne Titel (grau, blau, rot, weiss), 1924-1927

[cat. 302]

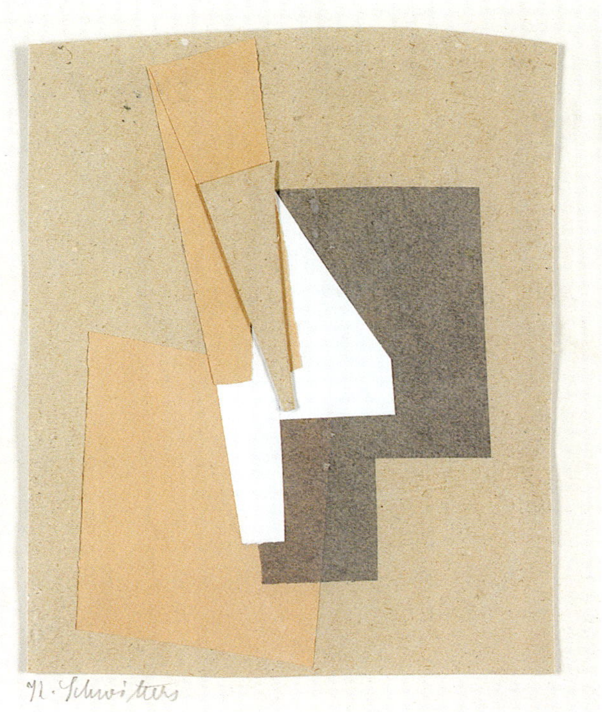

Kurt Schwitters

Abstraction No. 16 (Schlafender Kristall), 1919

[cat. 335]

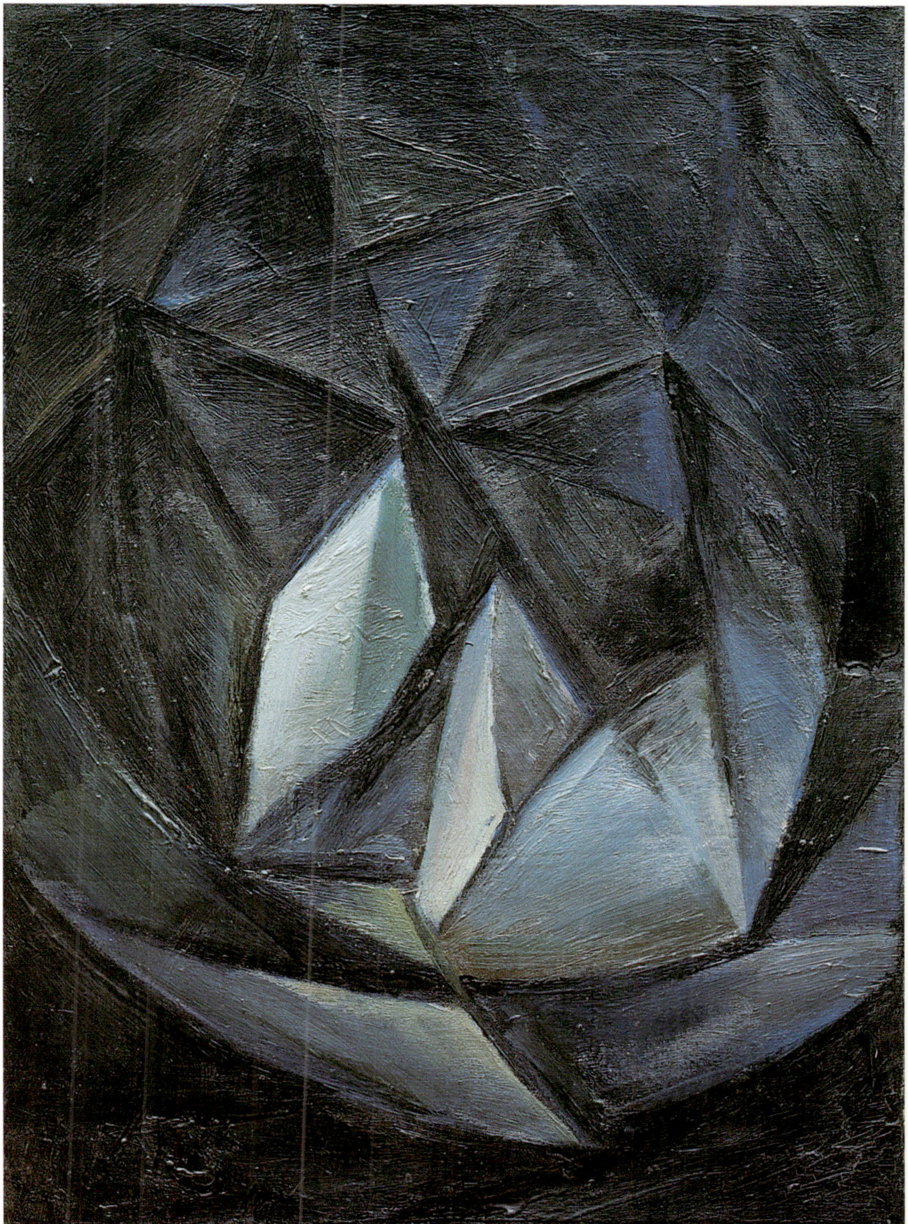

Any painterly plane is more alive than any face hung with a pair of eyes and a smile.
A painted face in a picture is a pathetic parody of life, this allusion being a thin reminder of the living thing.
A plane, by contrast, is alive, for it has been born.
A coffin reminds us of a corpse, whereas a picture suggests a living thing.

Kasimir Malevich
"Du cubisme et du futurisme au suprématisme. Le nouveau réalisme pictural," 1915

Lioubov Popova

Pictorial architecture, 1918-1920

[cat. 365]

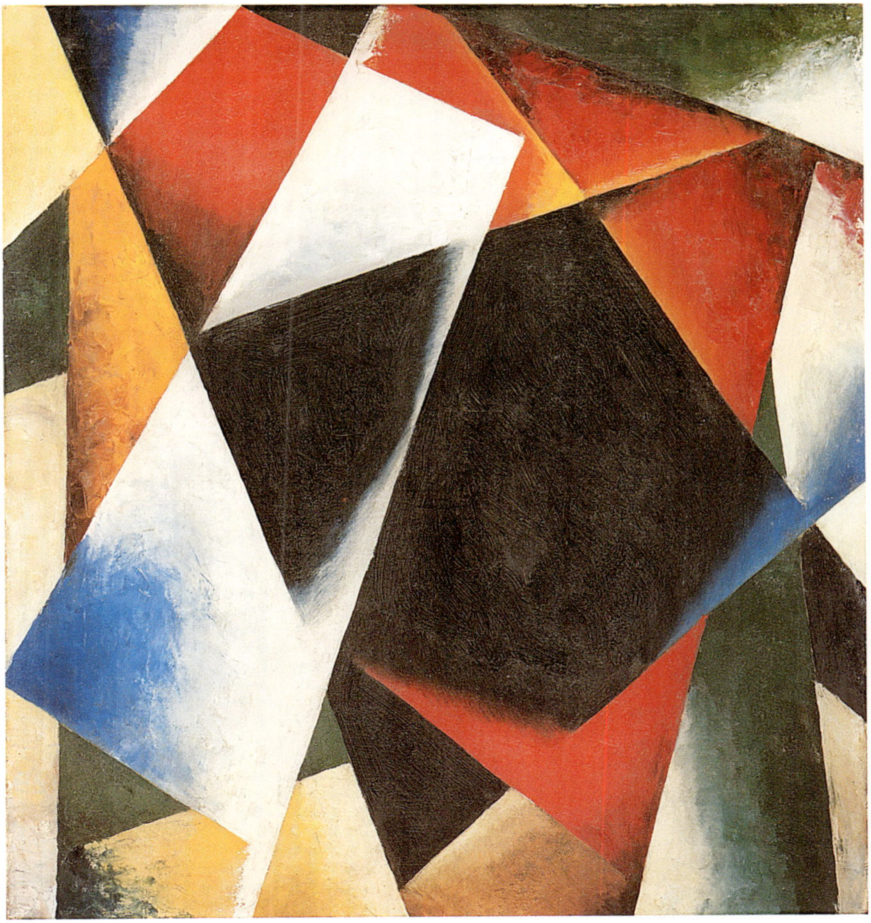

Ivan Puni

Schachmaty, 1917-1918
[cat. 364]

Novoie Iskusstvo, 1917-1918
[cat. 382]

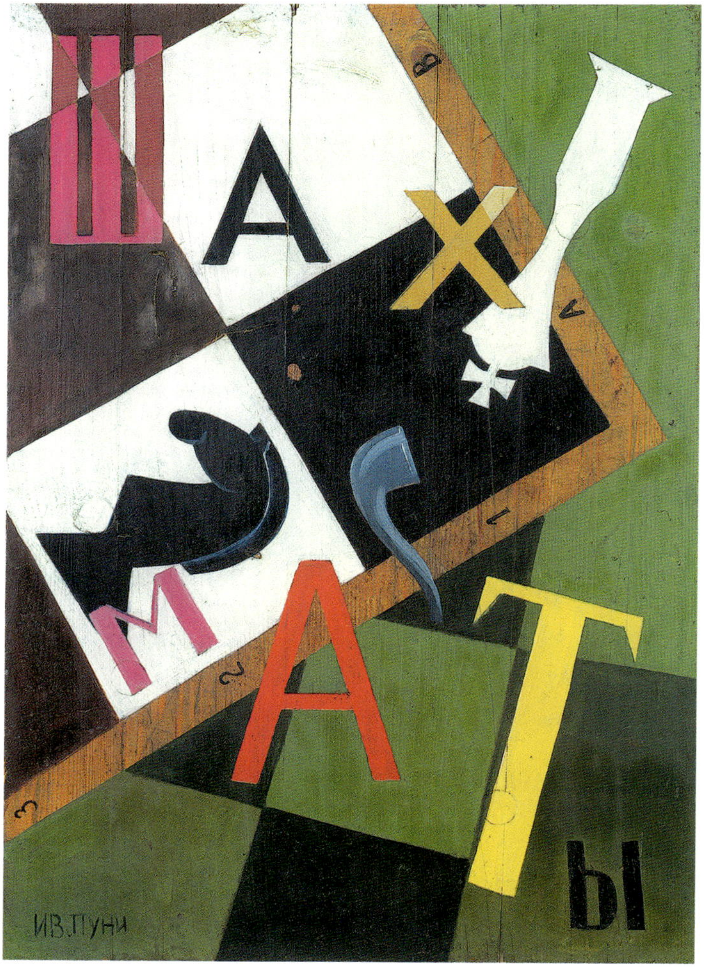

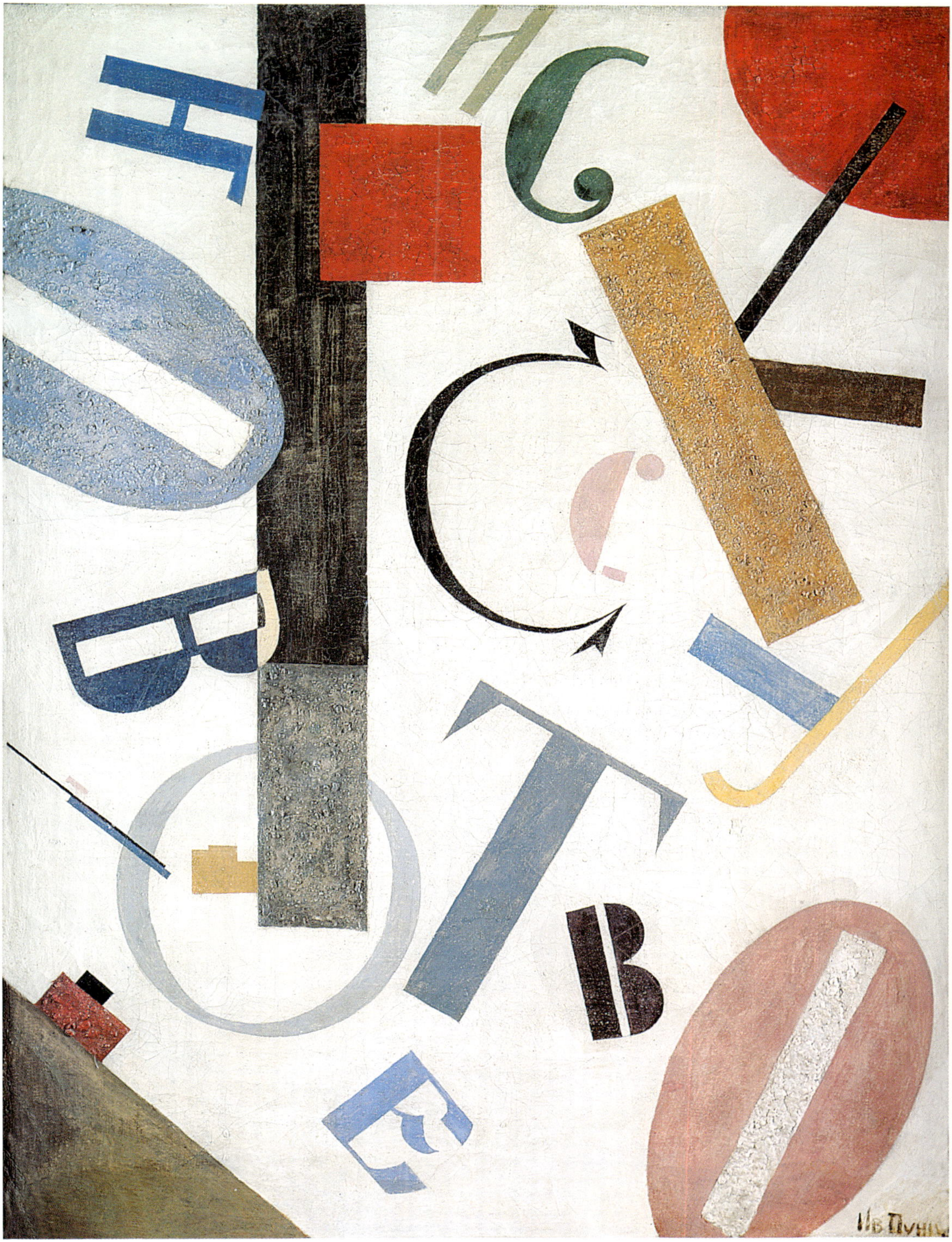
Ив Пуни

In Russia in the early 20th century, the book – the page – rather than the painter's canvas, was the support for a series of experimental works that combined poetic writing with the pictorial line, spurred by the invention of a "transrational" idiom known as *Zaum* (a neologism combining *za*, trans, with *um*, sense). Zaum is associated with the utopia of a fully spiritual universal language capable of reflecting the entire substance of the realm of the senses.

Zaum was cultivated by poets and artists: the great poet Velimir Khlebnikov, central figure in Russian futurist poetry, Aleksei Kruchenykh, Aliagrov (the linguist Roman Jakobson), Ilya Zdanevich (Ilyazd) and Kasimir Malevic. Of these writers, Kruchenykh was the one who took the greatest interest in pictorial works and collage. Today he is recognized as the author of the twelve illustrations for *Vselenskaia Voina* (Universal War), formerly attributed to Olga Rozanova. One of trademarks of these poetry-art books is their crudeness – in the materials as well as the techniques employed – in contrast with the elegance of the illustrated works of the Symbolist period. The books are also characterized by their innovative association between the gestuality of writing, chromatic fantasy and combinations of geometric forms free of any sort of functional rules. With Zaum, the page became a space for a rhythmic expansion of letters and words in correspondence with the energy of verbal expression.

Tsosa, accompanied by Kruchenykh's declaration, is, despite the humbleness of the object, and insofar as it summarizes all the elements of Zaum, the landmark work of the movement. The points of convergence between the poetic inventiveness catalyzed by Zaum and the dynamics of Suprematism are evidenced here in the work of two artists close to Malevic: Liubov Popova (6 etchings) and El Lissitzky (series of *Prouns*, contraction of *pro*, for, and *ounovis*, new). J.-F. C.

Declaration of Transrational Language

1 – Thought and speech cannot catch up with the emotional experience of someone inspired; therefore, the artist is free to express himself not only in a common language (concepts), but also in a private one (a creator is individual), as well as in a language that does not have a definite meaning (is not frozen), that is *transrational*. A common language is binding; a free one allows more complete expression. (Example: *go osnieg kaid*, etc.) *(This paragraph is transplanted from the "Declaration of the word as such", published in 1913)*

2 – *Zaum* is the primary (both historically and individually) form of poetry. At first comes a rhythmic, musical agitation, a protosound (a poet ought to write it down, because it may be forgotten in the course of further work).

3 – Transrational speech gives birth to a transrationnal protoimage (and vice versa), which cannot be defined precisely. For example: the amorphous bogey, gorgon, mormo ; the nebulous beauty Ylajali; Avoska and Neboska (the What-About and the How-About), and so on. *(This beautiful woman is from Hamsun's novel « Hunger»; the pair of names is from Russian folklore.)*

4 – Transrational language is resorted to

a) When the artists produces images that have not yet taken definite shape (in him or outside).

b) When it is not desired to name an object, but only to suggest it: "He is kind of like this," "He has a four-cornered soul"- here a common word is used in its transrational sense. Also belongings here are invented names of characters, nations, localities, cities, and the like. For example: Oile, Bleyana, Vudras and Baryba, Svidrigaylov, Karamazov, Chichikov, and others (not, however, the allegorical ones like Pravdin, Glupyshkin, where the meaning is clear and definite). *(The examples, respectively, refer to the names of imaginary lands in a poem by the symbolist poet Fedor Sologoud, and in a story by Myasoyedov in "Sadok sudi"e, and to the name of characters in Gorodietski, Dostoievski, and Gogol. Then in parentheses, are given the names of a character from Fonvizin's comedy, "The Mino"r, and of the funny characters in early Russian movies – something like Mr Truth and Mr Stupid.)*

c) When ones loses one's mind (hatred, jealousy, rage).

d) When one does not need it – religious, ecstasy, love (a gloss of an exclamation, interjections, purring, refrains, a child's babbling, affectionate names, nicknames – such *zaum* can be found in abundance inn the works of writers of every school).

5 – Zaum awakens and liberates creative, without offending it by anything concrete. Meaning makes the word contract, writhe, turn to stone; zaum, on the other hand, is wild, fiery, explosive (wild paradise, flaming tongues, glowing coal).

6 – Thus one should distinguish between three forms of word creation:

I. The transrational

a) sung and incanted magic.

b) "revelation (naming and depicting) of invisible things" – mysticism.

c) musical-phonetic word creation – orchestration, texture.

II. The rational (its opposite is the mad, the clinical, which has its own laws, establishable by science; what is however, beyond scientific cognition belongs to the area of aesthetics, of the aleatory.

III. The aleatory (alogical, fortuitous, a creative breakthrough, mechanical combination of words: slips of tongue, misprints, lapses; partly belonging here are shifts of songs and meaning, national accent, stuttering, baby talk, etc.).

7 – *Zaum* is the most compact art in the lens of the way from perception to reproduction, as well as in its form. For example: *Kuboa* (Hamsun), *Kho-bo-ro*, etc. *("Kuboa" is a word invented by the hero of Hamsun's Hunger. The last sequence of words is the beginning of Kruchenykh's own zaum poem printed in Learn Art).*

8 – Zaum is a universal art, though its origins and initial characters must be national. For example: "hurrah", "euhoe", and so on.

Transrational works may result in a worldwide poetic language, which is born organically, and not artificially like Esperanto.

Aleksei Khrutxenykh

Baku, 1921

Typed sheet included in *Tsosa*.

Translation and notes by Vladimir Markov, 1968

Wassili Kamenski, David Burljuk and Vladimir Burljuk

Tango s korovami. Jelezobetonnyïa poemy, 1914

[cat. 320]

босиком по крапиве

ДеТСВО (*этот стих написан в перми на пристани когда было мнѣ 11 лѣт*)

1884 на КАМЕ

на КАМНЕ

вася КАМЕНСКІЙ

апрель **5** *перед* ПАСХОЙ

с золотых пріисков

на буксирную пристань

любимова

свистки *пароходов*

по ночам

всплески плис

и на мачтах огни

мы одни

отдают якоря

от **чудес**

трое *жались*

под одним одеялом

вася алёша *и* **петя**

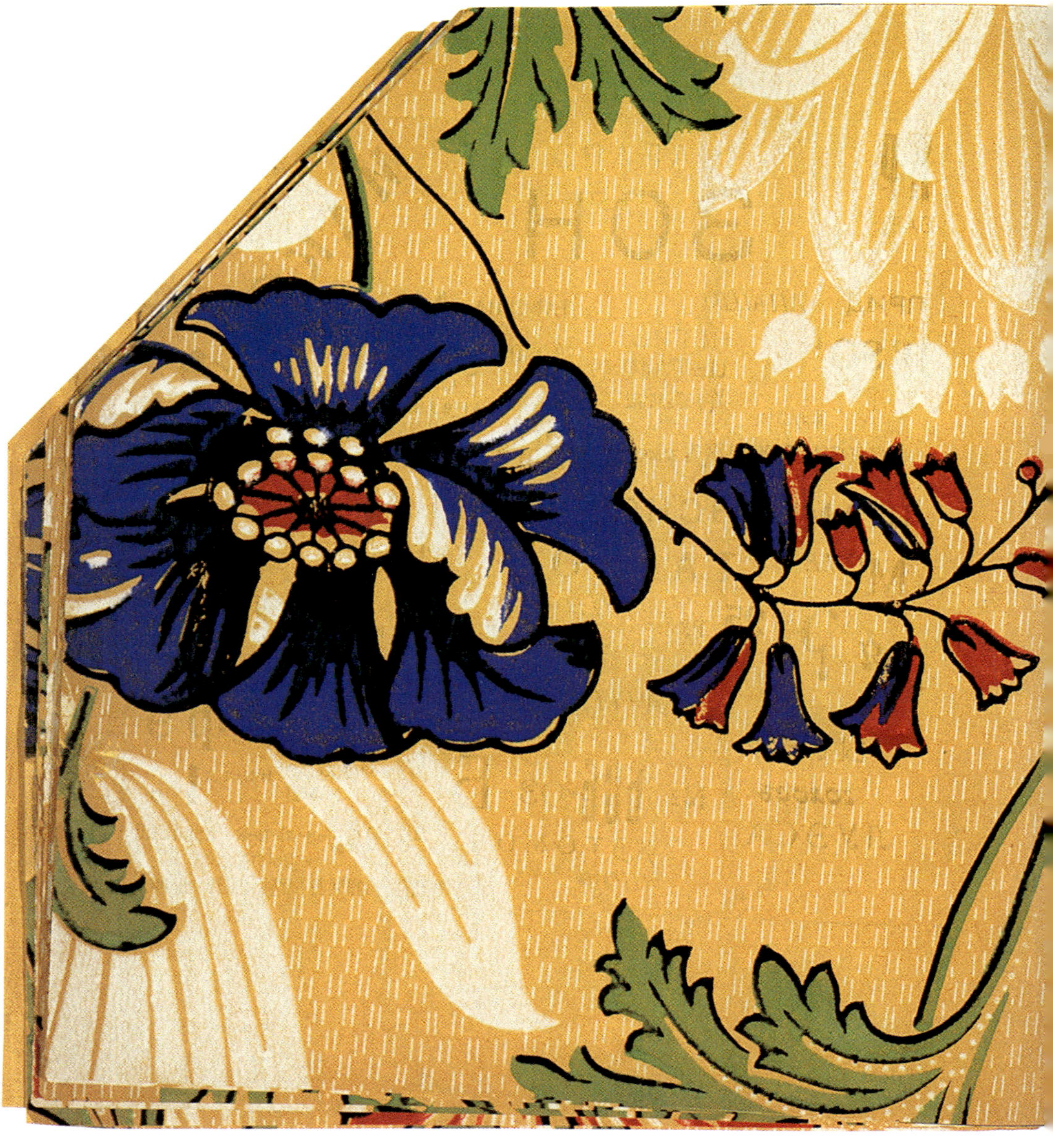

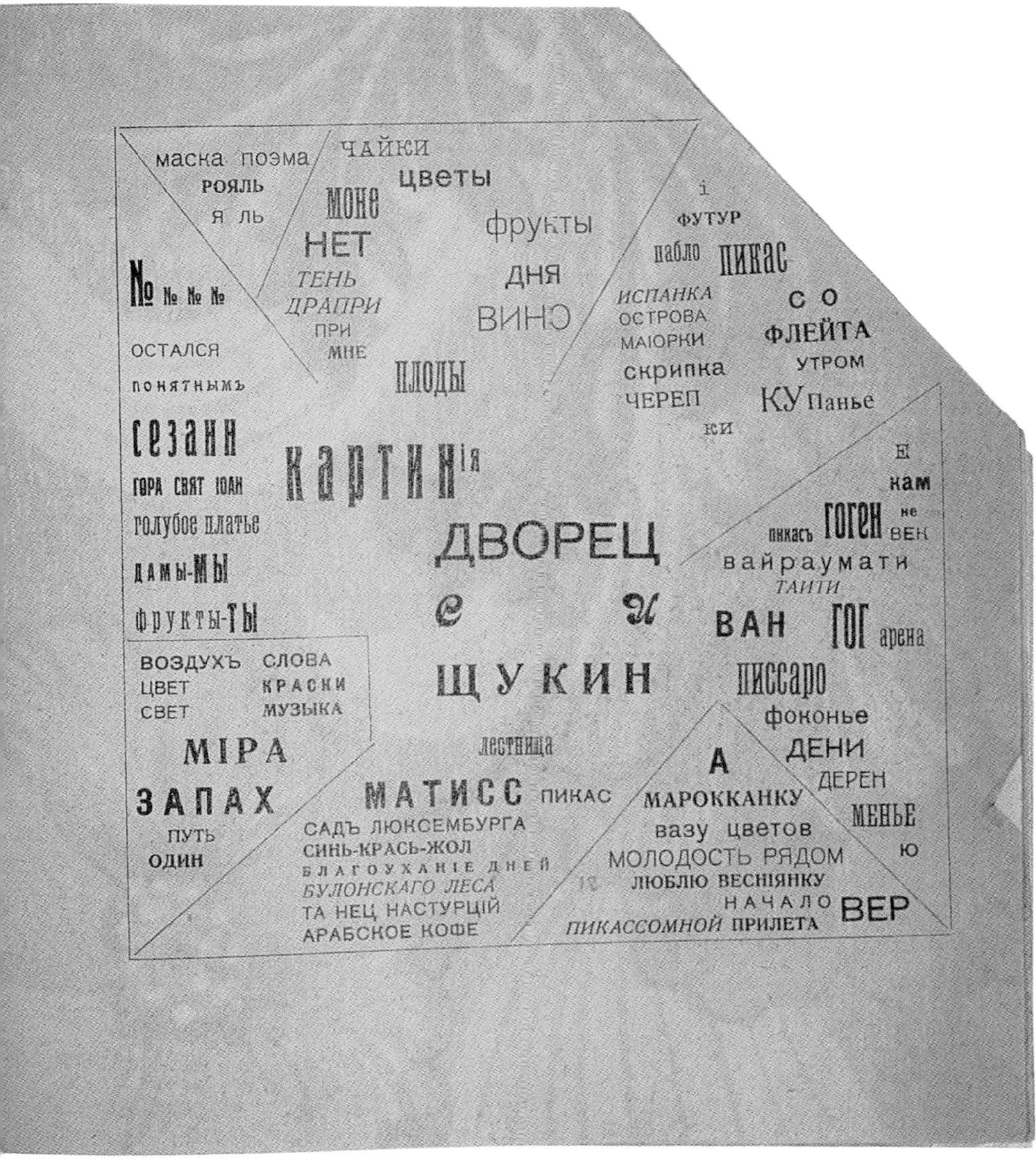

маска поэма
РОЯЛЬ
Я ЛЬ
ЧАЙКИ
цветы
МОНЕ
НЕТ
ТЕНЬ
ДРАПРИ
ПРИ
МНЕ
фрукты
ДНЯ
ВИНО
ПЛОДЫ
і
ФУТУР
пабло ПИКАС
ИСПАНКА
ОСТРОВА
МАІОРКИ
скрипка
ЧЕРЕП
КИ
С О
ФЛЕЙТА
УТРОМ
КУПанье
№ № № №
ОСТАЛСЯ
ПОНЯТНЫМЪ
СЕЗАНН
ГОРА СВЯТ ІОАН
голубое платье
ДАМЫ-МЫ
фрукты-ТЫ
КАРТИНія
ДВОРЕЦ
С И
ЩУКИН
Е
кам
пикасъ ГОГЕН не ВЕК
вайраумати
ТАИТИ
ВАН ГОГ арена
ПИССАРО
фоконье
ДЕНИ
ДЕРЕН
МЕНЬЕ
Ю
ВОЗДУХЪ СЛОВА
ЦВЕТ КРАСКИ
СВЕТ МУЗЫКА
МІРА
ЗАПАХ
ПУТЬ
ОДИН
лестница
МАТИСС ПИКАС
САДЪ ЛЮКСЕМБУРГА
СИНЬ-КРАСЬ-ЖОЛ
БЛАГОУХАНІЕ ДНЕЙ
БУЛОНСКАГО ЛЕСА
ТА НЕЦ НАСТУРЦІЙ
АРАБСКОЕ КОФЕ
А
МАРОККАНКУ
вазу цветов
МОЛОДОСТЬ РЯДОМ
ЛЮБЛЮ ВЕСНІЯНКУ
НАЧАЛО ВЕР
ПИКАССОМНОЙ ПРИЛЕТА

Kasimir Malevich

Cover of *Troe*, 1913.
Texts by Velimir Khebnikov, Aleksei Kruchenykh and Elena Gouro
[cat. 395]

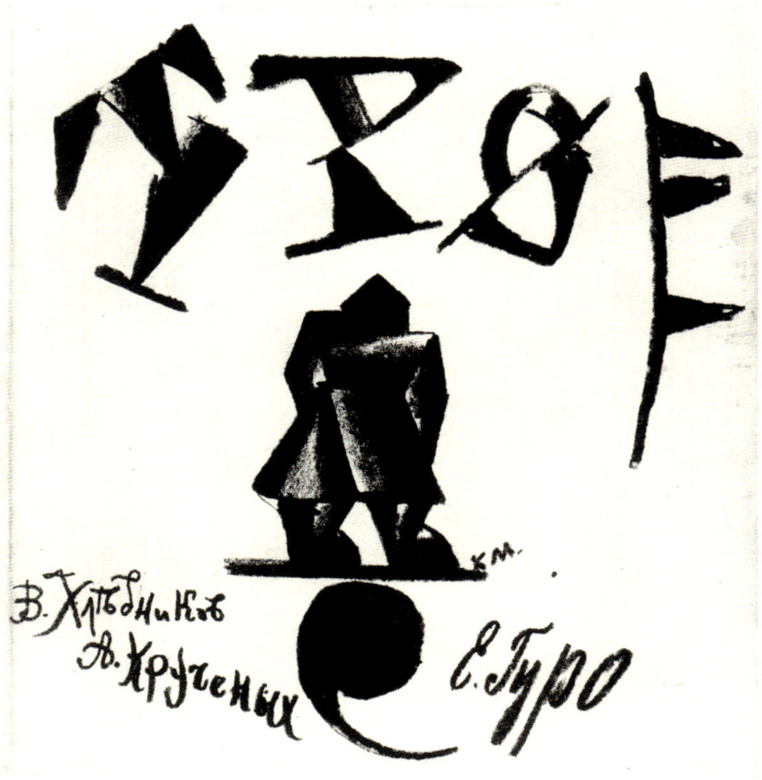

Olga Rozanova
Cover of *Zaumnaja gniga*, 1915-1916.
Texts by Aliagrov (Roman Jakobson) and Aleksei Kruchenykh
[cat. 389]

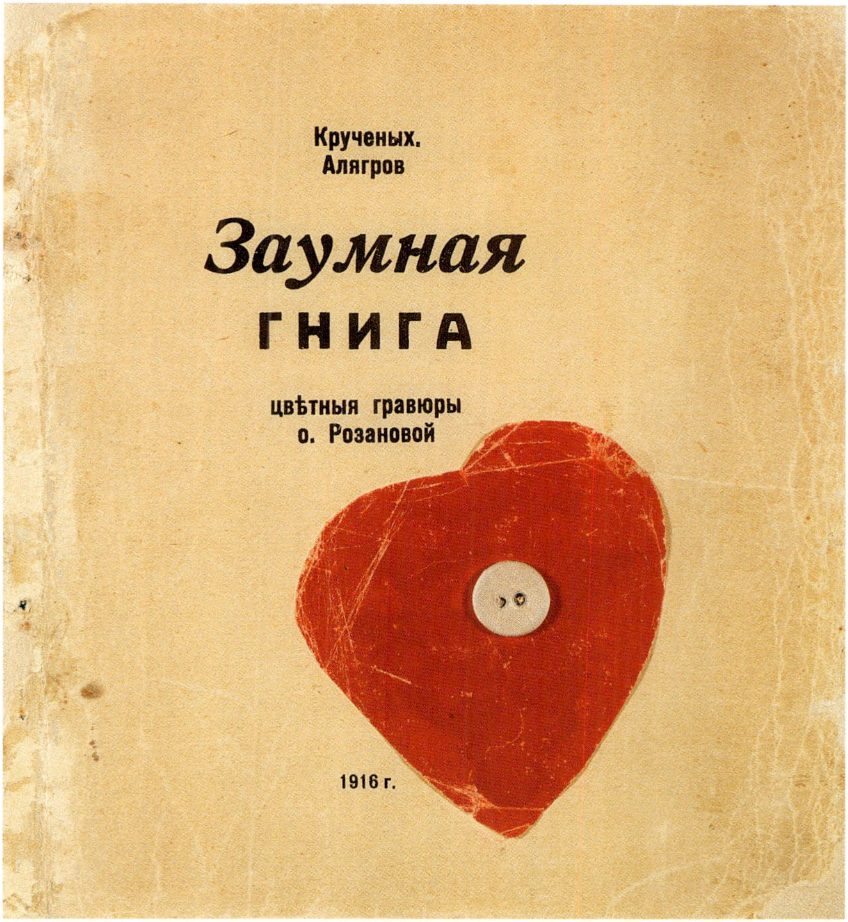

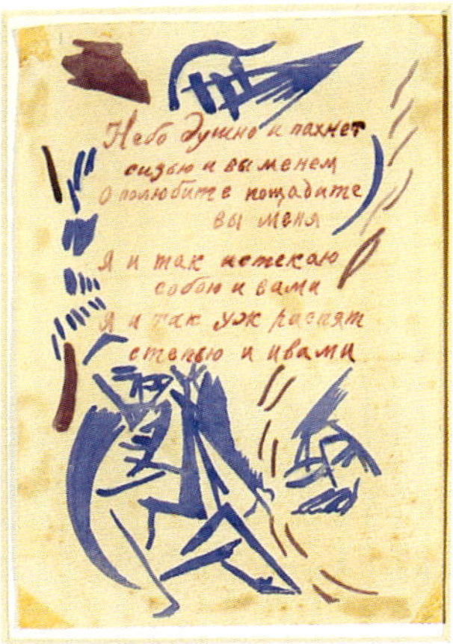
Небо душно и пахнет
сизью и вымeнем
О полюбите пощадите
вы меня
Я и так истекаю
собою и вами
Я и так уж распят
степью и ивами

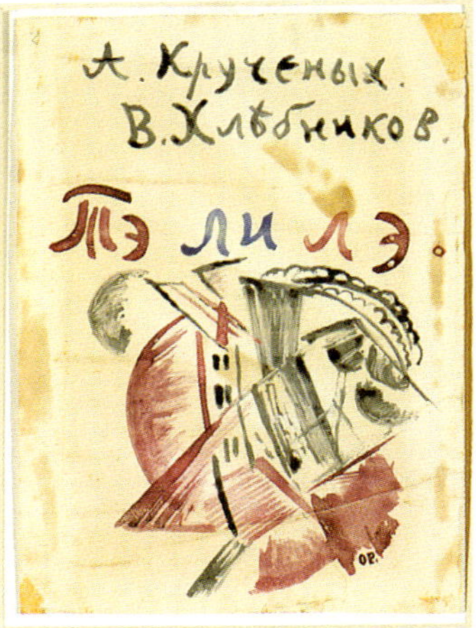
А. Крученых.
В. Хлѣбников.
ТЭ ЛИ ЛЭ.
ОР.

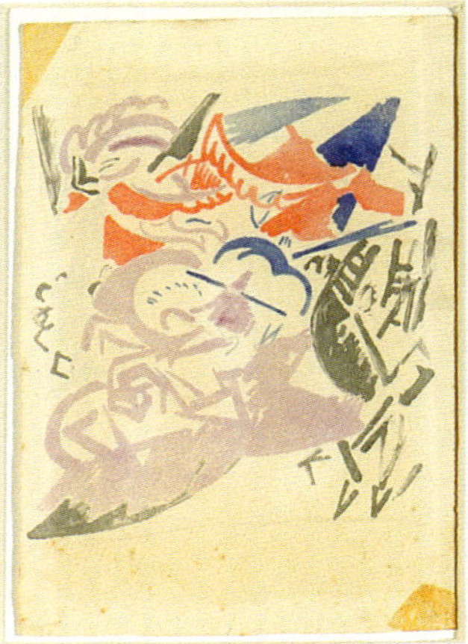

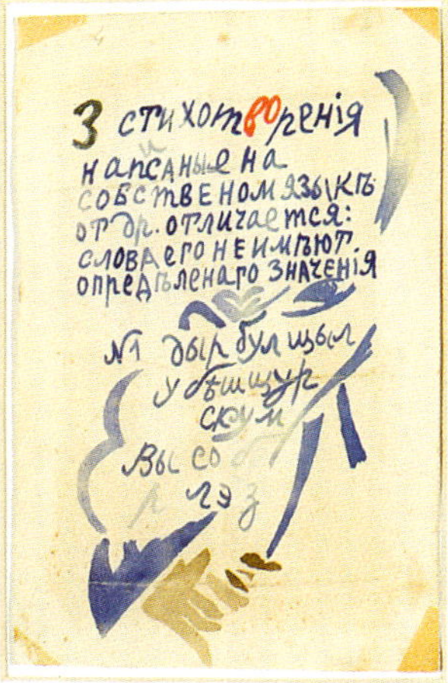
3 стихотворенія
написаные на
собственом языкѣ
от др. отличается:
слова его не имѣют
опредѣленаго значенія
№1 дыр бул щыл
убѣшщур
скум
вы со бу
р л эз

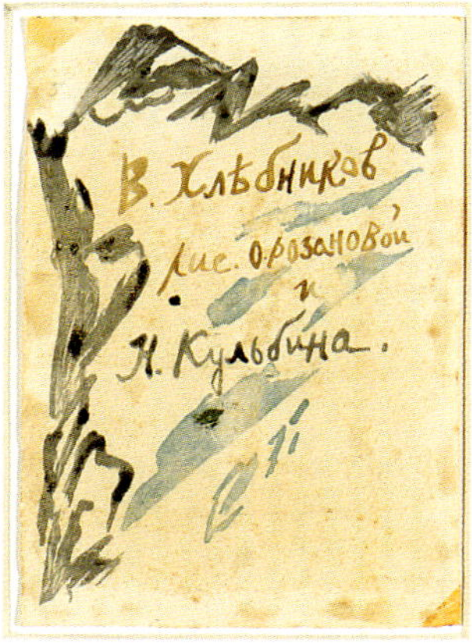
В. Хлѣбников
рис. О. Розановой
и
Н. Кульбина.

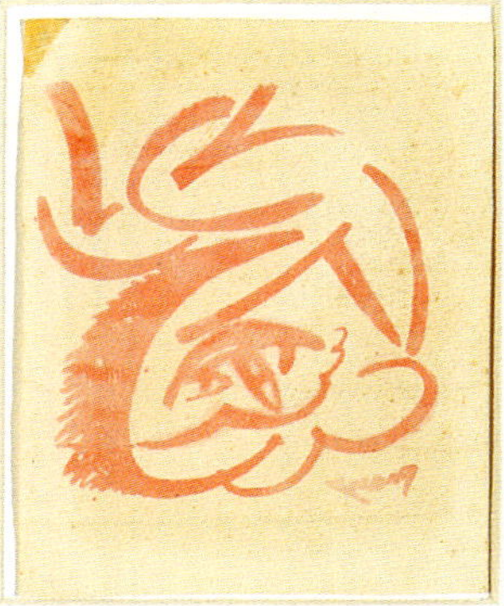

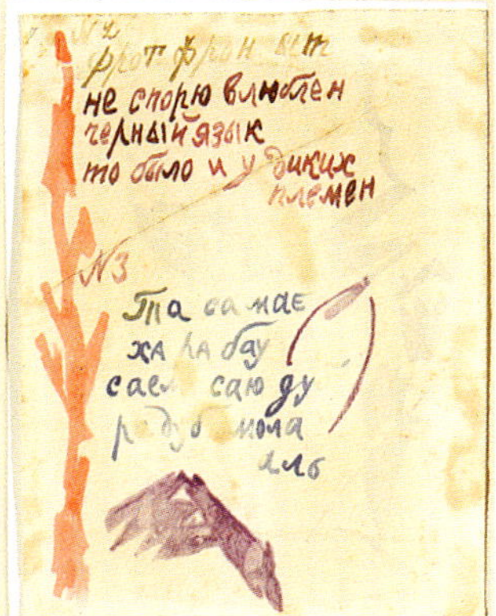
№2
фрот фрон вы
не спорю влюблен
черный язык
то было и у диких
племен
№3
Та са мае
ха ра бау
саем сию ду
р у б мола
альб

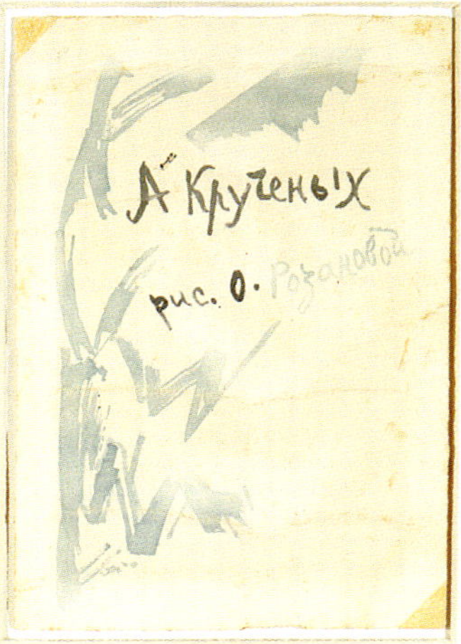
А. Крученых
рис. О. Розановой

Olga Rozanova, Nicolaï Kulbin
Cover and seven pages of *Té li lé*, 1914.
Poems by Vélimir Khlebnikov and Aleksei Kruchenykh
[cat. 396]

Olga Rozanova
Page of *Té li lé*, "Op. 13", 1908-1909.
Poem by Vélimir Khlebnikov
[cat. 396]

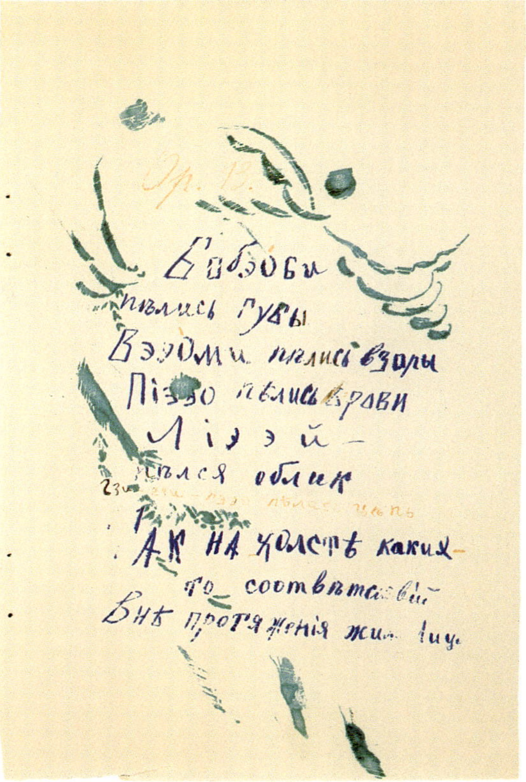

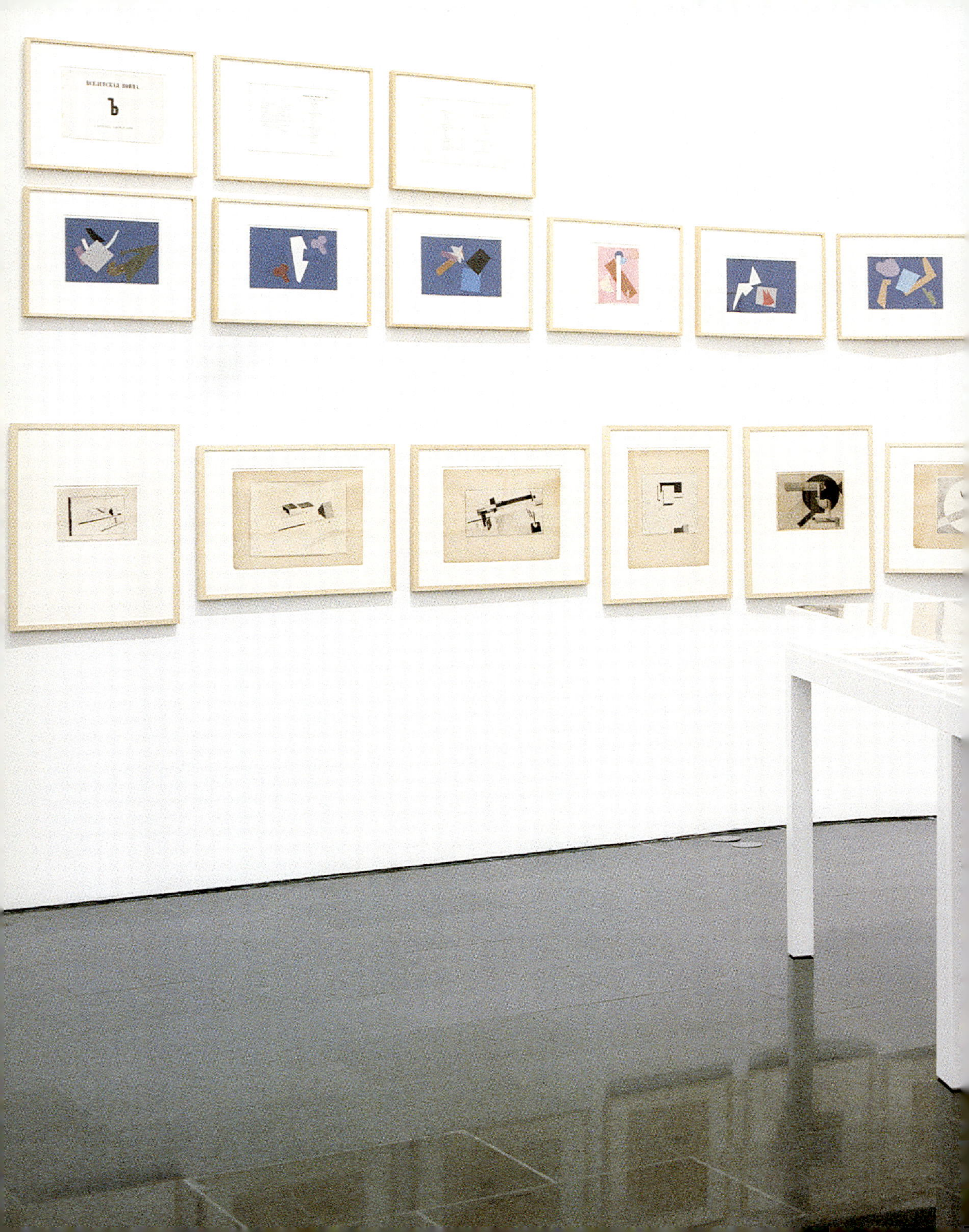

View of the exhibition rooms. Top row, Aleksei Khruchenykh, *Vselenskaia voina,* 1916 [cat. 383]; low row, El Lissitzky, *Proun 1,* 1920 [cat. 384]; showcase, Aleksei Khruchenykh / Olga Rozanova, *Utinoe gnezdyshko... durnykh slov...,* 1913 [cat. 387].

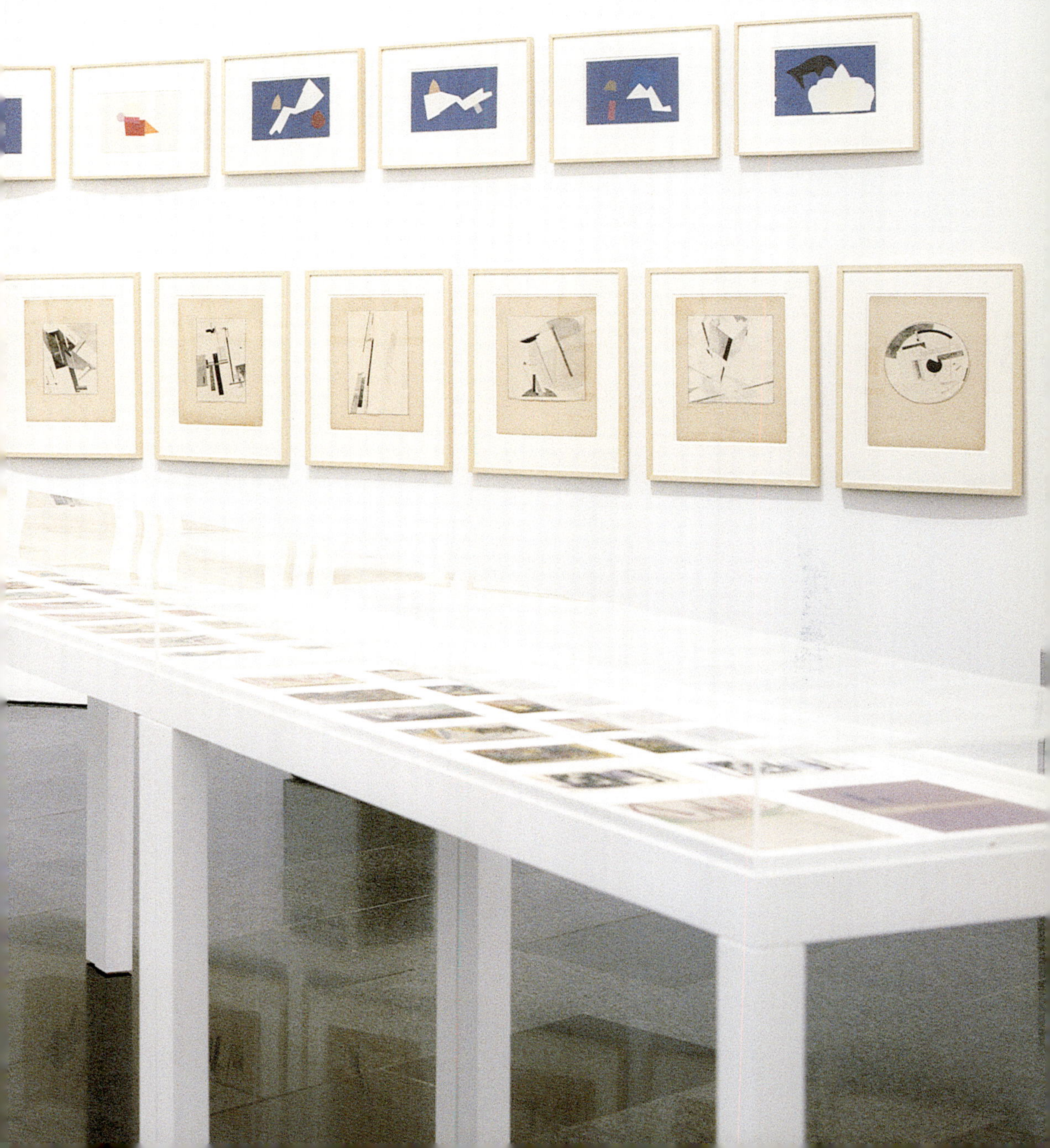

Aleksei Kruchenykh

Vselenskaia voina, 1916

"The Explosion of a Trunk"

[cat. 384]

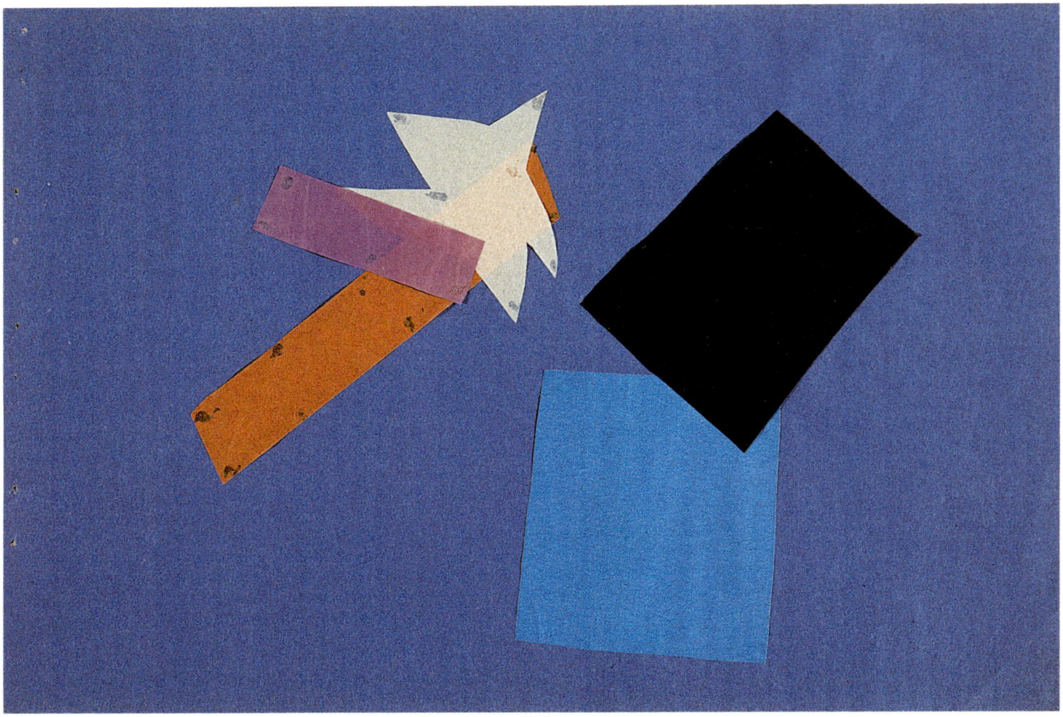

Aleksei Kruchenykh
Vselenskaia voina, 1916
"Battle with Ecuador"
[cat. 384]

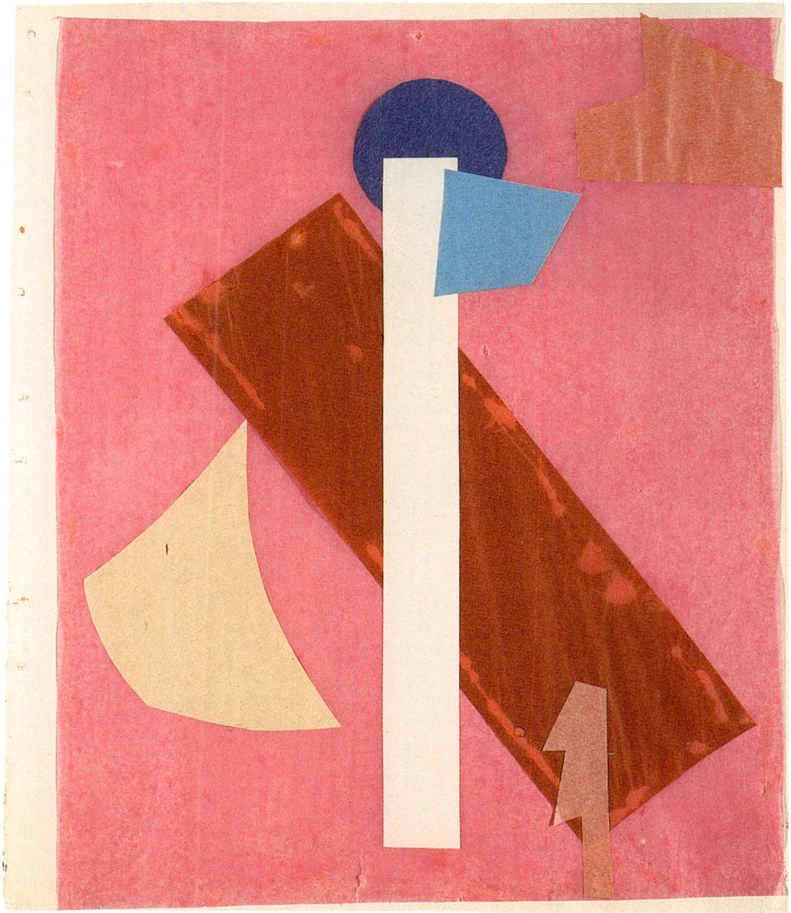

Iliazd (Ilia Zdanevitch)

Poster of a lecture by 41°, Borjom-Park, Tiflis, 1918

[cat. 361]

Newspaper by 41°, No. 1, Tiflis, 1919

[cat. 363]

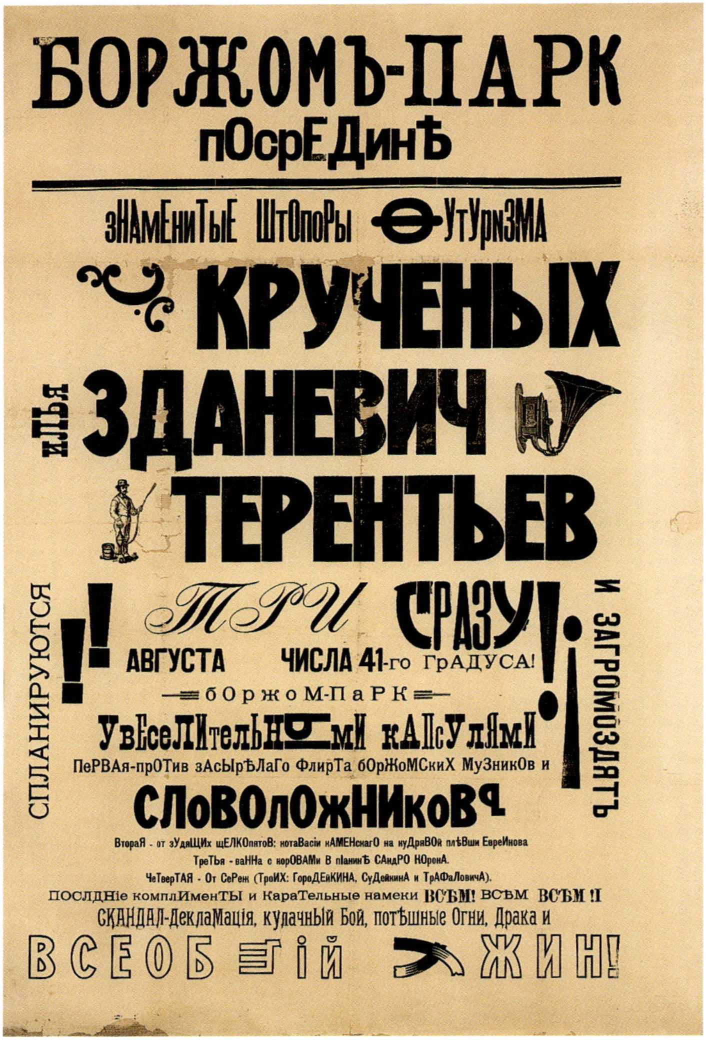
БОРЖОМЪ-ПАРК
пОсрЕДинѢ
зНАМЕниТыЕ ШТОпоРы УТУрнЗМА
КРУЧЕНЫХ
иЛЬя ЗДАНЕВИЧ
ТЕРЕНТЬЕВ
СПЛАНИРУЮТСЯ
ТРИ
СРАЗУ
АВГУСТА ЧИСЛА 41-го ГрАДУСА!
И ЗАГРОМОЗДЯТЬ
бОржоМ-ПаРК
УвЕселИтельНЫМИ КАПсУлЯМИ
ПеРВАя-прОТив зАсЫрѢЛаГо ФлирТа бОрЖоМСкиХ МуЗникОв и
СЛоВОлОжНИкоВЪ
ВтораЯ - от зУдяЩИх щЕЛКОпятоВ: нотаВасіи кАМЕНскагО на куДряВОй плѣВши ЕвреИнова
ТреТЬя - ваННа с корОВАМи В пІанинѢ САндРО НОронА.
ЧеТверТАЯ - От СеРеж (ТроИХ: ГороДЕйКИНА, СуДейкинА и ТрАФаЛовичА).
ПОСЛДНіе комплИменТЫ и КараТельные намеки ВСѢМ! ВСѢМ ВСѢМ !!
СКАНДАЛ-ДеклаМація, кУлачНЫЙ Бой, потѢшные Огни, Драка и
ВСЕОБЩІЙ ЖИН!

ЗА ТРУДОЛЮБИЕ И ИСКУСТВО КОМПАНИИ 41°

41°

№. 1

ЦѢНА 3 руб.

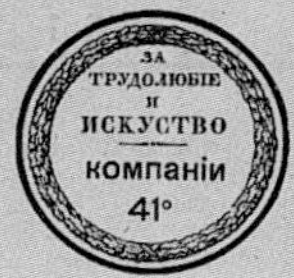

ЕЖЕНЕДѢЛЬНАЯ ГАЗЕТА

ПОНЕДѢЛЬНИКЪ–ВОСКРЕСЕНЬЕ 14–20 ІЮЛЯ 1919

Компанія 41° объединяет лѣвобережный футуризм, и утверждает **заумь** как обязательную форму воплощенія искусства.

Задача 41°—использовать всѣ великія открытія сотрудников и надѣть мір на новую ось.

Газета будет пристанью событій из жизни компаніи и причиной постоянных безпокойств.

Засучиваем рукава.

Аполлон в перепалкѣ.

(Живопись в поэзіи).

„Крученых
ногу втыкаешь ты
въ мяхково евнуха"
(Терентьев)

Рисунок—перпендикуляр сразмаху!

Необычное положеніе ноги: штопоръ или буравъ...

Композиція у Пушкина—естественное хожденіе, шатаніе из угла в угол и только смерть прекращала приводила необходимую для рисунка черту!..

А в приведенном Терентьевѣ—необычность живописной компановки!

„Пароход плывет по Волгѣ
По стѣнѣ верблюдъ ползетъ"!
(частушка)

Горизонталь пароходнаго рейса, пересеченная вертикалью карабканья верблюда—верблюд воткнутый в пароход!

Кажущаяся нелѣпость—мудрость рисунка!..

Живопись—проявитель такой композиціи поэта и начертаніе звуковъ: ударяемые **крученых** и **ты** дают звуковой **тык** штычек в отдувающагося как пуховик мяхково евнуха"!..

„Как памятник трезвый
Публично сплю"
(Терентьев).

(Человѣк не стѣсняющійся дѣлать публично все!)

Памятник ложится, но сейчас же протестует и встает, потому, что он „трезвый": рѣзкій, прямой, рѣзво вытянутый во фронт!

И тут же—„сплю"—распластанная постель (сравни: лежа бѣгаю)

Перпендикуляр мигающій!

Все изображается въ неприсвоенном положеніи и направленіи: вѣтеръ дуетъ **снизу**—„вой из войлочной туфли лихо радуй".
—лихо радуй и лихорадуя (лихорадочно и пр.)

„Пока не упрусь дощатой подошвой
Въ собственный каинный рост"
(Терентьев)

„Суп наголо"—
суп выдернутый наголо!

„Красота со взломом"—
лом продырявливающій икону!

„Совершенно неизвѣстно чего пожелает
Мой желудокъ
Хотябы через пять лѣтъ
С луком растянутаго бульдога
Ежа
Ваталіон телят
Или перепоротую кашу Лилилильню
Изъ фистали."
(Терентьевъ)

Построеніе: растянутый бульдогъ (растянутый куб!), воткнутый еж (нож), марширующій баталіон телят(!) и снова—каша разливная и перепоротая

„Поэзія что такое?
Укража дойное молоко
А корова?!!!!
Слово!
А быкъ????
Язык!"
(Терентьев)

Корова стоя читает газету. Ноги—четыре перпендикуляра. Бритва языка подкашивает тяжелаго быка—поэзія опредѣляется графически! Только при разборѣ я замѣтил что в рукописи послѣ четвероногих слов по четыре вопросит. и восклиц. знака!)

Каждое построеніе протыкается, проткнуто (проклято):

„Сливки мокко модница
Висла яблоко Николай угодник"
(Крученых-Терентьев)

Созвучныя слова. Общность их и в построеніи, которое выражается одним рисунком (—,1): поверхность сливок на тарелкѣ, рядом—стоящія жестянки и модница Яблоня повисла—а может рѣка Висла или висячая—и на берегу яблоко-ня, а повыше гладильной скриталью заушающій Никола Угодник—не подходи, а то выгладит!

В страхѣ бѣгут „дезертировавшіе меридіаны"—сухощавные поджарые спортсмены, растянутые в безконечность (лежачіе бѣгут)

Три названія перпендикуляра:
1) кличка „трезвый" (человѣк)
2) Николай Угодник (дух)
3) Дезертировавшіе мердіаны (вселенная)

„Птица тройка! Кто с ней угонится?!.

Наконец то Щедрин дождался, что (мы) стали к нему перпендикулярны—смотри его „будьте перпендикулярны" (сравни: я очен вам перпендикулярен")....

Воткнутый под прямым углом кинжал классической трагедіи не трогает современнаго сердца: онъ кажется холостым чертежом. По Аристотелю красота доканчивалась гибелью. Акробатическія выдумки стараго искуства не были сами по себѣ достаточно интересны почему публика вѣрить могла в основательность танца только послѣ сломанной шеи: это ее убѣждало восхищало!..

„Красота в погибели"
„Любовь и смерть"
„Философія трагедіи"

Веселье достигалось привѣшенным черепом

„Прими сей черепъ Делвиг, он
Принадлежит тебѣ по праву"

—Кубок—черепъ!

„Все, все, что гибелью грозит
Для сердца смертнаго таит
Неизъяснимы наслажденья"
(Пушкинъ)

Грубость вкуса, воспитанная старым искуством, требует искренности лирика и гибели въ трагедіи. Мы живем въ варварское время, когда „дѣло" ставится выше „слова", А у Терентьева: „цвѣтут какаисты Бревна смѣхом" воткнутая нога (кинжал)—цвѣтетъ сама (интересно осуществить все это на сценѣ!), а что дѣлается с продырявленным евнухом—для композитора не видно,—сажаемъ мудрецов на кол, устраивая громоотвод жизни

„Не упускайте случая
Сказать глупость,
Усыпительной пулей уносится
Всякая пакость".
(Терентьевъ из книги „Херувимы Свистят")

„Сорок соборов на одну Лизу"—
такой размах!..

В драмах Зданевича дан кинемотограф перпендикуляров—ежеминутно встает и падает:

В „Янко" частокол-разбойников, косая блоха и распяленный Янко, испускающій мало „бью".

В пьесѣ „Асел напрокат" вертикальные женихи с невѣстой (Зохной) и горизонтальный эсел. К концу всѣ ложатся въ слезах назель.

В третьей дра (!) „Островъ Пасхи" безпрерывныя смерть и воскрешеніе из пяти лиц: эффект выщербленнаго забора и спортивная комбинація пяти пальцевъ в сырное лицо смерти...

ВОЕННОЙ ВЫЗОВ

„У-у-а ме-гон э-бью".
(Крученых)

У-у—глухой рев внизу и затѣм рѣзкій перекод кверху (а)—раскрывшаяся пасть.

„Ом-чу гвут он
За-бью"
Опять „хлопасть"
Дальше: „гва-гва"—лягушачія трели и квак.
„[illegible]
„Зарья???
Качрюк!???!"—

графичность вопросительнаго знака—круженіе в военной пляскѣ. („вопросительный крючек"—выраженіе Пушкина)

ЗАДОРНЫЙ ВЫЗОВЪ

„Чхо-хоа"!
увей чипля!
злукон! злубоп!
шашимп!..
Фа-зу-зу-зу!..
(Крученых)

—шипѣнье брызги чахи, хлопанье лопнувшей камеры на всю Европу
Колючки осколки и брызги....

„Заюская гугулица"—(Фавни: юсь, высунуть как шерсть, молюски)—тонкая как волос блондинки, как математика. Гугулица—дикое у-у гу,—чудище на тонкой плюснѣ—ножкѣ...

РИСУНКИ СЛОВЪ: (Терентьева, Крученых, И. Зданевич)

1 **Свороченныя головы**—мочедан (чемодан), шрамное лицо, мрачья физіономія и др.

2 **Двухглавыя слова**—я не ягеній, вшпту исусами (отчаянно пьяный)

3 **Сломанное туловище**—мыслей (удареніе на е), Овделія (исковерк: офелія)

4 **Троичные в брюхѣ**—злостеболь (злость и боль), брендень (бред, дребень, раздробленный день). Вчимдѣла.

5 **Мохнатыя слова**—бѣден, как церковная лектриса (притягивает крысу), песчка (мягкое, круглое, пѣпистое). случайка и др.

6 **Третья нога**—летитот (летит от) во снѣ на Козерога.

7 **Однорельсныя**—жизь (вмѣсто: жизнь) нра (нравится)

8 **Трехрельсныя**—циркорій (вставная буква р)

9 **Свыжатой серединой**—сно (вмѣсто сов)

СЛОЖНЫЯ КОМПОЗИЦІЯ: (груз на кабелѣ. прикрѣпленном за кобуру горла)

Выбурив ка-горло
по кабелю
спускаюсь
на аптеки
в
сак—
вояж
(Крученых)

—Крѣпкая перекладина. По кап (б) елю, по каплѣ (ростянутое а). в саквояж—(сак—бряк, вояж—ляж—ка, пляж.

Еще возможны композиціи: из разных кривых, лучистая, симультане, пятиинстая и пр.

Карабкающ-іися
по прямому" проводу
птиц
Х Р Ж У Б

—Легкость (вертикальная фраза) и тяжесть (хржуб).

В заумных словах, освобожденных от груза смысла, наибольшая сила и самостоятельность звука, крайняя легкость (фьят, фьят; мечтаянный пюнь) и крайная тяжесть (дыр-бул-щыл, хряч сарча Крочо, хо-бо-ро, хружб.).

Чередованіе обычнаго и заумнаго языка—самое неожданная композиція и фактура (наслоеніе и раздробленіе звуков)—оркестровая поэзія, все сочетающая

Замауль! ..

А. Крученых

41°

КОМПАНІЯ

Основной капитал 1.000.000 руб.

Книгоиздательство

ГАЗЕТА
ТЕАТР
ВСЕУЧБИЩЕ
ОБРАЗЦОВАЯ ФЕРМА

Проспекты по первому требованію.

Изабеллѣ Седьмой

Открытое письмо

Madame!

Печально, что ваш недавній пріѣзд в Тифлис лишил вас возможности быть слушательницей футурвсеучбища прошлаго года и в частности моих докладов. Это дало бы вам возможность хотя бы нѣсколько ознакомиться с футуризмом и не писать несуразностей, помѣщенных в газетѣ „Новый День". Я имѣю в виду ваши разсужденія по поводу семитизма в футуризмѣ. Позвольте же вкратце указать вам поэтому.

Футуризм—заумный ставит задачей воплощеніе в словѣ таких сторон переживаній, которыя не могли быть никак воплощены нашими предшественниками, пока поэзія имѣла дѣло со словом, привязанным к смыслу. Для этой цѣли футуризм создает слово заумное. Слѣдовательно, он не только не отказывается от воплощенія Бога, но наоборот, стремится к этому и притом успѣшно, побѣждая скептицизм эстетов, разочаровавшихся в своих средствах—Тютчева с его Silentium и Фета („О если б без слова"). Примѣняя вашу концепцію могу сказать, что футуризм есть новое христіанство, а заумная поэзія во-

El Lissitzky, Vladimir Mayakovski

Cover and interior pages of *Dlia Golosa,* 1923

[cat. 329]

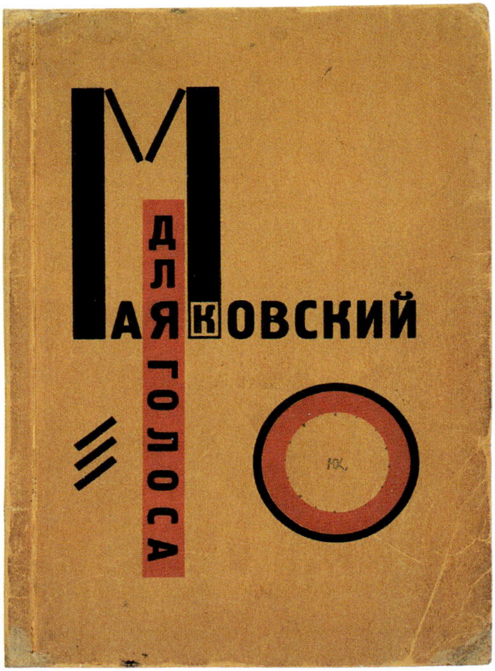

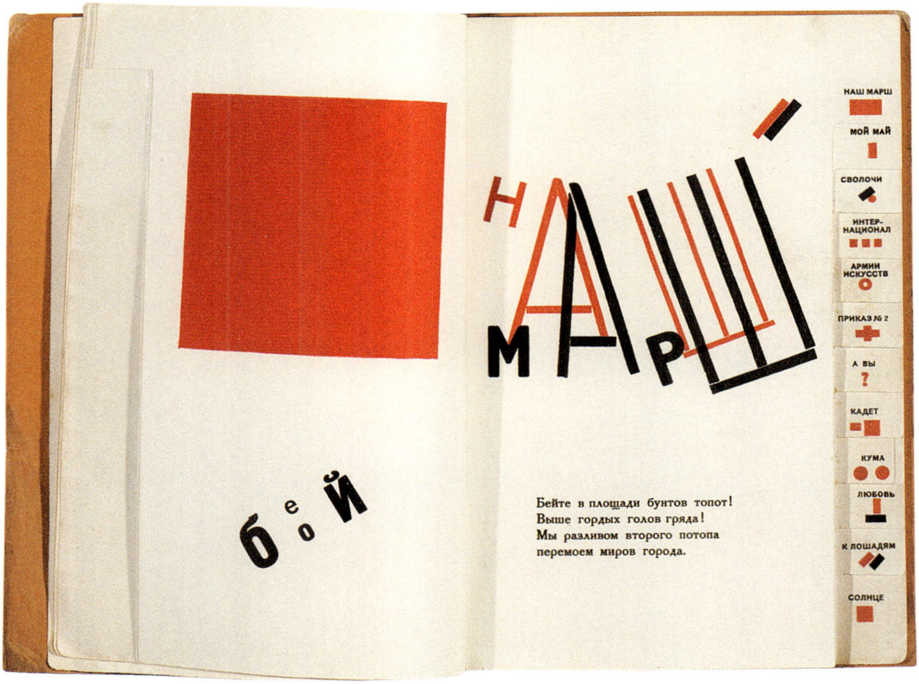
НАШ МАРШ
Бейте в площади бунтов топот!
Выше гордых голов гряда!
Мы разливом второго потопа
перемоем миров города.
НАШ МАРШ
МОЙ МАЙ
СВОЛОЧИ
ИНТЕР-НАЦИОНАЛ
АРМИИ ИСКУССТВ
ПРИКАЗ № 2
А ВЫ
КАДЕТ
КУМА
ЛЮБОВЬ
К ЛОШАДЯМ
СОЛНЦЕ

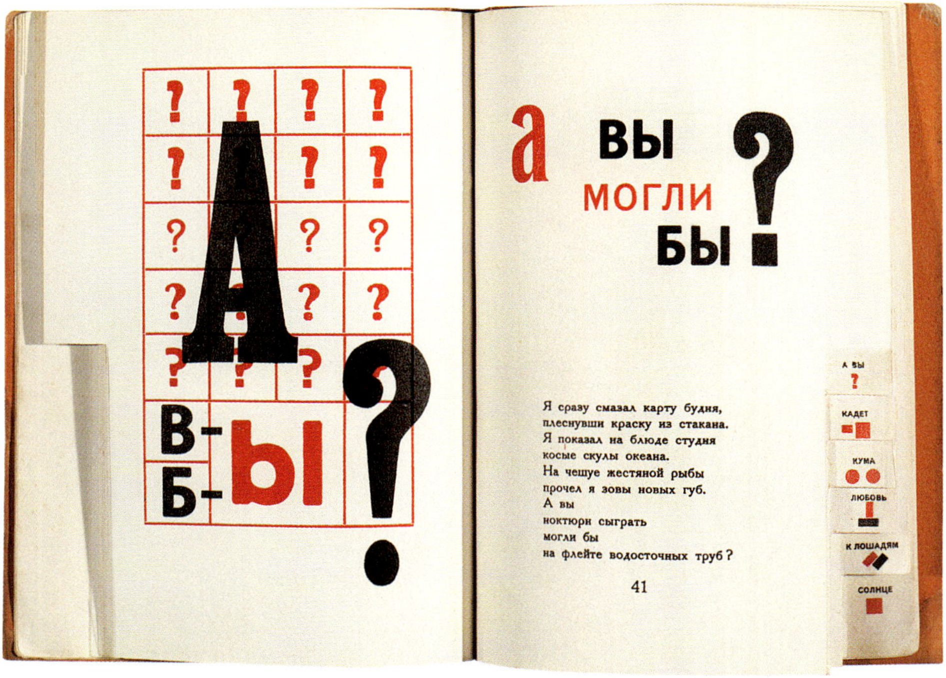
А
В-
Б-
Ы
а вы
могли
бы
Я сразу смазал карту будня,
плеснувши краску из стакана.
Я показал на блюде студня
косые скулы океана.
На чешуе жестяной рыбы
прочел я зовы новых губ.
А вы
ноктюрн сыграть
могли бы
на флейте водосточных труб?
41
А ВЫ
КАДЕТ
КУМА
ЛЮБОВЬ
К ЛОШАДЯМ
СОЛНЦЕ

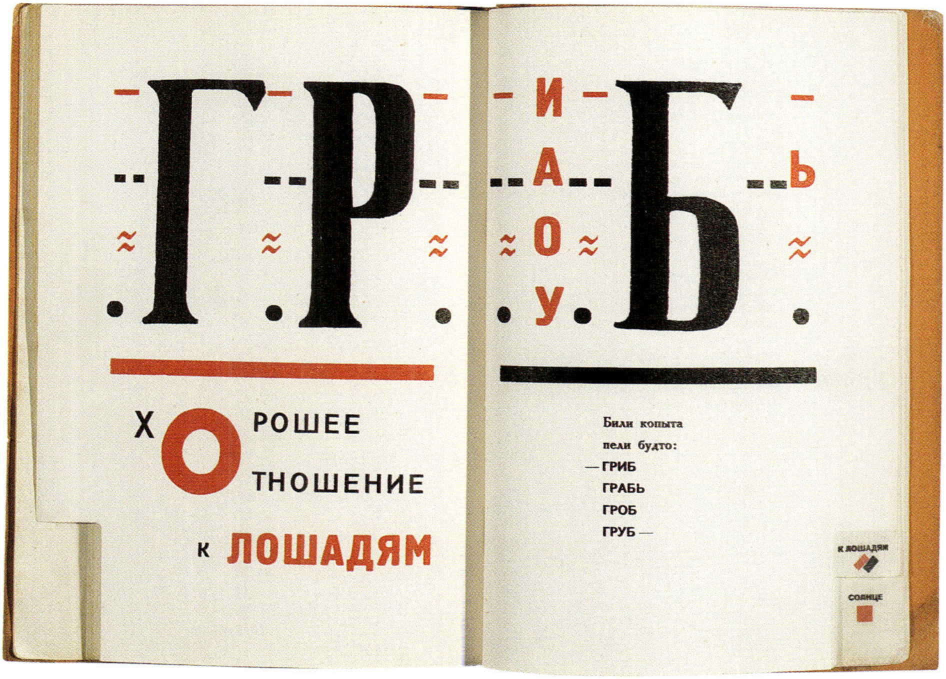
Г Р
И А О У
Б
Ь
Х О РОШЕЕ
О ТНОШЕНИЕ
К ЛОШАДЯМ
Били копыта
пели будто:
— ГРИБ
ГРАБЬ
ГРОБ
ГРУБ —
К ЛОШАДЯМ
СОЛНЦЕ

Constantin Brancusi

Portrait de James Joyce, 1929
[cat. 400]

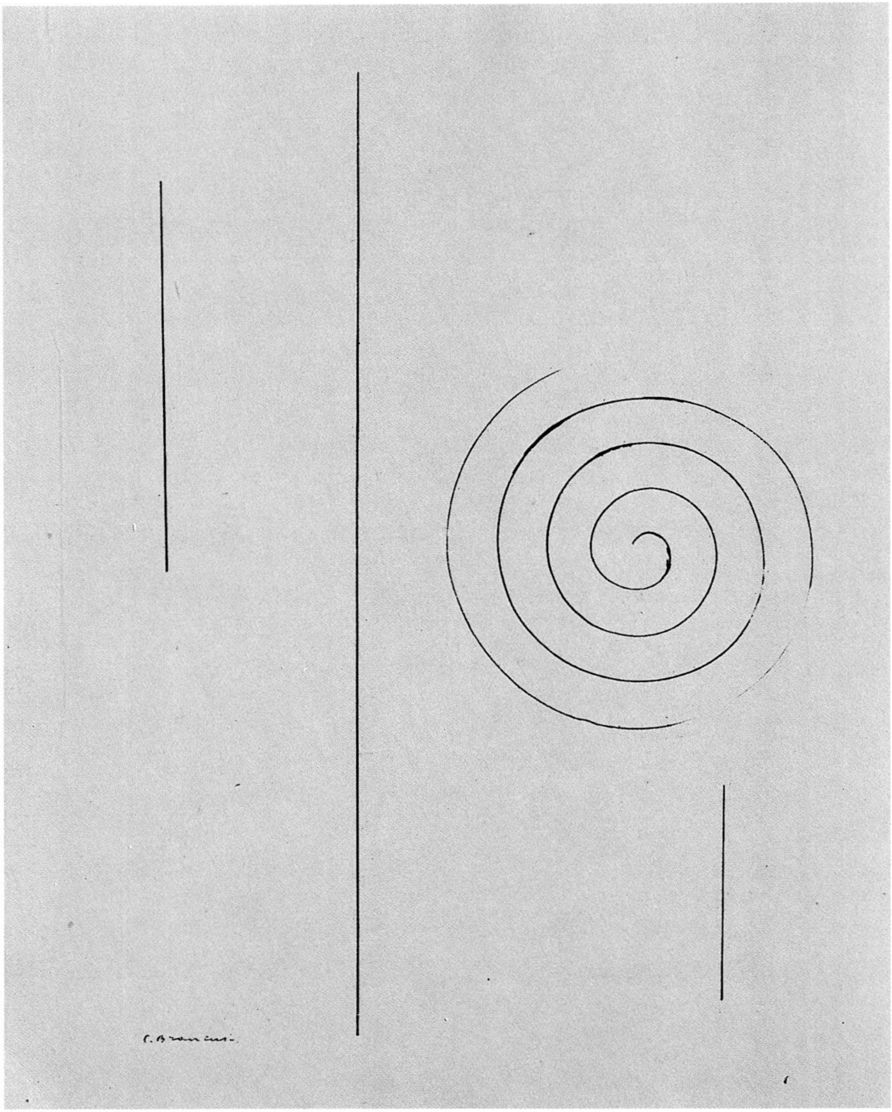

Can't hear with the waters of. The chittering waters of. Flittering bats, fieldmice bawk talk. Ho! Are you not gone ahome? What Tom Malone? Can't hear with bawk of bats, all the liffeying waters of. Ho, talk save us! My foos won't moos. I feel as old as yonder elm. A tale told of Shaun or Shem? All Livia's daughtersons. Dark hawks hear us. Night! Night! My ho head halls. I feel as heavy as yonder stone. Tell me of John or Shaun? Who were Shem and Shaun the living sons or daughters of? Night now! Tell me, tell me, tell me, elm! Night night! Tell me tale of stem or stone. Beside the rivering waters of, hitherandthithering waters of. Night!

James Joyce
Anna Livia Plurabelle. Fragment of Work in Progress, 1927

Hans Arp
Cover of *Transition*, No. 21, March 1932
[cat. 418]

Sophie Taeuber-Arp
Cover of *Transition*, No. 22, February 1933
[cat. 418]

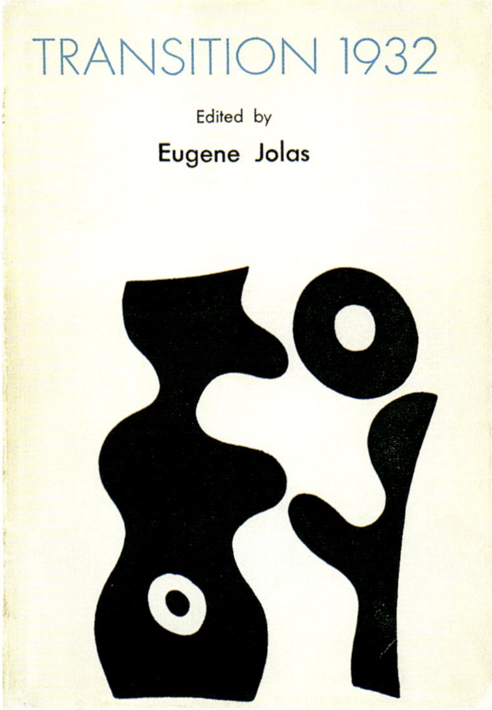

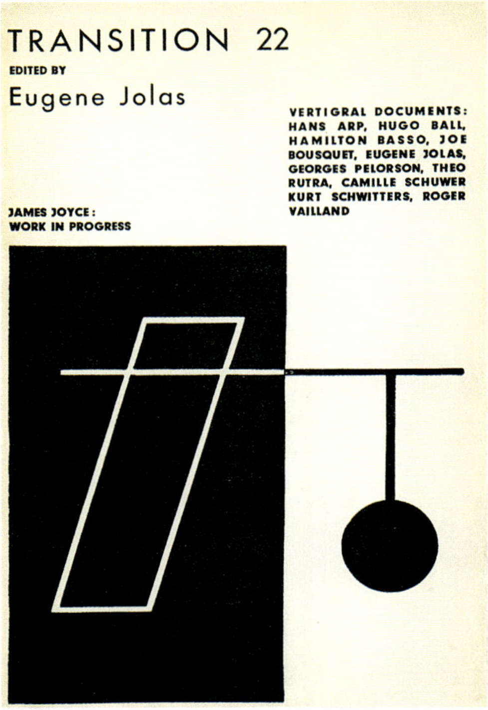

Joan Miró
Cover of *Transition,* No. 25, Fall 1936
[cat. 420]

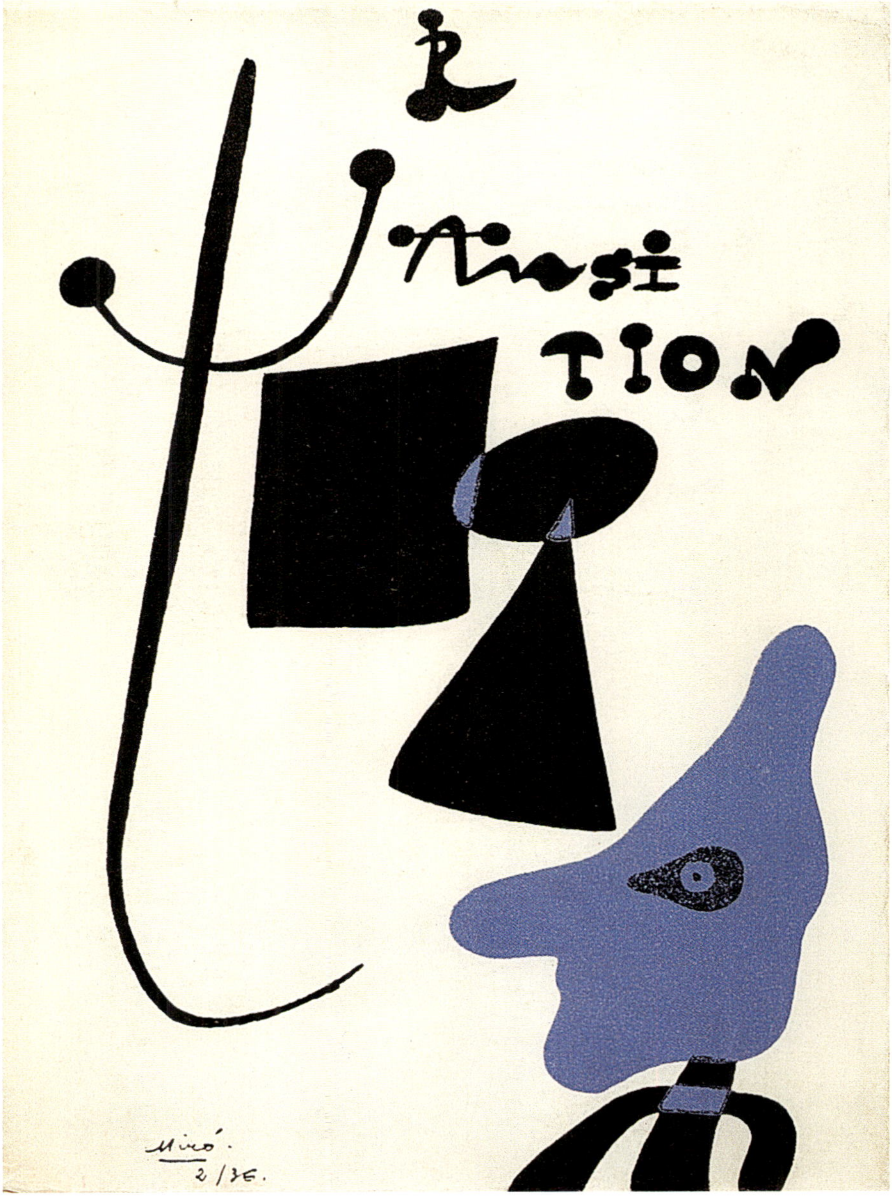

Marcel Duchamp
Cover of *Transition,* No. 26, Fall 1937
[cat. 420]

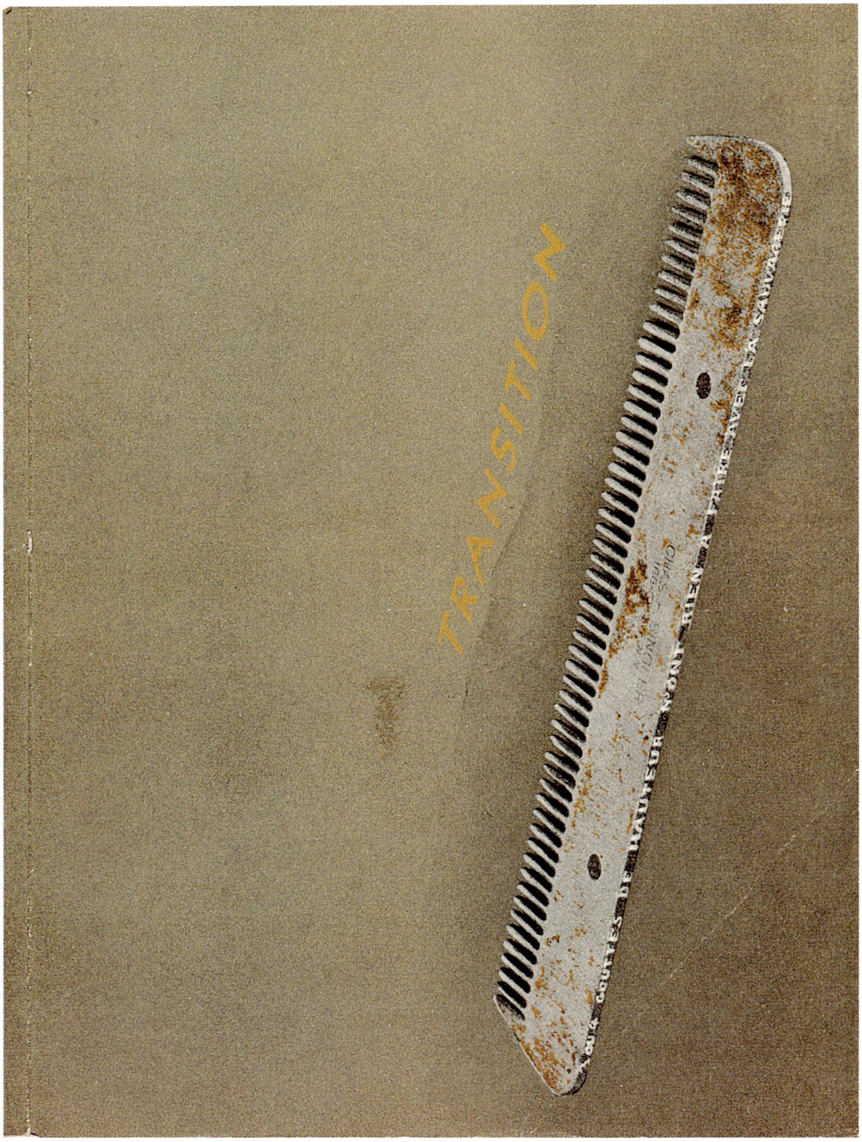

Poetry is not a special activity, but a state,
a becoming of the whole world.
The unconscious and its language – myth –
demonstrate the absence of any fit between
human events and ordinary reality.

Carl Einstein
Georges Braque, 1934

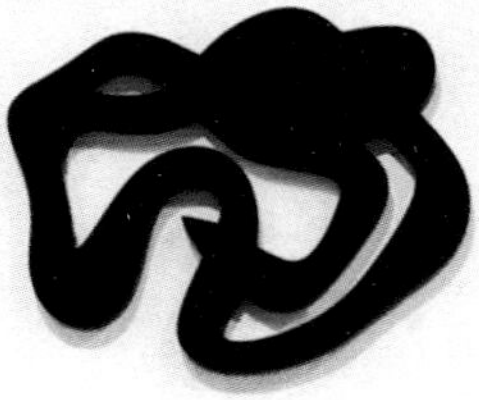

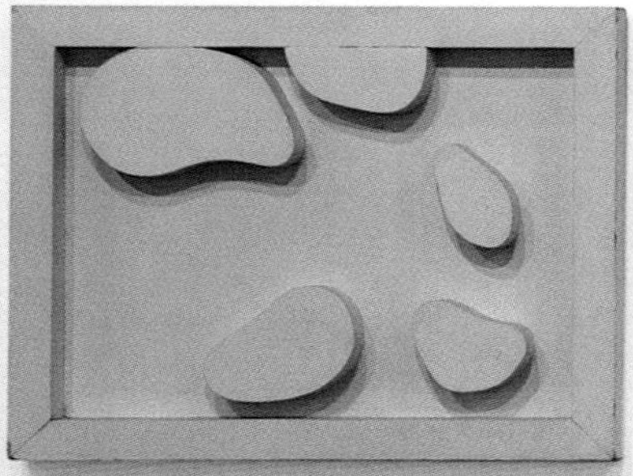

View of the exhibition rooms; left to right:
Hans Arp, *Constellation selon les lois du hasard,* 1932 [cat. 413];
Araignée, 1958 [cat. 414]; *Bläter IV,* 1930 [cat. 415];
Paul Klee, *Halme,* 1911 [cat. 416].

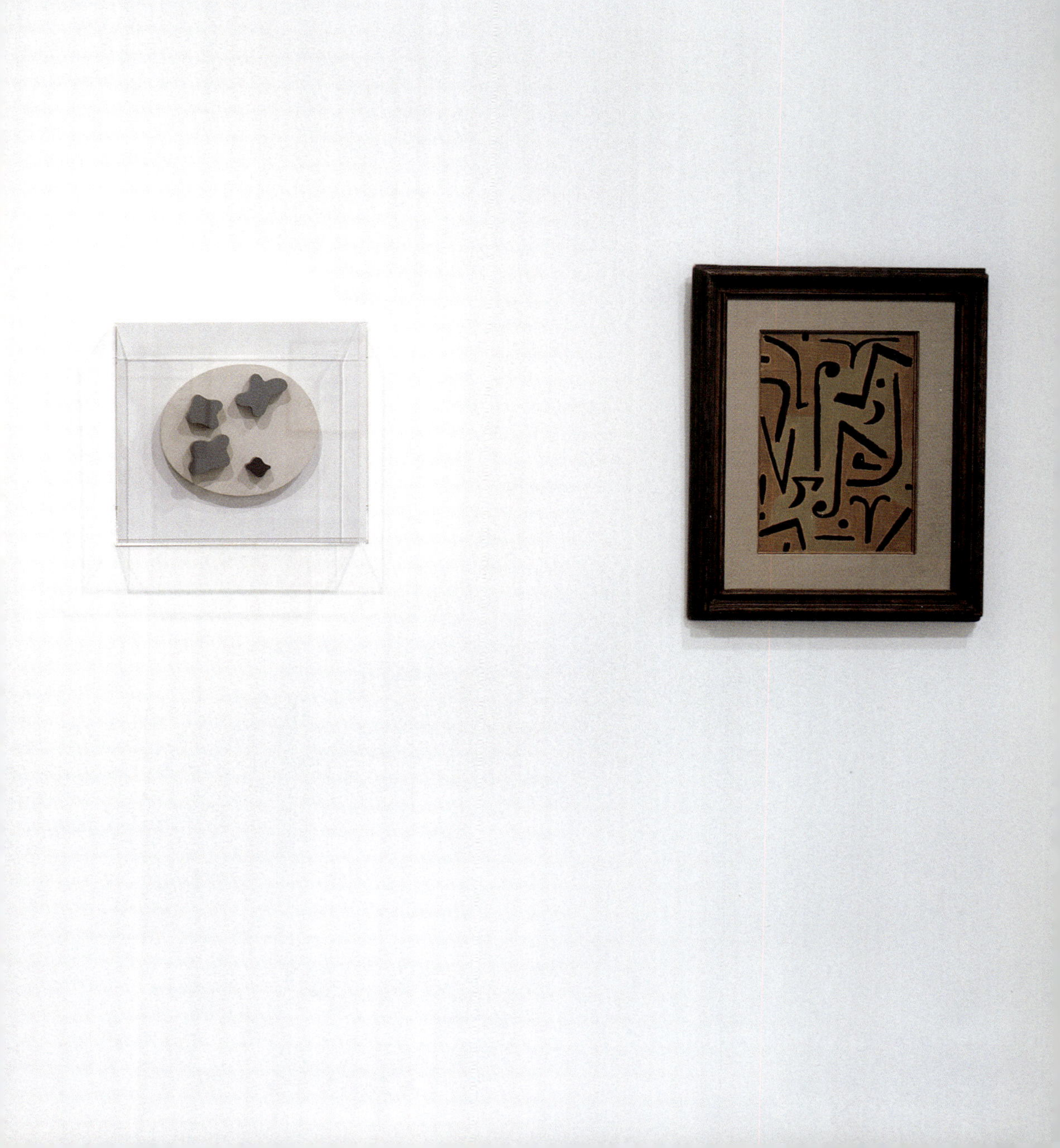

Hans Arp

Untitled, 1942

[cat. 402]

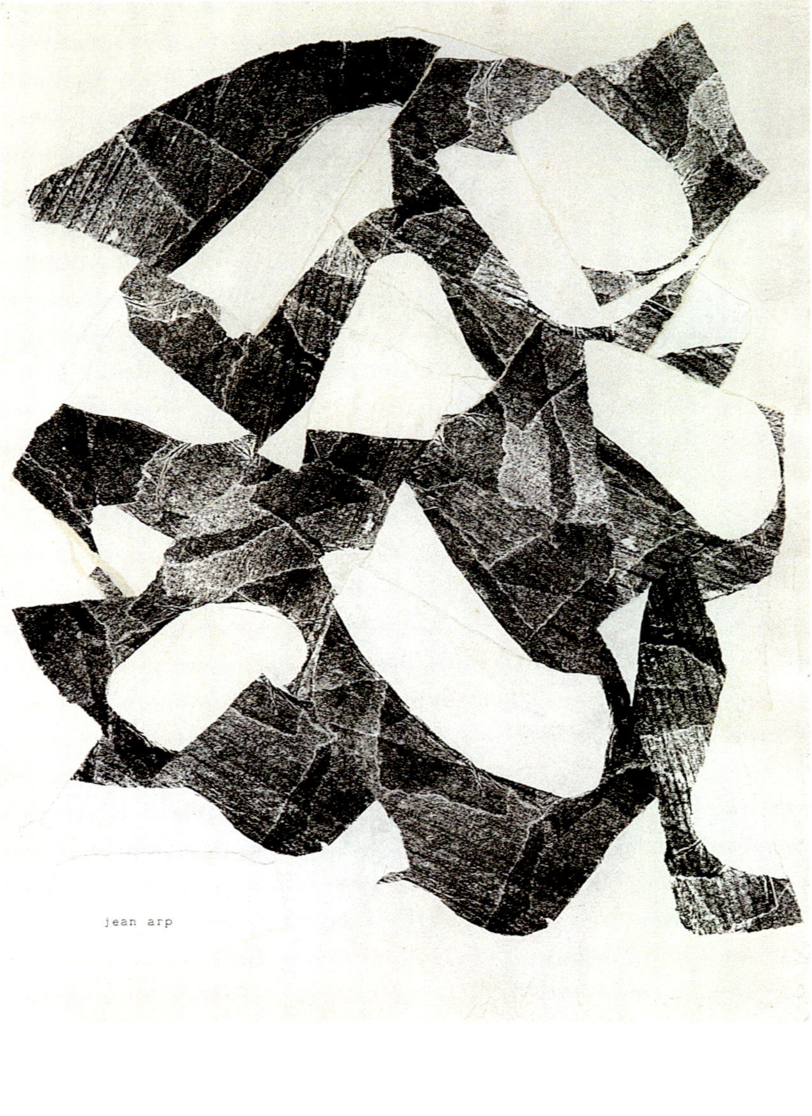

Julio González

Petite danseuse II, 1938-1940
[cat. 407]

Étude pour Danseuse à la palette, 1935
[cat. 408]

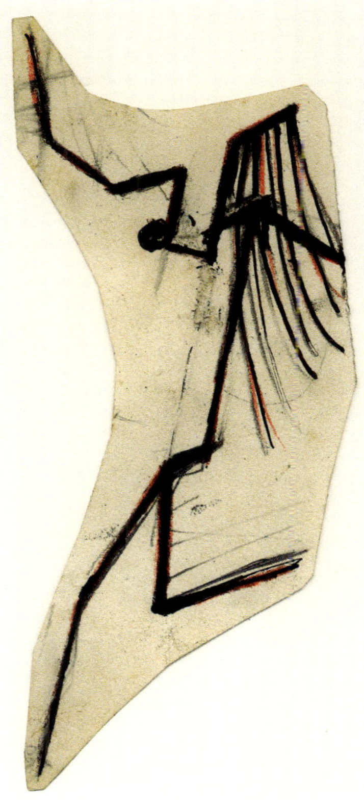

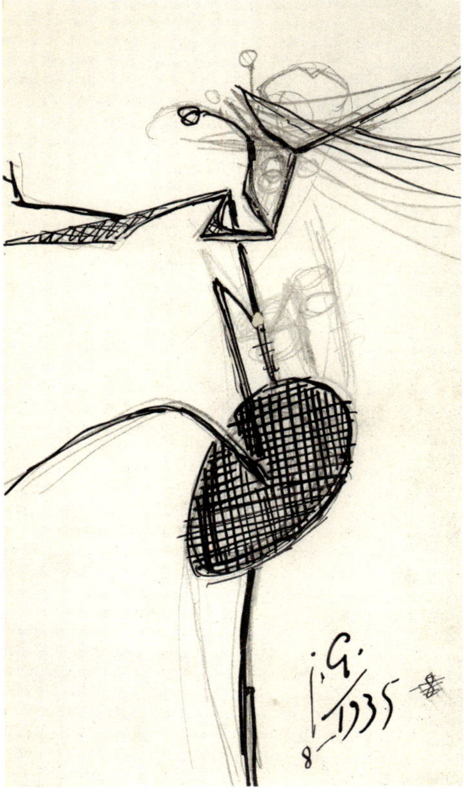

Hans Arp
Araignée, 1958
[cat. 790]

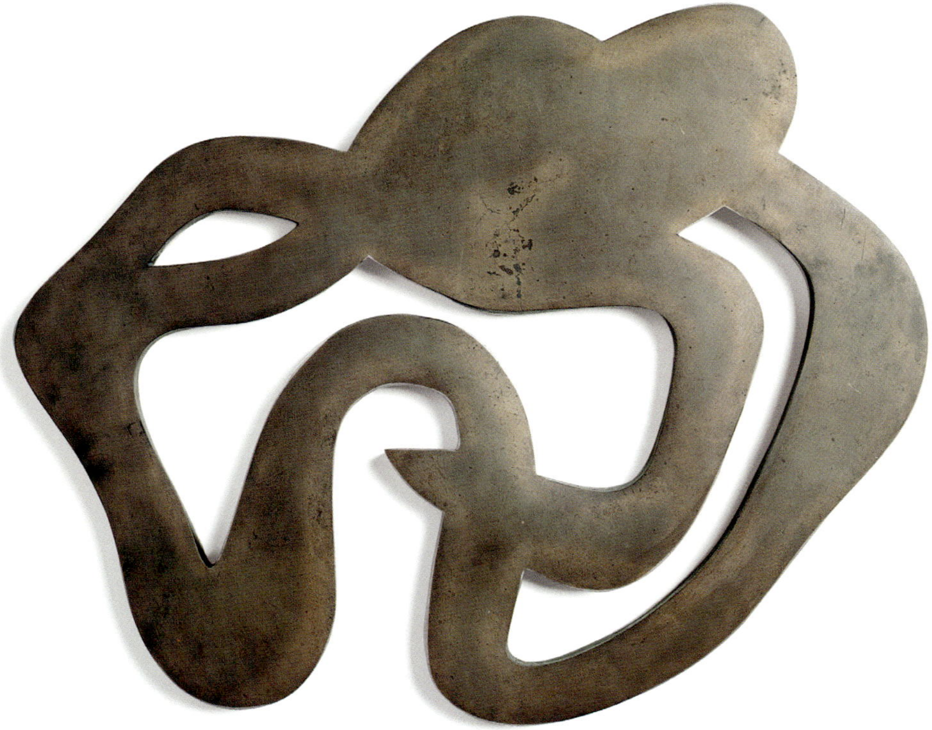

Sophie Taeuber-Arp

Échelonnement, 1934

[cat. 404]

Échelonnement, ca. 1934

[cat. 405]

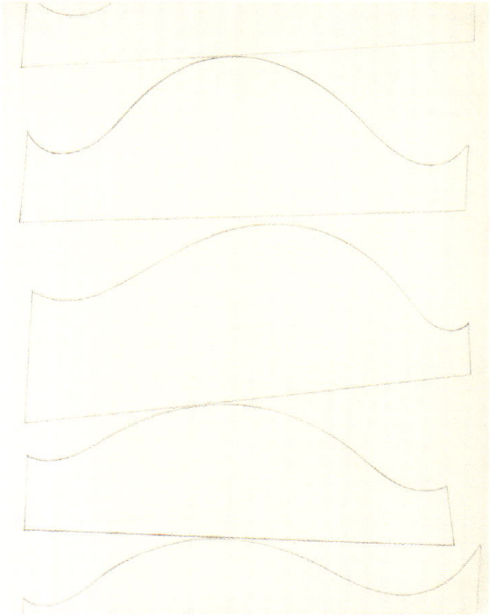

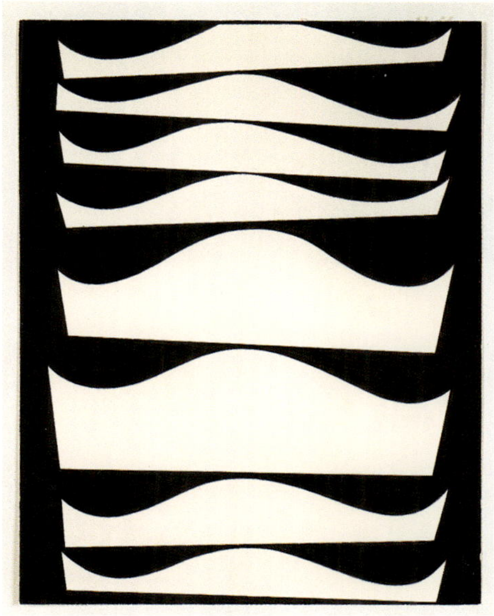

Josef Albers

Drei Behangen (3), 1931
[cat. 434]

Drei Behangen (2), 1931
[cat. 433]

Drei Behangen (1), 1931
[cat. 432]

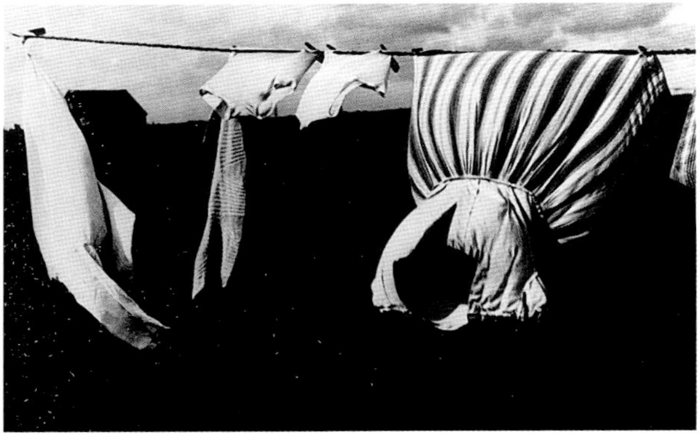

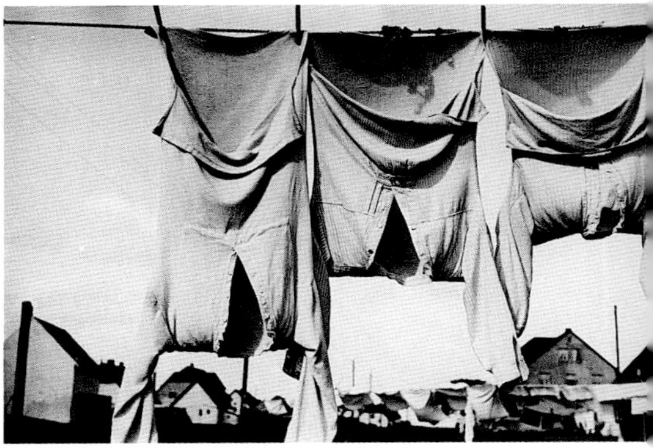

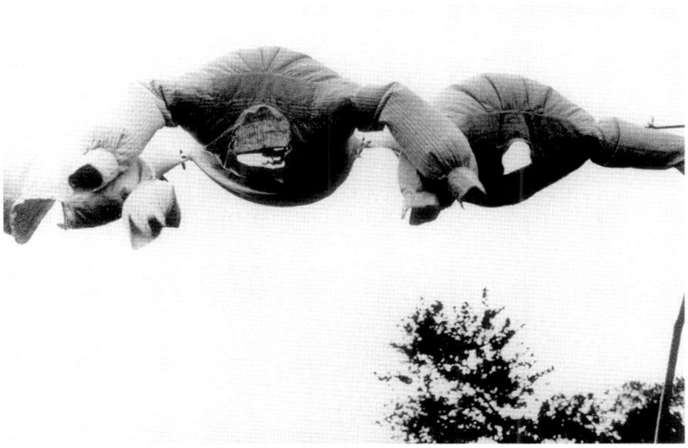

A truly creative vision is configured from the tensions and distensions of the basic relationships of a body, be it man, beast, plant, stone, machine, part or whole, big or small: the vision is never the centre coldly and mechanically observed.

Raoul Hausmann
"Nous me sommes pas des photographes," 1921

Josef Albers

Dessau, Flurstrasse während Neubauten, ca. 1931

[cat. 457]

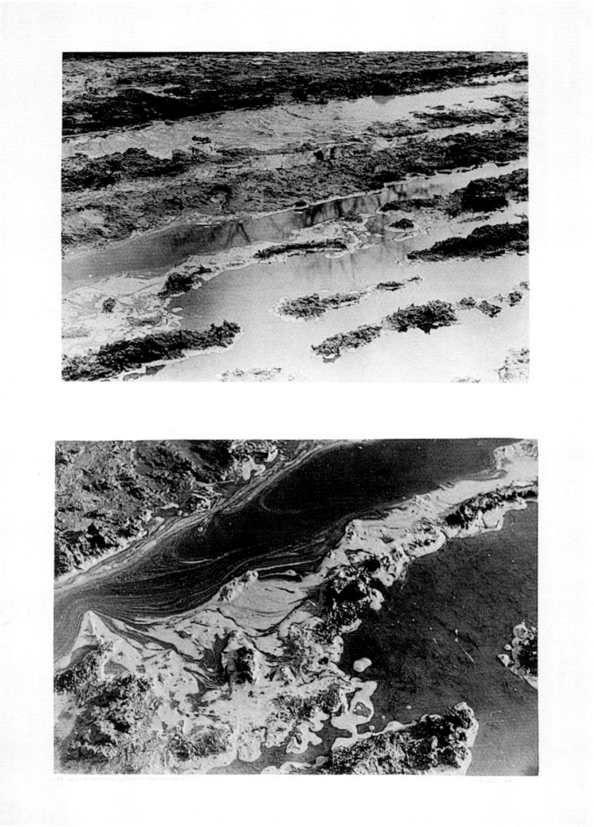

Josef Albers
Ozenfant, 1931
[cat. 462]

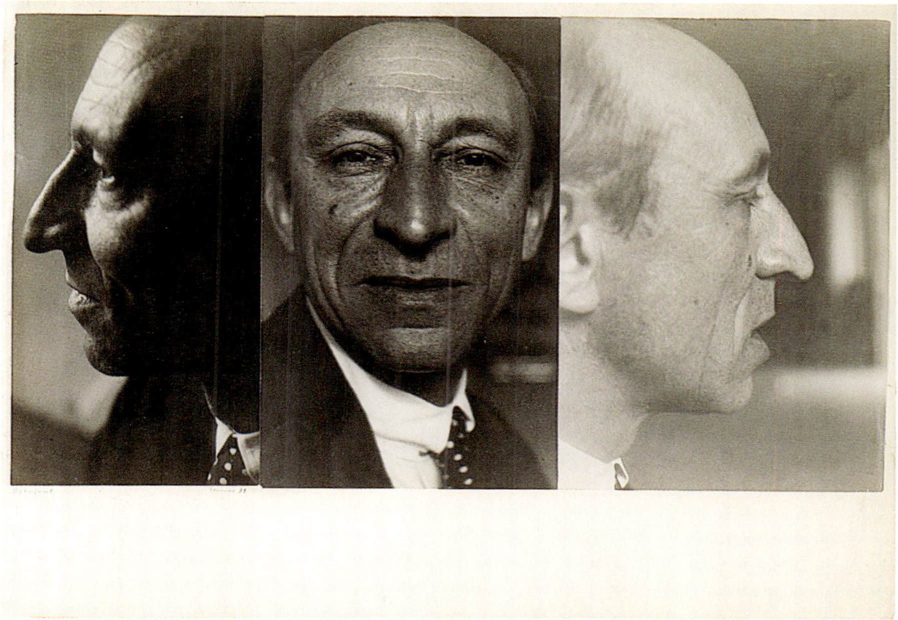

Josef Albers

Ohne Titel (Grosse Pyramide, Tenayuca, Mexico)

[cat. 455]

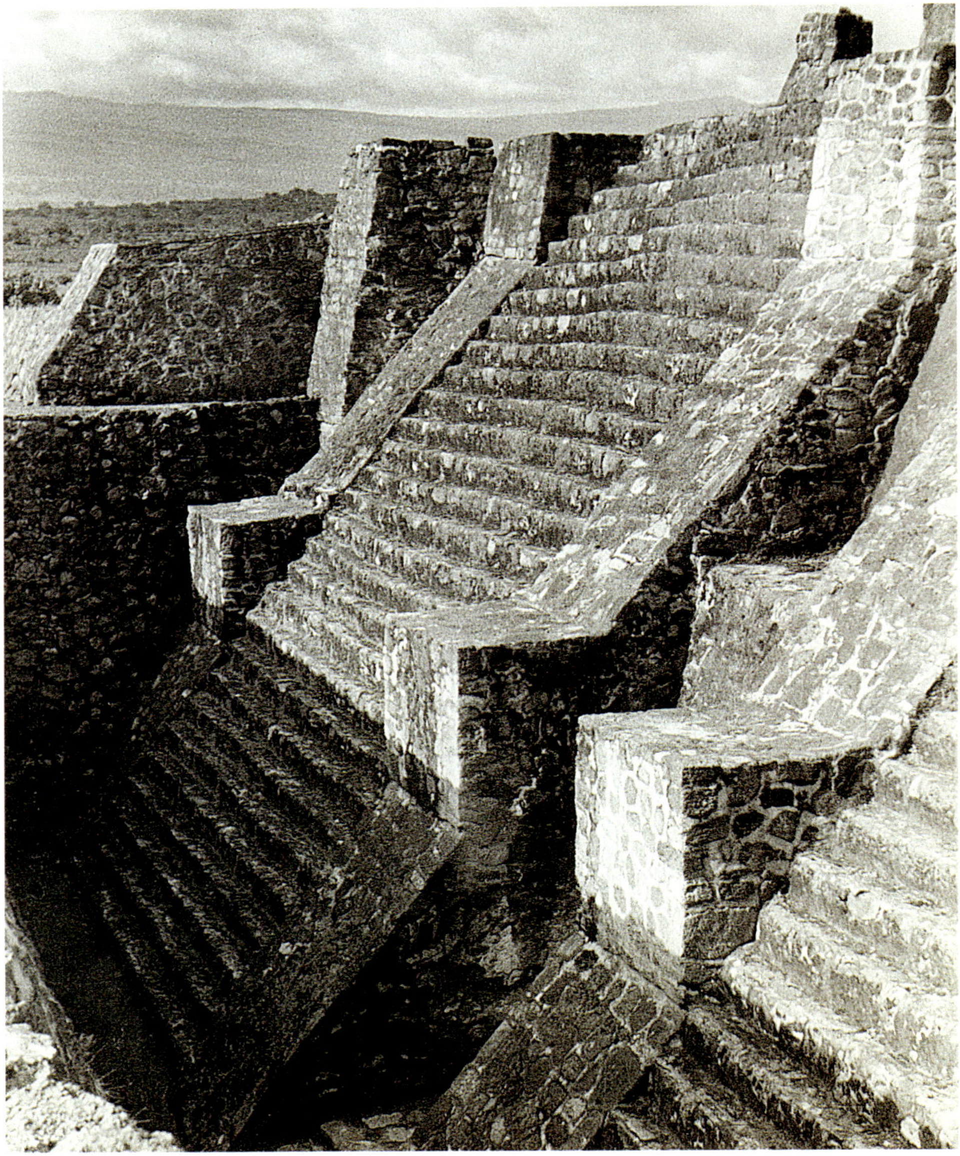

Josef Albers

Pachacamac (Peru), 1953

[cat. 456]

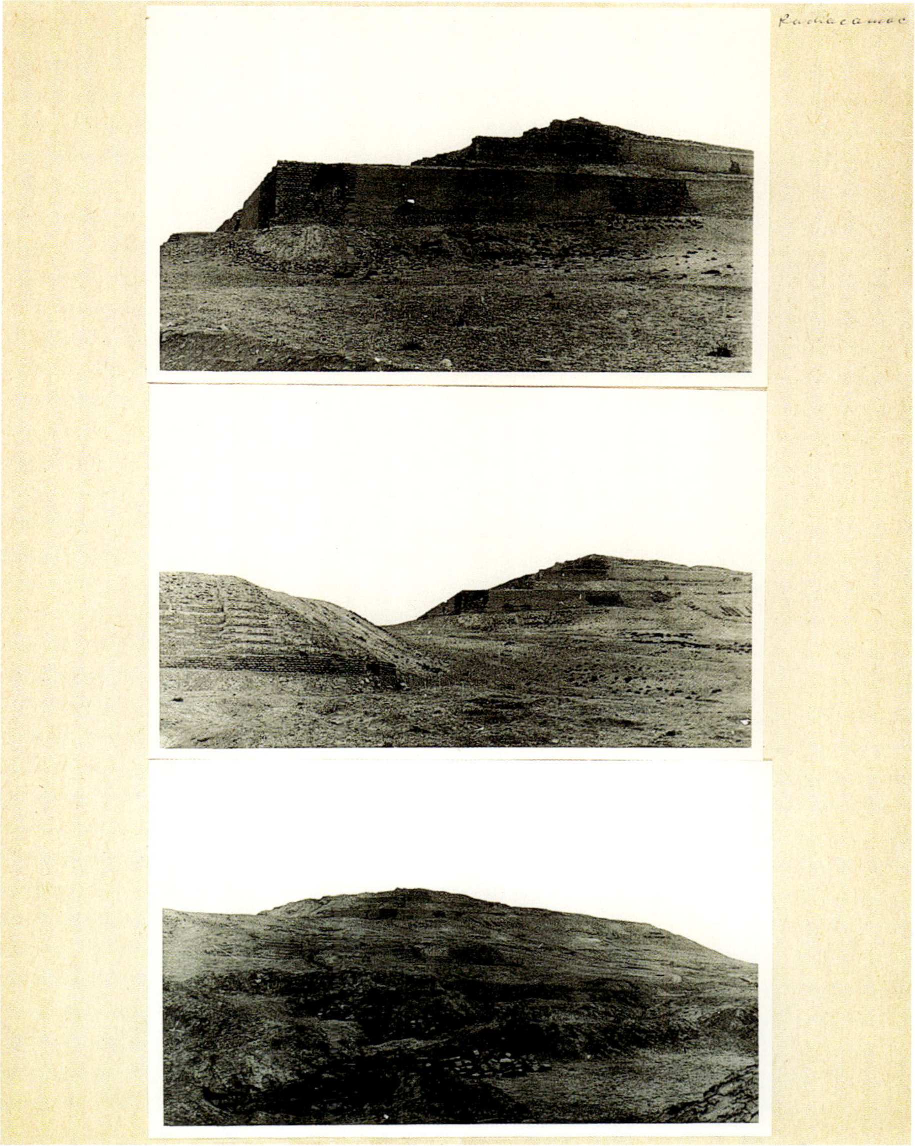

Impoverished, that is how we've ended up. We have been squandering one bit of mankind's birthright after another, we've had to pawn this treasure, often for a hundredth of its value, in exchange for the pitiful sum of that which is "current". The economic crisis is at the door and behind it lurks a shadow, the war that is brewing. Today resistance has become the prerogative of a handful of powerful men who, God knows, are no more human than the majority: they tend to be more barbarian, but not in the positive sense of the word. The rest have to make with what they have, begin anew and almost from scratch. They make common cause with those men who have striven to explore radically new possibilities, on the basis of discernment and renunciation.

Walter Benjamin
"Expérience et pauvreté", extract from the text written in Ibiza in 1933, the first period of Benjamin's exile after Hitler took power in Germany.

August Sander

Abbasanta, Alter Sarde,
"Eine Reise nach Sardinien" Series, 1927
[cat. 505]

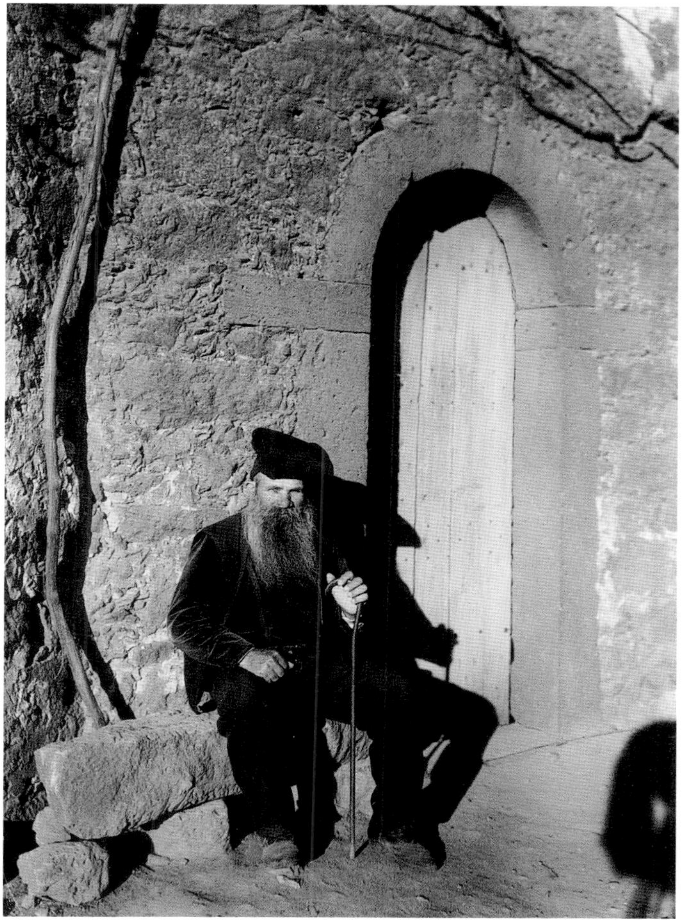

August Sander
Abbasanta, Vorraum eines gotisches Hauses,
"Eine Reise nach Sardinien" Series, 1927
[cat. 506]

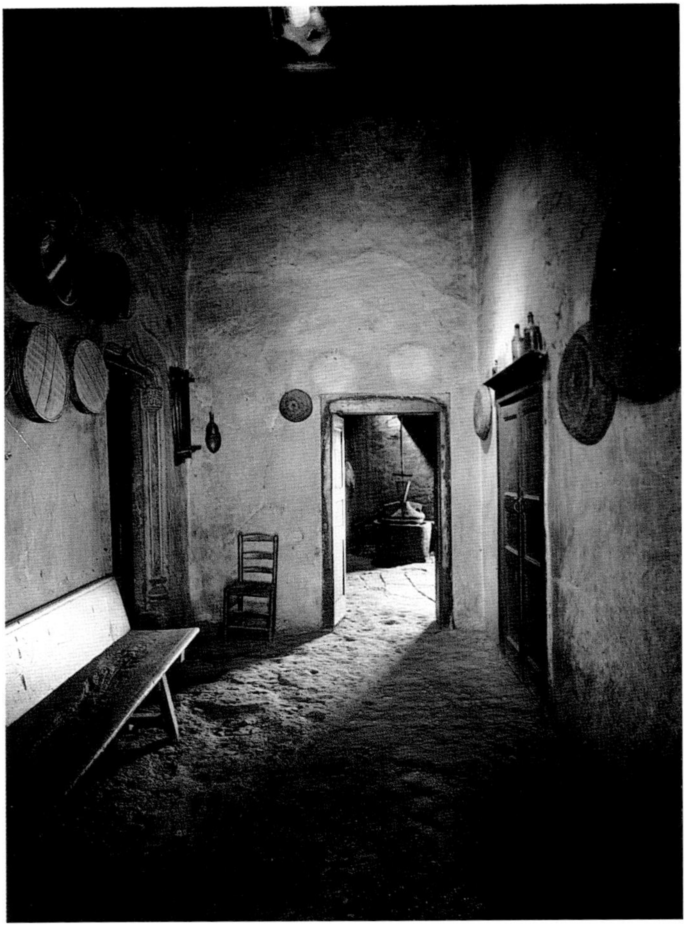

August Sander

Abbasanta, Gang in der Nuraghe Losa,

"Eine Reise nach Sardinien" Series, 1927

[cat. 502]

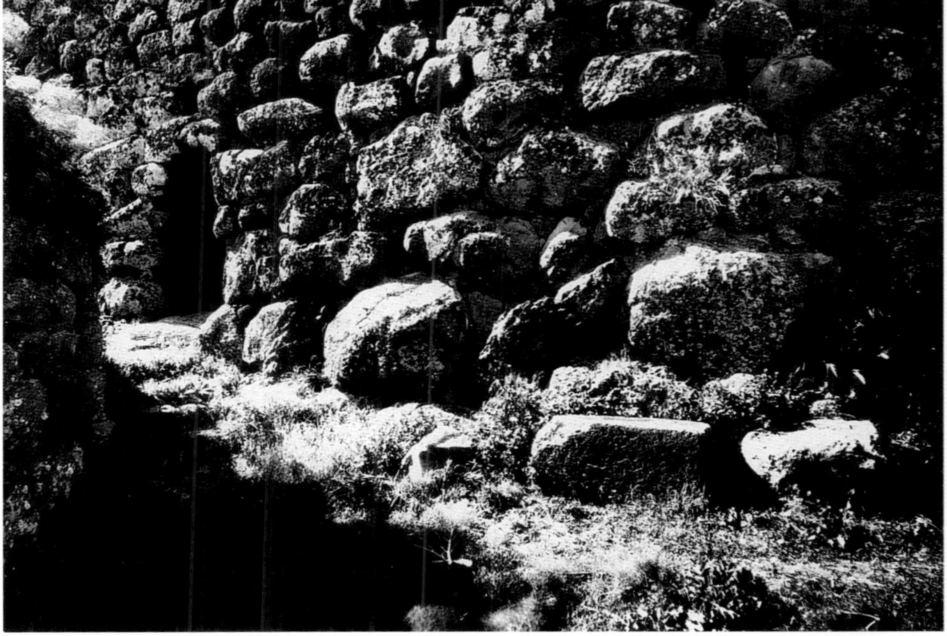

Raoul Hausmann

Au bord de la Mer Baltique, 1931

[cat. 490]

Kampen, 1927

[cat. 489]

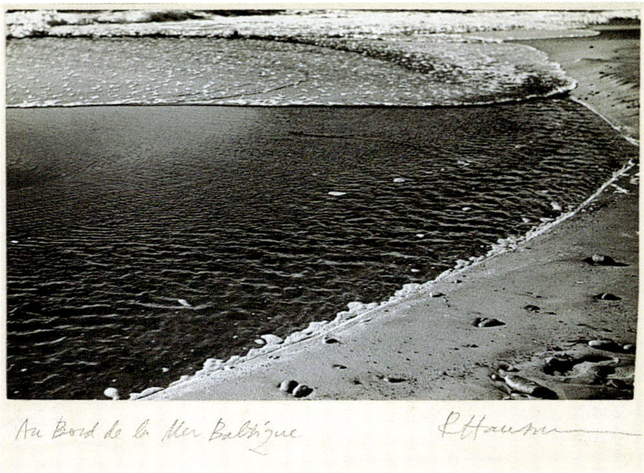

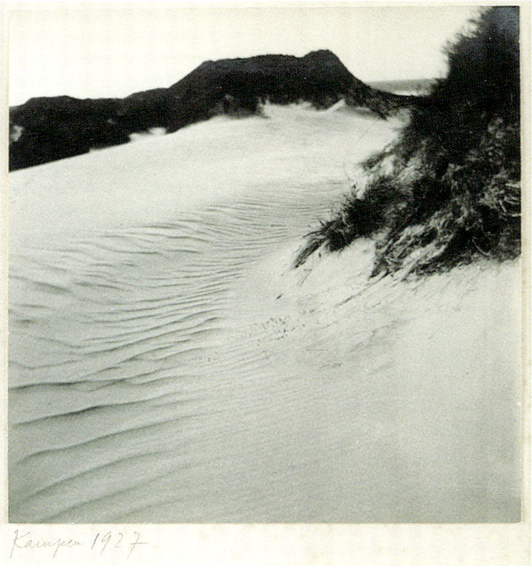

Raoul Hausmann

Composition 28 (Travaux de couture) 1930
[cat. 481]

Le Rêve, 1930
[cat. 484]

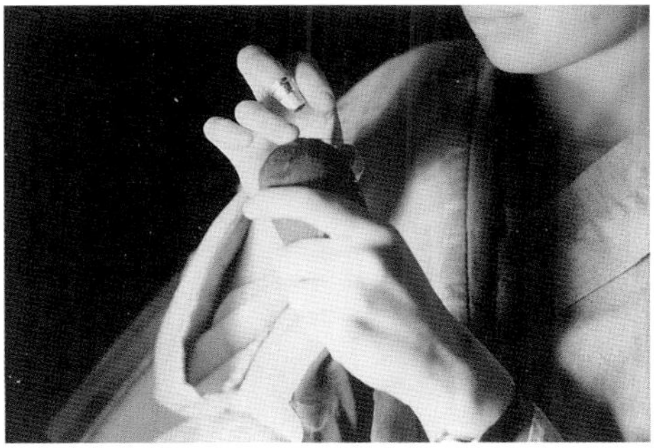

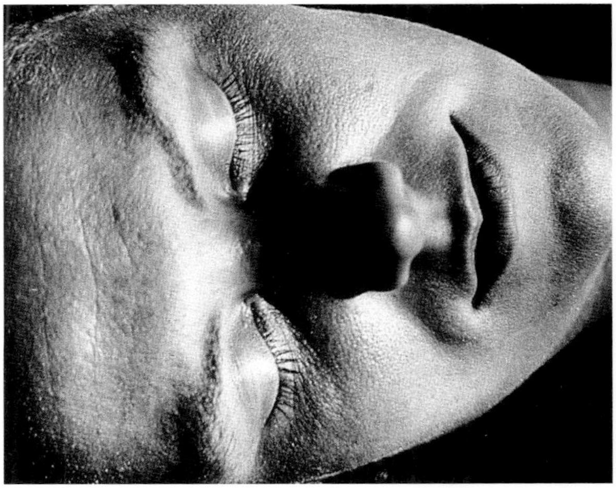

Raoul Hausmann

Señor Mariano Ribas, Ibiza, 1933
[cat. 493]

Can Rafal, 1934
[cat. 515]

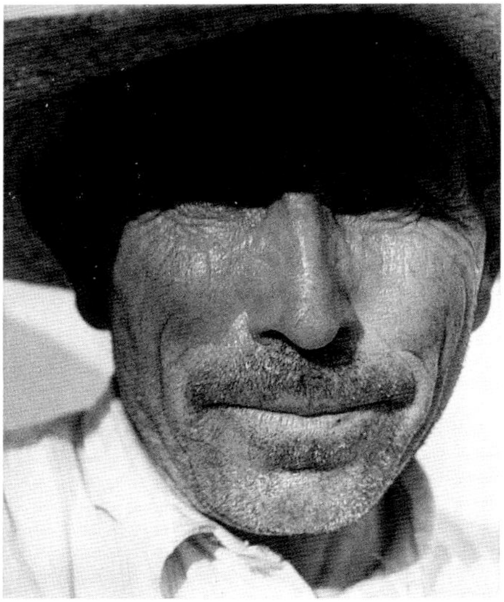

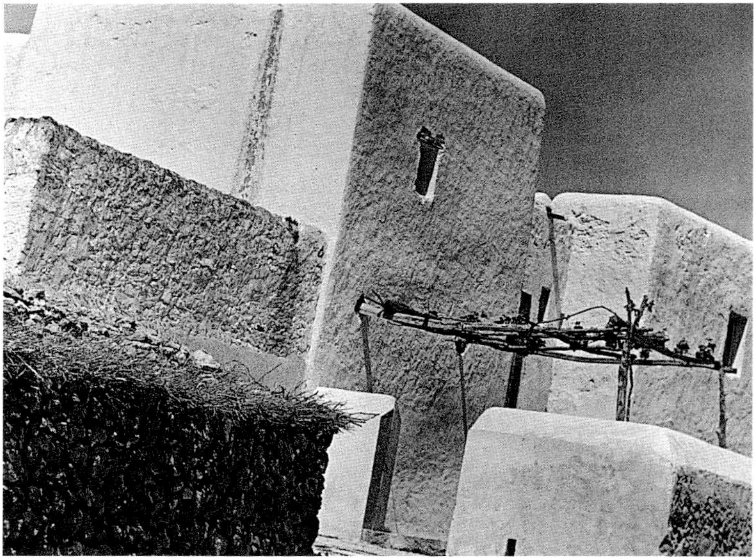

Raoul Hausmann

Trois chaises, Ibiza, 1934
[cat. 511]

Untitled, 1936
[cat. 512]

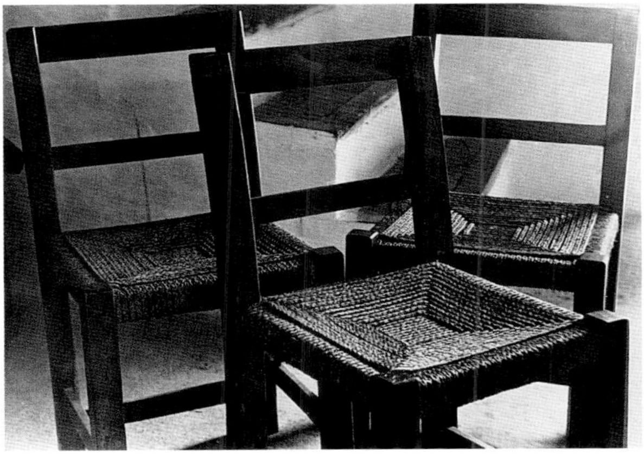

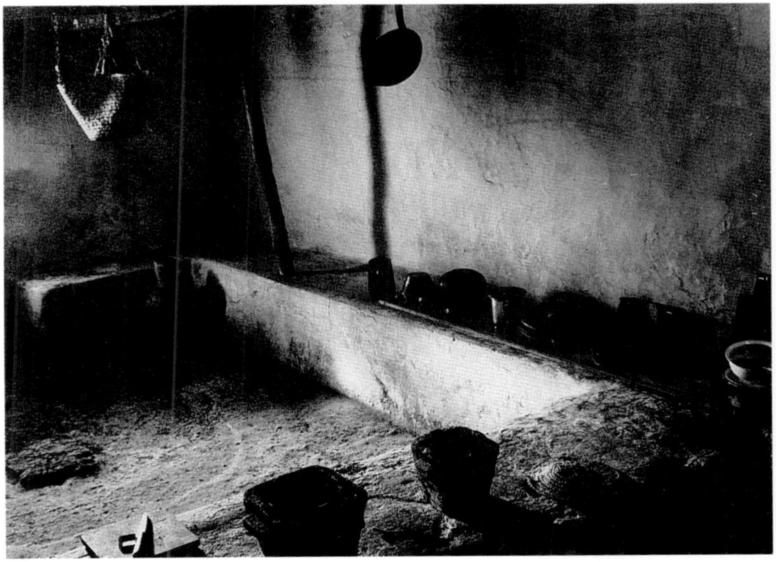

Walker Evans

Untitled (Independance Day, Terra Alta, West Virginia), 1935
[cat. 474]

Untitled (Subway Passengers, New York), 1938
[cat. 471]

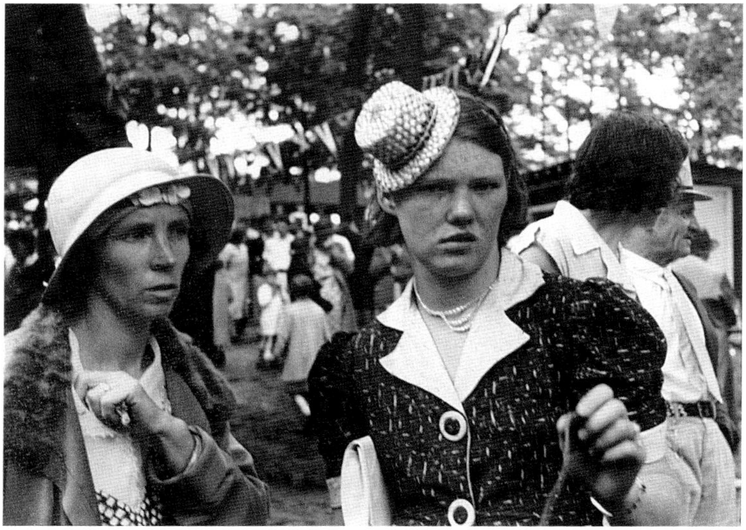

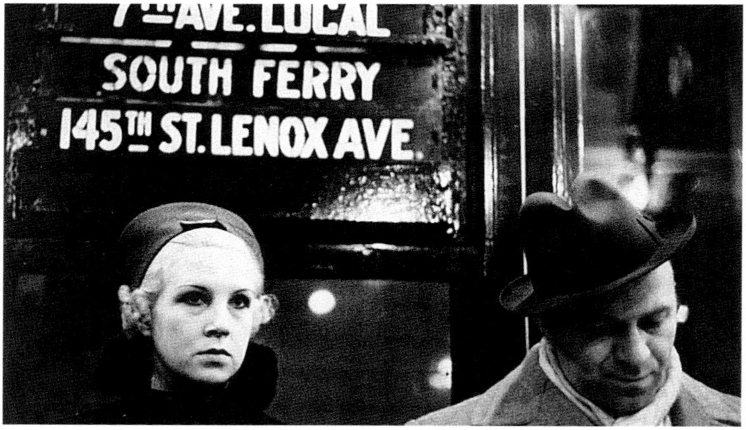

Walker Evans

Untitled (Bedroom, Biloxi, Mississippi), 1944-1945
[cat. 473]

Untitled (Trash Picture), 1968
[cat. 479]

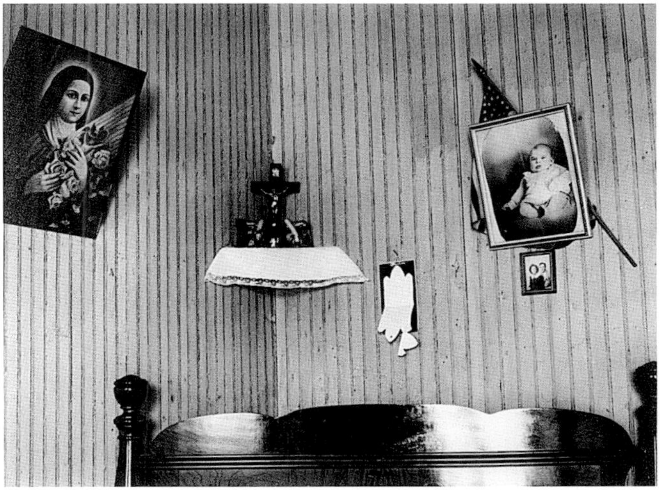

While removed from nature, this picture of a gutter is in a sense very human. It is Baudelairean. I wish he was alive to see it. The secret of photography is, the camera takes on the character and the personality of the handler. The mind works on the machine.

Walker Evans
Caption of a photo from the "Trash Pictures" Series, *Art in America*, April 1971

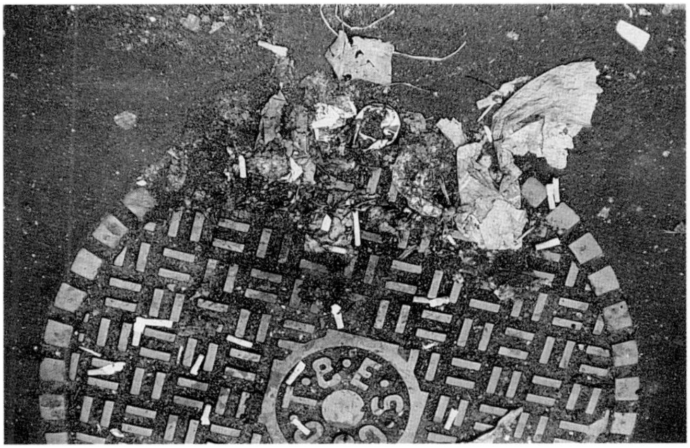

Helen Levitt

New York, Ribbon (From the City Pictures), ca. 1940

[cat. 441]

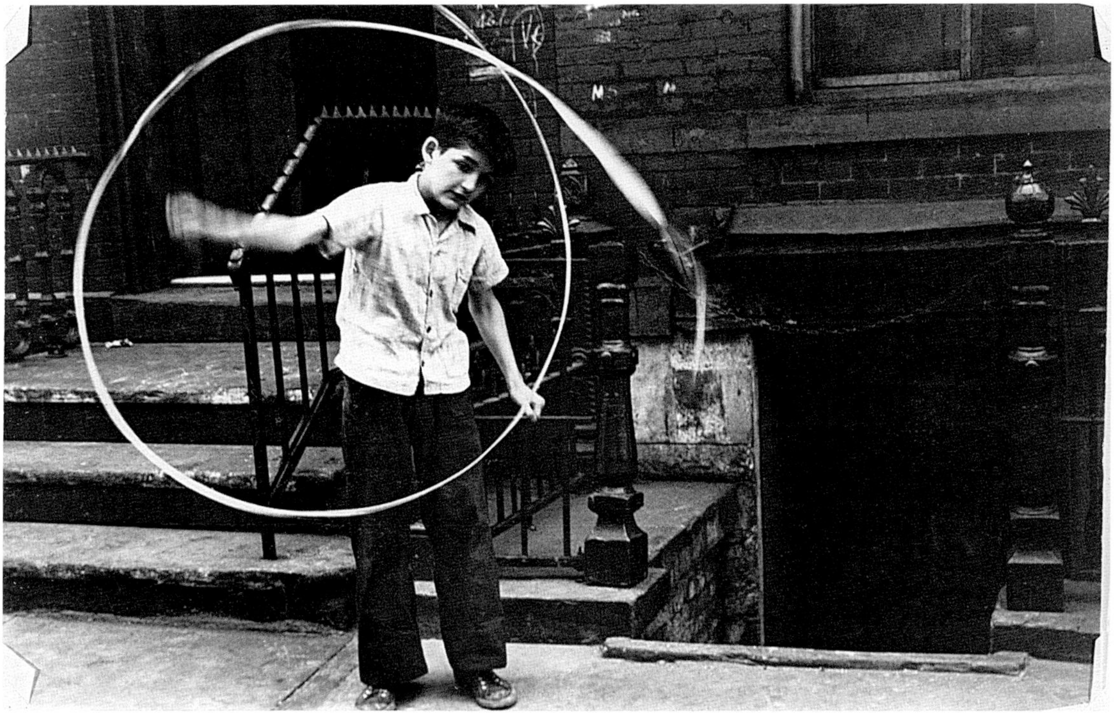

Helen Levitt

New York, Boy up Pole (From the City Pictures), ca. 1940

[cat. 442]

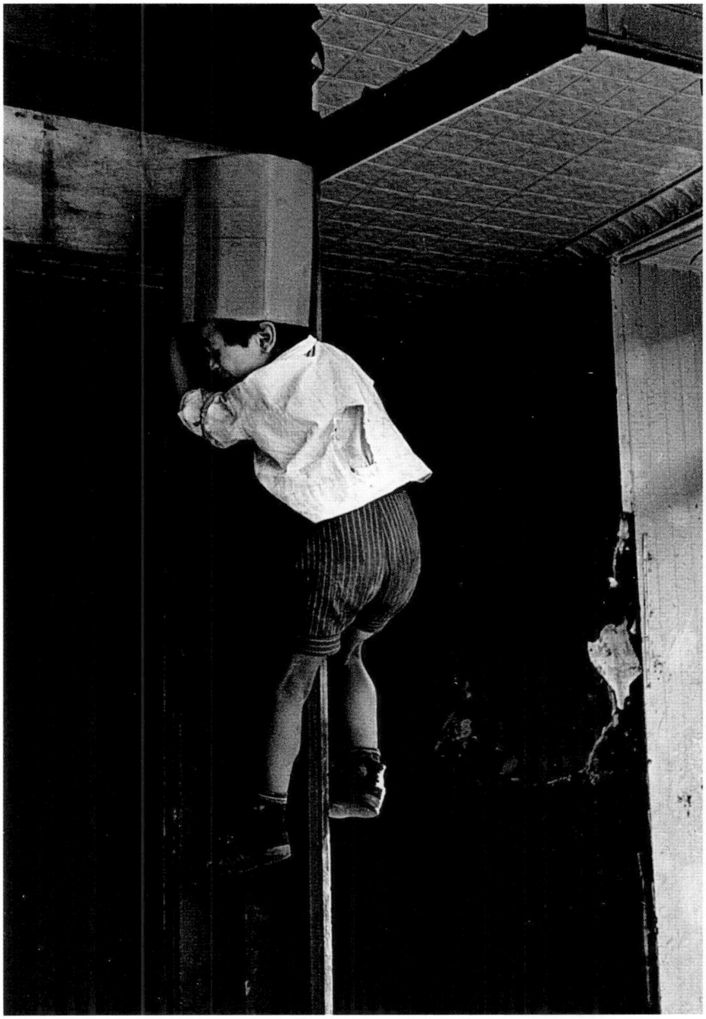

Wols

Clochards an der Seine, 1933

[cat. 538]

Stilleben mit Knoblauch, ca. 1937

[cat. 540]

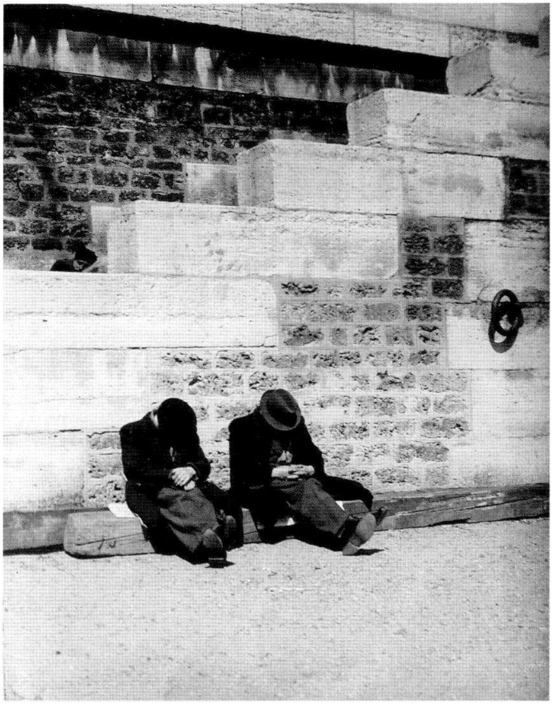

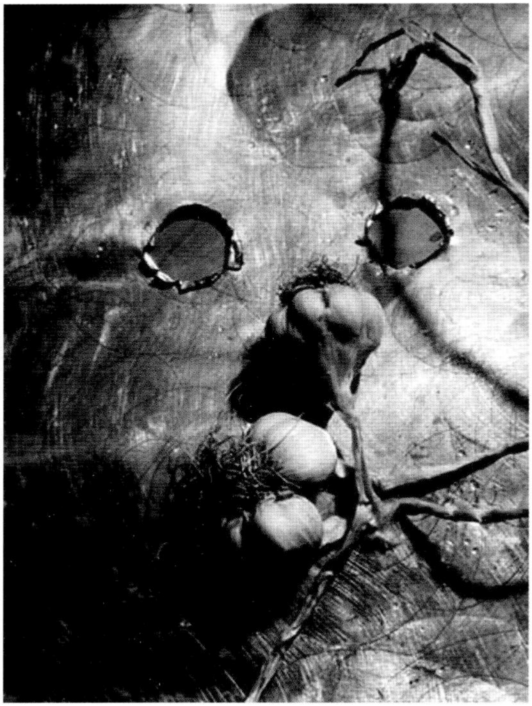

Wols

Schweinsniere, ca. 1937

[cat. 542]

Puppe und Auster im Rinnstein, ca. 1937

[cat. 539]

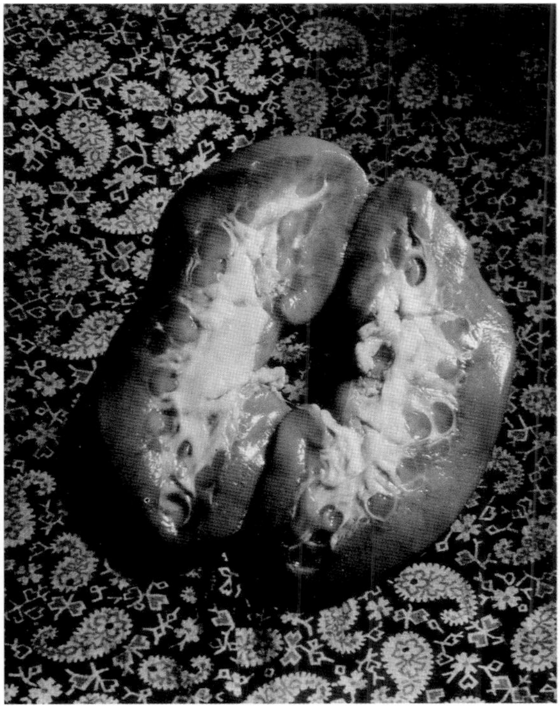

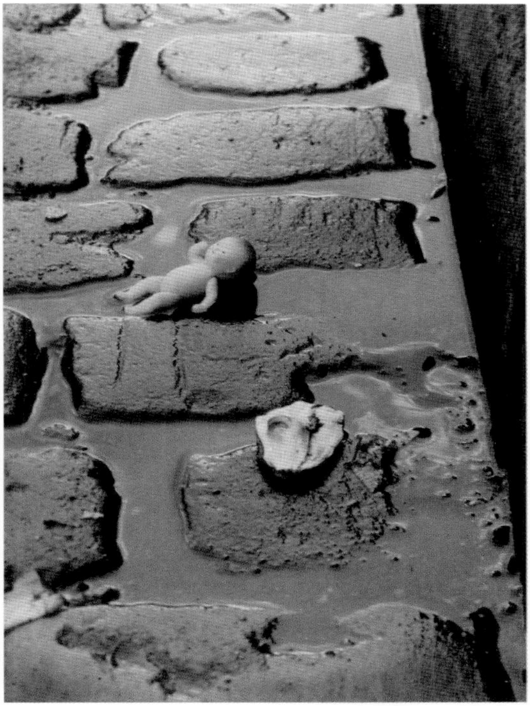

Wols

Grapefruit, ca. 1937
[cat. 541]

Kaninchen mit Kamm und Mundharmonika, ca. 1937
[cat. 543]

Komposition, ca. 1935
[cat. 544]

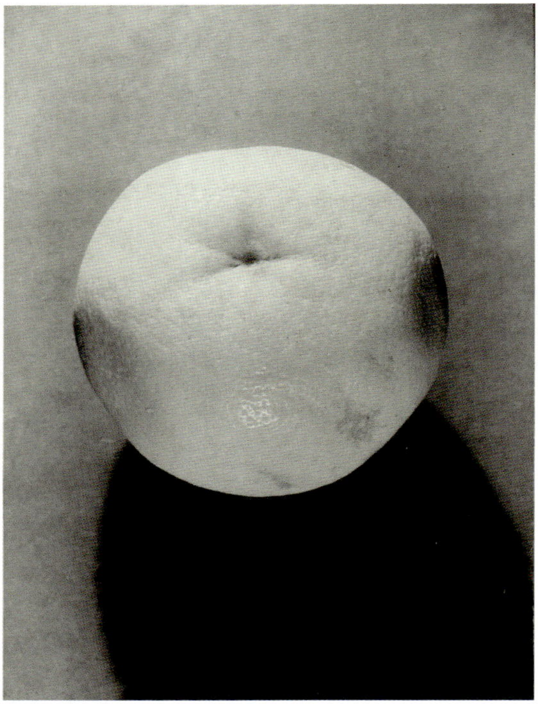

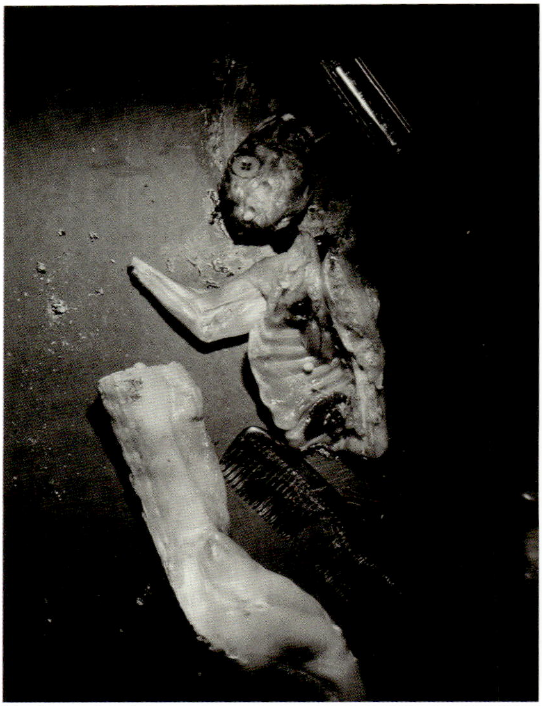

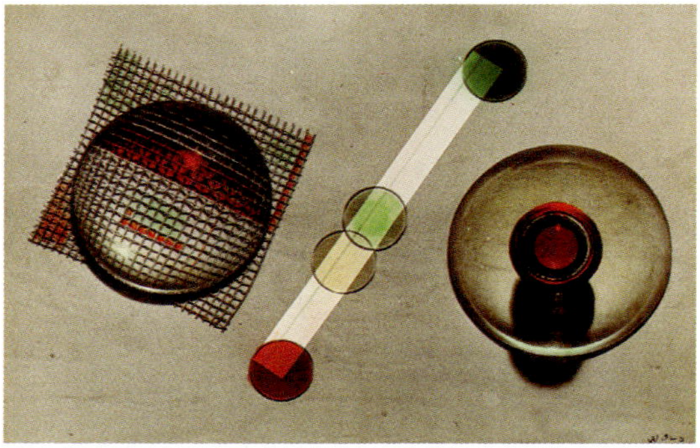

Wols

Le Cirque de météores, 1944-1945

[cat. 565]

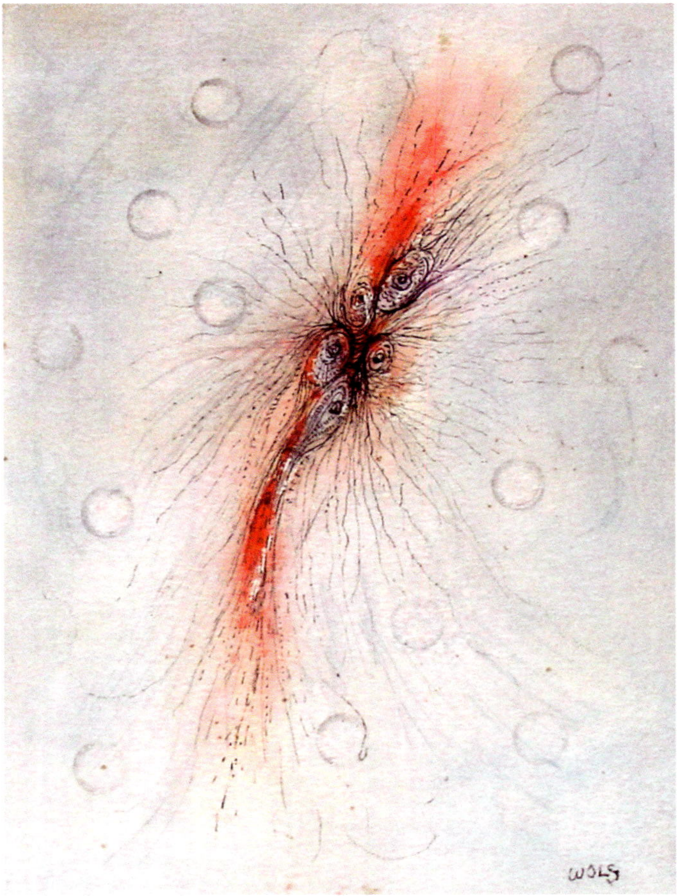

Wols

Nicole Boubant, ca. 1933
[cat. 537]

Tourbillon, 1947
[cat. 552]

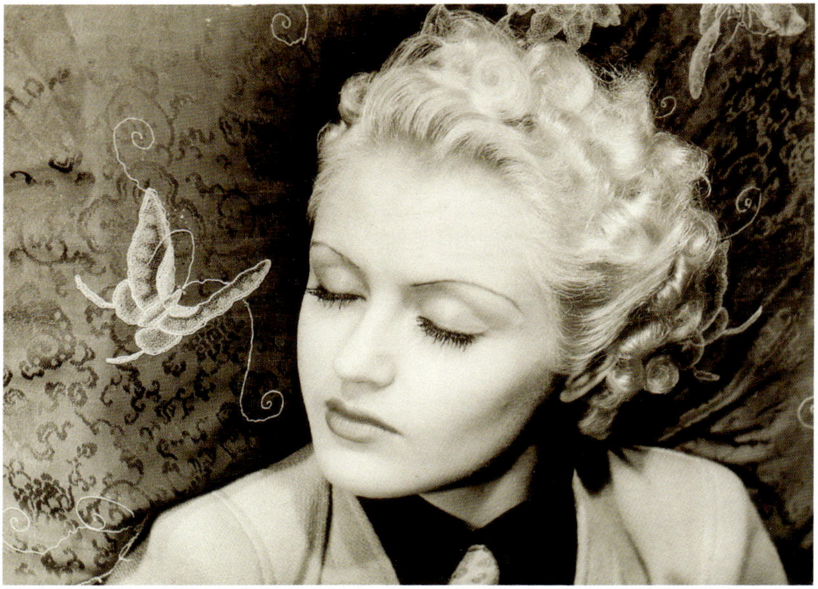

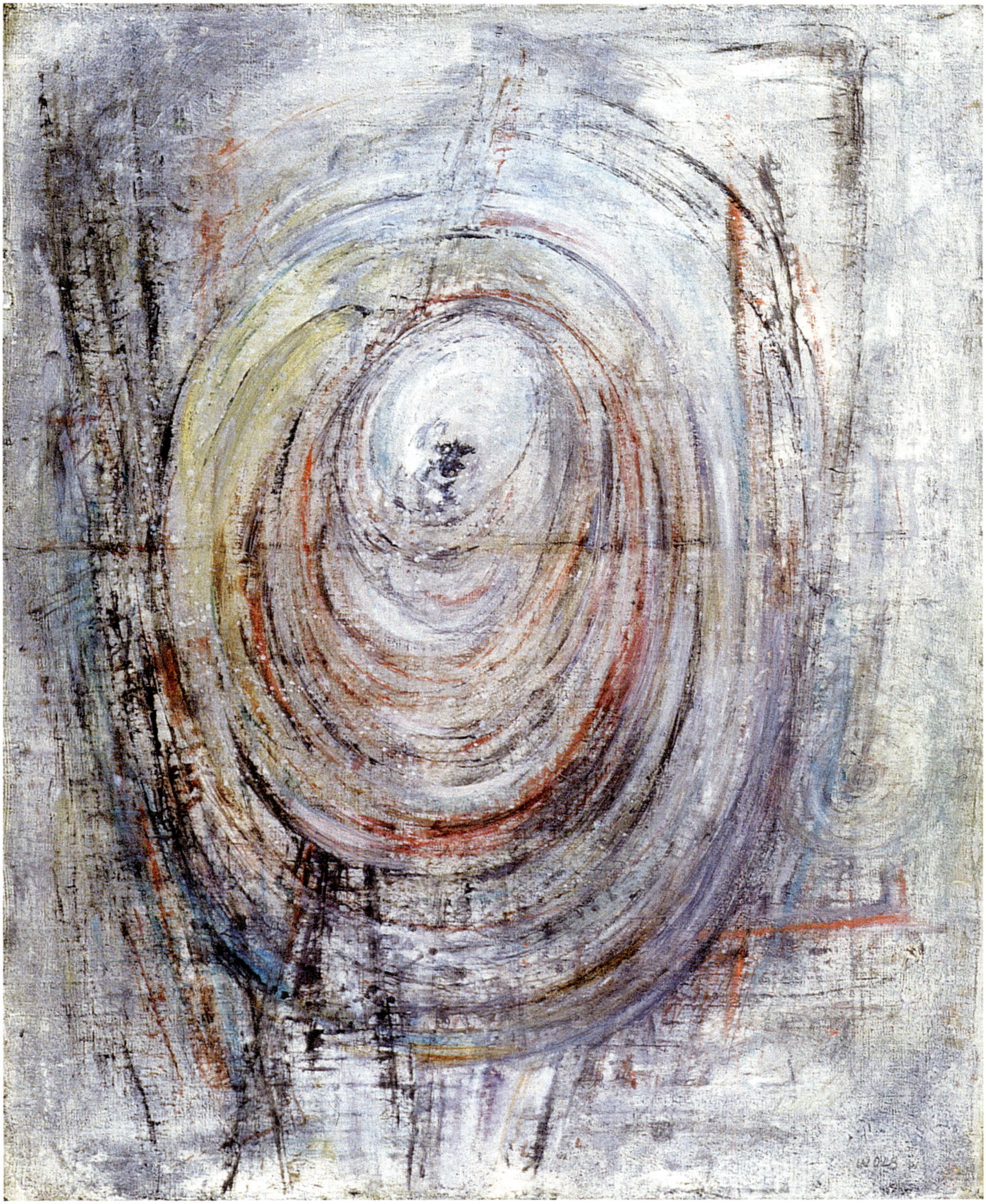

Antonin Artaud
La Potence du gouffre, 1945
[cat. 546]

kré
kré
pek
kre
e
pte

Il faut que tout
soit rangé
à un poil près
dans un ordre
fulminant.

puc te
puk te
li le
pek ti le
kruk

Antonin Artaud
Pour en finir avec le jugement de Dieu, 1947

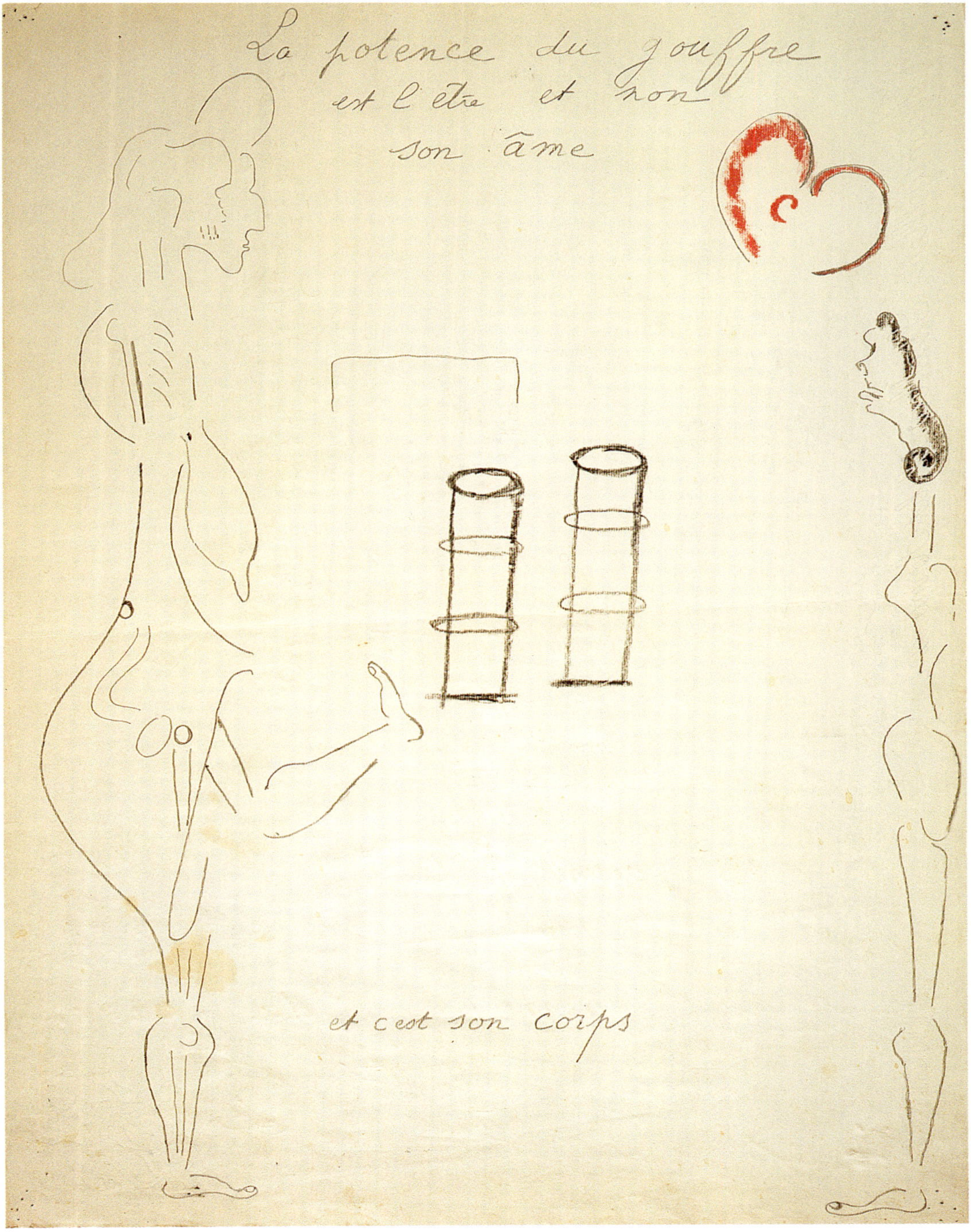
La potence du gouffre
est l'être et non
son âme
et c'est son corps

Antonin Artaud
Les Illusions de l'âme, 1946
[cat. 548]

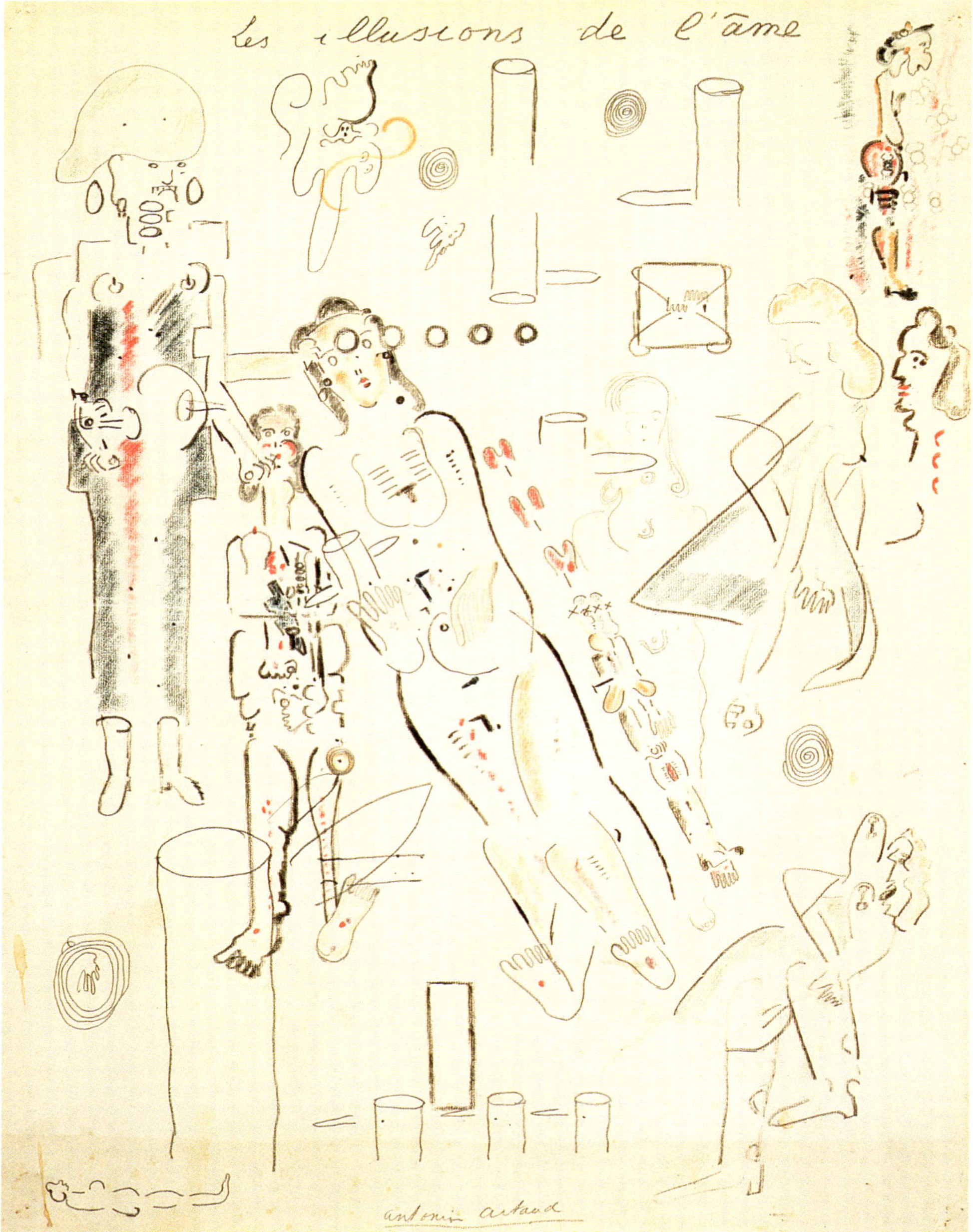

Antonin Artaud
L'Inca, 1946
[cat. 553]

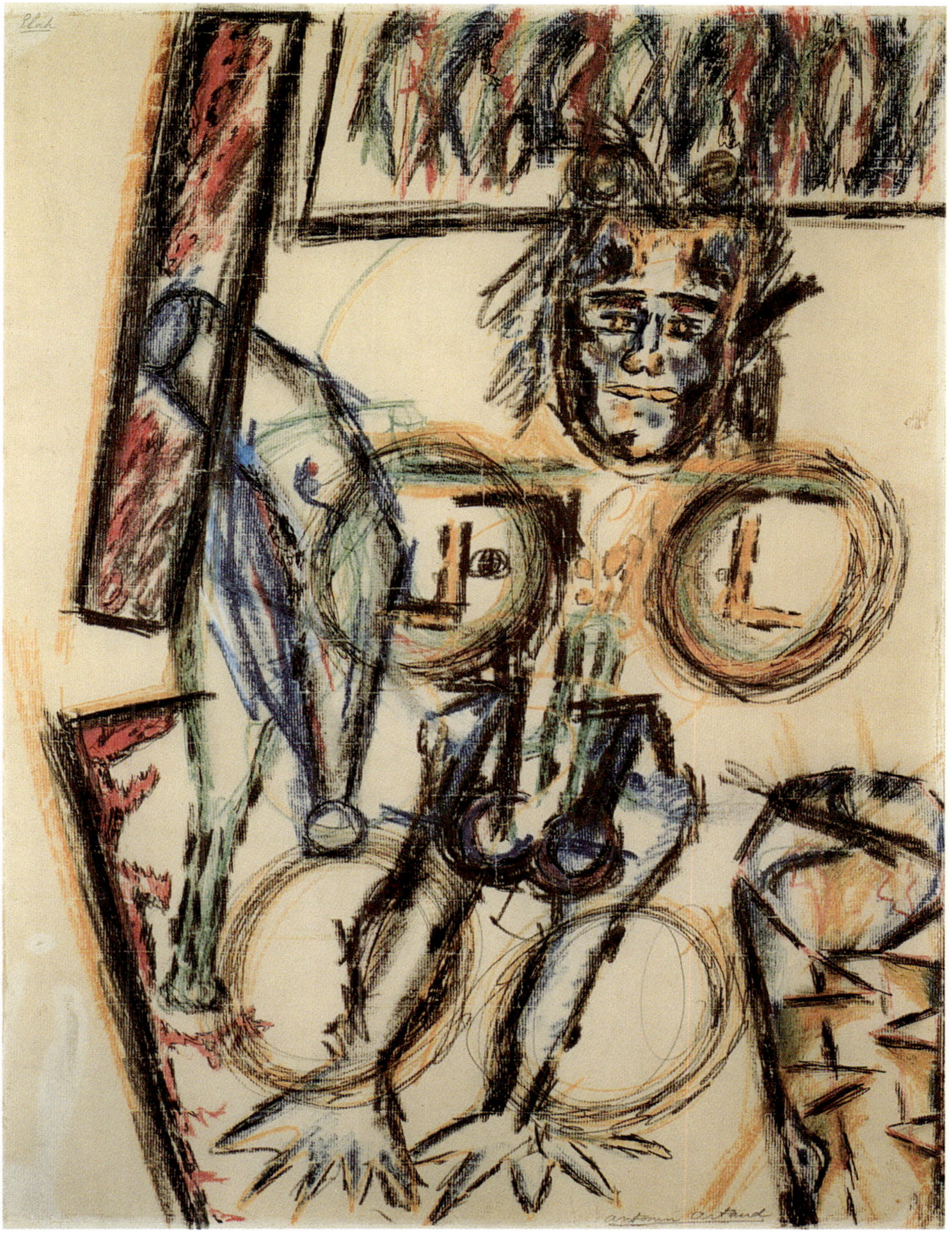

Antonin Artaud
Couti l'anatomie, 1945
[cat. 549]

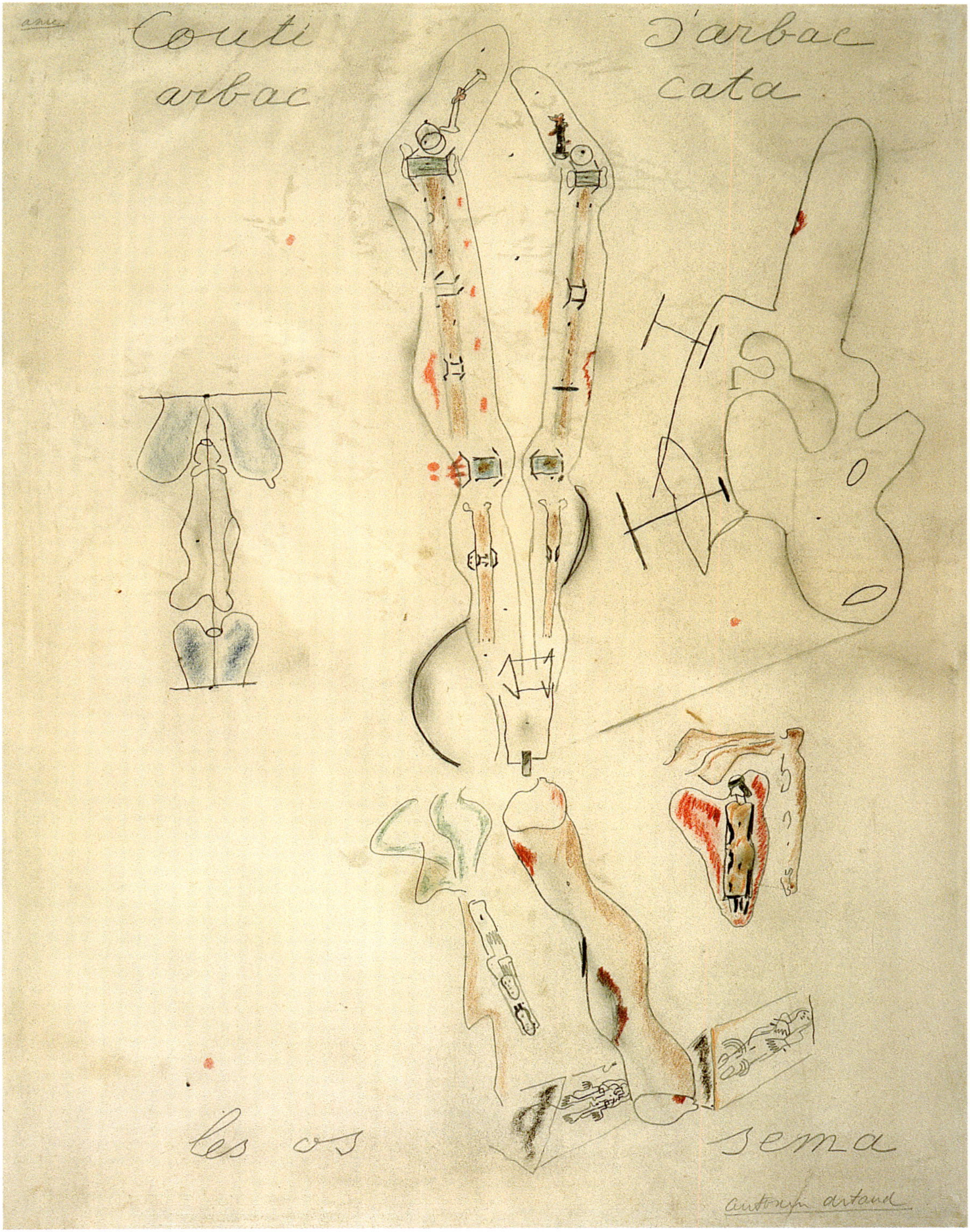
Couti
arbac
J'arbac
cata
les os
sema
antonin artaud

Pablo Picasso

Illustration for *Le Chant des morts* by Pierre Reverdy, 1948

[cat. 522]

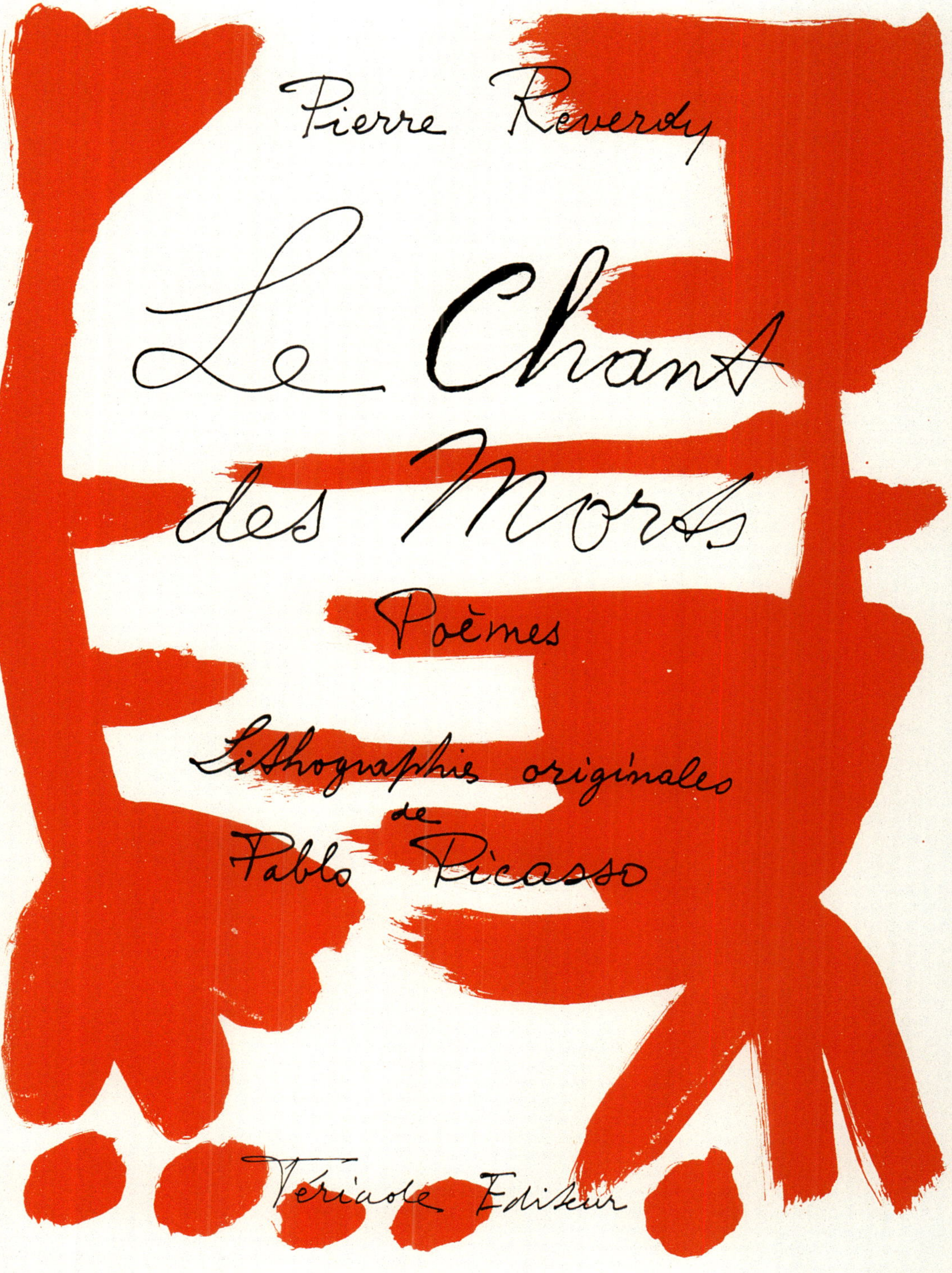
Pierre Reverdy
Le Chant des Morts
Poèmes
Lithographies originales de Pablo Picasso
Tériade Editeur

Wladislaw Strzeminski

"To My Friends the Jews" Series 1945

Vow and Oath to the Memory of Hands (Existences which are not with us)

The Sticky Spot of Crime

Stretched by the Strings of Legs

[cat. 521]

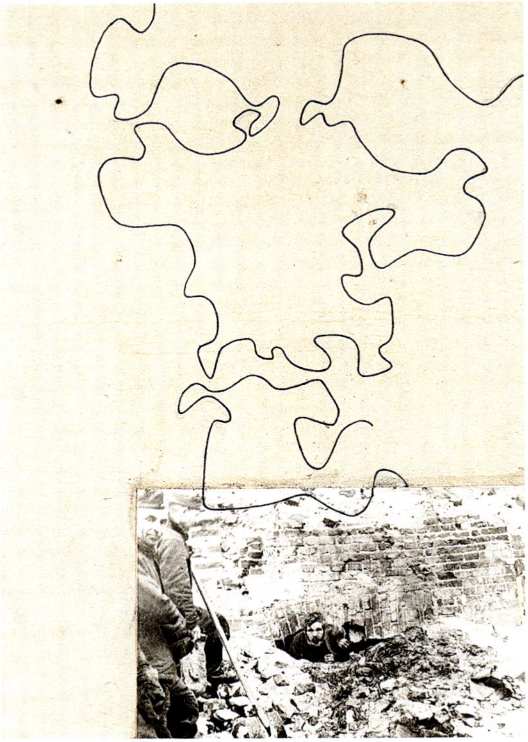

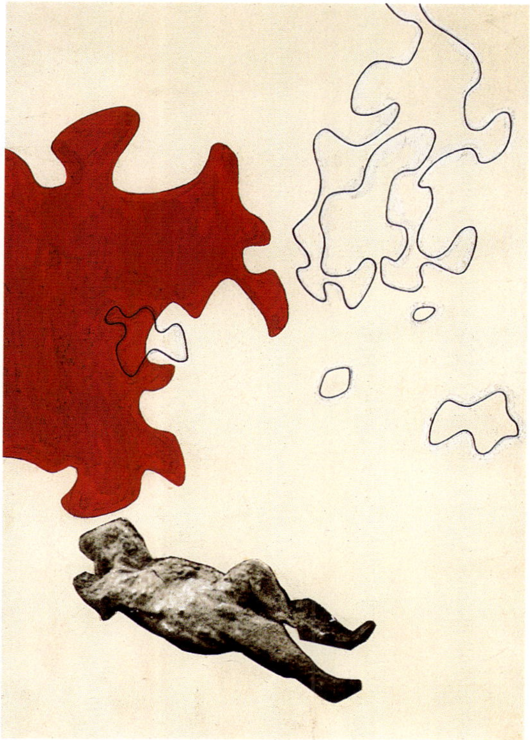

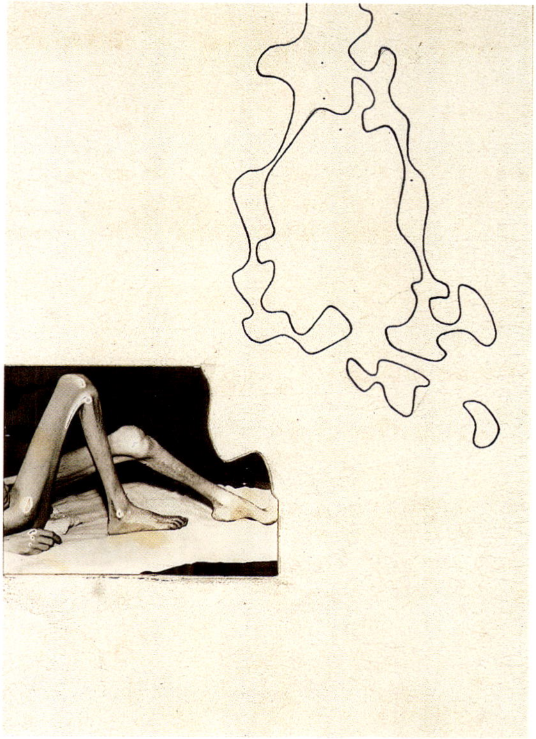

Some kind of protest had to be made against the intolerable idea of the torture of one man by another, of the human body and the face disfigured by man himself. The horror had to be registered, stigmatised for all eternity.
It had to be repeated in loathsome close-up, it had to be turned into something beautiful.
No gestures. No gesticulation. Just stunned reproach. No movement, apart from that of the image invading the mind, of the tortured face arising out of the depth of shadow, looming at us; apart from that of the faces of the martyrs wheeling through our heavens like stars, like satellites, like moons.

Francis Ponge
Note sur les Otages, peintures de Fautrier, 1945

Jean Fautrier
Tête d'otage n° 22, 1945
[cat. 518]

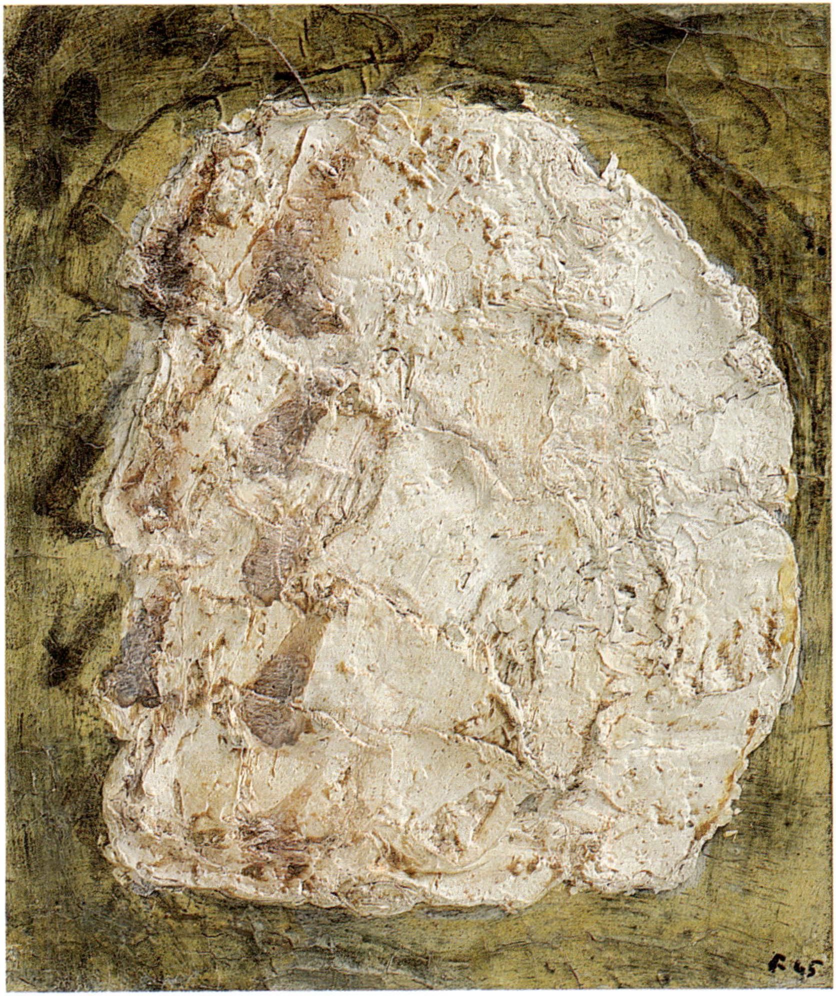

Antoni Tàpies

Collage de les creus, 1947

[cat. 791]

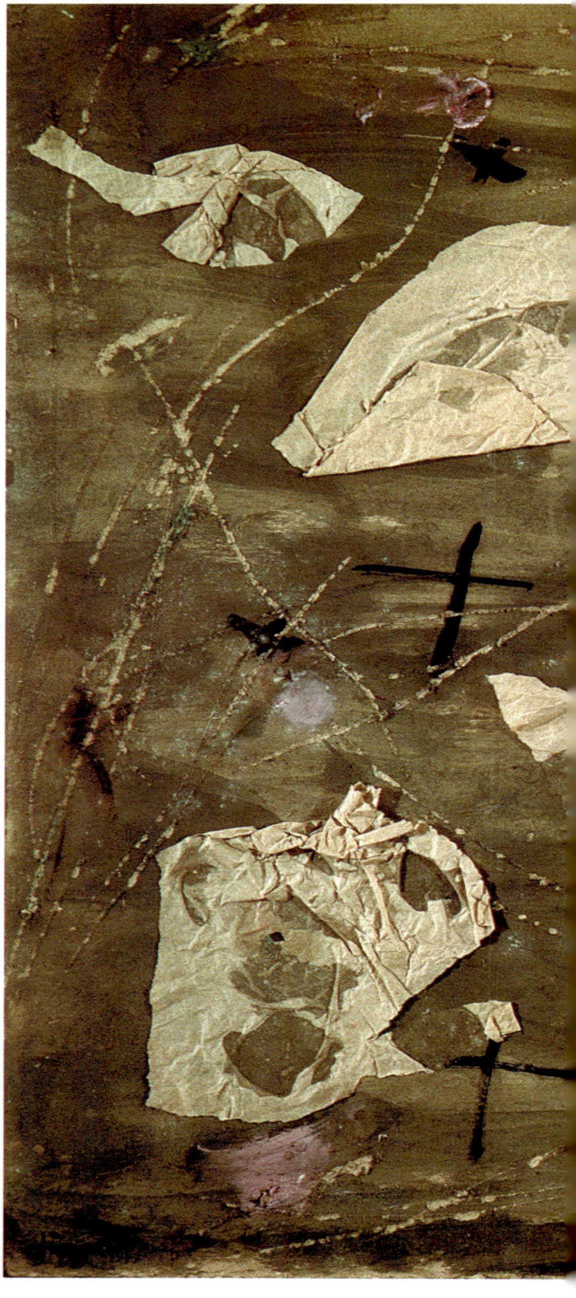

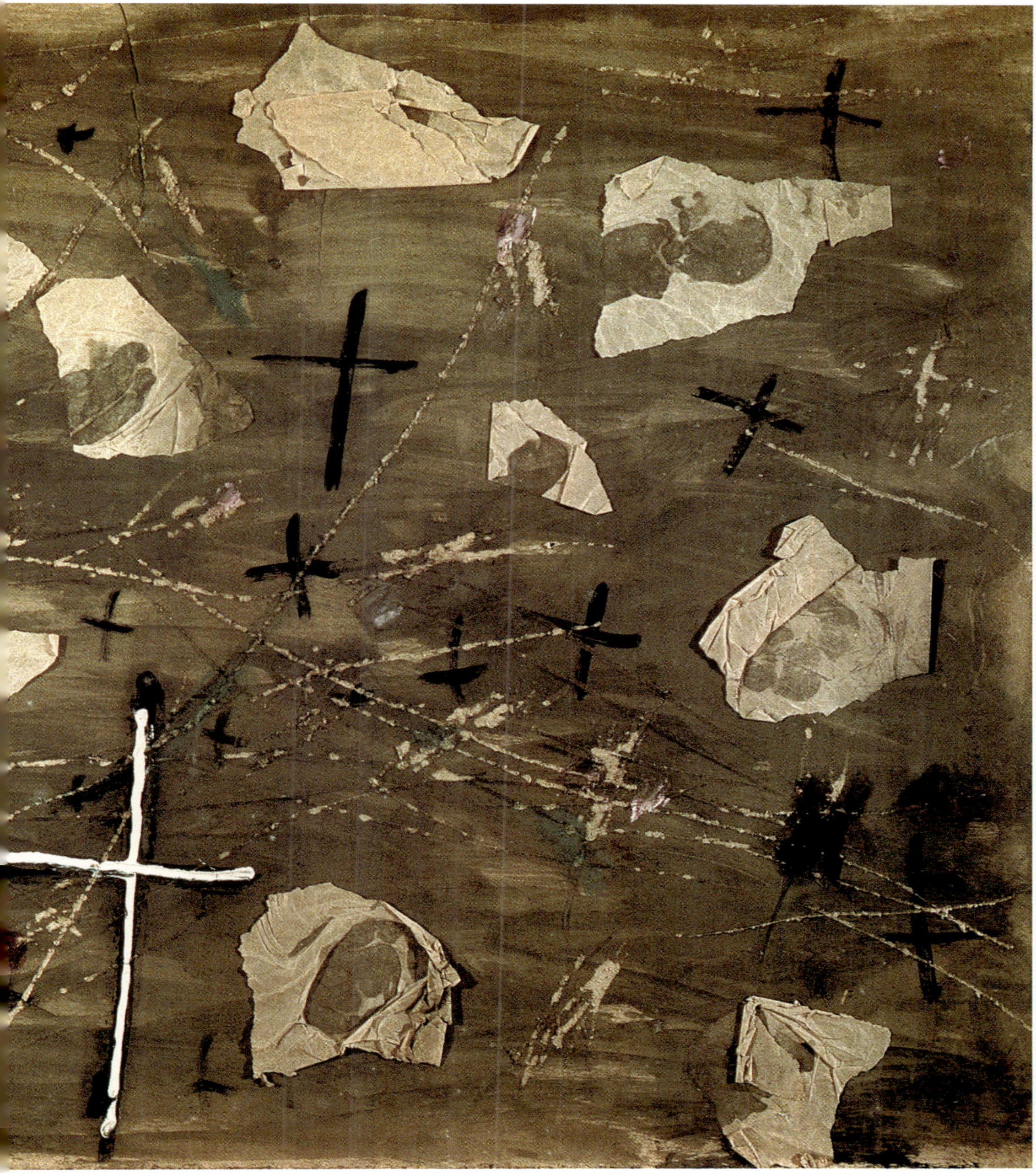

Henri Michaux

Sans titre (Alphabet), 1944
[cat. 523]

Sans titre (Alphabet), 1944
[cat. 524]

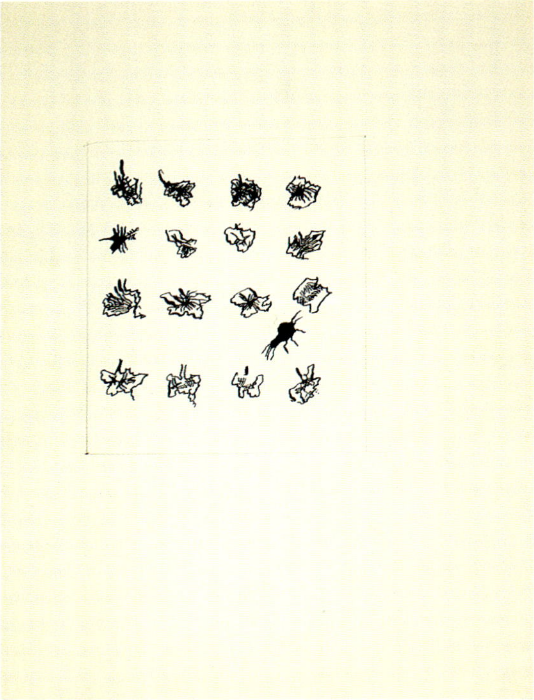

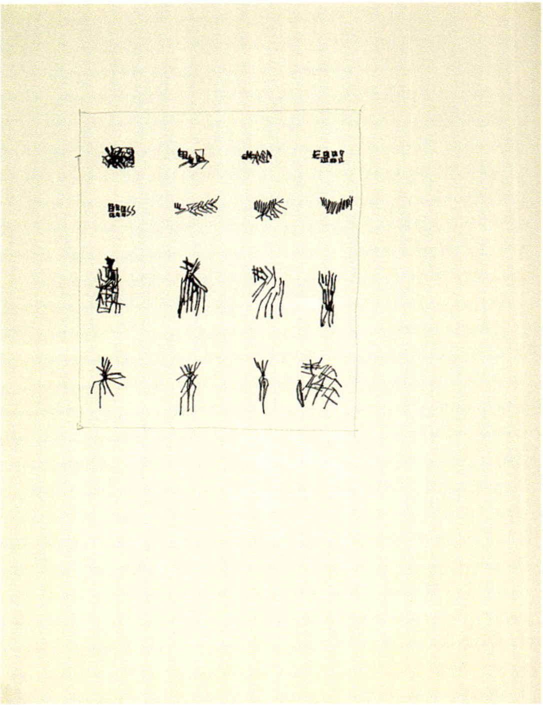

Henri Michaux
Untitled, 1948
[cat. 531]

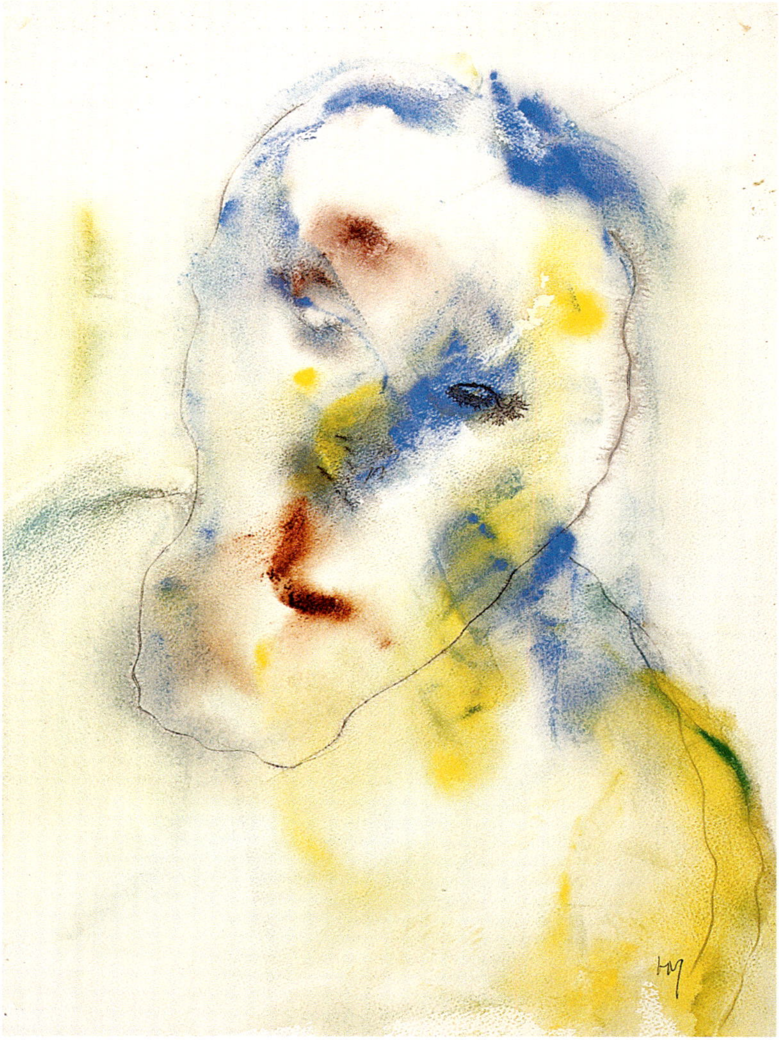

Henri Michaux

Untitled, 1944
[cat. 535]

Untitled, 1944
[cat. 534]

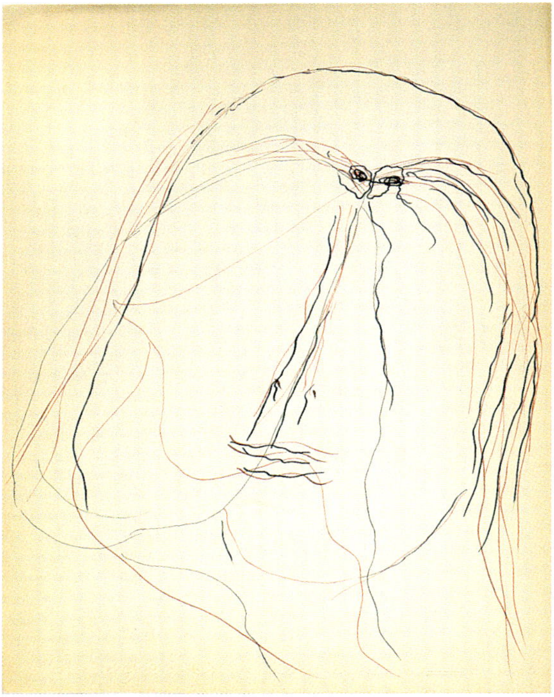

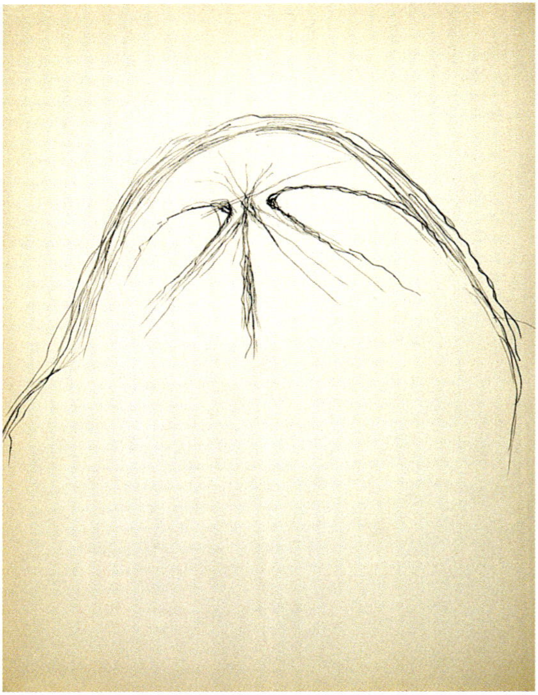

Henri Michaux
Untitled, 1982
[cat. 526]
Untitled, 1982
[cat. 527]
Untitled, 1982
[cat. 528]

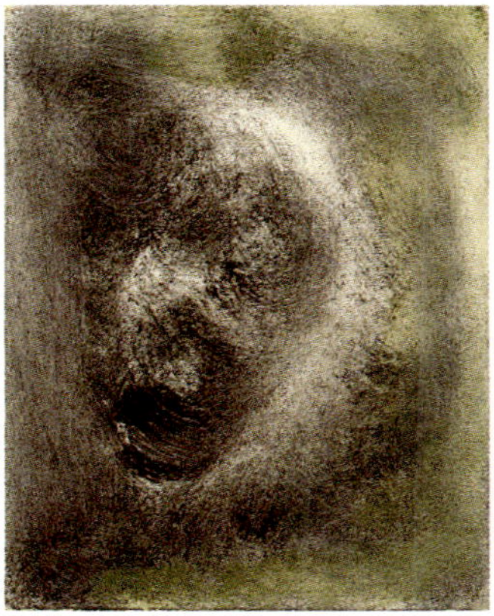

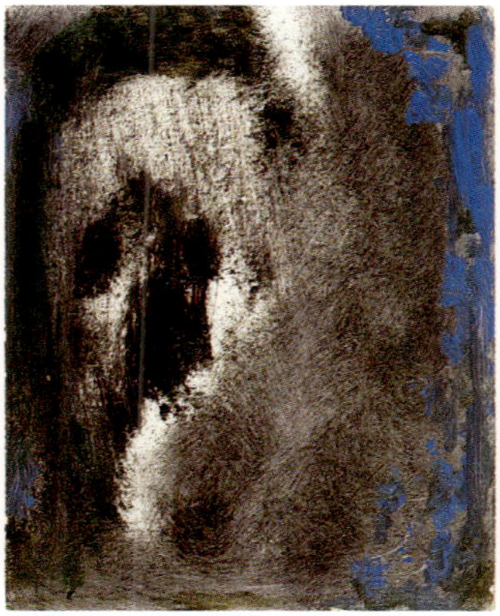

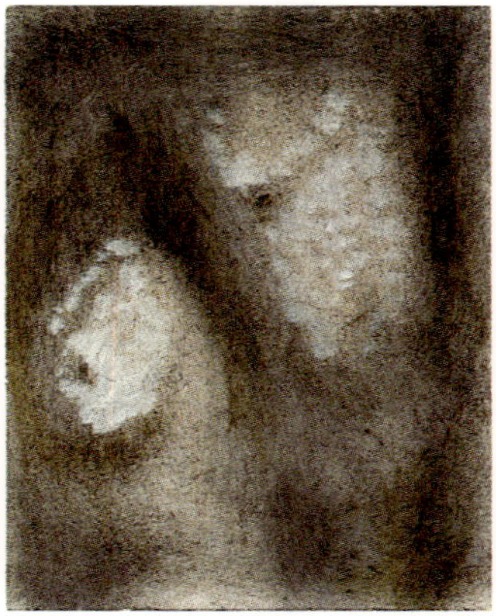

Exorcism – reacting powerfully, like a battering ram – is the prisoner's true poem.

Henri Michaux
Épreuves, exorcismes, 1945

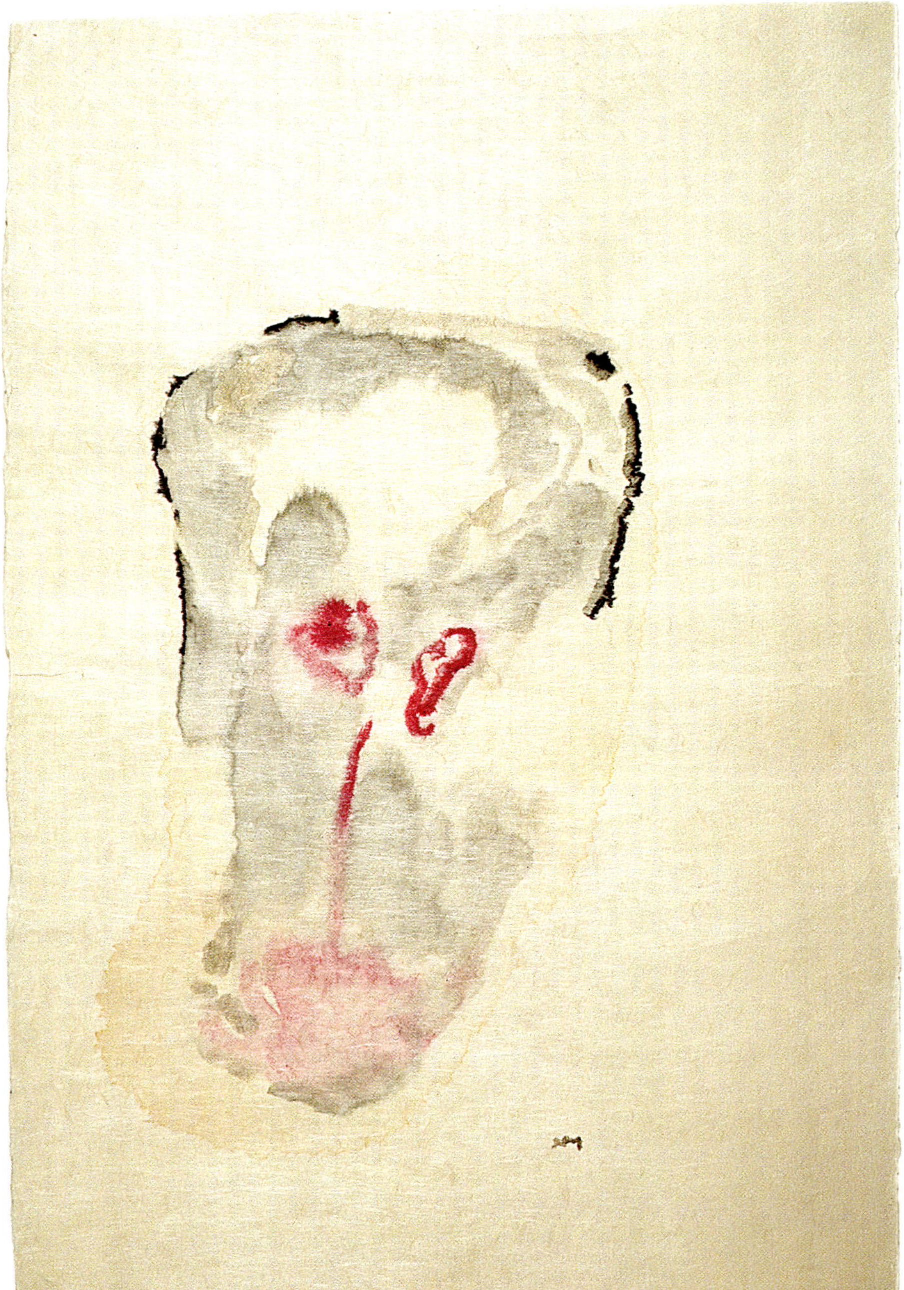

Henri Michaux

Untitled, ca. 1979

[cat. 533]

Untitled, ca. 1982-1983

[cat. 529]

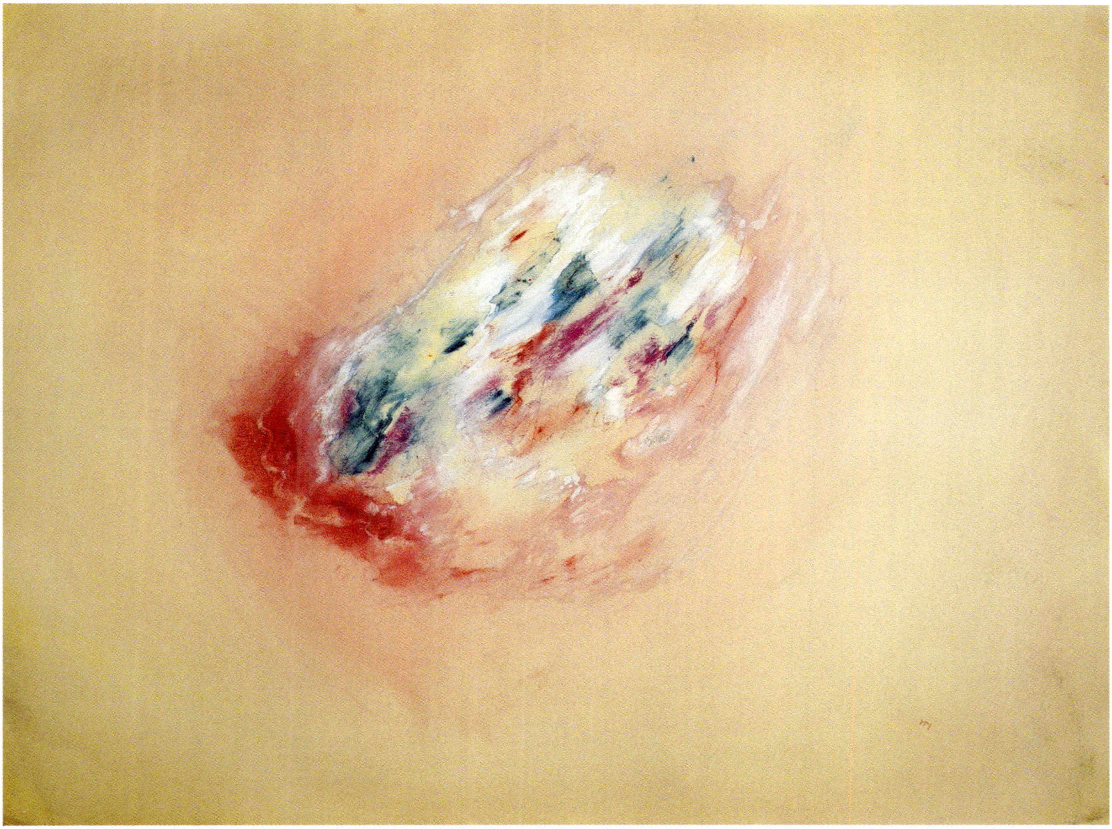

Roberto Matta

Untitled, 1941
[cat. 551]

The Blind Divers, 1946
[cat. 550]

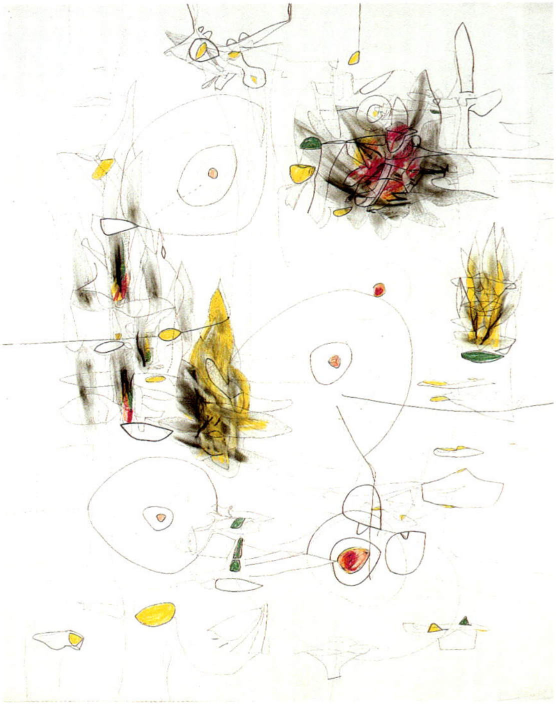

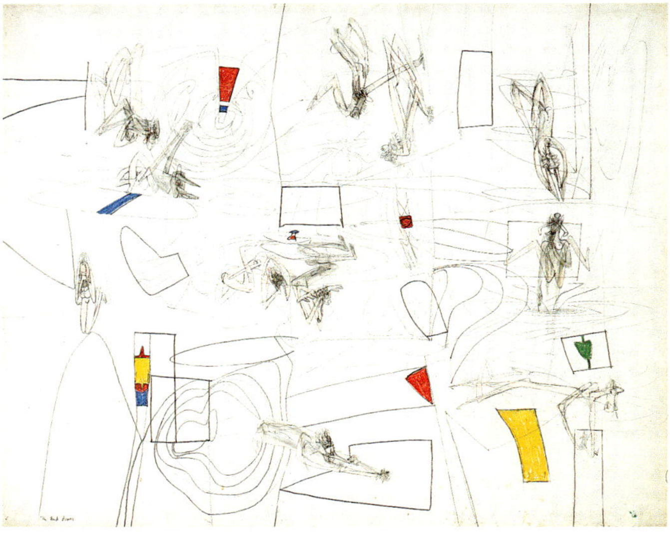

Roberto Matta

Por una bicicleta, 1946

[cat. 606]

Untitled, 1943

[cat. 607]

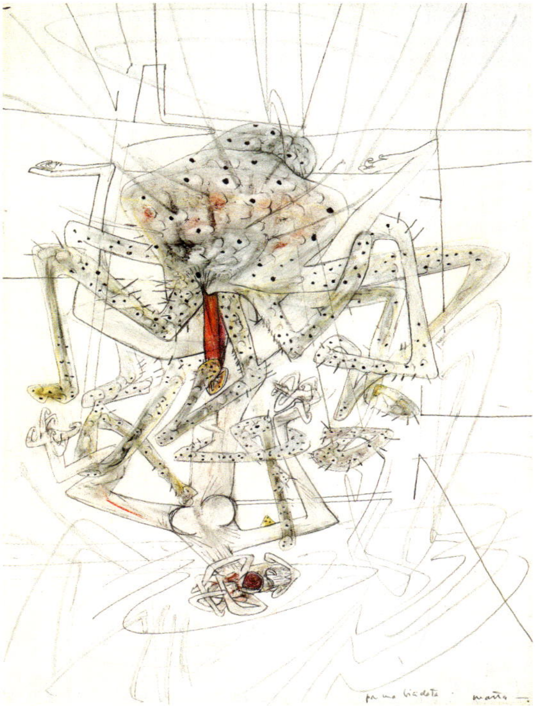

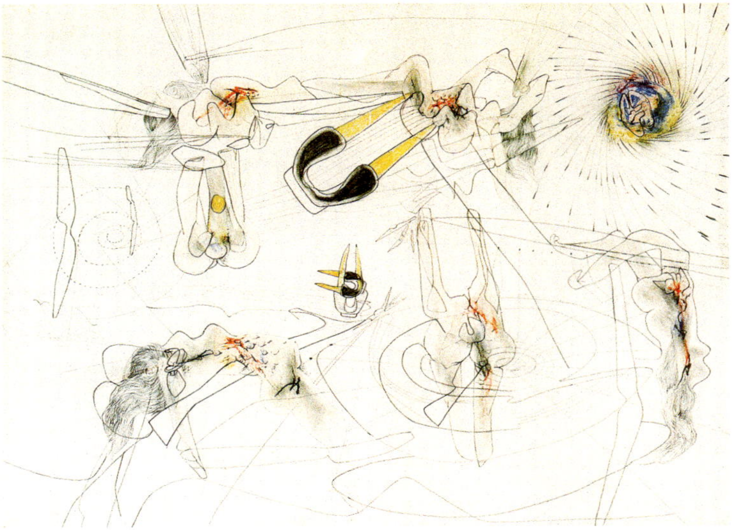

Marcel Duchamp

La Mariée mise à nu par ses célibataires même (Boîte verte), 1934

[cat. 609]

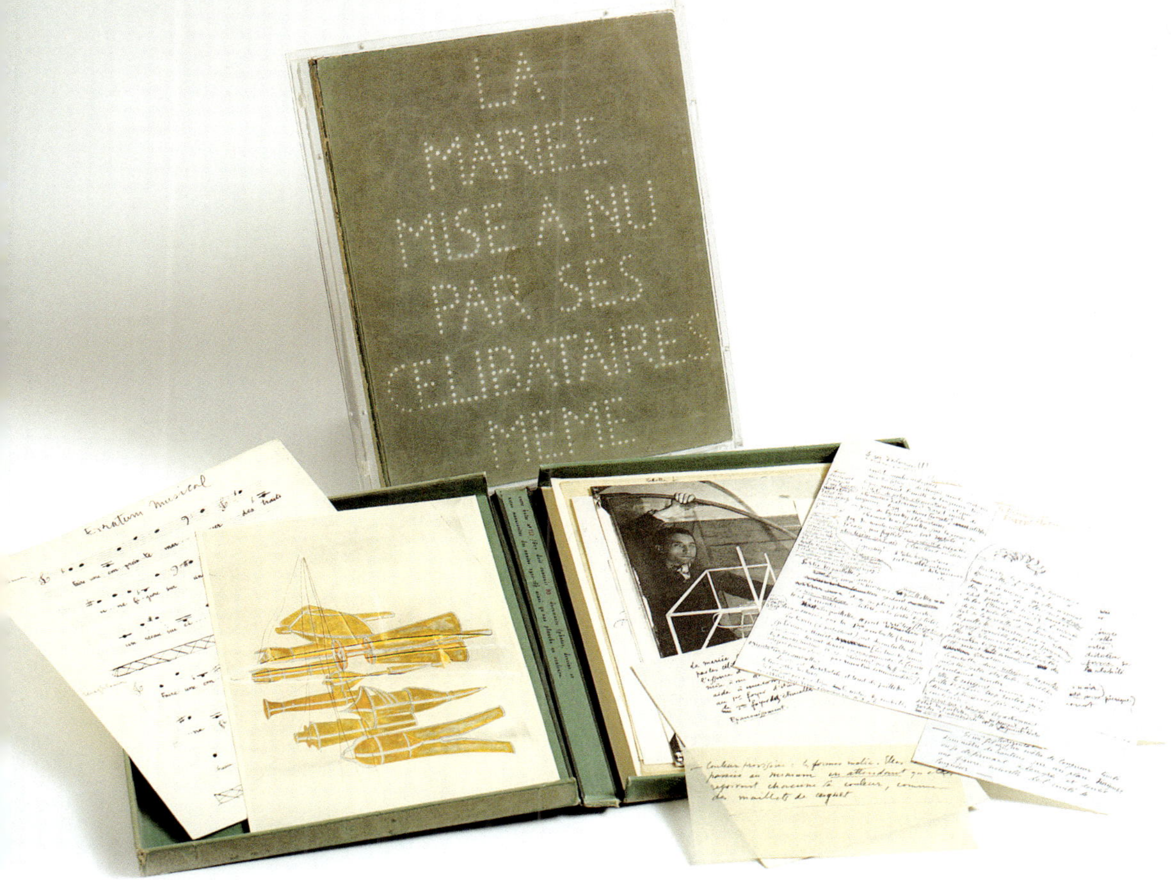
LA
MARIEE
MISE A NU
PAR SES
CELIBATAIRES
MEME

Marcel Duchamp
Boîte en valise (série c), 1958
[cat. 608]

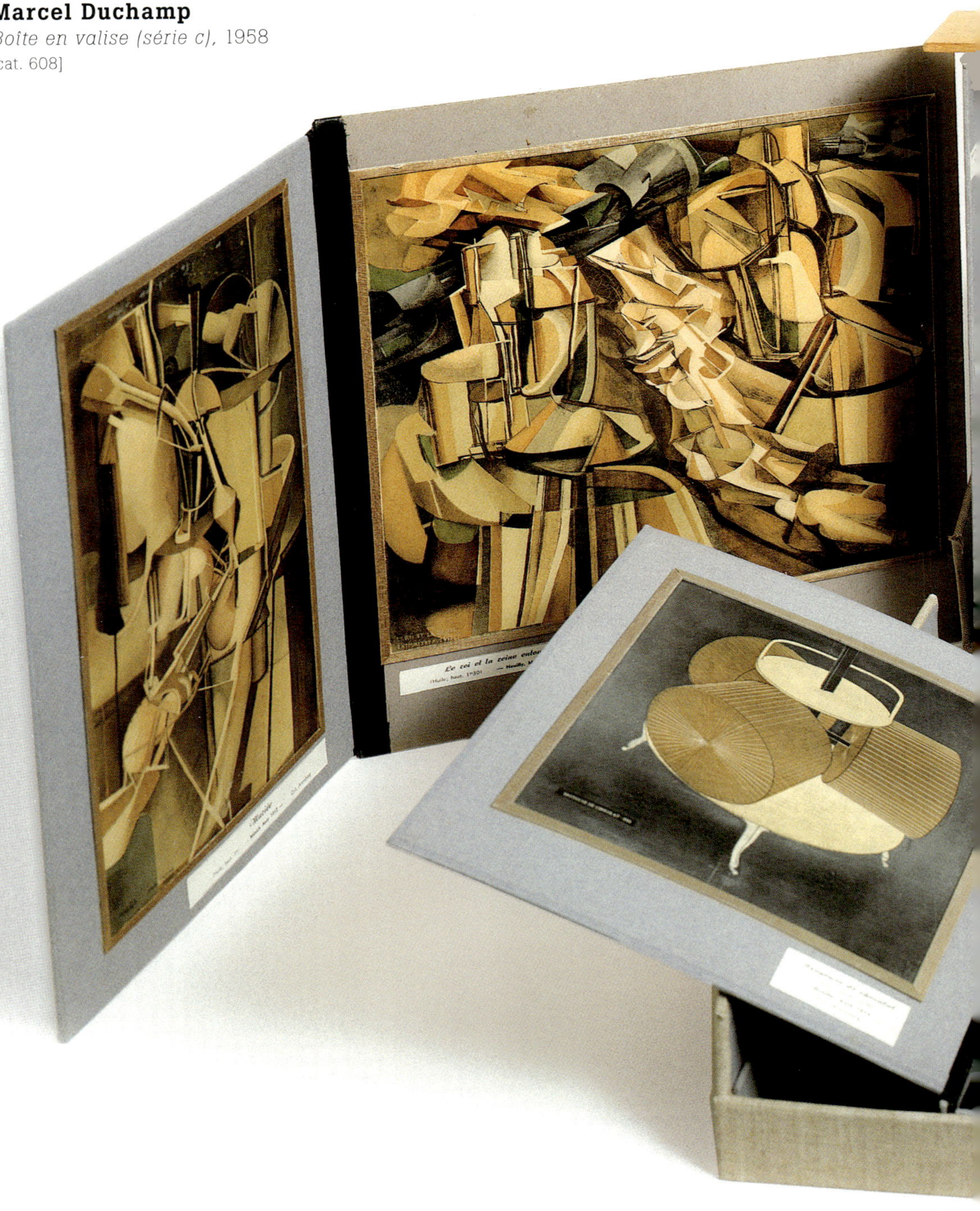

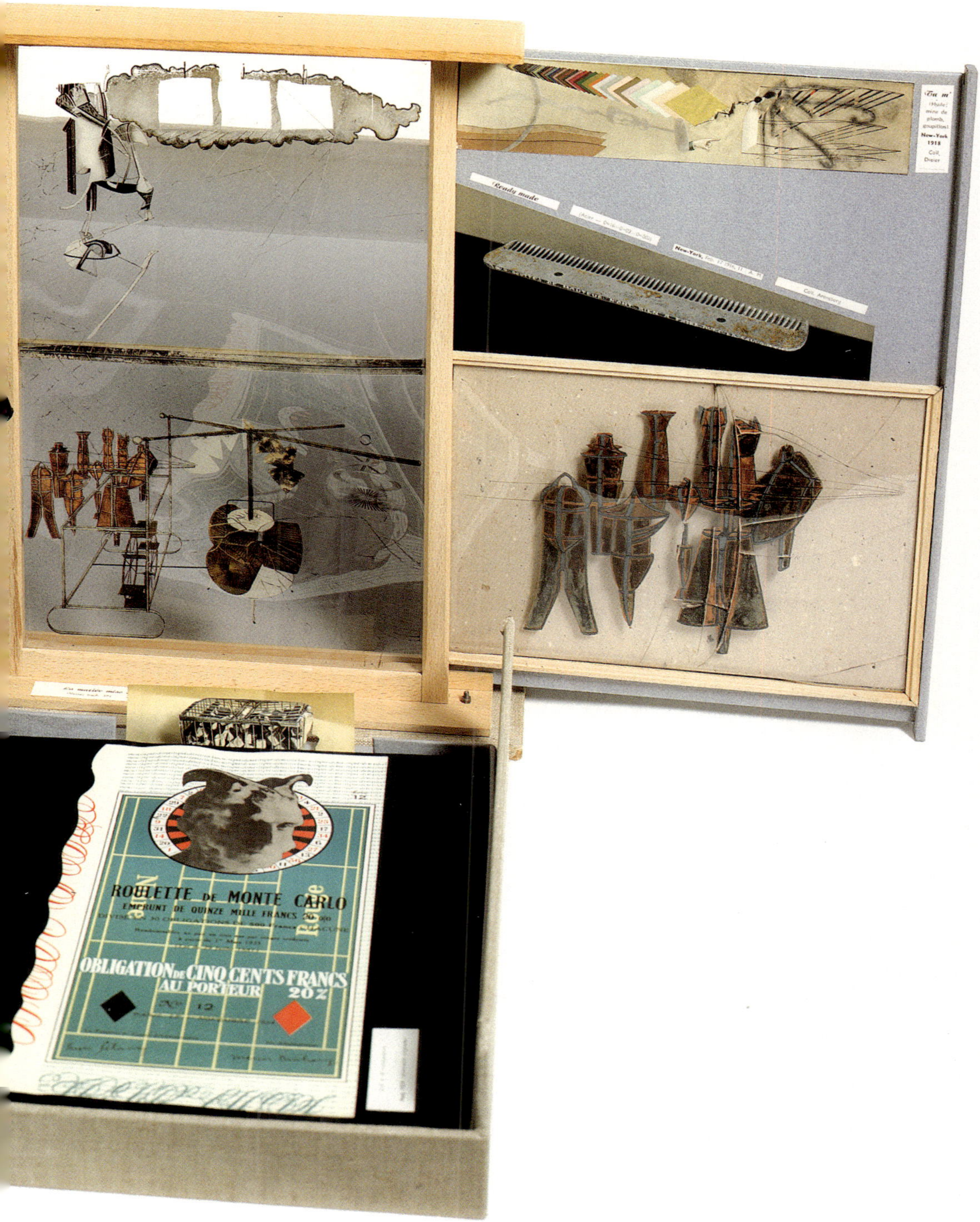
"Tu m'"
(Huile)
mine de
plomb,
goupillon)
New-York
1918
Coll.
Dreier
Ready made
New-York
Coll. Arensberg
ROULETTE DE MONTE CARLO
EMPRUNT DE QUINZE MILLE FRANCS
OBLIGATION DE CINQ CENTS FRANCS
AU PORTEUR
No 12
20%

Robert Rauschenberg
Untitled ("Scatole personali" Series), ca. 1952
[cat. 591]

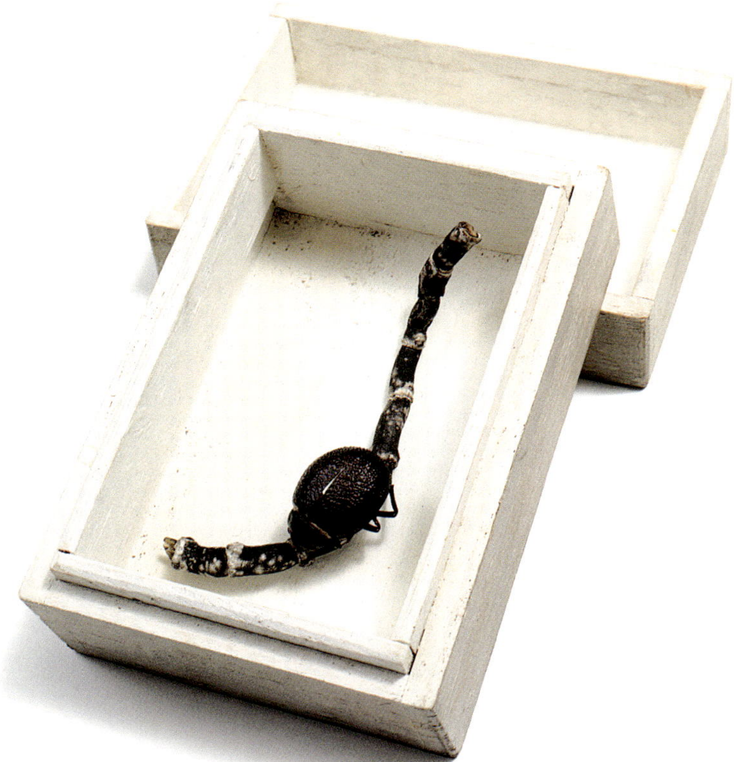

Robert Rauschenberg
Untitled ("Scatole personali" Series), ca. 1952
[cat. 593]

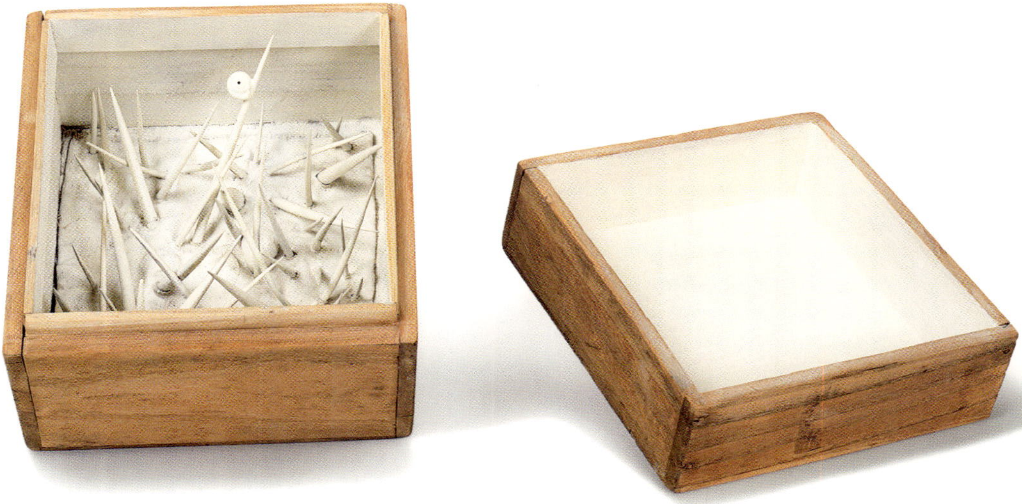

Robert Rauschenberg

Untitled (Inside of an Old Carriage), ca. 1979

[cat. 597]

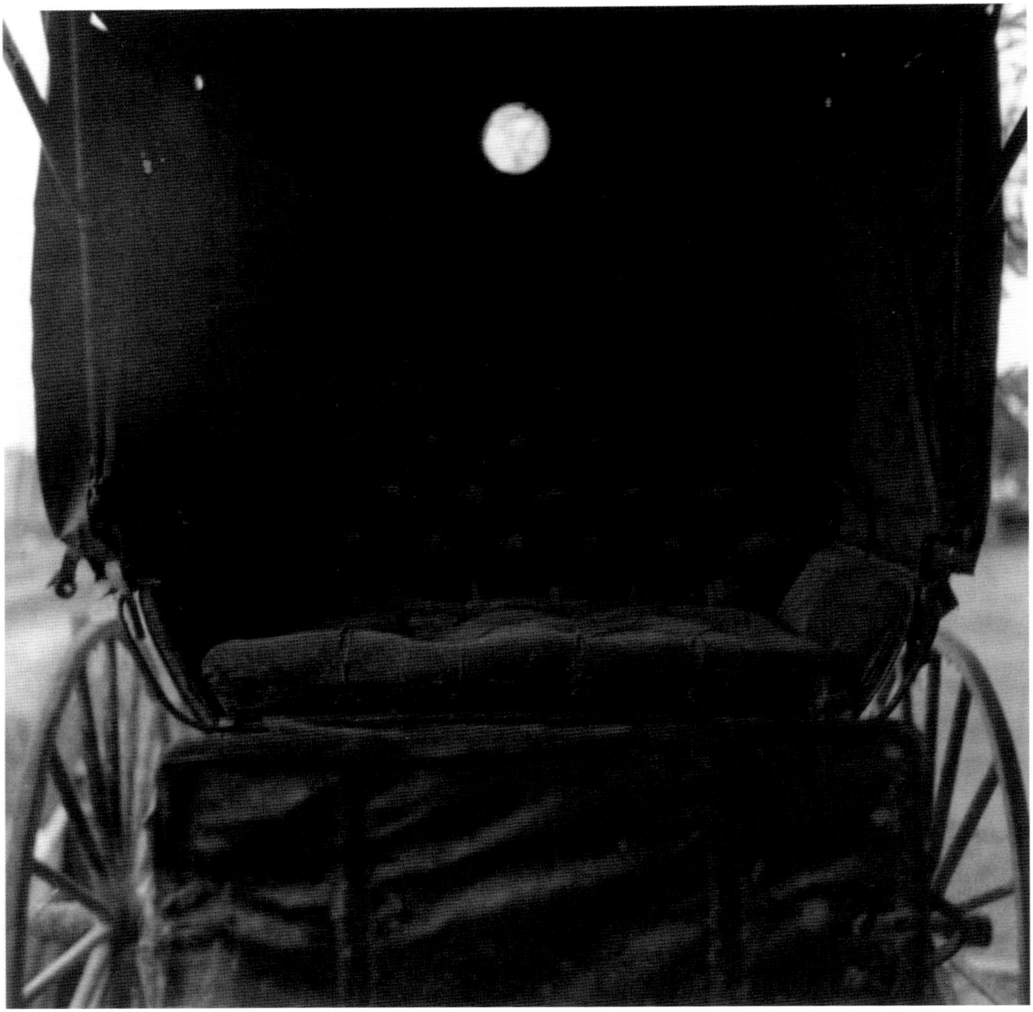

Robert Rauschenberg
Untitled (Matte Black with Fabric), ca. 1952
[cat. 599]

Robert Rauschenberg
Music Box (Elemental Sculpture), 1952
[cat. 592]

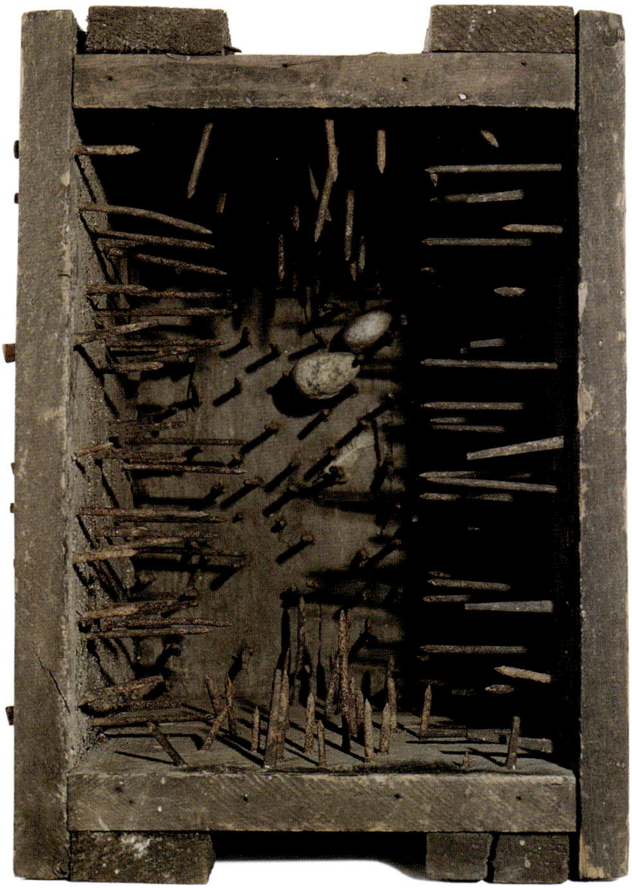

Robert Rauschenberg
Untitled (Elemental Sculpture), 1953
[cat. 594]

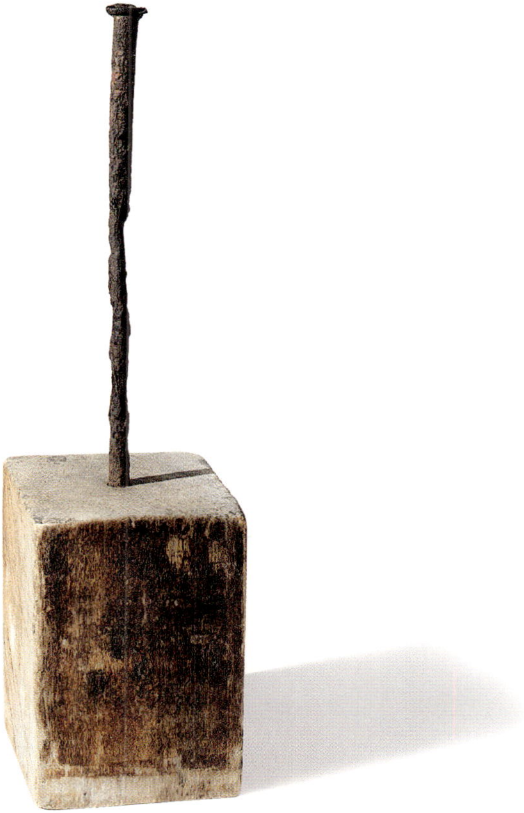

John Cage

"Writing for the Second Time through Finnegans Wake," 1977.
Text read by John Cage in *Roaratorio. Au Irish Circus on Finnegans Wake,* sound work, 1979.

duchaMp
and sAtie
aRe alone i'm glad to be with you
we Can look
at thE sceneries or have a conversation
is there anything you Like to say?

i've just talkeD my head off
my laUgh
what is that? an inCandescent lamp?
i've never seen sucH
A big one! what's it doing here
backstage? it Magrittes me think
it's using uP

all thE
eneRgy
there Is
looK! I'm right!

the other lightS
Are
noT
workIng
any longEr!

Richard Hamilton

d'Orientation, 1952

[cat. 621]

The title d'*orientation* will do for "about orientation". Its passage through French allows an allusion to the Golden Section and the mathematical science of the painters inspired mainly by Euclid. The idea of orientation associated with a perspective schema refers us to the work of the psychologist James J. Gibson, author of *Perception of the Visual World* (Boston, 1950). By placing the emphasis on the experience of orientation in a space of mobility (car driving, plane piloting) Gibson's theory opposes the abstract geometry of Euclidean space and redefines the field of perception as an environment.

The sinuous line that crosses the picture in the centre traces a biomorphic profile reminiscent of Duchamp's speculative figures for *Grand Verre*.

This apparition, inspired by the shape of an aquatic mollusc (jellyfish) is set in the transparency of a geometrical network. In 1952, Hamilton aimed at a new synthesis between speculations on a dynamic of vision in motion (Moholy-Nagy, *Vision in Motion*, 1948) and the formalisation of the processes of growth (d'Arcy Thompson, *On Growth and Forms*, 1917-1942). J.-F.C.

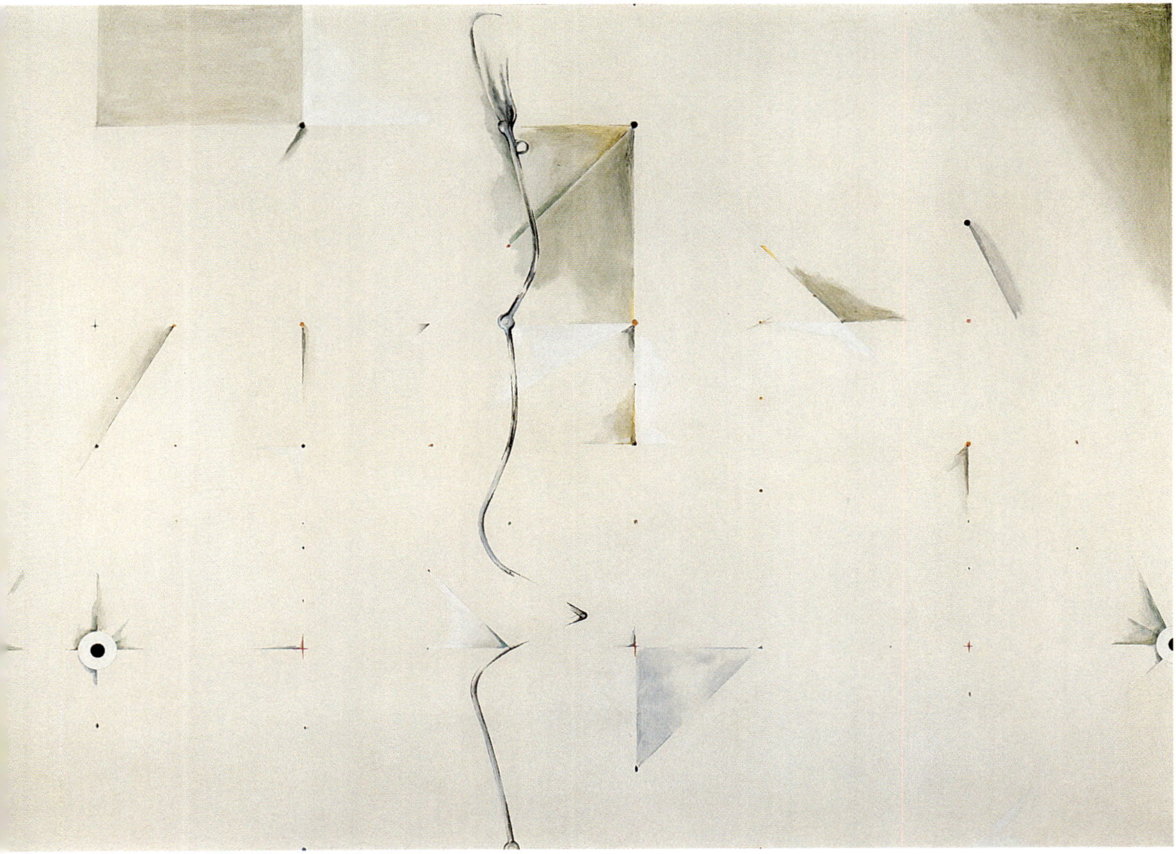

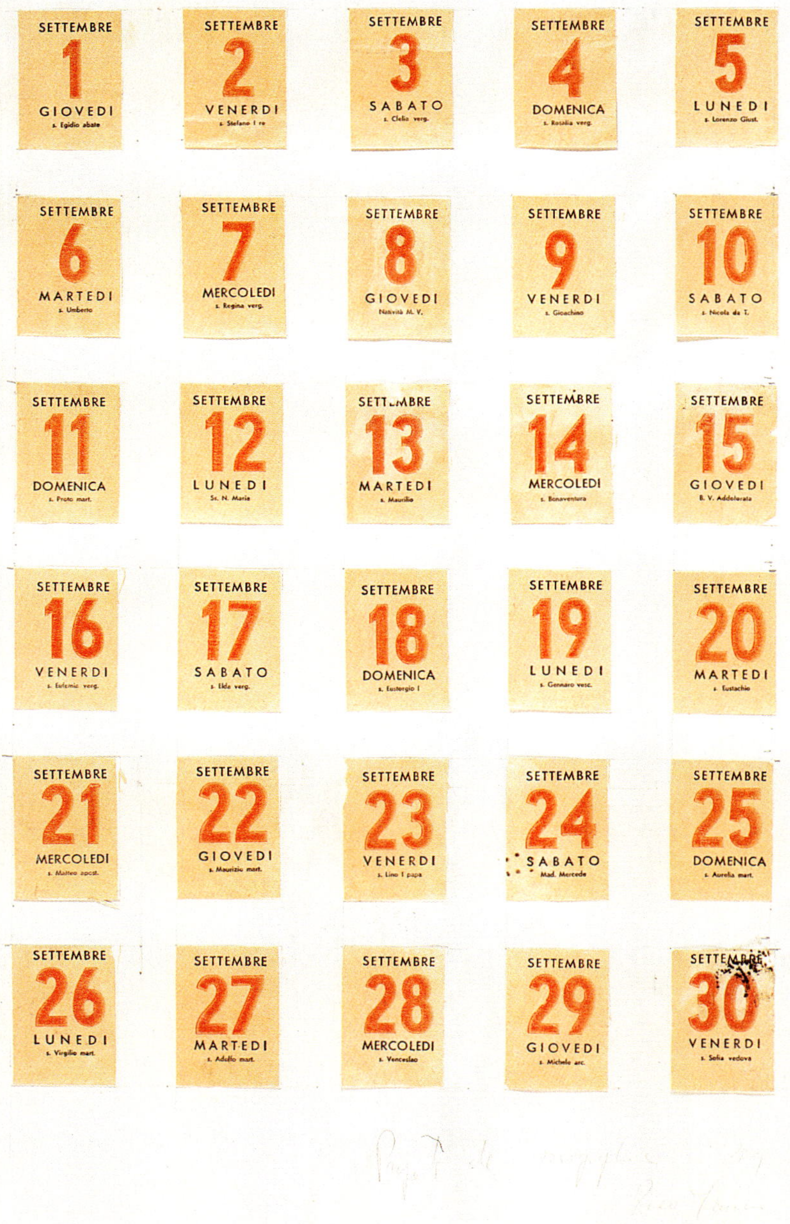
SETTEMBRE 1 GIOVEDI s. Egidio abate
SETTEMBRE 2 VENERDI s. Stefano I re
SETTEMBRE 3 SABATO s. Clelia verg.
SETTEMBRE 4 DOMENICA s. Rosalia verg.
SETTEMBRE 5 LUNEDI s. Lorenzo Giust.
SETTEMBRE 6 MARTEDI s. Umberto
SETTEMBRE 7 MERCOLEDI s. Regina verg.
SETTEMBRE 8 GIOVEDI Natività M. V.
SETTEMBRE 9 VENERDI s. Gioachino
SETTEMBRE 10 SABATO s. Nicola da T.
SETTEMBRE 11 DOMENICA s. Proto mart.
SETTEMBRE 12 LUNEDI Ss. N. Maria
SETTEMBRE 13 MARTEDI s. Maurilio
SETTEMBRE 14 MERCOLEDI s. Bonaventura
SETTEMBRE 15 GIOVEDI B. V. Addolorata
SETTEMBRE 16 VENERDI s. Eufemia verg.
SETTEMBRE 17 SABATO s. Elda verg.
SETTEMBRE 18 DOMENICA s. Eustorgio I
SETTEMBRE 19 LUNEDI s. Gennaro vesc.
SETTEMBRE 20 MARTEDI s. Eustachio
SETTEMBRE 21 MERCOLEDI s. Matteo apost.
SETTEMBRE 22 GIOVEDI s. Maurizio mart.
SETTEMBRE 23 VENERDI s. Lino I papa
SETTEMBRE 24 SABATO Mad. Mercede
SETTEMBRE 25 DOMENICA s. Aurelia mart.
SETTEMBRE 26 LUNEDI s. Virgilio mart.
SETTEMBRE 27 MARTEDI s. Adolfo mart.
SETTEMBRE 28 MERCOLEDI s. Venceslao
SETTEMBRE 29 GIOVEDI s. Michele arc.
SETTEMBRE 30 VENERDI s. Sofia vedova

Piero Manzoni

Calendario, 1-30 settembre 1959, 1959

[cat. 617]

Alfabeto, 1958

[cat. 615]

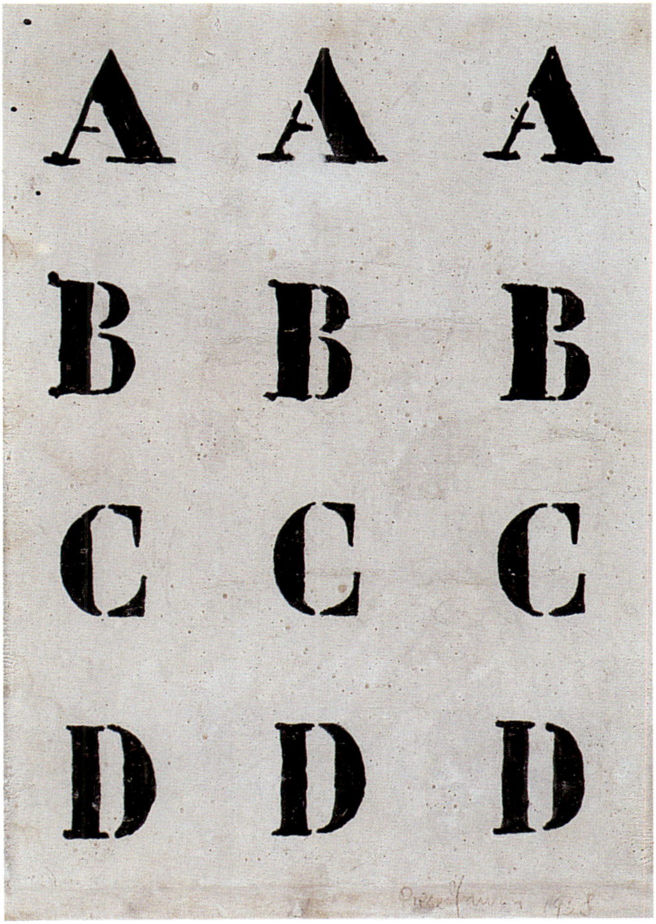

Tony Smith
Untitled, 1934-1936
[cat. 639]

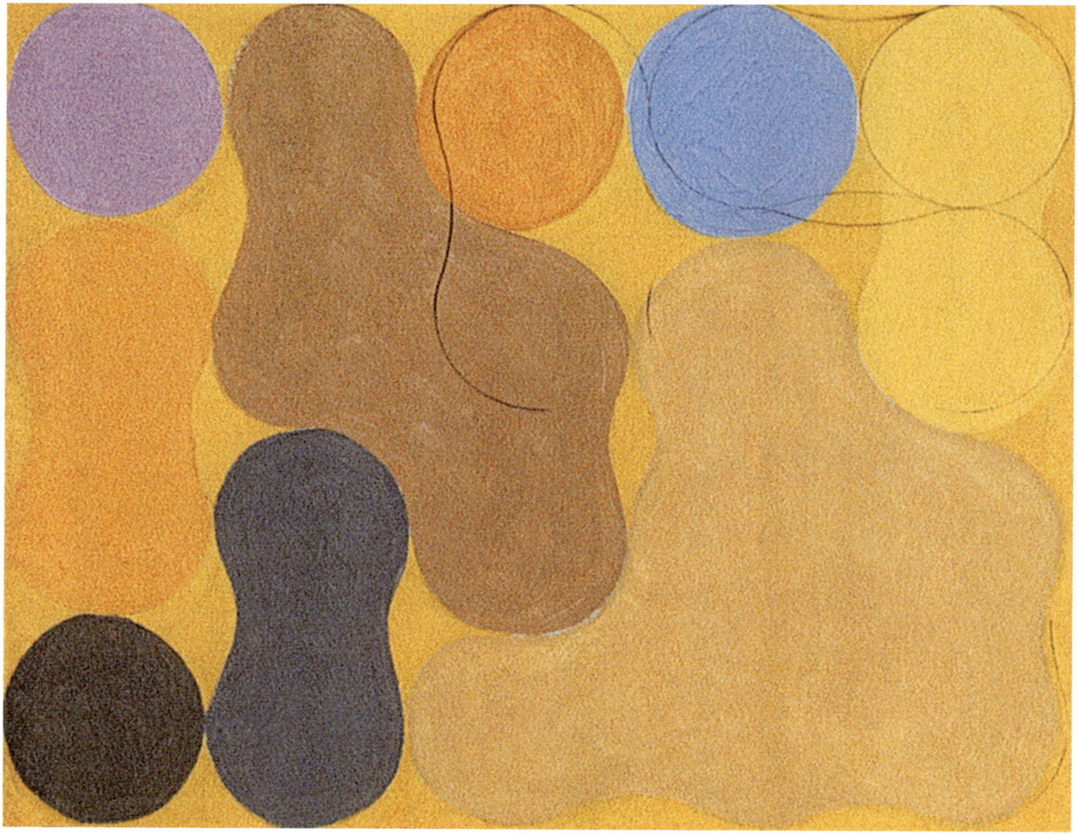

Tony Smith
Untitled, 1934-1936
[cat. 638]

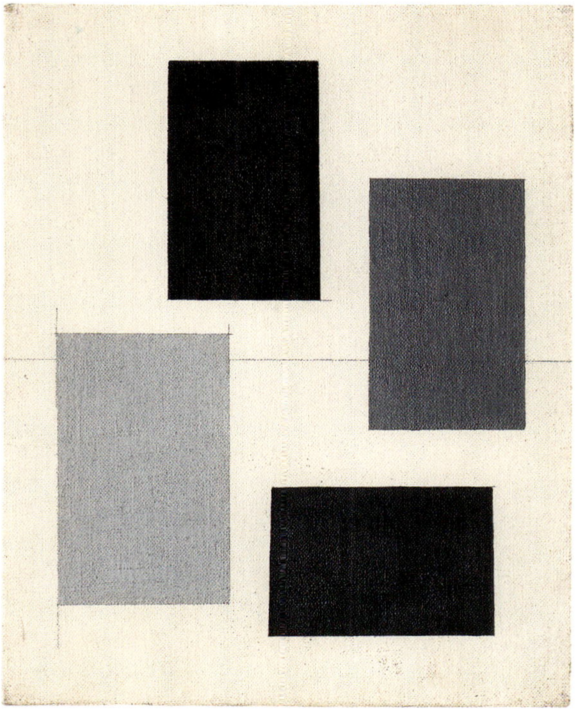

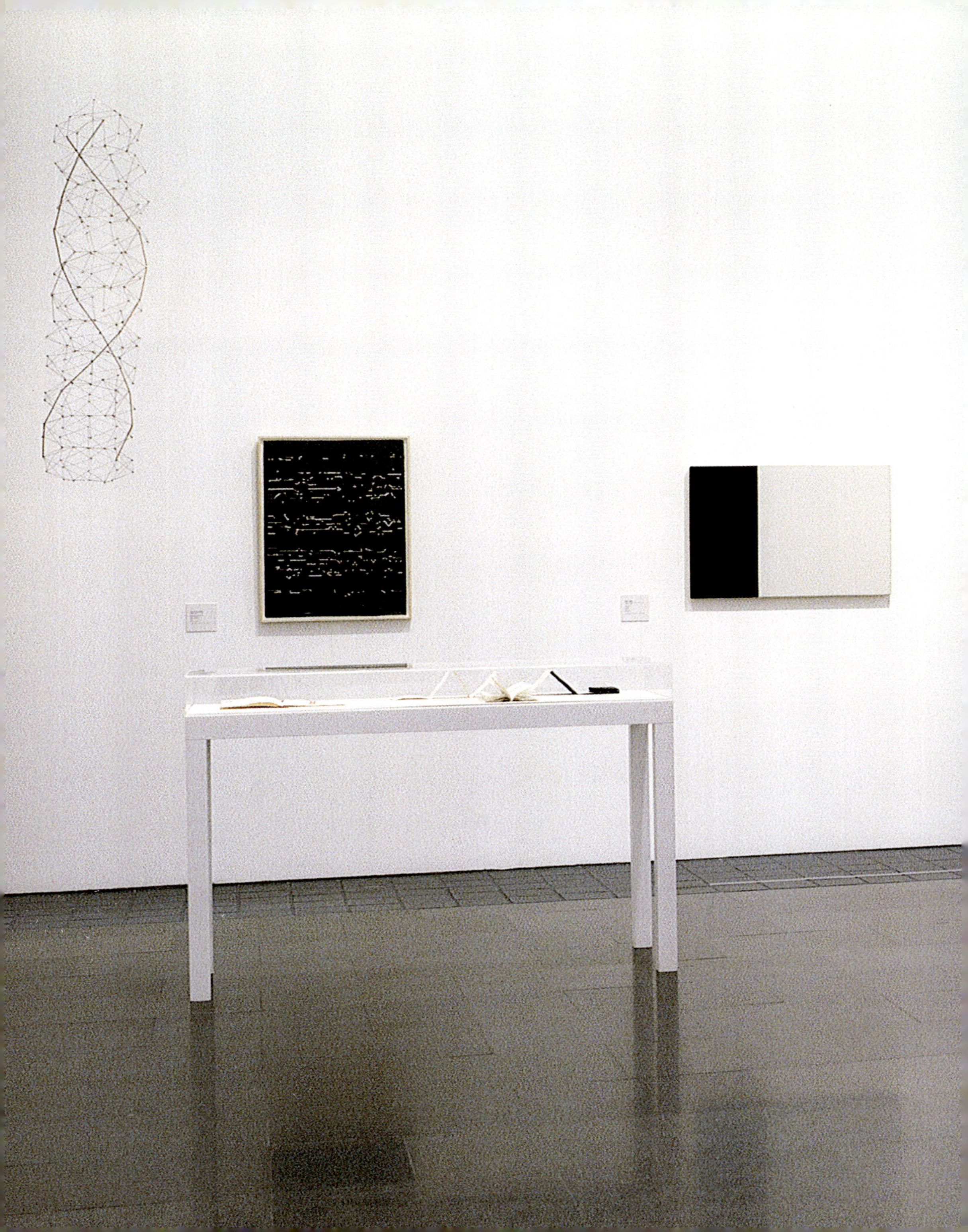

View of the exhibition rooms. In the background, left to right: Gego, *Tronco no. 2*, ca. 1975 [cat. 628]; Pablo Palazuelo, *Segundo cantoral II,* 1978 [cat. 632]; Tony Smith, *Untitled,* 1962-1963 [cat. 633], *Untitled,* 1962-1963 [cat. 634]; Georges Vantongerloo, *Deux zones de l'espace: action-réaction,* 1949 [cat. 636], *Radio-activité,* 1952 [cat. 635]. In the centre, left to right, Gego showcase and Georges Vantongerloo, *Le Dôme,* 1959 [cat. 637].

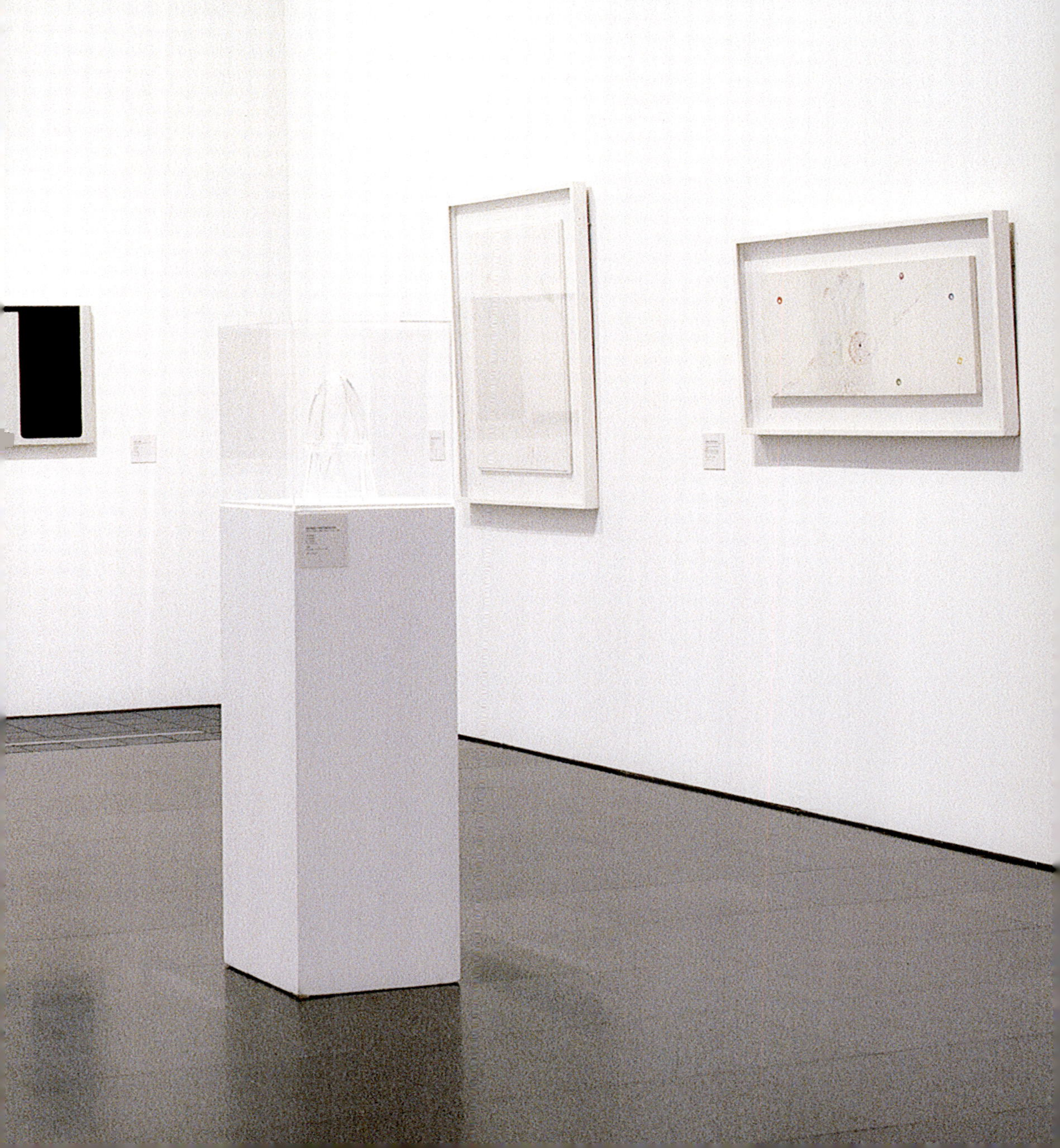

Gego

Dibujo sin papel 87/2, 1987

[cat. 604]

Tronco nº 2, ca. 1975

[cat. 628]

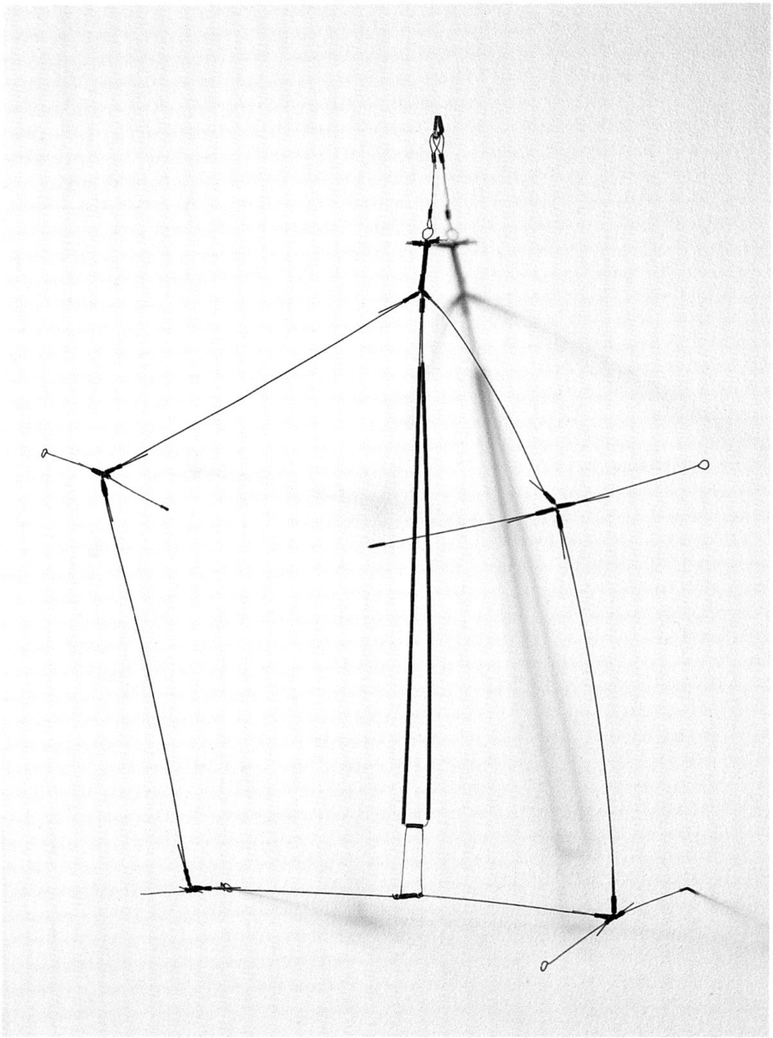

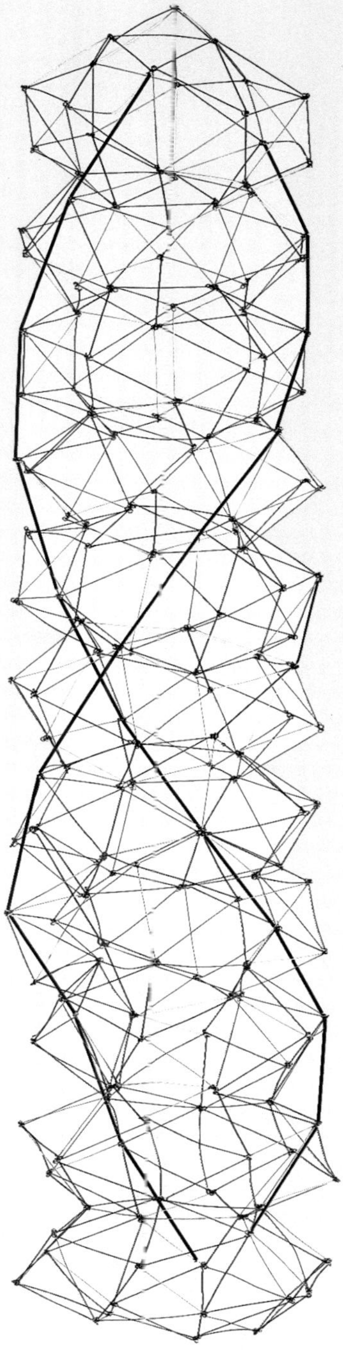

Pablo Palazuelo

Segundo cantoral II, 1978

[cat. 632]

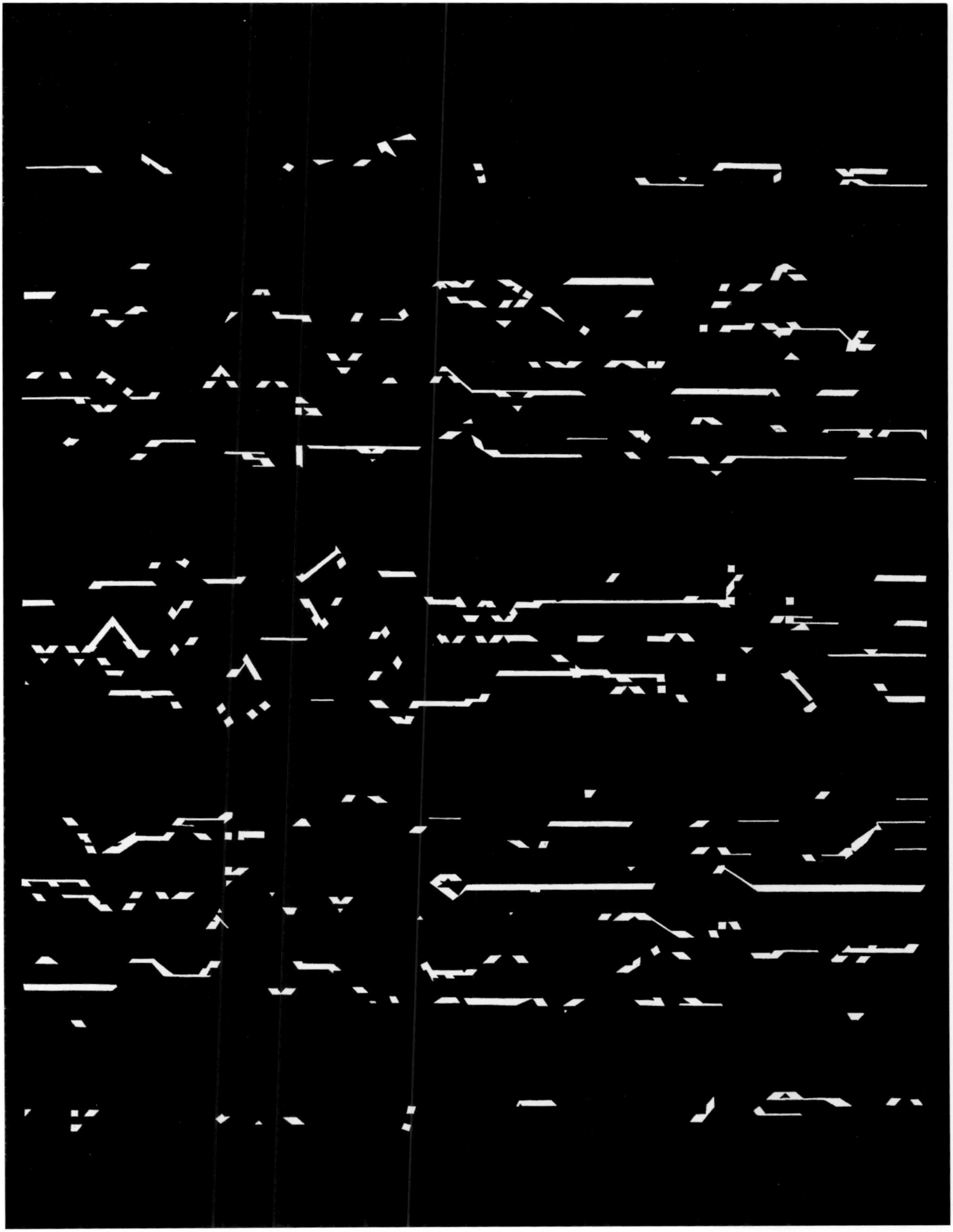

Georges Vantongerloo
Variante, 1939
[cat. 398]

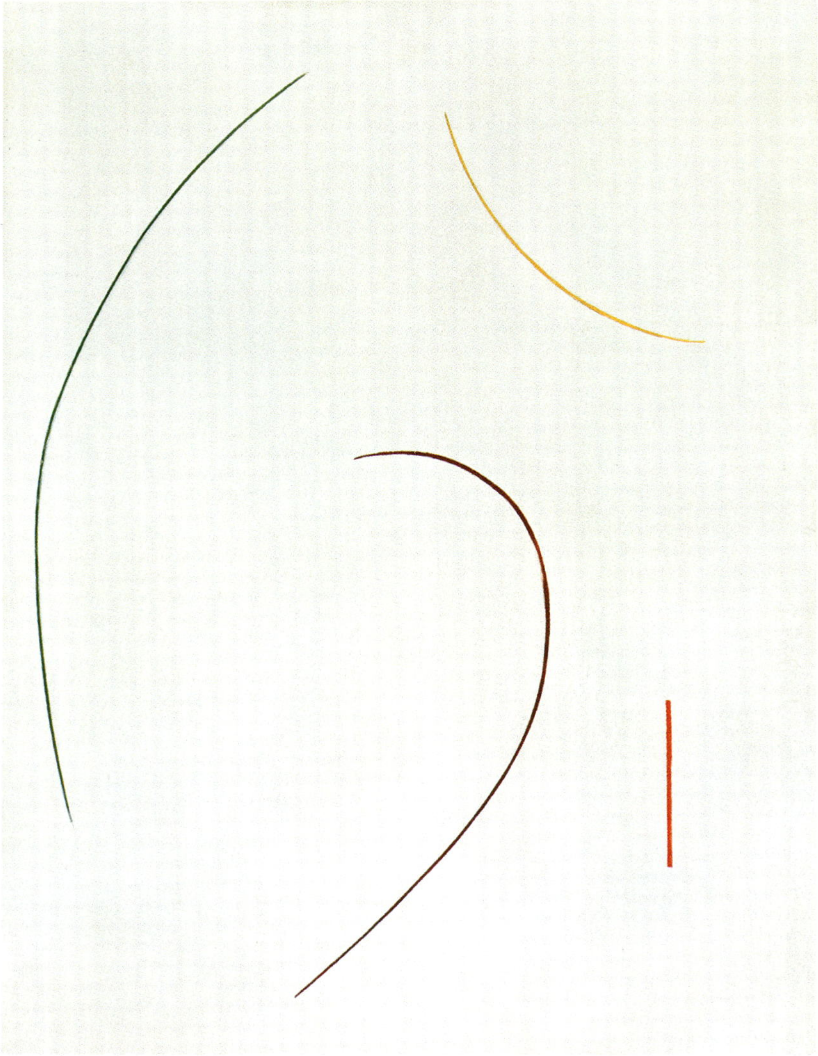

Georges Vantongerloo
Le Dôme, 1959
[cat. 637]

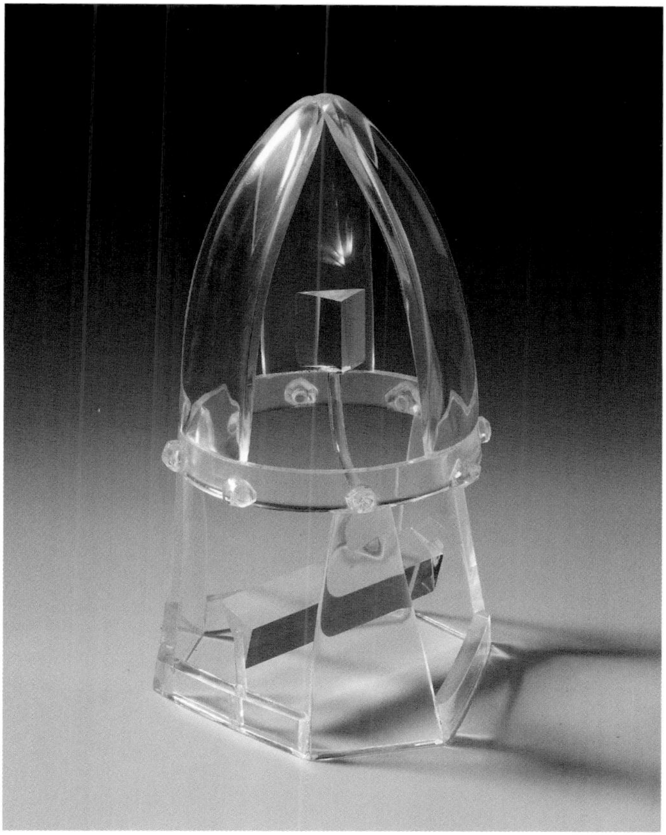

Next double page:
Carl Andre
Steel Lead Alloy Square, 1969
[cat. 644]

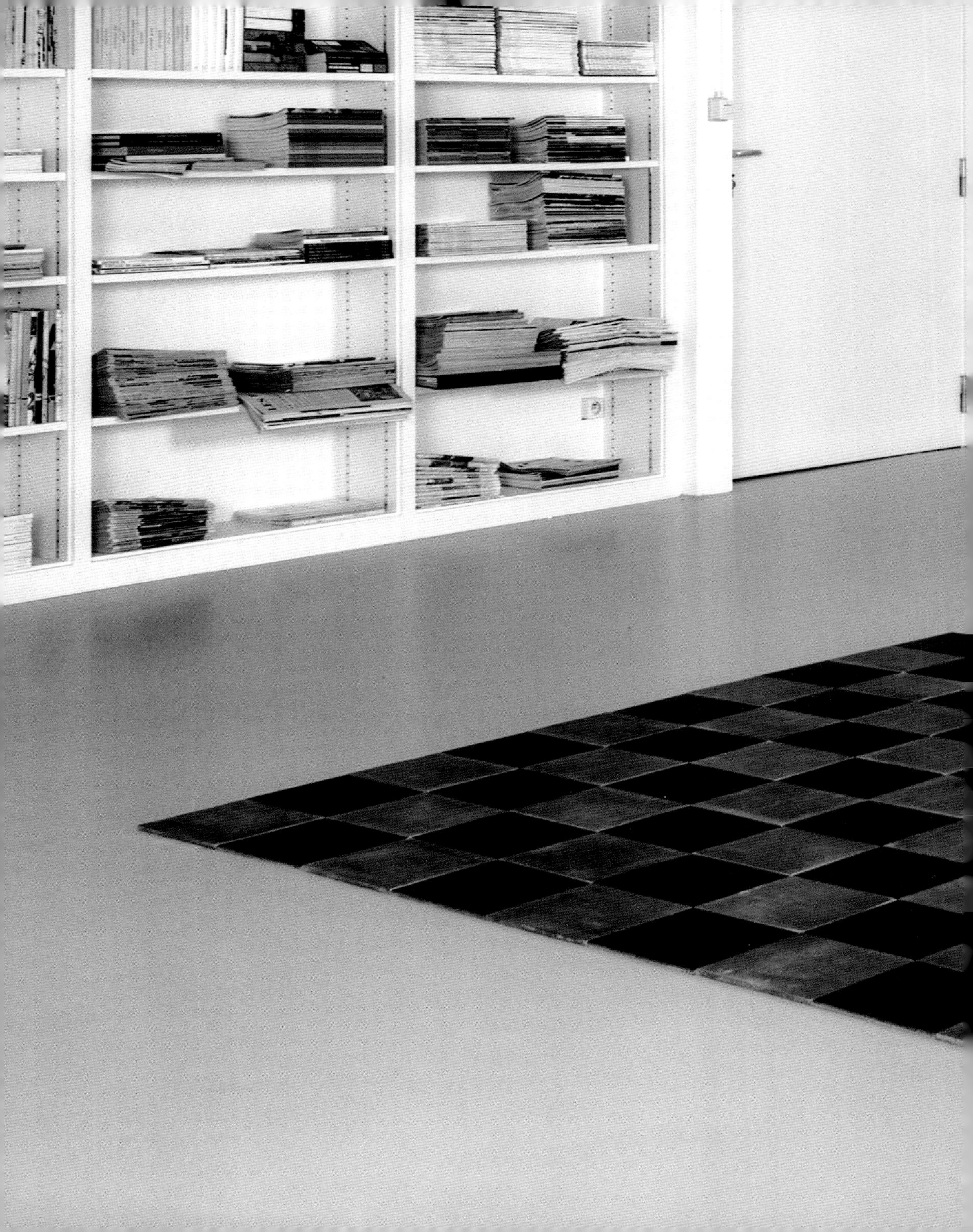

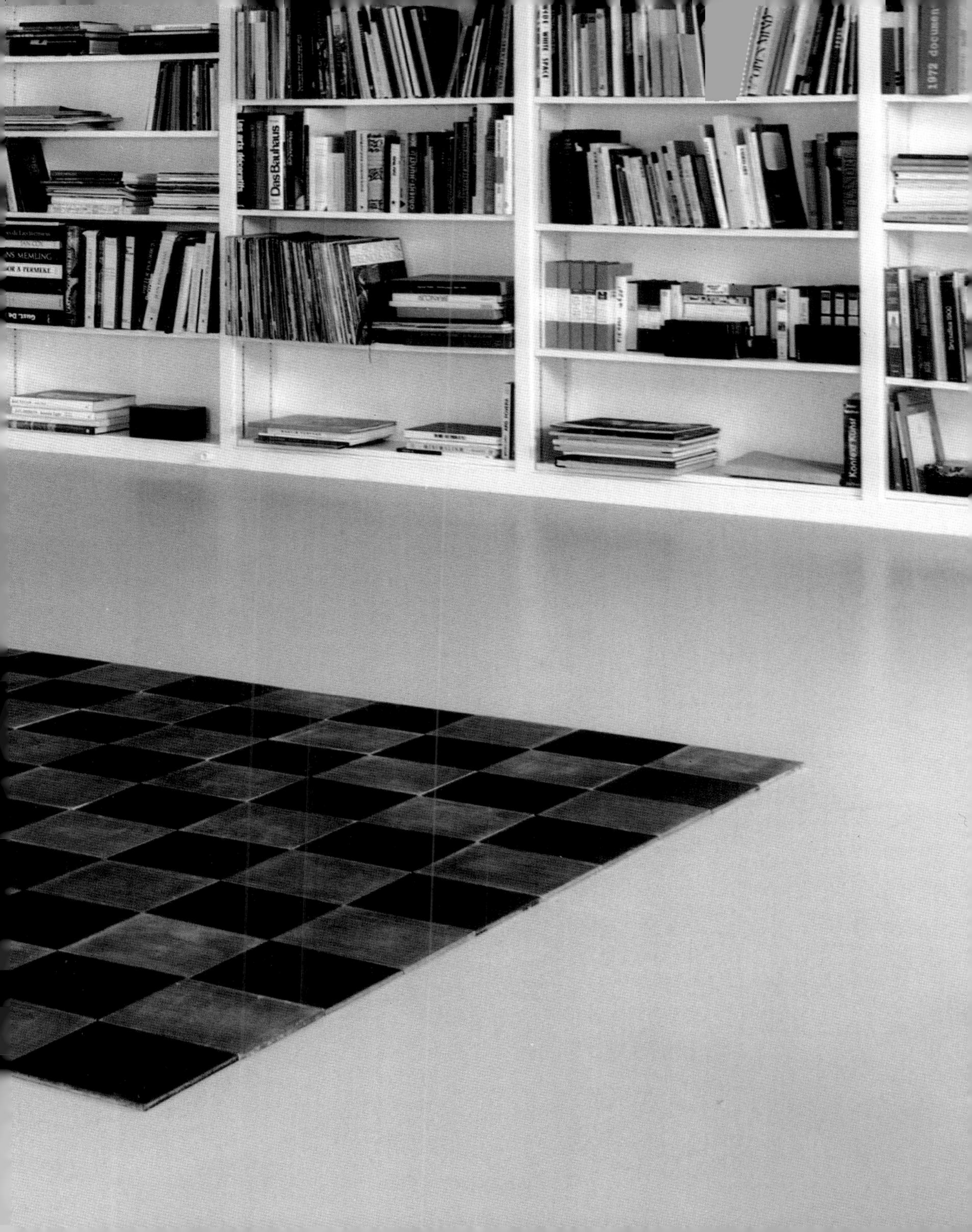
Das Bauhaus
Konkrete Kunst

Philip Guston

City, 1969

[cat. 646]

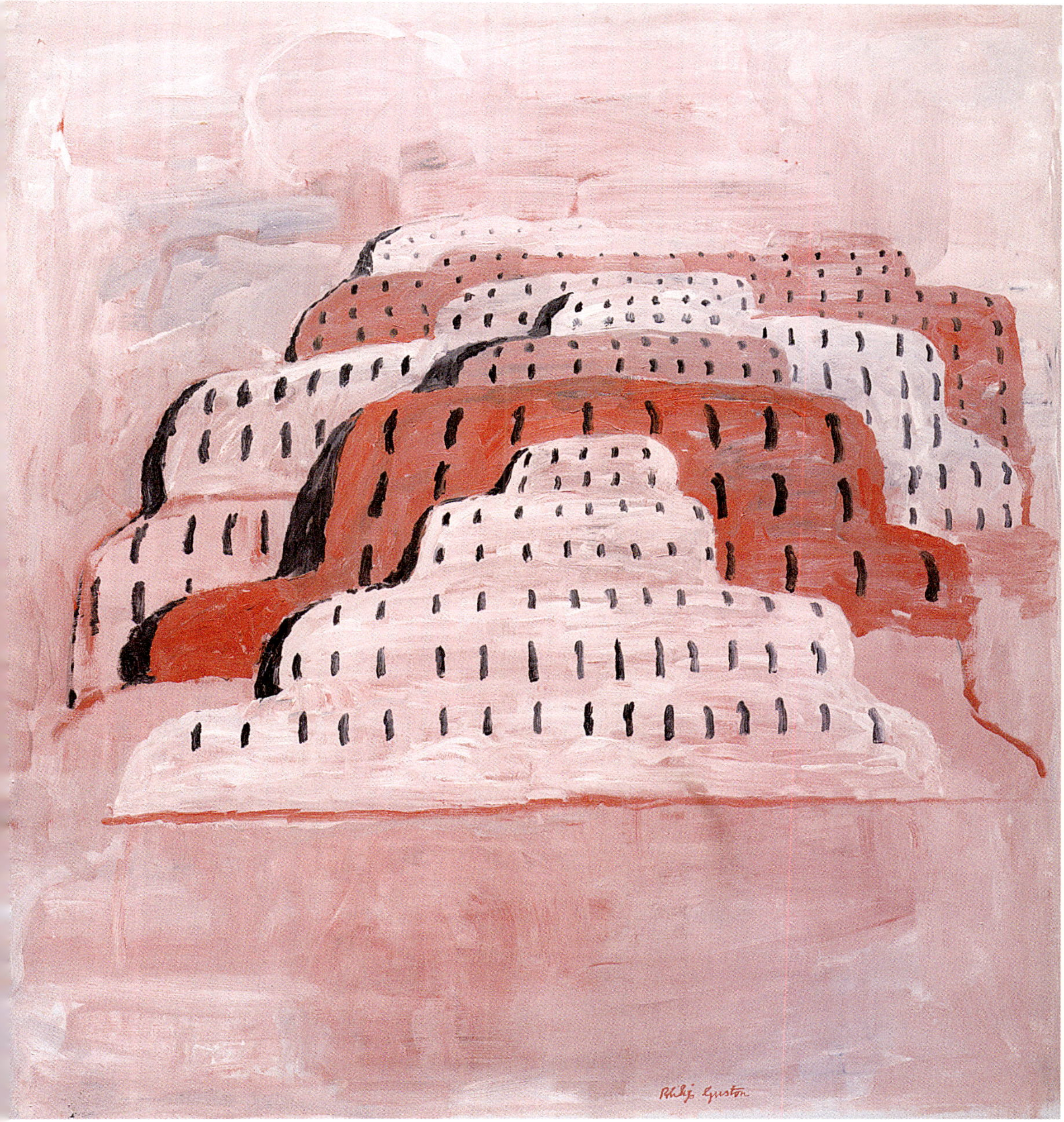
Philip Guston

Philip Guston

The Hill, 1965

[cat. 647]

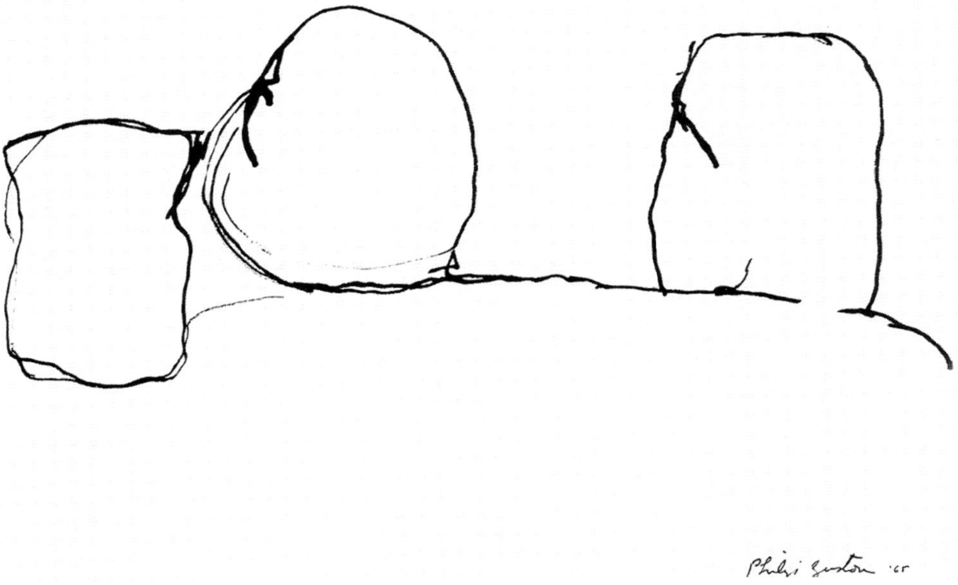

Philip Guston

Message, 1975

[cat. 650]

Untitled, 1975

[cat. 651]

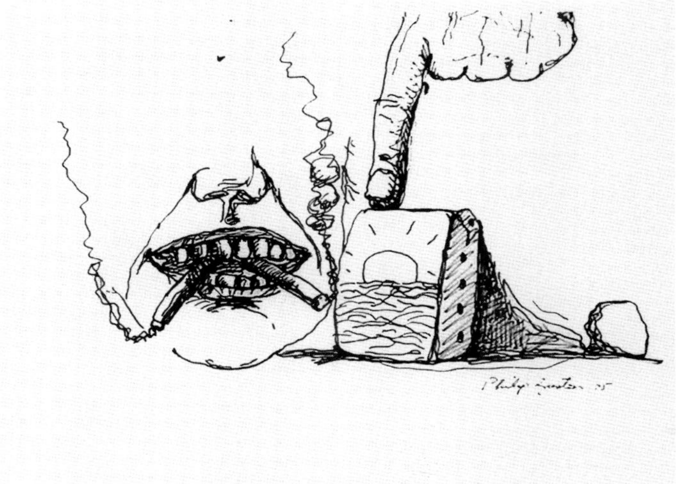

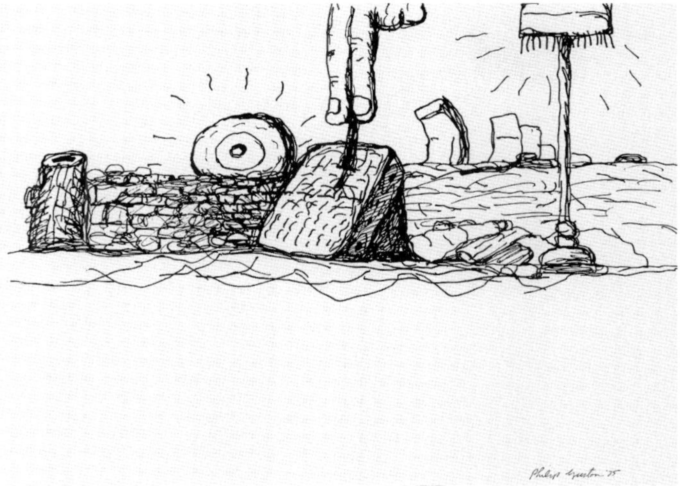

Philip Guston

Drawing for Web, 1975
[cat. 649]

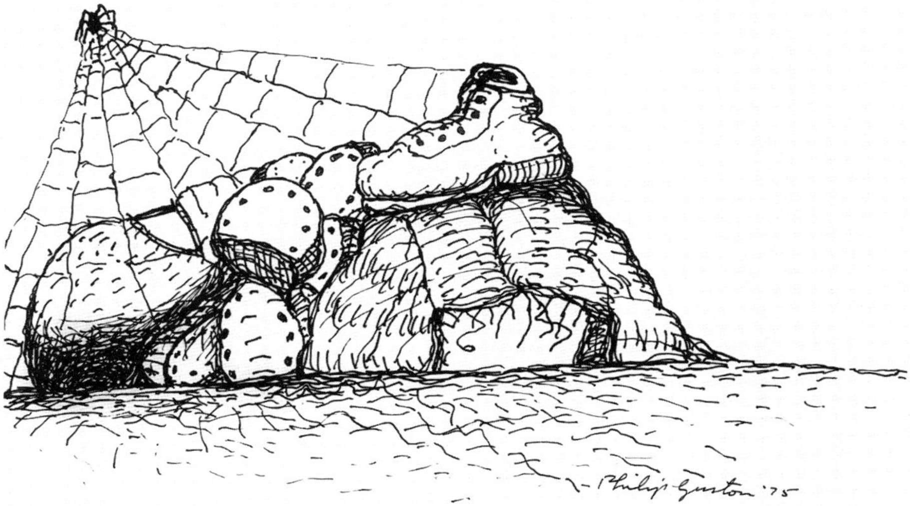

Philip Guston, Clark Coolidge

Untitled ("I Need to..."), 1976

[cat. 643]

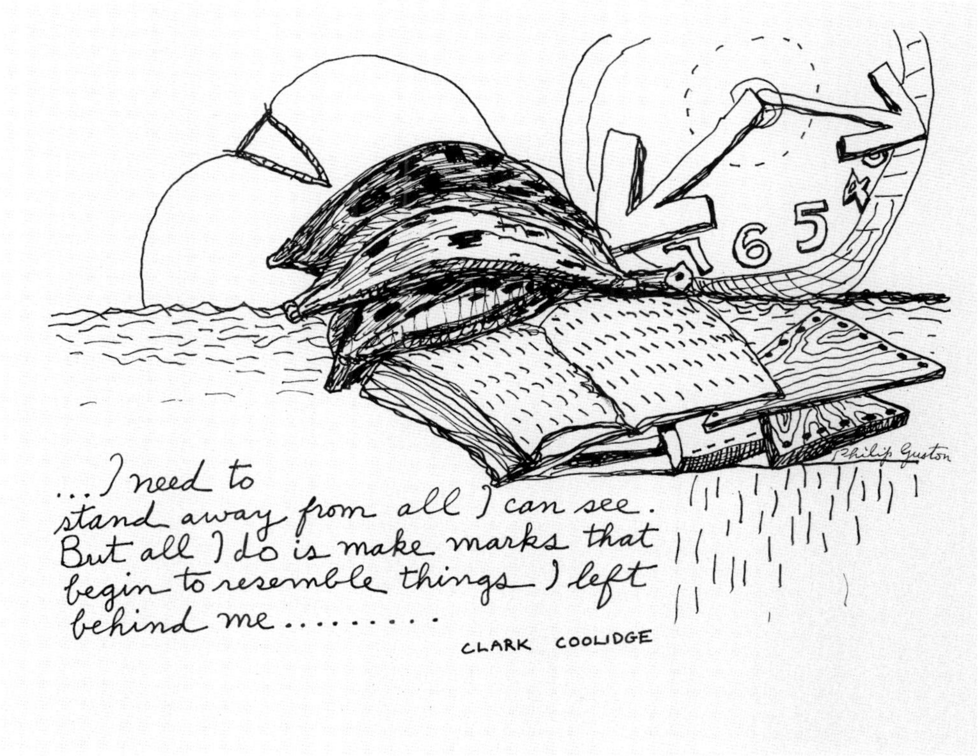

765
...I need to
stand away from all I can see.
But all I do is make marks that
begin to resemble things I left
behind me.........
CLARK COOLIDGE
Philip Guston

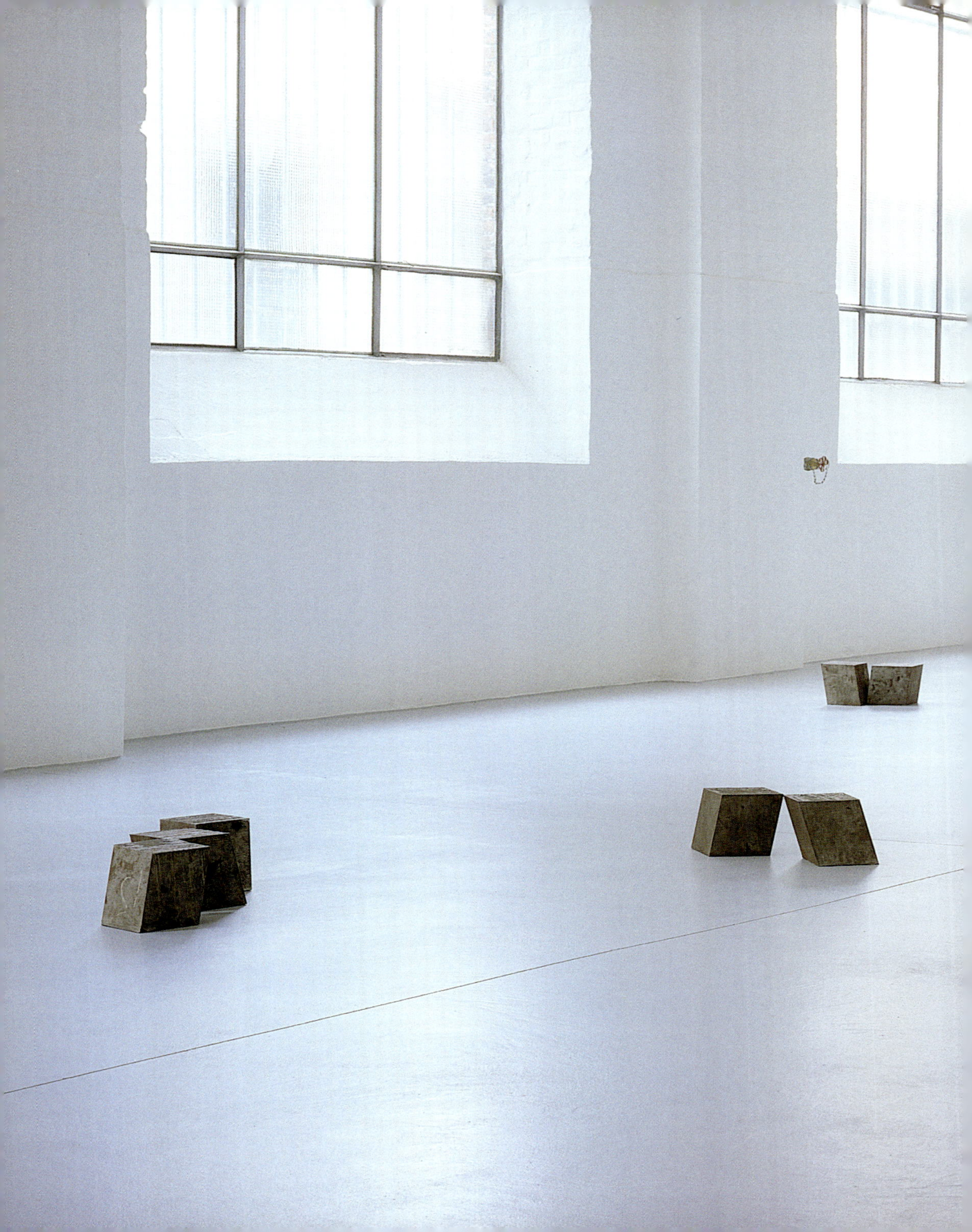

Bruce Nauman
White Breathing, 1976
[cat. 657]

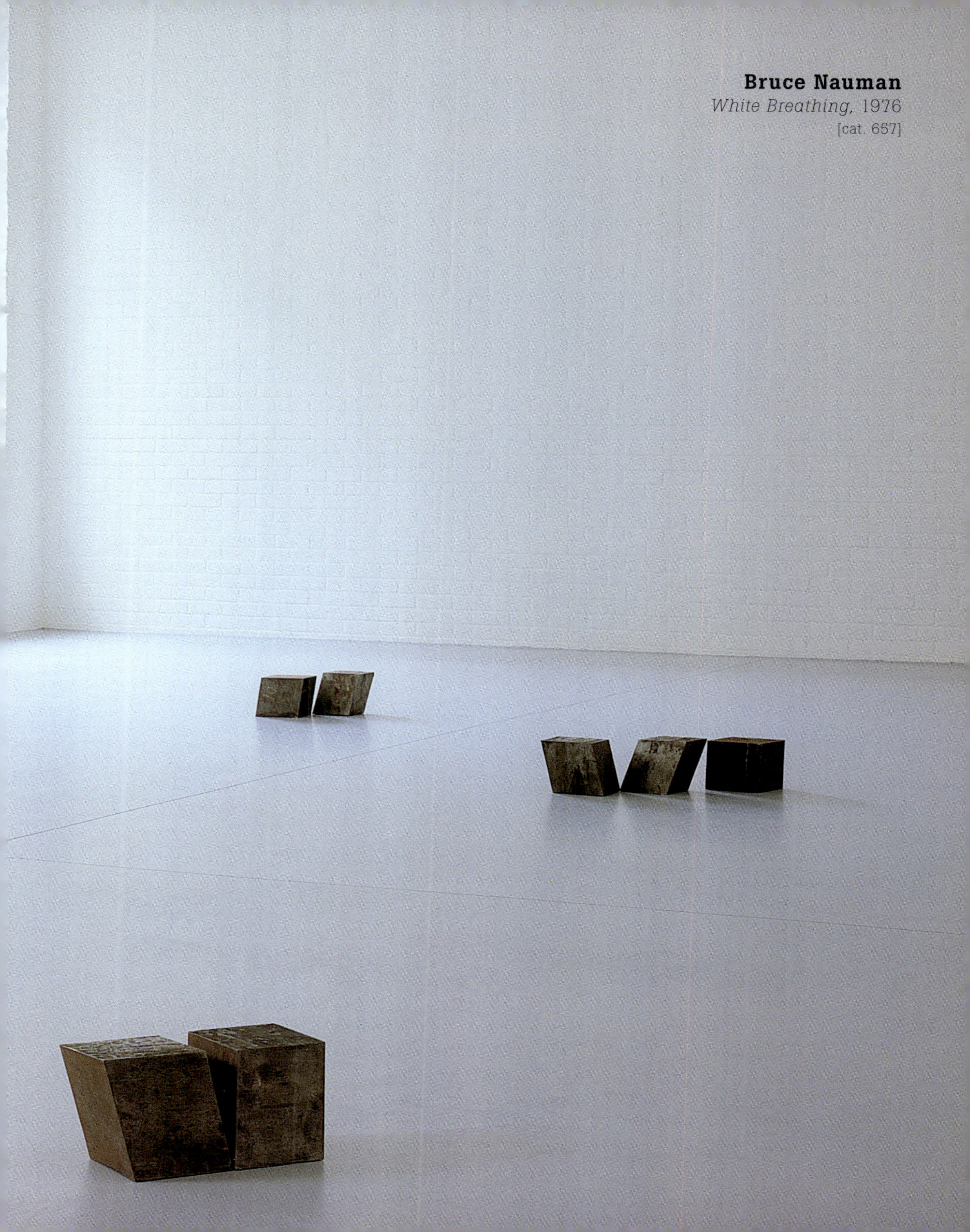

Bruce Nauman

White Breathing, Drawing #1, 1976

[cat. 654]

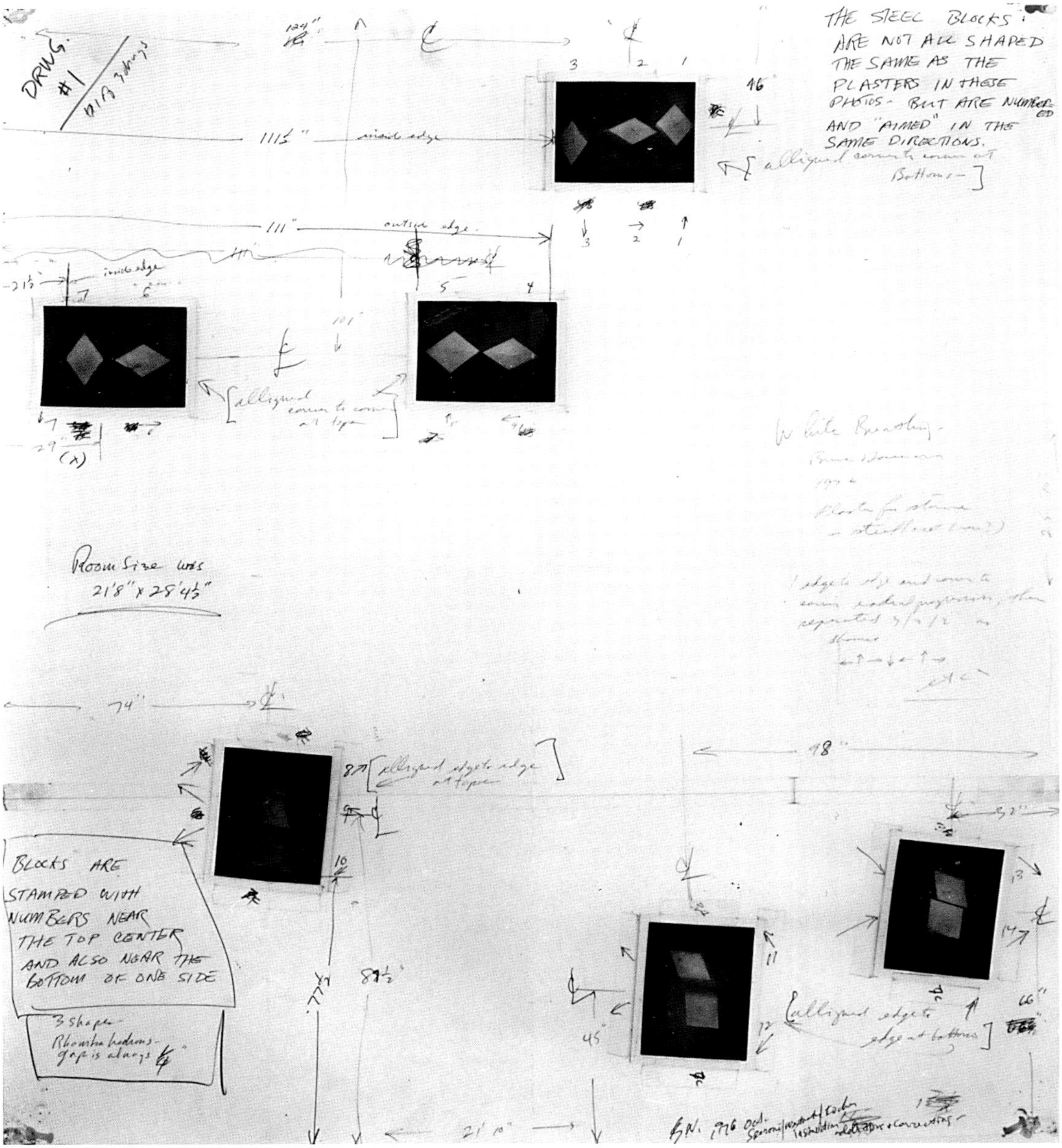

Bruce Nauman

White Breathing, Drawing #2, 1978

[cat. 655]

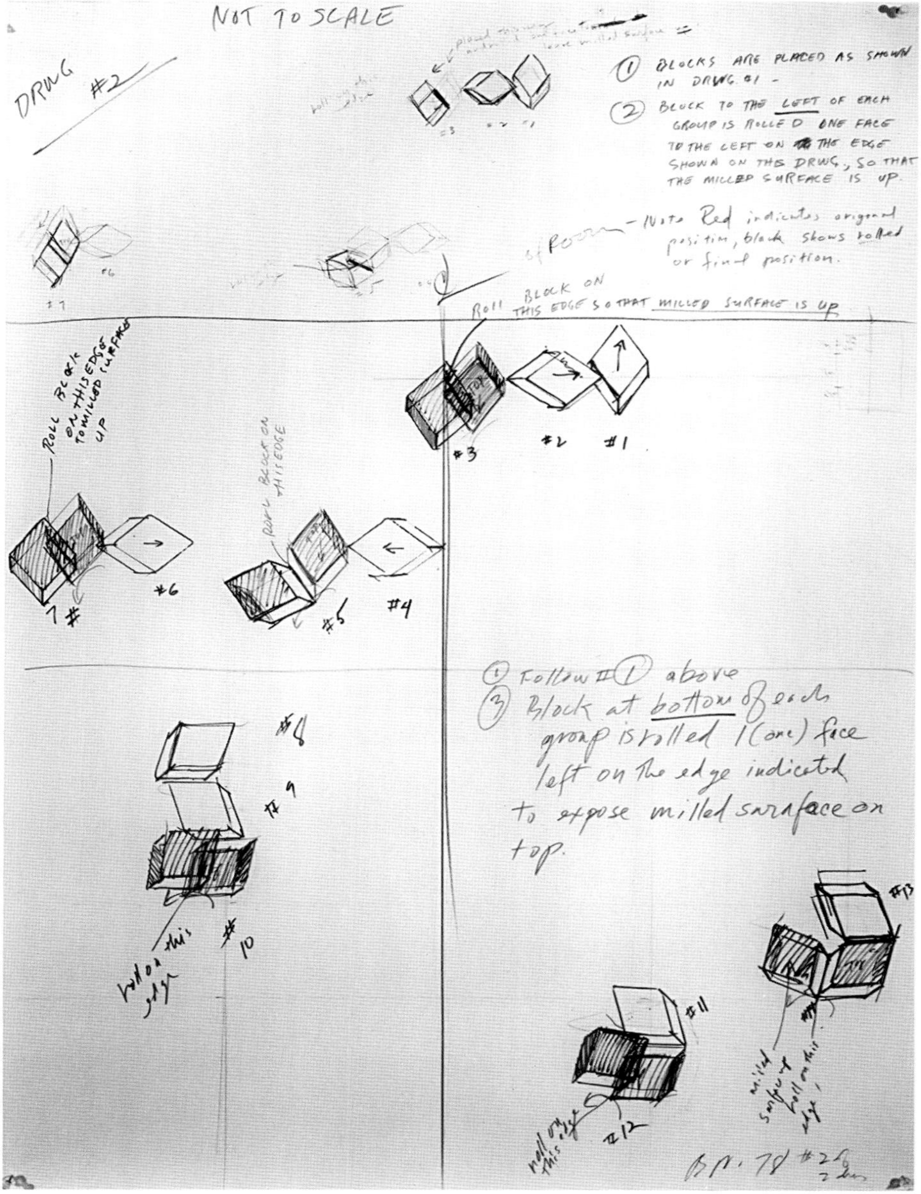

Sol LeWitt

Lines, Not Straight, From the Top and the Left Side, 1972

[cat. 658]

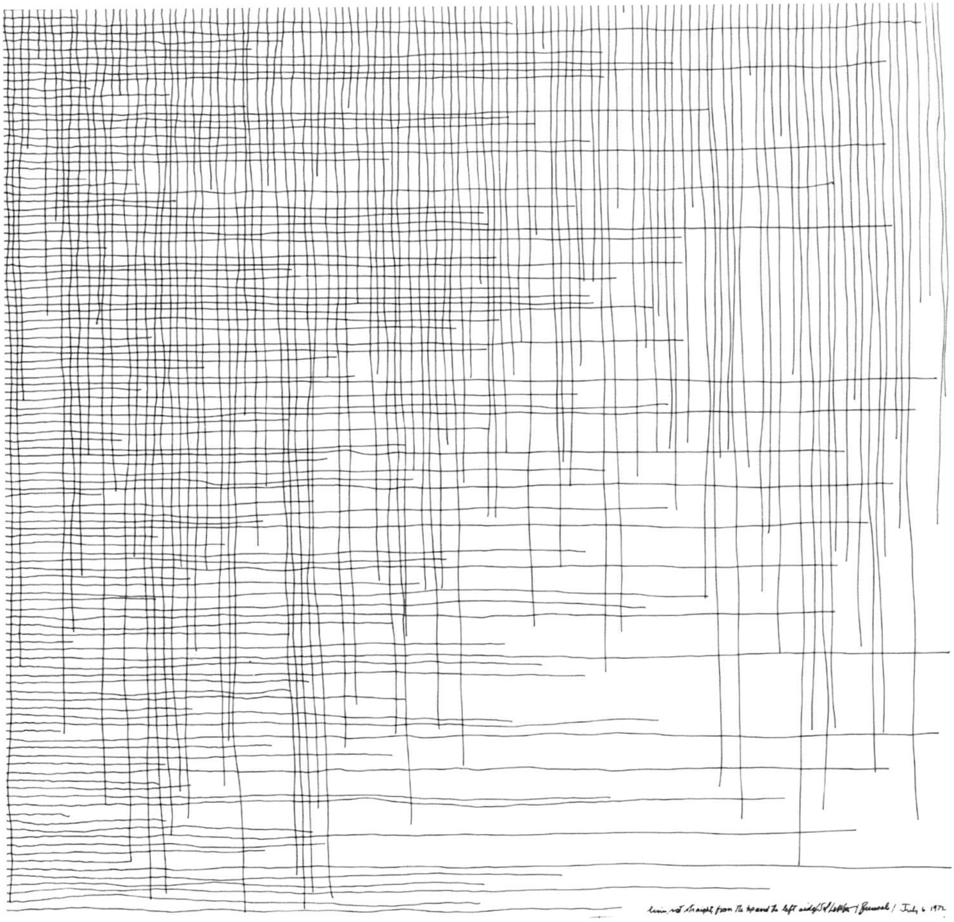

Sol LeWitt

Straight Lines, From the Left Side, 1972

[cat. 660]

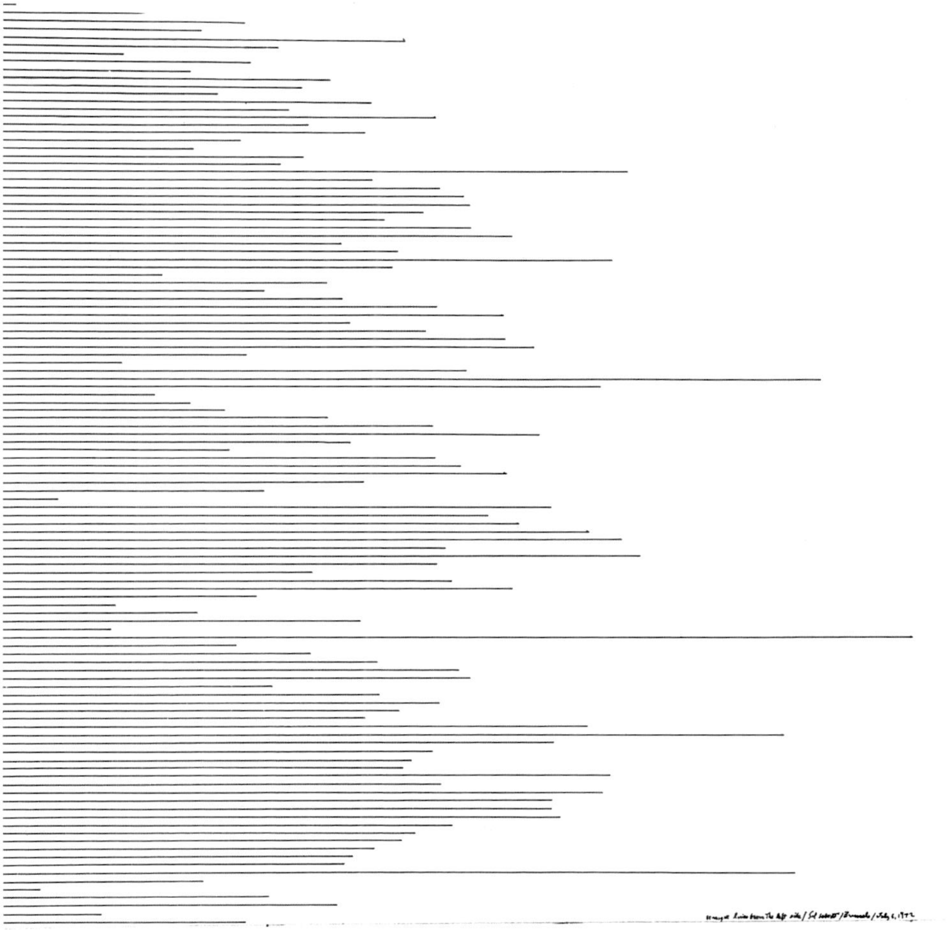

Cover of *Aspen,* No. 5-6, Fall–Winter 1967. Edited and designed by Brian O'Doherty, art direction by David Dalton and Lynn Letterman
[cat. 663]

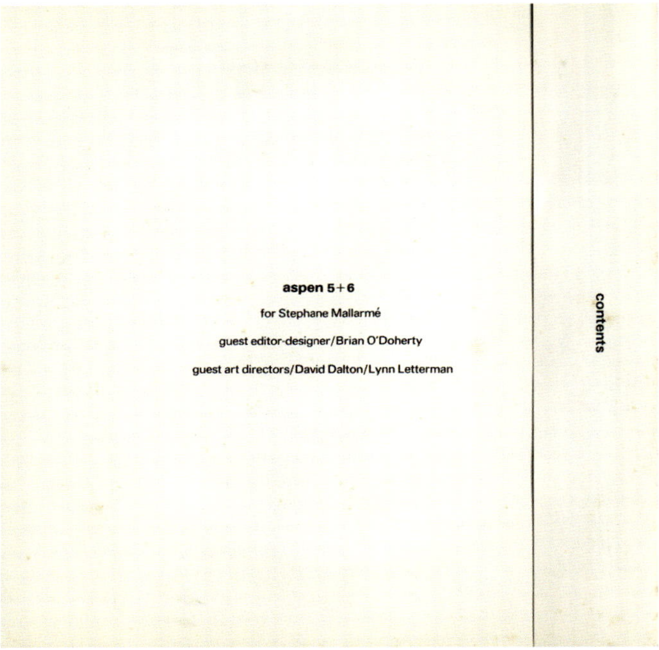

Contents page of *Aspen*, No. 5–6, Fall–Winter 1967. Edited and designed by Brian O'Doherty, art direction by David Dalton and Lynn Letterman
[cat. 663]

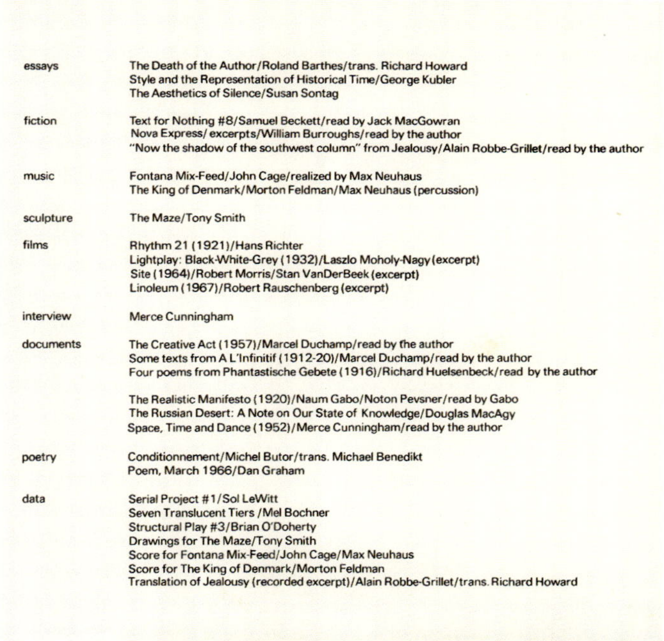

essays	The Death of the Author/Roland Barthes/trans. Richard Howard
	Style and the Representation of Historical Time/George Kubler
	The Aesthetics of Silence/Susan Sontag
fiction	Text for Nothing #8/Samuel Beckett/read by Jack MacGowran
	Nova Express/ excerpts/William Burroughs/read by the author
	"Now the shadow of the southwest column" from Jealousy/Alain Robbe-Grillet/read by the author
music	Fontana Mix-Feed/John Cage/realized by Max Neuhaus
	The King of Denmark/Morton Feldman/Max Neuhaus (percussion)
sculpture	The Maze/Tony Smith
films	Rhythm 21 (1921)/Hans Richter
	Lightplay: Black-White-Grey (1932)/Laszlo Moholy-Nagy (excerpt)
	Site (1964)/Robert Morris/Stan VanDerBeek (excerpt)
	Linoleum (1967)/Robert Rauschenberg (excerpt)
interview	Merce Cunningham
documents	The Creative Act (1957)/Marcel Duchamp/read by the author
	Some texts from A L'Infinitif (1912-20)/Marcel Duchamp/read by the author
	Four poems from Phantastische Gebete (1916)/Richard Huelsenbeck/read by the author
	The Realistic Manifesto (1920)/Naum Gabo/Noton Pevsner/read by Gabo
	The Russian Desert: A Note on Our State of Knowledge/Douglas MacAgy
	Space, Time and Dance (1952)/Merce Cunningham/read by the author
poetry	Conditionnement/Michel Butor/trans. Michael Benedikt
	Poem, March 1966/Dan Graham
data	Serial Project #1/Sol LeWitt
	Seven Translucent Tiers /Mel Bochner
	Structural Play #3/Brian O'Doherty
	Drawings for The Maze/Tony Smith
	Score for Fontana Mix-Feed/John Cage/Max Neuhaus
	Score for The King of Denmark/Morton Feldman
	Translation of Jealousy (recorded excerpt)/Alain Robbe-Grillet/trans. Richard Howard

Texts published in *Aspen*, No. 5-6, Fall–Winter 1967

For Mallarmé, as for us, it is language which speaks, not the author: to write is to reach, though a preexisting impersonality – never to be confused with the castrating objectivity of the realistic novelist – that point where language alone acts, 'performs', and not 'oneself'.

Roland Barthes
"The Death of the Author," 1967

The art of our time is noisy with appeals for silence.

Susan Sontag
"The Aesthetics of Silence," 1967

When flow and change are ignored, and when development is disregarded, style remains useful as a taxonomic convenience. But wherever the passage of time is under consideration, with its shifting identities and continuous transformations, the taxonomic notion, represented by the term style, becomes irrelevant.

George Kubler
"Style and Representation of Historical Time," 1967

Thence in painting we renounce color as a pictorial element; color is the idealized optical surface of objects; an exterior and superficial impression of them; color is accidental and it has nothing in common with the innermost essence of a thing. *We affirm* that the tone of a substance, i. e. its light-absorbing material body, is its only pictorial reality.

Naum Gabo, Noton Pevsner
"The Realistic Manifesto," 1920

For me, it seems enough that dancing is a spiritual exercise in physical form, and that what is seen, is what it is.

Merce Cunningham
"Space, Time and Dance," 1952

All in all, the creative act is not performed by the artist alone; the spectator brings the work in contact with the external world by deciphering and interpretating its inner qualifications and thus adds his contribution to the creative act.

Marcel Duchamp
"The Creative Act," 1957

The aim of the artist would not be to instruct the viewer but to give him information. Whether the viewer understands this information is incidental to the artist; he cannot foresee the understanding of all his viewers. He would follow his predetermined premise to its conclusion avoiding subjectivity. Chance, taste, or unconsciously remembered forms would play no part in the outcome.

Sol LeWitt
"Serial Project," 1966

Texts published in Aspen, No. 5-6, Fall-Winter, 1967

1. Graphed High, Middle and Low, with each box equal to MM 66-92. The top line or slightly above the top line, very high. The bottom line or slightly beneath, very low.
2. Numbers represent the amount of sounds to be played in each box.
3. All instruments to be played without sticks or mallets. The performer may use fingers, hand, or any part of his arm.
4. Dynamics are extremely low, and as equal as possible.
5. The thick horizontal line designates clusters. (Instruments should be varied when possible.)
6. Roman numerals represent simultaneous sounds.
7. Large numbers (encompassing High, Middle and Low) indicate single sounds to be played in all registers and in any time sequence.
8. Broken lines indicate sustained sounds.
9. Vibraphone is played without motor.

SYMBOLS USED:

B—Bell-line sounds
S—Skin Instruments
C—Cymbal
G—Gong

T—Bell-line sounds
T.R.—Skin Instruments
DELTA—Triangle
G.R.—Gong Roll

Morton Feldman

"The King of Denmark," 1964

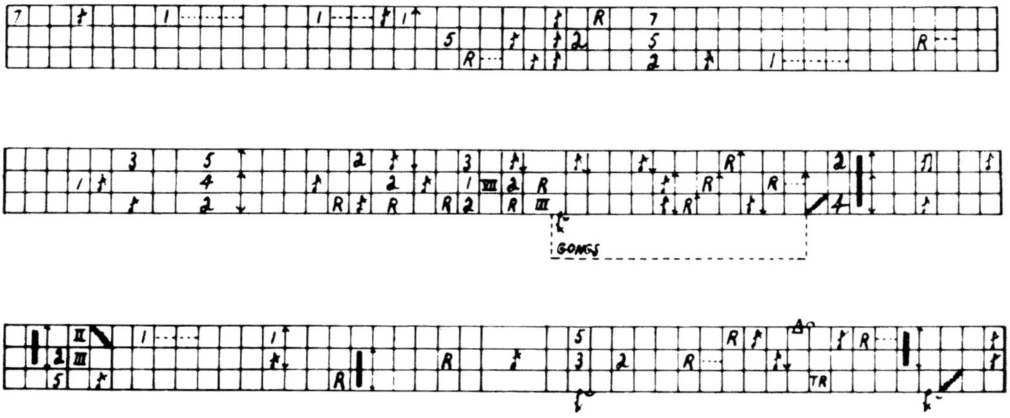

POEM

35 adjectives
7 adverbs
35,52% area not occupied by type
64,48% area occupied by type
1 columns
1 conjunctions
0 mms. depression of type into surface of page
0 gerunds
0 infinitives
247 letters of alphabet
28 lines
6 mathematical symbols
51 nouns
29 numbers
6 participles
8" x 8" page
36.287 g paper sheet
dull coated paper stock
0,01777 cm paper stock
3 prepositions
0 pronouns
10 size type
Universe 55 typeface
61 words
3 words capitalized
0 words italicized
58 words not capitalized
61 words not italicized

Dan Graham
"Poem Schema," 1966 -1967

Next double page:
Dan Graham
Homes for America, 1965-1970
[cat. 662]

Homes for America

D. GRAHAM

Belleplain	**Garden City**
Brooklawn	**Garden City Park**
Colonia	**Greenlawn**
Colonia Manor	**Island Park**
Fair Haven	**Levitown**
Fair Lawn	**Middleville**
Greenfields Village	**New City Park**
Green Village	**Pine Lawn**
Plainsboro	**Plainview**
Pleasant Grove	**Plandome Manor**
Pleasant Plains	**Pleasantside**
Sunset Hill Garden	**Pleasantville**

Large-scale 'tract' housing 'developments' constitute the new city. They are located everywhere. They are not particularly bound to existing communities; they fail to develop either regional characteristics or separate identity. These 'projects' date from the end of World War II when in southern California speculators or 'operative' builders adapted mass production techniques to quickly build many houses for the defense workers over-concentrated there. This 'California Method' consisted simply of determining in advance the exact amount and lengths of pieces of lumber and multiplying them by the number of standardized houses to be built. A cutting yard was set up near the site of the project to saw rough lumber into those sizes. By mass buying, greater use of machines and factory produced parts, assembly line standardization, multiple units were easily fabricated.

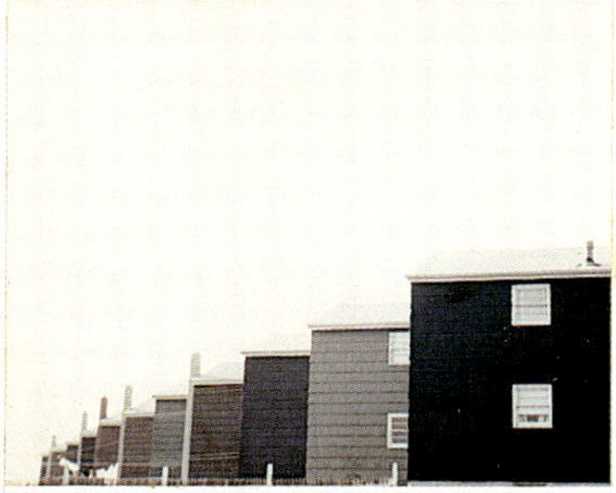

Housing Development, rear view, Bayonne, New Jersey

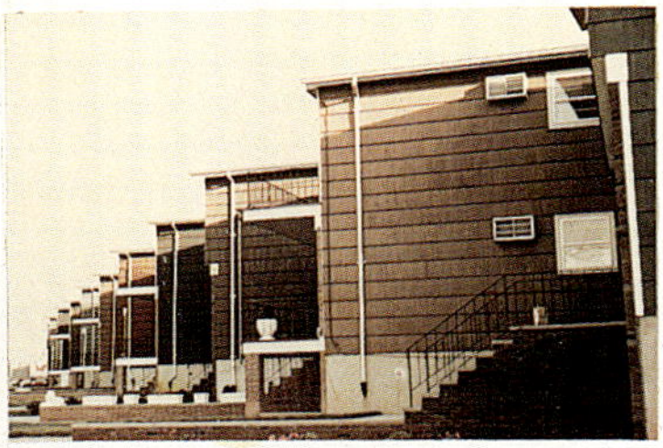

Housing Development, front view, Bayonne, New Jersey

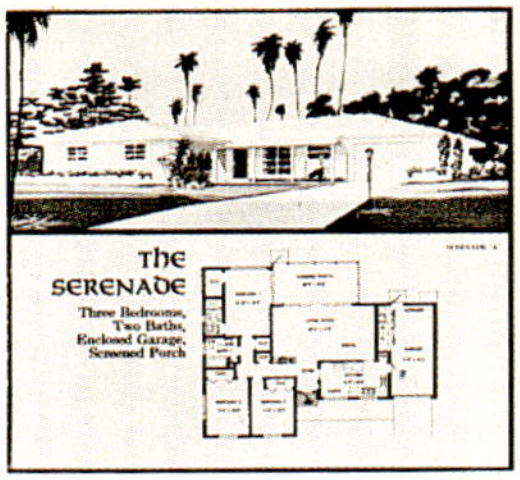

"The Serenade" - Cape Coral unit, Fla.

Each house in a development is a lightly constructed 'shell' although this fact is often concealed by fake (half-stone) brick walls. Shells can be added or subtracted easily. The standard unit is a box or a series of boxes, sometimes contemptuously called 'pillboxes.' When the box has a sharply oblique roof it is called a Cape Cod. When it is longer than wide it is a 'ranch.' A

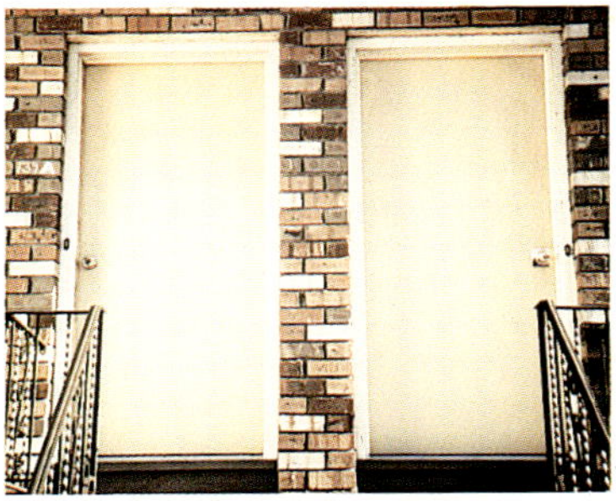

Two Entrance Doorways, 'Two Home Homes', Jersey City, N.J.

two-story house is usually called 'colonial.' If it consists of contiguous boxes with one slightly higher elevation it is a 'split level.' Such stylistic differentiation is advantageous to the basic structure (with the possible exception of the split level whose plan simplifies construction on discontinuous ground levels).

There is a recent trend toward 'two home homes' which are two boxes split by adjoining walls and having separate entrances. The left and right hand units are mirror reproductions of each other. Often sold as private units are strings of apartment-like, quasi-discrete cells formed by subdividing laterally an extended rectangular parallelopiped into as many as ten or twelve separate dwellings.

Developers usually build large groups of individual homes sharing similar floor plans and whose overall grouping possesses a discrete flow plan. Regional shopping centers and industrial parks are sometimes integrated as well into the general scheme. Each development is sectioned into blocked-out areas containing a series of identical or sequentially related types of houses all of which have uniform or staggered set-backs and land plots.

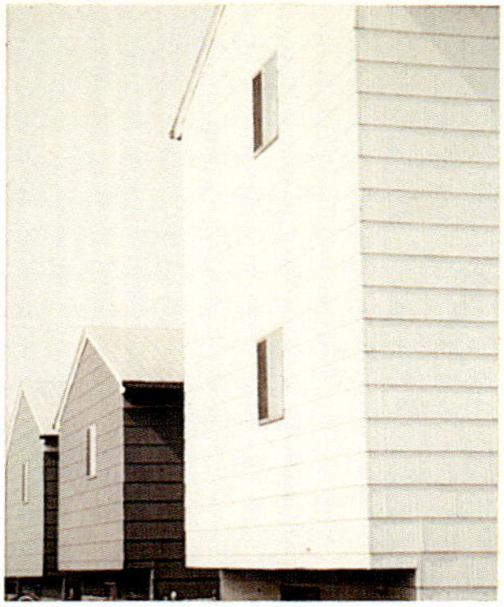

Set-back, Jersey City, New Jersey

The logic relating each sectioned part to the entire plan follows a systematic plan. A development contains a limited, set number of house models. For instance, Cape Coral, a Florida project, advertises eight different models:

A The Sonata
B The Concerto
C The Overture
D The Ballet
E The Prelude
F The Serenade
G The Noctune
H The Rhapsody

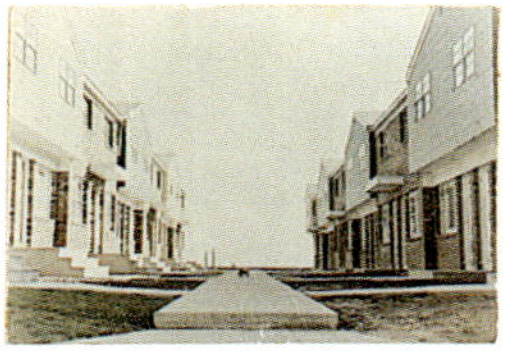

Center Court, Entrances, Development, Jersey City, N.J.

In addition, there is a choice of eight exterior colors:
1 White
2 Moonstone Grey
3 Nickle

LAWN GREEN

4 Seafoam Green
5 Lawn Green
6 Bamboo
7 Coral Pink
8 Colonial Red

As the color series usually varies independently of the model series, a block of eight houses utilizing four models and four colors might have forty-eight times forty-eight or 2,304 possible arrangements.

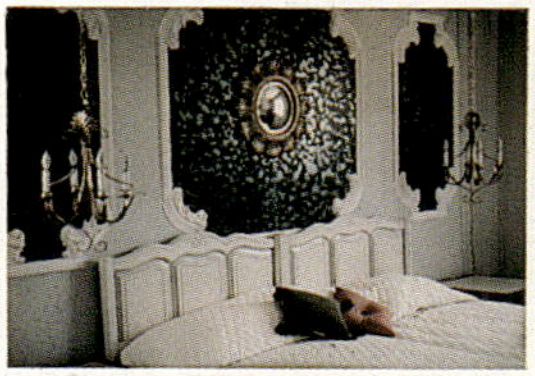

Interior of Model Home, Staten Island, N.Y.

Each block of houses is a self-contained sequence — there is no development — selected from the possible acceptable arrangements. As an example, if a section was to contain eight houses of which four model types were to be used, any of these permutational possibilities could be used:

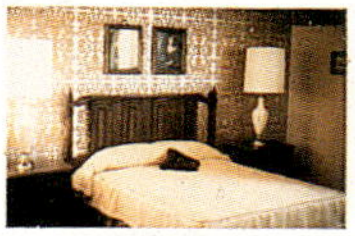

Bedroom of Model Home, S.I., N.Y.

AABBCCDD	ABCDABCD
AABBDDCC	ABDCABDC
AACCBBDD	ACBDACBD
AACCDDBB	ACDBACDB
AADDCCBB	ADBCADBC
AADDBBCC	ADCBADCB
BBAADDCC	BACDBACD
BBCCAADD	BCADBCAD
BBCCDDAA	BCDABCDA
BBDDAACC	BDACBDAC
BBDDCCAA	BDCABDCA
CCAABBDD	CABDCABD
CCAADDBB	CADBCADB
CCBBDDAA	CBADCBAD
CCBBAADD	CBDACBDA
CCDDAABB	CDABCDAB
CCDDBBAA	CDBACDBA
DDAABBCC	DACBDACB
DDAACCBB	DABCDABC
DDBBAACC	DBACDBAC
DDBBCCAA	DBCADBCA
DDCCAABB	DCABDCAB
DDCCBBAA	DCBADCBA

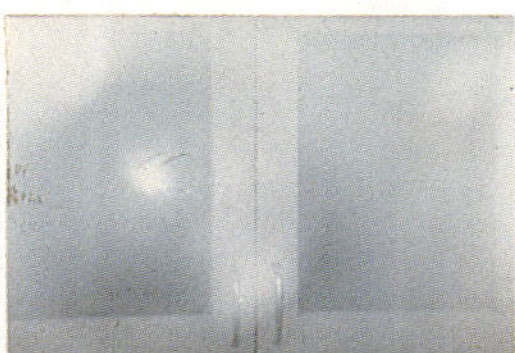

Basement Doors, Home, New Jersey

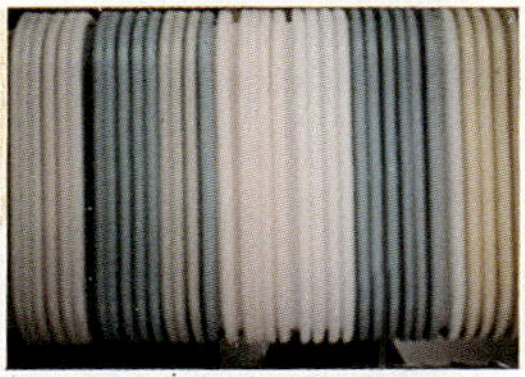

'Discount Store', Sweaters on Racks, New Jersey

The 8 color variables were equally distributed among the house exteriors. The first buyers were more likely to have obtained their first choice in color. Family units had to make a choice based on the available colors which also took account of both husband and wife's likes and dislikes. Adult male and female color likes and dislikes were compared in a survey of the homeowners:

'Like'

Male	Female
Skyway	Skyway Blue
Colonial Red	Lawn Green
Patio White	Nickle
Yellow Chiffon	Colonial Red
Lawn Green	Yellow Chiffon
Nickle	Patio White
Fawn	Moonstone Grey
Moonstone Grey	Fawn

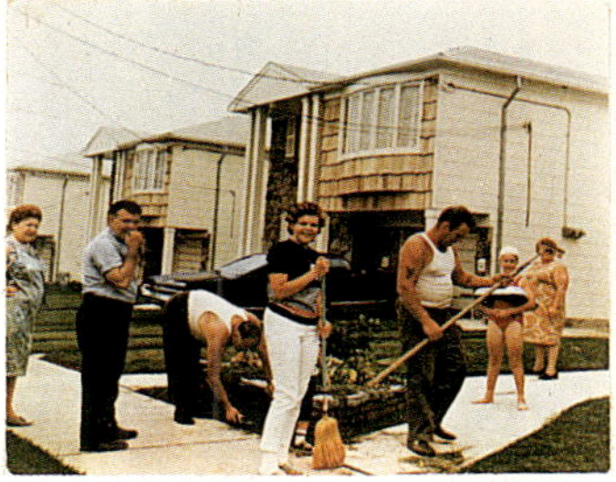

Two Family Units, Staten Island, N.Y.

'Dislike'

Male	Female
Lawn Green	Patio White
Colonial Red	Fawn
Patio White	Colonial Red
Moonstone Grey	Moonstone Grey
Fawn	Yellow Chiffon
Yellow Chiffon	Lawn Green
Nickle	Skyway blue
Skyway Blue	Nickle

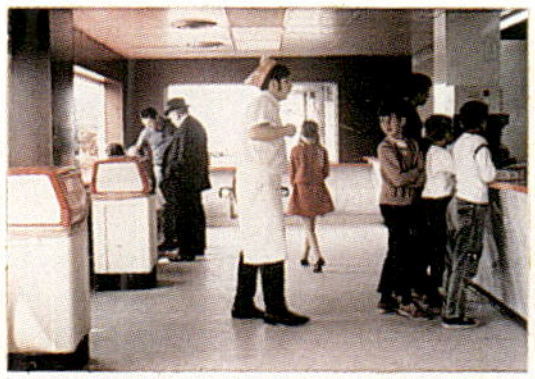

Car Hop, Jersey City, N.J.

A given development might use, perhaps, *four* of these possibilities as an arbitrary scheme for different sectors; then select four from another scheme which utilizes the remaining four unused models and colors; then select four from another scheme which utilizes all eight models and eight colors; then four from another scheme which utilizes a single model and all eight colors (or four or two colors); and finally utilize that single scheme for one model and one color. This serial logic might follow consistently until, at the edges, it is abruptly terminated by pre-existent highways, bowling alleys, shopping plazas, car hops, discount houses, lumber yards or factories.

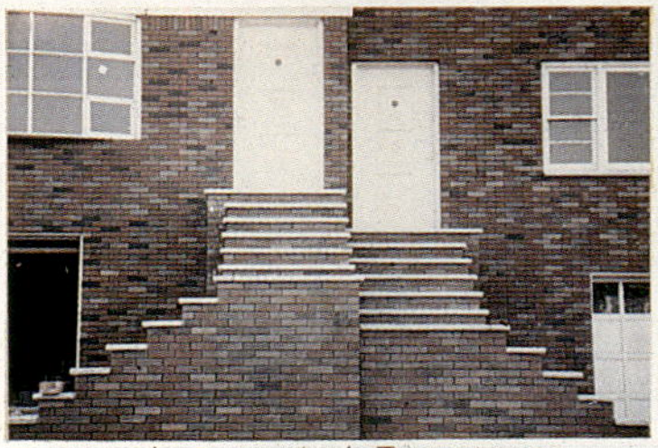

'Split-Level', 'Two Home Homes', Jersey City, N.J.

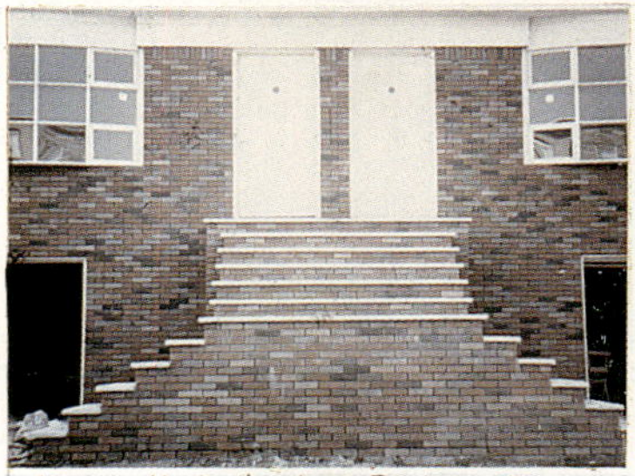

'Ground-Level', 'Two Home Homes', Jersey City, N.J.

Although there is perhaps some aesthetic precedence in the row houses which are indigenous to many older cities along the east coast, and built with uniform façades and set-backs early this century, housing developments as an architectural phenomenon seem peculiarly gratuitous. They exist apart from prior standards of 'good' architecture. They were not built to satisfy individual needs or tastes. The owner is completely tangential to the product's completion. His home isn't really possessable in the old sense; it wasn't designed to 'last for generations'; and outside of its immediate 'here and now' context it is useless, designed to be thrown away. Both architecture and craftsmanship as values are subverted by the dependence on simplified and easily duplicated techniques of fabrication and standardized modular plans. Contingencies such as mass production technology and land use economics make the final decisions, denying the architect his former 'unique' role. Developments stand in an altered relationship to their environment. Designed to fill in 'dead' land areas, the houses needn't adapt to or attempt to withstand Nature. There is no organic unity connecting the land site and the home. Both are without roots — separate parts in a larger, predetermined, synthetic order.

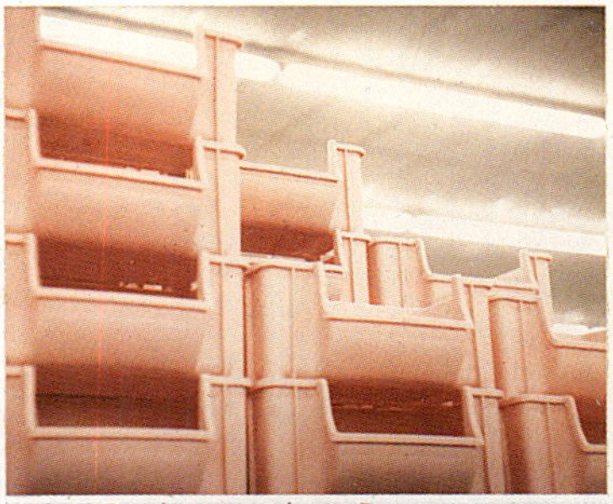

Kitchen Trays, 'Discount House', New Jersey

Dan Graham

Silence	Silence	Silence
Silence	Silence	Silence
Silence		Silence
Silence	Silence	Silence
Silence	Silence	Silence

Eugen Gomringer
Silence (Schweigen), 1960

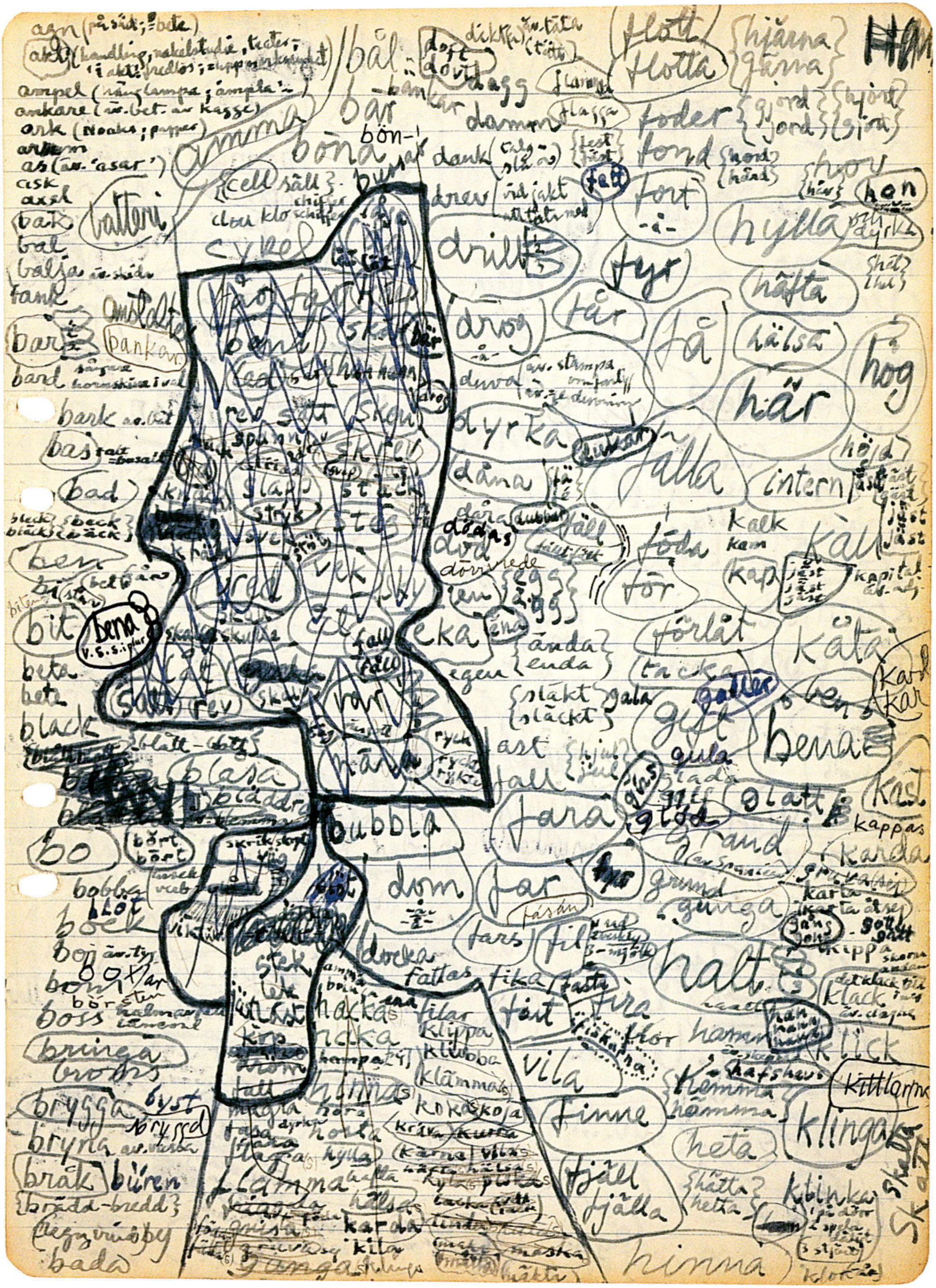
agn
akt
ampel
ankare
ark
as
ask
axel
bak
bal
balja
bank
bar
band
bark
bas
bad
ben
bit
bena
beta
black
blåsa
bladdra
bo
bobba
bock
boss
bringa
brygga
bryna
bråk
bada
bål
bar
böna
amma
batteri
cell
cykel
dank
drev
drill
drog
duva
dyrka
dåna
dövd
egen
ända
enda
släkt
släckt
last
fall
flott
flotta
hjärna
gärna
foder
fond
fort
hylla
fyr
får
få
häfta
hälsa
hög
här
fälla
intern
höjd
kalk
kam
kap
föda
för
kål
förlåt
kåta
tacka
gift
bena
gula
kast
fara
glatt
kappas
grand
karda
grund
gunga
bubbla
dom
far
fars
fil
fika
fast
fira
halt
klack
klick
hamn
klippa
klubba
klämma
koka
kittlarna
vila
finne
heta
klinga
fjäll
fjälla
klinka
hinna
kålla
hacka
kila

Öyvind Fahlström

Handwritten manuscript with word mutation inventories for concrete poetry, 1950

[cat. 684]

Sketch for *Whammo,* 1962

[cat. 686]

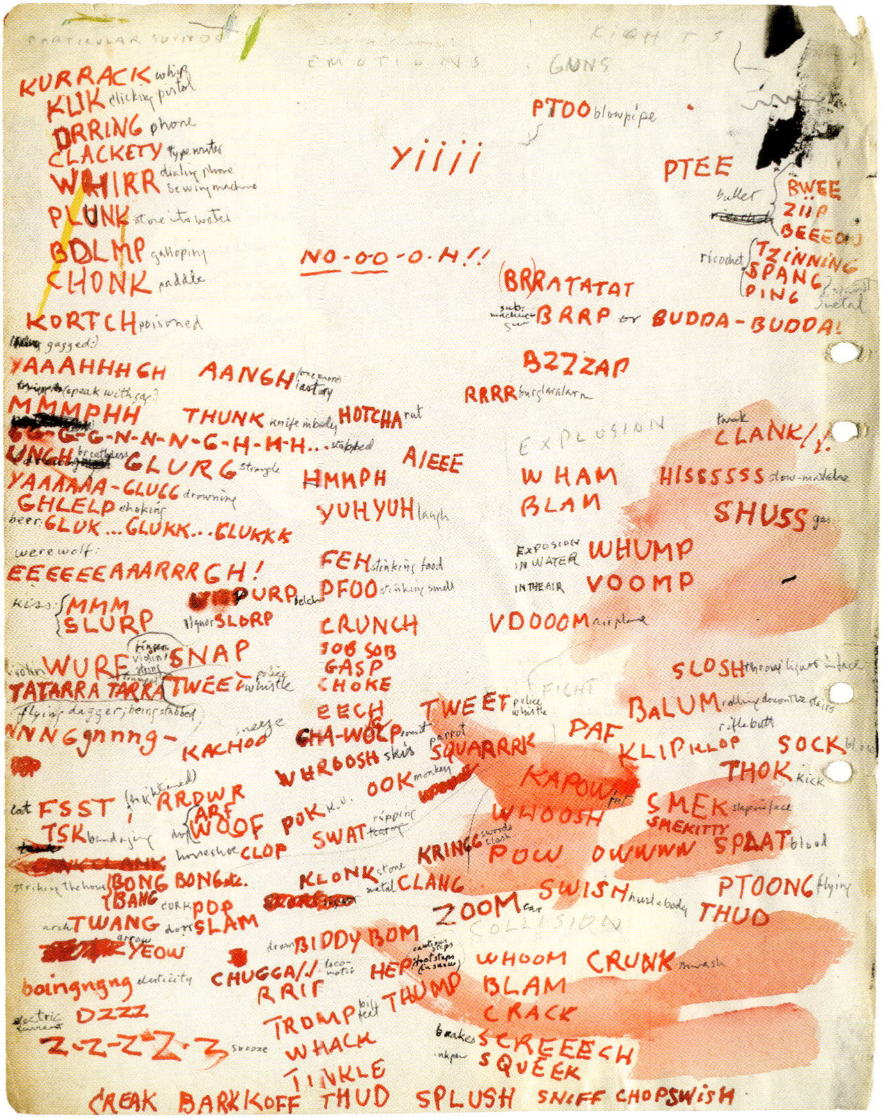

Raymond Hains

L'Affiche en yiddish, 1950

[cat. 695]

Cet homme est dangereux, 1957

[cat. 694]

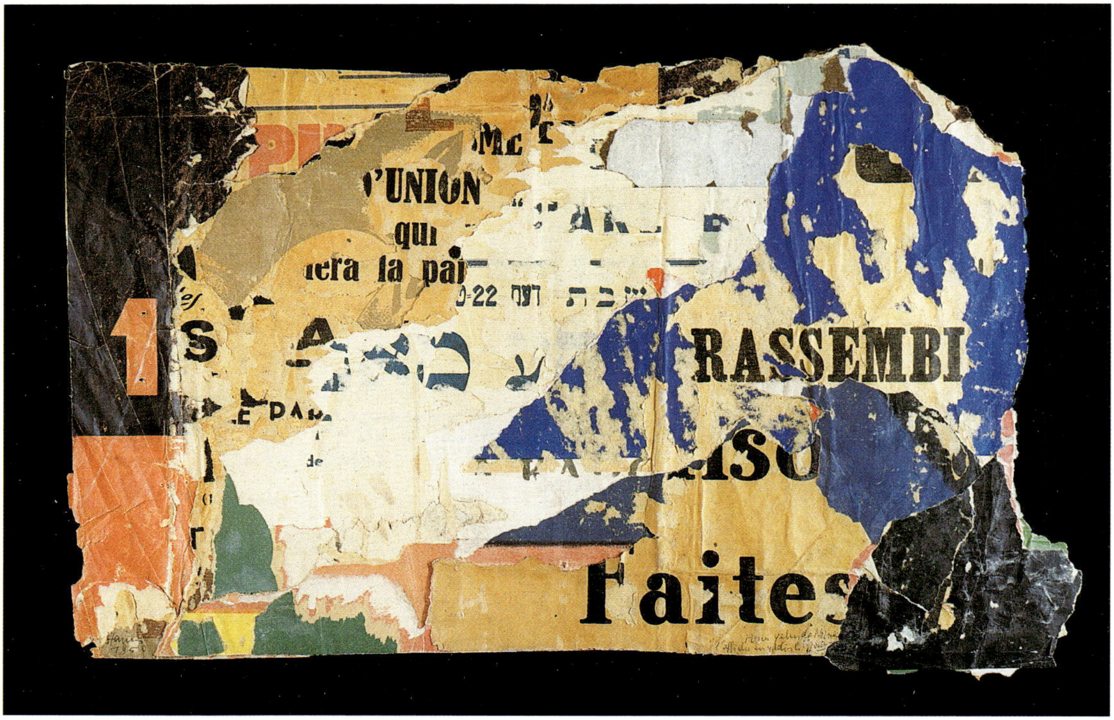

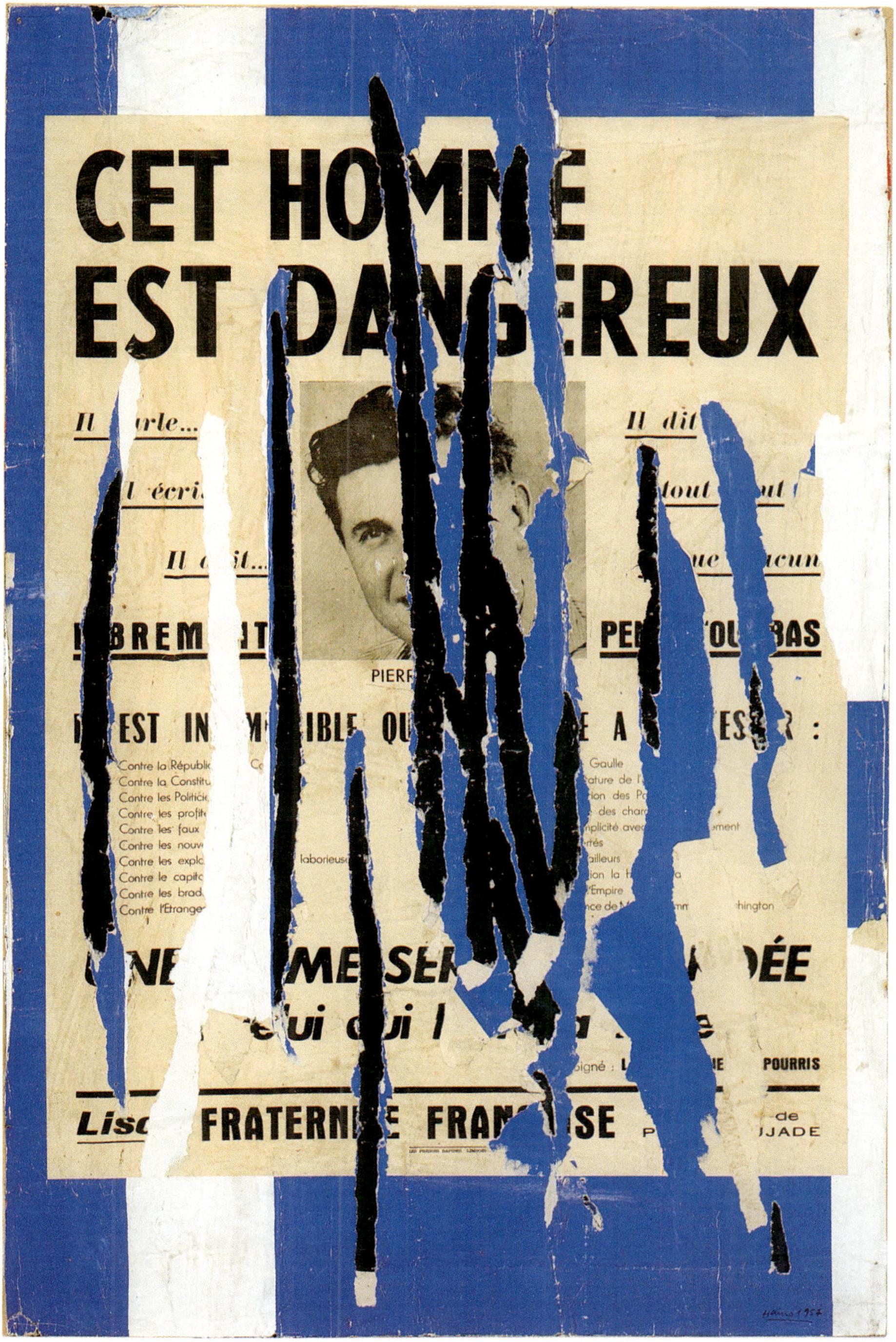
CET HOMME
EST DANGEREUX
PIERR
POURRIS

François Dufrêne

L'Inconnue ("L'Art c'est le vol" Series), 1961

[cat. 699]

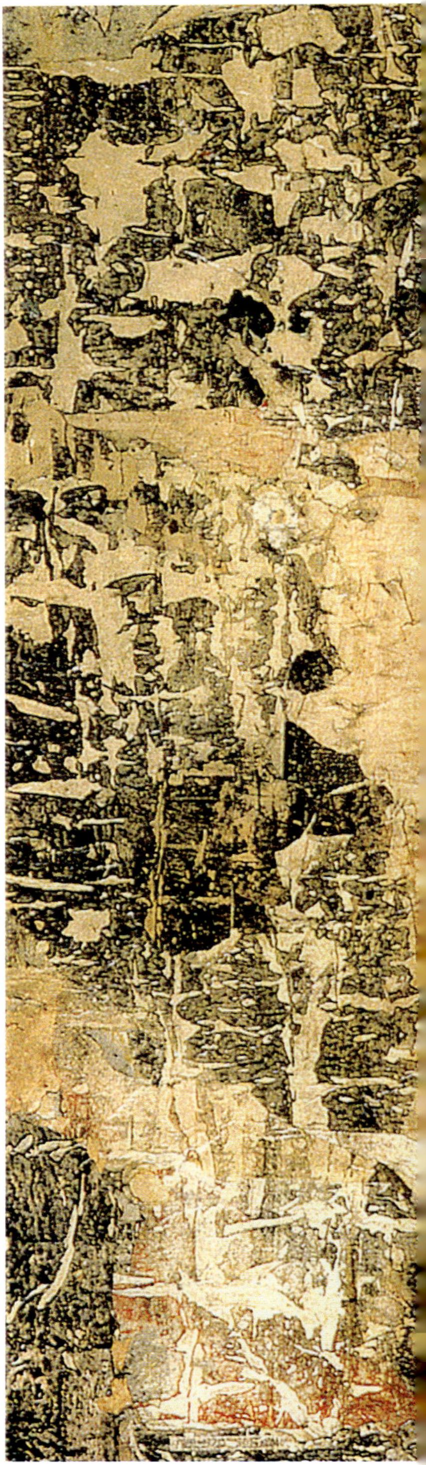

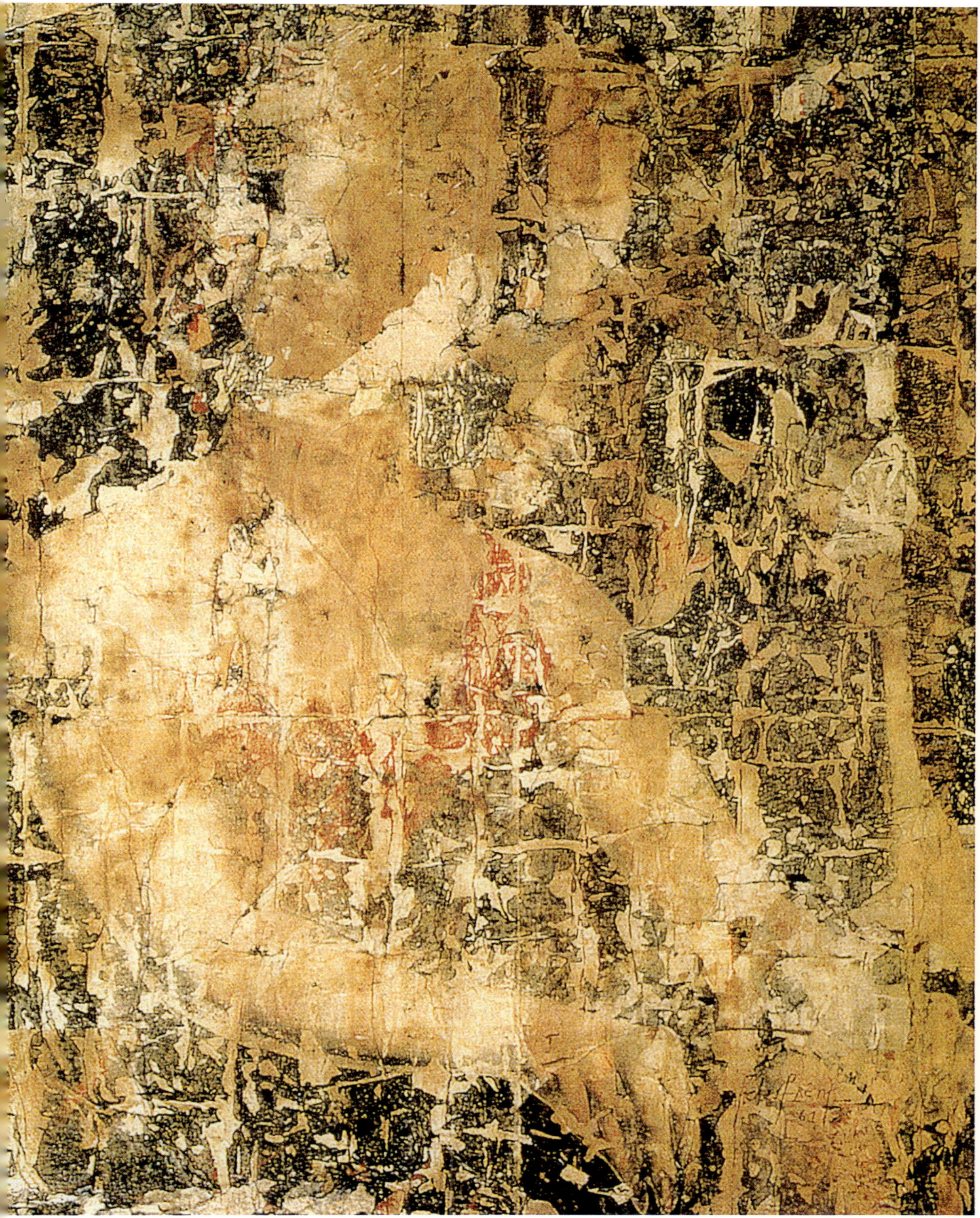

Dieter Roth

Stempelzeichnung zu Munduculum S. 299 (Alphabet), ca. 1965

[cat. 690]

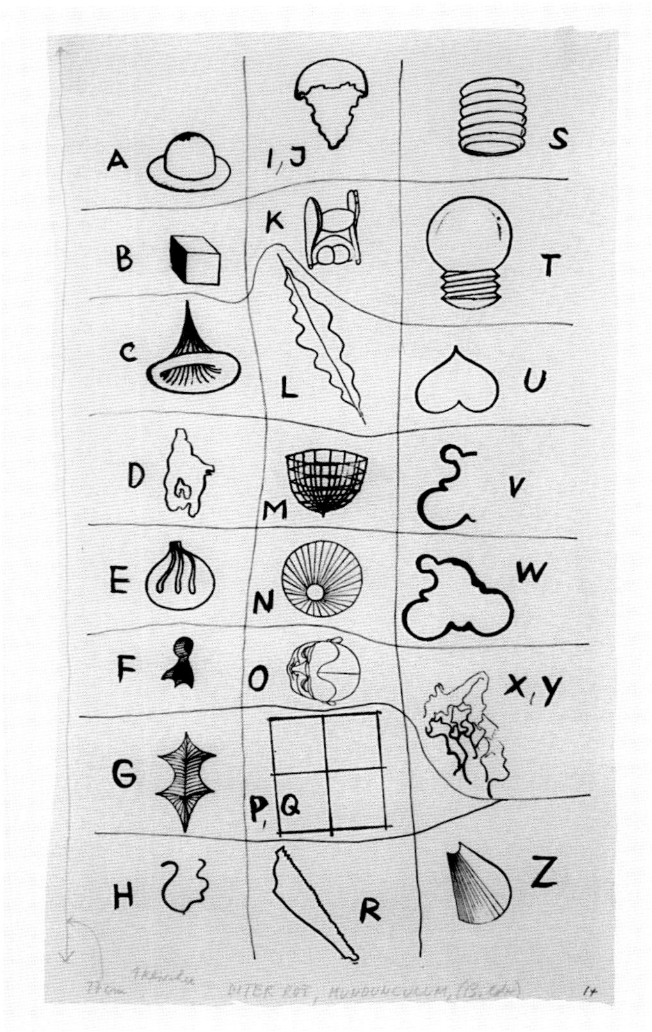

Dieter Roth

Stempelzeichnung zu Mundunculum S. 272/273, 1966
[cat. 690]

Stempelzeichnung zu Mundunculum, Umschlag, 1966
[cat. 690]

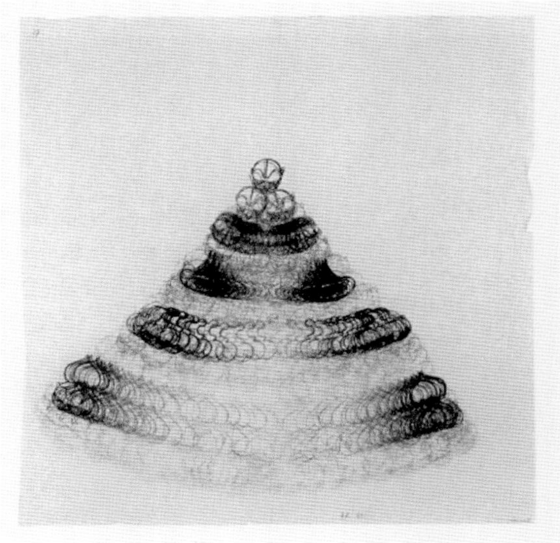

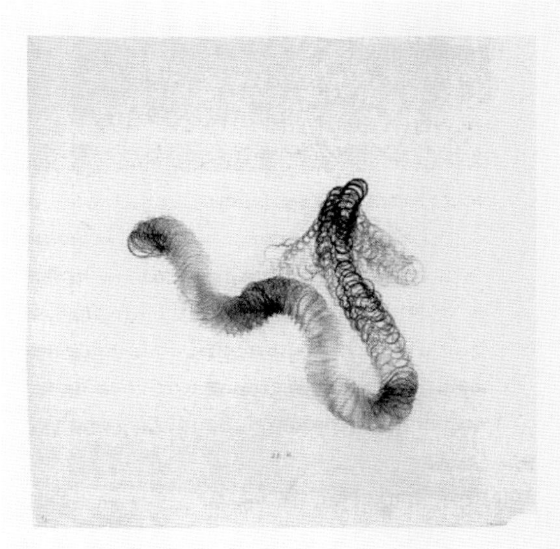

Dieter Roth

Stempelzeichnung zu Mundunculum S. 105 (Maerchen. Katalog der Tränen), ca. 1965
[cat. 690]

Stempelzeichnung zu Mundunculum S. 112/113 (Maerchen. Katalog der Tränen), ca. 1965
[cat. 690]

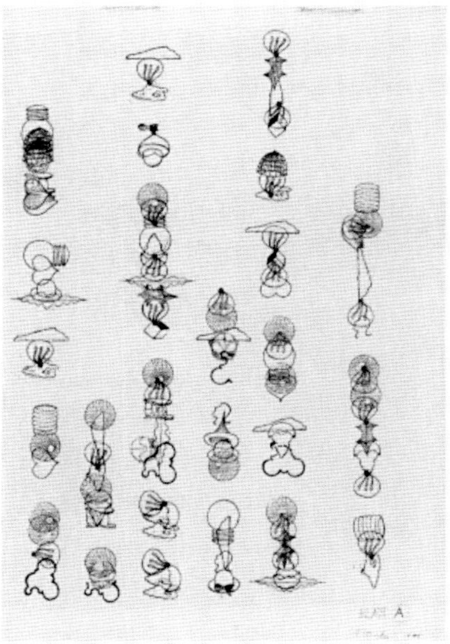

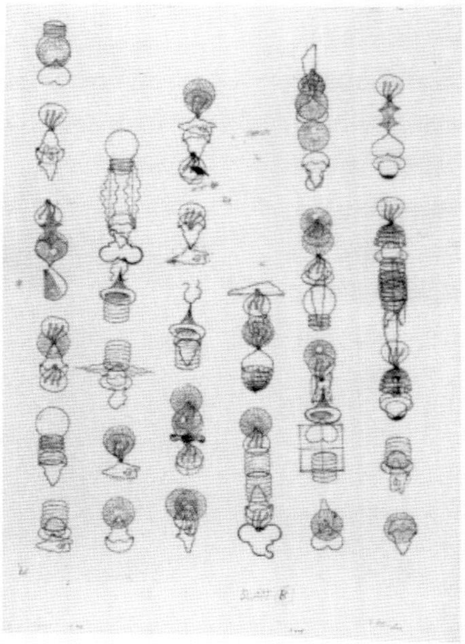

Dieter Roth

Stempelzeichnung zu Mundunculum S. 106/109 (Maerchen. Katalog der Tränen), ca. 1965
[cat. 690]

Stempelzeichnung zu Mundunculum S. 113/114 (Maerchen. Katalog der Tränen), ca. 1965
[cat. 690]

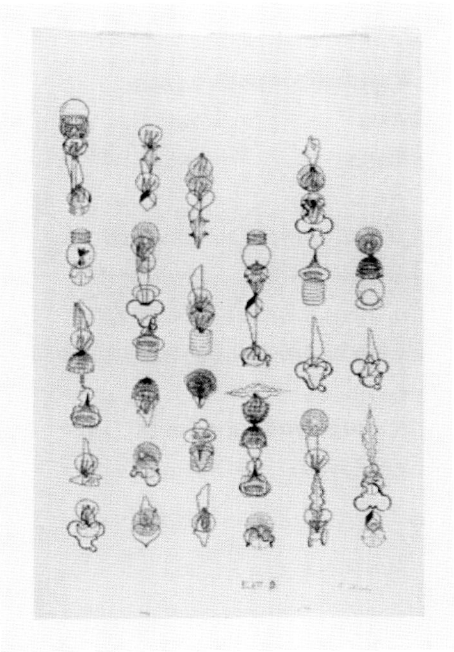

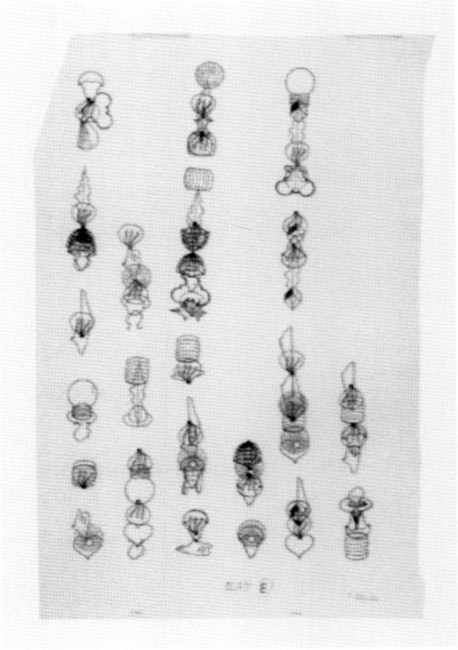

Julio Campal

Situación uno. Poesía N.O., 1959

[cat. 751]

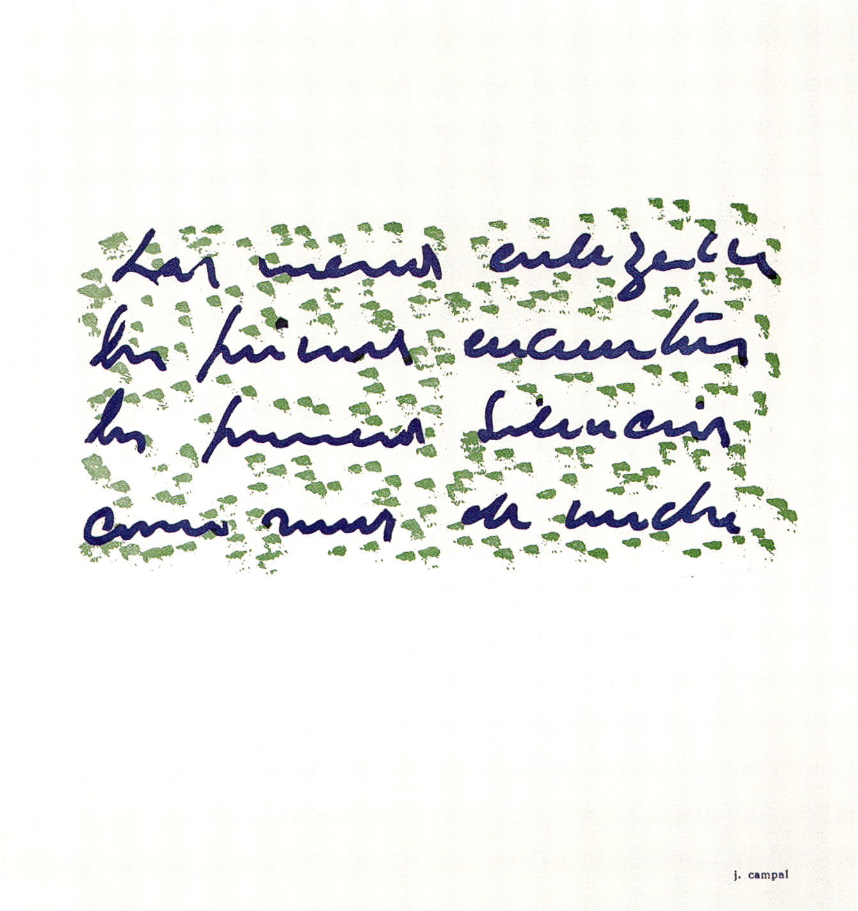

Fernando Millán

La depresión en España, 1993

[cat. 730]

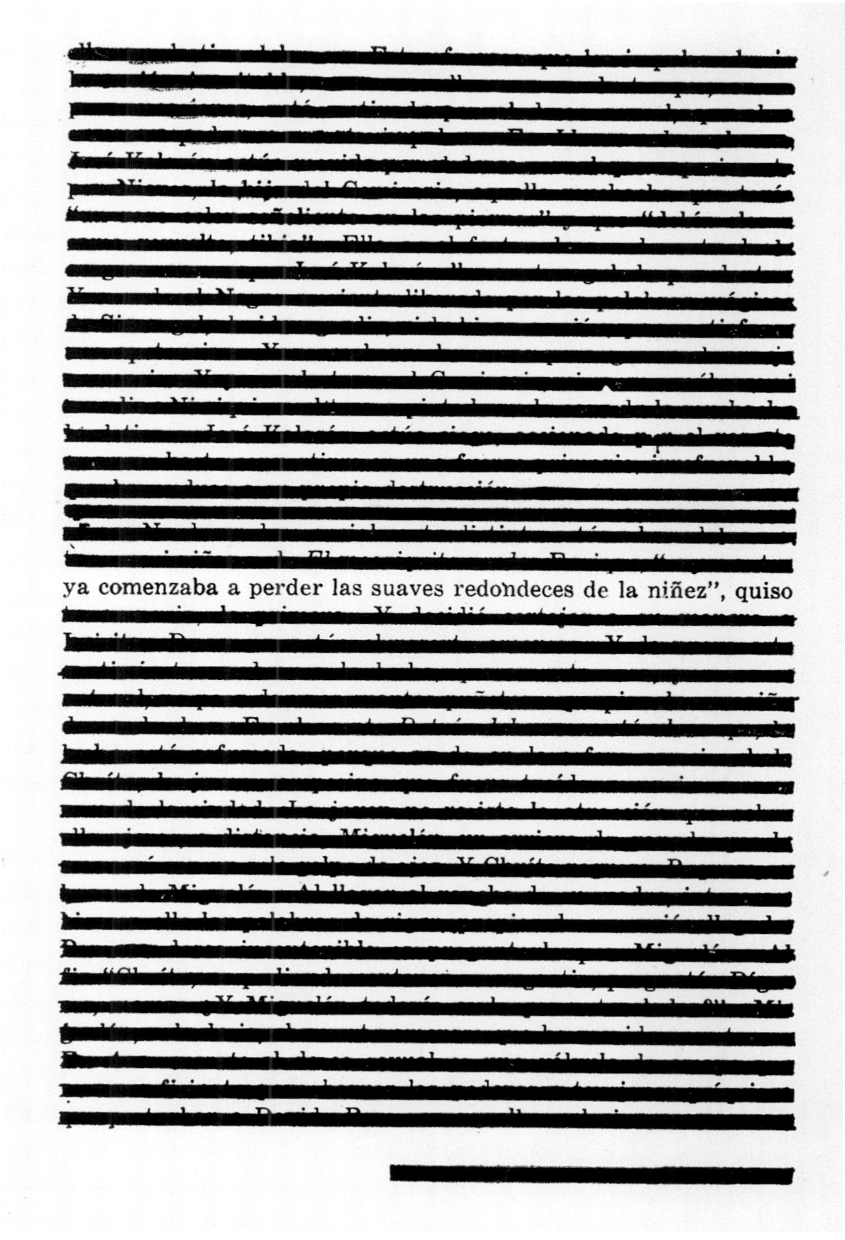

[redacted]

ya comenzaba a perder las suaves redondeces de la niñez", quiso

[redacted]

MALLARMÉ RÉVISÉ o MALARMADO REVISADO –
(Una acción de Esther Ferrer)

Se trata de realizar una acción con un adoquín marcado como un dado de juego.

Una versión, puede haber tantas como se quiera :
"Colocarse un adoquín sobre la cabeza - previamente marcado como un dado de juego - salir ante el público, pasearse o no, pero en cualquier caso, dejarlo caer al suelo (cuanto más sonoro sea éste, mejor). Agacharse, recogerlo, decir en alta voz el número y enseñarlo a la audiencia, para que comprueben que no hay trampa. Repetir la operación cuantas veces se dese, o hasta que por casualidad le caiga sobre el pié. Cuando se vaya, deje el adoquín en el centro del espacio, por si alguien desea repetir la experiencia".

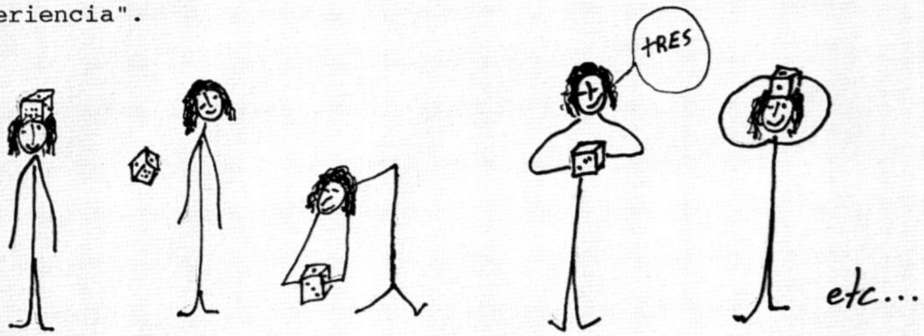

La acción puede ir acompañada de una grabación o una persona con un micrófono que repite incansablemente :

Un coup de dés, jamais n'abolira pas le hazard

Toute pensée émets un coup de dés

Esther Ferrer

Mallarmé révisé o Mallarmado revisado, 1992

[cat. 737]

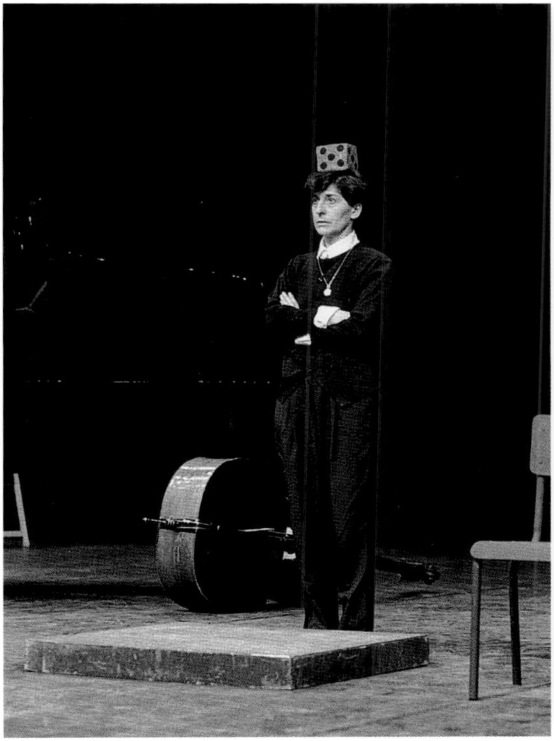

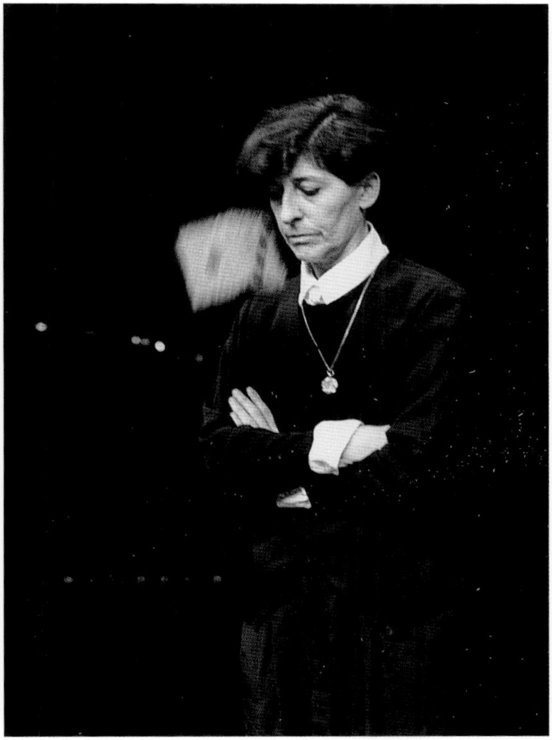

Trisha Brown

Untitled (1 of 16 drawings), 1994

[cat. 767]

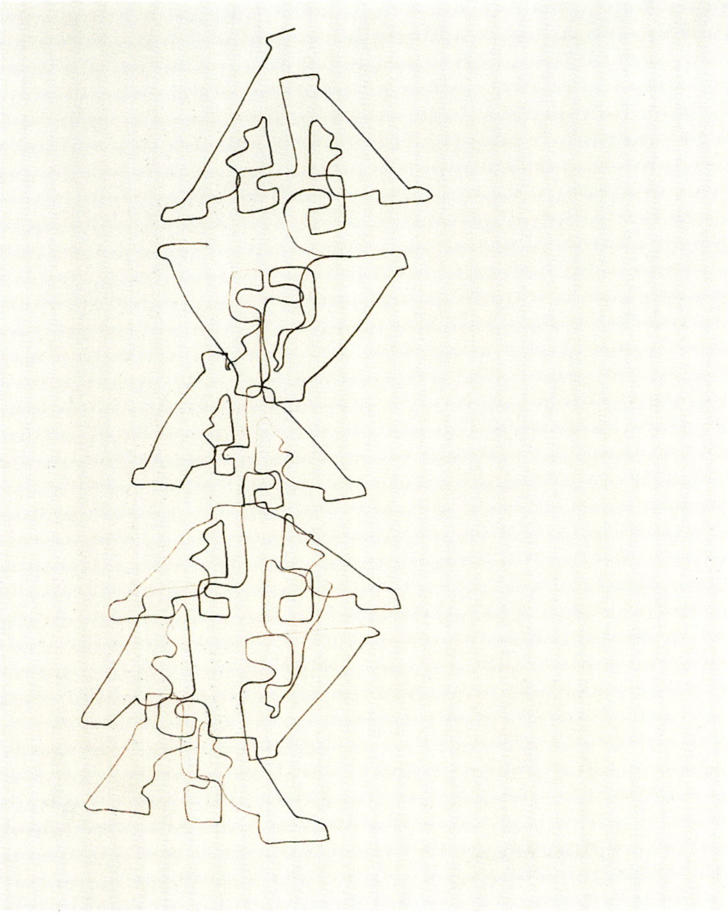

Trisha Brown
Untitled (1 of 16 drawings), 1994
[cat. 767]

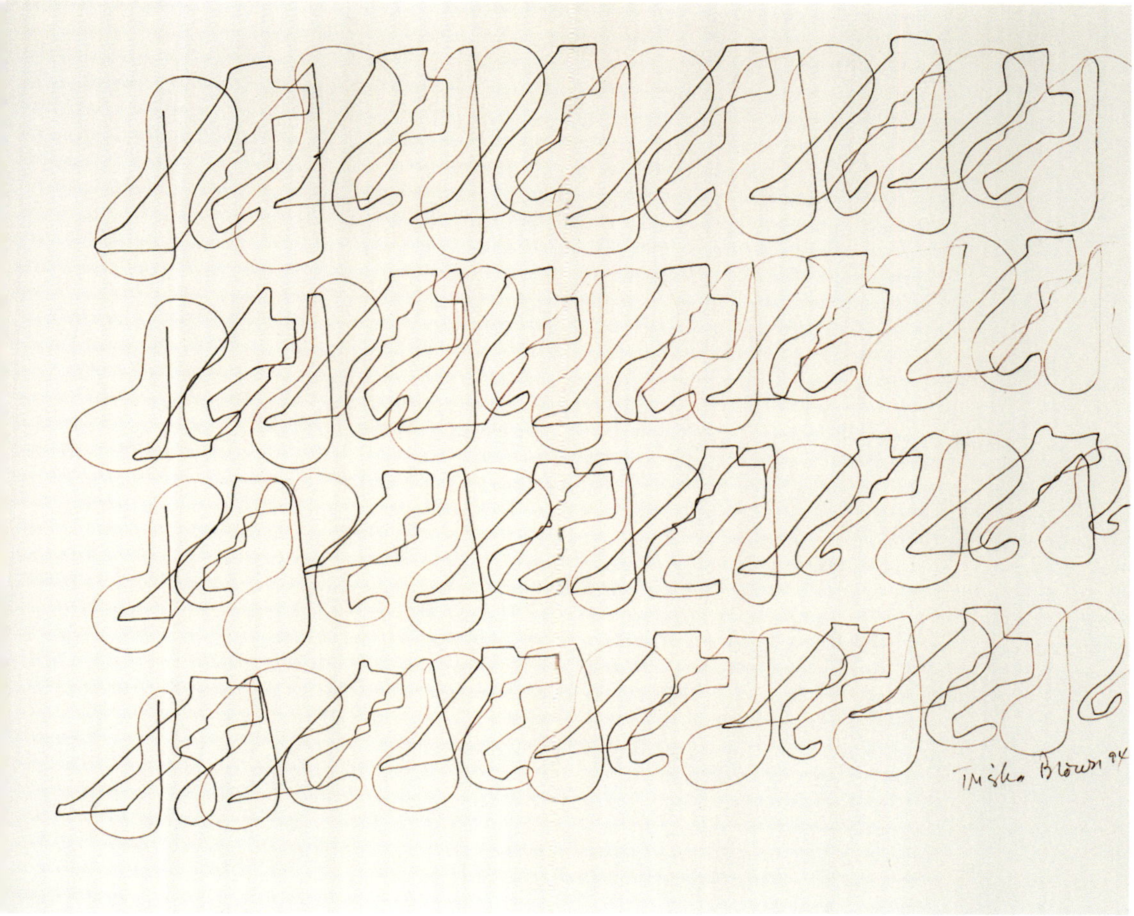

Nancy Spero

Un nœud d'asphyxie centrale ("Artaud Paintings" Series), 1969-1970

[cat. 777]

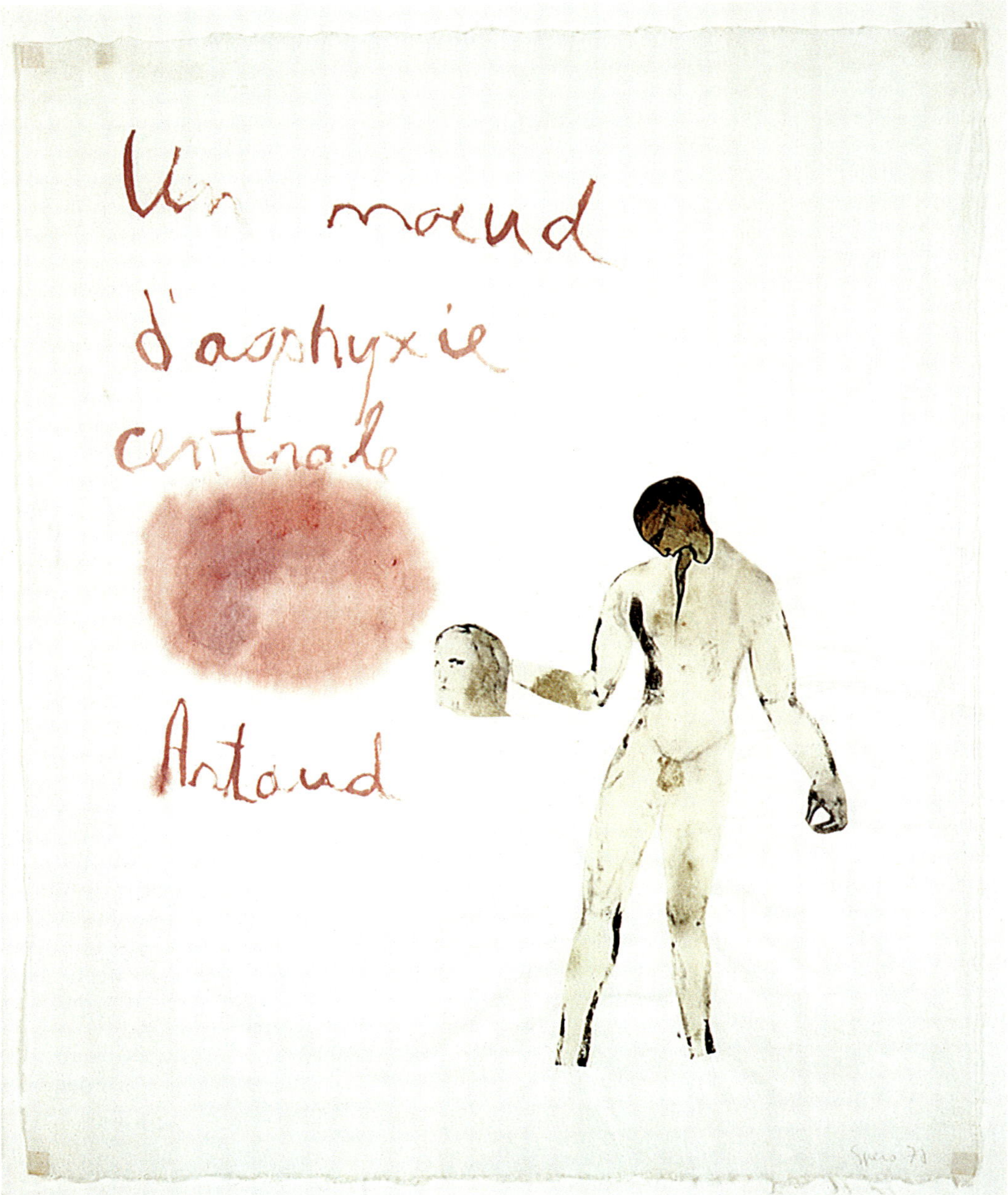

Nancy Spero

Une fatigue de commencement du monde ("Artaud Paintings" Series), 1969-1970

[cat. 777]

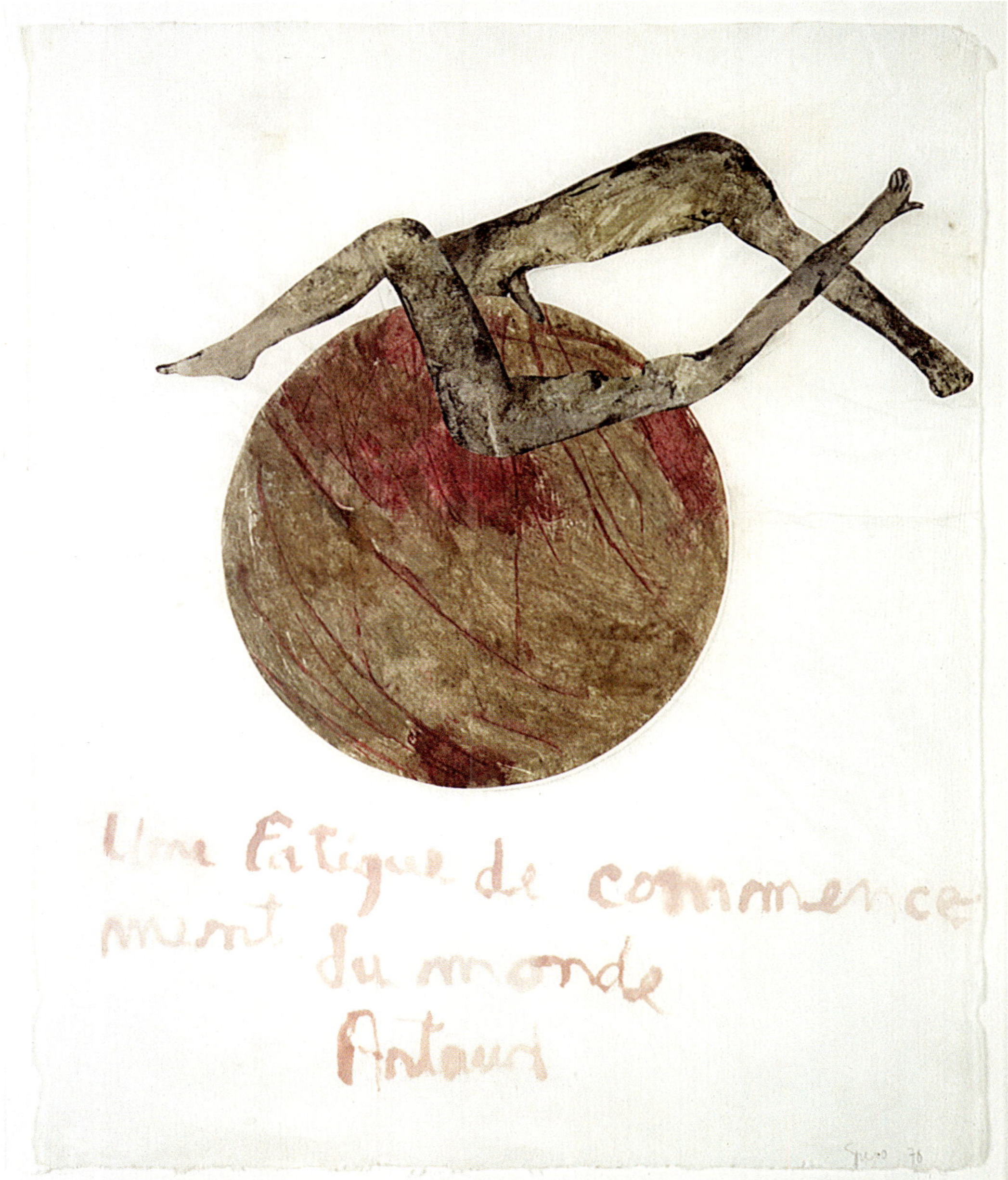

The Venal Muse

Muse of my heart, of palaces the lover,
Where will you, when the blast of winter blows
In the black boredom of snowed lights, discover
A glowing brand to warm your violet toes?

How will you there revive your marbled skin
At the chill rays your shutters then disperse?
The gold of azure heavens will you win
When empty are your palate and your purse?

You'll need each evening, then, to earn your bread,
As choirboys swinging censers that are dead
Who sing *Te Deums* which they disbelieve:

Or, fasting pierrette, trade your loveliness
And laughter, soaked in tears that none can guess,
The boredom of the vulgar to relieve.

Charles Baudelaire
"La Muse vénale," *Les Fleurs du mal,* 1857

René Daniels
La Muse vénale, 1979
[cat. 773]

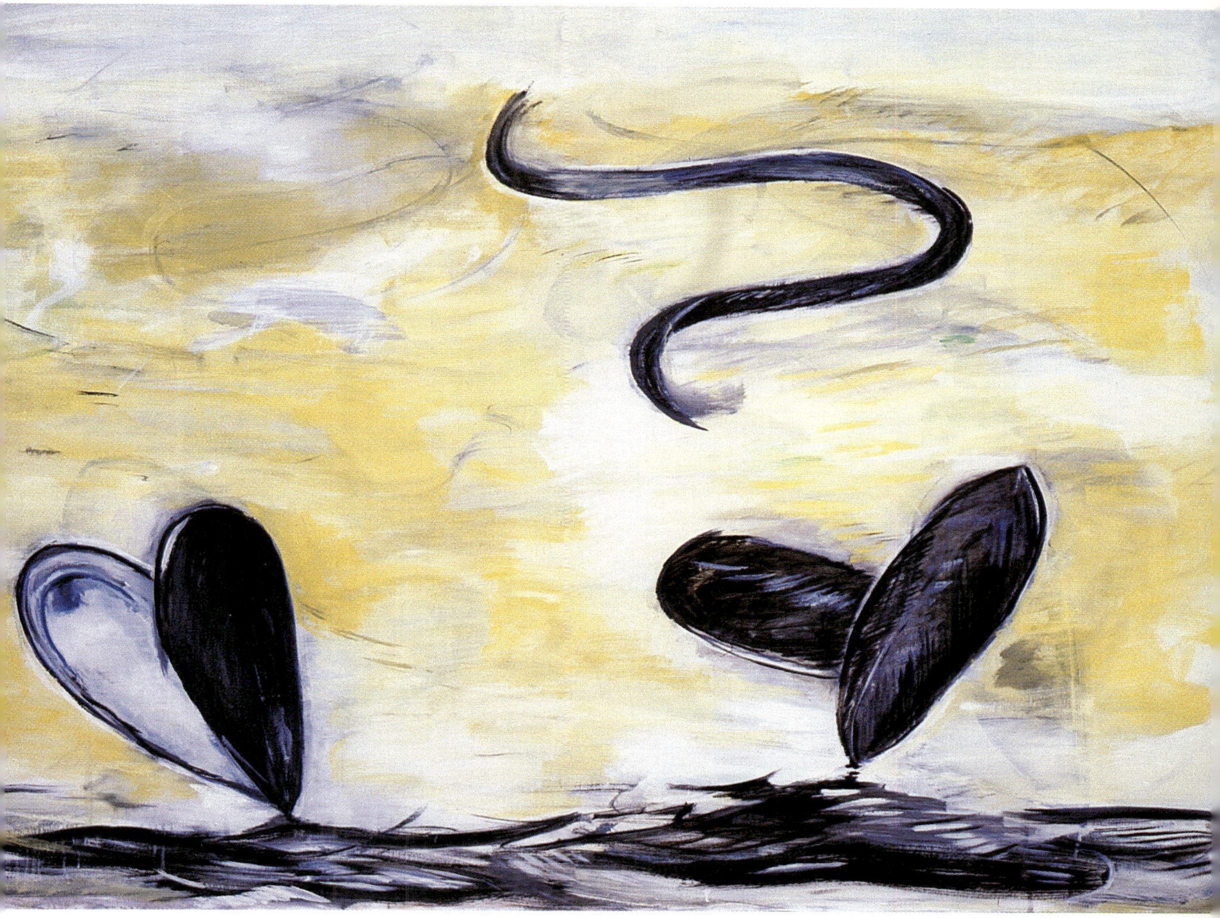

Marcel Broodthaers

Tapis de sable, 1974

[cat. 772]

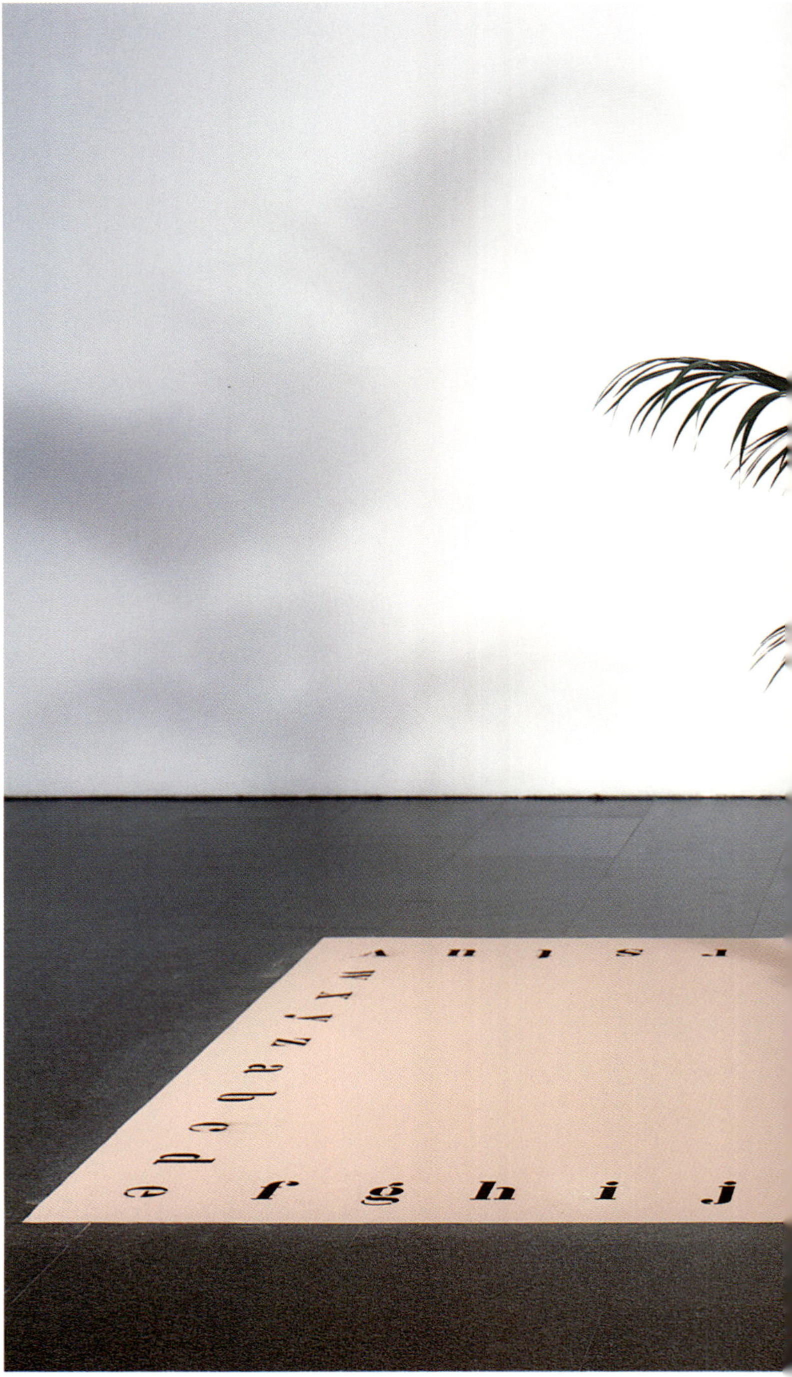

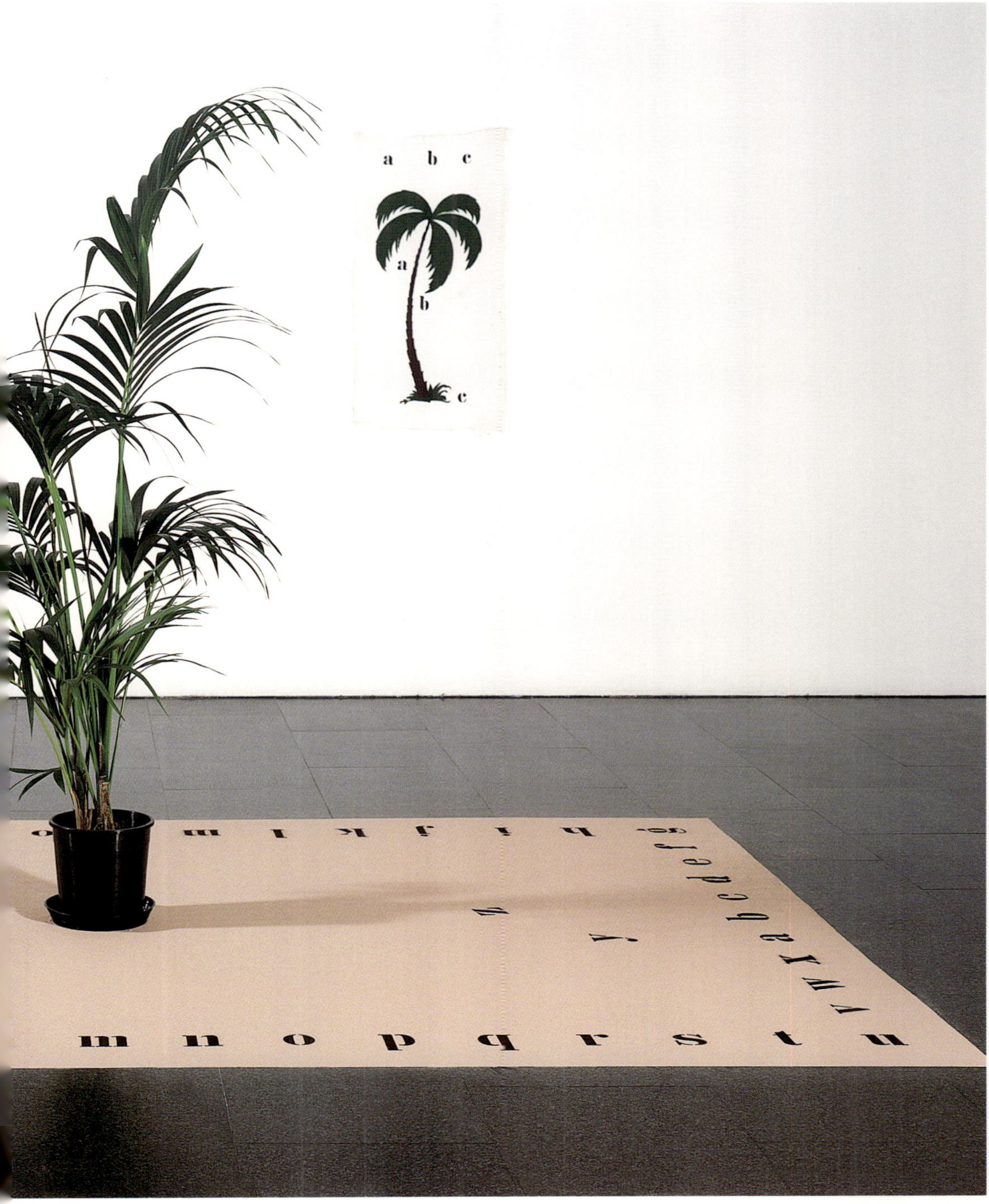
a b c
a
b
c

Alighiero Boetti

Regola Regolarsi, 1979

[cat. 771]

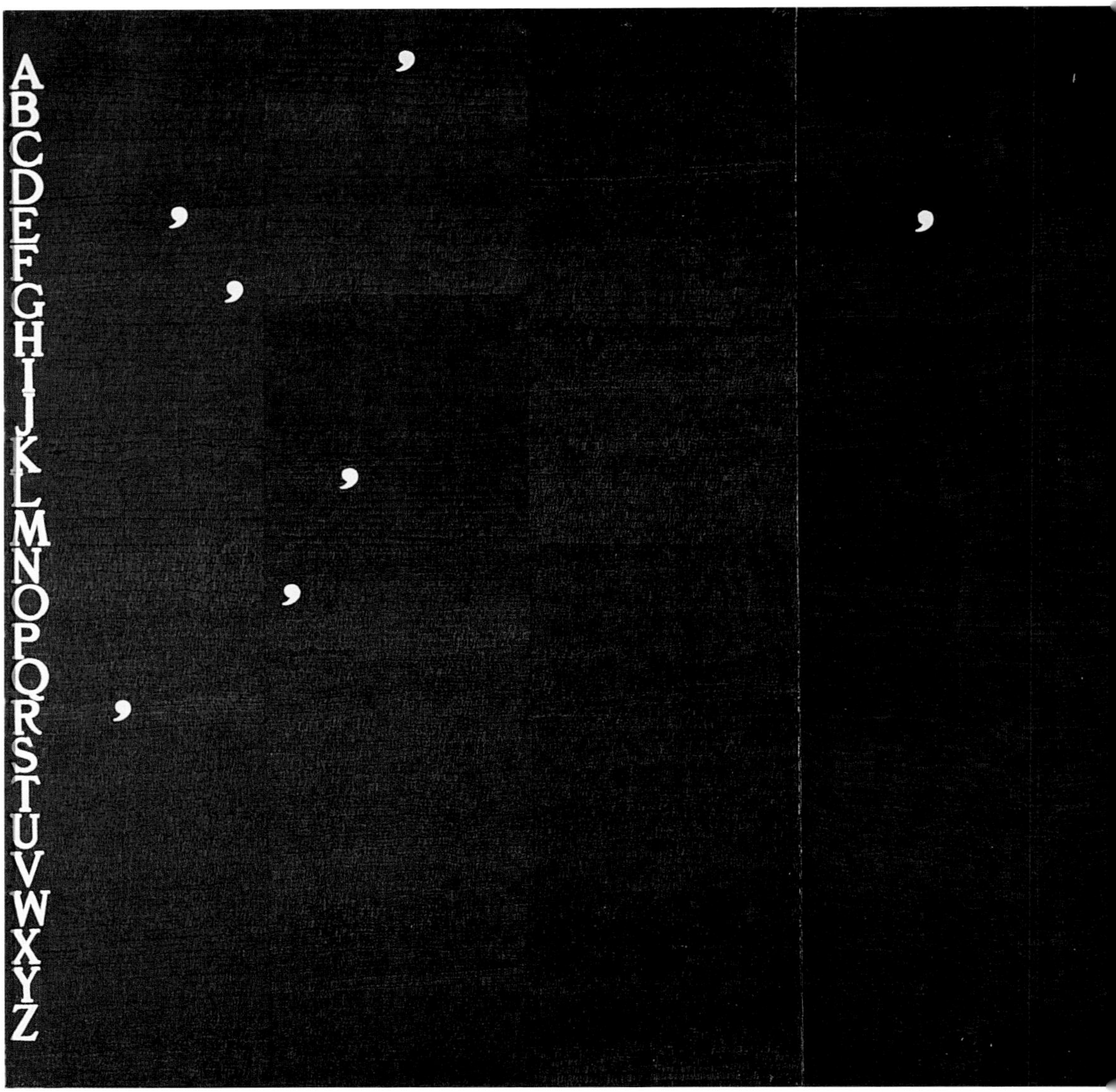

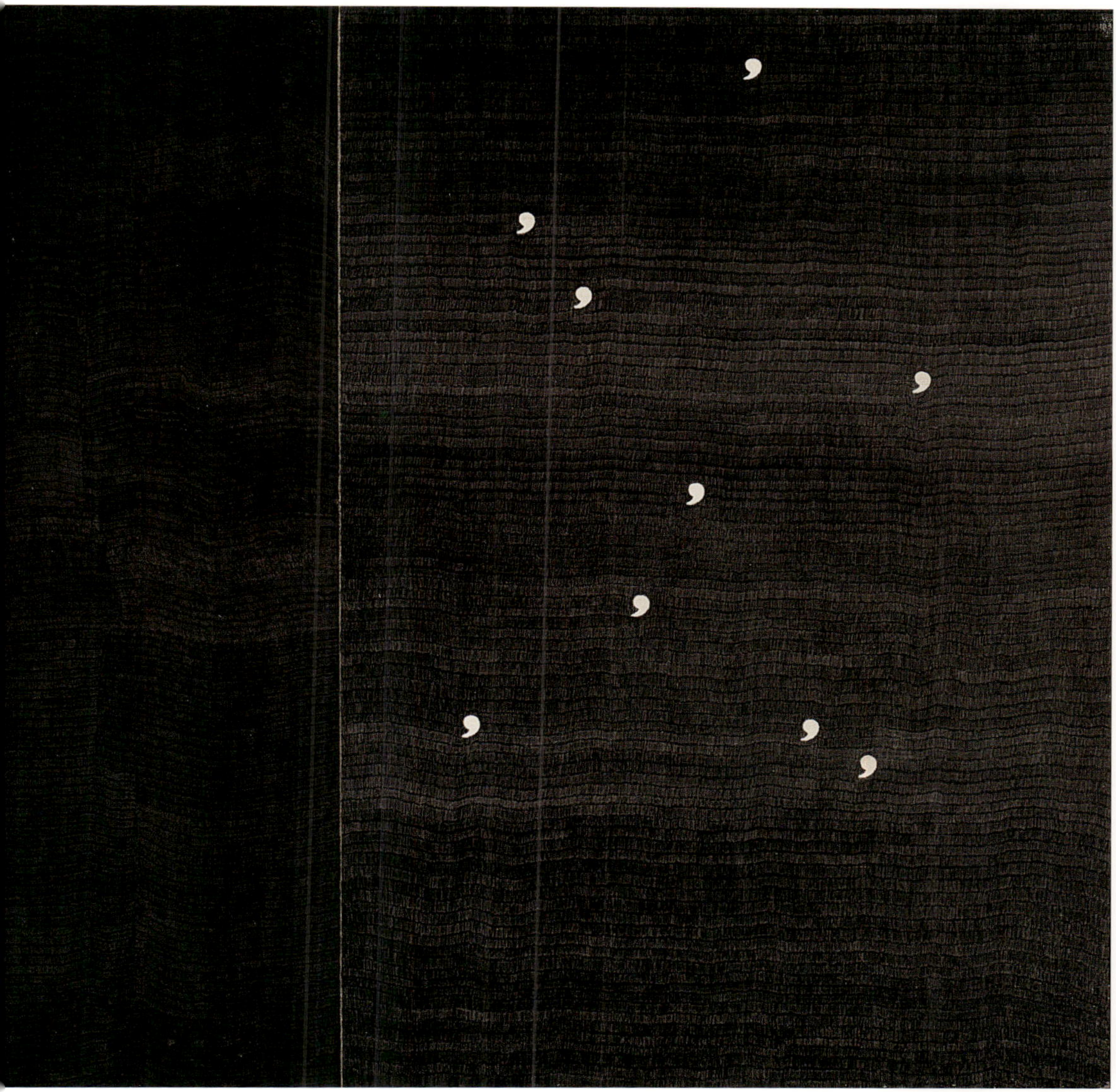

Alighiero Boetti

Mappa, 1989

[cat. 784]

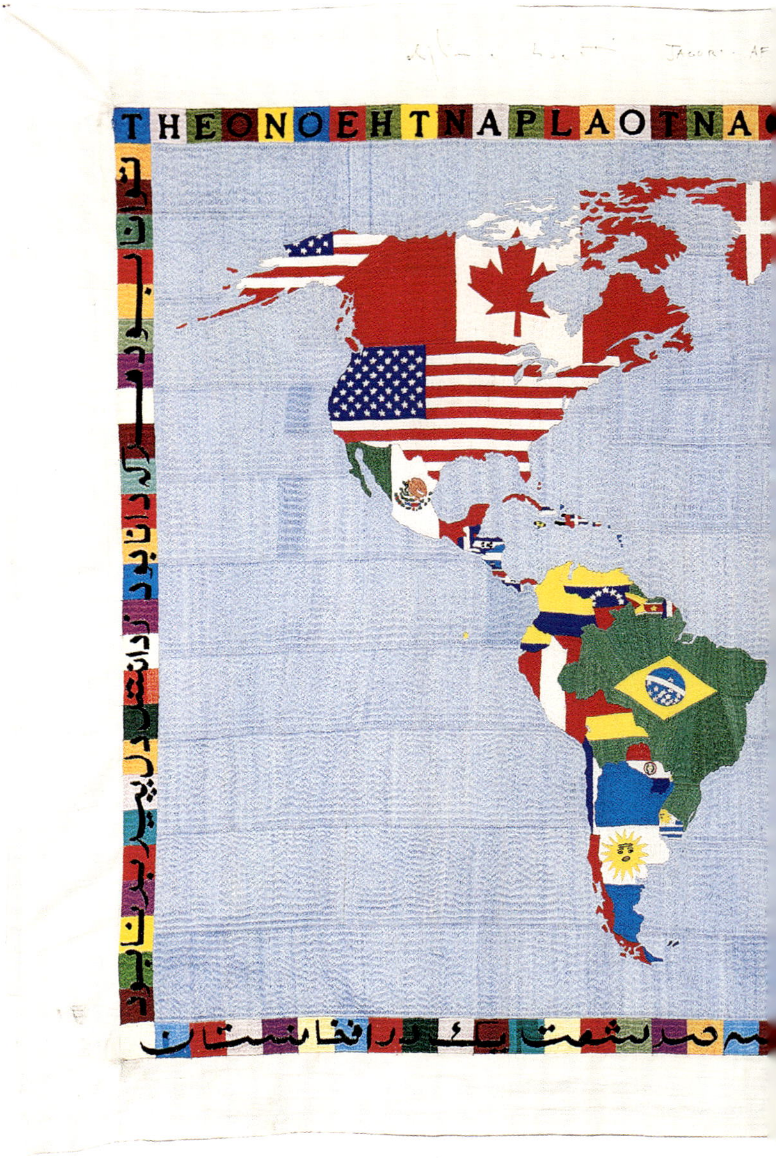

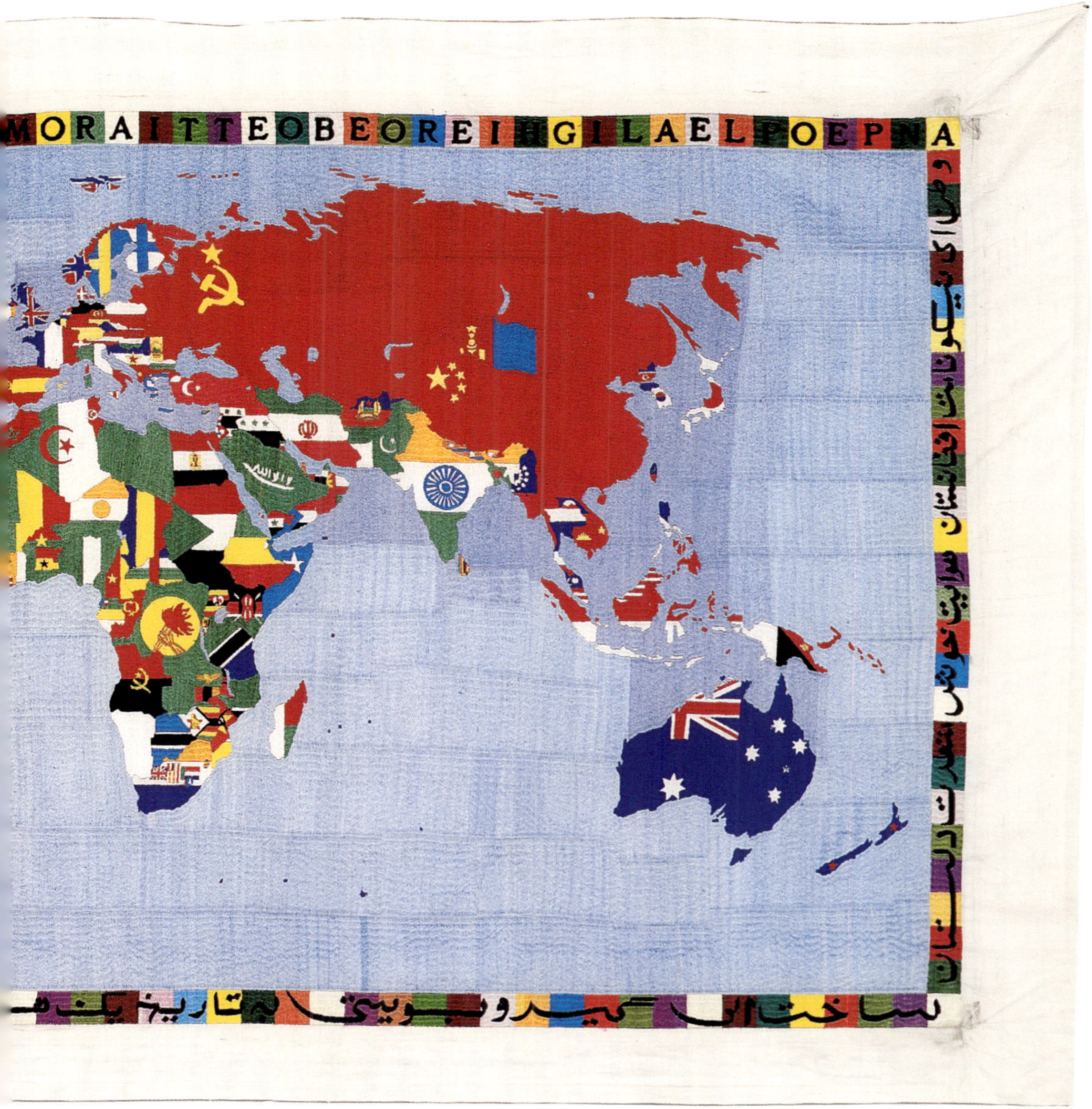
MORAITTEOBEOREIHGILAELPOEPNA

I don't write my scripts. I improvise as shooting goes on. But this improvisation can only be the result of previous inner preparation, which presupposes concentration. And in fact I make my films not only when I'm shooting but as I dream, eat, read, talk to you.
Deux ou trois choses que je sais d'elle is much more ambitious (than *Made in U.S.A.*), both on the documentary level, since it is about the replanning of the Parisian area, and on the level of pure research, since it is a film in which I am continually asking myself what I'm doing. There is, of course, the pretext of life itself – and sometimes prostitution – in the new housing complexes. But the real purpose of the film is to observe a huge mutation.
For me, to describe modern life is to observe mutations, and not simply to describe, as certain newspapers do, the new gadgets and industrial progress.
Basically, what I am doing is making the spectator share the arbitrary nature of my choices, and the quest for general rules which might justify a particular choice. Why am I making this film, why am I making it this way? Is the character played by Marina Vlady representative of the inhabitants of these housing complexes? I am constantly asking questions. I watch myself filming, and you hear me thinking aloud. In other words it isn't a film, it's an attempt

at film and is presented as such. It really forms part of my personal research. It is not a story, but hopefully a document to a degree where I think Paul Delouvrier himself [General Delegate for planning the Paris region in] should have commissioned the film.

[...]

During the course of the film – in its discourse, its discontinuous course, that is – I want to include everything, sport, politics, even groceries. Look at a man like Edouard Leclerc, a really extraordinary man whom I would love to do a film with or about. Everything can be put into a film. Everything should be put into a film. When people ask me why I talk – or have my characters talk – about Vietnam, about Jacques Anquetil, or about a woman who deceives her husband, I refer the questioner to his own newspaper. It's all there. And it's all mixed up. This is why I am so attracted by television. A televised newspaper made up of carefully prepared documents would be extraordinary. Even more so if one could get newspaper editors to take turns at editing these televised newspapers.

This is why, rather than speak of cinema and television, I prefer to use the more generalised terms of images and sounds.

Jean-Luc Godard

"On doit tout mettre dans un film," *Deux ou trois choses que je sais d'elle*, 1971

Rémy Zaugg

Esquisses perceptives - Tableaux; nº 1 ("La Maison du pendu"), 1970

[cat. 779]

Rémy Zaugg

Esquisses perceptives - Tableaux; nº 9, 1970-1983

[cat. 780]

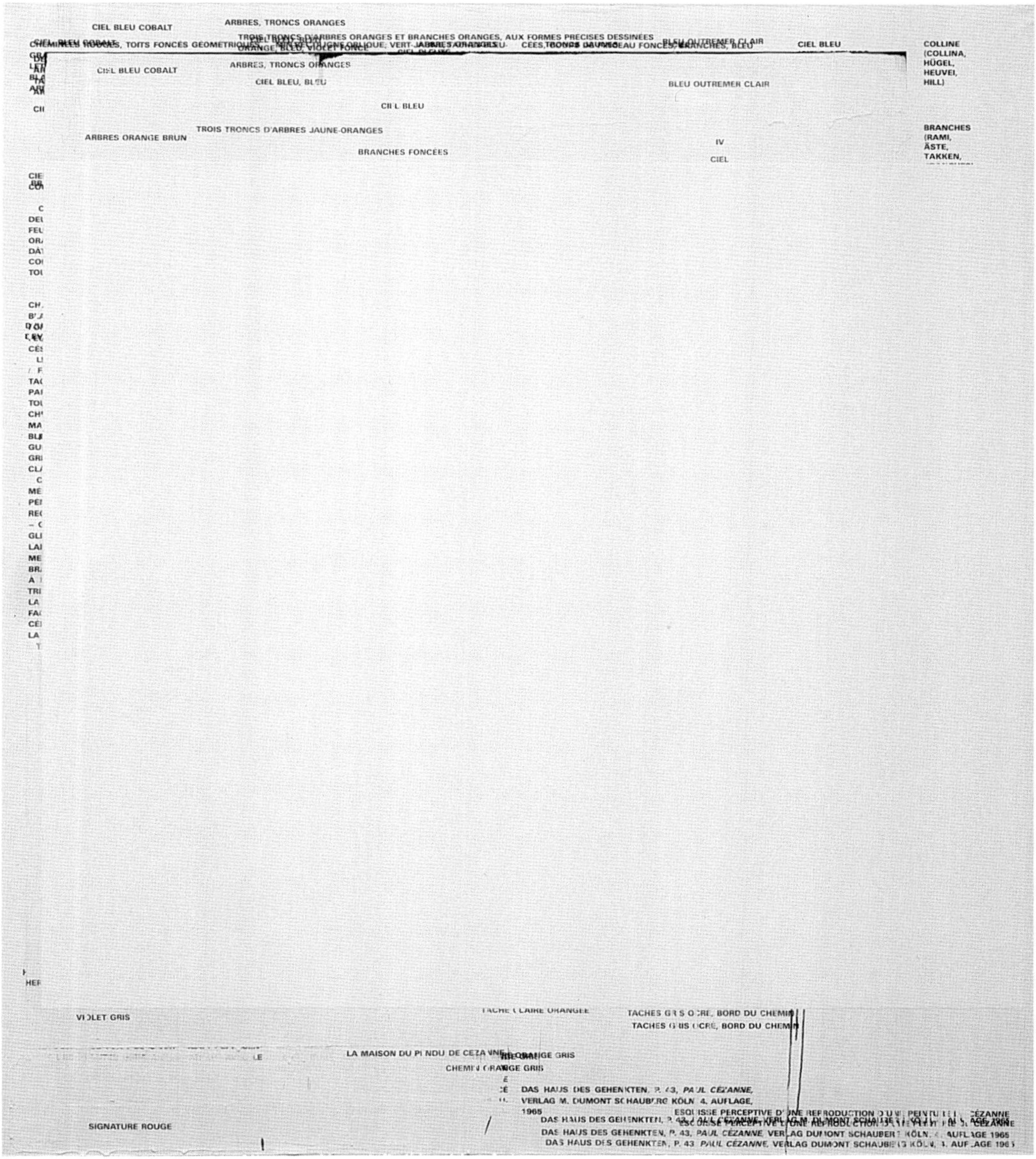

Rémy Zaugg

Esquisses perceptives - Tableaux; nº 14, 1970-1988

[cat. 781]

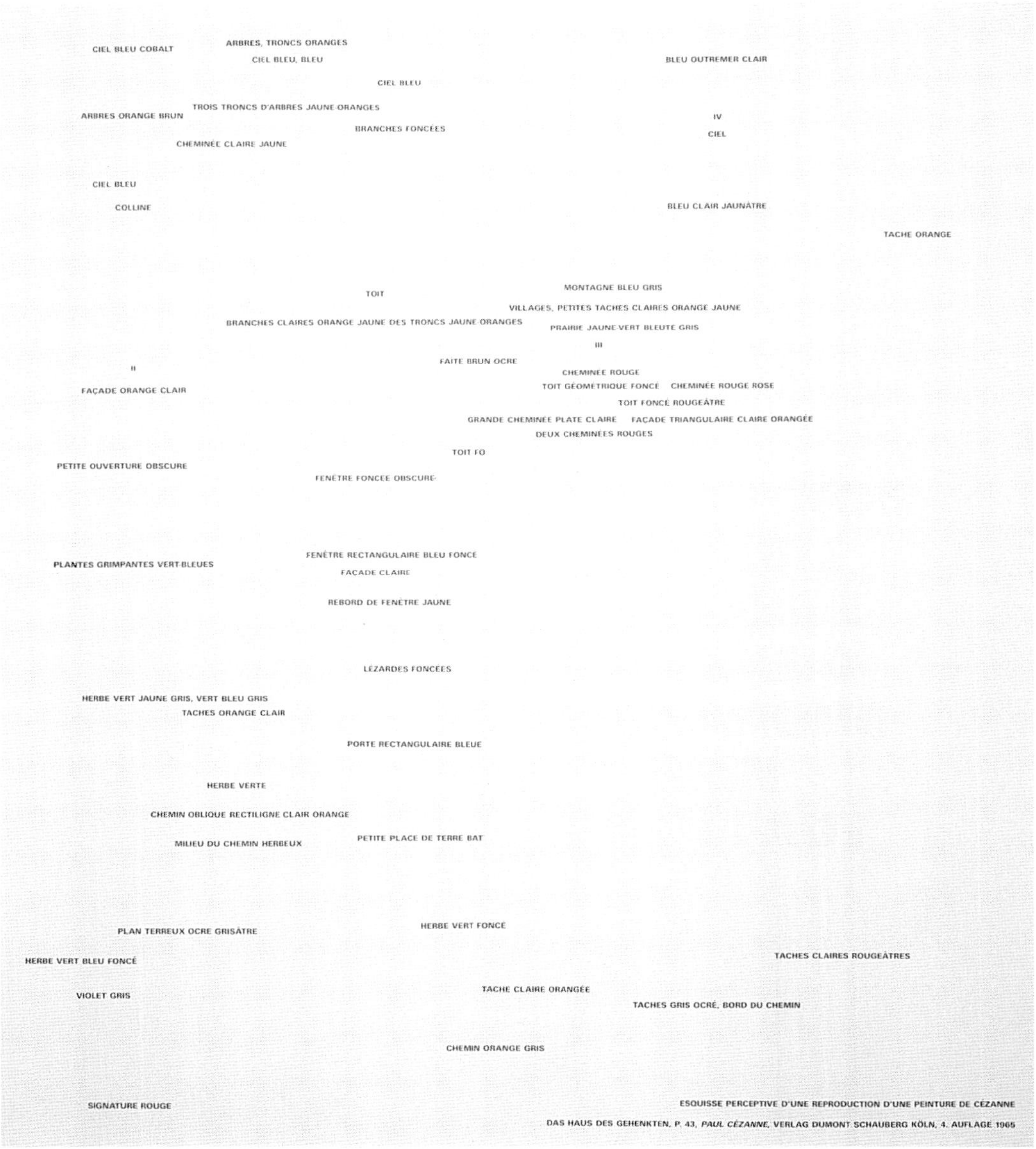
CIEL BLEU COBALT
ARBRES, TRONCS ORANGES
CIEL BLEU, BLEU
BLEU OUTREMER CLAIR
CIEL BLEU
TROIS TRONCS D'ARBRES JAUNE-ORANGES
ARBRES ORANGE BRUN
IV
BRANCHES FONCÉES
CIEL
CHEMINÉE CLAIRE JAUNE
CIEL BLEU
COLLINE
BLEU CLAIR JAUNÂTRE
TACHE ORANGE
MONTAGNE BLEU GRIS
TOIT
VILLAGES, PETITES TACHES CLAIRES ORANGE JAUNE
BRANCHES CLAIRES ORANGE JAUNE DES TRONCS JAUNE-ORANGES
PRAIRIE JAUNE-VERT BLEUTE GRIS
III
FAÎTE BRUN OCRE
II
CHEMINÉE ROUGE
FAÇADE ORANGE CLAIR
TOIT GÉOMÉTRIQUE FONCÉ
CHEMINÉE ROUGE ROSE
TOIT FONCÉ ROUGEÂTRE
GRANDE CHEMINÉE PLATE CLAIRE
FAÇADE TRIANGULAIRE CLAIRE ORANGÉE
DEUX CHEMINÉES ROUGES
TOIT FO
PETITE OUVERTURE OBSCURE
FENÊTRE FONCÉE OBSCURE
FENÊTRE RECTANGULAIRE BLEU FONCÉ
PLANTES GRIMPANTES VERT-BLEUES
FAÇADE CLAIRE
REBORD DE FENÊTRE JAUNE
LÉZARDES FONCÉES
HERBE VERT JAUNE GRIS, VERT BLEU GRIS
TACHES ORANGE CLAIR
PORTE RECTANGULAIRE BLEUE
HERBE VERTE
CHEMIN OBLIQUE RECTILIGNE CLAIR ORANGE
PETITE PLACE DE TERRE BAT
MILIEU DU CHEMIN HERBEUX
HERBE VERT FONCÉ
PLAN TERREUX OCRE GRISÂTRE
TACHES CLAIRES ROUGEÂTRES
HERBE VERT BLEU FONCÉ
TACHE CLAIRE ORANGÉE
VIOLET GRIS
TACHES GRIS OCRÉ, BORD DU CHEMIN
CHEMIN ORANGE GRIS
SIGNATURE ROUGE
ESQUISSE PERCEPTIVE D'UNE REPRODUCTION D'UNE PEINTURE DE CÉZANNE
DAS HAUS DES GEHENKTEN, P. 43, PAUL CÉZANNE, VERLAG DUMONT SCHAUBERG KÖLN, 4. AUFLAGE 1965

Rémy Zaugg

Esquisses perceptives - Tableaux; nº 16, 1973-1988

[cat. 782]

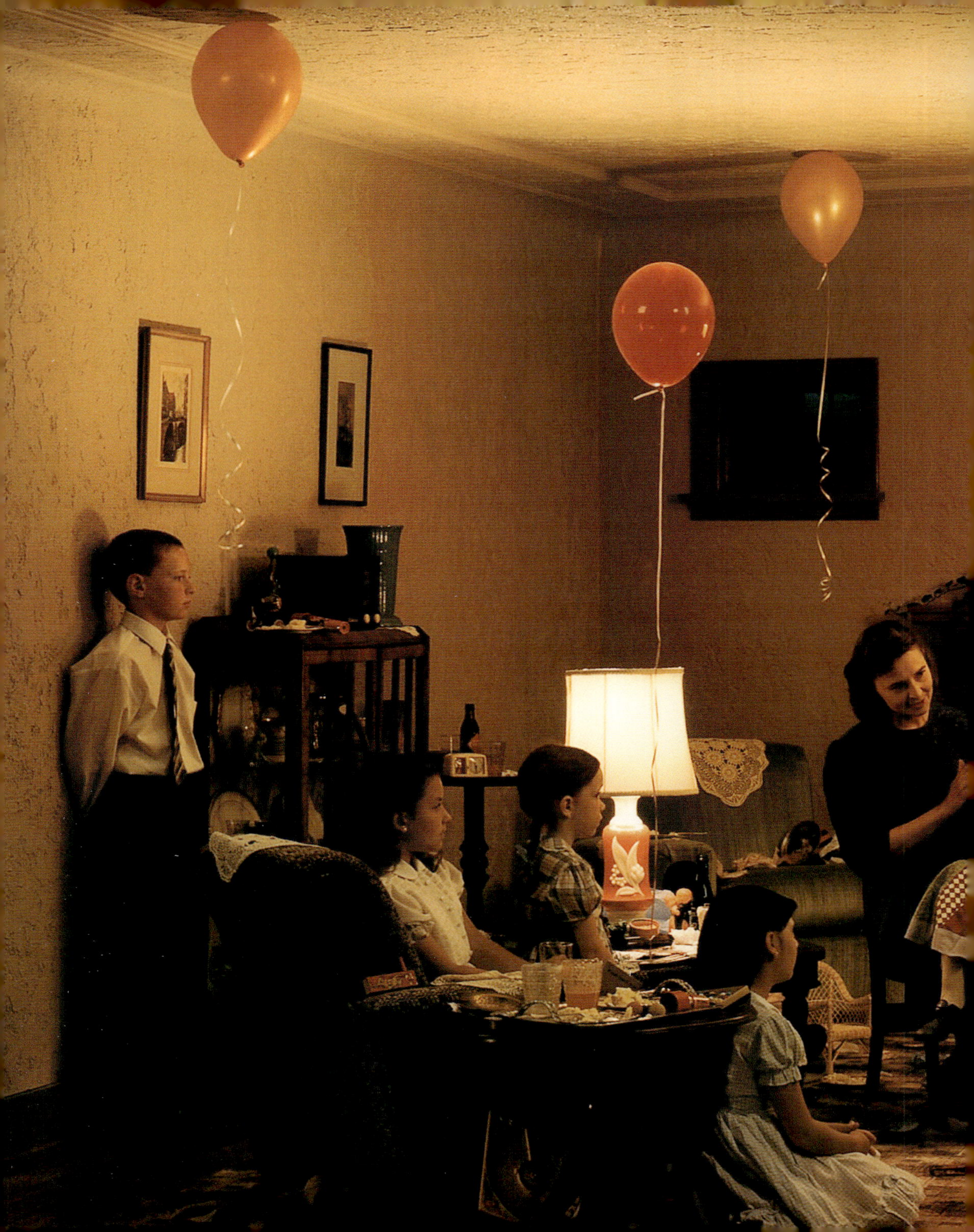

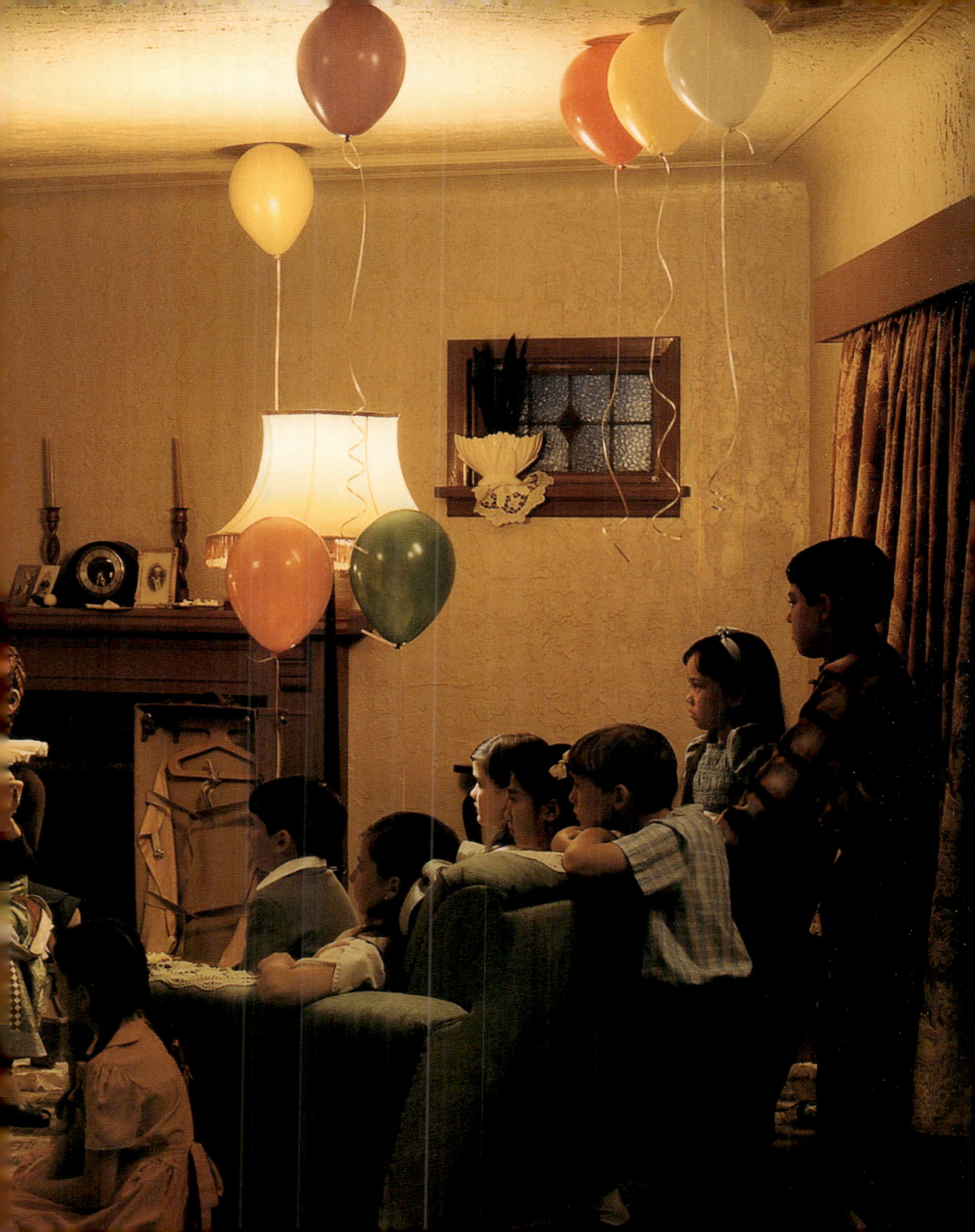

Hans Haacke
Manet-PROJEKT '74, 1974
[cat. 786]

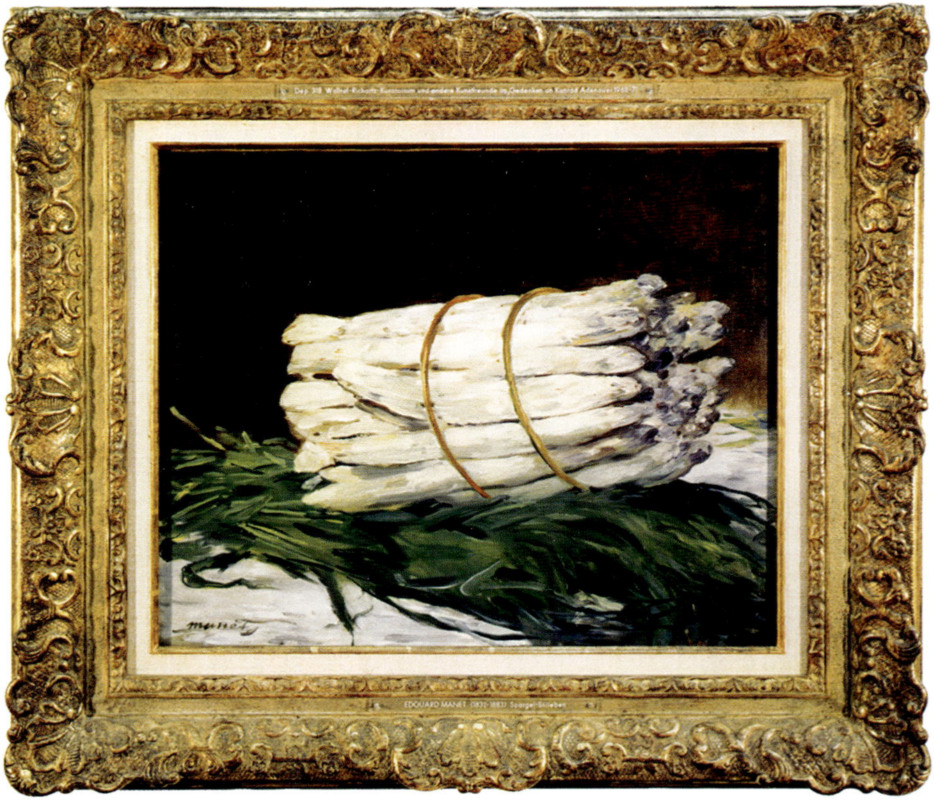

Previous double page:
Jeff Wall
A Ventriloquist at a Birthday Party in October 1947, 1990
[cat. 785]

Ten panels, each 20 x 31 in. (52 x 80 cm); color photo reproduction of Manet's *La botte d'asperges* (Bunch of Asparagus), with frame (actual size), 32 x 37 in. (83 x 94 cm); in black frames under glass. Color reproduction by Fotofachlabor Rolf Lillig, Cologne.
First exhibited in one-person exhibition at Galerie Paul Maenz, Cologne, July 4-31, 1974.
Collection of Dr. Roger Matthys, Deurle, Belgium.
Copy of the artist.

PROJEKT '74 was an exhibition billed as representing "aspects of international art at the beginning of the seventies." It was staged in the summer of 1974 by the Wallraf-Richartz-Museum in Cologne (now Wallraf-Richartz-Museum/Museum Ludwig), on the occasion of its 150th anniversary. It was promoted with the slogan, "Art Remains Art." The Cologne Kunsthalle (like the museum, a city institution) and the local Kunstverein (a private institution with subsidies from the city) joined the Wallraf-Richartz-Museum in presenting this exhibition.

Invited to participate in the exhibition, Haacke submitted a general outline for a new work: Manet's *Bunch of Asparagus* of 1880, collection Wallraf-Richartz-Museum, is on a studio easel in an approx. 6 x 8 meter room of *PROJEKT '74*. Panels on the walls present the social and economic position of the persons who have owned the painting over the years and the prices paid for it.

Dr. Evelyn Weiss, the modern art curator of the Wallraf-Richartz-Museum (1995, senior curator and deputy director of the Museum Ludwig) and one of the six members of the *PROJEKT '74* organizing team, responded that this plan was "one of the best projects submitted," but that it could not be executed in the exhibition or printed in the catalogue.

This decision was reached in what was described as a "democratic vote" by the organizing team; the vote was three to three. Voting for the work's exhibition were Dr. Evelyn Weiss; Dr. Manfred Schneckenburger, then director of the Kunsthalle (organizer of *Documenta* in 1977 and 1987); and Dr. Wulf Herzongenrath, director of the Kunstverein (now director of the Kunstverein of Bremen). The votes against the work were cast by Dr. Horst Keller, then director of the Wallraf-Richartz-Museum; Dr. Albert Schug, the museum's librarian; and Dr. Dieter Ronte, the personal aide of Prof. Dr. Gert von der Osten, who was head of all Cologne municipal museums and co-director of the Wallraf-Richartz-Museum until his retirement in 1975 (Ronte is now the director of the Städtisches Kunstmuseum, Bonn). With the exception of the director of the private Kunstverein, all team members were subordinates of Prof. von der Osten.

Dr. Keller objected to listing Hermann J. Abs' nineteen positions on boards of directors. Information about his social and economic standing was provided in the work because, in his capacity as chairman, he represented the Wallraf-Richartz-Kuratorium (Association of the Friends of the Museum), when it acquired the Manet painting. In a letter to the artist, Dr. Keller elaborated on his position. After explaining that the museum, although financially carried by the city and the state, depends on private donations for major acquisitions, he continued:

"It would mean giving an absolutely inadequate evaluation of the spiritual initiative of a man if one were to relate in any way the host of offices he holds in totally different walks of life with such an idealistic engagement... A grateful museum, however, and a grateful city, or one ready to be moved to gratefulness, must protect initiatives of such an extraordinary character from any other interpretation which might later throw even the slightest shadow on it..."

He also remarked:

"A museum knows nothing about economic power; it does indeed, however, know something about spiritual power."

Dr. Keller and Prof. Dr. von der Osten never saw or showed an interest in seeing the work before they rejected it. Instead, on July 4, the day of the press opening of *PROJEKT '74*, *Manet-PROJEKT '74* went on exhibition at Galerie Paul Maenz in Cologne, with a full-size color reproduction in place of the original *La Botte d'asperges*.

Daniel Buren incorporated in his own work in *PROJEKT '74* a scaled-down facsimile of *Manet-PROJEKT '74*, which Haacke had provided at his request. He also attached to it a poster entitled, "Art Remains Politics" —referring to the exhibition's official slogan, "Art Remains Art"— with an excerpt from "Limites Critiques," an essay Buren had written in 1970:

"...Art, whatever else it may be, is exclusively political. What is called for is the *analysis of formal and cultural limits* (and not one *or* the other) within which art exists and struggles. These limits are many and of different intensities. Although the prevailing ideology and the associated artists try in every way *to camouflage* them, and although it is too early – the conditions are not met – to blow them up, the time has come *to unveil* them."

On the morning after the opening, Prof. von der Osten had those parts of Buren's work which had been provided by Haacke (including a color reproduction of the Manet still life) pasted over with double layers of white paper.

Several artists, among them Antonio Diaz, Frank Gillette, and Newton and Helen Harrison, temporarily or permanently closed down their works in protest. Carl Andre, Robert Filliou, and Sol LeWitt had previously withdrawn from the exhibition, after hearing that *Manet-PROJEKT '74* would not be admitted.

In preparation for an article in *Art in America*, Prof. Dr. Carl R. Baldwin asked Dr. Keller in a letter: "Do you have reason to believe that Dr. Abs himself would have minded the objective presentation of facts regarding his professional involvements?" Dr. Keller's answer was: "I have to answer this question with a definite yes, as I had already explained clearly in a letter to Hans Haacke."

After his retirement, and until his death in 1994, Hermann J. Abs was associated with the Deutsche Bank and with cultural politics. He represented a German consortium at a 1983 Sotheby Parke-Bernet auction in London where he successfully bid for an old German illuminated manuscript, the Gospels of Henry the Lion, for $11.7 million (32 million DM, or 16 million euro). He proved his reputation as the "secret head of the Department of Culture" of the city of Frankfurt (a title conferred on him by the actual head of the city's cultural department), when Klaus Gallwitz, the director of the publicly financed Frankfurt Staedelsches Kunstinstitut, was forced into early retirement after incurring the wrath of Abs in 1992. Abs also managed to block the appointment of the leading candidate for the vacated museum directorship, a civil service position, and have his own protégé selected instead.

In 1982, after the Vatican Bank's entanglement in the scandal with Banco Ambrosiano of Milan, Abs was appointed by Pope John Paul II to the advisory board of the Institute of Religious works in order to straighten out the Vatican's finances. The appointment drew strong protests from the Simon Wiesenthal Center at Yeshiva University in Los Angeles. Because the Deutsche Bank, under the management of Abs, had played a central role in the "Aryanization" of Jewish property under the Nazis, Abs had been put on a U.S. Government "watch list" and was prohibited from entering the United States.

Hans Haacke
1974

Das Spargel-Stilleben

1880 gemalt von

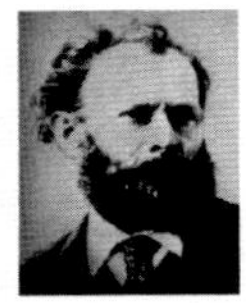

Edouard Manet

Lebt von 1832 bis 1883 in Paris. – Entstammt einer katholischen Familie des franz. Großbürgertums. Vater Auguste Manet Jurist, Personalchef im Justizministerium, später Richter (magistrat) am Cour d'appel de Paris (Berufungsgericht). Republikaner. Ritter der Ehrenlegion. – Großvater Clément Manet Bürgermeister von Gennevilliers an der Seine, vor Paris. Familie besitzt dort ein 54 Hektar großes Landgut. – Mutter Eugénie Désirée Fournier, Tochter eines franz. Diplomaten, der die Wahl Marschall Bernadottes zum schwedischen König betrieb. Karl XIV. von Schweden ihr Pate. – Ihr Bruder Clément Fournier Artillerieoberst. Demissioniert während der Revolution 1848. – Zwei Brüder Manets im Staatsdienst.

Manet besucht renommiertes Collège Rollin (Mitschüler Antonin Proust, späterer Politiker und Schriftsteller). Entgegen dem väterlichen Wunsch nach einem Jurastudium fährt er für kurze Zeit zur See. Fällt bei der Aufnahmeprüfung zur Seekadettenanstalt durch.

1850–56 Kunststudium im Privatatelier von Thomas Couture, einem erfolgreichen Salonmaler. Studienreisen nach Italien, Deutschland, Österreich, der Schweiz, Belgien, Holland, Spanien.

Finanziell unabhängig. Nicht auf den Verkauf seiner Bilder angewiesen. Wohnt in großen standesgemäß eingerichteten Häusern in Paris, mit Dienerschaft.

Stellt ab 1861 mit wechselndem Erfolg im Salon und in Kunsthandlungen aus. 1863 Beteiligung am „Salon des Réfusés" (Salon der Zurückgewiesenen). Bilder werden wegen Verstössen gegen die Konvention von der offiziellen Kritik bekämpft. Kritische Unterstützung durch Zola, Mallarmé, Rimbaud.

Heiratet 1863 nach dem Tod seines Vaters Suzanne Leenhoff, seine ehemalige Klavierlehrerin, die Tochter eines holländischen Musikers. Léon Edouard Koëlla, ihr 1852 geborener Sohn, ist ein illegitimes Kind Manets; wird von ihm adoptiert.

Stellt 1867 aus Protest gegen die konservative Jury 50 Bilder in einer für 18 000 Francs selbstfinanzierten Baracke auf einem Grundstück des Marquis de Pomereu in der Nähe der Weltausstellung in Paris aus. Anhänger unter jüngeren, besonders impressionistischen Künstlern.

Als Nationalgardist 1870 bei der Verteidigung von Paris im Deutsch-Französischen Krieg, Meldegänger im Regimentsstab. Während der Pariser Kommune bei seiner Familie in Südfrankreich. – Antiroyalist. Bewunderer des Republikaners Léon Gambetta, des späteren Ministerpräsidenten.

1871 umfangreiche Bilderkäufe durch den Kunsthändler Durand-Ruel, einem Freund impressionistischer Malerei. Findet Anerkennung in den für künstlerische Neuerungen aufgeschlossenen Kreisen der Pariser Gesellschaft. Zahlreiche Porträtaufträge. 1881 Gewinn der 2. Medaille des Salons. Auf Vorschlag Antonin Prousts Ernennung zum Ritter der Ehrenlegion.

Während seiner tödlichen Krankheit Behandlung durch früheren Leibarzt Napoleon III.

1883 Gedächtnisausstellung in der Ecole des Beaux-Arts Paris. Katalogvorwort von Emile Zola. Verkaufserlös zugunsten der Erben 116 637 Francs.

Das Spargel-Stilleben erworben mit Stiftungen von

Hermann J. Abs, Frankfurt
Viktor Achter, Mönchengladbach
Agrippina Rückversicherungs AG., Köln
Allianz Versicherung AG., Köln
Heinrich Auer Mühlenwerke, Köln
Bankhaus Heinz Ansmann, Köln
Bankhaus Delbrück von der Heydt & Co., Köln
Bankhaus Sal. Oppenheim jr. & Cie., Köln
Bankhaus C. G. Trinkaus, Düsseldorf
Dr. Walter Berndorff, Köln
Firma Felix Böttcher, Köln
Robert Bosch GmbH, Köln
Central Krankenversicherungs AG., Köln
Colonia Versicherungs-Gruppe, Köln
Commerzbank AG., Düsseldorf
Concordia Lebensversicherungs AG., Köln
Daimler Benz AG., Stuttgart-Untertürkheim
Demag AG., Duisburg
Deutsch-Atlantische Telegraphenges., Köln
Deutsche Bank AG., Frankfurt
Deutsche Centralbodenkredit AG., Köln
Deutsche Continental-Gas-Ges., Düsseldorf
Deutsche Krankenversicherungs AG., Köln
Deutsche Libby-Owens-Ges. AG., Gelsenkirchen
Deutsche Solvay-Werke GmbH, Solingen-Ohligs
Dortmunder Union-Brauerei, Dortmund
Dresdner Bank AG., Düsseldorf
Farbenfabriken Bayer AG., Leverkusen
Gisela Fitting, Köln
Autohaus Jacob Fleischhauer K. G., Köln
Glanzstoff AG., Wuppertal
Graf Rüdiger von der Goltz, Düsseldorf
Dr. Paul Gülker, Köln
Gottfried Hagen AG., Köln
Hein. Lehmann & Co. AG., Düsseldorf
Hilgers AG., Rheinbrohl
Hoesch AG., Dortmund
Helmut Horten GmbH, Düsseldorf
Hubertus Brauerei GmbH, Köln
Karstadt-Peters GmbH, Köln
Kaufhalle GmbH, Köln
Kaufhof AG, Köln
Kleinwanzlebener Saatzucht AG., Einbeck
Klöckner Werke AG., Duisburg
Kölnische Lebens- und Sachvers. AG., Köln
Viktor Langen, Düsseldorf-Meerbusch
Margarine Union AG., Hamburg
Mauser-Werke GmbH, Köln
Josef Mayr K. G., Hagen
Michel Brennstoffhandel GmbH, Düsseldorf
Gert von der Osten, Köln
Kurt Pauli, Lövenich
Pfeifer & Langen, Köln
Preussag AG., Hannover
William Prym Werke AG., Stolberg
Karl-Gustav Ratjen, Königstein (Taunus)
Dr. Hans Reuter, Duisburg
Rheinisch-Westf. Bodenkreditbank, Köln
Rhein.-Westf. Isolatorenwerke GmbH, Siegburg
Rhein.-Westf. Kalkwerke AG., Dornap
Sachtleben AG., Köln
Servais-Werke AG., Witterschlick
Siemag Siegener Maschinenbau GmbH, Dahlbruch
Dr. F. E. Shinnar, Tel-Ganim (Israel)
Sparkasse der Stadt Köln, Köln
Schlesische Feuervers.-Ges., Köln
Ewald Schneider, Köln
Schoellersche Kammgarnspinnerei AG., Eitorf
Stahlwerke Bochum AG., Bochum
Dr. Josef Steegmann, Köln-Zürich
Strabag Bau AG., Köln
Dr. Nikolaus Graf Strasoldo, Burg Gudenau
Cornelius Stüssgen AG., Köln
August Thyssen-Hütte AG., Düsseldorf
Union Rhein. Braunkohlen AG., Wesseling
Vereinigte Aluminium-Werke AG., Bonn
Vereinigte Glaswerke, Aachen
Volkshilfe Lebensversicherungs AG., Köln
Jos. Voss GmbH & Co. KG., Brühl
Walther & Cie. AG., Köln
Wessel-Werk GmbH, Bonn
Westdeutsche Bodenkreditanstalt, Köln
Westd. Landesbank Girozentrale, Düsseldorf
Westfalenbank AG., Bochum
Rud. Siedersleben'sche O. Wolff-Stiftg., Köln

vererbt an

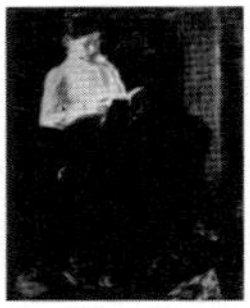

Käthe Riezler

Geboren 1885 in Berlin, gestorben 1951 in New York.

Tochter des Malers Max Liebermann und seiner Frau Martha Marckwald.

Heiratet 1915 in Berlin Dr. phil. Kurt Riezler. 1917 Geburt der Tochter Maria Riezler.

Dr. Kurt Riezler, geboren 1882 in München, Sohn eines Kaufmanns. Studium der Klassischen Antike an der Universität München. 1905 Dissertation : „Das zweite Buch der pseudoaristotelischen Ökonomie".

1906 Eintritt ins Auswärtige Amt in Berlin. Legationsrat, später Gesandter. Arbeitet im Stab des Reichskanzlers von Bethmann-Hollweg. 1919/20 Leiter des Büros des Reichspräsidenten Friedrich Ebert.

1913 unter dem Decknamen J. J. Ruedorffer Veröffentlichung der „Prolegomena zu einer Theorie der Politik", 1914 „Grundzüge der Weltpolitik in der Gegenwart". – Später Publikationen zur Geschichtsphilosophie, zur politischen Theorie und Ästhetik.

1927 Honorarprofessor, stellvertretender Geschäftsführer und Vorsitzender des Kuratoriums an der Goethe Universität in Frankfurt am Main.

1933 Entlassung durch Nazis.

Umzug der Familie nach Berlin in das Haus Max Liebermanns, Pariser Platz 7. – Erben 1935 seine Kunstsammlung, die Liebermann 1933 dem Kunsthaus Zürich in Obhut gegeben hatte.

1938 Emigration der Familie nach New York. Sammlung folgt dorthin.

1939 erhält Dr. Riezler eine Professur für Philosophie an der New School for Social Research in New York, einer von Emigranten gegründeten Universität. Gastprofessuren an der University of Chicago und der Columbia University in New York.

Käthe Riezler stirbt 1951. Dr. Riezler emeritiert 1952, stirbt in München 1956.

Pastell von Max Liebermann, „Die Tochter des Künstlers" 1901

Das Spargel-Stilleben erworben durch die Initiative des Vorsitzenden des Wallraf-Richartz-Kuratoriums

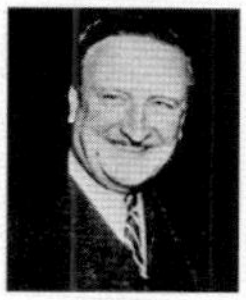

Hermann J. Abs

Geboren 1901 in Bonn. – Entstammt wohlhabender katholischer Familie. Vater Dr. Josef Abs, Rechtsanwalt und Justizrat, Mitinhaber der Hubertus Braunkohlen AG. Brüggen, Erft. Mutter Katharina Lückerath.

Abitur 1919 Realgymnasium Bonn. – Ein Sem. Jurastudium Universität Bonn. – Banklehre im Kölner Bankhaus Delbrück von der Heydt & Co. Erwirbt internationale Bankerfahrung in Amsterdam, London, Paris, USA.

Heiratet 1928 Inez Schnitzler. Ihr Vater mit Georg von Schnitzler vom Vorstand des IG. Farben-Konzerns verwandt. Tante verheiratet mit Baron Alfred Neven du Mont. Schwester verheiratet mit Georg Graf von der Goltz. – Geburt der Kinder Thomas und Marion Abs.

Mitglied der Zentrumspartei. – 1929 Prokura im Bankhaus Delbrück, Schickler & Co., Berlin. 1935-37 einer der 5 Teilhaber der Bank.

1937 im Vorstand und Aufsichtsrat der Deutschen Bank, Berlin. Leiter der Auslandsabteilung. – 1939 von Reichswirtschaftsminister Funk in den Beirat der Deutschen Reichsbank berufen. – Mitglied in Ausschüssen der Reichsbank, Reichsgruppe Industrie, Reichsgruppe Banken, Reichswirtschaftskammer und einem Arbeitskreis im Reichswirtschaftsministerium. – 1944 in über 50 Aufsichts- und Verwaltungsräten großer Unternehmen. Mitgliedschaft in Gesellschaften zur Wahrnehmung deutscher Wirtschaftsinteressen im Ausland.

1946 für 6 Wochen in britischer Haft. – Von der Alliierten Entnazifizierungsbehörde als entlastet (5) eingestuft.

1948 bei der Gründung der Kreditanstalt für Wiederaufbau. Maßgeblich an der Wirtschaftsplanung der Bundesregierung beteiligt. Wirtschaftsberater Konrad Adenauers. – Leiter der deutschen Delegation bei der Londoner Schuldenkonferenz 1951-53. Berater bei den Wiedergutmachungsverhandlungen mit Israel in Den Haag. 1954 Mitglied der CDU.

1952 im Aufsichtsrat der Süddeutschen Bank AG. – 1957-67 Vorstandssprecher der Deutschen Bank AG. Seit 1967 Vorsitzender des Aufsichtsrats.

Ehrenvorsitzender des Aufsichtsrats:
Deutsche Überseeische Bank, Hamburg – Pittler Maschinenfabrik AG, Langen (Hessen)
Vorsitzender des Aufsichtsrats:
Dahlbusch Verwaltungs-AG, Gelsenkirchen – Daimler Benz AG, Stuttgart-Untertürkheim – Deutsche Bank AG, Frankfurt – Deutsche Lufthansa AG, Köln – Philipp Holzmann AG, Frankfurt – Phoenix Gummiwerke AG, Hamburg-Harburg – RWE Elektrizitätswerk AG, Essen – Vereinigte Glanzstoff AG, Wuppertal-Elberfeld – Zellstoff-Fabrik Waldhof AG, Mannheim

Ehrenvorsitzender:
Salamander AG, Kornwestheim – Gebr. Stumm GmbH, Brambauer (Westf.) – Süddeutsche Zucker-AG, Mannheim
Stellvertr. Vors. des Aufsichtsrats:
Badische Anilin- und Sodafabrik AG, Ludwigshafen – Siemens AG, Berlin-München
Mitglied des Aufsichtsrats:
Metallgesellschaft AG, Frankfurt
Präsident des Verwaltungsrats:
Kreditanstalt für Wiederaufbau – Deutsche Bundesbahn

Großes Bundesverdienstkreuz mit Stern, Päpstl. Stern zum Komturkreuz, Großkreuz Isabella die Katholische von Spanien, Cruzeiro do Sul von Brasilien. – Ritter des Ordens vom Heiligen Grabe. – Dr. h.c. der Univ. Göttingen, Sofia, Tokio und der Wirtschaftshochschule Mannheim.

Lebt in Kronberg (Taunus) und auf dem Bentgerhof bei Remagen.

Photo aus Current Biography Yearbook 1970 New York

Das Spargel-Stilleben

vererbt an

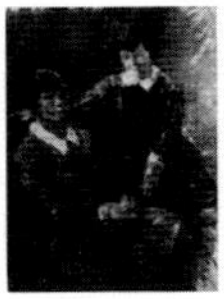

Maria White

Geboren 1917 in Berlin. – Tochter von Prof. Dr. Kurt Riezler und Käthe Liebermann.

Emigriert 1938 mit ihren Eltern nach New York.

Heiratet Howard Burton White.

Howard B. White, geboren 1912 in Montclair, N. J., studiert 1934–38 an der New School for Social Research in New York, wo Dr. Kurt Riezler lehrt. 1941 Rockefeller Stipendium. Promoviert 1943 an der New School zum Doctor of Science.

Unterrichtet an der Lehigh University und am Coe College. Gegenwärtig Professor im Graduate Department of Political and Social Science der New School for Social Research. Lehrt Political Philosophy.

Veröffentlichungen u. a. „Peace Among the Willows – The Political Philosophy of Francis Bacon", den Haag 1968. „Copp'd Hills Towards Heaven – Shakespeare and the Classical Polity," den Haag 1968.

Maria und Howard B. White leben in Northport, N. Y. Sie haben zwei Kinder.

Ölbild von Max Liebermann „Tochter und Enkelin des Künstlers" (Maria Riezler im Bild rechts), um 1930

Das Spargel-Stilleben

für 24 300,– RM gekauft durch

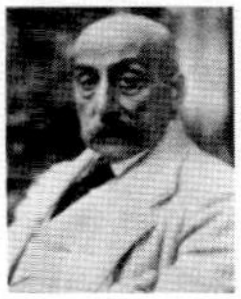

Max Liebermann

Maler, lebt von 1847 bis 1935 in Berlin. – Entstammt einer jüdischen Fabrikantenfamilie. Vater Louis Liebermann Textilindustrieller in Berlin. Besitzt ebenfalls Eisengießerei Wilhelmshütte in Sprottau, Schlesien. – Mutter Philipine Haller, Tochter eines Berliner Juweliers (Gründer der Firma Haller & Rathenau). – Bruder Prof. Felix Liebermann, bekannter Historiker. – Vetter Walther Rathenau, Industrieller (AEG), Reichsaußenminister (1922 ermordet).

Liebermann besucht renommiertes Friedrich-Werdersches Gymnasium in Berlin zusammen mit Söhnen Bismarcks. – Kunststudium im Privatatelier Steffeck, Berlin, und auf der Kunstakademie Weimar. Längere Arbeitsaufenthalte in Paris, Holland, München. – Freiwilliger Krankenpfleger im Deutsch-Französischen Krieg 1870/71.

Heiratet 1884 Martha Marckwald, zieht nach Berlin zurück. 1885 Geburt der Tochter Käthe Liebermann.

Erbt 1894 väterliches Palais am Pariser Platz 7 (Brandenburger Tor). Baut 1910 Sommersitz am Wannsee, Große Seestraße 27 (seit 1971 Clubhaus des Deutschen Unterwasserclubs e.V.). Finanziell unabhängig. Lebt nicht vom Verkauf seiner Werke.

1897 Gesamtausstellung in der Berliner Akademie der Künste. Große Goldene Medaille. Seine durch Realismus und franz. Impressionismus beeinflußten Bilder werden von Wilhelm II. empört abgelehnt. – Malt Genreszenen, Stadtlandschaften, Strand- und Gartenszenen, Gesellschaftsporträts, Künstler, Wissenschaftler, Politiker. – Ausstellung und Verkauf durch Kunstsalon Paul Cassirer in Berlin. Werke in öffentlichen Sammlungen u. a. Wallraf-Richartz-Museum Köln.

Professorentitel 1897. – Präsident der „Berliner Sezession" (Künstlervereinigung gegen Hofkunst) 1898–1911, Rücktritt wegen Opposition jüngerer Künstler. – 1898 Mitglied, 1912 im Senat, 1920 Präsident der Preußischen Akademie der Künste. Rücktritt 1933. – Ehrendoktor der Universität Berlin. Ehrenbürger der Stadt Berlin. Ritter der franz. Ehrenlegion. Orden von Oranje-Nassau. Ritter des Ordens Pour le mérite und andere Auszeichnungen

Besitzt Werke von Cézanne, Daumier, Degas, Manet, Monet, Renoir. Deponiert seine Sammlung 1933 im Kunsthaus Zürich.

1933 von Nazis aus allen Ämtern entlassen. Ausstellungsverbot. Entfernung seiner Bilder aus öffentlichen Sammlungen.

Stirbt 1935 in Berlin. Frau Martha Liebermann begeht 1943 Selbstmord, um sich drohender Verhaftung zu entziehen.

Photo um 1930

Das Spargel-Stilleben

1880 für 800 Francs gekauft durch

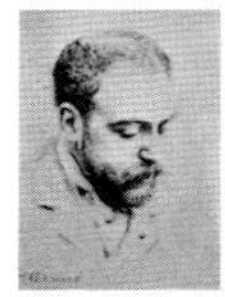

Charles Ephrussi

Geboren 1849 in Odessa, gestorben 1905 in Paris. – Entstammt jüdischer Bankiersfamilie mit Bankunternehmen in Odessa, Wien und Paris. Familiäre Beziehungen zur franz. Hochfinanz (Baron de Reinach, Baron de Rothschild).

Studiert in Odessa und Wien. – 1871 Übersiedlung nach Paris.

Eigene Bankgeschäfte. – Kunstschriftstellerische Arbeiten u. a. über Albrecht Dürer, Jacopo de Barbarij und Paul Baudry. 1875 Mitarbeit an der „Gazette des Beaux Arts", 1885 Mitinhaber, 1894 Herausgeber.

Mitglied zahlreicher kultureller Komitees und Salons der Pariser Gesellschaft. Organisiert mit Gustave Dreyfus, der Comtesse Greffulhes und der Prinzessin Mathilde Kunstausstellungen und Konzerte, u. a. von Werken Richard Wagners. – Zweites Vorbild für Marcel Prousts Swann.

Sammelt Kunst der Renaissance, des 18. Jahrhunderts, Albrecht Dürers, Ostasiatische Kunst und Werke zeitgenössischer Maler.

Zahlt Manet statt der vereinbarten 800 Francs für das „Spargel-Stilleben" insgesamt 1000 Francs. Aus Dankbarkeit schickt im Manet das Stilleben eines einzelnen Spargels (1880, Öl auf Leinwand, 16,5 x 21,5 cm, Paris Musée de l'Impressionisme) mit der Bemerkung: „Es fehlte noch in Ihrem Bündel".

Ritter (1882) und Offizier (1903) der Ehrenlegion.

Gravure von M. Patricot „Charles Ephrussi" aus „La Gazette des Beaux Arts", Paris 1905

Das Spargel-Stilleben
von unbekanntem Datum an im Besitz von oder
in Kommission bei

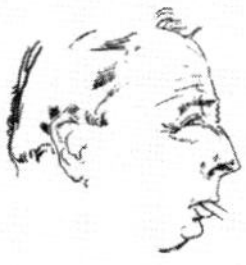

Paul Cassirer

Geboren 1871 in Görlitz, Selbstmord 1926 in Berlin. – Entstammt wohlhabender jüdischer Familie. Vater Louis Cassirer gründet mit 2 Söhnen die Firma Dr. Cassirer & Co., Kabelwerke in Berlin. – Bruder Prof. Richard Cassirer, Berliner Neurologe. – Vetter Prof. Ernst Cassirer bekannter Philosoph.

Kunstgeschichtsstudium in München. Mitredakteur des „Simplizissimus". Eigene literarische Arbeiten.

Gründet mit Vetter Bruno Cassirer 1898 in Berlin Verlags- und Kunsthandlung. 1901 Trennung. Weiterführung als Kunstsalon Paul Cassirer, Victoriastraße 35, in vornehmer Berliner Gegend.

Mit der Künstlervereinigung „Berliner Sezession" Kampf gegen offizielle Hofkunst. Trotz Unwillen des Kaisers Handel und publizistische Förderung des franz. Impressionismus. Enge Beziehungen zum Pariser Kunsthändler Durand-Ruel. Verhilft den Deutschen Malern Trübner, Liebermann, Corinth und Slevogt zum Erfolg.

1908 Gündung des Verlags Paul Cassirer für Kunstliteratur und Belletristik. Publikationen des literarischen Expressionismus. 1910 Gründung der Halbmonatsschrift „Pan" und „Pan"-Gesellschaft zur Förderung von Bühnenwerken, u. a. Wedekind.

Aus erster Ehe eine Tochter und ein Sohn (Selbstmord im 1. Weltkrieg). Heiratet 1910 in zweiter Ehe die Schauspielerin Tilla Durieux.

1914 Kriegsfreiwilliger. Erhält Eisernes Kreuz in Ypern. Wird Kriegsgegner.

Zeitweilig in Haft (beschuldigt, unrechtmäßig franz. Bilder verkauft zu haben). Flucht in die Schweiz und Aufenthalt in Bern und Zürich bis Kriegsende. Verhilft Harry Graf Keßler zu franz. Kontakten für Verhandlungen mit Frankreich im Auftrage Ludendorffs. Verlegt mit Max Rascher pazifistische Literatur.

Nach der Revolution 1918 in Berlin Eintritt in die USPD. Verlegt sozialistische Bücher, u. a. von Kautzky und Bernstein.

Grund für Selbstmord 1926 vermutlich Konflikt mit Tilla Durieux.

Weiterführung des Kunstsalons Paul Cassirer in Amsterdam, Zürich und London durch Dr. Walter Feilchenfeldt und Dr. Grete Ring, eine Nichte Max Liebermanns.

Lithographie von Max Oppenheimer, „Bildnis Paul Cassirer", um 1925.

Das Spargel-Stilleben

zwischen 1900 und 1902 gekauft durch

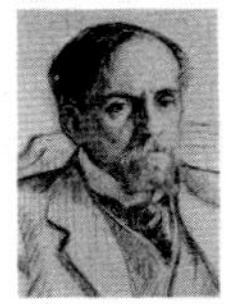

Alexandre Rosenberg

Geboren 1850 in Preßburg (Bratislava), Slowakei.- Entstammt jüdischer Familie. Emigration nach Paris im Alter von 9 Jahren.

1870 Gründung einer Kunst- und Antiquitätenhandlung in Paris.

Heiratet 1878 Mathilde Jellineck aus Wien. Sie haben drei Söhne und eine Tochter.

Fortführung der Firma nach seinem Tode 1913 durch den 1881 in Paris geborenen Sohn Paul Rosenberg. Spezialisierung auf die Kunst des 19. und 20. Jahrhunderts.- Gegenwärtig Paul Rosenberg und Co. in New York, geführt durch den Enkel Alexandre Rosenberg.

Kohlezeichnung von Louis Charlot "Alexandre Rosenberg" (Ausschnitt), 1913

Das Spargel-Stilleben
1968 über Frau Marianne Feilchenfeldt, Zürich
für 1 360 000,- DM erworben durch das

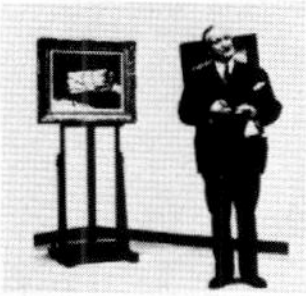

Wallraf-Richartz-Kuratorium und die Stadt Köln

Dem Wallraf-Richartz-Museum von Hermann J. Abs, dem Vorsitzenden des Kuratoriums, am 18. April 1968 im Andenken an Konrad Adenauer als Dauerleihgabe übergeben.

Das Wallraf-Richartz-Kuratorium und Förderer-Gesellschaft e. V.

Vorstand

Hermann J. Abs
Prof. Dr. Kurt Hansen
Dr. Dr. Günter Henle
Prof. Dr. Ernst Schneider
Prof. Dr. Otto H. Förster
Prof. Dr. Gert von der Osten (geschäftsführend)

Kuratorium

Prof. Dr. Viktor Achter
Dr. Max Adenauer
Fritz Berg
Dr. Walther Berndorff
Theo Burauen
Prof. Dr. Fritz Burgbacher
Dr. Fritz Butschkau
Dr. Felix Eckhardt
Frau Gisela Fitting
Prof. Dr. Kurt Forberg
Walter Franz
Dr. Hans Gerling
Dr. Herbert Girardet
Dr. Paul Gülker
Iwan D. Herstatt
Raymund Jörg
Eugen Gottlieb von Langen
Viktor Langen
Dr. Peter Ludwig
Prof. Dr. Heinz Mohnen
Cai Graf zu Rantzau
Karl Gustav Ratjen
Dr. Hans Reuter
Dr. Hans-Günther Sohl
Dr. Dr. Werner Schulz
Dr. Nikolaus Graf Strasoldo
Christoph Vowinckel
Otto Wolff von Amerongen

Hermann J. Abs bei der Übergabe des Bildes

Index of Names

18 **JULIO CAMPAL**
Montevideo, Uruguay, 1933 – Madrid, Spain, 1968

5 **FRANCESCO CANGIULLO**
Naples, Italy, 1884 – Livorno, Italy, 1977

2, 4, 5 **CARLO CARRÀ**
Quargnento, Italy, 1881 – Milan, Italy, 1966

3 **BLAISE CENDRARS**
Chaux-de-Fonds, Switzerland, 1887 – Paris, France, 1961

13 **AIMÉ CÉSAIRE**
Basse-Pointe, Martinica, 1913

1 **GIORGIO DE CHIRICO**
Volos, Greece, 1888 – Rome, Italy, 1978

11 **RENÉ CLAIR**
Paris, France, 1898 – Neuilly-sur-Seine, Île-de-France, France, 1981

15 **CLARK COOLIDGE**
Providence, Rhode-Island, United States, 1939

1 **JOSEPH CORNELL**
Nyack, New York, United States, 1903 – Flushing, New York, United States, 1972

18 **R. CORTES**

1 **EDWARD GORDON CRAIG**
Stevenage, United Kingdom, 1872 – Vence, France, 196[illegible]

17 **MERCE CUNNINGHAM**
Centralia, Washington, United States, 1919

19, 20 **RENÉ DANIELS**
Eindhoven, Netherlands, 1950

1 **CLAUDE DEBUSSY**
Saint-Germain-en-Laye, France, 1862 – Paris, France, 1918

4, 5 **ROBERT DELAUNAY**
Paris, France, 1885 – Montpellier, France, 1941

3, 7 **SONIA DELAUNAY**
Gradisk, Ukraine, 1885 – Paris, France, 1979

18 **JOKIN DIEZ DE FORTUNY**
San Sebastián, Spain, 1947

3 **EUGÈNE DRUET**
France, 1868 – 1917

[illegible], 11, 14 **MARCEL DUCHAMP**
Blainville, France, 1887 – Neuilly-sur-Seine, France, 1968

18 **FRANÇOIS DUFRÊNE**
Paris, France, 1930 – 1980

3 **THOMAS EDISON**
Milan, Ohio, United States, 1847 – West Orange, New Jersey, United States, 1931

11 **CARL EINSTEIN**
Berlin, Germany, 1885 – 1940

8 **SERGUEÏ EISENSTEIN**
Riga, Leetonia, 1898 – Moscow, Russia, 1948

3 **HARRY S. ELLIS**
Iowa, United States, 1855 – 1925

2, 6, 8 **MAX ERNST**
Brühl, Germany, 1891 – Paris, France, 1976

12 **WALKER EVANS**
St. Louis, Missouri, United States, 1903 – New Haven, United States, 1975

3 **ALEXANDRA EXTER**
Belestok, Russia, 1882 – Fontenay-aux-Roses, France, 1949

12 hallway, 18 **ÖYVIND FAHLSTRÖM**
São Paulo, Brazil, 1928 – Stockholm, Sweden, 1976

13 **JEAN FAUTRIER**
Paris, France, 1898 – 1964

17 **MORTON FELDMAN**
New York, United States, 1926 – Buffalo, United States, 1987

18 **ESTHER FERRER**
San Sebastián, Spain, 1937

1 **ALEXANDR FEVRAL'SKIJ**

2 **ROBERT FILLIOU**
Sauve, France, 1926 – Les Eyzies, France, 1987

8 **HERMANN FINSTERLIN**
Munich, Germany, 1887 – Stuttgart, Germany, 1973

12 **ROBERT FLAHERTY**
Iron Mountain, Michigan, United States, 1884 – Vermont, Montana, United States, 1951

11 **J.V. FOIX**
Barcelona, Spain, 1894 – 1987

19 **SIMONE FORTI**
Florence, Italy, 1936

1 **LYONEL FEININGER**
New York, United States, 1871 – 1956

3 **LOÏE FULLER**
Fullersburg, Illinois, United States, 1862 – Paris, France, 1928

2, 17 **NAUM GABO**
Bryansk, Russia, 1890 – Waterbury, Connecticut, United States, 1977

18 **JESÚS GARCÍA SÁNCHEZ**
Salamanca, Spain, 1943

14 **GEGO**
Hamburg, Germany, 1912 – Caracas, Venezuela, 1994

20 **JEAN-LUC GODARD**
Paris, France, 1930

5 **RAMÓN GÓMEZ DE LA SERNA**
Madrid, Spain, 1888 – Buenos Aires, Argentina, 1963

18 **EUGEN GOMRINGER**
Cachuela, Esperanza, Bolivia, 1925

3, 11 **JULIO GONZÁLEZ**
Barcelona, Spain, 1876 – Arcueil, France, 1942

10 **ELENA GOURO**
Saint Petersburg, Russia, 1877 – 1912

16,17 **DAN GRAHAM**
Illinois, United States, 1942

9 **NAOUM GRANOWSKI**

4 **JUAN GRIS**
Madrid, Spain, 1887 – Boulogne-sur-Seine, France, 1927

15 **PHILIP GUSTON**
Montreal, Canada, 1913 – Woodstock, New York, United States, 1980

20 hallway **HANS HAACKE**
Cologne, Germany, 1936

18 **RAYMOND HAINS**
Saint-Brieuc, France, 1926

14 **RICHARD HAMILTON**
London, United Kingdom, 1922

5, *6*, 9, 12, **RAOUL HAUSMANN**
Vienna, Austria, 1886 – Limoges, France, 1971

11 **LISE HIRTZ**
? – 1990

6 **HANNAH HÖCH**
Gotha, Turingen, Germany, 1889 – 1978

2 **FERDINAND HODLER**
Bern, Switzerland, 1853 – Geneva, Switzerland, 1918

17 **RICHARD HUELSENBECK**
Frankenau, Hessen, Germany, 1892 – Muralto, Switzerland, 1974

5 **VICENTE HUIDOBRO**
Santiago de Chile, Chile, 1893 – 1948

2 **DANIÈLE HUILLET**
Paris, France, 1936

9, 10,11 **ILIAZD (Ilia Zdanevitch)**
Tbilisi, Georgia, 1894 – Paris, France, 1975

4 **MAX JACOB**
Quimper, France, 1876 – Drancy, France, 1944

6 **MARCEL JANCO**
Bucarest, Romania, 1895 – Tel Aviv, Israel, 1984

1 **ALFRED JARRY**
Laval, France, 1873 – Paris, France, 1907

5 **JOSEP MARIA JUNOY**
Barcelona, Spain, 1887 – 1955

7, 10 **VASSILI KAMIENSKI**
Sarapoul, Russia, 1884 – Moscow, Russia, 1961

4, 8, 10, 11 **VASSILI KANDINSKY**
Moscow, Russia, 1866 – Paris, France, 1944

13 **EUGÈNE DE KERMADEC**
Paris, France, 1899 – 1976

6 **BUSTER KEATON**
Kansas, United States, 1895 – Los Angeles, California, United States, 1966

2 **ELLSWORTH KELLY**
Newburg, New York, United States, 1923

6, 11 **PAUL KLEE**
Münchenbuchsee, Switzerland, 1879 – Muralto Locarno, Switzerland, 1940

7, 10 **VELIMIR KHLEBNIKOV**
Turdutov, Astrakan, Russia, 1885 – Santalovo, Novgorod, Russia, 1922

10 **ALEXEI KRUCHENYKH**
Olevsk, Russia, 1886 – Moscow, Russia, 1968

17 **GEORGE KUBLER**
Los Angeles, United States, 1912 – Connecticut, United States, 1996

10 **NIKOLAÏ KUL'BIN**
1868 – 1917

2, 4 **FRANTISEK KUPKA**
Opocno, Bohemia, Czechoslovakia, 1871 – Puteaux, Hauts-de-Seine, France, 1957

3 **FERNAND LÉGER**
Argentan, France, 1881 – Gif-sur-Yvette, France, 195

12 **HELEN LEVITT**
New York, United States, 1914

16 **SOL LEWITT**
Hartfort, Connecticut, United States, 1928

6, 7, 10 **EL LISSITZKY**
Lazar Markovich, Russia, 1890 – Schodia, Russia, 1941

10 **BENEDIKT LIVSCHITZ**

3 **LOUISE LUMIÈRE**
Besaçon, Doubs, France, 1864 – Bandol, Var, France, 1948

4 **DORA MAAR**
Tours, France, 1907 – Paris, France, 1997

1, 8 **RENÉ MAGRITTE**
Lessines, Belgium, 1898 – Brussels, Belgium, 1967

7, 10 **VLADIMIR MAYAKOVSKI**
Bagdadi, Georgia, 1893 – Moscow, Russia, 1930

7, 10 **KASIMIR MALEVIC**
Kiev, Russia, 1878 – Leningrad, Russia, 1935

2 **STÉPHANE MALLARMÉ**
Paris, France, 1842 – 1898

5 **MAN RAY (Emmanuel Radnitzky)**
Philadelphia, United States, 1890 – Paris, France, 1976

2 **ÉDOUARD MANET**
Paris, France, 1832 – 1883

14 **PIERO MANZONI**
Cremona, Italy, 1933 – Milan, Italy, 1963

4 **FRANZ MARC**
Munich, Germany, 1880 – Verdun, France, 1916

18 **WALTER MARCHETTI**
Canosa di Puglia, Italy, 1931

5 **FILIPPO TOMMASO MARINETTI**
Alexandria, Egypt, 1876 – Como, Italy, 1944

13, 17 **ROBERTO MATTA**
Santiago de Chile, Chile, 1911 – 2002

8 **MIKHAÏL MATYUSHIN**
Nizhnii-Novgorod, Russia, 1861 –
Saint Petersburg, Russia, 1934

1 **VSEVOLOD MEYERHOLD**
Penza, Russia, 1874 – Moscow, Russia, 1940

13 **HENRI MICHAUX**
Namur, Belgium, 1889 – Paris, France, 1984

18 **AMADO RAMÓN MILLÁN**

18 **FERNANDO MILLÁN**
Villarodrigo, Jaén, Spain, 1944

9, 11, 13 **JOAN MIRÓ**
Barcelona, Spain, 1893 –Majorca, Spain, 1983

8, 17 **LÁSZLÓ MOHOLY-NAGY**
Bacsboro, Hungary, 1895 – Chicago, United States, 1946

3 **R. MOREAU**

17 **ROBERT MORRIS**
Kansas City, United States, 1931

8 **F. W. MURNAU**
Bielefeld, Germany, 1888 – Santa Barbara,
California, United States, 1931

16 **BRUCE NAUMAN**
Fort Wayne, Indiana, United States, 1941

2 **JORGE OTEIZA**
Orio, Spain, 1908 – Sant Sebastián,
Spain, 2003

4, 7 **AMÉDÉE OZENFANT**
Saint-Quentin, France, 1886 – Cannes, France, 1966

14 **PABLO PALAZUELO**
Madrid, Spain, 1916

11 **BENJAMIN PÉRET**
Rézé, France, 1899 – Paris, France, 1959

7 **GRIGORII PETNIKOV**
Petersburg, Russia, 1894 – Republic of Crimea, 1971

17, 2 **NOTON PEVSNER**
Orel, Russia, 1884 – Paris, France, 1962

5 **FRANCIS PICABIA**
Paris, France, 1879 – 1953

2, 3, 4, 13 **PABLO PICASSO**
Malaga, Spain, 1881 – Mougins, France, 1973

13 **HENRI PICHETTE**
Châteauroux, France, 1924 – 2000

13 **FRANCIS PONGE**
Montpellier, France, 1899 – Bar-sur-Loup, France, 1988

9, 10 **LIOUBOV POPOVA**
Ivanskoï, Moscow, Russia, 1889 – Moscow, Russia, 1924

5 **BALILLA PRATELLA**
Lugo di Romagna, Italy, 1880 – Ravenna, Italy, 1955

6, 9, 10 **IVAN PUNI**
Kuokkala, Finland, 1894 – Paris, France, 1956

4 **NIKOLAÏ PUNIN**
Helsinki, Finland, 1888 – Vorkuta, Siberia, 1953

19 **YVONNE RAINER**
San Francisco, California, United States, 1934

14, 17 **ROBERT RAUSCHENBERG**
Port Arthur, Texas, United States, 1925

2 **ODILON REDON**
Bordeaux, France, 1840 – Paris, France, 1916

13 **PIERRE REVERDY**
Narbonne, France, 1889 – Solesme, France, 1960

9 **GEORGES RIBEMONT-DESSAIGNES**
Montpellier, France, 1884 – Saint Jeannet, France, 1974

17 **HANS RICHTER**
Berlin, Germany, 1888 – Minusio, Locarno, Switzerland, 1976

17 **ALAIN ROBBE-GRILLET**
Brest, Finistère, France, 1922

7, 10 **ALEXANDER RODTXENKO**
Saint Petersburg, Russia, 1891 – Moscow, Russia, 1956

13 **ROBERTO ROSSELLINI**
Rome, Italy, 1906 – 1977

18 **DIETER ROTH**
Hanover, Germany, 1930 – Basel, Switzerland, 1998

3, 4, 10 **OLGA ROZANOVA**
Melenki, Russia, 1886 – Moscow, Russia, 1918

5 **LUIGI RUSSOLO**
Puortogruaro, Italy, 1885 – Cerro di Laveno, Italy, 1947

5 **JOAN SALVAT-PAPASSEIT**
Barcelona, Spain, 1894 – 1924

12 **AUGUST SANDER**
Herdorf, Germany, 1876 – Cologne, Germany, 1964

3 **ERIK SATIE**
Honfleur, France 1866 – Paris, France, 1925

2 **JACQUES SCHERER**
??? – 1997

4 **GINO SEVERINI**
Cortona, Italy, 1883 – Paris, France, 1966

6, 7, 8 **KURT SCHWITTERS**
Hanover, Germany, 1887 – Kendal, United Kingdom, 1948

11 **CARLES SINDREU**
Barcelona, Spain, 1900 – La Garriga, Spain, 1974

7 **MARIA SINIAKOVA**
1890 – 1984

1 **VICTOR SJÔSTRÔM**
Silbodal, Sweden, 1879 – Stockholm, Sweden, 1960

14 **TONY SMITH**
South Orange, New Jersey, United States, 1912
New York, United States, 1980

4 **ARDENGO SOFFICI**
Florence, Italy, 1879 – 1964

17 **SUSAN SONTAG**
New York, United States, 1933 – 2004

19 **NANCY SPERO**
Cleveland, Ohio, United States, 1926

7 **VARVARA STEPANOVA**
Kovno, Russia, 1894 – Moscow, Russia, 1958

2 **JEAN-MARIE STRAUB**
Metz, France, 1933

13 **WLADISLAW STRZEMINSKI**
Minsk, Byelorussia, 1893 – Lotz, Poland, 1952

6, 7, 11 **SOPHIE TAEUBER-ARP**
Davos, Switzerland, 1889 – Zurich, Switzerland, 194

2 **YVES TANGUY**
Paris, France, 1900 – Woodbury, Connecticut, United States, 1955

2, 13 **ANTONI TÀPIES**
Barcelona, Spain, 1923

4 **VLADIMIR TATLIN**
Kharkov, Russia, 1885 – Moscow, Russia, 1953

9 **IGOR TERENTIEV**

5 **GUILLERMO DE TORRE**
Madrid, Spain, 1900 – Buenos Aires, Argentina, 19

5 **JOAQUÍN TORRES-GARCÍA**
Montevideo, Uruguay, 1874 – 1949

5, 11 **TRISTAN TZARA**
Moinesti, Romania, 1896 – Paris, France, 1963

11 **BÈLA UITZ**
Temes, Mehala, Hungry, 1887 – Budapest, Hungry, 1972

18 **ENRIQUE URIBE**
Pamplona, Spain, 1942

13 **JACQUES VACHÉ**
Nantes, France, 1896 – 1919

7 **BART VAN DER LECK**
Utrecht, Netherlands, 1879 – Blaricum, Amsterdam, Netherlands, 1958

17 **STAN VANDERBEEK**
1927 – 1984

11, 14 **GEORGES VANTONGERLOO**
Antwerp, Belgium, 1886 – Paris, France, 1965

11 **JEAN VIGO**
Paris, France, 1905 – 1934

20 **JEFF WALL**
Vancouver, Canada, 1946

13 **WOLS (Alfred Otto Wolfgang Schulze)**
Berlin, Germany, 1913 – Paris, France, 1951

18 **FRANCISCO ZABALA**
Madrid, Spain, 1947

20 **RÉMY ZAUGG**
Courgenay, Switzerland, 1943

10 **KIRILL ZDANEVIC**
Tiflis, Georgia, 1892 – 1969

ROOM ASPEN

17 **ROLAND BARTHES**
Cherbourg, France, 1915 – Paris, France, 1980

17 **SAMUEL BECKETT**
Dublin, Ireland, 1906 – Paris, France, 1989

17 **WILLIAM BURROUGHS**
Saint Louis, Missouri, United States, 1914 – Lawrence, Kansas, United States, 1997

17, 18 **JOHN CAGE**
Los Angeles, United States, 1912 – New York, United States, 1992

17 **MERCE CUNNINGHAM**
Centralia, Washington, United States, 1919

17 **MARCEL DUCHAMP**
Blainville, France, 1887 – Paris, France, 1968

17 **MORTON FELDMAN**
New York, United States, 1926 – Buffalo, United States, 1987

2, 17 **NAUM GABO**
Bryansk, Russia, 1890 – Waterbury, Connecticut, United States, 1977

16, 17 **DAN GRAHAM**
Illinois, United States, 1942

17 **RICHARD HUELSENBECK**
Frankenau, Hessen, Germany, 1892 – Muralto, Switzerland, 1974

17 **GEORGE KUBLER**
Los Angeles, United States, 1912 – Connecticut, United States, 1996

16 **SOL LEWITT**
Hartfort, Connecticut, United States, 1928

17 **ROBERT MORRIS**
Kansas City, United States, 1931

2, 17 **NOTON PEVSNER**
Orel, Russia, 1884 – Paris, France, 1962

14, 17 **ROBERT RAUSCHENBERG**
Port Arthur, Texas, United States, 1925

17 **HANS RICHTER**
Berlin, Germany, 1888 – Minusio, Locarno, Switzerland, 1976

17 **ALAIN ROBBE-GRILLET**
Brest, Finistère, France, 1922

14 **TONY SMITH**
South Orange, New Jersey, United States, 1912 – New York, United States, 1980

17 **SUSAN SONTAG**
New York, United States, 1933 – 2004

17 **STAN VANDERBEEK**
1927 – 1984

Level 1. Rooms 1-11

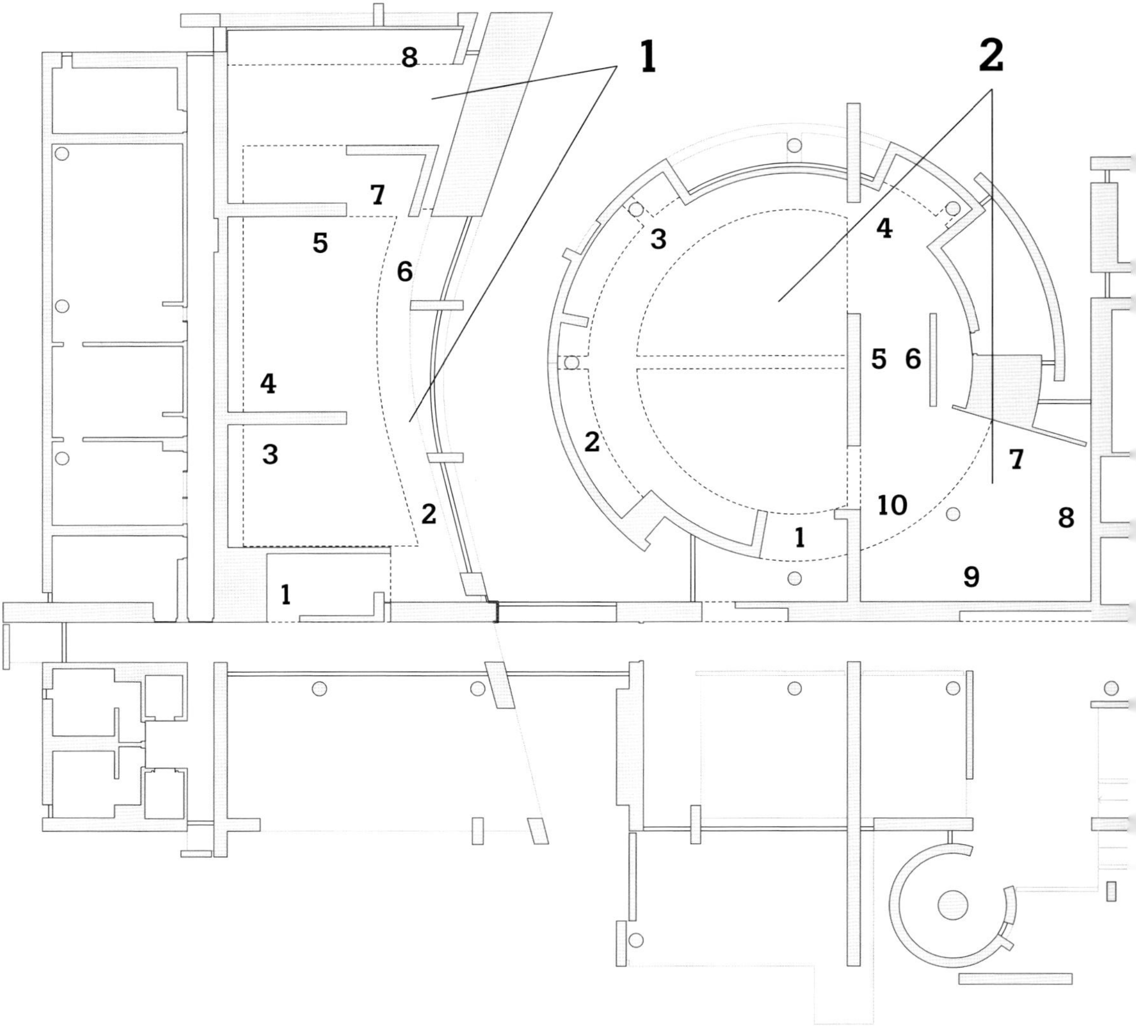

List of Works

Concept by Élia Pijollet; produced in conjunction with the MACBA

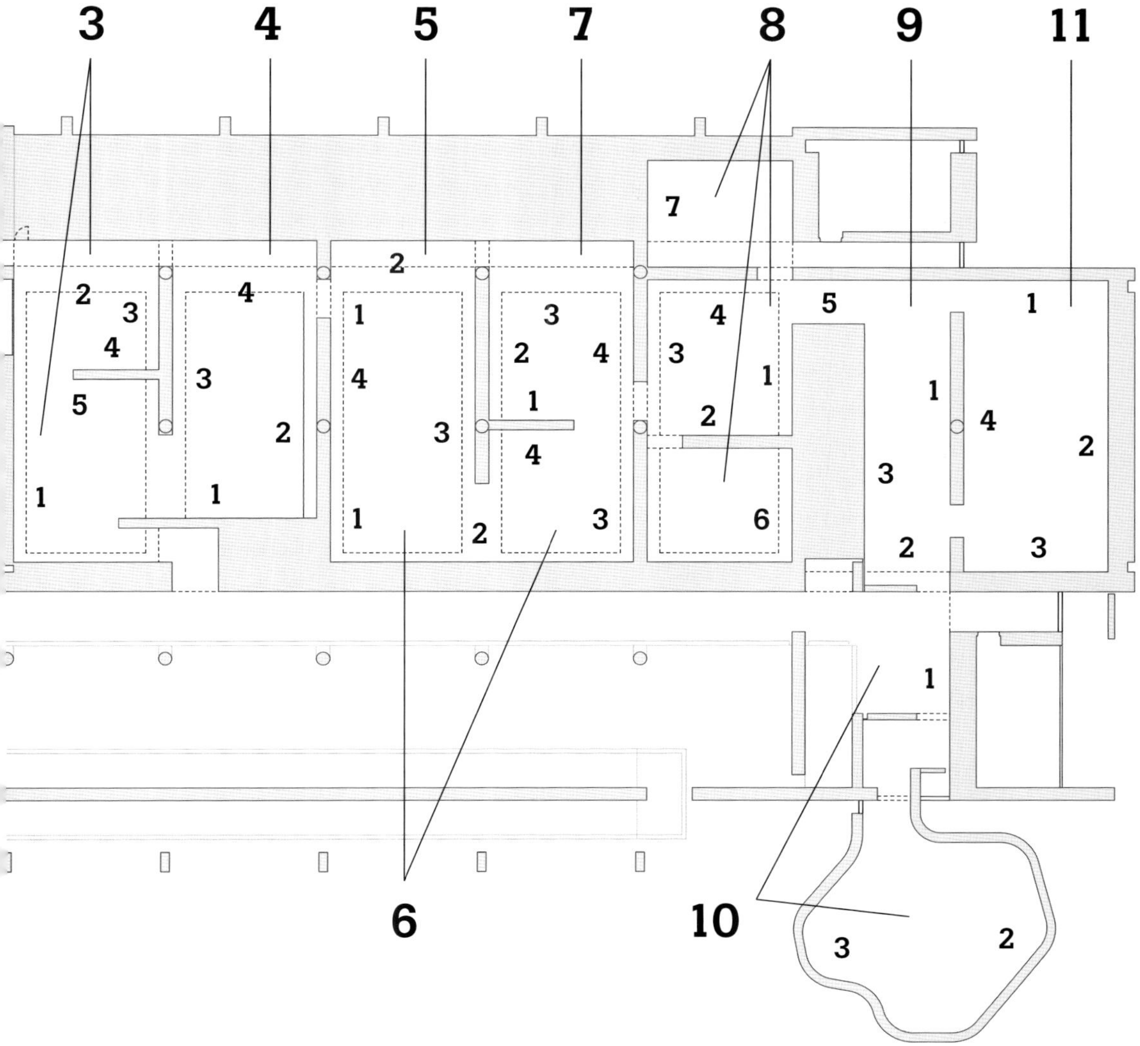

Level 1

Room 1: Prologue: The theatre of the mind

WALL 1

Giorgio de Chirico
1 *Le Printemps*
Spring
La primavera
1914
Oil paint on canvas
29 x 37 cm
Private collection

WALL 2

René Magritte
2 *Le Gouffre argenté*
The Silver Abyss
El abismo plateado
1926
Oil paint on canvas
75 x 65 cm
The Berardo Collection – Sintra Museum of Modern Art

WALL 3

Joseph Cornell
3 *Untitled (Apollinaris)*
Sin título (Apollinaris)
1953
Box construction
48,3 x 27,9 x 12,7 cm
The Robert Lehrman Art Trust

4 *Trade Winds Storm Warning*
Aviso de tormenta de vientos alisios
1958
Box construction
27,9 x 42,7 x 10,3 cm
The Robert Lehrman Art Trust

5 *Cloches à travers les feuilles*
Bells beyond the Leaves
Campanas a través de las hojas
ca. 1957
Silent film, 16 mm, USA, 4'15"

6 *Le Vierge, le vivace, le bel aujourd'hui...*
The Virgin, the Vivacious, the Beautiful Today...
Lo virgen, lo vivaz, lo bello hoy...
1970
Collage
35,5 x 30,6 cm
The Robert Lehrman Art Trust

BACKGROUND MUSIC

Claude Debussy
7 *Cloches à travers les feuilles*
Bells beyond the Leaves
Campanas a través de las hojas
Michelangeli, 1971
4'23''. Pianist: Martin Jones
Nimbus Records Limited, NI 1773

WALL 4

Edward Gordon Craig
8 *Set design for Hamlet*
Proyecto de decorado para Hamlet
Undated
Pastel on paper
29,2 x 45,3 cm
Bibliothèque nationale de France, Paris

9 *Unused set design for* Hamlet*, Act III, Scene 3*
Proyecto de decorado no utilizado para Hamlet, Act III, escena 3
Undated
Wash and white gouache
35,5 x 30 cm
Bibliothèque nationale de France, Paris

10 *Descending into Tomb*
Bajando a la tumba
1904
Preparatory drawing for an etching based on the final scene of Hamlet
28 x 20 cm
Bibliothèque nationale de France, Paris

11 *Study for Hamlet*
Estudio para Hamlet
1910
Pastel on paper
18 x 26 cm
Bibliothèque nationale de France, Paris

12 *Set design for Hamlet, Act I, Scene 1*
Proyecto de decorado para Hamlet, acto I, escena 1
Undated
Ink wash on paper
19,5 x 28 cm
Bibliothèque nationale de France, Paris

13 *Unused set design for* Hamlet*, Act III, Scene 3*
Proyecto de decorado no utilizado para Hamlet, Act III, escena 3
Undated
Pastel and white gouache on paper
36 x 27 cm
Bibliothèque nationale de France, Paris

14 *Set design for* Hamlet*, Act II, Scene 2*
Proyecto de decorado para Hamlet, acto II, escena 2
1904
Ink and watercolour on paper
30,5 x 25 cm
Bibliothèque nationale de France, Paris

WALL 5

Adolphe Appia
15 *Espace rythmique, "Avant qu'une main invisible ouvre la porte"*
Rhythmic Space, "Before an Invisible Hand Opens the Door"
Espacio rítmico, "Antes de que una mano invisible abra la puerta"
1909
Graphite, charcoal, stump work and red chalk on paper
47,7 x 63,5 cm
Musées d'art et d'histoire de la Ville de Genève Collection

16 *Espace rythmique, "La porte ouverte"*
Rhythmic Space, "The Open Door"
Espacio rítmico, "La puerta abierta"
1909
Charcoal and stump work on paper
47,7 x 63,5 cm
Musées d'art et d'histoire de la Ville de Genève Collection

17 *Espace rythmique, "Les Trois piliers"*
Rhythmic Space, "The Three Pillars"
Espacio rítmico, "Los tres pilares"
1909
Graphite, charcoal, stump work, white chalk and red chalk on paper
46,2 x 61,2 cm
Musées d'art et d'histoire de la Ville de Genève Collection

18 *Espace rythmique, "La ronde du soir"*
Rhythmic Space, "The Evening Patrol"
Espacio rítmico, "La ronda del anochecer"
1909
Graphite, charcoal and stump work on paper
49,9 x 71,7 cm
Musées d'art et d'histoire de la Ville de Genève Collection

19 *Décor pour "Tristan et Iseult" de Richard Wagner, acte II, final*
Set for "Tristan and Isolde" by Richard Wagner, Act II, End
Decorado para "Tristán e Isolda" de Richard Wagner,

acto II, final
1896
Graphite, charcoal, stump work, white chalk, charcoal and red chalk on paper
72,2 x 48,1 cm
Musées d'art et d'histoire Collection, Geneva

20 ***Espace rythmique, "Les Cyprès"***
Rhythmic Space, "The Cypresses"
Espacio rítmico, "Los cipreses"
1909
Charcoal, stump work, white chalk and red chalk on paper
48 x 62 cm
Musées d'art et d'histoire de la Ville de Genève Collection

21 ***Espace rythmique, "Neuf piliers"***
Rhythmic Space, "Nine Pillars"
Espacio rítmico, "Nueve pilares
1909
Charcoal and stump work on paper
50,2 x 72,4 cm
Musées d'art et d'histoire de la Ville de Genève Collection

22 ***Espace rythmique, "À la lisière"***
Rhythmic Space, "On the Edge"
Espacio rítmico, "En el lindero"
1909
Charcoal, stump work and red chalk on paper
52,5 x 72,4 cm
Musées d'art et d'histoire de la Ville de Genève Collection

23 ***Espace rythmique, "Cheminement"***
Rhythmic Space, "Progression"
Espacio rítmico, "Camino"
1909
Charcoal, stump work, white chalk and red chalk on paper
48 x 62 cm
Musées d'art et d'histoire de la Ville de Genève Collection

24 ***Espace rythmique, "La cascade"***
Rhythmic Space, "The Waterfall"
Espacio rítmico, "La cascada"
1909
Charcoal and stump work on paper
50,7 x 72,2 cm
Musées d'art et d'histoire de la Ville de Genève Collection

WALL 6

Vsevolod Meyerhold
25 ***The Inspector General, by N. Gogol. Photograph of a Scene from Episode 14: "A Party is a Party"***
El revisor, de N. Gogol. Fotografía de una escena del episodio 14: "Una fiesta es una fiesta"
GOSTIM (Meyerhold Theatre)
1926
Black-and-white photographic enlargement
130 x 195 cm
B. Picon-Vallin Archive (original)

26 ***Zemlja dybom***
The Rearing Earth
La tierra encabritada
TIM (Meyerhold Theatre), 1923
Montage of the text by S. Tre'jakov, according to M. Martinet
Photo of the stage set for episode 7, "A Knife on the Left of the Revolution". Construction by Liubov Popova
Black-and-white photographic enlargement
130 x 185 cm
Arxius B. Picon-Vallin (original)

WALL 7

Lyonel Feininger
27 ***Tortum I***
1923-1926
Oil paint on canvas
61 x 47,5 cm
Kunstmuseum Basel, Basel

VITRINE

Joseph Cornell
28 ***Untitled ("Hôtel de l'Étoile")***
Sin título ("Hôtel de l'Étoile")
ca. 1956
Box construction
45,5 x 30,7 x 10,4 cm
The Berardo Collection – Sintra Museum of Modern Art

VIDEO

Ingmar Bergman
29 ***Tystnaden***
The Silence
El silencio
1963
Black-and-white film, Sweden 96'

WALL 8

Victor Sjöström
30 ***The Wind***
El viento
1928
35 mm film, black and white, silent, 73'

VITRINES: EDWARD GORDON CRAIG: THE "SURMARIONNETTE"

Edward Gordon Craig and his Arena Goldoni students (Florence)
31 ***Untitled***
Sin título
Undated
Burmese-style puppet of gilded wood, with costume
69 x 26 x 13 cm
Bibliothèque nationale de France, Paris

32 ***Untitled***
Sin título
Undated
Studio puppet of painted woodwith mask of Pantalon
81 x 23 x 14 cm
Bibliothèque nationale de France, Paris

33 ***Untitled***
Sin título
Undated
7 fragments of studio puppets of carved wood.
17 x 13 x 5 cm; 33 x 31 x 3 cm; 40 x 10 x 8 cm; 17 x 15 x 6 cm; 17 x 15 x 6 cm; 19 x 17 x 7,5 cm; 40 x 12 x 5 cm;
1913
Bibliothèque nationale de France, Paris

34 ***Untitled***
Sin título
1913
2 headless studio puppetsof carved wood; 13 articulated elements: torso, legs in 6 segments, arms in 6 segments
Each one 62 x 22 x 10 cm
Bibliothèque nationale de France, Paris

VITRINE: "VSEVOLOD MEYERHOLD, DOCUMENTS: 1914-1934"

35 ***Ljubok' k trem appel'sinam***
Love for Three Oranges
Amor por tres naranjas
Journal of Doctor Dappertutto (alias Meyerhold)
Saint Petersburg, 1914
Cover by Yuri Budi

36 ***Erast Garin in the role of Pavel Guliachkin, in The Warrant (play by Nikolai Erdman), directed by V. Meyerhold, 1925***
Ernest Garine en el papel de Pavel Gouliatchkine, en Le Mandat (pieza de Nikolaï Erdman), puesta en escena de V. Meyerhold, 1925
Vintage copy
V. Meyerhold / Shostakovich, 1928
Black-and-white photograph, vintage copy

37 *Programme of Woe from Wit by Alexander Griboyedov, directed by V. Meyerhold*
Programa de la representación de Malheur à l'esprit, *de Griboïedov, puesta en escena de V. Meyerhold*
1928
Typographic print on paper

Alexander Fevralsky
38 10 let Teatra Mejerhol'da
10 Years of the Meyerhold Theatre
Los 10 años de Théâtre Meyerhold
Moscow, Federacija, 1931

39 *Programme of* The Government Inspector, *play by N. Gogol, directed by V. Meyerhold at the GOSTIM (Meyerhold State Theatre)*
Programa de Le Revizor, *pieza de N. Gogol, puesta en escena de V. Meyerhold en el GOSTIM (Teatre de Estado Meyerhold)*
1926

40 Le Revizor *de N. Gogol*
The Inspector by N. Gogol
El Revisor *de N. Gogol*
Photograph of a scene from episode 14, "A Holiday Is a Holiday"
GOSTIM (Meyerhold State Theatre)
1926
Vintage copy
TIM poster(Meyerhold Theatre Posters), no. 4, 1927
GOSTIM (Teatre d'Estat Meyerhold)
1926
Tiratge d'època
Aficha TIM (Cartell del Teatre Meyerhold), núm. 4, 1927

41 *V. Meyerhold, D. Shostakovich, V. Mayakovsky, A. Rodchenko during the preparation of The Bedbug (play by Mayakovsky), directed by V. Meyerhold*
V. Meyerhold, Chostakóvich, V. Mayakovski, A. Rodtchenko durante la preparación de La Punaise *(pieza de V. Mayakovski), puesta en escena de V. Meyerhold*
1928
Black-and-white photograph, vintage copy

42 *Biomechanical Exercice The Rifle 1, 2 and 3*
Ejercicio biomecánico
Le Rifle *1, 2 i 3*
ca. 1934
3 photographs in black-and-white, vintage copies

The documents in this vitrine come from the B. Picon-Vallin Archive

Room 2: First constellation, matrix

WALL 1

Marcel Broodthaers
43 *Ma collection*
My Collection
Mi colección
1971
Collage on paper
2 panels, each one 68 x 104 cm
Uli Knecht Collection

44 *Un coup de dés*
A Toss of the Dice
Una tirada de dados
1969
Paint on canvas
165 x 122 cm
Speck Collection, Cologne

GLASS CASE

Jorge Oteiza
45 *Desocupación no cúbica del espacio*
Non-Cubic Emptying of Space
1958-1959
Iron
40 x 43.8 x 38 cm
Col·lecció MACBA. Fundació Museu d'Art Contemporani de Barcelona. Gift of the Fundació Bertrán

Naum Gabo
46 *Spheric Theme: Black Variation*
Tema esférico: variación en negro
1937
Transparent celluloid acetate and black celluloid
Ø 42.5 cm
Galerie de France, Paris

WALL 2

Odilon Redon
47 *Three illustrations for "A Toss of the Dice," a poem by Stéphane Mallarmé, edition by Ambroise Vollard interrupted by Mallarmé's death.*
La femme à l'aigrette
The Woman with the Tuft
La mujer con el copete
1898
Lithograph, trial proof
36 x 27.5 cm
Bibliothèque nationale de France, Paris

48 *La Femme au hennin*
The Hooded Woman
La mujer con la capucha
1898
Lithograph, trial proof
35.5 x 27.3 cm
Bibliothèque nationale de France, Paris

49 *L'Enfant à l'arc-en-ciel (ex-libris)*
The Kid with the Rainbow
El niño con el arco iris
1898
Lithograph, trial proof
10.5 x 7.2 cm (design);
22.5 x 18.2 cm (paper)
Bibliothèque nationale de France, Paris

Pablo Picasso
50 *Bouteille, journal et verre sur une table ("Un coup de thé")*
Bottle, Newspaper and Glass on a Table ("A Blow of Tea")
Botella, periódico y vaso sobre una mesa ("Un golpe de té")
Paris, Autumn-Winter 1912
Charcoal, gouacheand glued pieces of paper on paper
62 x 48 cm
Centre Pompidou, Musée national d'art moderne / Centre de création industrielle, Paris

Stéphane Mallarmé / Edouard Manet
51 *L'Après-midi d'un faune, églogue*
The Eclogue Faun's Afternoon Nap
La siesta de un fauno, égloga
Alphonse Derenne Editeur, Paris, 1876
-Cover, 27.8 x 20 cm
-"Le faune", frontispiece, 17.4 x 24.2 cm
-"Feuilles dans l'herbe", ex-libris, 10.9 x 6.5 cm
-"Les Nymphes", fleuron, 28.4 x 18 cm
-"Grappes de raisin", vignette, 28.2 x 17.9 cm
4 illustrations, anonymous engravings after Manet, printed on Japan paper, the first two heightened with watercolour
195 copies
Bibliothèque nationale de France, Paris

Ferdinand Hodler
52 *Le Lac de Thoune et le massif du Stockhorn*
Lake Thun and the Stockhorn Massif
El lago de Thoune y el macizo del Stockhorn
1912
Oil paint on canvas
68 x 90.5 cm
Private collection, Switzerland

Edouard Manet
53 *Tête de corbeau de profil*
Raven's Head in Profile
Cabeza de cuervo de perfil
Poster for Le Corbeau [The Raven], poem by Edgar Allan Poe, translated into French by Stéphane Mallarmé
Ed. R. Lesclides, 1875
Parchment
59 x 40.2 cm
Bibliothèque nationale de France, Paris

54 *Six autographed brush illustrations for Edgar Allan Poe's poem "The Raven", translated into French by Stéphane Mallarmé*
Seis ilustraciones autógrafas, con pincel, para "Le corbeau [The Raven], poema de Edgar A. Poe, traducción al francés de Stéphane Mallarmé
240 copies, illustrations on riceor laid paper
Ed. R. Lesclides, 1875
Complete copy with "À la fenêtre" in its second state, number 45
-"Tête de corbeau", in profile, for the cover. Proof without text. Lithograph.
17.1 x 15.9 cm (design)
-"Le Corbeau volant", ex-libris on fine parchment
27.9 x 33.7 (dibuix); 29.9 x 36.6 cm (paper)
-"Sous la lampe", proof on rice paper, 38.9 x 55.1 cm
-"À la fenêtre", proof on rice paper, 45.8 x 35.6 cm
-"La chaise", proof on rice paper, 41 x 36 cm
-"Le corbeau sur le buste", proof on rice paper, 55.7 x 39 cm
Bibliothèque nationale de France, Paris

WALL 3

Marcel Broodththaers
55 *Le Corbeau et le Renard*
The Fox and the Crow
El cuervo y el zorro
1967
-Cardboard and fabric portfolio of drawings, 37/40
80 x 60.5 cm
-Silkscreen-printed projection screen
98.8 x 130 cm
-Tin box
Ø 19 cm, with adhesive label
-Silkscreen-printed projection screen and wood
61.2 x 81.2 x 4.5 cm
-16 mm film, colour; silent, 7'
-3 prints: 53.7 x 75.7 cm; 75.5 x 53.7 cm; 75.5 x 54 cm
-Typographic print on paper
56 x 75.8 cm
-Typographic print on cardboard
57.3 x 75.7 cm
-Photographic print on canvas
Col·lecció MACBA. Fundació Museu d'Art Contemporani de Barcelona

56 *Série de neuf tableaux*
Series of Nine Paintings
Serie de nueve cuadros
1972
Ink print on industrially prepared canvas
9 x 79.5 x 100 cm
Van Abbemuseum Collection, Eindhoven, The Netherlands

57 *Figures*
Figures
Figuras
1973
Typographic print on canvas
80 x 100 cm
Kewenig Galerie, Cologne

Robert Filliou
58 *Autobiographical*
Autobiográfico
1963-1973
Wooden box with 5 bricks and various materials
29 x 79 x 11 cm
Anne-Marie & Marc Robelin Collection

VITRINE

Robert Filliou
59 *Trois jeux: Apollinaire, Rimbaud, Baudelaire*
Three Games: Apollinaire, Rimbaud, Baudelaire
Tres juegos: Apollinaire, Rimbaud, Baudelaire
1961
Pieces of engraved wood in a wooden box (50 red, 50 green, 50 black)
Box: 7 x 60.5 x 12 cm
Neues Museum Weserburg Bremen, Gerstner Collection

WALL 4

Ellsworth Kelly
60 *The Mallarmé Suite*
La suite Mallarmé
1992
4 lithographs in a fabric-covered slipcase, each sheet 74 x 55 cm
Courtesy of the artist and the Matthew Marks Gallery, New York

VIDEO

Jean-Marie Straub / Danielle Huillet
61 *Toute révolution est un coup de dés*
All Revolutions are a Toss of the Dice
Toda revolución es un golpe de dados
France, 1977
VHS copy of a 16 mm film, 11'

WALL 5

Frantisek Kupka
62 *La Dormeuse*
The Sleeper
La durmiente
1909-1910
10 illustrations for the Edgar A llan Poe tale
Graphite, grease pencil and Indian ink wash on paper
Each sheet 32.8 x 25.4 cm
Private collection

WALL 6

Odilon Redon
63 *C'était une main de chair et de sang*
It Was a Hand of Flesh and Blood
Era una mano de carne y sangre
Àlbum *La Maison hantée*, ill. IV
1896
Lithograph on rice paper
24.6 x 17.9 cm (design);
44.7 x 31 cm (paper)
Bibliothèque nationale de France, Paris

64 *Lumière*
Light
Luz
1893
Lithograph on rice paper
39.3 x 27.4 cm (design);
62.4 x 45 cm (paper)
Bibliothèque nationale de France, Paris

65 *Il y eut aussi des êtres embryonnaires*
There Were also Embryonic Beings
También hubo seres embrio-narios
Àlbum *Hommage à Goya*, il. IV
1885
Lithograph on rice paper
23.8 x 19.8 cm (design) ;
33.2 x 28.2 cm (paper)

Bibliothèque nationale de France, Paris

VITRINE

Odilon Redon
66 ***La Tentation de saint Antoine***
The Temptation of St Antony
La tentación de san Antonio
1938
Text by Gustave Flaubert, 22 lithographs by Odilon Redon on sized rice paper
220 copies, in loose sheets, with illustrated cover, Paris, ed. Ambroise Vollard
73 x 44 x 7 cm (open)
Private collection, Barcelona

WALL 7

Yves Tanguy
67 ***Belomancie***
1927
Oil paint on canvas
55 x 38 cm
Museo Nacional Centro de Arte Reina Sofía, Madrid

Odilon Redon
68 ***Quadrige***
Chariot
Cuadriga
Undated
Oil paint on canvas
78.5 x 105 cm
Private collection

69 ***Tête d'Orphée sur la lyre***
Head of Orpheus on the Lyre
Cabeza de Orfeo sobre la lira
1880
Oil paint on canvas
32.2 x 40.3 cm
Musée Municipal de l'Evêché, Limoges (on loan from the Musée d'Orsay)

WALL 8

Günter Brus
70 ***Redon: die heilige Qual, Bild-Dichtung***
Redon: the Holy Martyr, Image-Poem
Redon: el martirio sagrado, imagen-poema
1981-1982
15 sheets. Conté crayon on paper
each sheet 29.7 x 21 cm
Centre Pompidou, Musée national d'art moderne / Centre de création industrielle, Paris

WALL 9

Odilon Redon
71 ***Dans mon rêve, je vis au ciel un visage de mystère***
In my Dream I saw a Mysterious Face in the Sky
En mi sueño he visto en el cielo un rostro de misterio
Àlbum *Hommage à Goya* ill. I
1885
Lithograph on rice paper
29.1 x 24.1 cm (design); 36.8 x 29.9 cm (paper)
Bibliothèque nationale de France, Paris

72 ***Un fou dans un morne paysage***
Madman in a Sad Landscape
Un loco en un paisaje triste
Àlbum *Hommage à Goya*, il. III
1885
Lithograph on rice paper
22.7 x 19.8 cm (design); 32.5 x 28.2 cm (paper)
Bibliot hèque nationale de France, Paris

73 ***L'Aile***
The Wing
El ala
1893
Litografia
32 x 24,5 cm (dibuix);
62 x 43,9 cm (paper)
Bibliothèque nationale de France, Paris

74 ***Il y eut peut-être une vision première essayée dans la fleur***
Perhaps there was a First Vision Tested in the Flower
Posiblemente hubo una primera visión ensayada en la flor
Àlbum *Les Origines*, il. II
1883
Lithograph on rice paper
22.3 x 17.6 cm (design); 48.8 x 35 cm (paper)
Bibliothèque nationale de France, Paris

75 ***Un étrange jongleur***
A Strange Juggler
Un malabarista extraño
Album *Hommage à Goya*, ill. V
1885
Lithograph on rice paper
19.9 x 19 cm (design); 29.5 x 27.7 cm (paper)
Bibliothèque nationale de France, Paris

76 ***Au réveil j'aperçus la déesse de l'intelligible au profil sévère et dur***
Upon Awakening I perceived the Goddess of the Intelligible with a Severe and Hard Profile
Al despertar percibí a la diosa de lo inteligible con perfil severo y duro
Album *Hommage à Goya*, ill. VI
1885
Lithograph on rice paper
27 x 21.6 cm (design); 36.9 x 30.3 cm (paper)
Bibliothèque nationale de France, Paris

77 ***Oannès: Moi, la première conscience du chaos, j'ai surgi de l'abîme pour durcir la matière, pour régler les formes***
Oannes: I, the First Consciousness of Chaos, Arose from the Abyss to Harden Matter to Regulate Forms.
Oannes: yo, la primera conciencia del caos, surgío del abismo para endurecer la materia, para regular las formas.
Album *La Tentation de saint Antoine*, 3rd series, ill. XIII
1896
Lithograph
27.8 x 21.7 cm (design); 56.2 x 39.9 cm (paper)
Bibliothèque nationale de France, Paris

78 ***L'Œil comme un ballon bizarre se dirige vers l'infini***
The Eye, like a Strange Balloon, Moves Towards Infinity
El ojo como un extraño balón se dirige hacia el infinito
Album *À Edgar A. Poe*, ill. I
1882
Lithograph on rice paper
26.2 x 20.1 cm (design); 27.7 x 28.8 cm (paper)
Bibliothèque nationale de France, Paris

79 ***Vision***
Vision
Visión
Album Dans le rêve, ill. VIII
1879
Lithograph on paper
27.6 x 19.8 cm (design); 37.2 x 29.7 cm (paper)
Bibliothèque nationale de France, Paris

80 ***La Fleur de marécage, une tête humaine et triste***
The Swamp Flower, a Sad and Human Head
La flor de ciénaga, una cabeza humana y triste
Album Hommage à Goya, ill. II
1885
Lithograph on rice paper
27.6 x 20.6 cm (design);

35.7 x 26.4 cm (paper)
Bibliothèque nationale de France, Paris

81 ***Germination***
Germination
Germinación
Album *Dans le rêve*, ill. II
1879
Lithograph on rice paper
27.2 x 19.3 cm (design); 36.2 x 28 cm (paper)
Bibliothèque nationale de France, Paris

82 ***Une longue chrysalide couleur de sang***
A Long Chrysalis the Colour of Blood
Una larga crisálida de color sangre
Color
Album *À Gustave Flaubert* (2nd series of *La Tentation de Saint-Antoine*), ill. II
1889
Lithograph on rice paper
21.8 x 18.7 cm (design); 50.3 x 34.3 cm (paper)
Bibliothèque nationale de France, Paris

83 ***La Mort: Mon ironie dépasse toutes les autres***
Death: My Irony Exceeds All Other
La muerte: mi ironía sobrepasa todas las demás
Album *À Gustave Flaubert* (2nd series of *La Tentation de Saint-Antoine*), ill. III
1889
Lithograph on rice paper
21.6 x 19.8 cm (design); 54.2 x 35.9 cm (paper)
Bibliothèque nationale de France, Paris

WALL 10

Max Ernst
84 ***Hommage à Rimbaud***
Tribute to Rimbaud
Homenaje a Rimbaud
1961
Drypoint
21 x 16 cm
Private collection, Barcelona

Antoni Tàpies
85 ***Personatges***
Characters
Personajes
1946
Ink on paper
78.5 x 59.5 cm
Fundació Antoni Tàpies Collection

86 ***Personatges amb el cap girat***
Characters with Their Heads Turned
Personajes con la cabeza vuelta
1945
Paris pencil on paper
40 x 59 cm
Col·lecció Fundació Antoni Tàpies

VITRINE: STÉPHANE MALLARMÉ

Stéphane Mallarmé
87 ***Cosmopolis,*** Vol VI
Armand-Collin, Paris, April-May-June 1897
Archives Martin-Malburet, Paris
First publication of the Stéphane Mallarmé poem *Un coup de dés jamais n'abolira le hasard*

88 ***Un coup de dés jamais n'abolira le hasard***
Poème (1898)
Ed. N. R. F., Paris, 1914
2 copies: Speck Collection, Cologne & Musée départemental Stéphane Mallarmé

89 ***Les Poésies***
Frontispiece by Félicien Rops, Brussels; Edmond Deman, Libraire, 1899

90 ***Minotaure,*** no. 9
Paris, October 1936
[André Breton, "Le Merveilleux contre le mystère. À propos du symbolisme"]

91 ***Pour un Tombeau d'Anatole***
Edited by Jean-Pierre Richard, Éditions du Seuil, Collection "Pierres vives", Paris, 1961
Private collection, Paris

Carlo Carrà
92 ***Un coup de dés et Igitur,***
1945
Poems by Stéphane Mallarmé illustrated by Carlo Carrà (lithographs)
Edited by Carlo & Massimo Carrà
M. Carrà, Milan

93 ***L'Après-midi d'un faune***
1949
Poem by Stéphane Mallarmé translated by Giuseppe Ungaretti (bilingual edition) illustrated with drawings by Carlo Carrà
M. Carrà, Milan

Jacques Scherer
94 ***Le "Livre" de Mallarmé. Premières recherches sur des documents inédits***
Ed. Gallimard, Paris, 1957
Private collection, Paris

Ellsworth Kelly
95 ***Un coup de dés jamais n'abolira le hasard***
1992
Book with 11 lithographs with fabric-covered slipcase, Number 208/300, 54 pages
Courtesy of the artist and the Matthew Marks Gallery, New York

VITRINE: MALLARMÉ AND BROODTHAERS

Marcel Broodthaers
96 ***Minuit***
Editor: George Houyoux, Brussels, 1960
Typographic print, ink and paint on paper
225 copies
MACBA Collection. Fundació Museu d'Art Contemporani de Barcelona

97 ***Pense-bête***
Memory Jogger
Recordatorio
1964
Typographic print on paper, ink and high-gloss paper.
Published by the artist, Brussels
720 copies, 32 pp
MACBA Collection. Fundació Museu d'Art Contemporani de Barcelona

98 ***Jamais***
Never
Nunca
1969
Ballpoint pen on paper
29.5 x 21 cm
Speck Collection, Cologne

99 ***Un coup de dés jamais n'abolira le hasard. Image***
Editor: Galerie Wide White Space, Anvers, i Galerie Michael Werner, Colònia, 1969
Typographic print on paper
300 copies
MACBA Collection. Fundació Museu d'Art Contemporani de Barcelona

100 ***Un coup de dés jamais n'abolira le hasard. Image***
Editor: Galerie Wide White Space, Anvers & Galerie Michael Werner, Cologne, 1969
Typographic print and ink on transparent paper
90 copies
MACBA Collection. Fundació Museu d'Art Contemporani de Barcelona

Room 3: Cubism 1: Prism and movement

BACKGROUND MUSIC

Erik Satie
101 ***Socrate***
Socrates
Sócrates
1918-1919
Symphonic drama withvoices, second movement: "Bords de l'Ilissus. Phédon" (7'37").
Hughes Cuenod, baritone; Geoffrey Parsons, piano
Nimbus Records Limited, 1985

WALL 1

Guillaume Apollinaire
102 ***La Mandoline, l'œillet et le bambou***
Mandolin, Carnation and Bamboo
La mandolina, el clavel y el bambú
ca. 1915-1917
Preparatory manuscript for *Calligrammes*
Ink on paper and fragment of newspaper
27.5 x 20.9 cm
Centre Pompidou, Musée national d'art moderne / Centre de création industrielle, Paris

103 Pablo Picasso
1917
Corrected proof for the magazine *SIC*, no. 17, May 1917
30.5 x 24.5 cm
Bibliothèque nationale de France, Paris

Marcel Duchamp
104 ***Apolinère enameled***
Apolinère esmaltado
1916/1917 – 1965
Cardboard and tin
24.5 x 34 cm
Galleria Nazionale d'Arte Moderna, Rome

105 ***L'équilibre***
Equilibrium
El equilibrio
1958
Drypoint on celluloid
16.8 x 23.3 cm
Galleria Nazionale d'Arte Moderna, Rome

106 ***Written, Wrotten / Morceaux moisis***
Escrito, putrefacción / Pedazos enmohecidos
1940
1940
Black ink on sheets of music paper
32 x 24.5 cm
Galleria Nazionale d'Arte Moderna, Rome

107 ***Obligation Monte-Carlo***
Monte Carlo Bond
Obligación MonteCarlo
1924
Photo-collage on typographic print mounted on cardboard
31.5 x 19.5 cm
Private collection

108 ***Étude pour Moulin à café***
Study for a Coffee Grinder
Estudio para Molinillo de café
1911
Ink on paper
20.5 x 14 cm
Private collection

VITRINE: MARCEL DUCHAMP

Marcel Duchamp
109 ***La Mariée***
1912
Black-and white reproduction
One of the 93 documents from *La Mariée mise à nu par ses célibataires même (Boîte Verte)*, Éditions Rrose Sélavy, Paris, 1934
Private collection, Milan

110 ***The Blind Man / P.B.T., no. 2***
New York, May 1917
Monthly magazine edited by Henri-Pierre Roché, Marcel Duchamp, Beatrice Wood (2 numbers, April & May 1917)
16 pages
Cover by Marcel Duchamp, *La Broyeuse de chocolat*, nº 2
2 copies: Bibliothèque Historique de la Ville de Paris, Fonds Apollinaire & Archives Martin-Marlburet, Paris

111 ***À Guillermo de Torre***
To Guillermo de Torre
A Guillermo de Torre
1927
Ink on paper
22.5 x 25 cm
Private collection, Milan

112 ***Reproduction du Moulin à café***
Reproduction of a Coffee Grinder
Reproducción de Molino de café
1938
Stencil on paper (created by Duchamp as part of the preparatory drawings for the *Boîte en valise*)
Private collection, Milan

Umberto Boccioni
113 ***Dinamismo di un ciclista***
Dynamism of a Cyclist
Dinamismo de un ciclista
1913
Pen and black ink on paper
18 x 30 cm
Estorick Collection, London

Giacomo Balla
114 ***Mercurio passa davanti al sole visto dal cannocchiale (studio)***
Mercury Passes in Front of the Sun Seen from the Telescope (study)
Mercurio pasa delante del sol visto desde el telescopio (estudio)
1914
24 x 18 cm
Tempera on paper
Private collection Futur-ism Associazione Culturale

Sonia Delaunay / Blaise Cendrars
115 ***La Prose du Transsibérien et de la petite Jehanne de France***
The Prose of the Trans-Siberian and Little Jehanne de France
La prosa del Transiberiano y de la pequeña Jehanne de Francia
1913
Gouache, oil and typography (folder with original drawing stencilled on the cover, another drawing mounted by its inner face, and four sheets with original drawings and text) on paper
52 x 37.7 cm (200 x 36 cm when unfolded)
IVAM, Instituto Valenciano de Arte Moderno, Generalitat Valenciana

Anonymous (Gaumont Production)
116 ***Danse serpentine***
Serpentine Dance
Danza serpentina
1900
1', black-and-white film, silent
[by an imitator of Loïe Fuller]
Association des Frères Lumière, Lobster Films & Cinémathèque de la Danse

Thomas Edison (attributed to)
117 ***Annabelle's Fire Dance***
Danza del fuego de Annabelle
1898
Black-and-white film, hand-coloured, silent, 20 seconds
[By an imitator of Loïe Fuller]
Association des frères

Lumière, Lobster Films & Cinémathèque de la Danse

Louis Lumière
118 ***Danse serpentine n° 765***
Serpentine Dance no. 765
Danza serpentina n° 765
1896
Black-and-white film, hand-coloured, silent, 1'15"
[By an imitator of Loïe Fuller]
Association des frères Lumière, Lobster Films & Cinémathèque de la Danse

George R. Busby
119 ***Le Lys. Prélude du Déluge de Saint-Saëns***
The Lily. Prelude to The Déluge *by Saint-Saëns*
El lirio. Preludio del Diluvio de Saint-Saëns
1934
Black-and-white film, sound, 1'45"
Ballarina: Miss Baker, to a choreography by Loïe Fuller
Association des frères Lumière, Lobster Films & Cinémathèque de la Danse

WALL 2

R. Moreau
120 ***Loïe Fuller dansant dans "Le Papillon"***
Loïe Fuller dancing in "The Butterfly"
Loïe Fuller bailando en "La mariposa"
Undated
Photograph (calotype)
16.5 x 12 cm
Gift of A. Rodin, 1916. Musée Rodin, Paris

Eugène Druet
121 ***Loïe Fuller dansant. Jardí a Neuilly-sur-Seine***
Loïe Fuller Dancing. Garden in Neuilly-sur-Seine
Loïe Fuller bailando. Jardín en Neuilly-sur-Seine
c. 1900
Photograph (gelatin silver print)
38.9 x 29 cm
Gift of A. Rodin, 1916. Musée Rodin, Paris

122 ***Loïe Fuller dansant. Jardí a Neuilly-sur-Seine***
Loïe Fuller Dancing. Garden in Neuilly-sur-Seine
Loïe Fuller bailando. Jardín en Neuilly-sur-Seine
c. 1900
Photograph (gelatin silver print)
39.6 x 29.6 cm
Gift of A. Rodin, 1916. Musée Rodin, Paris

Harry C. Ellis
123 ***Loïe Fuller dansant. Jardí a Neuilly-sur-Seine***
Loïe Fuller Dancing. Garden in Neuilly-sur-Seine
Loïe Fuller bailando. Jardín en Neuilly-sur-Seine
ca. 1900
Photographic salt print
18.8 x 24.2 cm
Gift of A. Rodin, 1916. Musée Rodin, Paris

WALL 3

Giacomo Balla
124 ***Rumoristica plastica BALTRR***
Plastic Rumouristic BALTRR
Rumorística plástica BALTRR
1914
Mixed media and collage on paper
112.5 x 98 cm
Private collection

Alexandra Exter
125 ***Composition dynamique***
Dynamic Composition
Composición dinámica
1916
Gouache on paper
65 x 50 cm
Private collection

WALL 4

Alexandra Exter
126 ***Dynamique de couleurs***
Colour Dynamic
Dinámica de colores
1916-1917
Oil paint on canvas
57 x 40 cm
Private collection. Courtesy the Galería Manuel Barbié

Olga Rozanova
127 ***Colour Compositions***
Composiciones de color
1916-1918
Oil paint on canvas
49.5 x 49.5 cm
Private collection, Milan

128 ***Colour Compositions***
Composiciones de color
1916-1918
Oil paint on canvas
36 x 34 cm
Private collection, Milan

WALL 5

Fernand Léger
129 ***Les Trois femmes et la nature morte***
Three Women and a Still-Life
Las tres mujeres y la naturaleza muerta
1921
Oil paint on canvas
60 x 92 cm
FondationBeyeler, Riehen/ Basel

130 ***Étude pour* La ville**
Study for The City
Estudio para La ciudad
1919
Gouache
38 x 28 cm
Private collection, Paris

WALL 6

Julio González
131 ***Le Baiser I***
The Kiss I
El beso I
1930
Wrought and soldered iron
28.5 x 26.7 x 9.5 cm
Staatsgalerie Stuttgart, loaned by the Stuttgart Galerie Association

Drawings
Dibujos
ca. 1931-1935

132 ***Le Baiser n° 1***
The Kiss no. 1
El beso n° 1
Pen and Indian ink on Bristol board
5.2 x 6.5 cm

133 ***Le Baiser n° 2***
The Kiss no. 2
El beso n° 2
Pen and Indian ink on Bristol board
8 x 9.4 cm

134 ***Le Baiser n° 3***
The Kiss no. 3
El beso n° 3
Pen and Indian ink on Bristol board
8 x 8.4 cm

135 ***Le Baiser n° 4***
The Kiss no. 4
El beso n° 4
Pen and Indian ink, black pencil on Bristol board
13 x 13.7 cm

136 ***Le Baiser n° 5***
The Kiss no. 5
El beso n° 5
Pen and Indian ink, black pencil on Bristol board
8 x 7.4 cm

137 ***Masque étrange***
Strange Mask
Máscara extraña
Pen and Indian ink, black pencil on Bristol board
8 x 8.4 cm

138 ***Double visage***
Double Face
Doble rostro

Pen and Indian ink, black pencil on Bristol board
4.4 x 5.5 cm
Private collection, Paris. Courtesy the Galerie de France, Paris

Room 4: Cubism 2: The painting, the object

WALL 1

Frantisek Kupka
139 *Étude pour "Amorpha – Chromatique chaude"*
Study for "Amorpha – Warm Chromatics"
Estudio para "Amorfa – Cromática caliente"
1912-1914
Pastel on paper
27.2 x 27.2 cm
Galerie Cazeau-Béraudière, Paris

140 *Étude pour "Autour d'un point"*
Study for "Around a Point"
Estudio para "Alrededor de un punto"
1920-1925
Gouache on paper
24 x 24 cm
Galerie Cazeau-Béraudière, Paris

Olga Rozanova
141 *Colour Compositions*
Composiciones de color
1916-1918
Oil paint on canvas
50 x 50 cm
Private collection, Milan

Carlo Carrà
142 *Gravitazione spaziale*
Spatial Gravitation
Gravitación espacial
1910
Pencil on paper
19.8 x 16.7 cm
Private collection, Milan

Gino Severini
143 *Untitled*
Sin título
1913
Pencil on paper
22.7 x 13.7 cm
Private collection, Milan

Georges Braque
144 *Compotier, bouteille et verre*
Fruit Jar, Bottle and Glass
Frutero, botella y vaso
1912
Oil paint and sand on canvas
60 x 73 cm
Centre Pompidou, Musée national d'art moderne / Centre de création industrielle, Paris. Gift of Louise & Michel Leiris

145 *Bass*
1911
Drypoint. Black etching. Proof no. 28/50, signed, with autograph by Braque in black and white
45.5 x 33 cm
Bibliothèque nationale de France, Paris

146 *Composition (Nature morte aux verres)*
Composition (Still Life with Glasses)
Composición (Naturaleza muerta con vasos)
1912
Black etching. Signed proof, signed, with autograph by Braque in black and white, not verified
Drypoint
34.5 x 21 cm
Bibliothèque nationale de France, Paris

WALL 2

Georges Braque
147 *Le Petit éclaireur*
The Little Scout
El pequeño explorador
1913
Paper mounted on canvas
92.5 x 60.5 cm
Gift of Geneviève & Jean Masurel, Musée d'art moderne Lille Métropole, Villeneuve d'Ascq

Pablo Picasso
148 *Mur de l'atelier du 242 bd Raspail*
Wall of the Studio at 242 bd Raspail
Pared del estudio del nº 242 del bd Raspail
November-December, 1912
Black-and-white photograph
Modern copy
16 x 22 cm
Musée Picasso, Paris

149 *Photographie de "Guitare et bouteille de Bass"*
Photograph of Guitar and Bottle of Bass
Fotografía de "Guitarra y botella de Bass"
Paris, Autumn 1913
Black-and-white photograph
Photo: Henry Kahnweiler; vintage copy
13 x 9 cm
Musée Picasso, Paris

150 *Papier Collé*
Paper Collage
Papel encolado
1913
Black-and-white photograph
Vintage copy
17 x 12 cm
Musée Picasso, Paris

151 *Tête d'Arlequin*
Head of Harlequin
Cabeza de arlequín
Céret, 1913
Watercolour and charcoal on paper
62.7 x 47 cm
Musée Picasso, Paris

152 *Verre et dé*
Glass and Die
Vaso y dado
1914
Construction in painted wood
17 x 16.2 x 5.5 cm
Musée Picasso, Paris

153 *Étude pour Mademoiselle Léonie*
Study for Mademoiselle Léonie
Estudio para Mademoiselle Léonie
1910
Pencil and Indian ink on paper
64.3 x 49.5 cm
[Mademoiselle Léonie is a character in Max Jacob's Saint-Matorel]
Marina Picasso Collection. Courtesy the Galerie Jan Krugier, Ditesheim & Cie, Geneva

154 *Figure assise*
Seated Figure
Figura sentada
1910-1911
Drawing on a presentation foldout of Max Jacob's Saint-Matorel
30 x 42 cm
Musée Picasso, Paris

155 *Construction photographique au joeur de guitare*
Photographic Construction of a Guitarist
Construcción fotográfica con guitarrista
1913
Black-and-white photograph
Musée Picasso, Paris

WALL 3

Dora Maar
156 *Portrait de Picasso dans l'atelier*
Portrait of Picasso in the Studio
Retrato de Picasso en el

estudio
Royan, Villa Les Voiliers, 1940
Vintage copy
15.5 x 12 cm
Documentation from the Musée Picasso, Paris. Gift of Sir Roland Penrose

Pablo Picasso
157 ***Bouteille de vieux marc et journal***
Bottle of Vieux Marc and Newspaper
Botella de Vieux Marc y periódico
Céret, Spring 1913
Watercolour, white chalk and charcoal on paper
47.8 x 62 cm
Musée Picasso, Paris

158 ***Guillaume Apollinaire dans l'atelier de Picasso, 11 bd de Clichy, Paris***
Guillaume Apollinaire in Picasso's Studio, 11 Boulevard de Clichy, Paris
Guillaume Apollinaire en el estudio de Picasso, 11 bd de Clichy, Paris
Autumn-Winter 1910
Black-and-white photograph
Modern copy
24 x 18 cm
Musée Picasso, Paris

159 ***Ramon Pichot dans l'atelier de Picasso, 11 Boulevard de Clichy, Paris***
Ramon Pichot in Picasso's Studio, 11 Boulevard de Clichy, Paris
Ramon Pichot en el estudio de Picasso, 11 Boulevard de Clichy, París
Autumn-Winter 1910
Vintage copy, silver bromide print
29.9 x 24 cm
Musée Picasso, Paris

160 ***Portrait de Ricardo Canals***
Portrait of Ricardo Canals
Retrato de Ricardo Canals
Paris, 1904
Vintage copy, silver bromide print
On the back, a hand-written annotation by Picasso: "Portrait of the painter Ricardo Canals from Barcelona / In the mirror, me, Picasso / On the mantelpiece a photo of Benedetta Ricardo Canals' wife. Photo taken in Paris in Canals' atelier in 1904"
22.8 x 40 cm
Musée Picasso, Paris

161 ***Le Bock***
The Jar
La jarra
Autumn 1909
Oil paint on canvas
81 x 65.5 cm
Gift of Geneviève & Jean Masurel, Musée d'art moderne Lille Métropole, Villeneuve d'Ascq

Robert Delaunay
162 ***Fenêtres ouvertes simultanément (1ère partie, 3ème motif)***
Windows Open Simultaneously (First Part, Third Motif)
Ventanas abiertas simultá-neamente (1ª parte, 3r motivo)
1912
Oil paint on canvas
45.7 x 37.5 cm
Tate. Acquired 1967

WALL 4

Amédée Ozenfant
163 ***Nature morte au casque***
Still Life with Helmet
Naturaleza muerta con casco
1916
Oil paint on canvas
70 x 90
Larock Granoff Collection

Juan Gris
164 ***Verres, journal et bouteille de vin***
Glasses, Newspaper and Bottle of Wine
Vasos, periódico y botella de vino
1913
Collage, gouache, coloured pencils and charcoal on paper
45 x 29.5 cm
La Colección de Arte de Telefónica

165 ***Nature morte au livre (Saint Matorel)***
Still Life with Book (Saint-Matorel)
Naturaleza muerta con libro (Saint Matorel)
1912-1913
Oil paint on canvas
46 x 30 cm
Centre Pompidou, Musée national d'art moderne / Centre de création industrielle, Paris

VITRINE: APOLLINAIRE AND CUBISM

Pablo Picasso / Max Jacob
166 ***Saint-Matorel***
Ed. Daniel-Henry Kahnweiler, Paris, 1911
Text by Max Jacob, 4 etchings by Picasso
101 pages
Musée Picasso, Paris

Wassily Kandinsky
167 ***Über das Geistige in der Kunst insbesondere in der Malerei***
Concerning the Spiritual in Art, Particularly in Painting
De lo espiritual en el arte y en la pintura en particular
R. Piper & Co Verlag, Munich, 1911 [dated 1912]
Bibliothèque Historique de la Ville de Paris, Fonds Apollinaire

168 ***Klänge***
Sounds
Sonidos
R. Piper & Co Verlag, Munich, 1913
40 wood engravings; original in black-and-white and 12 colours
300 copies numbered and signed by the artist
Guillaume Apollinaire's (unsigned and unnumbered) copy
Bibliothèque Historique de la Ville de Paris, Fonds Apollinaire

Wassily Kandinsky / Franz Marc (eds)
169 ***Der Blaue Reiter***
The Blue Rider
El jinete azul
R. Piper & Co Verlag, Munich, 1912
Bibliothèque Historique de la Ville de Paris, Fons Apollinaire

170 ***Exposició d'art cubista***
Ed. Galerie Dalmau, Barcelona, 20 April – 10 May 1912
Preface by Jacques Nayral [reproduction of Sonata by Marcel Duchamp]
2 copies: Museo Nacional Centro de Arte Reina Sofía. Biblioteca & Bibliothèque Historique de la Ville de Paris, Fonds Apollinaire

Ardengo Soffici
171 ***Cubismo et oltre***
Libreria della Voce, Florence, 1913
Bibliothèque Historique de la Ville de Paris, Fonds Apollinaire

172 ***Arlecchino***
Lacerba Edizioni, Florence, 1914
Bibliothèque Historique de la Ville de Paris, Fonds Apollinaire

173 *Les Soirées de París*
Magazine edited by Serge Férat, Baron d'Oettingen (Jean Cérusse) & Guillaume Apollinaire; monthly, 27 numbers; 1st series: February 1912 –Summer 1913 [nos. 1-17]; 2nd series: November 1913 – July/ August 1914)
-No. 25, 2nd series, June 1914. Bibliothèque Historique de la Ville de Paris, Fonds Apollinaire
-No. 26-27, 2nd series, 1914. Archives Martin-Malburet, Paris

Guillaume Apollinaire
174 ***La Première exposition des "Soirées de Paris", Survage. Iréne Lagut/ Apollinaire***
Undated
Foldout catalogue
Archives Martin-Malburet, Paris

175 ***L'anti-tradition futuriste. Manifeste-synthèse***
Direction du Mouvement futuriste, Milan, 29 June 1913
2 copies: Bibliothèque Historique de la Ville de Paris, Fonds Apollinaire & Archives Martin-Malburet, Paris

176 ***Prova relligada de* Et mois [sic] aussi je suis peintre! *amb anotacions d'Apollinaire***
With a wood engraving portrait by Pierre Roy, after Giorgio De Chirico
This first design for a compilation of Calligrammes never appeared
Bibliothèque Historique de la Ville de Paris, Fonds Apollinaire

177 ***Calligrammes (Poèmes de la paix et de la guerre. 1913-1916)***
Ed. Mercure de France, Paris, 1918
Archives Martin-Malburet, Paris

Nikolaï Punin
178 ***Tatlin protiv kubizma / Pamiatnik III Internationala***
Tatlin Versus Cubism / Monument to the Third International
Tatlin contra el cubismo / Monumento a la Tercera Internacional
Ed. Gosudarstvennoe Izdatel'stvo, Petersburg, 1921
Print run unknown, 25 pages, 13 colour illustrations
Private collection, Barcelona

Room 5: Words in freedom

WALL 1

Rafael Barradas
179 ***Calle de Barcelona a la 1 del mediodía***
Barcelona Street at 1 pm
1918
Oil paint on canvas
50.7 x 60.5 cm
Contemprary Art Collection – Museo Patio Herreriano, Valladolid

WALL 2

Francis Picabia
180 ***Portrait d'Apollinaire***
Portrait of Apollinaire
Retrato de Apollinaire
1918
Ink and watercolour on paper
58 x 45.7 cm
Private collection. Courtesy the Galerie Seroussi

181 ***Réveil-matin***
Alarm Clock
Despertador
1919
Ink on paper
32 x 24 cm
Private collection

182 ***Brouette***
Wheelbarrow
Carretilla
1922
Gouache and Indian ink on cardboard
78,2 x 54 cm
Museo Nacional Centro de Arte Reina Sofía, Madrid

Man Ray
183 ***L'Atelier à New York***
The Studio in New York
El taller en Nueva York
1920
Photograph (copy)
22.6 x 28.4 cm
Kunsthaus Zürich Photography Collection

184 ***L'Impossibilité***
Impossibility
La imposibilidad
1917
Black-and-white photograph
16.5 x 11.3 cm
Private collection, Milan

WALL 3

Robert Delaunay
185 ***Alchimie du verbe***
Alchemy of the Verb
Alquimia del verbo
1914
Calligraphic research based on Arthur Rimbaud's poem "Les Voyelles", watercolour on cardboard
24.7 x 30.7 cm
Bibliothèque nationale de France, Paris

Pierre Albert-Birot
186 ***Étude finale pour "La Guerre"***
Final study for "The War"
Estudio final para "La Guerra"
1916
Oil paint on wood
42.5 x 42 cm
Centre Georges Pompidou, Musée national d'art moderne / Centre de création industrielle, Paris; gift of Arlette Albert-Birot, 1978

187 ***Dentelle***
Lace
Encaje
1922
White letters traced with a brush on paper
43 x 27.5 cm
Fonds Albert-Birot

188 ***La Fleur de lys***
The Fleur de Lys
La flor de lis
1922
Gold letters traced with a brush on paper
43 x 27.5 cm
Fonds Albert-Birot

Joaquín Torres-García
189 ***Hoy***
Today
c. 1921
Tempera and collage on cardboard
45 x 61.5 cm
IVAM, Instituto Valenciano de Arte Moderno, Generalitat Valenciana

Vicente Huidobro
190 ***Couchant***
Sunset
Poniente
1920-1922
Painted poem
Gouache on paper, mounted on cardboard
60 x 48 cm
IVAM, Instituto Valenciano de Arte Moderno, Generalitat Valenciana

Filippo Marinetti
191 ***I paroliberi futuristi / Les Mots en liberté futuristes***
Futurist Words-in-Freedom
Las palabras en libertad futuristas
1919
Futurist number of Poesia, Milan
19 x 12.5 cm, with four folding sheets
IVAM, Instituto Valenciano de Arte Moderno, Generalitat Valenciana. Library

192 ***5 proves per a "I paroliberi futuristi / Les mots en liberté futuristes"***
5 Sketches for "I paroliberi futuristi/ Les mots en liberté futuristes"
5 pruebas para "I paroliberi futuristi/ Les mots en liberté futuristes"
1915
Typographic print, annotations by the author
- Cover, "Chair"
- Sheet no.8, "XXX"
- Sheet no. 2, "My friend, my dear"
- Sheet no. 10, "Summum of analogical colours and forms"
- Sheet no. 38, "Logic of the niiight"
33 x 21 cm c/u
Private collection

193 ***Ami. N° 64***
Friend. No. 64
Amigo. N° 64
1915
Words-in-Freedom manus-cript, Indian ink on paper
22 x 27.9 cm
Compagnie Martin-Malburet Collection, Paris

Francesco Cangiullo
194 ***Pisa (Tavole parolibere)***
Pisa (Sheet of Words-in-Freedom)
Pisa (Tabla de palabras en libertad)
1914
Tempera on paper
57 x 74 cm
Private collection, Milan

WALL 4

Carlo Carrà
195 ***Rapporto di un nottambule milanese. Parole in libertà***
Report by a Milanese Night Owl. Words-in-Freedom
Informe de un noctámbulo milanés. Palabras en libertad
1914
Ink and collage on paper
37.4 x 28 cm
Private collection, Milan

196 ***13 introspezioni***
13 Introspections
13 introspecciones
1914
Pencil, ink and collage on paper
26.5 x 21 cm
Private collection

197 ***Cineamore***
Cinelove
Cineamor
1914
Ink and pencil on paper
26 x 37 cm
M. Carrà Collection, Milan

198 ***Arrolepimento atmosferici. Scoppio di un obice***
Atmospheric Swirls. A Bursting Shell
Remolinos atmosféricos. Explosión de un obús
1914
Ink and collage on paper
26.5 x 37 cm
Estorick Collection, London

Francesco Cangiullo
199 ***Grande foule sur la Piazza del Popolo***
Large Crowd in the Piazza del Popolo
Gran multitud en la Piazza del Popolo
1914
Watercolour on paper
58 x 74 cm
Private collection

200 *4 proofs for* Piedigrotta
4 pruebas para Piedigrotta
1916
1916
4 typographic sheets with hand-written annotations
Each one approx 33 x 21 cm
- Cover
- Sheet no. 8 ("In bocca suonotore apice del conosuono", "Tarentella")
- Sheet no. 12 ("Fantasia")
- Sheet no. 16 ("Trombetoni")
Private collection

Giacomo Balla
201 ***Cartolina a Carrà con linee di velocità***
Postcard to Carrà with Speed Lines
Postal a Carrà con líneas de velocidad
1915
Watercolour
9 x 14 cm
Private collection, Milan

202 ***Partenza di Sironi per Milano. Parole in libertà***
Leaving Sironi for Milan. Words-in-Freedom
Partida de Sironi hacia Milán. Palabras en libertad
1914
Ink on paper
28 x 22 cm
Private collection, Milan

VITRINE: PICABIA IN CATALONIA

203 ***391***
Magazine edited by Francis Picabia; bi-monthly to begin with, 19 numbers (nos. 1-4, January-March 1917, Barcelona; nos. 5-7, June-August 1917, New York; no. 8, February 1919, Zurich; no. 9-19, November 1919 - November 1924, Paris)
-No. 1, 25 January 1917, Barcelona

-No. 2, February 1917, Barcelona
-No. 3, February 1917, Barcelona
-No. 4, March 1917, Barcelona
Private collection, Barcelona

204 ***Cannibale***, no. 1
Paris, 25 April 1920
- No. 2, Paris 25 May 1920
Monthly magazine edited by Francis Picabia.
Museo Nacional Centro de Arte Reina Sofía. Biblioteca

VITRINE: CATALAN VISUAL POETRY

J. M. Junoy
205 ***Troços***, no. 1-4
Imprenta Oliva de Vilanova, Barcelona, 1916-1918
Biblioteca de Catalunya

206 ***Arc Voltaic***, no. 1
Barcelona, February 1918
Drawings by Miró and Barradas, texts by J. Torres-García
Editor: Papasseit
IVAM, Instituto Valenciano de Arte Moderno, Generalitat Valenciana. Library.

207 ***Poemes & Cal·ligrames***
Llibreria Nacional Catalana, Barcelona, 1920
Letter-preface by Guillaume Apollinaire
Private collection, Barcelona

Joan Salvat-Papasseit
208 ***Un enemic del poble: full de subversió espiritual***, no. 16
March 1919
IVAM, Instituto Valenciano de Arte Moderno, Generalitat Valenciana. Library.

209 *L'irradiador del port i les gavines*
Editorial Atenes, Barcelona, 1921
Biblioteca de Catalunya

210 *El poema de la rosa als llavis*
Llibreria Nacional Catalana, Barcelona, 1923
Frontispiece of the Josep Obiols cover, 66 copies on Japanese vellum, signed by the author
Biblioteca de Catalunya

211 *L'Esport Català*
no. 29 & no. 46
1926
With calligrammes by Sindreu
Private collection, Barcelona

VITRINE: PIERRE ALBERT-BIROT / SIC

Pierre Albert-Birot
212 *SIC*
Magzine edited by Pierre Albert-Birot; monthly, bi-monthly from no. 31onwards
54 numbers, January 1916 –December 1919. 28 x 22 cm
-No. 2, February 1916, Paris. Fonds Albert-Birot
-No. 3, March 1916 [2 texts by Pierre Albert-Birot, "OUI" and "Réflexions"]. Fonds Albert-Birot
-No. 4, April 1916, Paris [Gino Severini, "Dans le Nord-Sud. Compénétration simultanéité d'idées-images"]. Fonds Albert-Birot
-No. 12, December 1916 [Guillaume Apollinaire, "Il pleut" and Pierre Albert-Birot, "Intimité"]. Archives Martin-Malburet, Paris
-No. 17, May 1917 [Guillaume Apollinaire, "Pablo Picasso", calligramme]. Fonds Albert-Birot
-No. 23, November 1917. Fonds Albert-Birot

213 *4 proofs for Ode, 1922*
Visual poem
Typographic print on paper
Fonds Albert-Birot

VITRINES: MADRID

Ramón Gómez de la Serna
214 *Greguerías*
Madrid, 1917
Llibrería Gulliver, Madrid

Vicente Huidobro / Robert Delaunay
215 *Tour Eiffel*
Madrid, 1918
14 pages
Museo Nacional Centro de Arte Reina Sofía. Library

216 *Grecia*, no. 18
Seville, June 1919
Print
Biblioteca de la Residencia de Estudiantes, Madrid

217 *Grecia*, year II
Seville, 1919
Edited by Isaac del Vando Villar
Interiors pages
-No. 27, calligrammes "Poema N especial" by Eugenio Montes & "Otoño" by Juan Larrea
-No. 31, calligramme "En el infierno de una noche" by Isaac del Vando
-No. 35, calligrammes "Viaje orbicular" by Luis de Mosquera & "Atrás" by Gerardo Diego
-No. 36, calligramme "Signos celestes"by Adriano del Valle
Archivo Rafael Cansinos Asséns, Madrid

218 *Ultra*, no. 10
Madrid, 1921
IVAM, Instituto Valenciano de Arte Moderno, Generalitat Valenciana. Library.

Guillermo de Torre
219 *Hélices*
1923
2 copies: Biblioteca de la Residencia de Estudiantes, Madrid & Museo Nacional Centro de Arte Reina Sofía. Library

220 *Der Sturm*, no. 10
Berlin, 1923
Magazine edited by Herwarth Walden
(March 1910 – June 1932, monthly magazine, bi-monthly from 1912 onwards, later quarterly)
Buendía Collection, Madrid

221 *Literaturas europeas de vanguardia*
Caro Raggio, Madrid, 1925
390 pages
Museo Nacional Centro de Arte Reina Sofía, Library

222 *L'Amic de les Arts*, no. 21
Ed. Gaseta de Sitges, Barcelona, 1927
No. 1- 31 (1926-1929)
Printed matter
Biblioteca de la Residencia de Estudiantes, Madrid

VITRINE: FUTURISMS

Gabriel Alomar
223 *El futurisme*
1904
Lecture given to the Ateneu Barcelonès the night of 18 June 1904
Private collection, Barcelona

224 *Peintres futuristes italiens*
Galeria Bernheim Jeune, Paris, 5-24 February 1912
Exhibition catalogue
Bibliothèque Historique de la Ville de Paris, Fonds Apollinaire

225 *Zweite Ausstellung: die Futuristen (Boccioni, Carra, Russolo, Severini)*
Second Exhibition of the Futurists (Boccioni, Carra, Russolo, Severini)
Galeria Sturm, Berlin, 12 April – 31 May 1912
Exhibition catalogue
Archives Martin-Malburet, Paris

226 *The Futurist Painter Severini exhibits his latest works*
Marlborough Gallery, London, April 1913
Bibliothèque Historique de la Ville de Paris, Fonds Apollinaire

Guillaume Apollinaire
227 *L'Antitradizione futurista. Manifesto-sintesi*
Direzione del Movimento Futurista, Milan, 20 June 1913
4 pages
Archives Martin-Malburet, Paris

228 *Lacerba*, no. 22, year I
Florence, 15 November 1913
Magazine edited by Ardengo Soffici & Giovanni Papini; bi-monthly, weekly from 1915 onwards
70 numbers; 16 pages
Archives Martin-Malburet, Paris

Filippo Marinetti
229 *Manifeste technique de la littérature futuriste (destruction de la syntaxe)*
Milan, 11 May 1912
Archives Martin-Malburet, Paris

230 *Futuristische Dichtungen*
Ed. Der Sturm, Berlin, 1912
Cover illustrated with a Carlo Carrà engraving
Archives Martin-Malburet, Paris

231 *Zang Tumb Tumb*
Edizioni Futuriste di "Poesia", Milan, 1914
Archives Martin-Malburet, Paris

232 *Zang Tumb Tumb*
Edizioni Futuriste di "Poesia", Milan, 1914
Bibliothèque Historique de la Ville de Paris, Fonds Apollinaire

233 *Les Mots en liberté futuristes*
Edizioni futuriste di "Poesia", Milan, 1919
4 folding sheets
Archives Martin-Malburet, Paris

234 *Les Mots en liberté futuristes*
Edizioni futuriste di "Poesia", Milan, 1919
4 folding sheets
Archives Martin-Malburet, Paris

235 *Lacerba*, no. 15, year II
Florence, 1 August 1914
Magazine edited by Ardengo Soffici & Giovanni Papini; bi-monthly, weekly from 1915 onwards
70 numbers
Archives Martin-Malburet, Paris

236 *Parole in libertà*
11 February 1915
Manifesto of the "Direzione del movimento futurista", Milan, announcing the imminenet publication of volume I of *Paroliberi futuristi*. In the end this work did not appear until 1919 as *Les Mots en liberté futuristes*
4 pages
Archives Martin-Malburet, Paris

Pierre Albert-Birot
237 *SIC*, no. 4
April 1916
Magazine edited by Pierre Albert-Birot; monthly, bi-monthly from no. 31onwards
54 numbers, January 1916 – December 1919
[Cover by Pierre Albert-Birot]
Archives Martin-Malburet, Paris

J. M. Junoy
238 *Estela. Hommage funèbre à Umberto Boccioni*
1916
Poem published in Poemes & Cal·ligrames, Llibreria Nacional Catalana, Barcelona, 1920
Letter-preface by Guillaume Apollinaire
Biblioteca Nacional de Catalunya

Joan Salvat-Papasseit
239 *Contra els poetes amb minúscula. Primer manifest català futurista*
c. 1920
Included in the magazine Un enemic del poble. Fulla de subversió..., final number
Biblioteca Nacional de Catalunya

240 *L'irradiador del port i les gavines*
Editorial Atenes, Barcelona, 1921
IVAM, Instituto Valenciano de Arte Moderno, Generalitat Valenciana. Library.

VITRINE: ITALIAN FUTURISM

241 *Lacerba*
Magazine edited by Ardengo Soffici & Giovanni Papini; bi-monthly, weekly from 1915 onwards
70 numbers
-No. 20, 15 October 1913, Florence. Bibliothèque Historique de la Ville de Paris, Fonds Apollinaire
-No. 2, 15 January 1914, year II, Florence. [Soffici, "Bicchier d'acqua", visual poem]. Archives Martin-Malburet, Paris
-No. 7, 1 April 1914, year II, Florence. Archives Martin-Malburet, Paris
-No. 10, any II, 15 maig 1914, Florence
2 copies: Archives Martin-Malburet, Paris & Bibliothèque Historique de la Ville de Paris, Fonds Apollinaire
-No. 12, March 1915, year III, Florence [Stéphane Mallarmé, "Conflitto", translation of "Conflits" by A. Soffici, (based on the text in La Revue blanche, 1 August 1895, and not from the collection Divagations, Fasquelle, Paris, 1898]. Archives Martin-Malburet, Paris

242 *L'Italia Futurista*, no. 4, year I
Florence, 1916
Bi-monthly magazine edited by Bruno Corra & Enrico Settinelli
4 pages
Archives Martin-Malburet, Paris

243 *Vela Latina*, no. 7, year IV
Naples, 4 March 1916
4 pages (words-in-liberty by Guglielmo Janelli & Pasqualino Cangiullo)
Archives Martin-Malburet, Paris

Francesco Cangiullo
244 *Piedigrotta*
Edizioni futuriste di "Poesia", collection "Manifesto sulla declamazione dinamica sinottica di Marinetti", Milan, 1916
Compilation of words-in-freedom by Francesco Cangiullo [Cover by Cangiullo]
Archives Martin-Malburet, Paris

VITRINE: FUTURISM AND DADA

Balilla Pratella
245 *La Musica futurista. Manifesto tecnico*
Redazione di "Poesia", Milan, 11 March 1911
[Cover by Umberto Boccioni]
Private collection, Milan

Luigi Russolo
246 *L'Arte dei Rumori. Manifesto futurista*
Direzione del Movimento Futurista, Milan, 11 March 1913
4 pp-
Archives Martin-Malburet, Paris

247 *Lacerba*, no. 13, year II
Florence, July 1914
Archives Martin-Malburet, Paris

248 *L'arte dei rumori*
Edizioni futuriste di "Poesia", Milan, 1916
[Contains the Russolo text " L'Arte dei Rumori. Manifesto-futurista", 11 March 1913]
Archives Martin-Malburet, Paris

249 *La folgore futurista*
February 1917
Printed by A. Rognoni, G. Saggeti
12 pages
Archives Martin-Malburet, Paris

Tristan Tzara
250 *Cabaret Voltaire (Recueil littéraire et artistique)*
Zurich, May 1916
Magzine edited by Hugo Ball
2 copies: Bibliothèque Historique de la Ville de Paris, Fonds Apollinaire & Archives Martin-Malburet, Paris

Raoul Hausmann
251 ***Programme of the Dada celebration of 15 May 1919***
Typography on paper
Musée départemental, Rochechouart

252 ***Boletin Dada***, no. 6
1920
Typography on paper
Archivo Rafael Cansinos Assens

Guillermo de Torre
253 ***Manifiesto vertical ultraísta***
Supplement to the magazine Grecia no. 50, Madrid, 1 November 1920
With a vignette by Rafael Barradas ; text by Guillermo de la Torre
Biblioteca de la Residencia de Estudiantes, Madrid

Room 6: Klee and Dada

WALL 1

Paul Klee
254 ***Revolving House***
Casa giratoria
1921
Gouache on cheesecloth mounted on paper
37.7 x 52.2 cm
Museo Thyssen-Bornemisza, Madrid

Buster Keaton
255 ***One Week***
Una semana
1920
Black-and-white silent film, 20'11", USA

WALL 2

Raoul Hausmann
256 ***L'Inconnu***
The Unknown Man
El desconocido
1919
Pencil on paper
27 x 20.5 cm
Musée départemental, Rochechouart

257 ***Grün***
Green
Verde
1918
Pencil on the verso of a printed Berlin Dada manifesto, torn and repaired
28.2 x 21.9 cm
Centre Pompidou, Musée national d'art moderne / Centre de création industrielle, Paris

258 ***Kp'erioUM Manifest von der Gesetzmässigkeit des Lautes***
Manifesto for the Sound Ordinance
Manifiesto del orden del sonido
1919
Typography on paper
47.5 x 66 cm
Musée départemental, Rochechouart

Max Ernst
259 ***Lächeln Sie nicht !***
Don't Smile!
¡No sonriáis!
1919
Photographic print and graphite frottage of typographic elements, pencil and charcoal on paper
47 x 32 cm
Private collection; courtesy Blondeau & Associés, Paris

260 ***La danseuse, Gertrud Leistikow***
The Dancer Gertrud Leistikow
La bailarina, Getrud Leistikow
1913
Pen and Indian ink on paper
24.5 x 16.5 cm
Private collection; courtesy Blondeau & Associés, Paris

Hans Arp
261 ***Dessin dada***
Dada Drawing
Dibujo dadá
1916
Indian ink and pencil on paper
17.8 x 22.1 cm
Fondation Hans Arp & Sophie Taeuber- Arp e. V., Rolandseck

262 ***Hombre, bigote y ombligo***
Man, Moustache and Navel
1928
Paint and lead pencil on paper
66.5 x 73.5 cm
Private collection, Barcelona

263 ***Grasse***
1941-1942
Indian ink on paper
25 x 20 cm
Fondation Arp Collection, Clamart

Sophie Taeuber-Arp
264 ***Sophie Taeuber dancing in a Marcel Janco mask at the Cabaret Voltaire, Zurich***
Sophie Taeuber bailando con una máscara de Marcel Janco en el Cabaret Voltaire de Zúrich
1916
Black-and-white photograph, modern copy
25 x 15 cm
Fondation Arp Collection, Clamart (original)

265 ***Four Dancers in Dada Costume (dance performance of a poem by Hugo Ball)***
Cuatro bailarinas con vestido dadá (interpretación bailada de un poema de Hugo Ball)
1918
Black-and-white photograph, modern copy
25 x 16 cm
Fondation Arp Collection, Clamart (original)

266 ***The Deramo Puppet, a character from King Stag, a theatrical piece by Carlo Gozzi***
La marioneta de Deramo, un personaje de "König Hirsch" (El rey ciervo), pieza teatral de Carlo Gozzi
1918
Black-and-white photograph, modern copy
31 x 10 cm
Fondation Arp Collection, Clamart (original)

267 ***Hans Arp and Sophie Taeuber in Sophie Taeuber's study, in front of the marionettes for König Hirsch (King Stag), Carlo Gozzi's spectacle, Zurich, 1918***
Hans Arp y Sophie Taeuber en el estudio de Sophie Taeuber, ante las marionetas para "König Hirsch" (El rey ciervo), espectáculo de Carlo Gozzi, Zúrich, 1918
Black-and-white photograph, vintage copy
12.5 x 16 cm
Kunsthaus Zürich

268 ***Sophie Taueber with a cardboard Dada costume, in Ascona***
Sophie Taueber con un vestido dadá de cartón, en Ascona
c. 1918
Black-and-white photograph, modern copy (unknown photographer)
25 x 16 cm
Fondation Arp Collection, Clamart (Original)

Ivan Puni
269 ***Double page taken from the newspaper Die Dame: "The painter Xenia Boguslavskaja in a Futurist costume designed by the painter Puni"***
Dos páginas enfrentadas extraídas del periódico Die Dame: "La pintora Xenia Boguslavskaja con un vestido futurista

diseñado por el pintor Puni"
ca. 1921
16.7 x 21.5 cm
Ivan Puni Archive, Zurich

270 ***Futurist (also called "Cubist") costumes worn in the street by sandwich-board men to advertise an exhibition at Der Sturm Gallery***
Vestidos futuristas (llamados también "cubistas") que llevaban por la calle unos hombres anuncio para hacer propaganda de su exposición en la galería Der Sturm
Berlin, February 1921
Photography
18 x 24 cm
Ivan Puni Archive, Zurich

271 ***La Neige (Vitebsk)***
Snow (Vitebsk)
La nieve (Vitebsk)
1919
Indian ink and pencil on paper
32 x 22.5 cm
Ivan Puni Archive, Zurich

Kurt Schwitters
272 ***Merz 3. Merz Mappe***
Merz 3. Merz portfolio
Merz 3. Carpeta Merz
1923
The Merz Verlag's first portfolio
6 lithographs
Each one 55.5 x 44.4 cm
Kurt & Ernst Schwitters Foundation , Hanover

WALL 3

Hannah Höch
273 ***Filigran***
Watermark
Filigrana
1925
Collage on cardboard
23.2 x 18.9 cm
Kunsthaus Zürich, Graphic Art Collection

Raoul Hausmann
274 ***Ventre de carrosse ou Dupont-Durand fait des poèmes***
Carriage Stomach or Dupont-Durand Makes Poems
Vientre de carroza o Dupont-Durand hace poemas
1920
Ink and watercolour on paper
42.2 x 32 cm
Musée d'Art Moderne, Saint-Étienne Métropole

Hannah Höch
275 ***Hochfinanz***
High Finance
Altas finanzas
1923
Photomontage and collage
36 x 31 cm
Galerie Berinson, Berlin

276 ***Astronomie***
Astronomy
Astronomía
1922
Collage
25.7 x 20.5 cm
James Mayor & Andrew Murray, London

277 ***Dada/Constructivist Komposition***
Dada/Constructivist Composition
Dada/Composición constructivista
1924
Collage of fragments of black-and-white ink drawings and gouache
26 x 18.5 cm
James Mayor & Andrew Murray, London

Kurt Schwitters
278 ***Ohne Titel (Bild mit grosser Kreuzspinne)***
Untitled (Image with a Large Garden Spider)
Sin título (imagen con una gran araña de la cruz)
1921
Collage, paper on paper
15.1 x 11.6 cm
Kurt & Ernst Schwitters Foundation, Hanover

279 ***MZ 308 Grau***
MZ 308 Grey
MZ 308 Gris
1921
Collage, coloured pencil, paper and cloth on paper
17.9 x 14.4 cm
Kurt & Ernst Schwitters Foundation, Hanover

LISTENING POST

280 ***Ursonate (Sonata in Urlanten)***
Sonata original
1932
Spoken by Kurt Schwitters, recorded Frankfurt, 5 May 1932, 3'24''
CD: Lunapark 0,10. Production: Sub Rosa. Edited by Marc Dachy

WALL 4

Paul Klee
281 ***Weissteufel, die Weld beherrschend***
White Evil, Dominating the World
Diablo blanco, dominando el mundo
1921
Watercolour on paper
46 x 28 cm
Private collection, Barcelona

282 ***Komödie***
Comedy
Comedia
1921
Watercolour and oil paint on paper
30.5 x 45.4 cm
Tate. Adquired 1946

283 ***Braunes Rechtw. Strebendes Dreieck***
Brown Right-Angled Triangle
Triángulo rectángulo marrón
1915
Watercolour on a layer of plaster on paper and cardboard
21.3 x 13.2 cm
Kunstsammlung Nordrhein-Westfalen, Düsseldorf

284 ***Dogmatische Komposition***
Dogmatic Composition
Composición dogmática
1918
Black lead fixed in watercolour on two white Bristol boards, on yellowish cardboard
26.5 x 20.3 cm
Staatsgalerie Stuttgart, Graphic Art Collection

VITRINE: DADA / HANS ARP

Hans Arp / Richard Huelsenbeck
285 ***Phantastische Gebete***
Fantastic Prayers
Oraciones Fantásticas
Zurich, September 1916
Typography and wood engravings by Hans Arp
IVAM, Instituto Valenciano de Arte Moderno, Generalitat Valenciana

Tristan Tzara / Marcel Janco
286 ***La première aventure céleste de Monsieur Antipyrine***
Monsieur Antipyrine's First Celestial Adventure
La primera aventura celeste del senyor Aspirina
Collection Dada, Zurich, 1916
Text by Tristan Tzara, coloured wood engravings by Marcel Janco
4 pages folded in the middle
6wood engravings, of which 5 are two-colour (black and blue)
Bibliothèque Historique de la Ville de Paris, Fonds Apollinaire

287 ***Dada*** (Recueil littéraire et artistique), no. 1
Zurich, July 1917
Magazine edited by Tristan Tzara
Bibliothèque Historique de la Ville de Paris, Fonds Apollinaire

288 ***Dada*** (Recueil littéraire et artistique), no. 2
Zurich, December 1917
Magazine edited by Tristan Tzara
(8 numbers, variable dates of publication, July 1917 - September 1921)
Guillaume Apollinaire's copy, with a poem in homage to Tristan Tzara on the back cover: "Hommage, Tristan Tzara"
Bibliothèque Historique de la Ville de Paris, Fonds Apollinaire

Tristan Tzara / Hans Arp
289 ***Vingt-cinq poèmes***
Twenty-five Poems
Veinticinco poemas
Collection Dada, Zurich, 1918
Poems by Tristan Tzara, 10 wood engravings by Hans Arp
No pagination, 13 pages folded in two and stapled, untrimmed
Guillaume Apollinaire's copy
Bibliothèque Historique de la Ville de Paris, Fonds Apollinaire

Kurt Schwitters
290 ***Die Kathedrale***
The Cathedral
La catedral
Paul Steegemann Verlag, Hanover, 1920
Lithographed cover
IVAM, Instituto Valenciano de Arte Moderno, Generalitat Valenciana

Raoul Hausmann
291 ***Hurrah! hurrah! hurrah! 12 Satiren***
Hurrah! hurrah! hurrah! 12 Satires
Der Malik Verlag, Berlin, 1921
Relief printing and typography
12 texos, 1 watercolour and 2 drawings
2 copies: IVAM, Instituto Valenciano de Arte Moderno, Generalitat Valenciana & Musée départemental, Rochechouart

292 ***Mécano***, no. blue 2
Leiden, 1922
Magazine edited by Theo Van Doesburg [I.K. Bonset]
(5 numbers, February 1922-1923, variable format)
Musée départemental, Rochechouart

Kurt Schwitters
293 ***Die Blume Anna – Die neue Anna Blume***
The Anna Flower - the New Anna Flower
Verlag Der Sturm, Berlin, 1922
2 copies: Archives Martin-Malburet, Paris & IVAM, Instituto Valenciano de Arte Moderno, Generalitat Valenciana

El Lissitzky / Kurt Schwitters
294 ***Merz***, no. 8/9
April – July 1924
Magazine edited by Kurt Schwitters
(Quarterly, 24 numbers, January 1923-1932)
[Cover by El Lissitzky, relief printing and typography using 2 inks]
IVAM, Instituto Valenciano de Arte Moderno, Generalitat Valenciana

Tristan Tzara
295 ***Sept Manifestes Dada***
Seven Dada Manifestos
Siete manifiestos dadá
Jean Budry, Paris, 1924
Private collection, Barcelona

Paul Klee
296 ***Pädagogischen Skizzenbuch*** (Bauhausbücher n° 2)
Notebook of Pedagogical Sketches
Langen, Munich 1925
51 pages, illustrations
IVAM, Instituto Valenciano de Arte Moderno, Generalitat Valenciana

297 ***Merz***, no. 24
Hanover, 1932
Magazine edited by Kurt Schwitters; quarterly, 24 numbers, 1923-1932
First publication of the final version of Ursonate
IVAM, Instituto Valenciano de Arte Moderno, Generalitat Valenciana

298 ***Le surréalisme au service de la révolution***, no. 6 (Hans Arp, "L'Air est une racine")
May 1933
Monsieur Bernard Loliée

Room 7: Hans Arp - Sophie Taeuber

WALL 1

Bart van der Leck
299 ***Compositie (Bloesemtak)***
Composition (Flowering Branch)
Composición (Rama en flor)
1921
Oil paint on canvas
38.5 x 56 cm
Van Abbemuseum Collection, Eindhoven, Holland

Kurt Schwitters
300 ***Aufschlag ("Tempera-Fart")***
Impact ("Tempera-Fart")
Impacto ("Tempera-Fart")
1928
Collage on paper
20 x 14.5 cm
Private collection, Milan

301 ***Herz (Mz 253)***
Heart (Mz 253)
Corazón (Mz 253)
1921
Collage
32.7 x 24 cm
Private collection, Milan

WALL 2

Kurt Schwitters
302 ***Ohne Titel (grau, blau, rot, weiss)***
Untitled (Grey, Blue, Red, White)
Sin título (gris, azul, rojo, blanco)
1924-1927
1924-1927
Collage, paper on paper
20 x 16 cm
Kurt & Ernst Schwitters Foundation , Hanover

303 ***MZ 439***
1922
Collage, paper on paper
19 x 17,5 cm
Kurt & Ernst Schwitters Foundation , Hanover

Sonia Delaunay
304 ***Composition abstraite***
Abstract Composition
Composición abstracta
1924
Gouache on cardboard
46.5 x 30 cm
Private collection; courtesy the Galería Manuel Barbié

WALL 3

Hans Arp
305 ***Éclosion***
Blooming
Eclosión
1927
Collage on paper
32.7 x 25 cm
Landes Rheinland-Pfalz Collection for theArp-Museum Rolandseck

306 ***Die Lippen***
Lips
Los labios
1926
Relief. Painted cardboard
42.5 x 40.5 cm
Landes Rheinland-Pfalz Collection for theArp-Museum Rolandseck

307 ***Formes géométriques-biologiques***
Geometrical-Biological Forms
Formas geométricas-biológicas
1917
Embroidery with cotton thread
12 x 7.2 cm
Georges Jollès Collection

Anonymous
308 ***Portrait of Hans Arp***
Retrato de Hans Arp
1924
Black-and-white photograph
18 x 12.9 cm
Galerie Berinson, Berlin

Nic Aluf
309 ***Portrait of Sophie Taeuber Arp with her "Cap dadà"***
Retrato de Sophie Taeuber Arp con su "Cabeza dadá"
1920
silver bromide photograph
14.8 x 11.6 cm
Galerie Berinson, Berlin

Sophie Taeuber-Arp
310 ***Composition verticale-horizontale***
Vertical-Horizontal Composition
Composición vertical-horizontal
1916
Gouache
21 x 21 cm
Fondation Hans Arp & Sophie Taeuber- Arp e. V., Rolandseck

311 ***Composition verticale-horizontale à éléments d'objets***
Vertical-Horizontal Composition with Object Elements
Composición vertical-horizontal con elementos de objetos
1919
Collage
20.2 x 20.2 cm
Fondation Hans Arp & Sophie Taeuber- Arp e. V., Rolandseck

312 ***Composition à forme de "U"***
"U" Shaped Composition
Composición en forma de "U"
1918
Watercolour and collage
24.8 x 28.8 cm
Fondation Hans Arp & Sophie Taeuber- Arp e. V., Rolandseck

WALL 4

Sophie Taeuber-Arp
313 ***Composition à forme de "S"***
"S" Shaped Composition
Composición en forma de "S"
1927
Gouache
26 x 32.5 cm
Fondation Hans Arp & Sophie Taeuber- Arp e. V., Rolandseck

314 ***Composition verticale-horizontale***
Vertical-Horizontal Composition
Composición vertical-horizontal
1916
Coloured pencils on paper
23.6 x 19.3 cm
Fondation Hans Arp & Sophie Taeuber- Arp e. V., Rolandseck

315 ***Grand triangle. Composition verticale-horizontale***
Large triangle. Vertical-Horizontal Composition
Gran triángulo. Composición vertical-horizontal
1916
Coloured pencils on paper
19.3 x 23.6 cm
Fondation Hans Arp & Sophie Taeuber- Arp e. V., Rolandseck

316 ***Composition à rectangles et bras angulaires***
Composition with Rectangles and Angular Arms
Composición con rectángulos y brazos angulares
1928
Gouache on paper
25 x 28 cm
Fondation Arp Collection, Clamart

Amédée Ozenfant
317 ***Pot et pipe II***
Pot and Pipe II
Bote y pipa II
1918
Pencil on paper
45 x 32 cm
Larock-Granoff Collection, Paris

318 ***Reds, Rome***
Rojos, Roma
1920-1925
Oil paint on canvas
81 x 100 cm
Larock-Granoff Collection, Paris

319 ***Église d'Andernos***
Andernos Church
Iglesia de Andernos
1918
Pencil on paper
27 x 34 cm
Larock-Granoff Collection, Paris

VITRINE: FUTURISM AND RUSSIAN CONSTRUCTIVISM

Wasilii Kamenskii / David Burljuk' / Vladimir Burljuk'
320 ***Tango s korovami. Jelezobetonnyïa poemy***
Tangoing With the Cows. Poems in Reinforced Concrete
Moscow, 1914
300 copies, 16 pages
Wallpaper cover with typographic design mounted on the inside; the text includes poems "in reinforced concrete" and typographic designs by Kamensky, 3 typographic illustration s (1 by Vladimir Burliuk and 2 by David Burliuk); all this printed on the back of sheets of wallpaper
Archives Martin-Malburet, Paris

Vélimir Khlebnikov / Mariia Siniakova / Grigorii Petnikov / Nicolai Aseev
321 ***Truba Marsiian***
Trumpet of the Martians
Liren, Moscow, 1916
300 copies, 8 pages
Archives Martian Trumpet, Paris

Kasimir Malevic
322 ***Ot kubizma i futurizma k suprematizmu. Novyi zhivopisnyi realizm***, 3rd edition
From Cubism and Futurism to Suprematism: The New Pictorial Realism
Moscow, 1916
Unknown print run, 31 pages
Cover with photolithoed illustration on the front; 2

photolithoed illustrations
Private collection, Barcelona

Kasimir Malevic / El Lissitsky
323 *O novykh systemakh v iskusstve. Statika i skorost'*
On New Systems in Art.Statics and Speed
Artel' khudozhestvennogo truda pri Vitsvomas (Vitebskikh svobodnykh masterskikh), Vitebsk, 1919
1,000 copies, 32 pages
Cover with illustrations and hand-written text by Lissitzky lithographed on the inside and on the rear cover; 6 lithographed illustrations by Malevich; lithographed hand-written text
IVAM, Instituto Valenciano de Arte Moderno, Generalitat Valenciana. Library.

Nikolaï Punin
324 *Pamjatnik III Internacionala*
Monument to the Third International
Ed. Izdanie Otdela Izobrazitel. Nyh Iskusstv NKP, Petersburg, 1920
Unknown print run, 8 pages
Archives Martin-Malburet, Paris

El Lissitzky
325 *Wendingen*, no. 36
Amsterdam, 1921
Engraving
IVAM, Instituto Valenciano de Arte Moderno, Generalitat Valenciana

326 *Pro Dva Kvadrata. Suprematichskii skaz v 6-ti postroikakh*
Apropos of Two Squares. A Suprematist Tale in Six Constructions
Skify, Berlin, 1922
Unknown print run, 20 pages
Cover with typographic illustrations on the front and rear covers; 6 typographic illustrations; text with typographic lettering and typographic designs, plus a final page printed black
IVAM, Instituto Valenciano de Arte Moderno, Generalitat Valenciana

327 *Das entfesselte Theater* by Alexander Tairoff
The Free Theatre
Gustav Kiepenheuer, Potsdam, 1923
Unknown print run, 122 pages, 11 illustrations
Cover with typographic lettering on the front surface
IVAM, Instituto Valenciano de Arte Moderno, Generalitat Valenciana

328 *Zapiski poeta. Povest', d'Ilia Sel'vinskii*
Notes of a Poet. A Tale
Gosudarstvennoe izdatel'stvo, Moscow, Leningrad, 1928
3,000 copies, 91 pages and 1 unfolding page
Wraparound cover with typographic lettering and photomontage
IVAM, Instituto Valenciano de Arte Moderno, Generalitat Valenciana

Vladimir Tatlin
Catalogue of the Moderna Museet exhibition, Stockholm, 1968
Moderna Museet, Stockholm

El Lissitzky / Vladimir Maïakovski
329 *Dlia Golosa*
For the Voice
Gosudarstvennoe izdatel'stvo, Moscow / Lutze & Vogt GMBH, Berlin, 1923
2,000 – 3,000 copies, 61 pages
A compilation of Mayakovsky's 13 most popular poems
Overall design; cover in orange paperr with a typographic design on the front cover; 24typographic illustrations ; the typographic text includes typographic designs and a thumb index
4 copies: Private collection, Milan; Private collection, Barcelona; Archives Martin-Malburet, Paris; Private collection, Barcelona

Vladimir Maïakovski / Alexander Rodtxenko
330 *Pro Eto. Ei i mne*
About That: To Her and to Me
Gosudarstvennoe Izdatel'stvo, Moscow, 1923
3,000 copies, 43 pages
Cover with typographic lettering/photomontage on the front cover and typographic lettering (industrial logo) on the back cover; 8 typographic-photomontage illustrations
Copieswith hand-written annotations by Lilia Borix
Private collection, Barcelona

Alexander Rodchenko / Varvara Stepanova
331 *LEF. Zhurnal levogo fronta iskusstv*
LEF: Magazine of the Left Front in Art
Moscow / Leningrad: Gosudarstvennoe izdatel'stvo
-No. 2, 1923, relief engraving and two-colour typography
2 copies: IVAM, Instituto Valenciano de Arte Moderno, Generalitat Valenciana & Archives Martin-Malburet, Paris
-No. 3, 1923, typography
2 copies: IVAM, Instituto Valenciano de Arte Moderno, Generalitat Valenciana. Library & Archives Martin-Malburet, Paris
-No. 10, 1928, photogram
Archives Martin-Malburet, Paris

El Lissitzky / Hans Arp
332 *Die Kunstismen / Les ismes de l'art / The Isms of Art / Kunstismus, 1914-1924*
Eugen Rentsch, Zurich, Munich & Leipzig, 1925
Unknown print run, 48 pages
Cover with typographic lettering on the front cover; the typographic text includes typographic designs
IVAM, Instituto Valenciano de Arte Moderno, Generalitat Valenciana. Library

Vladimir Maïakovski
333 *15. 000.000*
Prague, 1925
Czech edition of Mayakovsky's text
Book with airbrushed page design
21.5 x 13.5 x 1 cm
Private collection, Milan

Vladimir Maïakovski / Alexander Rodtxenko
334 *Razgovor s fininspektorom o poezii*
A Conversation with the Tax Inspector About Poetry
Zakkniga, Tiflis, 1926
5,000 copies, 14 pages
Cover with typographic lettering/photomontage on the front cover and typographic/photomontage illustration on the back cover; 1 typographic/ photomonta-geillustration
Private collection, Barcelona

Room 8: **The myth of the crystal and the castle question**

WALL 1

Kurt Schwitters
335 ***Abstraction No. 16 (Schlafender Kristall)***
Abstraction No. 16 (Sleeping Glass)
Abstracción nº 16 (Cristal durmiente)
1919
Oil paint on canvas
73.5 x 51.5 cm
Kurt & Ernst Schwitters Foundation , Hanover

Wassily Kandinsky
336 ***Acht Mal***
Eight Times
Ocho veces
1929
1929
Oil paint on a preparation imitating granite on plywood
24.3 x 40 cm
Centre Pompidou, Musée national d'art moderne / Centre de création industrielle, Paris

WALL 2

László Moholy-Nagy
337 ***Untitled***
Sin título
Weimar, March 1923-1925
Photogram, gelatin silver print
17.8 x 13 cm
Vintage copy; (inv. 9/95)
Museum Folkwang, Essen

338 ***Untitled***
Sin título
Dessau 1925-1928
Photogram, gelatin silver print
23.9 x 17.8 cm
Vintage copy; (inv. 63/95)
Museum Folkwang, Essen

339 ***Untitled***
Sin título
Weimar, 1923-25
Photogram, gelatin silver print
18.1 x 12.7 cm
Vintage copy; (inv. 5/95)
Museum Folkwang, Essen

340 ***Untitled***
Sin título
Dessau 1925-1928
Photogram, gelatin silver print
23.8 x 17.9 cm
Vintage copy; (inv. 40/95)
Museum Folkwang, Essen

341 ***Untitled***
Sin título
Dessau 1925-1928
Photogram, gelatin silver print
23.9 x 17.9 cm
Vintage copy; (inv. 33/95)
Museum Folkwang, Essen

342 ***Untitled***
Sin título
Weimar, 1925-1928.
Photogram, gelatin silver print
24 x 18 cm
Vintage copy; (inv. 15/95)
Museum Folkwang, Essen

343 ***Photograma***
Fotograma
1928
Gelatin silver print, made that year by the artist
23.4 x 17.8 cm
Galerie Berinson, Berlin / UBU Gallery, New York

344 ***Verre de vin***
Glass of Wine
Vaso de vino
1938
Photogram, made that year by the artist
25.3 x 20.5 cm
Hattula Moholy-Nagy, Ann Arbor, Michigan, USA

345 ***Project for the cover for the magazine Broom***, no. 4
Proyecto de portada para la revista *Broom*, nº 4
March 1922
Photogram
18 x 31 cm
Vintage copy
Hattula Moholy-Nagy, Ann Arbor, Michigan, USA

VITRINE

Max Ernst / André Breton
346 ***Le Château étoilé***
The Starry Castle
El castillo estrellado
1937
Offprint of Minotaure, no. 8; 50 numbered copies; text by'André Breton, illustrations by Max Ernst (1 original frottage and 8 reproductions)
32 x 25 cm
Galleria Nazionale d'Arte Moderna, Rome

WALL 3

Max Ernst
347 ***Entre dans les continents***
Enter into the Continents
Entra en los continentes
1925
Frottage, graphite
42 x 26.5 cm
Private collection, Geneva

348 ***Au-dessus des nuages marche la minuit. Au-dessus de la minuit plane l'oiseau invisible du jour. Un peu plus haut que l'oiseau l'éther pousse et les murs et les toits flottent.***
Above the clouds walks midnight. Above midnight hovers the invisible bird of day. A little higher than the bird, the ether grows and the walls and roofs float.
Por encima de las nubes camina la medianoche. Por encima de la medianoche se cierne el pájaro invisible del día. Un poco más alto que el pájaro sube el éter, y flotan las paredes y los tejados.
1920
Enlarged photograph, print
1/5
73 x 55 cm
Kunsthaus Zürich, Graphic Art Collection

349 ***Un autre monde***
Another World
Otro mundo
1965
Frottage, graphite
22.5 x 21 cm
Private collection, Geneva

Hermann Finsterlin
350 ***Theaterbau – Voluptarium***
Theatre – Voluptarium
Teatro – Voluptarium
1919
Watercolour with opaque white paint on pencil fixed onyellowish paper
39.4 x 29.1 cm
Staatsgalerie Stuttgart, Graphic Art Collection

351 ***Architektur – Austellungsbau***
Architecture – Exhibition Building
Arquitectura – Edificio para exposiciones
1919
Watercolour onpencil fixed on brown paper
21 x 20.8 cm & 19.3 x 23.3 cm
Staatsgalerie Stuttgart, Graphic Art Collection

352 ***Die Stadt***
The City
La ciudad
1920-1924
Watercolour on pencil fixed on handmade off-white paper
31 x 48 cm
Staatsgalerie Stuttgart, Graphic Art Collection

WALL 4

Max Ernst
353 ***Untitled [Sun over the Forest]***
Sin título [Sol sobre el bosque]
1927
Gouache
36 x 24.8 cm
Courtesy of Daniel Malingue, Paris

Mikhaïl Matyushin
354 ***"Crystal" Self-Portrait***
Autorretrato "Cristal"
1917
Oil paint on canvas
70 x 37.3 cm
Museum Ludwig, Cologne; Ludwig Collection

WALL 5

F. W. Murnau
355 ***Nosferatu, eine Symphonie des Grauens***
Nosferatu, A Symphony of Horrors
Nosferatu, una sinfonía de horrores
1922
Black-and-white film, silent, Germany, 110'

WALL 6

Sergueï Eisenstein
356 ***Kniaz Potiomkin***
Battleship Potemkin
El acorazado Potemkim
1925
Soviet Union, produced by the Goskino Studios
Black-and-white film, 80'

WALL 7

René Magritte
357 ***Le Corps bleu***
The Blue Body
El cuerpo azul
1928
Oil paint on canvas
73 x 54 cm
Private collection, London

VITRINE

358 ***La Révolution surréaliste***, Paris
(12 numbers, 1 December 1924 – 15 December 1929. Editors: Pierre Naville & Benjamin Péret [nos 1- 3]; André Breton [nos 4- 12])
-No. 1, "Il faut aboutir à une nouvelle déclaration des droits de l'homme", 1 December 1924, Collection Museo Nacional Centro de Arte Reina Sofía. Library
-No. 2, "Art français, début du XXe siècle", 15 January 1925 Collection Museo Nacional Centro de Arte Reina Sofía. Library
-No. 3, "1925: fin de l'ère chrétienne", 15 April 1925. [Exposition of the projects and interventions of the Bureau central de Recherches surréalistes, opened on 1December 1924, closed to the public on 30 January 1925, after this date by Antonin Artaud] Collection Museo Nacional Centro de Arte Reina Sofía. Biblioteca
-No. 4, "Et guerre au travail", 15 July 1925. Collection Museo Nacional Centro de Arte Reina Sofía. Library
-No. 5, "Le passé", 15 October 1925. Collection Museo Nacional Centro de Arte Reina Sofía. Library
-No. 8, "Ce qui manque à tous ces messieurs c'est la dialectique (Engels)", 1 December 1926 Collection Museo Nacional Centro de Arte Reina Sofía. Library
-No. 11, "La prochaine chambre", 15 March 1928. Collection Museo Nacional Centro de Arte Reina Sofía. Library
-No. 12, "Quelle sorte d'espoir mettez-vous dans l'amour ?", 15 Decmber 1929. Collection Museo Nacional Centro de Arte Reina Sofía. Library

359 ***Variétés***
-15 January
-15 December
1929, Brussels
Private collection, Barcelona

André Breton
360 ***L'Amour fou*** (1935)
Gallimard, Collection "Métamorphoses" III, Paris, 1937
180 pages
Museo Nacional Centro de Arte Reina Sofía. Library

Room 9: Iliazd

WALL 1

Iliazd (Ilia Zdanevitch)
361 ***Poster for a Conference of the 41°, Borjom-Park, Tiflis***
Cartel de una conferencia del 41°, Borjom-Park, Tiflis
1918
Typography on paper
106 x 69.5 cm
François & Michel Mairé, France

362 ***Poésie de mots inconnus***
Poetry of Unknown Words
Poesía de palabras desconocidas
Éditions Le Degré 41, Paris, 1949
158 copies
26 folded sheets; each one 4.3 x 24.5 cm
Box: 18.2 x 15.5 x 6 cm
Woodcuts and linocuts, etchings, copperplate engravings, lithographs.
Pagination byIliazd
Poems by Akinsemoyin, Albert-Birot, Arp, Artaud, Bryen, Dermée, Hausmann, Huidobro, Iliazd, Jolas, Khlebnikov, Kruchenykh, Picasso, Poplavsky, Schwitters, Seuphor, Terentiev, Tzara
Illustrations by Arp, Braque, Bryen, Chagall, Domínguez, Ferat, Giacometti, Gleizes, Hausmann, Laurens, Léger, Magnelli, Masson, Matisse, Metzinger, Miró, Picasso, Ribemont-Dessaignes, Survage, Taeuber-Arp, Tytgat, Villon, Wols
François & Michel Mairé, France

Iliazd (Ilia Zdanevitch) / Combined editorial team
363 ***Journal du 41°***
Newspaper of the 41°
Periódico del 41°
No. 1, Tiflis, 1919
4 pages
58 x 42 cm unfolded
François & Michel Mairé, France

WALL 2

Ivan Puni
364 ***Schachmaty***
Checkmate
Jaque y mate
1917-1918
Oil paint on wood
70.3 x 49 cm
Ivan Puni Archive, Zurich

WALL 3

Lioubov Popova
365 ***Pictorial Architecture***
Arquitectura pictórica
c. 1918-1920
Oil paint on canvas
55.5 x 50 cm
Private collection, Italy; courtesy Manuel Barbié

Ivan Puni
366 ***Composition (aux lettres J R JA)***
Composition (With letters J R J A)
Composición (con las letras J R J A)
1922
Linocut on Van Gelder Zonen laid paper
22.1 x 16.7 cm
Cabinet des estampes du Musée d'art et d'histoire, Geneva

367 ***Composition (au cercle détaché)***
Composition (With Detached Circle)
Composición (con círculo suelto)
1922
Linocut on Van Gelder Zonen laid paper
24.9 x 15.6 cm
Cabinet des estampes du Musée d'art et d'histoire, Geneva

368 ***Composition (à la virgule)***
Composition (With Comma)
Composición (con coma)
1922
Linocut on Van Gelder Zonen laid paper
23.4 x 19.8 cm
Cabinet des estampes du Musée d'art et d'histoire, Geneva

369 ***Composition***
Composition
Composición
1922
Linocut on Van Gelder Zonen laid paper
21.8 x 12.3 cm
Cabinet des estampes du Musée d'art et d'histoire, Geneva

370 ***Composition***
Composition
Composición
1922
Linocut on Van Gelder Zonen laid paper
25.5 x 18.7 cm
Cabinet des estampes du Musée d'art et d'histoire, Geneva

Raoul Hausmann
371 ***Material der Malerei, Plastik, Architektur***
The Material of Painting, Sculpture, and Architecture
Material de la pintura, el plástico y la arquitectura
1918
Cover collage
32 x 18 cm
Musée départemental, Rochechouart

372 ***Untitled (Sketch for an inside page of "Material der Malerei, Plastik, Architektur")***
Sin título (prueba para una página interior de "Material der Malerei, Plastik, Architektur")
1917
Wood engraving on paper
31.1 x 19 cm
Musée d'Art Moderne, Saint-Étienne Métropole

373 ***Untitled (Sketch for an inside page of "Material der Malerei, Plastik, Architektur")***
Sin título (prueba para una página interior de "Material der Malerei, Plastik, Architektur")
1918
Wood engraving on paper
30.5 x 15
Musée départemental, Rochechouart

374 ***Untitled (Sketch for an inside page of "Material der Malerei, Plastik, Architektur")***
Sin título (prueba para una página interior de "Material der Malerei, Plastik, Architektur")
1918
Wood engraving on paper
26 x 16 cm
Musée d'Art Moderne, Saint-Étienne Métropole

375 ***Untitled (Sketch for an inside page of "Material der Malerei, Plastik, Architektur")***
Sin título (prueba para una página interior de "Material der Malerei, Plastik, Architektur")
1918
Wood engraving on paper
33 x 24 cm
Musée départemental, Rochechouart

VITRINES

Iliazd (Ilia Zdanevitch)
376 ***Ostraf paskhi***
Easter Eyeland
Ed. 41°, Tiflis, 1919
Approx 200 copies, 31 pages
Front cover with typographic lettering; the typographic text includes typographic designs
François & Michel Mairé, France

Igor Terentiev / Iliazd (Ilia Zdanevitch)
377 ***Fakt***
Fact
Ed. 41°, Tiflis, 1919
Approx 250 copies, 30 pages
Text by Terentiev, cover and layout by Iliazd
Front cover with typographic lettering; the typographic text includes typographic designs; all the pages are printed in pink
François & Michel Mairé, France

Iliazd (Ilia Zdanevitch)
378 ***Soirée du coeur à barbe***
Heart to Beard Soirée
Velada de corazón a barba
1923
Announcement of a soirée at the Théâtre Michel, Paris
Refief engraving and typography
IVAM, Instituto Valenciano de Arte Moderno, Generalitat Valenciana

Iliazd (Ilia Zdanevitch) / Naoum Granowski
379 ***Lidantiu faram***
Ledentu as a Beacon
Ed. 41°, Paris, 1923
530 copies (of which some 150 were put on sale, the remainder being destroyed), 61 pages
Wrapping-paper with typographic lettering and collage illustrations by Granowski on the front; the text includes typographic designs by Iliazd
2 copies: IVAM, Instituto Valenciano de Arte Moderno, Generalitat Valenciana & François & Michel Mairé, France

Iliazd (Ilia Zdanevitch) / Georges Ribemont-Dessaignes
380 Leaflet announcing ***Ledentu le phare***, a dramatic poem in zaoum
Paris, 1947
8 pages
François & Michel Mairé, France

Iliazd (Ilia Zdanevitch) / Joan Miró / Adrian de Montluc (dit Comte de Cramail)
381 ***Le Courtisan grotesque***
Ed. 41°, Paris, 1974
110 copies, 16 full-page and 7 double-page colour illustrations

Layout and illustration by Iliazd, engravings by Joan Miró, 30 sheets of Auvergne paper folded in two, parchment cover
François & Michel Mairé, France

Room 10: The word as such (the Russian Futurist book in the collection of the Cabinet des estampes du Musée d'Art et d'Histoire de Genève)

WALL 1

Ivan Puni
382 *Novoie Iskusstvo*
New Art
Nuevo arte
1917-1918
Oil paint on canvas
60.5 x 80.5 cm
Private collection. Courtesy the Galería Manuel Barbié

WALL 2

Olga Rozanova
383 *8 Sketches for Té li lé*
8 esbozos para Té li lé
Watercolour sketches
22 x 15 cm; 23 x 16.3 cm; 22 x 15.2 cm; 23.5 x 14.6 cm; 21.3 x 14.6 cm; 18.3 x 14.3 cm; 21.5 x 15.2 cm; 23.3 x 16 cm.
Framed together: 88 x 70.5 cm
Private collection, Milan

WALL 3

Aleksei Krutxenykh
384 *Vselenskaia voina*
Universal War
Ed. Yrei Shemshurin, Petrograd, 1916
100 copies (12 known copies), 14 pages
12 collage illustrations (9 on blue paper, 2 on white paper & 1 on purple paper), printed cover; preface and poem-table
Each page approx 22.5 x 32.9 cm
Unbound book, framed plates
-Plate 1: "A Futurist's Battle Against the Ocean"
-Plate 2: "Battle of Mars Against Scorpio"
-Plate 3: "Explosion of a Trunk"
-Plate 4: "Battle with the Equator"
-Plate 5: "Treachery"
-Plate 6: "Destruction of Gardens"
-Plate 7: "The Battle of India and Europe"
-Plate 8: "Heavy Artillery"
-Plate 9: "Fervent Germany"
-Plate 10: "Germany in the Dust""
-Plate 11: "Call for Victory"
-Plate 12: "Military State"
Cabinet des estampes du Musée d'art et d'histoire, Geneva

El Lissitzky
385 *Proun 1 (Construction Floating in Space)*
Proun 1 (Construcción flotante en el espacio)
Vitebsk, 1920
Wood engraving on old vellum
12.9 x 17.8 cm
Cabinet des estampes du Musée d'art et d'histoire, Geneva

386 *Proun*
Vitebsk, 1920
Vitebsk, 1920
11 plates:
-Proun 1 (25.5 x 33.8 cm)
-Proun 1A (17.1 x 30.2 cm)
-Proun 1C (23.3 x 23.4 cm)
-Proun 1D (21.5 x 26.8 cm)
-Proun 1E the city (22.7 x 27.5 cm)
-Proun 2B (26.4 x 20.5 cm)
-Proun 2C (29.9 x 20.2 cm)
-Proun 2D (35.9 x 22.6 cm)
-Proun 3A (27.5 x 26.4 cm)
-Proun 5A (27.6 x 26.8 cm)
-Proun 6B (Ø 25 cm)
Lithograph y on old vellum
Cabinet des estampes du Musée d'art et d'histoire, Geneva

Aleksei Kruchenykh / Vassily Kamenskii / Kirill Zdanevitx
387 *1918*
Tiflis, 1917
Unknown print run (6 complete copies known), 13 sheets
24 x 37 cm (irregular format)
Unbound book, framed plates
Wrapping-paper cover withtypographic text and collage-title by Kruchenykh mounted on the front; 2 lithographed poems in "reinforced concrete" (1 by Kamensky, and 1 by Kamensky and Zdanevich) mounted on wrapping paper; 4 lithographed illustrations (3 with collage elements) by Zdanevich alongside 4 lithographed zaum poems (1 by Kamensky and 3 by Kruchenykh) on wrapping paper; and 7 collage illustrations by Kruchenykh (4 on wrapping paper, 1 on blue paper, 1 on cream paper and one on ivory paper) manuscript text by Zdanevich
Cabinet des estampes du Musée d'art et d'histoire, Geneva

VITRINE

Aleksei Kruchenykh / Olga Rozanova
388 *Utinoe gnezdyshko.... durnykh slov...*
Duck's Nest. . . Bad Words. . .
Saint Petersburg, 1913
500 copies (100 retouched by hand), 22 pages, unbound.
Cover with watercolour and gouache retouches on the front; 14 lithographed illustrations with watercolour and/or gouache retouches; hand-written lithographed text with watercolour and/or gouache retouches
2 copies: 1 with hand-written cover and 1 with a typographic cover
Cabinet des estampes du Musée d'art et d'histoire, Geneva

Aliagrov (Roman Jakobson) / Aleksei Krutxenykh / Olga Rozanova
389 *Zaumnaja gniga*
The Transrational Book
Moscow, 1915-1916
140 copies, 21 pages
22 x 18.8 cm
Front cover with collage in green glossy paper and button; 9 linocut illustrations and 1collage illustration with stamped text
Texts by Aliagrov & Alexei Kruchenykh, wngravings by Olga Rozanova
Unbound book, framed plates
Cabinet des estampes du Musée d'art et d'histoire, Geneva

WALL 4

Lioubov Popova
390 *6 graviur'*
6 prints
6 grabados
1917
Coloured linocuts in

gouache cover on linoleum on cardboard
Each one approx 34.5 x 26 cm
Cabinet des estampes du Musée d'art et d'histoire, Geneva

ANGLE VITRINE

Aleksei Krutxenykh / Alexander Rodtxenko
391 *Tsotsa*
Baku, 1921
Unknown print run, 13 double pages
Collage cover and coloured-pencil drawing (Rodchenko); "Declaration on the ZaumLanguage", typography by Kruchenykh; hectographed poems "drawn" by Kruchenykh, a poem reproduced on charcoal-blue paper, a typographic foldout
Cabinet des estampes du Musée d'art et d'histoire, Geneva

392 *Tsotsa*
Baku, 1921
3 unused covers, zaum graphisms by Alexei Kruchenykh
Collage and coloured-pencil drawing
Each one 22 x 16 cm
Cabinet des estampes du Musée d'art et d'histoire, Geneva

Olga Rozanova
393 *Ingra v adu*
A Game in Hell
Juego en el infierno
2nd edicion, Saint Petersburg, 1914
800 copies, 40 pages
Coever with lithographed illustrations by Malevich on the front and back; 26 lithographed illustrations (23 by Rozanova and 3 by Malevich); lithographed hand-written text
6.2 x 12.5 cm (lithographs 1 & 2, pp. 2-3)
8 x 11.5 cm (lithograph 3, p. 38)
Cabinet des estampes du Musée d'art et d'histoire, Geneva

VITRINE

David Burliuk' / Nikola Burliuk' / Wassily Kandinsky / Vélimir Klhebnikov / Aleksei Krutxenykh / Benedikt Livchitz / Vladimir Maïakovski
394 ***Poshchechina obshchestvennomu vkusu. V zashchitu svobodnogo iskousstva. Stokhi, proza, stat'i***
A Slap in the Face of Public Taste: In Defence of Free Art, Poetry, Prose, and Essays
G. L. Kuzmin, Moscow, 1912
600 copies,112 pages
Cover in brown sackcloth with typographic text on the front; pages printed on wrapping paper
Cabinet des estampes du Musée d'art et d'histoire, Geneva

Velimir Khlebnikov / Aleksei Krutxenykh / Elena Gouro / Kasimir Malevic
395 *Troe*
Three
Zhuravl', Saint Petersburg, 1913
500 copies, 96 pages
Cover with lithographed hand-written design and illustration on the front and lithographed hand-written text on the back; 4 photomechanical reproductions; all pages printed on pale green paper
Cabinet des estampes du Musée d'art et d'histoire, Geneva

Vélimir Khlebnikov / Aleksei Krutxenykh / Olga Rozanova / Nikolaï Kul'bin
396 *Té li lé*
Saint Petersburg, 1914
Number 18/50, 15 pages
Cover with hectographed hand-written text and illustration on the front, and hectographed twxt on the back, all this by Rozanova; 14 hectographed illustrations (11 by Rozanova and 3 by Kulbin); hectographed hand-written text, poems by V. Khlebnikov and A. Kruchenykh
Don Ena Abensur, Suzanne de Agostini Mairet, RMM, Morris Pinto
Cabinet des estampes du Musée d'art et d'histoire, Geneva

Room 11: Transition, the 1930s

WALL 1

Wassily Kandinsky
397 *Dreizehn Rechtecke*
Thirteen Rectangles
Trece rectángulos
1930
Oil paint on cardboard
70 x 60 cm
Centre Pompidou, Musée national d'art moderne/ Centre de création industrielle, Paris

Georges Vantongerloo
398 *Variante*
Variant
Variante
1939
Oil paint on masonite
52.5 x 40 cm
IVAM, Instituto Valenciano de Arte Moderno, Generalitat Valenciana

399 *Courbes*
Curves
Curvas
1939
Oil paint on masonite
60 x 42 cm
Chantal & Jakob Bill

VITRINE

Constantin Brancusi
400 *Portrait de James Joyce*
Portrit of James Joyce
Retrato de James Joyce
1929
First page of "Tales Told of Shem and Shaum. Three Fragments from Work in Progress" by James Joyce
Paris, The Black Sun Press, 1929
21 x 16 cm
Private collection, Barcelona

WALL 2

Marcel Duchamp
401 *Deux ou trois gouttes de hauteur n'ont rien à faire avec la sauvagerie*
3 or 4 drops of height have nothing to do with savagery
Dos o tres gotas de altura no tienen nada que hacer con el salvajismo
1937
Enlargement of the cover of no. 26 of the magazine Transition
Ink-jet printing

Hans Arp
402 *Untitled*
Sin título
1942
Printed paper torn and mounted on paper
37.5 x 25 cm
Private collection, Milan

Sophie Taeuber-Arp
403 *Échelonnement*
Escalation
Escalonamiento
1934
Gouache on paper
27.1 x 20.7 cm
Fondation Hans Arp & Sophie Taeuber- Arp e. V., Rolandseck

404 *Échelonnement*
Escalation
Escalonamiento
c. 1934
Pencil on paper
26.9 x 20.8 cm
Fondation Hans Arp & Sophie Taeuber- Arp e. V., Rolandseck

405 *Échelonnement*
Escalation
Escalonamiento
c. 1934
Pencil on paper
26.9 x 20.8 cm
Fondation Hans Arp & Sophie Taeuber- Arp e. V., Rolandseck

Julio González
406 *Petite maternité n° 2*
Little Motherhood no. 2
Pequeña maternidad n° 2
1934
Green ink, graphite on paper
20.5 x 12 cm
Galerie de France, Paris

407 *Petite danseuse II*
Little Dancer II
Pequeña bailarina II
1938-1940
Indian ink and coloured pencil on paper
20.8 x 8.7 cm
Galerie de France, Paris

408 *Étude pour Danseuse à la palette*
Study for Dancer with Palette
Estudio para Bailarina con la paleta
1935
Indian ink, graphite on paper
21.2 x 12.3 cm
Galerie de France, Paris

409 *Étude pour la Tête de Montserrat no 2*
Study for Montserrat's Head no. 2
Estudio para Cabeza de Montserrat n° 2
1917-1939
Black pencil on paper
25 x 16.5 cm
Galerie de France, Paris

Béla Uitz
410 *Analisi di un'icona*
Analysis of an Icon
Análisis de un icono
1921
Oilpaint on canvas
160 x 145 cm
Private collection

WALL 3

Jean Vigo
411 *À propos de Nice*
À propos de Nice
A propósito de Niza
1930
Black-and-white film, silent, 24', France. Director of photography: Boris Kaufman; soundtrack: Marc Perrone, 2001

WALL 4

Joan Miró
412 *Peinture-poème ("Bonheur d'aimer ma brune")*
Painting-Poem ("The Happiness of Loving My Brunette")
Pintura-poema ("La dicha de amar a mi morena")
1925
Oil paint and hand-written inscription on canvas
73 x 92 cm
Formerly in the Raymond Queneau Collection. Private collection

Hans Arp
413 *Constellation selon les lois du hasard*
Constellation According to the Laws of Chance
Constelación según las leyes del azar
1932
Painted wood
50 x 70 cm
Private collection, Paris

414 *Araignée*
Spider
Araña
1958
Bronze
36 x 45 cm
Fondation Hans Arp & Sophie Taeuber- Arp e. V., Rolandseck

415 *Blätter IV*
Leaves IV
Hojas IV
1930
Relief. Painted wood
19 x 34 cm
Fondation Hans Arp & Sophie Taeuber- Arp e. V., Rolandseck

Paul Klee
416 *Halme*
Straw
Paja
1938
Coloured paste on paper mounted on cardboard
50 x 35 cm
FondationBeyeler, Riehen/Basel

VITRINE: TRANSITION

417 *Transition. An International Quarterly for Creative Experiment*
Edited by Eugène Jolas & Elliot Paul, Paris:
-No. 1, April 1927. Editors: Eugène Jolas, Elliot Paul, 158 pages [James Joyce, "Opening Pages of a Work in Progress"]
-No. 8, November 1927, Paris, 184 pages [James Joyce, "Continuation of a Work in Progress" ("Anna Livia Plurabelle")]
-No. 11, February 1928, 152 pages
Edited by Eugène Jolas, Paris:
-No. 13, Summer 1928. "American Number", 277 pages. Cover by Pablo Picasso
-No. 14, Autumn 1928, 279 pages. Cover by Stuart Davis
-No. 15, February 1929. 298 pages. Cover by Man Ray
-No. 16-17, June 1929 , "Revolution of the Word", 328 pages. Cover by Gretchen Powel ("Synthesis")
-No. 18, November 1929, "From Instinct to New Composition, Word Lore Totality, Magic Synthetism", 291 pages. Cover by Kurt Schwitters
-No. 19-20, June 1929, "We Want Myths and More Myths", 398 pages. Cover by Eli Lotar

418 *Transition. An International Workshop for Orphic Creation*
Edited by Eugène Jolas, The Hague (Holland)
-No. 21, March 1932, "The Vertical Age", 325 pages. Cover by Hans Arp
-No. 22, February 1933, "The Vertigal Age", 179 pages. Cover by Sophie Taeuber-Arp

419 *Transition. Intercontinental Workshop for Vertigralist Transmutation*
Edited by Eugène Jolas, The Hague (Holland)
-No. 23, "Vertigral", July 1935, 205 pages. Cover by Paul Klee
-Supplent of Transition, no. 23: Transition Pamphlet no. 1, "Testimony Against Gertude Stein", 1934-1935, 15 pages. Georges Braque, Eugène Jolas, Maria Jolas, Henri Matisse, André Salmon, Tristan Tzara.

420 *Transition. A Quarterly Review*
Edited by Eugène Jolas, associate editor: James J. Sweeney

-No. 24, June 1936, The Hague (Holland)), 150 pages. Cover by Fernand Léger
-No. 25, Autumn 1936, New York, 216 pages. Cover by Joan Miró
-No. 26, Autumn 1937, New York, 208 pages. Cover by Marcel Duchamp: "3 or 4 drops of height have nothing to do with savagery"
-No. 27, March-April 1938, New York, "Tenth Anniversary", 382 pages. Cover by Vassily Kandinsky
Private collection, Paris

VITRINE: JOAN MIRÓ

Iliazd (Ilya Zdanevitch) / Tristan Tzara / Joan Miró
421 *Poésie de mots inconnus*
Éd. 41°, Paris, 1949
158 copies
26 sheets folded in four in a parchment slipcase
Fundació Joan Miró, Barcelona

Tristan Tzara / Joan Miró
422 *L'Arbre des voyageurs*
Éditions de la Montagne, Paris, 1930
Text by Tristan Tzara, illustrated with 4 lithographs by Miró
Fundació Joan Miró, Barcelona

Joan Miró
423 Hand-written note, undated
Ballpoint pen on paper
Fundació Joan Miró, Barcelona

Lithograph inserted into the *Anthologie de l'humour noir*, 1950
Fundació Joan Miró, Barcelona

André Breton
424 *Anthologie de l'humour noir*
Éditions du Sagittaire, Paris, 1950
Cover by Pierre Faucheux
Fundació Joan Miró, Barcelona

J.V. Foix / Joan Miró
425 *KRTU*
Edicions de l'Amic de les Arts, Barcelona, 1932
Original drawings by Joan Miró around the frontispiece in thewhite spaces of the doublecontents page (signed and dated"2-41")
Text by J.V. Foix, illustrations by Joan Miró
Gouache and ink
Fundació Joan Miró, Barcelona

Tristan Tzara / Joan Miró
426 *L'Antitête*
Éditions Bordas, Paris, 1949
200 copies
Text by Tristan Tzara, 8 etchings by Joan Miró heightened with gouache
Fundació Joan Miró, Barcelona

Lise Hirtz / Joan Miró
427 *Il était une petite pie*
Éditions Jeanne Bucher, Paris, 1928
Texts by Lise Hirtz: 10 songs for children, illustratinos by Joan Miró
Miró's personal copy, number 71, stapled
Fundació Joan Miró, Barcelona

J.V. Foix / Joan Miró
428 *Gertrudis*
Edicions de l'Amic de les Arts, Barcelona, 1927
Text by J.V. Foix, illustrations by Joan Miró
Original drawing by Joan Miró (1940) on the 1927 frontispiece. Pencil and gouache
Fundació Joan Miró, Barcelona

Benjamin Péret / Joan Miró
429 *...Et les seins mouraient...*
Éditions Les Cahiers du Sud, Collection "Nouvelles", 1929
Text by Benjamin Péret, edition embellished with a frontispiece by Miró
Original drawing by Joan Miró on the endpaper, October 1940
Watercolour and ink
Fundació Joan Miró, Barcelona

Carles Sindreu / Joan Miró
430 *Darrera el vidre*
Edicions de l'Amic de les Arts, Barcelona, 1933
Text by Carles Sindreu, illustrations by Joan Miró
Original drawing by Joan Miró on the endpaper, signed and dated "1-3-41"
Pen and watercolour
Fundació Joan Miró, Barcelona

Joan Miró / René Clair
431 *Flux de l'aimant*
Maeght Editeur, Paris, 1964
95 copies
Text by René Clair, 17 lithographs by Miró (drypoint)
Fundació Joan Miró, Barcelona

Level 2. Rooms 12-20

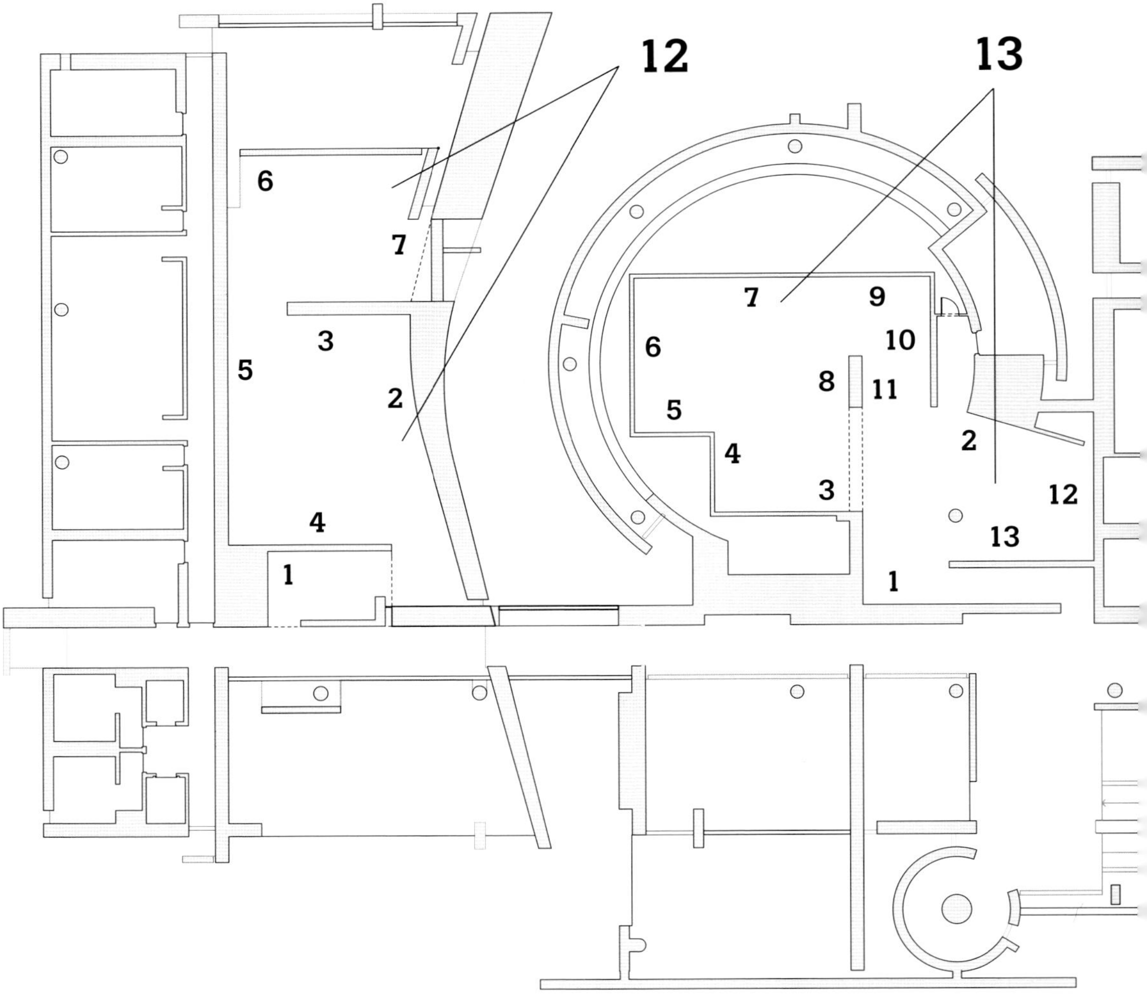

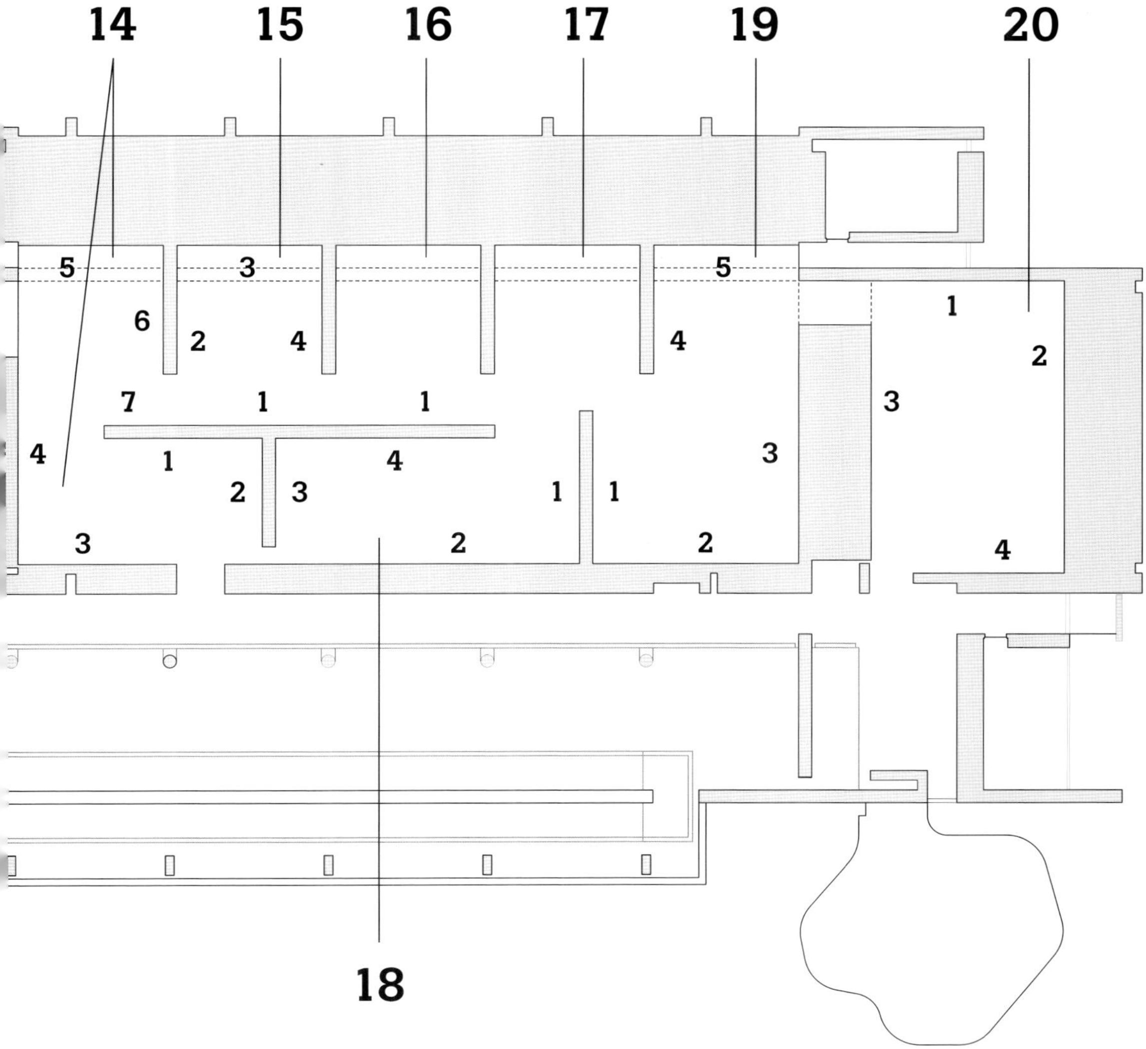
14
15
16
17
19
20
18

Room 12: Anthropology for photography (the poetic document)

WALL 1

Josef Albers
432 *Drei Behangen (1)*
Hanging Clothes (I)
Ropa colgada (1)
Undated
Silver gel print run
12.7 x 20.32 cm approx.
Josef and Anni Albers Foundation, Bethany, Connecticut, United States

433 *Drei Behangen (2)*
Hanging Clothes (2)
Ropa colgada (2)
Undated
Silver gel print run
12.7 x 20.32 cm approx.
Josef and Anni Albers Foundation, Bethany, Connecticut, United States

434 *Drei Behangen (3)*
Hanging Clothes (3)
Ropa colgada (3)
Undated
Silver gel print run
12.7 x 20.32 cm approx.
Josef and Anni Albers Foundation, Bethany, Connecticut, United States

WALL 2

Helen Levitt
435 *New York*
Nueva York
1971
Colour photography
40 x 50 cm
Courtesy of Laurence Miller Gallery, New York

436 *New York*
Nueva York
1972
Colour photography
40 x 50 cm
Courtesy of Laurence Miller Gallery, New York

437 *New York*
Nueva York
1979
Colour photography
35 x 23 cm
Courtesy of Laurence Miller Gallery, New York

438 *New York*
Nueva York
1980
Colour photography
22 x 31 cm
Courtesy of Laurence Miller Gallery, New York

439 *Untitled (New York)*
Sin título (Nueva York)
1945
Black and white photographic proof with gelatine emulsion of silver bromide
11.5 x 17 cm
Sandra Álvarez de Toledo Collection, Paris

440 *Untitled (Woman on a Porch)*
Sin título (Mujer en un porche)
1940
Black and white photographic proof with gelatine emulsion of silver bromide
11.5 x 16 cm
Sandra Álvarez de Toledo Collection, Paris

441 *New York, Ribbon (From the City Pictures)*
Nueva York, cinta (de las fotos de la ciudad)
ca. 1940
Black and white photo
18.5 x 24.5 cm
Courtesy of Laurence Miller Gallery, New York

442 *New York, Boy up Pole (From the City Pictures)*
Nueva York, niño en lo alto del poste (de las fotos de la ciudad)
ca. 1940
Black and white photo
21.75 x 14.5 cm
Courtesy of Laurence Miller Gallery, New York

443 *New York*
Nueva York
1940
Black and white photographic proof with gelatine emulsion of silver bromide
19 x 20.5 cm
Sandra Álvarez de Toledo Collection, Paris

444 *Untitled (Children Playing in Water Spraying from Fire Hydrant)*
Sin título (niños jugando a salpicar agua de una boca de incendios)
ca. 1945
Black and white photographic proof with gelatine emulsion of silver bromide
22.5 x 15.3 cm
Sandra Álvarez de Toledo Collection, Paris

445 *Mexico City (1)*
México D. F. (1)
1941
Black and white photos
Various sizes
Courtesy of Laurence Miller Gallery, New York

446 *Mexico City (2)*
México D. F. (2)
1941
Black and white photos
Various sizes
Courtesy of Laurence Miller Gallery, New York

447 *Mexico City (3)*
México D. F. (3)
1941
Black and white photos
Various sizes
Courtesy of Laurence Miller Gallery, New York

448 *Mexico City (4)*
México D. F. (4)
1941
Black and white photos
Various sizes
Courtesy of Laurence Miller Gallery, New York

449 *Mexico City (5)*
México D. F. (5)
1941
Black and white photos
Various sizes
Courtesy of Laurence Miller Gallery, New York

450 *Mexico City (6)*
México D. F. (6)
1941
Black and white photos
Various sizes
Courtesy of Laurence Miller Gallery, New York

451 *Mexico City (7)*
México D. F. (7)
1941
Black and white photos
Various sizes
Courtesy of Laurence Miller Gallery, New York

452 *Mexico City (8)*
México D. F. (8)
1941
Black and white photos
Various sizes
Courtesy of Laurence Miller Gallery, New York

Josef Albers
453 *Biarritz, Miramare + Grande plage VIII'29*
Biarritz, Miramare + Long Beach VIII'29
Biarritz, Miramar + Gran playa VIII'29

1929
Two photos on cardboard
41.9 x 29.7 cm
Josef and Anni Albers
Foundation, Bethany,
Connecticut, United States

454 *Brackwasser*
High Tide
Marea
Biarritz, 1929
Photo collage
27.94 x 40.64 cm
Josef and Anni Albers
Foundation, Bethany,
Connecticut, United States

455 *Ohne Titel (Grosse Pyramide, Tenayuca, Mexico)*
Untitled (Big Pyramid, Tenayuca, Mexico)
Sin título (gran pirámide, Tenayuca, México)
Undated
Silver gel print run
24.5 x 19.5 cm
Josef and Anni Albers
Foundation, Bethany,
Connecticut, United States

456 *Pachacamac (Peru)*
Pachacamac (Perú)
Undated
Three photos on cardboard (photo collage)
25.6 x 20.1 cm
Josef and Anni Albers
Foundation, Bethany,
Connecticut, United States

457 *Dessau, Flurstrasse während Neubauten*
Dessau, Flurstrasse Under Construction
Dessau, calle Flurstrasse durante la construcción
1931
Two photos on cardboard
Josef and Anni Albers
Foundation, Bethany,
Connecticut, United States

WALL 3

458 Josef Albers
Paris, Tour Eiffel, VIII'29
Paris, Eiffel Tower, VIII'29
París, Torre Eiffel, VIII'29
1929
Two photos on cardboard
29.7 x 41.7 cm
Josef and Anni Albers
Foundation, Bethany,
Connecticut, United States

459 *Anni, summer 1928*
Anni, verano de 1928
Two photos on cardboard
29.7 x 41.7 cm
Josef and Anni Albers
Foundation, Bethany,
Connecticut, United States

460 *Biarritz, VIII'29*
1929
Two photos on cardboard
29.7 x 41.7 cm
Josef and Anni Albers
Foundation, Bethany,
Connecticut, United States

461 *Hotel Staircase*
Escalera de hotel
Geneva, 1929
Photo collage
27.94 x 40.64 cm
Josef and Anni Albers
Foundation, Bethany,
Connecticut, United States

462 *Ozenfant*
1931
Photo collage
27.94 x 40.64 cm
Josef and Anni Albers
Foundation, Bethany,
Connecticut, United States

WALL 4

Helen Levitt
463 *New York, Tadpole (From the Grafittis)*
Nueva York, renacuajo (de los grafitos)
ca. 1939
Black and white photo
12 x 20 cm
Courtesy of Laurence Miller
Gallery, New York

464 *Untitled (Graffiti – Couple – New York City)*
Sin título (grafiti –pareja – Nueva York)
1940
ca. 23.5 x 15.5 cm
Black and white photographic proof with gelatine emulsion of silver bromide
Sandra Álvarez de Toledo
Collection, Paris

465 *Untitled (graffiti)*
Sín título (grafiti)
1940
Black and white photographic proof with gelatine emulsion of silver bromide
15 x 20 cm
Sandra Álvarez de Toledo
Collection, Paris

466 *New York, Haystack (From the Grafittis)*
Nueva York, pajar (de grafitis)
1939
Black and white photo
24 x 19 cm
Courtesy of Laurence Miller
Gallery, New York

467 *Untitled (New York)*
Sin título (Nueva York)
Black and white photo
Copy from the period
11 x 17 cm
Courtesy of Mikael Levin

468 *New York, Woman's Figure (From the Grafittis)*
Nueva York, figura de mujer
ca.1939
Fotografia en blanc i negre
25,25 x 17,25 cm
Cortesia Laurence Miller
Gallery, Nova York

469 *New York, African (From the Grafittis)*
Nueva York, africano
ca. 1939
Black and white photo
20 x 12 cm
Courtesy of Laurence Miller
Gallery, New York
Walker Evans

Walker Evans
470 *Untitled (Subway Passengers, New York)*
Sin título (pasajeros del metro, Nueva York)
1938-1941
Black and white photographic proof with gelatine emulsion of silver bromide
10 x 17.6 cm
Sandra Álvarez de Toledo
Collection, Paris

471 *Untitled (Subway Passengers, New York)*
Sin título (pasajeros del metro, Nueva York)
1938
Black and white photographic proof with gelatine emulsion of silver bromide
10.7 x 15.3 cm
Sandra Álvarez de Toledo
Collection, Paris

472 *Untitled (Industrial Elevators)*
Sin título (ascensores industriales)
ca. 1929
Black and white photographic proof with gelatine emulsion of silver bromide
22 x 16.5 cm
Sandra Álvarez de Toledo
Collection, Paris

473 *Untitled (Bedroom, Biloxi, Mississippi),*
Sin título (dormitorio, Biloxi, Mississipi)
1944-1945
Black and white photographic proof with gelatine emulsion of silver bromide
17 x 22 cm
Sandra Álvarez de Toledo
Collection, Paris

474 ***Untitled (Independence Day, Terra Alta, West Virginia)***
Sin título (Día de la Independencia, Terra Alta, West Virginia)
1935
Black and white photographic proof with gelatine emulsion of silver bromide
20 x 21 cm
Sandra Álvarez de Toledo Collection, Paris

475 ***Untitled (Sidewalk in Vicksburg, Mississippi)***
Sin título (acera en Vicksburg, Misisipi)
1936
Black and white photographic proof with gelatine emulsion of silver bromide
19.5 x 24.5 cm
Sandra Álvarez de Toledo Collection, Paris

476 *Shoe Shine Stand*
Puesto de limpiabotas
Mississippi, 1935
Black and white photographic proof with gelatine emulsion of silver bromide
14 x 16.5 cm
Sandra Álvarez de Toledo Collection, Paris

477 ***Untitled (Men seated in front of Coca-Cola Sign, Mississippi)***
Sin título (hombres sentados delante de un anuncio de Coca-Cola, Misisipi)
1936
Black and white photographic proof with gelatine emulsion of silver bromide
11.5 cm x 18.5 cm
Sandra Álvarez de Toledo Collection, Paris

478 *The Home Organ, Nova Scotia, Canada*
El órgano familiar, Nueva Escocia, Canadá
1969
Black and white photographic proof with gelatine emulsion of silver bromide
18 x 18 cm
Sandra Álvarez de Toledo Collection, Paris

479 *Untitled (Trash Picture)*
Sin título (imagen basura)
1968
Black and white photographic proof with gelatine emulsion of silver bromide
15.8 x 23.4 cm
Sandra Álvarez de Toledo Collection, Paris

WALL 5

Raoul Hausmann

480 *Alt-Berlin*
Old Berlin
Berlín antiguo
1931
Black and white photo
30.5 x 40 cm
Musée départemental, Rochechouart

481 ***Composition 28 (Travaux de couture)***
Composition 28 (Dressmaking)
Composición 28 (labores de costura)
Germany, 1930
6.3 cm x 8.5 cm
Black and white photographic proofs with gelatine emulsion of silver bromide on paper
Sandra Álvarez de Toledo Collection, Paris

482 *Nu 19*
Nude 19
Desnudo 19
Germany, 1930
6.1 x 8.6 cm
Black and white photographic proofs with gelatine emulsion of silver bromide on paper
Sandra Álvarez de Toledo Collection, Paris

483 *Nu 36 (la toilette)*
Nude 36 (Toilet)
Desnudo 36 (arreglándose)
1927
6 x 8.4 cm
Black and white photographic proofs with gelatine emulsion of silver bromide on paper
Sandra Álvarez de Toledo Collection, Paris

484 *Le Rêve*
The Dream
El sueño
1930
Black and white photo
11.3 x 13.9 cm
Musée départemental, Rochechouart

485 *Femme étendue*
Woman Lying Down
Mujer tumbada
1931
Black and white photo
22.2 x 17 cm
Musée départemental, Rochechouart

486 *Composition 35*
Composición 35
1927-1933
Black and white photographic proof with gelatine emulsion of silver bromide on Agfa Lupex paper
7.8 x 10.8 cm
Sandra Álvarez de Toledo Collection, Paris

487 *Sense títol (Vera Broïdo)*
Untitled (Vera Broïdo)
Sin título (Vera Broïdo)
1931
Black and white photo
13.5 x 12.8 cm
Musée départemental, Rochechouart

488 *Vera*
Germany, 1931
Black and white photographic proof with gelatine emulsion of silver bromide on Agfa Brovira paper
17.8 x 23.5 cm
Sandra Álvarez de Toledo Collection, Paris

489 *Kampen*
1927
Black and white photo
25 x 28 cm
Musée départemental, Rochechouart

490 ***Au bord de la mer Baltique***
On the Shores of the Baltic Sea
A la orilla del mar del Báltico
1931
Black and white photo
15 x 23 cm
Musée départemental, Rochechouart

491 *Cala Corral, Ibiza*
1934
Black and white photo
29 x 39 cm
Musée départemental, Rochechouart

492 ***Ca'n Racó de la Torre, Ibiza***
Can Racó de la Torre, Ibiza
1935
Black and white photo
28.5 x 38.2 cm
Musée départemental, Rochechouart

493 ***Señor Mariano Ribas, Ibiza***
Mr. Mariano Ribas, Ibiza
1933
Black and white photo
29 x 23.2 cm
Musée départemental, Rochechouart

494 ***Ca'n Nadal de Baix, San José, Ibiza***
Can Nadal de Baix, Sant Josep, Ibiza
1936
Black and white photo
30 x 42 cm
Musée départemental, Rochechouart

495 *Petit vaurien de la ville, Ibiza*
Street Urchin, Ibiza
Golfillo de la ciudad, Ibiza
1933
Black and white photo
17.2 x 23 cm
Musée départemental, Rochechouart

496 *Ca'n Nadal de Baix, San José, Ibiza*
Can Nadal de Baix, San Josep, Ibiza
1936
Black and white photo
30 x 42 cm
Musée départemental, Rochechouart
August Sander

August Sander
497 *11 fotografies de la sèrie: "Eine Reise nach Sardinien" (Viatge a Sardenya)*
11 photographs from the series "Journey to Sardinia"
11 fotografías de la serie: "Viaje a Cerdeña"

498 *Atzara, Palmsonntag, In der Dorfstrasse*
Atzara, Palm Sunday, Village Street
Atzara, Domingo de Ramos, calle del pueblo
16,5 x 22,4 cm

499 *Ploaghe, Landschaft im Frühling*
Ploaghe, Landscape in Spring
Ploaghe, paisaje en primavera
15,9 x 23 cm

500 *Abbasanta, Dorfstrasse*
Abbasanta, Village Street
Abbasanta, calle del pueblo
11,3 x 16,2 cm

501 *Bauernjunge mit Esel*
Young Peasant with Donkey
Joven campesino con asno
11,7 x 16,2 cm

502 *Abbasanta, Gang in der Nuraghe Losa*
Abbasanta, Excursion to Nuraghe Losa
Abbasanta, excursión a Nuraghe Losa
20,7 x 15 cm

503 *Abbasanta, Eingang zur Nurhage Losa*
Abbasanta, Entrance to Nuraghe Losa
Abbasanta, entrada a Nuraghe Losa
17,3 x 23 cm

504 *Porto Tórres, Kapitell, Basilika San Gavino*
Porto Tórres, capital, Church of San Gavino
Porto Tórres, capitel, Basílica de San Gavino
22 x 16,6 cm

505 *Abbasanta, Alter Sarde*
Abbasanta, Sardinian Old Age
Abbasanta, vejez sarda
15,9 x 11,3 cm

506 *Abbasanta, Vorraum eines gotisches Hauses*
Abbasanta, Hall of a Gothic house
Abbasanta, vestíbulo de una casa gótica
1927
20,2 x 14,6 cm

507 *Atzara, Palmsonntags-prozession*
Atzara, Palm Sunday Procession
Atzara, procesión del Domingo de Ramos
16,5 x 22,4cm

508 *Abbasanta, Bauer in spätgotische Tür*
Abbasanta, Peasant by a Late Gothic Door
Abbasanta, campesino en puerta tardogótica
16,7 x 11,7 cm
1927
Period prints, baryta paper
Sprengel Museum Hannover, Ann and Jürgen Wilde Collection

WALL 6

Raoul Hausmann
509 *Ibiza (Portrait d'homme)*
Ibiza (Portrait of a Man)
Ibiza (Retrato de hombre)
1933-1936
Black and white photo
27.8 x 36 cm
Musée départemental, Rochechouart

510 *Porche de Ca'n Nadal de Baix, San José, Ibiza*
Porch at Can Nadal de Baix, Sant Josep, Ibiza
1936
Black and white photo
39.5 x 29 cm
Musée départemental, Rochechouart

511 *Trois chaises, Ibiza*
Three Chairs, Ibiza
Tres sillas, Ibiza
1934
Black and white photo
18 x 23.8 cm
Musée départemental, Rochechouart

512 *Untitled*
Sin título
1936
Black and white photo
29.4 x 39.3 cm
Musée départemental, Rochechouart

513 *Construcción del techo, Ca'n Palerm, San José*
Building the Roof, Can Palerm, Sant Josep
1934
Black and white photo
28.5 x 38.5 cm
Musée départemental, Rochechouart

514 *Capillita de Santa Inés, San Antonio Abad, Ibiza*
St Agnes Chapel, Sant Antoni Abat, Ibiza
1935
Black and white photo
29.2 x 41.5 cm
Musée départemental, Rochechouart

515 *Ca'n Rafal, Ibiza*
Can Rafal, Ibiza
1934
Black and white photo
30 x 39 cm
Musée départemental, Rochechouart

WALL 7

Robert Flaherty
516 *Man of Aran*
El hombre de Aran
1934
Black and white film, Great Britain, 80'

HALLWAY

Öyvind Fahlström
517 *Night Music 4: Protein Race Scenario (Words by Trackl, Lorca, Pietri and Plath)*
Música nocturna 4: guión para una carrera de proteínas (letra de Trackl, Lorca, Pietri y Plath)
1976
Variable painting. Acrylic paint and Indian ink on vinyl, magnets and metal panel
161 x 224 cm
Sharon Avery-Fahlström Collection

Room 13: Second constellation, around Antonin Artaud

WALL 1

Jean Fautrier
518 ***Tête d'Otage, no 22***
Hostage's Head, No. 22
Cabeza de rehén, nº 22
1945
Oil on paper marouflé to canvas
27 x 22 cm
Private collection, Paris

WALL 2

Antonin Artaud
519 ***Pour en finir avec le jugement de Dieu***
To Put an End to God's Judgement
Para acabar de una vez con el juicio de Dios
1947
Antonin Artaud recorded this programme for Radiodiffusion Française (Paris) in several sessions between 22 and 29 November 1947. The day before its scheduled broadcast, Monday 2 February 1948 at 10:45pm, the head of Radiodiffusion Française prohibited it from being aired.
Extract aired: "Conclusion", ca. 10 minutes
Voice and percussion: Antonin Artaud and Roger Blin
Archives of Radio France / INA

VIDEO

Roberto Rosselini
520 ***Germania anno zero***
Germany Year Zero
Alemania año cero
1947
35mm film transferred to DVD, black and white, sound, 75'
Tevere film, production Salvo d'Angelo
MACBA Collection. Museu d'Art Contemporani de Barcelona Foundation

WALL 3

Wladislaw Strzeminski
521 ***To My Friends the Jews***
A mis amigos los judíos
1945
Series of 9 drawings:
-Father's Skull, 33 x 23 cm
-I Accuse the Crime of Cain and the Sin of Ham, 30 x 21 cm
-Following the Existence of
-Feet Which Tread a Path, 33 x 23 cm
-Vow and Oath to the Memory of Hands (Existences which are not with us), 30 x 21.5 cm
-The Sticky Spot of Crime, 33 x 23 cm
-Stretched by the Strings of Legs, 30 x 21 cm
-Veins Strung Taut by Shinbones, 30 x 21 cm
-The Empty Shinbones of the Crematoria, 33 x 23 cm
-With the Ruins of Demolished Eye Sockets / Paved With Stones Like Heads, 30 x 21 cm
Collage and ink on paper
Yad Vashem Art Museum, Jerusalem, Israel

VITRINE

Pablo Picasso / Pierre Reverdy
522 ***Le Chant des morts***
Éditions Tériade, Paris, 1948
270 copies (20 not put up for sale), 68 sheets folded in half, unbound
Cartoné cover, sleeve and case
Poems by Pierre Reverdy, 125 original lithographs by Pablo Picasso
Musée Picasso, Paris

WALL 4

Henri Michaux
523 ***Sans titre (Alphabet)***
Untitled (Alphabet)
Sin título (alfabeto)
1944
Ink on paper, pen drawing
32 x 24 cm
Private collection

524 ***Sans titre (Alphabet)***
Untitled (Alphabet)
Sin título (alfabeto)
1944
Ink on paper, pen drawing
32 x 24 cm
Private collection

525 ***Alphabet***
Alfabeto
1927
Ink on paper
35.5 x 25.5 cm
Private collection

WALL 5

Henri Michaux
526 ***Untitled***
Sin título
1982
Oli sobre cartró tela
18 x 14 cm
Col·lecció privada

527 ***Untitled***
Sin título
1982
Oil on canvasboard
18 x 14 cm
Private collection

528 ***Untitled***
Sin título
1982
Oil on canvasboard
18 x 14 cm
Private collection

WALL 6

Henri Michaux
529 ***Untitled***
Sin título
1982-1983
Oil and acrylic paint
50 x 65.3 cm
Private collection

530 ***Untitled***
Sin título
1982
Oil and acrylic paint on canvasboard
26.5 x 18.5 cm
Private collection

531 ***Untitled***
Sin título
1948
Watercolour on paper
39.5 x 28.2 cm
Private collection

532 ***Untitled***
Sin título
1959
Wash, watercolour and pen on paper
27 x 19 cm
Private collection

533 ***Untitled***
Sin título
ca. 1979
Watercolour on iridescent Japan paper
51 x 33 cm
Private collection

534 ***Untitled***
Sin título
1944
Ink on paper, pen drawing
31.7 x 23.8 cm
Private collection

535 ***Untitled***
Sin título
1944
Ink on paper, pen drawing
31.7 x 24 cm
Private collection

536 *Untitled*
Sin título
1975-1976
Watercolour on paper
52.7 x 33.7 cm
Private collection

Wols
537 *Nicole Boubant*
ca. 1933
Silver gel print run
17.9 x 24.2 cm
Galerie Berinson, Berlin

538 *Clochards an der Seine*
Tramps on the Seine
Vagabundos en el Sena
1933
Tiratge a la gelatina de plata
17 x 12 cm
Galerie Berinson, Berlín

539 *Puppe und Auster im Rinnstein*
Doll and Oyster in the Creek
Muñeca y ostra en el arroyo
ca. 1937
Silver gel print run
23 x 17 cm
Galerie Berinson, Berlin

540 *Stilleben mit Knoblauch*
Still life with Garlic
Naturaleza muerta con ajo
ca. 1937
Silver gel print run
24.4 x 17.7 cm
Galerie Berinson, Berlin

541 *Grapefruit*
Pomelo
ca. 1937
Silver gel print run
23.5 x 17.4 cm
Galerie Berinson, Berlin

542 *Schweinsniere*
Pig's Kidney
Riñón de cerdo
ca. 1937
Silver gel print run
23.2 x 18 cm
Galerie Berinson, Berlin

543 *Kaninchen mit Kamm und Mundharmonika*
Rabbits with Comb and Harmonica
Conejos con peine y armónica
ca. 1937
Silver gel print run
24.1 x 18 cm
Galerie Berinson, Berlin

544 *Komposition*
Composition
Composición
ca. 1935
Silver gel print run, hand-painted
15.8 x 24 cm
Galerie Berinson, Berlin

WALL 7

Antonin Artaud
545 *Le Minotaure*
The Minotaur
El Minotauro
1946
Colour pencil and chalk
63 x 48 cm
Private collection, Paris

546 *La Potence du gouffre*
The Gallows of the Abyss
La horca del precipicio
October 1945
Colour pencil and chalk on paper
62.6 x 47.8 cm
Centre Pompidou, Musée national d'art moderne / Centre de création industrielle, Paris

547 *La Pendue*
The Hanged Woman
La ahorcada
1945
Colour pencil and chalk on paper
65 x 50 cm
Private collection, Paris

548 *Les Illusions de l'âme*
The Illusions of the Soul
Las ilusiones del alma
January 1946
Colour pencil and chalk on paper
62.5 x 47.8 cm
Centre Pompidou, Musée national d'art moderne / Centre de création industrielle, Paris

549 *Couti l'anatomie*
Couti the Anatomy
Couti la anatomía
September 1945
Colour pencil and chalk on paper
65.5 x 50 cm
Centre Pompidou, Musée national d'art moderne / Centre de création industrielle, Paris
Roberto Matta

Roberto Matta
550 *The Blind Divers*
Los submarinistas ciegos
1946
Lead and colour pencil on paper
58.5 x 73.8 cm
Private collection; courtesy of Galerie de France, Paris

551 *Untitled*
Sin título
1941
Lead and colour pencil on paper
65 x 50 cm
Galerie de France, Paris

WALL 8

Wols
552 *Tourbillon*
Whirlpool
Remolino
1947
Oil on canvas
41.5 x 32 cm
Courtesy of Galleria Blu, Milan

WALL 9

Antonin Artaud
553 *L'Inca*
The Inca
El inca
ca. March 1946
Colour chalk on laid paper
62 x 46 cm
Centre Pompidou, Musée national d'art moderne / Centre de création industrielle, Paris

WALL 10

Antonin Artaud
554 *Autoportrait*
Self-portrait
Autoretrato
1946
Pencil on paper
62 x 46 cm
Florence Loeb Collection

WALL 11

Antonin Artaud
555 *Portrait de Florence Loeb*
Portrait of Florence Loeb
Retrato de Florence Loeb
1946
Pencil on paper
68 x 53 cm
Florence Loeb Collection

WALL 12

Antoni Tàpies
556 *Box of Strings*
Caja de cordeles
1946
Mixed technique on cardboard
48 x 40 cm
Antoni Tàpies Foundation Collection

557 *Tinfoil Collage*
Collage del papel de plata
1946
Mixed technique on cardboard
73 x 105 cm
Private collection, Barcelona

WALL 13

Jean Fautrier
558 *Formes*
Forms
Formas
1937
Tempera, wash and ink
17 x 22 cm
Musée d'art moderne de la Ville de Paris

559 *Untitled*
Sin título
1938
Tempera and wash
11 x 20 cm
Musée d'art moderne de la ville de Paris

560 *Petit paysage*
Small Landscape
Pequeño paisaje
1935
Wash and ink
15 x 25 cm
Musée d'art moderne de

la Ville de Paris

561 *Untitled*
Sin título
1928
Pastel and pencil
16 x 21 cm
Musée d'art moderne de la Ville de Paris

562 *Untitled*
Sin título
1942
Tempera, wash and ink on cardboard
9 x 15 cm
Musée d'art moderne de la Ville de Paris

563 *Paysage mouvementé*
Landscape in Motion
Paisaje movido
1937
Wash and ink
16 x 24 cm
Musée d'art moderne de la Ville de Paris

Wols
564 *Dessin*
Drawing
Dibujo
1937
Drawing on paper
24 x 15.5 cm
Private collection

565 *Le Cirque de météores*
The Meteor Circus
El circo de meteoros
1944-1945
Ink, watercolour and wash on paper
15.5 x 11.5 cm
Courtesy of Galleria Blu, Milan

VITRINE: ÉDITIONS K, PARÍS

Georges Bataille (Lord Auch)
566 *Histoire de l'œil* (1928)
K Éditeur, Sevilla, 1940
199 copies
New edition, with 6 original etchings by Hans Bellmer
Numbered copy (no. 74) on rag paper (vélin fil pur Johannot, cheminé et emboité, sous emboitage blanc muet)
26.5 x 17 cm
Léon Aichelbaum Collection
Benjamin Péret

Benjamin Péret
567 *Le Déshonneur des poètes. Mexico, Poésie et Révolution*
K Éditeur, Paris, 1945
1,020 copies (20 on vélin fil pur paper)
Numbered copy (no. 737) on lightweight paper due to publishing considerations
Léon Aichelbaum Collection

568 *Feu central*
K Éditeur, Paris, 1947
1,030 copies, 107 pages
Text by Benjamin Péret, with illustrations by Yves Tanguy
Numbered copy (no. 127) on Crèvecœme de Marais vélin paper, special cover for deluxe copies
Léon Aichelbaum Collection
Georges Bataille

Georges Bataille
569 *L'Alleluiah. Catéchisme de Dianus*
K Éditeur, Paris, 1947
1,220 copies (20 on vélin fil pur paper; 400 on high-quality paper vergé)
89 pages; all copies numbered
Copy not put up for sale
Léon Aichelbaum Collection
Antonin Artaud

Antonin Artaud
570 *Ci-gît précédé de La Culture indienne*
K Éditeur, Paris, 1947
450 copies (435 on vélin paper), 44 pages
Léon Aichelbaum Collection

571 *Pour en finir avec le jugement de Dieu*
K Éditeur, Paris, 1948
2,000 copies, 111 pages
Numbered copy (no. 293) on Chiffon de Marais paper
Léon Aichelbaum Collection

572 *Van Gogh, le suicidé de la société*
K Éditeur, Paris, 1948
2,000 copies, 111 pages
Numbered copy (no. 293) on Chiffon de Marais paper
Léon Aichelbaum Collection

573 *K, revue de la poésie,* no. double 1-2
Paris, June 1948: "Antonin Artaud, textes, témoignages, documents"
148 pages
Magazine edited by Alain Gheerbrant and Henri Parísot
Léon Aichelbaum Collection

Henri Pichette
574 *Les Épiphanies*
K Éditeur, Paris, 1948
215 copies, 142 pages
Numbered copy (no. 73) on Crèvecœme de Marais vélin paper
Léon Aichelbaum Collection

Hans Arp
575 *Le Siège de l'air. Poèmes, 1915-1945*
Le Quadrangle Collection, Vrille, Paris, 1946
With 8 duo-dessins by Hans Arp and Sophie Taeuber-Arp and prologue by Alain Gheerbrant
Léon Aichelbaum Collection

Aimé Césaire
576 *Soleil Cou-coupé*
K Éditeur, Paris, 1948
2,050 copies, 125 pages
Numbered copy (no. 1335) on alfa de Marais paper
Léon Aichelbaum Collection
Camille Bryen

Camille Bryen
577 *La Chair et les mots. Journal poétique*
K Éditeur, Paris, 1948
1,000 copies (50 on Chiffon Crèvecœme de Marais paper), 48 pages
Portrait of Bryen by Zadkine, original lithograph
Léon Aichelbaum Collection

578 *La Poésie naturelle*
K Éditeur, Paris, 1949
175 copies, 175 pages
Documents collected and presented by Camille Bryen and Alain Gheerbrant, with 8 photos by Brassaï. On the cover, "Le Palais du Facteur Cheval"
Copy not for sale on Chiffon Navarra paper
2 copies: Léon Aichelbaum Collection and private collection, Paris

Jacques Vaché
579 *Lettres de guerre*
K Éditeur, Paris, 1949

500 copies, with 4 prefaces by André Breton, and drawing by Jacques Vaché on the cover
Banner conserved, 4 unbound facsimiles
Léon Aichelbaum Collection

580 *K, revue de la poésie*, núm. 3
May 1949, Paris: "De l'humour à la terreur, hommage à Kurt Schwitters"
Unknown print run, 72 pages
Magazine edited by Alain Gheerbrant and Henri Parísot
Léon Aichelbaum Collection

VITRINE

Henri Michaux
581 *Connaissance par les gouffres*
N.R.F., Paris, 1967
Unknown print run, 283 pages
Private collection, Paris

582 *Poteaux d'angle*
L'Herne, Paris, 1971
Unknown print run, 35 pages
Paperbound, collection of poems
Private collection, Paris

583 *Parcours*
Édition Le Point Cardinal, Paris, 1965
Unknown print run
Suite of 12 etchings
Introduction by René Bertelé
Private collection

584 *Misérable miracle*
Éditions du Rocher, Monaco, 1956
Unknown print run
With reproductions of 48 drawings by Michaux
Sandra Álvarez de Toledo Collection

Antonin Artaud
585 *Les danses à Bali*
Huit Collection, ed. Robert Delpire, 1954
Unknown print run, 121 pages
Photos by Henri Cartier-Bresson; text by Antonin Artaud, "Sur le Théâtre balinais"
Private collection, Paris

586 *Pour en finir avec le jugement de Dieu*
París, K Éditeur, 1948
2,000 copies, 111 pages
Sharon Avery-Fahlström Collection

Jean Fautrier / Francis Ponge
587 *L'Asparagus*
Éditions Mermod, Paris, 1963
Unknown print run
Private collection, Paris

Francis Ponge / Eugène de Kermadec
588 *Le Verre d'eau*
Ed. de la Galerie Louise Leiris, París, 1949
unpaginated, copy 91/100, on Arches paper
Compilation of notes and lithographs by Eugène de Kermadec, Paris
Private collection, Paris

589 *La Tour de feu*, núm. 63-61
"Antonin Artaud ou la Santé des poètes", December 1959
Unknown print run, 227 pages
Magazine edited by Pierre Boujut
Private collection, Paris

VITRINE: "CONSTEL·LACIONS"

Joan Miró / André Breton
590 *Constellations*
Editions Pierre Matisse, New York, 1959
23 plates (reproductions of the series from 1940-1941); unbound
Introduction and *proses parallèles* by André Breton
[L'Oiseau migrateur]
Fundació Joan Miró, Barcelona

Room 14: Duchampian Spaces

URNS

Robert Rauschenberg
591 *Untitled ("Scatole Personali" series)*
Sin título (serie "Scatole Personali")
1952
Assemblage: painted wooden box with twig and beetle
3.8 x 7.6 x 5.4 cm
Courtesy of the artist

592 *Music Box (Elemental Sculpture)*
Caja de música (escultura elemental)
ca. 1953
Wooden cage with metallic paint details, keys, three loose stones and a feather
27.9 x 19.1 x 23.5 cm
Collection Jasper Johns

593 *Untitled ("Scatole Personali" series)*
Sin título (serie "Scatole Personali")
ca. 1952
Assemblage: painted wooden box with cover with printed fabrics, thorns and snail shells
12.7 x 14 x 13.6 cm
Collection Jasper Johns

WALL 1

Robert Rauschenberg
594 *Untitled (Elemental Sculpture)*
Sin título (escultura elemental)
ca. 1953
Iron stake and wood
29.8 x 7.9 x 7.3 cm
Courtesy of the artist

595 *Ceiling + Light Bulb*
Techo + bombilla
1950
Silver gel print run
29.2 x 29.2 cm (drawing); 34 x 34 cm (sheet)
Courtesy of the artist

596 *Central Park*
1950-1980
Silver gel print run
29.2 x 29.2 cm (drawing); 34 x 34 cm (sheet)
Courtesy of the artist

597 *Untitled (Inside of an Old Carriage)*
Sin título (interior de un viejo carruaje)
ca. 1949
Silver gel print run
29.2 x 29.2 cm (drawing); 34 x 34 cm (sheet)
Courtesy of the artist

598 *Quiet House (Black Mountain College)*
Casa tranquila (Black Mountain College)
ca. 1949-1980
Silver gel print run
29.2 x 29.2 cm (drawing); 34 x 34 cm (sheet)
Courtesy of the artist

599 *Untitled (Matte Black With Fabric)*
Sín título (negro mate con tela)
ca. 1952
Oil and fabric on canvas
76,5 x 76,2 cm
Courtesy of the artist

600 *30 Scatole Personali Roma, 1953*
30 Objects from the Scatole Personali series, 1953
30 objetos de la serie Scatole Personali, 1953
Thirty objects from the

Scatole Personali series, arranged and photographed by the artist, floor of the Pensione Allegi
Silver gel print run
30 x 37.5 cm (drawing); 50.5 x 40.3 cm (sheet)
Courtesy of the artist

601 *The Man with Two Souls*
El hombre con dos almas
1950
Silver gel print run
37.5 x 37.5 cm (drawing); 40.3 x 50.5 cm (sheet)
Courtesy of the artist

WALL 2

Robert Rauschenberg
602 *Pincio Garden, Rome*
Jardín Pincio, Roma
1953
9 hanging assemblages from the Fettici Personali series
Silver gel print run
30 x 37.5 cm (drawing); 50.5 x 40.3 cm (paper)
Courtesy of the artist

603 *Pincio Garden, Rome*
Jardín Pincio, Roma
1953
8 hanging assemblages from the Fettici Personali series
Silver gel print run
37.5 x 37.5 cm (drawing); 50.5 x 40.3 cm (sheet)
Courtesy of the artist

WALL 3

Gego
604 *Dibujo sin papel 87/2*
Drawing without Paper 87/2
1987
Steel, iron and bronze
45 x 47 x 30 cm
Daros Latin America Collection, Zurich

Roberto Matta
605 *Le Troisième ciel*
The Third Sky
El tercer cielo
1946
Lead and colour pencil on paper
20.5 x 30 cm
Private collection, Paris.
Courtesy of Galerie de France, Paris

606 *Pour une bicyclette*
For a Bicycle
Por una bicicleta
1946
Colour and lead pencil on paper
50.5 x 36.8 cm
Philippe Morane, Paris

607 *Sense títol*
Untitled
1943
Wax and lead pencil on paper
39.3 x 52.1 cm
Philippe Morane, Paris

VITRINE: MARCEL DUCHAMP

Marcel Duchamp
608 *Boîte en valise (Série C)*
París, 1958
30 copies, unnumbered, unsigned, linen (natural colour), grey-blue ruled Ingres and wooden suitcase
40 x 37.5 x 9 cm
La Boîte was to contain 68 objects. For this series, Duchamp added a label for the Arensberg Collection, pasted into a black folder
In December 1954 Ilyazd (Ilya Zdanevich) began work on the the Boîte. The series was finished in 1958
Private collection, Milan

609 *La Mariée mise à nu par ses célibataires même (Boîte Verte)*
Edition Rrose Sélavy, Paris, 1934
320 copies (20 deluxe and 300 normal)
1 colour illustration and 93 documents (notes, drawings, photos and/or facsimiles) used by Duchamp in Large Glass, inside a green-flecked, self-hinged cardboard box
Private collection, Milan

610 *View*, vol. 5, núm. 1
Ed. Ch.H. Ford, New York, March 1945
54 pages
Special issue devoted to Duchamp, front and back cover by Duchamp; etching in relief and typography on paper
IVAM, Instituto Valenciano de Arte Moderno, Generalitat Valenciana

611 *Marchand du Sel*
Le Terrain Vague, París, 1959
232 pages
Texts by Marcel Duchamp, compiled and presented by Michel Sanouillet, loose insert: Grand Verre reproduction on 2 foldout transparent plastic sheets
Private collection, Paris

612 *Marchand du Sel*
Le Terrain Vague, París, 1959
232 pages
Texts by Marcel Duchamp, compiled and presented by Michel Sanouillet; loose insert: Grand Verre reproduction on 2 cellulose acetate sheets
Copy by Marcel Duchamp (copy A of 10 not for sale, specially printed by Duchamp), uncut, dedicated: "Chère Berthe, cher Bernard / l'auteur amoureux de sa virginité"
Private collection, Milan
Pierre Cabanne

Pierre Cabanne
613 *Entretiens avec Marcel Duchamp*
Belfond, París, 1967
218 pages
5 interviews; book with dedication to Julie and Man Ray with annotations by Man Ray
Private collection, Milan

WALL 4

Marcel Duchamp
614 *Plan du Porte-bouteilles*
Plan of the Bottle Rack
Plano del Botellero
1964
Work drawing, heliographic paper
118 x 49 cm
Berardo Collection – Sintra Museum of Modern Art
Piero Manzoni

Piero Manzoni
615 *Alfabeto*
Alphabet
1958
Ink and kaolin on canvas
25 x 18 cm
Private collection, Milan

616 *Alfabeto (ABCDE)*
Alphabet (ABCDE)
1959
Silkscreen project, collage on paper
65 x 48 cm
Private collection, Milan

617 *Calendario, 1-30 settembre 1959*
Calendar, 1-30 September 1959
Calendario, 1-30 de septiembre 1959
1959
Silkscreen project, collage on paper
65 x 48 cm
Private collection, Milan

VITRINE: PIERO MANZONI

Piero Manzoni
618 *Manifesto contra niente (per l'esposizione Internazionale di niente)*
1960
Printed on paper
Private collection, Milan

619 *8 Tavole di accertamento*
Edizioni di Vanni Scheiwiller, Milà, 1962
Fotolitografia, 8 plates in a pouch
Copy no. 43/60
Private collection, Milan

Richard Hamilton
620 *Self-portrait b*
Autorretrato b
1951
Soft varnish etching with drypoint
30 x 20 cm
Private collection, London

621 *Of Orientation*
De Orientación
1952
Oil on cardboard
117 x 160 cm
Private collection, London

622 *Reaper h*
Segadora h
1949
Drypoint and roller
17.5 x 25 cm
Private collection, London

623 *Reaper c-Study I*
Segadora c-Estudio I
1949
Pencil on paper
20.4 x 33 cm
Private collection, London

624 *Reaper b*
Segadora b
1949
Drypoint and roller
16.2 x 23.6 cm
Private collection, London

625 *Reaper f (I)*
Segadora f (I)
1949
Pencil on paper
20.4 x 33 cm
Private collection, London

626 *Reaper l*
Segadora I
1949
Etching, aquatint and drypoint
16.5 x 24.7 cm
Private collection, London

627 *Reaper (Harvester Study)*
Segadora (Estudio para cosechadora)
1949
Etching with three-sheet colour
19.7 x 14.8 cm
Private collection, London

IN SUSPENSION

Gego
628 *Tronco nº 2*
Trunk no. 2
ca. 1975
Stainless steel and bronze
144 x 30.5 x 35 cm
Daros Latin America Collection, Zurich

VITRINE

Gego
629 *Red bands, text*
1963
Ink on paper, brown thread. Posterboard cover
Fundación Gego Collection

630 *Poesía*
1963
Posterboard; foldout (inkless etching) on paper BFK Rives
Fundación Gego Collection

631 *One-line autobiography*
1963
Indian ink on Japan paper, lithograph, threads, white posterboard
Fundación Gego Collection

WALL 5

Pablo Palazuelo
632 *Segundo cantoral II*
Second Hymnal II
1978
Wash on paper
79 x 58 cm
Private collection; courtesy of Galería Manuel Barbié
Tony Smith

Tony Smith
633 *Untitled*
Sin título
1962-1963
Oil on canvas
61 x 91 cm
Jean Smith Collection, New York; courtesy of Matthew Mark Gallery, New York

634 *Untitled*
Sin título
1962-1963
Oil on canvas
61 x 91 cm
Jean Smith Collection, New York; courtesy of Matthew Mark Gallery, New York

WALL 6

Georges Vantongerloo
635 *Radio-activité*
Radio-Activity
Radio-actividad
1952
Paint on masonite
66 x 95 cm
Chantal & Jakob Bill

636 *Deux zones de l'espace; action-réaction*
Two Zones in Space; Action-Reaction
Dos zonas del espacio; acción-reacción
1949
Oil paint on masonite
40 x 98 cm
Chantal & Jakob Bill

URN

Georges Vantongerloo
637 *Le dôme*
The Dome
La cúpula
1959
Plexiglass
32 x 17 x 17 cm
Chantal & Jakob Bill

WALL 7

Tony Smith
638 *Untitled*
Sin título
1934-1936
Oil and pencil on canvasboard
25.4 x 20.3 cm
Jean Smith Collection, New York; courtesy of Matthew Mark Gallery, New York

639 *Untitled*
Sin título
1953-1954
Oil on cardboard
40 x 50 cm
Jean Smith Collection, New York; courtesy of Matthew Mark Gallery, New York

Room 15: Year 1967, Philip Guston

WALL 1

Philip Guston
640 *Mark*
Marca
1967
Ink on paper
35.6 x 41.9 cm
The Estate of Philip Guston; courtesy of McKee Gallery, New York

641 *Edge*
Borde
1967

Ink on paper
34.3 x 42.5 cm
The Estate of Philip Guston; courtesy of McKee Gallery, New York

642 *Horizon*
Horizonte
1967
Ink on paper
45.7 x 54.6 cm
The Estate of Philip Guston; courtesy of McKee Gallery, New York
Philip Guston / Clark Coolidge

Philip Guston / Clark Coolidge
643 *Untitled ("I need to...")*
Sin título ("Necesito...")
1976
Drawing and poem
48.4 x 61.2 cm
Clark Coolidge Collection

ON THE FLOOR

Carl Andre
644 *Steel Lead Alloy Square*
Cuadrado de aleación de acero y plomo
1969
Steel and lead
200 x 200 x 0.8 cm
Herbert Collection, Gant

WALL 2

Philip Guston
645 *Painting, Smoking, Eating*
Pintando, fumando, comiendo
1973
Oil on canvas
196.85 x 262.89 cm
Stedelijk Museum, Amsterdam

WALL 3

Philip Guston
646 *City*
Ciudad
1969
Oil on canvas
182.9 x 171.5 cm
The Estate of Philip Guston; courtesy of McKee Gallery, New York

647 *The Hill*
La colina
1965
Pen, ink on paper
44.5 x 59.7 cm
The Estate of Philip Guston; courtesy of McKee Gallery, New York

WALL 4

Philip Guston
648 *Air*
Aire
1967
Pen, ink on paper
45,7 x 58,4 cm
The Estate of Philip Guston; courtesy of McKee Gallery, New York

649 *Drawing for Web*
Dibujo para Telaraña
1975
Ink on paper
48.3 x 61 cm
Private collection

650 *Message*
Mensaje
1975
Ink on paper
47 x 62.2 cm
Jennifer and David Stockman

651 *Untitled*
Sin título
1975
Ink on paper
45.4 x 61.9 cm
Private collection

Philip Guston / Clark Coolidge
652 *The Act of Painting*
El acto de pintar
Drawing and poem
Undated
48 x 61.2 cm
Clark Coolidge Collection

653 *Whobody*
Quién
1973
Drawing and poem
60 x 48.4 cm
Clark Coolidge Collection

Room 16

WALL 1

Bruce Nauman
654 *White Breathing, Drawing # 1*
Respiración blanca, dibujo nº 1
1976
Pencil and black and white photos on paper
82 x 72 cm
Herbert Collection, Gant

655 *White Breathing, Drawing # 2*
Respiració blanca, dibuix núm. 2
Respiración blanca, dibujo nº 2
1978
Pencil on paper
102 x 76 cm
Herbert Collection, Gant

656 *White Breathing, Drawing # 3*
Respiración blanca, dibujo nº 3
1978
Pencil on paper
102 x 76 cm
Herbert Collection, Gant

ON THE FLOOR

Bruce Nauman
657 *White Breathing*
Respiración blanca
1976
Solid steel sheet
14 rhombohedrons: 15.2 x 15.2 x 15.2 cm each; set: ca. 600 x 700 cm
Herbert Collection, Gant

WALL 1

Sol Lewitt

658 *Lines, Not Straight, From the Top and the Left Side*
Líneas, no rectas, desde la parte de arriba y el lado izquierdo
Brussels, 6 July 1972
Ink on paper
36 x 36 cm
Herbert Collection, Gant

659 *Straight Pencil Lines, From the Left Side & Straight Ink Lines from the Top*
Líneas rectas a lápiz desde la izquierda, y líneas rectas a tinta desde la parte de arriba
Brussels, 6 July 1972
Ink on paper
36 x 36 cm
Herbert Collection, Gant

660 *Lines, Not Straight, From the Left Side*
Líneas, no rectas, desde el lado izquierdo
Brussels, 6 July 1972
Ink on paper
36 x 36 cm
Herbert Collection, Gant

661 *Straight Lines, From the Left Side*
Líneas rectas, desde el lado izquierdo
Brussels, 6 July 1972
Ink on paper
36 x 36 cm
Herbert Collection, Gant

Dan Graham
662 *Homes for America*
Casas para América
1965-1970
2 panels
Black and white and colour photos
102 x 77 cm each
Daled Collection, Brussels

Room 17: *Aspen*, no. 5-6, autumn 1967

All the works shown in this room are from the MACBA Collection. Fundació Museu d'Art Contemporani de Barcelona

VITRINE

663 *Aspen*, no. 5-6 ("For Stéphane Mallarmé"), autumn-winter 1967
28 numbered pieces, including promotional archives. Edited and designed by Brian O'Doherty. Artistic direction: David Dalton and Lynn Letterman. Published by Phyllis Johnson, Roaring Fork Press
MACBA Collection. Fundació Museu d'Art Contemporani de Barcelona

RADIO BROADCAST RECORDINGS TRANSFERRED TO CD FOR THE EXHIBITION

Naum Gabo / Noton Pevsner
664 *The Realist Manifesto*
El Manifiesto Realista
Moscow, 1920
17'24''
Read by Naum Gabo

Samuel Beckett
665 *Text for Nothing # 8*
Texto para nada, nº 8
1958
12'45''
Passage read by Jack MacGowan

William Burroughs
666 Nova Express
1965
Passages read by the autor

Alain Robbe-Grillet
667 *Jalousie*
Jealousy
Celos
1957
10'7''
Passage read by the author

Morton Feldman
668 *The King of Denmark*
El rey de Dinamarca
1964
7'23''
Played by Max Neuhaus, 1967

John Cage
669 *Fontana Mix-Feed*
6 November 1967
9'57''
Directed by Max Neuhaus

Merce Cunningham
670 *Space, Time and Dance*
Espacio, tiempo y danza
A *Trans/formation*, 1:3, 1952
8'11''
Read by the author

671 *Further Thoughts*
Más pensamientos
1967
9'22''
Interview with Merce Cunningham

Marcel Duchamp
672 *The Creative Act*
El acto creativo
1957
7'17''
Read by the author

673 *Some Texts from "À l'infinitif"*
Algunos textos de "À l'infinitif"
1912-1920
3'58''
Read by the author

Richard Huelsenbeck
674 *Four poems from "Phantastische Gebete"*
Cuatro poemas de "Oraciones fantásticas"
1916
4'10''
Read by the author

SUPER 8 FILMS TRANSFERRED TO CD FOR THE EXHIBITION

Hans Richter
675 *Rhythm 21*
Ritmo 21
Germany, 1921
3'36'', 16 mm, black and white, silent

László Moholy-Nagy
676 *Lichtspiel, Schwarz-Weiss-Grau*
Lightplay, Black-White-Grey
Juego de luz, negro-blanco-gris
Germany, 1930
5'30'', 16 mm, black and white, silent (fragment shown: 1'40'')

Robert Morris / Stan Vanderbeek
677 *Site*
Sitio
United States, 1964
7', black and white, silent (fragment shown: 5'11'')

Robert Rauschenberg
678 *Linoleum*
Linóleo
United States, 1966
13', 16mm, black and white, sound (fragment shown: 4'12'')

Room 18: Concrete poetry and décollages

WALL 1

Joan Brossa
679 *Poema experimental*
Experimental Poem
Poema experimental
1947
Pencil and pins on paper
35 x 24.5 cm
Museu Abelló. Fundació Municipal d'Art, Mollet del Vallès

Öyvind Fahlström
680 *Column no. 2 (Picasso 90)*
Columna nº 2 (Picasso 90)
1973
Silkscreen (26 colors)
77 x 57 cm
120 copies
Printing: Domberger KG, Bonlanden, Germany (Luitpold Domberger, master printer)
Published by Propyläen Verlag, Berlin
Sharon Avery-Fahlström Collection

VITRINE: ÖYVIND FAHLSTRÖM

Öyvind Fahlström
681 *Un livre instructif*
Unpublished manuscript
Ink, colour ink and pencil on paper
1946
Öyvind Fahlström Archive, MACBA

Pierre Schaeffer
682 *À la recherche d'une musique concrète*
Concrete Poetry Manifesto
Éditions du Seuil, París, 1952
Manuscript annotations by Öyvind Fahlström
Öyvind Fahlström Archive, MACBA

Öyvind Fahlström
683 *Hätila Ragulpr Pa Fatskliaben*
Manifesto for concrete poetry
Published in Odyssé (Stockholm), no. 2-3, 1954
Mimeograph on paper
Öyvind Fahlström Archive, MACBA

684 *Manuscript for concrete poetry with word mutation inventories*
Late 1940s – early 1950s
Öyvind Fahlström Archive, MACBA

685 *Bord-Dikter 1952-55*
Bonniers, Stockholm, 1966
Öyvind Fahlström Archive, MACBA

686 Preliminary study for *Whammo*
1962
Ink on paper
Öyvind Fahlström Archive, MACBA

687 *Whammo*
1962
Ink, colour ink and corrective fluid on paper Öyvind Fahlström Archive, MACBA

688 *Sitting...Directory*
Ink, pencil, tempera and colour pencil on paper
Öyvind Fahlström Archive, MACBA

BACKGROUND MUSIC

John Cage
689 *Roaratorio. An Irish Circus on Finnegans Wake*
Roaratorio. Un circo irlandés sobre Finnegans Wake
1979
John Cage, voice; Joe Heaney, singer; Seamus Ennis, bagpipe; Paddy Glackin, violin; Matt Malloy, flute; Peadher Mercier, Mell Mercier, bodhrán (Celtic drum)
First part: 26'46"; second part: 16'14"; third part:14'17"; fourth part: 3'13"
John Cage: Roaratorio
Henmar Press Inc., Peters Edition Limited, London

WALL 2

Dieter Roth
690 *Stampelzeichnungen zu Mundunculum*
22 stamped drawings for Mundunculum
22 dibujos hechos con un sello de caucho para Mundunculum
1965-1966
Stamps on transparent paper
Various sizes
Staatsgalerie Stuttgart. Archiv Sohm

VITRINE ROTH

Dieter Roth
691 *Stempelkasten*
Stamp Container
Caja de sellos
1963-1967
Box with 23 stamps for Mundunculum
Rubber stamps, ink pads, ink, and stamp print on paper
Box: 27.9 x 27.9 x 7 cm; ed. 111
Staatsgalerie Stuttgart. Archiv Sohm

692 *MUNDUNCULUM. Ein tentatives Logico-Poeticum, dargestellt wie Plan und Programm oder Traum zu einem provisorischen Mytherbarium für Visionspflanzen. Band 1: Das rot'sche VIDEUM*
DuMont Schauberg, Cologne, 1967
1,000 copies, 336 pages
Typography, text, drawings, stamps, rustic binding, sleeve
21.2 x 15.5 cm
Staatsgalerie Stuttgart. Archiv Sohm

WALL 3

Raymond Hains
693 *Avec le grand concours de l'humanité et la nation française*
With the Help of Humanity and the French Nation
Con la gran ayuda de la humanidad y la nación francesa
1956
Torn bill on canvas
100 x 216 cm
Private collection, Brussels

WALL 4

Raymond Hains
694 *Cet homme est dangereux*
This Man is Dangerous
Este hombre es peligroso
1957
Torn bill on canvas
95 x 61 cm
Dufrêne Collection-Marcuzzi

695 *L'affiche en yiddish*
The Poster in Yiddish
El cartel en yidish
1950
Torn bills
34 x 54 cm
Yehuda Neiman Collection

696 *De Gaulle veut un bain de sang il l'aura*
De Gaulle wants a bloodbath which he will have
De Gaulle quiere un baño de sangre que tendrá
ca. 1960
Torn bill on canvas
70 x 50 cm
Private collection, Brussels

697 *Paix en Algérie*
Peace in Algeria
Paz en Argelia
1956
Torn bills on canvas
39 x 33 cm
Dufrêne Collection

698 *Hépérile éclaté*
Burst Hépérile
Hépérile reventado
1989
Silkscreen on 2 panels
128 x 100 cm each
Musée des Baux-Arts, Nantes

François Dufrêne
699 *L'Inconnue (série "L'art c'est le vol")*
The Unknown Woman ("Art is Flight" series)
La desconocida (serie "El arte es el vuelo")
1961
Bill backs on canvas
150 x 170 cm
Dufrêne Collection

700 *Hommage à Camille Bryen*
Tribute to Camille Bryen
Homenaje a Camille Bryen
1959
Torn bill backs
110 x 90 cm
Musée des Beaux-Arts, Nantes

VITRINE: CONCRETE POETRY 1

Camille Bryen
701 *Hépérile*
Alès, 1950
Phonetic poem published by Pierre Albert-Birot
17 línies
Musée des Beaux-Arts, Nantes

Raymond Hains / Jacques Villeglé
702 *Hépérile éclaté*
Librairie Lutétia, Paris, 1953
According to the phonic poem "Hépérile" by Camille Bryen (1950)
Musée des Beaux-Arts, Nantes

François Dufrêne
703 *Grâmmes*, no. 2
Paris, 1958
Magazine by the group Ultra-lettriste (Dufrêne, Estivals, Wolman, Brau)
"L'après demain d'un phenomène"; "D'un prélettriste à l'ultralettirsme"
Dufrêne Collection

704 *Brazilian Cultural Magazine*
All issues

Madrid 1963-1969
Published by the propaganda and commercial expansion services of the embassy of Brazil in Madrid
Magazine
Library of the Museu d'Art Contemporani de Barcelona, MACBA

705 *OU, Cinquième Saison*, no. 28-29
1966
Magazine-disc directed by Henri Chopin; Sceaux (Paris), 1964-1972
Text by François Dufrêne, "Pragmatisme du cri-rythme", republished in the magazine
Dufrêne Collection

Walter Marchetti / ZAJ
706 *Respire, Otra vez, Más*
Breathe, Again, More
Leaflet Madrid 1965-1966
Library of the Museu d'Art Contemporani de Barcelona, MACBA

ZAJ
707 *Zaj presents Alison Knowles and Dick Higgins*
Leaflet
Madrid, November 1966
Library of the Museu d'Art Contemporani de Barcelona, MACBA

R. Cortes / ZAJ
708 *ZUJ*
Leaflet
Madrid, 1968
Library of the Museu d'Art Contemporani de Barcelona, MACBA

ZAJ
709 *Bigger Than Life*
Undated
Leaflet
Library of the Museu d'Art Contemporani de Barcelona, MACBA

710 *YO*
Undated
Leaflet
Library of the Museu d'Art Contemporani de Barcelona, MACBA

711 *Diga ¡ZAJ!*
Undated
Leaflet
Library of the Museu d'Art Contemporani de Barcelona, MACBA

712 *Cuando usted no sepa que decir...*
When you don't know what to say...
Undated
Leaflet
Library of the Museu d'Art Contemporani de Barcelona, MACBA

713 *Table avec Nature Morte "Demoiselle"*
Undated
Leaflet
Library of the Museu d'Art Contemporani de Barcelona, MACBA

714 *Black, White, Red, Yellow*
Undated
Leaflet
Library of the Museu d'Art Contemporani de Barcelona, MACBA

715 *C IV*
Undated
Leaflet
Library of the Museu d'Art Contemporani de Barcelona, MACBA

Amado Ramón Millán
716 *NNNNO*
Gráficas San Enrique, Madrid 1969
Book
Fernando Millán Collection

Francisco Zabala
717 *Science NO*
Madrid, 1969
Visual poem
Fernando Millán Collection

718 *Este Protervo Zas*
Ediciones N.O., Madrid, April 1969
Handmade copy, bound sheets
Fernando Millán Collection

Fernando Millán
719 *Esto protervo zas*
Ediciones N.O., Madrid, April 1969
Original book
Fernando Millán Collection
Fernando Millán

720 *Relatos 3*
Stories 3
Madrid, February 1969
Story, handmade edition of 20 copies
Fernando Millán Collection

721 *Textos y antitextos*
Texts and antitexts
Ed. Parnaso 70, collection "El anillo del cocodrilo", Madrid 1970
Fernando Millán Collection

722 *Ariadna o la búsqueda*
Ariadne or The Search
Colección Detextos, Informaciones y Producciones S. L, Madrid 1971-1973
Bound sheets
Fernando Millán Collection

723 *Fablas. Magazine of poetry and criticism*, no. 22-23
Editorial Domingo Velázquez Las Palmas de Gran Canaria, September - October 1971
Magazine
Fernando Millán Collection

724 *International exhibition of visual poetry*
Casa de la Cultura, Burgos, 1972
Leaflet from the exhibition
Fernando Millán Collection

725 *Mitogramas (1968-1976)*
Mythograms
Ediciones Turner, colección Beltenebros, Libros de Poesía, Madrid, 1978
Fernando Millán Collection

726 *Prosae*
Colección Metaphora, Editorial Garsi, Madrid 1981
Fernando Millán Collection

727 *DOC(K)S L'avant-garde poétique en Espagne (1963-1981)*
France, 1982
Magazine
Fernando Millán Collection

728 *Vitalidad*
Vitality
June 1983
Copy no. 1 (2-copy run)
Work sampled by Fernando Millán
Fernando Millán Collection

729 *La depresión en España*
Depression in Spain
Madrid 1993
Work sampled by Fernando Millán
Fernando Millán Collection

730 *La depresión en España*
Editorial Amargord, no. 2 of the collection, separate from no. 5, magazine Abreojos, Madrid, October 1993
Fernando Millán Collection

731 *Poemas NO (1965-1975)*
Detextos y Producciones S.L, Madrid 1997
Col·lecció Fernando Millán

732 *Parnaso 70 "El anillo del Cocodrilo"*
Undated
Leaflet
Fernando Millán Collection

733 *Amaya*
Undated
Original poem
Typewritten page
Fernando Millán Collection

Fernando Millán / Jesús García Sánchez
734 *La escritura en libertad. Antología de poesía experimental.*
Writing in freedom. Anthology of experimental poetry.
Alianza editorial, Madrid, 1975
Fernando Millán Collection

Haroldo de Campos
735 *Mallarmé*
Colección Signos, Editorial Perspectiva, 1970
Sergio Bessa Collection

736 *Galáxias*
1984
Collection Sergio Bessa

Esther Ferrer
737 *Mallarmé révisé o Malarmado revisado*
1992
Documentation of the action by the MNAM / Centre Georges Pompidou
2 black and white photos
Courtesy of the artist

Felipe Boso
738 *The Concrete Poems*
Editorial La Fábrica. Arte Contemporáneo, Abarca de campos (Palencia), 1994
Book printed on paper couché
Fernando Millán Collection

739 *An Anthology of Concrete Poetry*
Edited by Emmet Williams, Something Else Press INC, New York, 1967
Book
Library of the Museu d'Art Contemporani de Barcelona, MACBA

VITRINA: CONCRETE POETRY 2

Fernando Millán
740 *Problemática 63, bulletin no. 3*
Madrid, March 1964
11 typewritten pages
Fernando Millán Collection

741 *Aulas, Educación y Cultura 64, I Rev no. 7- Poesía*
November, 1964
Magazine
Fernando Millán Collection

742 *Poesía visual, fónica, espacial y concreta*
Visual, phonic, spatial and concrete poetry
Sociedad Dante Alighieri and the O.P.I, Zaragoza, November 1965
Leaflet from the exhibition
Fernando Millán Collection

743 *Problemática 63*
Juventudes musicales de Madrid, Instituto Francés, Madrid, March 1966
Leaflet
Fernando Millán Collection

744 *Avant-garde poetry week*
San Sebastián, August 1966
Leaflet
Fernando Millán Collection

745 *Avant-garde poetry week*
San Sebastián, September 1966
Leaflet
Fernando Millán Collection

746 *International avant-garde poetry exhibition*
Galería Juana Mordó, 1966
Exhibition catalogue
Fernando Millán Collection

747 *Seminar of avant-garde lyrical information*
Faculty of Philosophy and Letters, Madrid, February 1967
Leaflet
Fernando Millán Collection

748 *Problemática 63*
Juventudes Musicales de Madrid, Instituto Francés, Madrid, May 1968
Leaflet
Fernando Millán Collection

749 *No es fácil*
It's not easy
1968
Visual poem
Fernando Millán Collection

J.C. Aberásturi / Jokin Díez / F. Millán / J. García Sánchez / E. Uribe
750 *Carta: "Estimado amigo..."/ "Dear Friend ..."*
May 1968 (2 pages)
2 typewritten pages
Spanish and English version
Fernando Millán Collection

751 *Situación uno. Poesía N.O.*
Situation one. Poetry N.O.
Madrid 1969
Leaflet
Fernando Millán Collection

752 *Situación tres*
Situation three
Madrid, 1969
Leaflet
Fernando Millán Collection

753 *Situación cuatro*
Situation four
Madrid 1969
Leaflets
Fernando Millán Collection

754 *Situación cinco. Poesía N.O.*
Situation five. Poetry N.O.
Madrid 1969
Leaflet
Fernando Millán Collection

755 *Sessions on documentation of avant-garde poetry*
International Exhibition, Zaragoza, 20-24 May 1969
Exhibition leaflet
Fernando Millán Collection

756 *International Exhibition of Visual Poetry*
Oficina poética internacional, Sociedad Dante Alighieri, 20-24 May 1969
Fernando Millán Collection

757 *International Exhibition of Visual Poetry*
Jornadas de Documentación sobre Poesía de Vanguardia, Oficina Poética Internacional, Sociedad Dante Alighieri, 20-24 May 1969
Leaflet
Fernando Millán Collection

Fernando Millán
758 *Noticia sobre A. Petronio*
News of A. Petronio
May 1969
2 pages typewritten
Fernando Millán Collection

759 *Seminar on phonetic poetry "International Extension of Phonetic Poetry I"*
Juventudes musicales de Madrid, Instituto Francés, Madrid, April 1971
Leaflet
Fernando Millán Collection

760 *Seminar on phonetic poetry "Genesis and Foundations of Phonetic Poetry"*
Juventudes Musicales de Madrid, Instituto Francés, Madrid, 1971
Leaflet
Fernando Millán Collection

761 *Signs, space, art*
Club Pueblo, Madrid 1973
Leaflet
Fernando Millán Collection

762 *Urgent problems in art today*
Talk by Julio Campal, Cuenca, 1976
Leaflet
Fernando Millán Collection

763 *7 Caligrams*
Colemenar Viejo, 1998
Book
Fernando Millán Collection

764 *You still don't know 'n.o. poetry': Tribute to Julio Campal*
Undated
Leaflet
Fernando Millán Collection

765 *Prima mostra individuale di Jokin Diez*
Undated
Exhibition leaflet
Fernando Millán Collection

Julio Campal
766 *Post-symbolism I*
Series organized by Problemática 63, undated
Book
Fernando Millán Collection

Room 19: Alphabets (dance and decoration)

WALL 1

Trisha Brown
767 *16 Untitled Drawings*
16 dibujos sin título
1994
16 drawings; ink on paper
35.6 x 43 cm (6), 27.8 x 35.4 cm (5), 35.4 x 27.8 cm (5)
Collection Trisha Brown

VIDEO

768 *Roof Piece*
Pieza del techo
1973 (first screened 1971)
Video, ambience sound, ca. 30'
Camera: Babette Mangolte
12 dancers on rooftops over a ten-block area. The video contains more or less immobile improvised gestures, beginning at 53 Wooster Street and thereafter imitated by each dancer one after the other. The wave of movement arrived at 381 Lafayette Street 15 minutes later, were stopped and changed directions for another 15 minutes
First screening: 53 Wooster Street and 381 Lafayette Street, New York, 11 May 1971
Courtesy of Trisha Brown Company

769 *Newark (Niweweorce)*
1987
Vídeo D. Studio, New York (1990), vídeo, 32'
Work done during a stay at the Centre National de la Danse Contemporaine d'Angers, France, by the Trisha Brown Company, in collaboration with Donald Judd (stage design, costumes, sound concept, visual presentation)
Courtesy of Trisha Brown Company

WALL 2

Alighiero Boetti
770 *Positivo Negativo*
Positive Negative
1988-1989
Tela brodada
100 x 100 cm
Collection Berardo – Sintra Museum of Modern Art

771 *Regola Regolarsi*
Rule and Regulate Oneself
Regla y regularse
1979
Different materials on canvas (mixed technique, "marouflé", paper and fabric)
100 x 200 cm
Berardo Collection – Sintra Museum of Modern Art

FLOOR AND WALL 3

Marcel Broodthaers
772 *Tapis de sable*
Sand Carpet
Alfombra de arena
1974
Installation made with coloured sand, Kentia forsteriana and printed towel
340 x 217 cm (floor); 108 x 52 (wall)
Van Abbemuseum Collection, Eindhoven, Holland

WALL 3

René Daniels
773 *La Muse vénale*
The Venous Muse
La musa venal
1979
Oil on canvas
152 x 212 cm
Van Abbemuseum Collection, Eindhoven, Holland

WALL 4 / VIDEO

Simone Forti
774 *Three Grizzlies*
Tres osos pardos
1974
Short film, 16'40"

775 *Solo no. 1*
Solo nº 1
1975
Short film, 18'

VIDEO

Yvonne Rainer
776 *Five Easy Pieces*
Cinco piezas sencillas
1966
Film, 48'

WALL 5

Nancy Spero
777 14 drawings from the Artaud Paintings series
1969-1970
Wash, ink and collage on paper
Galerie de France, Paris

-"Sous cette croute d'os et de peau qui est ma tête...", 62.2 x 49.5 cm
-"From this pain ...", 63.5 x 52.7 cm
-"Un nœud d'asphyxie centrale...", 62.2 x 49.5 cm
-"The human face carried a kind of...", 63.5 x 50 cm
-"This crucible of fine and real meat...", 63.5 x 50.2 cm
-"Je n'ai plus de point d'appui, plus de base...", 63 x 50 cm
-"Why couldn't it have been some world...", 69.9 x 50.8 cm
-"C'est un couteau a mi chemin dans les rêves...", 62.2 x 49.5 cm
-"Me, Antonin Artaud, born on September 4th 1896...", 63.5 x 50.2 cm
-"L'Angoisse fait les demons...", 61.6 x 49.5 cm
-"Une fatigue de commencement du monde...", 61.6 x 49.5 cm
-"Et voici le triangle d'eau qui marche...", 62.2 x 49.5 cm
-"L'Angoisse qui pince la corde ombilicale de la vie...", 62.2 x 49.5 cm
-"That thick hemp in the neck of the priest about to be hung...", 62.9 x 50.8 cm

Room 20: Epilogue

WALL 1

René Daniels
778 *Painting on the Bullfight*
Pintura sobre la corrida de toros
1985
Oil on canvas
170.4 x 240.5 cm
Van Abbemuseum Collection, Eindhoven, Holland

WALL 2

Rémy Zaugg
779 *Esquisses perceptives - Tableaux; n°1 ("La Maison du pendu")*
Perceptive Sketches - Pictures, No. 1 ("The House of the Hanged One")
781 y 782. cambiar 'A Target' a 'A Blank'
Esbozos perceptivos – Cuadros; n° 1 ("La casa del colgado")
1970
Acrylic on oil and silkscreen
200 x 175 x 2 cm
From the artist's collection

780 *Esquisses perceptives - Tableaux; n° 9*
Perceptive Sketches - Pictures; No. 9
Esbozos perceptivos - Cuadros; n° 9
1970-1983
Paper on cotton; acrylic and silkscreen
200 x 175 x 2 cm
From the artist's collection

781 *Esquisses perceptives - Tableaux; n° 14 ("Une absence / Un oubli / Personne / Un blanc / Un manque / Rien / Un défaut")*
Perceptive Sketches - Pictures; No. 14 ("An Absence / An Oblivion / Nobody / A Target / A Lack / Nothing / A Fault")
Esbozos perceptivos - Cuadros; n° 14 ("Una ausencia / Un olvido / Nadie / Un blanco / Una carencia / Nada / Un defecto")
1970-1988
Paper on cotton; acrylic and silkscreen
200 x 175 x 2 cm
From the artist's collection

782 *Esquisses perceptives – Tableaux; n° 16 ("Un Manque / Un vide / Une lacune / Un blanc / Une cécité / Un défaut")*
Perceptive Sketches - Paintings; no. 16 ("A Lack / An Emptiness / A Lagoon / A Target / A Blindness / 'A Defect')
Esbozos perceptivos - Cuadros; n° 16 ("Una carencia / Un vacío / Una laguna / Un blanco / Una ceguera / Un defecto")
1973-1988
Acrylic on laminated paper on cotton canvas. Silkscreen
200 x 175 x 2 cm
Private collection, Switzerland

WALL 3

VIDEO

Jean-Luc Godard
783 *Le Scénario du film Passion*
The script for the film Passion
El guión de la película Passion
1982
Production: JLG Films, Studio Transvidéo, Télévision Suisse Romande
In collaboration with Jean-Bernard Menoud, Anne-Marie Miéville with Pierre Binggeli
Colour video, with sound, in French, English subtitles. 54'. With Jean-Luc Godard, Isabelle Huppert, Hanna Schygulla and Jerzy Radziwilowicz, Michel Piccoli and László Szabo

Alighiero Boetti
784 *Mappa*
Map
Mapa
1989
Embroidered linen
121 x 221 cm
Private collection

WALL 4

Jeff Wall
785 *A Ventriloquist at a Birthday party in October, 1947*
Un ventrílocuo en una fiesta de cumpleaños en octubre, 1947
1990
Slide in light box
229 x 352 cm
Groupe Lhoist Collection

HALL

Hans Haacke
786 *Manet Projekt'74*
1974
Ten 52 x 80 cm panels; color photo of La botte d'asperges de Manet, with frame (83 x 94 cm); in black frames with glass. Shown for the first time at an individual show, at the Galerie Paul Maenz in Cologne, 4-31 July 1974
Artist's copy

The following works are reproduced in this catalogue but were not exhibited

Marcel Broodthaers
787 *Un coup de dés jamais n'abolira le hasard*
A toss of the dice never abolishes chance
Una tirada de dados no abolirá nunca el azar
Ed. Galerie Wide White Space, Anvers i Galerie Michael Werner, Colònia, 1969
Impressió tipogràfica i tinta impresa sobre paper transparent
Ed. 90, 32 pàgines
32,5 x 25 cm
Col·lecció MACBA. Fundació Museu d'Art Contemporani de Barcelona

Georges Braque
788 *La Mandore*
The Mandolin
La mandolina
1909-1910
Oli sobre tela
71,1 x 55,9 cm
Tate Gallery, Londres

Hans Arp
789 *Araignée*
The Spider
Araña
1958
Bronze
36 x 45 x 2,7 cm
Fundació Marguerite Arp, Locarno

Raoul Hausmann
790 *"fmsbw..."*
1918
Poema cartell imprès sobre paper
33 x 48 cm
Musée national d'art moderne / Centre Georges Pompidou, París

Antoni Tàpies
791 *Collage de les creus*
Collage of the Crosses
Collage de las cruces
1947
Pintura i collage sobre cartró
52,5 x 73,5 cm
Städtische Galerie im Städelschen Kunstinstitut, Graphische Sammlung, Frankfurt

Stéphane Mallarmé's texts

"L'action restreinte", first part of "Quant au livre", *Divagations*. Paris: Bibliothèque Charpentier, Eugène Fasquelle éditeur, 1897. The first version of this text appeared in February 1895 entitled "L'Action", in *La Revue blanche*, marking the start of Mallarmé's monthly chronicles, under the general heading of "Variations sur un sujet". Recent editions: *Œuvres complètes*, vol. II. Paris: Gallimard, Collection "Bibliothèque de la Pléiade", 2003, p. 214-218; *Igitur, Divagations, Un coup de dés*. Paris: Gallimard, Poésie collection, 1976, p. 253-258. Spanish edition: "La acción restringida", in *Divagaciones, vol. III* Lima: Pontificia Universidad Católica del Perú, 1998. English edition: "Limited Action", in *Stéphane Mallarmé. Selected Poetry and Prose*. New York: New Directions Books, 1982 [edited and translated by Mary Ann Caws].

"Hamlet", in *La Revue indépendante*, Paris, 1 November 1886; reproduced in "Crayonné au théâtre", *Divagations*. Paris: Bibliothèque Charpentier, Eugène Fasquelle éditeur, 1897. Recent editions: *Œuvres complètes*, vol. II. Paris: Gallimard, Collection "Bibliothèque de la Pléiade", 2003, p. 166-169 [edition prefaced, set and annotated by Bertrand Marchal]; *Igitur, Divagations, Un coup de dés*. Paris: Gallimard, Collection "Poésie", 1976, p. 185-191. Spanish edition: "Hamlet", *Divagaciones*. Lima: Pontificia Universidad Católica del Perú, 1998.

"Une dentelle s'abolit...", in *La Revue Indépendante*, Paris, January 1887; reproduced in *Les Poésies de Stéphane Mallarmé*. Paris: Éditions de la Revue Indépendante, 1887 [photolithographs of the final manuscript of 40 numbered copies, with ex-libris etching by Félicien Rops]. Recent editions: *Œuvres complètes*, vol. I. Paris: Gallimard, Collection "Bibliothèque de la Pléiade", 2001, p. 42 [edition prefaced, set and annotated by Bertrand Marchal]; *Poésies*. Paris: Gallimard, Collection *Poésies*, p. 68. Catalan edition: "Aquesta randa...", in *Vint-i-cinc poemes*. Barcelona: Quaderns Crema, collection of poetry, 1986. Spanish edition: "Un encaje se abuele", in *Poesía completa*, vol. 1. Barcelona: 2001 (corrected and enlarged edition) Edicions 29. English edition: "Lace passes into nothingness...", in Selected Poetry and Prose. New York: New Direction Books, 1982 [Mary Ann Caws (ed.)].

"Autre étude de danse. Les Fonds dans le ballet, d'après une indication récente", in *National Observer*, London, 13 March 1893; reproduced in "Crayonné au théâtre", in *Divagations*. Paris: Bibliothèque Charpentier, Eugène Fasquelle éditeur, 1897. Recent editions: *Œuvres complètes*, vol. II. Paris: Gallimard, Collection "Bibliothèque de la Pléiade", 2003, p. 174-175 [edition prefaced, set and annotated by Bertrand Marchal]; *Igitur, Divagations, Un coup de dés*. Paris: Gallimard, Collection "Poésie", 1976, p. 198.

"Un coup de dés jamais n'abolira le hasard", in *Cosmopolis*, London, May 1897 [pre-original edition]; *Un coup de dés jamais n'abolira le hasard. Poème*. Paris: Éditions de la Nouvelle Revue Française, 1914. Recent editions: *Un coup de dés jamais n'abolira le hasard. Poème*. Paris: Imprimerie nationale, 1987; reproduced in *Œuvres complètes*, vol. II. Paris, Gallimard, Collection "Bibliothèque de la Pléiade", 2003, p. 363-387 [edition prefaced, set and annotated by Bertrand Marchal]; *Igitur, Divagations, Un coup de dés*. Paris: Gallimard, Collection "Poésie", 1976, p. 409-429. Spanish edition: "Una tirada de dados", in *Poesía completa*, vol. 2. Barcelona: Edicions 29, 2001 (corrected and enlarged edition). English edition: "Dice Thrown", in *Selected Poetry and Prose*. New York: New Direction Books, 1982 [Mary Ann Caws (ed.)].

Other texts reproduced in this book, in alphabetical order by author

Anonymous. "Cubisme", in *Les Marges* (magazine), vol. X, Paris, June – December 1912, p. 246.

Apollinaire Guillaume. "Les Fenêtres", in *Calligrammes. Poèmes de la paix et de la guerre (1913-1916)*. Paris: Mercure de France, 1918. French courante edition: *Calligrammes*. Paris:

Gallimard, Collection "Poésie", 1966 [prologue by Michel Butor]. Catalan edition: *Poemes*. Barcelona: Edicions dels Quaderns Crema, 1983 [bilingual edition]. Spanish edition: *Obra poética*. Sant Cugat del Vallés (Barcelona): Ediciones 29, 1999.

Arp, Hans. "Collage", in *Arp collages*. Paris: Galerie Berggruen, 1955 [booklet]; reproduced in Hans Arp, *Jours effeuillés (Poèmes, essais, souvenirs, 1920-1965)*. Paris: Gallimard, 1966 [prologue By Marcel Jean].

————"Dadaland", in *On my Way. Poetry and Essays, 1912-1947*. New York: Wittenborn, Schultz, 1948. German edition: *Unseren täglichen Traum... Erinnerungen, Dichtungen und Betrachtungen aus den Jahren 1914-1954*. Zurich: Arche, 1955. Reproduced in French in *Jours effeuillés. (Poèmes, essais, souvenirs, 1920-1965)*. Paris: Gallimard, 1966.

Artaud, Antonin. *Pour en finir avec le jugement de Dieu* (1947). Paris: K éditeur, 1948. French edition: Paris: Gallimard, Collection "Poésies", 2003 [revised and corrected edition]. Spanish edition: *Para terminar con el juicio de Dios y otros poemas*. Buenos Aires: Ediciones Calden, 1975 [trad. María Irene Bordaberry].

————"Note sur Mallarmé" (1933), one-page manuscript in verse by Antonin Artaud. *Héliogabale ou l'anarchiste couronné*. Paris: Gallimard, 1979.

Ball, Hugo. Note from 24 May 1916, *Die Flucht aus der Zeit. Tagebuch 1913-1921*. Lucerne: J. Stocker, 1946. English edition: *Flight out of Time: A Dada Diary*. New York: Viking Press, 1974. French edition: *La Fuite hors du temps. Journal 1913-1921*. Monaco: Éditions du Rocher, 1993.

Baudelaire, Charles. "La Muse vénale", in *Les Fleurs du mal*. Paris: Poulet-Malassis, 1857 (1st ed.). Catalan edition: *Les flors del mal*. Barcelona: Edicions del Mall, 1987 [trad. Xavier Benguerol]. Spanish edition: *Las flores del mal*. Barcelona: Editorial Mateu, 1966 [trad. Anna Maria Moix]. English edition: *Flowers of Evil*. New York: Bantam Books, 1964.

Barthes, Roland. "The Death of The Author", *Aspen*, no. 5-6, "For Stéphane Mallarmé", autumn-winter 1967, edited and designed by Brian O'Doherty, artistic direction David Dalton and Lynn Letterman. Published by Phyllis Johnson, Roaring Fork Press. Reproduced in French, "La mort de l'auteur", in *Manteia*, no. V, 1968. French edition: Roland Barthes. *Essais critiques IV. Le Bruissement de la langue*. Paris: Seuil, 1984. Spanish edition: "La muerte del autor", in *El susurro del lenguaje*. Barcelona: Paidós, 1999.

Boccioni, Umberto. "Sculpture futuriste," in *Première exposition de sculpture futuriste*. Paris: Galerie La Boëtie, June 1913 [exhibition catalogue]. Italian edition in *Lacerba*, no. 13, Florence, 1 July 1913 and the catalogue from the exhibition at the Galleria Sprovieri, Rome, December 1913. English edition: catalogue from the exhibition at the Doré Gallery, London, May 1914. Reproduced in French in Giovanni Lista. *Futurisme. Manifestes, Documents, Proclamations*. Lausanne: L'Âge d'Homme, 1973.

Braque, Georges. *Les Peintres vous parlent*. Paris: Les Éditions du Temps, 1964 [posthumous publication; research by Louis Goldaine and Pierre Astrer].

Breton, André. "Limites non-frontières du surréalisme", in *La Nouvelle Revue Française*, no. 48, 1937; reproduced in André Breton. *La Clé des champs*. Paris: Éditions du Sagittaire, 1953.

Broodthaers, Marcel. Extract from a manuscript sheet from the exhibition *Tractatus Logico-Catalogicus*. Brussels: Galerie MTL, 13 March – 10 April 1970.

Cage, John. "26 Statements on Marcel Duchamp", in *Silence. Lectures and Writings*. Long Lane, Middletown: Wesleyan University Press, 1961.

French edition: "26 déclarations au sujet de Marcel Duchamp", in *Silence. Discours et écrits*. Paris: Denoël, 1970. Spanish edition: *Silencio: conferencias y escritos*. Madrid: Ardora Ediciones 2002 [trad. Marina Pedraza].

Cornell, Joseph. Note from 9 October 1968, reproduced in *Theatre of the Mind. Selected Diaries, Letters, and Films*. New York: Thames and Hudson, 1993, [Mary Ann Cows (ed.)].

Craig, Edward Gordon. *On the Art of the Theatre* (1912). Boston: Small Maynard, 1925. French edition: *De l'art du théâtre*. Paris: O. Lieutier, 1942.

Cunningham, Merce. "Space, Time and Dance", *Trans/formation* 1:3 (1952), and in *Aspen* no. 5+6, item 12, autumn – winter 1967 [recording of the author reading the text, 8 min. 11 sec.].

Delaunay, Robert. Letter to Sam Halpert, 1924, reproduced in *Du cubisme à l'art abstrait*. Paris: S.E.V.P.E.N., 1957 [unedited documents published by Pierre Francastel].

Duchamp, Marcel. "L'Acte créatif", in English "The Creative Act" (1957), *Aspen* no. 5+6, item 13, autumn – winter 1967 [text read by the author, presented at the Convention of the American Federation of the Arts at Houston, Texas, April 1957, 7 min. 17 sec.]. Reproduced in *Art-news*, vol. 56, no. 4 (summer 1957); and in Robert Lebel. *Marcel Duchamp*. New York: Paragraphic Books, 1959. "The Creative Act", in Michel Sanouillet; Elmer Peterson (eds.). *Salt Seller: The Writings of Marcel Duchamp*. New York: Oxford University Press, 1973. Spoken edition including the lecture: *The Creative Act*, Sub Rosa (Belgium), 2000 (CD).

Feldman, Morton. "The King of Denmark" (1964), *Aspen* no. 5+6, item 6, autumn – winter 1967 [text that goes with the recording of the piece of the same name, 7 min. 23 sec.]. Reproduced by RCA Red Seal, 1977.

Gabo, Naum; Pevsner, Noton. "The Realistic Manifesto" (1920), *Aspen* no. 5+6, item 4, autumn – winter 1967 [recording of Naum Gabo reading the manifesto, 17 min. 24 sec.] Reproduced in J. E. Bowlt (ed.). *Russian Art of the Avant-Garde: Theory and Criticism, 1902–1934, The Documents of Twentieth-Century Art*. New York, 1976. Also in Charles Harrison; Paul Wood (eds). *Art in theory, 1900-2000: An Anthology of Changing Ideas*. Malden, MA: Blackwell, 2003.

Gris, Juan. "Des possibilités de la peinture", lecture given 15 May 1924 at the Groupe d'Études Philosophiques et Scientifiques, founded by Dr Allendy at the Université de la Sorbonne, Paris. Text reproduced in *Juan Gris*. Paris: Éditions des Musées Nationaux, 1974 [exhibition catalogue]. Spanish edition: *De las posibilidades de la pintura y otros escritos*. Barcelona: Gustavo Gili, 1971.

Godard, Jean-Luc. "On doit tout mettre dans un film", *Deux ou trois choses que je sais d'elle*. Paris: Seuil, Collection "Avant-scène", 1971. Spanish edition in: *Jean-Luc Godard por Jean-Luc Godard*. Barcelona: Barral, 1971 [trad. Gustavo Londoño].

Gomringer, Eugen. "Schweigen" (1957), *Vom Rand nach Innen. Die Konstellationnen, 1951-1995*, vol. 1. Vienna: Splitter, 1995.

Graham, Dan. "Poem" (March 1966), *Aspen* no. 5+6, item 16, autumn – winter 1967.

Hausmann, Raoul. "Nous ne sommes pas des photographes" (1921), first appeared in Raoul Hausmann. *Courrier Dada*. Paris: Le Terrain Vague, 1958. New edition, set, enlarged and annotated by Marc Dachy, Paris: Allia, 1992.

Jarry, Alfred. *Les Minutes de sable mémorial*. Paris: Mercure de France, 1894. French edition: Paris: *Les Minutes de sable mémorial. César-Antechrist*. Paris: Gallimard, Collection "Poésie", 1977 [edition prefaced and annotated by Philippe Audoin].

Joyce, James. *Anna Livia Plurabelle*. New York: Crosby Gaige, 1928. *Anna Livia Plurabelle. Fragment of Work in progress*. London: Faber & Faber, 1932. A first version of the text appeared as "Continuation of a Work in Progress", in *Transition, An International Quarterly for Creative Experiment*, no. 8, Paris, November 1927 [Eugène Jolas and Elliot Paul (eds.)]. Spanish edition: *Anna Livia Plurabelle*. Madrid: Ediciones Cátedra, 1992.

Kahnweiler, Daniel-Henry. "Mallarmé et la peinture", *Les Lettres* (magazine), Paris, 1948. Reproduced in D.-H. Kahnweiler. *Confessions esthétiques*. Paris: Gallimard, 1963.

Khlebnikov, Vélimir. "Opus 13", 1908-1909; reproduced in Velimir Khlebnikov and Aleksei Kruchenykh. *Té li lé*, Sant-Petersbourg, 1914 (illustrations by Olga Rozanova and Nikolaï Kul'bin; trad. Yvan Mignot].

Klee, Paul. *Tagebücher, 1898-1918*. Zurich: Europa Verlag, 1957 [Felix Klee (ed.)]. Spanish edition: *Diarios. 1898-1918*. Madrid: Alianza Editorial, 1998. [trad. Jas Reuter]. English edition: *The Diaries of Paul Klee, 1898-1918*. California: University of California Press, 1964. French edition: *Journal*. Paris: Éditions Grasset, Collection "Les Cahiers Rouges", 1959 [trad. Pierre Klossowski].

Kruchenykh, Aleksei. "Déclaration du langage transrationnel", manifesto included in Aleksei Kruchenykh. *Tsotsa*, Baku, 1921 (cover by Alexander Rodchenko). English edition: *Russian Futurism, A History*. Berkeley / Los Angeles: University of California Press, 1968 [trad. and notes by Vladimir Markov].

Kubler, George. "Style and Representation of Historical Time", *Aspen* no. 5+6, item 3, autumn – winter 1967.

LeWitt, Sol. "Serial Project #1" (1966), *Aspen* no. 5+6, item 17, autumn – winter 1967. Reproduced in Gary Garrels (ed.). *Sol LeWitt: A Retrospective*. San Francisco: San Francisco Museum of Modern Art / Yale University Press, New Haven, Connecticut, 2000.

Malevich, Kasimir. "Du cubisme et du futurisme au suprématisme. Le nouveau réalisme pictural" (1915), in *De Cézanne au suprématisme*. Lausanne: L'Âge d'Homme, 1974 [trad. Jean-Claude and Valentine Marcadé].

Meyerhold, Vsevolod. "Le Théâtre de foire" (1912), reproduced in Vsevolod Meyerhold, *Écrits sur le théâtre. Tome 1. 1891-1917*. Lausanne: La Cité – L'Âge d'Homme, 1973 [translated and prefaced by Béatrice Picon-Vallin].

Motherwell, Robert. "Preliminary Notice", from the American edition of the work by Marcel Raymond. *From Baudelaire to Surrealism* (1933). New York: George Wittenborn, 1949; reproduced in *The Collected Writings of Robert Motherwell*. New York: Oxford University Press, 1992 [Stephanie Terenzio, ed.].

Michaux, Henri. *Épreuves, exorcismes, 1940-1944*. Paris: Gallimard, 1945.

Ponge, Francis. *Note sur les Otages, peintures de Fautrier* (January 1945). Paris: Seghers, 1946; reproduced in *L'Atelier contemporain*. Paris: Gallimard, 1977.

Prinzhorn, Hans. *Bildnerei der Geisterkranken*. Berlin: J. Springer Verlag, 1922. French edition: *Expressions de la folie* (1922). Paris: Gallimard, Collection "Connaissance de l'inconscient", 1984 [trad. Alain Brousse and Marielène Weber].

Severini, Gino. "Symbolisme plastique, symbolisme littéraire", *Mercure de France* (magazine), Paris, 1 February 1916. Reproduced in Gino Severini. *Écrits sur l'art*. Paris: Cercle d'art, 1987.

Sontag, Susan. "The Aesthetics of Silence", *Aspen* no. 5+6, item 3, autumn – winter 1967; reproduced in *Styles of Radical Will*. London: Secker, 1969. Spanish edition: "La estética del silencio", in *Estilos radicales* (1969). Madrid: Taurus, 1997 [trad. Eduardo Goligorsky].

Schwitters, Kurt. "Merz", in *Der Ararat* (magazine), Munich, 19 December 1920. French edition: *Merz. Écrits de Kurt Schwitters*. Paris: Gérard Lebovici, 1990 [compiled and prefaced by Marc Dachy].

La acción restringida
Stéphane Mallarmé, 1897

Varias veces llegó un Camarada, el mismo, este otro, para confiarme la necesidad de actuar: ¿qué pretendía? Como el dirigirse a mí anunció por su parte, también, en él, joven, la ocupación de crear, que parece suprema y triunfar con palabras; insisto, ¿qué quería decir expresamente?
Aflojar los puños, en ruptura de sueño sedentario, para un enfrentamiento a puntapiés con la idea, así como brota un ansia o moverse: pero esta generación parece poco agitada, más allá del desinterés político, por el afán de hacer disparates con el cuerpo. Salvo la monotonía, claro está, de enrollar, entre las corvas, sobre la calzada, con el instrumento favorito, la ficción de un deslumbrante riel continuo.
Actuar, sin esto y para quien no cree que el ejercicio empiece en el fumar, significó, te comprendo visitante, filosóficamente, producir en muchos un movimiento que te da, a cambio, la emoción de sentir que tú fuiste su principio, y por lo tanto existes: algo de lo cual nadie de antemano cree estar seguro. Esta práctica comprende dos maneras; o, por una voluntad, ignorada, que dura toda una vida hasta el múltiple estallido – pensar, esto: de otro modo, los vertederos ahora al alcance para una previsión, periódicos y su torbellino, determinar en ellos una fuerza de sentido, cualquiera contrariada por muchos, con la inmunidad del resultado nulo.
Al gusto, según la disposición, plenitud, prontitud. Tu acto siempre se aplica al papel; pues meditar, sin huellas, se vuelve evanescente, por más que se exalte el instinto en algún gesto vehemente y perdido que buscaste.

Escribir –
El tintero, cristal como una conciencia, con su gota, en el fondo, de tinieblas relativa a que alguna cosa sea: luego, aparta la lámpara.
Te diste cuenta, no se escribe, luminosamente, sobre un campo oscuro, el alfabeto de los astros, solo, se indica así, esbozado o interrumpido; el hombre prosigue negro sobre blanco.
Este pliegue de encaje oscuro, que contiene el infinito, tejido por mil, cada uno según el hilo o prolongamiento, ignorado su secreto, reúne arabescos distantes donde duerme un lujo por inventariar, estrige, nudo, follajes y presentar.
Con tan escaso misterio, indispensable, que subiste, expresado, un poco.
Ignoro si el Huésped circunscribe perspicazmente su predio de esfuerzo: me gustaría señalarle, también, ciertas condiciones. El derecho a no consumar nada excepcional o que rehuya las maniobras vulgares, se paga, en todos los casos, con la omisión de sí y, se diría, con la muerte como tal. Proezas, las ejecuta en el sueño, para no importunar a nadie; pero todavía el programa continúa expuesto para los que no le hacen caso.
El escritor, con sus males, dragones que ha mimado, o con un regocijo, debe instituirse, en el texto, como histrión espiritual.
Piso, araña de cristal, obnubilación de telas y licuefacción de espejos, en el orden real, hasta los saltos excesivos de nuestra forma encubierta en derredor de una detención, de pie, de la estatura viril, un Lugar se presenta, escena, engrandecimiento ante todos del espectáculo de Sí mismo; allí, en razón de los intermediarios de la luz, de la carne y de las risas el sacrificio que hace el inspirador, con respecto a su personalidad, culmina completo o bien, en una extraña resurrección, acaba con él: cuyo verbo repercutido e vano en lo sucesivo se exhala por medio de la quimera orquestal.
Una sala, él se celebra, anónimo, en el héroe.
Todo, como funcionamiento de fiestas: un pueblo da testimonio de su transfiguración en verdad.

Honor.
Buscad, por donde sea, algo semejante –
Se le reconocerá en estos inmuebles sospechosos que se destacan, por una sobrecarga en lo trivial, del común alineamiento, con pretensión de sintetizar los sucesos de un barrio; o, si algún frontispicio, conforme al gusto adivinatorio francés, aísla, en una plaza, su espectro, yo saludo. Indiferente a lo que, aquí y allá, se esparza como la llama de reducidas lenguas a lo largo de tuberías.
Así la Acción, en la forma convenida, literaria, no vulnera el Teatro; se limita en él a la repre-

sentación... inmediato desvanecimiento de lo escrito. Que acabe, en la calle, en otro lugar, esta, la máscara cae, nada tengo que ver con el poeta: perjura tu verso, solo está dotado de un débil poder exterior, preferiste alimentar el resto de intrigas cometidas al individuo. Para qué sirve precisarte, sabiendo desde niño, como yo, que solo conservé noción de ello por una cualidad o un defecto exclusivos de la infancia, este punto al que todo, vehículo o colocación, se ofrece ahora al ideal es contrario a él – casi una especulación, sobre tu pudor, para tu silencio – o defectuoso, no directo y legítimo en el sentido que hace un momento ha querido un impulso y viciado. Como nunca basta el malestar, voy a aclarar, seguramente, con digresiones próximas en cantidad necesaria, esta recíproca contaminación de la obra y de los medios: pero, antes, ¿no convino ampliamente que se expresaría, al igual que un cigarro, mediante juegos circunvolutorios, cuya vaguedad, cuando menos, se trazara sobre la luz eléctrica y cruda?
Un delicado ha padecido, así lo espero – Exteriormente, como el clamor de la inmensidad, el viajero percibe la angustia del silbato. "Sin duda", se convence: "atravesamos un túnel – *la época* – este, largo el último, que se arrastra bajo la ciudad antes de la estación omnipotente del virginal palacio central, que corona." El subterráneo ha de durar, oh impaciente, lo que tu recogimiento en preparar el edificio de alto cristal enjugado con un impulso de la Justicia.
El suicidio o abstención, no hacer nada, ¿para qué? – Por única vez en el mundo, pues siempre en virtud de un acontecimiento siempre que explicaré, no hay Presente, no – no existe un presente. Por falta de que se manifieste la Muchedumbre, por falta – de todo. Mal informado quien se proclamase su propio contemporáneo, desertando, usurpando, con el mismo descaro, cuando ya cesó el pasado y tarda un futuro o ambos vuelven a entremezclarse en forma perpleja con el designio de enmascarar el distanciamiento. Fuera de los editoriales de los periódicos encargados de divulgar una fe en la nada cotidiana e inexpertos si el período de la calamidad es un fragmento, importante o no, de siglo.

Defiéndete, entonces, y mantén tu presencia.
La poesía, consagración; que intenta, en castas crisis y en aislamiento, mientras avanza la otra gestación en curso.

Publica.
El Libro, donde vive el espíritu satisfecho, en caso de malentendido, obligado uno por cierta pureza de retozo a sacudir lo importante del momento. Impersonificado, el volumen, igual que de él te separas como autor, no reclama aproximación de lector. Él, que te conste, entre los accesorios humanos, tiene lugar solo: hecho, siendo. El sentido soterrado se mueve y dispone, en coro, unas hojas.
Lejos, la soberbia de poner en entredicho, incluso en cuanto a los fastos, el instante: se comprueba que un azar niega en él los materiales de confrontación con ciertos sueños; o ayuda a una especial actitud.
Tú, Amigo mío, a quien no hay que deducir años ya que paralelos a la sorda labor general, el caso es extraño: te pido, sin juicio, por carencia de considerandos súbitos, que trates mi indicación como una locura, no lo escondo, rara. Sin embargo, la modera ya esta sabiduría, o discernimiento, de si no es mejor – en vez de arriesgar sobre un estado circundante cuando menos incompleto, ciertas conclusiones acerca del arte extremas que pueden deslumbrar, diamantinamente, desde ahora para siempre, en la integridad del Libro – ejecutarlas, pero y por un trastorno triunfal, con el mandato tácito de que no exista nada, que palpite en el flanco inconsciente de la hora, mostrado en las páginas, diáfano, evidente, no la encuentre dispuesta; aunque, tal vez, no sea en otra donde deba iluminar.

¡A quien quiera!

Jean-François Chevrier

Al estudiar los orígenes de la abstracción, son muchos los historiadores del arte que han trabajado sobre el telón de fondo simbolista del modernismo. En esta construcción, la obra de Mallarmé resulta central. Durante los años sesenta imperó más bien la tendencia de extraer a Mallarmé del simbolismo, mostrando que su pensamiento iba mucho más allá de la estética o la ideología del movimiento literario y artístico que se impuso en la década de 1880. En torno a 1910, numerosos actores u observadores del arte de vanguardia habían relacionado ya la poética mallarmeana con las formas más avanzadas del arte poscezanniano, y en particular con el cubismo. Hoy en día no es posible volver a reflexionar sobre los efectos de la poética mallarmeana en el arte moderno –que es lo que se propone esta exposición– sin tener en cuenta esos dos momentos de la interpretación llamada modernista en las décadas de 1960 y 1910. Pero también hay que tener en cuenta aquello que esta interpretación había descartado o mantenido al margen. Para ello, no basta invocar el simbolismo como un sistema alternativo. Hay que intentar destacar los "casos" más significativos. Odilon Redon, por ejemplo, había sido casi sistemáticamente excluido por lo teóricos del modernismo. Y sin embargo Mallarmé no solo fue muy amigo de Manet, sino que también se mostró muy interesado por el arte sugestivo de Redon, del cual pueden descubrirse muchísimos ecos a lo largo de todo el siglo XX.

Los efectos de la poética mallarmeana no pueden reducirse al mito o a la leyenda de un poeta a la búsqueda de lo absoluto, aunque esa imagen haya gozado de una larga tradición inventada en el siglo XIX, en el momento del primer romanticismo. El efecto de la poética mallarmeana estriba sobre todo en su extraordinaria abertura, de la cual la teoría modernista tan solo representa una interpretación restrictiva. Mallarmé no es el heraldo de la "poesía pura" celebrado por Paul Valéry. Cualquiera que haya sido su eficacia, la tesis modernista de una poesía cuyo objeto esencial cuando no exclusivo era el propio lenguaje reduce y petrifica la poética mallarmeana. En realidad, la fuerza de esa poética fue descubrir, tras la gran explosión romántica, una tensión entre la idea y la actualidad. Esta tensión queda solo parcialmente reflejada en la oposición entre lo ideal y lo cotidiano. La idea mallarmeana es una interpretación del poder de abstracción del lenguaje *concretado* en la escritura poética. Se resume en la famosa frase: "Digo: ¡una flor!, Y fuera del olvido al que mi voz relega todo contorno, en tanto que algo distinto de los consabidos cálices, se alza musicalmente, idea también y suave, la ausente de todos los ramos." Pero no nos engañemos: a Mallarmé le gustaban las flores. La flor poética no solo es un hecho retórico; es una síntesis de la experiencia de todos los ramos. La actualidad, por su parte, hay que entenderla en el sentido en que Émile Zola habla de "actualismo" a propósito del impresionismo. Para Mallarmé, también es una dimensión de la experiencia que remite al desconocimiento del sujeto y a su imposibilidad de definirse enteramente en las formas convencionales de lo cotidiano. La actualidad mallarmeana es una crítica de lo cotidiano y de la presencia ante uno mismo. "Mal informado quien se proclamase su propio contemporáneo."

Los efectos de la poética mallarmeana también se ejercieron negativamente. La crítica del actualismo en nombre de la idea podía interpretarse en el sentido de una superación del presente y una utopía, pero apareció también como un replegarse del artista en su torre de marfil. Las vanguardias (todos los "ismos" del arte desde el futurismo) tuvieron la tentación de contraponer a Mallarmé la idea de una proyección inmediata en el futuro, como una transfiguración, una irradiación utópica del presente. Estas utopías estéticas y políticas se desarrollaron a menudo a través de una interpretación del modelo de la obra de arte total (la *Gesamtkunstwerk*) propuesto por Wagner. Mallarmé no creía en la solución wagneriana. Su escepticismo resulta de la convicción de que el nihilismo derivado de la muerte de Dios no puede superarse con la reconstitución de un sistema de creencias fundador de una nueva comunidad. Este escepticismo es la condición irreductible de un pensamiento utópico que reinventa constantemente la ruptura, contra la tentación de una clausura imaginaria. La poética mallarmeana es, pues, la vara crítica para medir las utopías vanguardistas. Implica una voluntad de reconciliación antropológica (la comunidad humana tiene que poder prescindir de la idea de Dios), pero todo ser humano en su singularidad múltiple –una singularidad construida sobre la multiplicidad de las pulsiones internas–, todo individuo vive sin cesar la experiencia de su finitud y de la insatisfacción que ello produce. Esta experiencia individual es la base –despojada de todo fundamento teológico– de una interacción entre lo uno y lo múltiple, entre el individuo y la multitud. La utopía tiende a resolver esta interacción en un imaginario de la comunidad. Para Mallarmé, la comunidad es algo por llegar, pero el artista la vislumbra en el relámpago –el verso, "trazo del rayo"– que ilumina el fondo oscuro de las virtualidades. La gran tradición del "arte concreto" en el siglo XX, cualesquiera que sean las utopías subyacentes, se basa en esta posibilidad de actualizar una riqueza virtual.

Las utopías de la vanguardia siempre movilizaron restos mitológicos o, de forma más ambiciosa aún, la perspectiva de una nueva mitología. André Breton, al imaginar la constitución de un mito moderno, prescinde de Mallarmé, en quien inicialmente se había inspirado en gran medida. Antes del surrealismo, para Apollinaire y para los futuristas, el mito moderno quedó resumido en la figura de un Ícaro triunfador del destino y de la gravedad. El ser humano –o, mejor dicho, el hombre sin la mujer– iba por fin a poder transfigurar su peso de carne y su finitud proyectándose en un Edén repleto de máquinas. Pero ya previamente Mallarmé había reducido el politeísmo de los "dioses antiguos" a un drama solar de muerte y de resurrección. Esta reducción corresponde a una búsqueda de sobriedad opuesta a la elocuencia romántica y a los entusiasmos utópicos. Es una disolución de los mitos, una evacuación de la iconografía y de los accesorios de la representación mitológica en aras de los elementos fundamentales de una acción restringida al escenario de la escritura. Todo el *atrezzo* de los mitos es sustituido por la mesa, la hoja de papel en blanco (modelo del "vacío papel" en el que se forma y dibuja el poema), la pluma y el tintero ("con su gota, en el fondo, de tinieblas relativa a que alguna cosa sea"). Este escenario de la escritura es el "teatro de nuestro espíritu". Es el descubrimiento de un vacío matricial que responde a la nada de las creencias abolidas. Tras la Segunda Guerra Mundial, en 1947, Artaud radicalizó la postura mallarmeana negándose a participar en la exposición esotérica organizada por Breton. Él, que en los años treinta había imaginado que la potencia de la anarquía revolucionaria se plasmaría en un "teatro de la crueldad", concentra ahora su acción poética en el trazado y la proferación. Ocupado en "rehacer un cuerpo", encarna la poesía concreta de Mallarmé en una experiencia del sufrimiento como trabajo de la carne. Esta actualización de "la acción restringida" se desmarca de cualquier apelación a un fondo irracional, que ahora evoca las ideologías fascistas y el terror nazi. Con la violencia precisa, aplicada por Artaud, la sobriedad mallarmeana se cumple en el exorcismo del terror.

Se ha discutido mucho, en los parajes de la poética mallarmeana, sobre el arte como sustituto de la religión o esbozo de un nuevo vínculo comunitario, sobre el enigma y lo oculto, el valor o la legitimidad de la "oscuridad", el misterio y lo maravilloso, lo hermético, los cenáculos y las sociedades secretas. Pero las utopías modernas tienen en cuenta el gran número y la individualidad de masa, al pensar normas, estándares y prototipos. Adaptándose a los criterios de la sociedad industrial y al triunfo de la mecanización, las utopías han querido ser constructivas y productivas. Fue Marcel Duchamp quien transpuso el misterio mallarmeano a la imagen y a los circuitos metafóricos de la máquina. Al hacerlo, el autor del *Grand Verre*, experto en mistificaciones de todo tipo, no cesó de regular pequeñas máquinas antiutópicas, proponiendo una versión irónica del eclecticismo *fin du siècle* al que se opusieron los ideólogos del "estilo moderno". Duchamp fue considerado, por lo tanto, el padre del posmodernismo. Pero este papel le corresponde tan poco como a Mallarmé el de precursor del modernismo.

En realidad, lo que perdura de Mallarmé a Duchamp –pero también, en una historia más larga, de Baudelaire a Jeff Wall, pasando por Marcel Broodthaers– es esa libertad anárquica del arte opuesta a la búsqueda de un estilo colectivo. Esta libertad se había afirmado con la gran innovación del simbolismo literario: el polimorfismo del verso libre, que rompió con las normas de la tradición prosódica. En 1967 George Kubler, el autor de *The Shape of Time* (1962), señaló: "Cuando el flujo y el cambio se ignoran, y cuando se desecha el desarrollo, el estilo sigue siendo útil a modo de comodidad taxonómica. Pero siempre que se tiene en cuenta el transcurso del tiempo, con sus identidades cambiantes y sus constantes transformaciones, la noción taxonómica, representada por el término 'estilo', deja de ser importante." Ello explica que el arte moderno haya concentrado una mística de la innovación formal en la idea de *ritmo*. Al exceder la cadencia de las actividades productivas, el ritmo –orgánico o biomecánico, pero también lírico y cósmico– ha sido celebrado como alternativa al proyecto de un estilo moderno dotado presuntamente de la misma capacidad de síntesis que los grandes estilos del pasado. A diferencia del estilo, el ritmo permitía integrar la diversidad anárquica de las libertades individuales así como el juego de las diferencias, empezando por la diferencia sexual. Al asociar la poesía con la danza y la música, el ritmo es la condición de un espacio del lenguaje que desborda la fijación espacial del objeto y la cosificación de la imagen. La movilidad de la lectura de *Un coup de dés* manifiesta el principio de incertidumbre y de variaciones que caracteriza el aspecto público de la obra moderna. Mallarmé admite que esa relación participa de la "comunicación", pero añade que la obra, más que forzar la atención o suponer un público a la medida, se dirige "a quien quiera".

Arte y utopía. La acción restringida

En 1897, Stéphane Mallarmé (1842-1898) publicó su ensayo "La acción restringida" ("L'action restreinte") en *Divagations*. En él describe tanto los límites como la concentración de la acción poética. A finales del siglo XIX, tras la muerte de Victor Hugo, el poeta ya no puede pretender actuar directamente en la escena política, ni siquiera erigirse en conciencia moral. Puede nombrar el mundo, dar del mundo una equivalencia verbal, pero no cambiarlo. Su actividad, no obstante, no es puramente contemplativa. Realiza una acción en un campo "restringido" pero ilimitado, que no le pertenece pero que él puede recalificar e incluso redefinir. Este campo es el de la lengua y los lenguajes, es la escena de la escritura y el espacio del libro como "instrumento espiritual".
En una era en la que el progreso se basa en la información, el libro se asimila a veces al periódico y debe distinguirse de él, del mismo modo que el lenguaje poético se distingue de la definición instrumental de la lengua como medio de comunicación o de propaganda. En 1921, el poeta ruso Ossip Mandelstam coincide con Mallarmé cuando escribe, en el contexto de una sociedad y una cultura posrevolucionarias: "Las diferencias sociales y los antagonismos de clase son poca cosa comparados con la separación que existe actualmente entre los amigos y los enemigos del verbo."

La exposición pasa revista a algunos momentos clave de los intercambios entre arte y poesía en el siglo XX, hasta finales de los años setenta. La poética mallarmeana sirve como hilo conductor de una historia del arte moderno en su relación con el lenguaje y su diseminación. En marzo de 1970, el artista y poeta belga Marcel Broodthaers declaró: "Mallarmé es la fuente del arte contemporáneo. Inventa inconscientemente el espacio moderno." Broodthaers pensaba sobre todo en la constelación verbal construida en *Un coup de dés* (1897). Tras su publicación tardía en forma de libro en 1914, este poema se impuso, en efecto, como el prototipo de todas las investigaciones en la confluencia entre poesía, tipografía y artes visuales. Los caligramas de Apollinaire, contemporáneos de los *papiers collés* cubistas, las *parole in libertà* futuristas y "la palabra como tal" de los poetas rusos (Velimir Khlebnikov y Alexei Kruchenykh) derivan más o menos directamente de ese poema, o se desmarcan de él dentro de una dinámica de radicalización vanguardista. Es una genealogía que continúa con la aparición de la poesía "concreta" en los años cincuenta.
El *plein air* impresionista desde Manet y la estructura prismática del cuadro cubista poscezaniano representan dos polos de la poética mallarmeana, que ya se habían manifestado en la forma concentrada del soneto (especialmente en *Une dentelle s'abolit*), al menos diez años antes del *Coup de dés*. El cubismo de Braque y de Picasso fue calificado

de "hermético", igual que las poesías de Mallarmé. Gino Severini habla de un "divisionismo de las formas" y de una "compenetración de los planos" semejantes al trabajo de la palabra en poesía. La colaboración entre Juan Gris y Pierre Reverdy participa de esa bipolaridad de la escritura plástica. Paralelamente, lo fantástico de Odilon Redon recurrió a la idea de sugestión, definida por el simbolismo, en contraposición a la óptica impresionista, así como a la descripción y al relato literario. El auge de la imaginación onírica en el siglo XX se inscribe en esa tensión entre lo óptico y lo simbólico. Los procedimientos del collage y del montaje, ambos derivados del movimiento dadá y utilizados por el constructivismo poscubista y el surrealismo, hallan aquí una profundidad histórica. El diálogo entre arte y poesía, que se condensa ejemplarmente en las pinturas-poema de Joan Miró, se abre también a otras formas de creación visual como la fotografía y el cine. Rodtchenko ilustra el *Pro Eto* de Maiakovski con fotomontajes, y los signos abreviados de Paul Klee se asemejan a las desarticulaciones de lo burlesco. Más allá de la abstracción llamada "geométrica", el énfasis en los constituyentes esenciales de la pintura –el punto, la línea, el plano, el color– participa de una especulación sobre la génesis de las formas que tiene mucho que ver con el lenguaje poético. Con Marcel Duchamp, émulo de Mallarmé y lector de Jules Laforgue, la sugestión simbolista se actualizó en una ironía mecanomorfa.

Sin embargo, como indican las actividades extrapictóricas de Duchamp, las resonancias de la poética mallarmeana desbordan la genealogía de la poesía y de las artes visuales. Mallarmé también se interesó por la música y las artes escénicas, el teatro y la danza, refutando el modelo wagneriano de la obra de arte total. Es más: la exigencia especulativa del autor del *Coup de dés* pretendía reinstaurar el misterio en la experiencia poética, entre los vestigios de la fe y los ornamentos de lo cotidiano. Esta brecha define la abertura del espacio moderno, desde las grandes reformas teatrales de Edward Gordon Craig y Adolphe Appia hasta las "actividades" de la *post-modern dance* americana, pasando por la asociación de la biomecánica y lo grotesco en Vsevolod Meyerhold, sobre un trasfondo de simbolismo.

En 1925, la colaboración de Hans Arp y El Lissitsky para *Die Kunstismen (Les ismes de l'art, The -isms of Art. 1924-1909)*, atestigua una búsqueda común de síntesis del arte moderno en los dos extremos del continente europeo y salvando la diferencia de lenguas. Asimismo, la ejemplaridad de la trayectoria de Sophie Taeuber se explica por la forma en que supera la división entre creación y artes aplicadas, estableciendo una nueva continuidad entre espacios tradicionalmente separados: el taller, el ámbito doméstico, el escenario y la pista de baile, a escala corporal o a escala reducida. Esta trayectoria se corresponde con las investigaciones formales más exigentes sobre las artes de lo cotidiano en la Rusia posrevolucionaria.
Mallarmé ya había imaginado una reconciliación antropológica del arte moderno, liberado de las representaciones religiosas. Pero ese anclaje se reveló tan precario como el ejercicio de la poesía. A propósito de Georges Braque, Carl Einstein escribía a principios de los años treinta: "El arte solo tiene significación en la medida en que con él se define y se crea también una visión del mundo, un mito. Hacía mucho tiempo que la vieja óptica no correspondía ya a la estructura psíquica." El mismo autor confirmaba "el desmoronamiento del hombre racionalizado" y denunciaba la creencia supersticiosa en una utopía del progreso tecnológico. En los años treinta, la presión angustiosa de la época trajo el modelo del mito de vuelta a los debates, así como a las tentativas de síntesis entre las utopías racionalistas y un neoprimitivismo más o menos razonado, entre constructivismo y surrealismo. Haciéndose eco de la obra de James Joyce, la fotografía (Evans, Sander, Hausmann, Albers, Levitt) se convirtió en el medio privilegiado de una antropología poética de lo cotidiano y lo sagrado.
Inmediatamente después de la Segunda Guerra Mundial, el regreso de Antonin Artaud a la poesía, tras el fracaso de sus incursiones teatrales en los años treinta, corresponde a una condensación necesaria del mito en la "acción restringida" de línea (trazo) y expresión. En 1933 Artaud había definido la ejemplaridad de Mallarmé: "Una nada que se resuelve en infinito después de pasar por lo finito, lo concreto y lo inmediato; una música basada en la nada ya que a uno le impresiona la sonoridad de las sílabas antes de comprender su

sentido." Con la guerra y los campos de concentración, la nada adquirió la resonancia del terror y lo inhumano. Wladyslaw Strzeminski produce la serie de collages *A mis amigos los judíos* y Rossellini realiza *Alemania año cero*. En los círculos del arte europeo denominado "informal", debajo del primitivismo subyace más que nunca una necesidad de exorcismo (Henry Michaux, Wols, Jean Fautrier). Antoni Tàpies dramatiza la escritura de Miró. En Estados Unidos, lo que resurge en Rauschenberg desde finales de los años cuarenta es más bien la herencia de dadá y de Duchamp, transmitida por John Cage, mientras otro pintor americano afincado en Francia, Ellsworth Kelly, sigue la trayectoria del arte concreto.

En los años cincuenta y sesenta, la ampliación del corpus mallarmeano (con la publicación de la *Correspondance* y de *Écrits sur le livre*) coincide con la introducción del modelo lingüístico en las humanidades y emergencia de la cultura artística de las neovanguardias. Roland Barthes describe una "actividad estructuralista" común en la literatura, la música y las artes visuales. La impersonalidad propugnada por Mallarmé desemboca en "la muerte del autor": fórmula-eslogan para el arte conceptual de inspiración estructuralista, del cual el número 5-6 de la revista *Aspen*, en 1967, muestra algunas piezas representativas seleccionadas entre diversas disciplinas. Inspirándose en la teoría de la información y en las estructuras de la música serial, Umberto Eco reemplaza la sugestión simbolista por "la obra abierta", que él define como "un campo de posibilidades interpretativas". Pero la acción restringida aún tiene que desmarcarse de las nuevas utopías tecnológicas de una era de expansión económica. En *La Ricotta* (1963), Pier Paolo Pasolini le hace decir a Orson Welles: "Soy una fuerza del pasado." Desde su retiro en la avenida Utopia Parkway (Queens, Nueva York), Joseph Cornell actualiza la poética del objeto y lo maravilloso surrealistas relacionándolos con el imaginario simbolista.
El libro, al que Mallarmé llama "expansión total de la letra", sigue siendo el contramodelo de los medios de comunicación de masas, pero ha perdido por contaminación su dimensión sagrada: se ha vulgarizado. La lógica inclusiva resumida en la fórmula de Jean-Luc Godard, "Hay que ponerlo todo en una película", contrasta con el "silencio arcaico del libro" (Walter Benjamin), cuyo equivalente plástico es el cubo negro de Tony Smith, (1962). Paralelamente a Broodthaers y sus *Peintures littéraires*, otro poeta artista, Öyvind Fahlström, propone una síntesis de la tradición mallarmeana transformada por el surrealismo (Roberto Matta) y divulgada por el pop. Las piruetas del juego y del humor perturban la confrontación entre lo pictórico y lo conceptual. El *Mundunculum* de Dieter Roth responde a los *Alphabets figés* de Piero Manzoni. Con sus *décollages* de carteles, Raymond Hains encuentra en la calle las pruebas de una alianza Matisse-Duchamp-Schwitters bajo el signo de Mallarmé.
A finales de los años setenta el cuadro de René Daniels titulado *La Muse vénale*, como un poema de Baudelaire, marca el agotamiento de las alternativas culturales propuestas por los neovanguardistas. También indica la actualidad de una mirada poética que sabe detectar los anacronismos del presente. "Mal informado –escribía Mallarmé– quien se proclamase su propio contemporáneo." Artaud denunciaba la "mentira del ser". *Mettere il mondo al mondo* (Alighiero e Boetti) no participa de la producción de bienes materiales o de signos: la invención formal es una actividad simbólica, un trabajo concreto dentro del lenguaje. El dibujo participa de esa actividad, como lo demuestra la obra gráfica de Philip Guston a partir de 1967, realizada a menudo en colaboración con poetas; y como lo prueban también las variaciones de Nancy Spero en 1969 sobre los "dibujos escritos" de Artaud, y la Imagen-poema de Günter Brus en homenaje a Odilon Redon. En sus cuadros fotográficos desde 1978, Jeff Wall retoma la tradición del teatro pintado para interpretar las condiciones del habla y de la narración, así como de todo acto de expresión poética, en el entorno enigmático de lo cotidiano.

p. 20
El adolescente desvanecido de nosotros en el comienzo de la vida y que acosará los espíritus superiores o pensativos con el luto que le place llevar, lo reconozco, pues se debate bajo el mal de aparecer: porque Hamlet exterioriza, sobre las tablas, a ese personaje único de una tragedia íntima y oculta, su propio nombre exhibido ejerce sobre mí, sobre ti que lo lees, una fascinación, cercana a la angustia.
[...]
La obra de Shakespeare está tan bien construida de acuerdo con el único teatro de nuestro espíritu, prototipo de los demás, que se acomoda a la escenificación actual, o la pasa por alto, con indiferencia.
Stéphane Mallarmé
"Hamlet", *La Revue indépendante,* 1886

p. 22
9.10.68 miércoles. Duchamp / Delacroix
asunto: un "primo lejano" del sueño de Debussy pregunta en la vida real sobre si Debussy le veía o le conocía Duchamp ha hablado de su inaccesibilidad, "como Einstein".
considera el sueño interpretándolo (garantizando su significado más allá de lo enigmático) a la luz del "OBJETO" ("l'objet") observado curiosamente bajo una forma de perspectiva, de tradición Delacroix—Redon—Duchamp
Redon siguió una noche a Delacroix por admiración (MELLERIO)
Duchamp reconoce abiertamente la influencia de Redon "le royaume de l'objet"
surrealismo
propia inclinación a coleccionar desde una trayectoria anterior que conduce a la preocupación por "l'objet"
Duchamp, Delacroix # 2
nota: propia y espontánea admiración inicial hacia Delacroix —los 3 tomos de Escholier antes de conocer el periodo de trabajo de Duchamp en el sótano-taller sobre los "Journals" de Delacroix de los 50. La reproducción de Nadar en el boletín de anuncios —los "Journal" entrando en el tejido de la vida diaria — tardes en Flushing Main St. — tentempié + modelo de librería (la vieja librería mismo lugar)
"Delacroix's Handkerchief" ["El pañuelo de Delacroix"] considerar como título para una visión cristalizada de las notas aleatorias como artículo
Joseph Cornell
Nota del 9 de octubre de 1968

p. 28
Deseo que entre Hamlet y el resto del mundo no haya ni un solo punto de acuerdo, ni la menor esperanza de reconciliación.
Edward Gordon Craig
On the Art of the Theatre, 1912

p. 38
Lo fantástico se afirmará en el juego con su propia originalidad; habrá alegría de vivir tanto en lo cómico como en lo trágico; un aspecto demoníaco en la más profunda ironía; lo tragicómico en lo cotidiano; aspiraremos a la inverosimilitud convencional, a las alusiones misteriosas, a las sustituciones y las transformaciones; ahogaremos el lado sentimental y debilucho del romanticismo. La disonancia se erigirá en armoniosa belleza, y en lo cotidiano derrotaremos lo cotidiano.
Vsevolod Meyerhold
"Le Théâtre de foire", *Écrits sur le théatre,* 1912

p. 42
Mallarmé es la fuente del arte contemporáneo... Inventa inconscientemente el espacio moderno.
Marcel Broodthaers
Tractatus Logico-Catalogicus, 1970 (extracto)

p. 62
Un encaje se abuele
en la duda del Juego supremo
al no entreabrir como una blasfemia
más que una ausencia eterna de lecho

este unánime conflicto blanco
de una guirnalda con la misma
huido contra el cristal descolorido
flota más que se sepulta.

Mas, en quien con el sueño se dora
tristemente duerme una mandora
en la hueca nada del músico

tal como hacía alguna ventana
según no más vientre que el suyo
filial se habría podido nacer.

Stéphane Mallarmé
"Une detelle s'abolit...", *La Revue indépendante*, 1887

p. 63
El punto de partida es la nada, una armonía en la que las palabras van más lejos, tienen un significado. Cuando alcanzamos esa nada intelectual, esa "hueca nada que hace música", como escribía Mallarmé, hemos llegado a la Pintura.
Georges Braque
Les Peintres vous parlent, 1964

p. 66
Una nada que se resuelve en infinito después de haber pasado por lo finito, lo concreto y lo inmediato, música basada en la nada pues la sonoridad de las sílabas nos impresiona antes de comprender su sentido, bella, es decir tan bella que uno querría, que uno creería, que uno desearía ser su hijo, nacer hijo suyo, pues su presencia significa, simboliza la imagen misma de la creación que empieza en el cero, en la nada sin sonido, y con sonido, pues a imagen de la nada y de ninguna cosa resuena pese a todo, y todo parece nacido de nada, y allí donde no hay nada hay en primer lugar sonido, y el sonido puede nacer pese a todo, y también es la imagen de la armonía y de los números según los cuales todo se crea.
Hay en Mallarmé la estética de una poesía transcendente y de la poesía misma, pero también hay claramente y de forma absolutamente consciente y voluntaria la idea de varias realidades concretas que están ahí y al mismo tiempo se presentan evocadas.
Antonin Artaud
Manuscrito al verso de una página de *Héliogabale ou l'anarchiste couroné*, 1933

p. 74
La esfera es la forma perfecta. El sol es el astro perfecto. En nosotros no hay nada tan perfecto como la cabeza, siempre levantada hacia el sol, y tendiendo a su forma; salvo el ojo, espejo de ese astro y parecido a él.

Alfred Jarry
Les Minutes de sable mémorial, 1894

p. 84
Todas las convicciones me incitan a buscar en la escultura no la forma pura, sino el *ritmo plástico puro*; no la construcción de los cuerpos, sino *la construcción de la acción de los cuerpos*. Así pues, mi ideal no es una arquitectura piramidal (estado estático), sino una arquitectura espirálica (dinamismo).
Umberto Boccioni
"Sculpture futuriste", *Première exposition de sculpture futuriste*, 1913

p. 86
Respecto a Loïe Fuller en la medida que ella misma se propaga en derredor, con telas restituidas a su persona, por acción de una danza, todo se ha dicho, en artículos algunos de ellos poemas.
El ejercicio, como invención, sin aplicarse, permite una embriaguez de arte y. simultáneo, un acabado industrial.
En el baño terrible de las telas se pasma, radiante, fría la figurante que ilustra muchos temas giratorios en los cuales se extiende una trama derramada en la distancia, pétalo y mariposa gigantes, desplegamiento, todo con orden nítido y elemental. Su fusión con los veloces matices transformando su fantasmagoría axihídrica de crepúsculo y de gruta, tales ímpetus de pasiones, delicia, congoja, cólera: es necesario para moverlos, prismáticos, con violencia o diluidos, el vértigo de un alma como colocado en el aire mediante un artificio.
Que una mujer asocie el vuelo de los vestidos en la danza potente o vasta hasta el punto de sostenerlos, hasta lo infinito, como su expansión ˆ
La lección cumple en este efecto espiritual ˆ
Stéphane Mallarmé
"Autre étude de danse. Les Fonds dans le ballet, d'après une indication récente", *National Observer*, 1893

p. 96
Pero, a fin de cuentas, ¿por qué no nos va a poder dar el cubismo un pintor que, pese a pintar cosas del todo insignificantes, sea un artista que, con una

especie de magia, comunique un encanto al caos y al absurdo? El mallarmismo nos dio a Mallarmé, cuyos versos más vacíos de contenido y poemas más opacos desprenden, sin embargo, una auténtica seducción gracias a la selección de las palabras, a un sentimiento refinado de la música verbal.
Anónimo
"Cubisme", *Les Marges*, 1912

p. 96
La literatura se adelantó a las artes plásticas a la hora de expresar una estética acorde con nuestra psicología moderna.
La expresión de dicha estética, en consonancia con ese idealismo que hunde sus raíces profundas en la vida de la materia, la encontramos, en sus inicios, en Mallarmé y los poetas simbolistas.
Por tal motivo, hemos encontrado en los poetas modernos simpatía, comprensión y la mejor crítica. Porque hasta hoy no hemos tenido una obra plástica acorde con la obra poética de Mallarmé. [...]
Las palabras, escogidas por Mallarmé según su cualidad complementaria, y utilizadas en grupos o separadas, constituyen una técnica para expresar una subdivisión prismática de la idea, una compenetración simultánea de imágenes.
Gino Severini
"Symbolisme plastique, symbolisme littéraire", *Mercure de France*, 1916

p. 98
Con el análisis no se construye. Es la época caótica, dramática, del cubismo. La poesía no es ajena a ello. Hay unas relaciones entre esta época pictórica y la poesía de un Mallarmé (*Tristement dort une mandore au creux néant musicien* [Tristemente duerme una mandolina en la hueca nada que hace música]).
Robert Delaunay
Carta a Sam Halpert, 1924

p. 98
En mi opinión, fue a partir de 1907 cuando la poesía de Stéphane Mallarmé ejerció una profunda influencia en el arte plástico, una influencia que se enlaza con la de la pintura de Paul Cézanne. El arte de nuestro tiempo tiene una gran deuda para con estos dos hombres, que no se conocieron y que, sin lugar a dudas, no tuvieron ocasión de intercambiar sus ideas.
El *cubismo*, origen del arte actual, encontró en Cézanne el ejemplo que le permitió edificar unas *arquitecturas plásticas*. La lectura de Mallarmé fue lo que dio a los pintores cubistas la audacia de inventar libremente unos *signos*, con la convicción de que tarde o temprano dichos signos *serían* para los espectadores los objetos significados.
Daniel-Henry Kahnweiler
"Mallarmé et la peinture", *Les Lettres*, 1948

p. 98
La actual pintura moderna tiene una limitación, frecuente sobre todo en la tradición "constructivista", que es inherente al hecho de asumir o inventar unas formas "abstractas" que no están suficientemente arraigadas en lo concreto, en el mundo de los sentimientos en el que nace el arte y del que la poesía francesa es una expresión. La pintura moderna no ha evolucionado únicamente en función de la estructura interna de la pintura; no tan sólo es legítimo sino también necesario incluir, entre los documentos del arte moderno, una referencia a la poesía francesa desde Baudelaire hasta el surrealismo. Por ejemplo, es evidente que el cubismo no se habría desarrollado tan aprisa y de un modo tan idéntico en los casos de Picasso y Braque si no hubieran dispuesto de la superficie de Cézanne como modelo; no obstante, lo cierto es que Kahnweiler tiene razón cuando, en su notable libro sobre *Juan Gris* (Nueva York, 1947), afirma que el poeta Mallarmé creó la atmósfera en la que llegó a ser posible el cubismo.
Robert Motherwell
"Preliminary Notice", Marcel Raymond, *De Baudelaire au surréalisme*, 1933

p. 102
Para utilizar una imagen. Diré que un espectáculo es comparable a un juego de cartas. Las cartas son los elementos que componen el espectáculo. El que se ha emocionado ante el espectáculo es porque ha modificado para él la disposición de las cartas, de los elementos. Sin abolirlos, sin cambiarlos, les ha dado una nueva ordenación. Ha mezclado las cartas y las ha visto presentados de una manera nueva.

Juan Gris
"Des possiblités de la peinture", 1924 (extracto de una conferencia)

p. 118
"...de rojo al verde todo el amarillo muere
Paris Vancouver Hyères Maintenon Nueva-York
y las Antillas
la ventana se abre como una naranja
el hermoso fruto de la luz"
Guillaume Apollinaire
"Les Fenêtres", *Calligrammes. Poèmes de la paix et de la guerre (1913-1916)*, 1918

p. 146
En Zúrich, asqueados por la carnicería de la Primera Guerra Mundial, nos dedicábamos a las bellas artes. Mientras en la lejanía resonaba el trueno de los cañonazos, pegábamos, recitábamos, escribíamos versos y cantábamos con toda el alma. Buscábamos un arte elemental que, creíamos, salvaría a los hombres de la violenta locura de la época, y un nuevo orden que restablecería el equilibrio entre el cielo y el infierno.
Hans Arp
"Dadaland", *On my Way. Poetry and Essays, 1912-1947*, 1948

p. 146
Los elementos del arte poético son las letras, las sílabas, las palabras, las frases. La poesía nace de la eclosión conjunta de dichos elementos. La razón sólo es importante si se le da el mismo valor que a los demás factores. El valor que le doy a la razón depende de la sinrazón. Prefiero la sinrazón, pero es una cuestión muy personal. La sinrazón me da lástima ya que raramente se le ha dado una forma en arte, y precisamente por eso me gusta la sinrazón.
Kurt Schwitters
"Merz", *Der Ararat*, 1920

p. 146
En un mundo en el que ya no tuviéramos necesidad de ser los dominadores por miedo, no osaríamos imponer nuestro pequeño ego corporal como juez óptico de las realidades espirituales de un mundo que no está compuesto de límites corporales.
Raoul Hausmann
"Nous ne sommes pas des photographes", 1921

p. 152
Para la nueva Fiesta, Janco elaboró varias máscaras que ponen de manifiesto algo más que un simple talento. Si bien recuerdan el teatro japonés y el de la antigua Grecia, son plenamente modernas. Pensadas para surtir efecto a una gran distancia, en el espacio relativamente reducido del Cabaret producen una impresión verdaderamente asombrosa. Todos estábamos allí cuando llegó Janco con las máscaras y, en el acto, cada cual se apresuró a elegir una. Entonces sucedió algo extraño. La máscara no solo exigía un vestuario, sino que también imponía una determinada manera de moverse y prescribía una gestualidad dramática muy particular que llegaba a rayar en la locura. Sin preverlo en absoluto, ni siquiera unos minutos antes, empezamos a movernos, representando las figuras más extrañas, vestidos y cubiertos con objetos inimaginables, en tanto que cada uno de nosotros superaba a los demás en inventiva. La fuerza motriz de esas máscaras se nos había contagiado de modo irresistible.
De repente, captamos el significado de una tal máscara para mimo, el teatro. Las máscaras exigían ni más ni menos que quienes las llevaban ejecutasen una danza trágica y absurda.
Entonces observamos más de cerca esas cosas recortadas en cartón, pintadas y recubiertas de papeles pegados y, a partir de sus significados originales y múltiples, creamos una serie de danzas, para las que compuse inmediatamente un pequeño fragmento de música. A una de esas danzas la llamamos "Atrapar moscas". Para esa máscara solo se precisaban unos pasos algo lentos y torpes y algunas poses de gestos pausados, precipitados de pronto y acompañados de una música estridente y nerviosa; a la segunda danza la llamamos "Pesadilla". Partiendo de una posición en cuclillas, la intérprete se levanta poco a poco y va creciendo a medida que avanza hacia la parte delantera del escenario. La boca de la máscara está abierta, y la nariz es chata y está descentrada. Una especie de tubos alargan los

brazos levantados y amenazadores de la bailarina. La tercera danza se llamaba "Desesperación solemne". De los brazos, ligeramente curvados, pendían unas manos largas, recortadas y doradas. La figura se vuelve varias veces hacia la izquierda y la derecha, luego poco a poco gira en torno a su propio eje y, de pronto, rápida como un rayo, se desploma para reanudar lentamente sus primeros movimientos.
Lo que nos fascinaba de todas esas máscaras era que no representaban personajes humanos, sino unos personajes heroicos y más allá de las pasiones. En ellas era visible el horror de esta época, su trasfondo paralizante.
Hugo Ball
Nota del 24 de mayo de 1916

p. 163
Ha llegado a ser normal no reservar el término *ritmo* a la sucesión de elementos similares, como en música, y calificar generalmente de rítmica, en alusión al sentido etimológico de "flujo", el desarrollo estructurado de un movimiento expresivo. Ello equivale a definir todos los movimientos estructurados y sus materializaciones como soportes de procesos vitales, y a distinguirlos de los fenómenos cuya regularidad se puede medir, tanto si se trata de una regularidad geométrica como si es una sucesión rigurosamente idéntica de elementos formales, curvas, etc. [...]
El que nos hayamos acostumbrado a la uniformidad industrial es la principal causa de que hoy seamos tan poco sensibles a los valores rítmicos vivos.
Hans Prinzhorn
Bildnerei der Geisterkranken, 1922

p. 163
Sueño. Volé a casa, dónde está el principio. Comenzó con meditación y mordida de uñas. Lugo olí algo o gusté algo. El olfato me liberó. De repente me sentí libre y pasé de un estado al otro, como el azúcar en el agua. También mi corazón tomaba parte en el juego, desde hacía tiempo era demasiado grande, y ahora se hinchaba terriblemente. Pero no asomo de opresión. Fue llevado a lugares donde ya no se busca la voluptuosidad. Si ahora llegase una diputación y se inclinase solemnemente ante el artista señalando con agradecimiento sus obras, poco me extrañaría. Pues yo me encontraba allí donde es el principio. Estaba con mi adorada Madame Célula Original, lo que significaba tanto como ser productivo.
Paul Klee
Nota de enero de 1906

p. 168
Conocí a Sophie Taeuber en 1915. Me influyeron la grandiosidad y pureza de sus obras, así como el sorprendente y atrevido uso de rectángulos. Hoy día es difícil lograr que las jóvenes generaciones entiendan lo que significaba ese descubrimiento del rectángulo.
Hans Arp
"Collage", *Arp collages*, 1955

p. 178
El psiquismo humano, en lo que tiene de más universal, ha encontrado en el castillo gótico y sus accesorios un lugar de fijación tan preciso que sería imprescindible saber qué es para nuestra época el equivalente de tal lugar. (Todo hace pensar que no se trata de una fábrica.)
André Breton
"Limites non-frontières du surréalisme", *Nouvelle Revue Française*, 1937

p. 186
Todo plano pictórico es más vivo que cualquier cara en que sobresalen un par de ojos y una sonrisa.
Un rostro pintado en el cuadro ofrece una triste parodia de la vida. Y esta alusión sólo es un recuerdo de lo vivo.
El plano es vivo, pues ha nacido. El ataúd nos hace recordar al muerto y el cuadro, al vivo.
Kasimir Malévich
"Du cubisme et du futurisme au suprématisme. Le nouveau réalisme pictural", 1915

p. 190
En Rusia, en la década de 1910, el libro, es decir, primero la página, fue, más que la tela del pintor, el soporte de múltiples experimentaciones que asociaban la escritura poética y el trazo pictó-

rico. La invención de un lenguaje "transracional" (llamado "zaum", palabra compuesta de "za", más allá, y "um", el espíritu, la razón) catalizó estas investigaciones. El *zaum* está vinculado a la utopía de un lenguaje universal plenamente espiritual e impregnado a un tiempo de toda la sustancia del mundo sensible.
Poetas y artistas cultivaron el *zaum*: el gran poeta Velimir Khlebnikov, figura central de la poesía futurista rusa, y Alexei Kruchenykh, pero también Aliagrov (el lingüista Roman Jakobson), Ilia Zdanevich (Iliazd) y Kasimir Malevich. De estos autores Kruchenykh era el que estaba más interesado en la grafía pictórica y el collage. Actualmente se le atribuyen las 12 láminas de *Vselenskaia voina*, durante largo tiempo asociadas a la obra de Olga Rozanova. Una de las características de estos libros de poetas y artistas es una tosquedad –tanto en los materiales como en las técnicas– que contrasta con la elegancia de las obras ilustradas del periodo simbolista. También se caracterizan por la asociación inédita entre la gestualidad y la escritura, la fantasía cromática y las combinaciones de formas geométricas liberadas de cualquier pauta funcional. La página se convirtió en el espacio de una expansión rítmica de la letra y la palabra que se correspondía con la energía de la expresión verbal.
Tsosta, acompañado de una declaración de Kruchenykh, es, pese a la modestia del objeto, el monumento que resume el movimiento *zaum*. Las coincidencias entre la invención poética catalizada por el *zaum* y la dinámica del suprematismo se evidencian en esta sala a través de la presencia de dos artistas próximos a Malévich: Liubov Popova (*6 grabados*) y El Lissitzky (serie de *Prouns*, de la contracción de *pro*, para, y *ounovis*, nuevo). J.-F. C.

p. 191
DECLARACIÓN DEL LENGUAJE TRANSRACIONAL
1. El pensamiento y el habla no pueden transmitir la experiencia emocional cuando se está inspirado; por lo tanto, el artista tiene derecho a expresarse no sólo en un lenguaje común (conceptos), sino también en uno privado (un creador es individual), y en un lenguaje que carezca de significado definido (que no esté petrificado), que sea *transracional*. Un lenguaje común ata, en tanto que uno libre permite una expresión más completa. (Ejemplo: *go osnieg kaid*, etc.) *(Este párrafo proviene de la "Declaración de la palabra como tal", publicada en 1913.)*
2. El zaum es la principal forma de poesía (tanto desde el punto de vista histórico como individual). Primero se produce una agitación rítmica, musical, un protosonido (el poeta debe anotarlo dado que se le podría olvidar luego al seguir trabajando).
3. El habla transracional engendra una protoimagen transracional (y viceversa) que no se puede definir con precisión. Por ejemplo, el amorfo terror, la gorgona, la pesadilla; la nebulosa belleza Ylajali; Avoska y Neboska (el Qué y el Cómo), etc. *(Esta bella mujer procede de la novela de Hamsun Hambre; los dos nombres corresponden al folklore ruso.)*
4. Se recurre al lenguaje transracional:
a) Cuando el artista produce imágenes que aún no han adoptado una forma definitiva (dentro o fuera de sí mismo).
b) Cuando no se quiere nombrar un objeto sino sólo sugerirlo: "Él es así", "tiene un alma bien plantada" –aquí hay una palabra corriente que se usa en su sentido transnacional–. En este apartado se incluyen también los nombres inventados de personajes, naciones, poblaciones, ciudades, etc., como Oile, Bleyana, Vudras y Baryba, Svidrigailov, Karamazov, Chichikov y otros (pero no los alegóricos, como Pravdin, Glupishkin, que tienen un significado claro y definido). *(Los ejemplos se refieren respectivamente a los nombres de países imaginarios en un poema del poeta simbolista Fedor Sologud y en un cuento de Miasoyedov en "Sadok sudie", así como al nombre de personajes de Gorodietski, Dostoyevski y Gogol. Los nombres entre paréntesis corresponden a un personaje de la comedia de Fonvizin "El menor" y a los personajes cómicos de las primeras películas rusas; algo así como el Sr. Verdad y el Sr. Estúpido.)*
c) Cuando alguien pierde el control de sí mismo (odio, celos, cólera).
d) Cuando no se necesita dicho control: éxtasis religioso, amor (la glosa de una exclamación, interjecciones, ronroneos, estribillos, un balbuceo infantil, apelativos cariñosos, apodos: este *zaum* se puede encontrar en abundancia en las obras de escritores de todas las escuelas).
5. El *zaum* despierta y libera la creatividad sin ofenderla con nada concreto. El significado

hace que la palabra se contraiga, se retuerza, se convierta en piedra; por otra parte, el *zaum* es salvaje, fogoso, explosivo (paraíso salvaje, lenguas en llamas, carbón incandescente).

6. Así pues, hay que distinguir tres tipos de creación de palabras:

I. La transracional
   a. Magia cantada y hechizada.
   b. "Revelación de cosas invisibles" (darles nombre y describirlas): misticismo.
   c. Creación de palabras musicales y fonéticas: orquestación, textura.

II. La racional (la antítesis es la palabra de la locura, de lo clínico, que tiene unas leyes propias que la ciencia puede establecer; sin embargo, lo que está más allá del conocimiento científico pertenece al área de la estética, de lo aleatorio.

III. La aleatoria (ilógica, fortuita, un gran salto creativo, la combinación mecánica de palabras: lapsos lingüísticos, erratas de imprenta, errores; aquí se incluyen en parte los cambios de sonido y significado, los acentos nacionales, el tartamudeo, el parloteo infantil, etc.).

7. El *zaum* es el arte más compacto en cuanto al objetivo que capta el proceso de la percepción a la reproducción, así como por lo que se refiere a su forma: *Kuboa* (Hamsun), *Kho-bo-ro*, etc. (*"Kuboa" es una palabra inventada por el héroe de* Hambre, *de Hamsun. La última secuencia de palabras es el comienzo del poema zaum del propio Kruchenij impreso en* Learn Art).

8. El *Zaum* es un arte universal, si bien sus orígenes y personajes iniciales deben ser nacionales. Por ejemplo, "hurrah", "euhoe", etc.

Tal vez las obras transracionales den lugar a un lenguaje poético mundial, nacido de modo natural y no artificial, a diferencia del esperanto.

Alexei Kruchenykh,
Baku, 1921
Hoja mecanografiada incluida en *Tsosa*. Traducción y notas de la versión inglesa de Vladimir Markov, 1968

p. 211

No oigo las aguas de. Las cojijosas aguas de. Aleteantes murciélagos, garla de guarros guarenes. ¡Fu! ¿No te vas a casa? ¿Que Tom Malone se casa? No oigo con el pandeo de pandiques, todas las linfas de fina lifia. Fu, ¡el parlosanto nos guarde! Mis pies no se mueven. Me siento tan vieja como aquel olmo. ¿Cómo, un cuento que cuenta de Shaun y de Shem? Todos los hijoshijas de. Los foscos halcones escuchan. ¡La noche! ¡La noche! Mi carca chola se hunde. Me siento pesada como aquel penón. ¿Me hablas de Joan o Shuan? ¿Quién eran Shem y Shaun los hijos o hijas vivientes de? ¡Llega la noche! Dime, dime, dime, dagame! ¡La noche noche! Táblame de rocas o raigones. Junto a las ondas riberas de, másallámurmurantes olas de. ¡La noche!

James Joyce
Anna Livia Plurabelle. Fragment of Work in Progress, 1927

p. 215

La poesía no es una especialidad, sino un estado, un devenir del mundo entero. El inconsciente y su lenguaje, que es el mito, muestran la no concordancia de los acontecimientos humanos con lo real ordinario.

Carl Einstein
Georges Braque, 1934

p. 223

La visión, si es una visión creadora, es la conformación de toda clase de tensiones y distensiones en las relaciones esenciales de un cuerpo, sea él hombre, animal, planta, piedra, máquina, parte o todo, grande o pequeño. Él no es nunca el centro, fría y mecánicamente considerado.

Raoul Hausmann
"Nous ne sommes pas de photographes", 1921

p. 228

Pobres, así es como hemos acabado. Hemos ido dilapidando una parcela tras otra de la herencia de la humanidad, hemos tenido que dejar este tesoro en el monte de piedad, a menudo por una centésima parte de su valor, a cambio de la pequeña moneda de lo "actual". La crisis económica está en puertas y tras ella hay una sombra, la guerra que se prepara. Hoy en día resistir se ha convertido en prerrogativa de un puñado de poderosos que, Dios bien lo sabe, no son más humanos que la mayoría: acostumbran a ser más bárbaros, y no en el buen sentido de la palabra. Los demás deben apañárselas como

pueden, volver a empezar desde otro punto de partida y con bien poca cosa. Hacen causa común con los hombres que se han esforzado en explorar posibilidades radicalmente nuevas, basadas en el discernimiento y la renuncia.
Walter Benjamin
"Expérience et pauvreté", extracto del texto escrito en 1933 en Ibiza, primera etapa del exilio de Benjamin después de la llegada al poder de Hitler en Alemania

p. 246

Kré	todo	puc te
Kré	debe	pukte
pek	colocarse	lile
Kré	en un orden	pek tile
e	casi fulminante	ktuk
pte		

Antonin Artaud
Pour en finir avec le jugement de Dieu, 1947

p. 256
A la idea intolerable de la tortura del hombre por el propio hombre, del cuerpo y del rostro humanos desfigurados por obra del propio hombre, había que oponerle algo. Había que constatar el horror y al tiempo estigmatizarlo, eternizarlo.
Había que plasmarlo execrándolo, había que transformarlo en belleza.
Sin gestos. Ninguna gesticulación. La estupefacción, el reproche. Ningún movimiento, salvo el movimiento de la imagen que invade el campo del espíritu; de la cara torturada que sube desde el fondo de la sombra, que se acerca en primer plano; salvo el movimiento giratorio de los rostros de los mártires en nuestro cielo como astros, como satélites, como lunas.
Francis Ponge
Note sur les Otages, peintures de Fautrier, 1945

p. 263
El exorcismo, reacción forzuda, como un ataque de morueco, es el verdadero poema del prisionero.
Henri Michaux
Épreuves, Exorcismes, 1945

p. 271

duchaMp
y sAtie
están solos me alegRa estar contigo
podemos Contemplar
los dEcorados o tener una
conversación ¿hay aLgo que quieras decir?

acabo De romper a hablar
Una risa mía
¿qué es esto? ¿una luz inCandescente?
¡nunca Había visto una
así de grAnde! ¿qué está haciendo
entre bastidores? me enMagritta
Pensar que está agotando

Toda Esa
eneRgia
ahÍ está
mira! oK, tengo razón!

¡las otras LuceS
yA
no esTán
funcIonando
En absoluto!

John Cage
"Writing for he Second Time through *Finnegans Wake*", texto leído por John Cage en *Roaratorio. An Irish Circus on Finnegans Wake*, pieza sonora, 1979

p. 280
El título d'Orientation equivale a about orientation. El paso por el francés permite una alusión a la Sección de Oro y a la ciencia matemática de los pintores, inspirada sobre todo en Euclides.
La idea de orientación asociada a un esquema de perspectiva remite a las obras del psicólogo James J. Gibson, autor de *Perception of the Visual World* (Boston, 1950). Al hacer hincapié en la experiencia de la orientación en un espacio de movilidad (conducción automovilística, pilotaje aéreo), la teoría de Gibson se opone a la geometría abstracta del espacio euclidiano y redefine el campo perceptivo como un entorno.
La línea sinuosa que atraviesa el cuadro por el centro dibuja un perfil biomórfico emparentado con las figuras especulativas de Duchamp para el

Grand Verre. Esta aparición, inspirada en la forma de un molusco acuático (jellyfish), se inscribe en la transparencia de una red geométrica. En 1952, Hamilton busca una nueva síntesis entre las especulaciones sobre la dinámica de la visión en movimiento (Moholy-Nagy, Vision on Motion, 1948) y la formalización de los procesos de crecimiento (de Arcy Thompson, On Growth and Forms 1917-1942). J.-F.C.

p. 310
Tanto para Mallarmé como para nosotros, el lenguaje es el que habla y no el autor: escribir es alcanzar, mediante una impersonalidad preexistente ˆque no debe ser nunca confundida con la objetividad castrante del novelista realista˝ ese punto en el que el lenguaje solo actúa, "interpreta", y no a "uno mismo".
Roland Barthes
"The Death of The Author", 1967

p. 310
El arte de nuestro tiempo es ruidoso con llamamientos al silencio.
Susan Sontag
"The Aesthetics of Silence", 1967

p. 310
Cuando el flujo y el cambio se ignoran, y cuando se hace caso omiso del desarrollo, el estilo resulta útil como conveniencia taxonómica. Pero allá donde el paso del tiempo se toma en consideración, con sus identidades cambiantes y sus continuas transformaciones, la noción taxonómica, representada por el término estilo, se vuelve irrelevante.
George Kubler
"Style and Representation of Historical Time", 1967

p. 311
Rechazamos en la pintura el color como elemento pictórico.
El color es la cara óptica idealizada de las cosas. Es su expresión exterior y superficial. El color es accidental y no tiene nada en común con el contenido interno del cuerpo.
Afirmamos que el TONO del cuerpo, es decir su capacidad material para absorber la luz, es la única realidad pictórica.
Naum Gabo, Noton Pevsner
"The Realistic Manifesto", 1920

p. 311
A mí, me resulta claro que la danza es un ejercicio espiritual que se presenta bajo una forma física, y que lo que se ve, es lo que es.
Merce Cunningham
"Space, Time and Dance", 1952

p. 311
Bien mirado, el acto creativo no lo lleva a cabo sólo el artista; el espectador pone la obra en contacto con el mundo externo al descifrar e interpretar sus atributos íntimos y así añade su contribución al acto creativo.
Marcel Duchamp
"The Creative Act", 1957

p. 311
El objetivo del artista no debería ser instruir al espectador sino darle información. Que el espectador entienda dicha información es algo secundario para el artista; no puede prever la comprensión por parte de todos sus espectadores. Debería seguir su hipótesis predeterminada hasta la conclusión de la misma, evitando la subjetividad. Suerte, gusto, o formas recordadas inconscientemente no deberían jugar ningún papel en el resultado.
Sol LeWitt
"Serial Project #1", 1966

p. 312
1. Partitura con Alto, Medio y Bajo, con cada caja igual a MM66ˆ92. En la línea superior o ligeramente por encima, muy alto. En la línea inferior o ligeramente por debajo, muy bajo.
2. Los números representan la cantidad de sonidos que deben tocarse en cada caja.
3. Ningún instrumento debe tocarse con palillos o mazos. El intérprete utilizará los dedos, las manos, o cualquier otra parte de su brazo.
4. Intensidad extremadamente baja, y lo más uniforme posible.

5. La gruesa línea horizontal señala grupos. (Se deben variar los instrumentos cuando sea posible).
6. Los números romanos representan sonidos simultáneos.
7. Los números grandes (que abarcan Alto, Medio y Bajo) indican sonidos sencillos que deben tocarse en todos los registros y siguiendo cualquier secuencia temporal.
8. Las líneas quebradas indican sonidos sostenidos.
9. Se toca el vibráfono sin motor.

SÍMBOLOS UTILIZADOS:
B—Sonidos de campana
T— Sonidos de campana
S—Instrumentos de percusión
T.R.—Instrumentos de percusión
C—Platillo
DELTA—Triángulo
G—Gong
G.R.—Gong cilíndrico
Morton Feldman
"The King of Denmark", 1964

p. 313
POEMA

35 adjetivos
7 adverbios
35,52% de la superficie no ocupada por letras
64,48% de la superficie ocupada por letras
1 columna
1 conjunción
0 mms. de profundidad de la letra en la superficie de la página
0 gerundios
0 infinitivos
247 letras del alfabeto
28 líneas
6 símbolos matemáticos
51 nombres
29 números
6 participios
20,32 x 20,32 cm la página
36.287 g la hoja de papel
reserva de papel mate
0,017777 cm reserva de papel
3 preposiciones
0 pronombres
10 tamaños de letra
tipografía Universe 55
61 palabras
3 palabras en mayúscula
0 palabras en cursiva
58 palabras sin mayúsculas
61 palabras sin cursiva
Dan Graham
"Poem Schema", 1967

p. 336
LA MUSA VENAL

Musa de mi corazón, enamorada de los palacios,
¿tendrás, cuando enero llegue con sus Bóreas,
en las noches de invierno de negras penas llenas,
un tizón para calentar tus pies morados?

¿Reanimarás tus hombros ˆcomo mármoles heladosˆ
con los rayos nocturnos que a través de tus tules
pasarás?
Al sentir la boca seca y los bolsillos vacíos,
¿recogerás el oro de las azuladas bóvedas?

Es necesario, para ganar el pan de cada día, hacer
como el niño del coro, mover el incensario,
cantar Tedeum, aunque no sientas nada,

o saltimbanqui en ayunas, tus destrezas mostrar,
y con risas que son ahogos de lágrimas,
servir de evasión a la gente vulgar.
Charles Baudelaire
"La Muse vénale", *Les Fleurs du mal*, 1857

p. 344
Jean-Luc Godard: "En un film debemos ponerlo todo". Yo no escribo mis guiones, sino que improviso a medida que voy filmando. Ahora bien, esta improvisación solo puede ser el resultado de un trabajo interior previo, que supone una concentración. De hecho, no hago cine únicamente cuando filmo, sino cuando sueño, cuando almuerzo, cuando leo, cuando hablo con usted. *Deux ou trois choses que je sais d'elle* es mucho más ambicioso (que *Made in U.S.A.*). A la vez sobre el plan documental, ya que retrata de los trabajos de urbanización de la región de París, y sobre el plan de la búsqueda pura, ya que es un

film en que me pregunto constantemente qué cosa voy a hacer. Claro está que hay un pretexto, que es la vida y, a veces la prostitución en los grandes conjuntos; pero el objetivo real es observar una gran mutación. Para mí, describir la vida moderna no es describir, como lo hacen ciertos periódicos, los gadgets o el desarrollo de los negocios, sino observar las mutaciones. En una palabra, hago que el espectador participe de la arbitrariedad de mis decisiones y de la búsqueda de aquellas leyes particulares que podrían justificar una determinada decisión. ¿Por qué hago este film, y por qué lo hago de esta manera precisa? ¿Marina Vlady encarna realmente a una heroína representativa de los habitantes de los grandes conjuntos urbanísticos? Continuamente planteo este problema. Me miro filmar y se me oye pensar. En suma, no se trata de un film, sino de un intento de film que se presenta, además, como tal. Se sitúa, más exactamente, en el terreno de mi búsqueda personal. No es una historia, sino que busca ser un documento. A fin de cuentas, pienso que es el propio Paul Delouvrier quien ha debido encargarme este film. Por otra parte, mi sueño más caro es convertirme un día en director de las actualidades francesas. Todos mis films constituyen informes sobre la situación del país, documentos de actualidad, tratados tal vez de manera particular, pero en función de la actualidad moderna. Volviendo al film sobre los grandes conjuntos de vivienda, lo que me resultó más incitante fue que la anécdota que describe responde, en el fondo, a una de mis más arraigadas ideas. La idea de que para vivir en la sociedad parisiense de hoy uno se ve obligado, al nivel que sea, a prostituirse de una manera u otra, o a vivir de acuerdo con leyes que recuerdan las de la prostitución. En el curso de un film ˆen su discurso, es decir, su curso discontinuo- siento deseos de hacerlo todo, respecto a los deportes, la política o incluso las ventas de comestibles. Por ejemplo creo que un hombre como Edouard Leclerc es alguien verdaderamente apasionante, y me gustaría mucho hacer un film sobre él o con él. En un film hay que ponerlo todo. Cuando se me pregunta porqué hablo o hago hablar de Vietnam, de Jacques Anquetil o de una señora que engaña a su marido, remito a la persona que me hace esa pregunta a su periódico acostumbrado. Allí está todo. Y todo está allí yuxtapuesto. Es por eso que me atrae tanto la televisión. Un periódico televisado hecho de documentos muy cuidados sería algo extraordinario. Y todavía mejor sería encargar a los directores de los diferentes periódicos de hacer por turno esos diarios televisados. Es por eso que, mejor que hablar de cine o de televisión prefiero emplear los términos más generales de imágenes y sonidos. (*L'Avant-Scène du Cinema*, nº 70, mayo de 1967)

Jean-Luc Godard

"On doit tout mettre dans un film", *Deux ou trois choses que je sais d'elle*, 1971

p. 353

Manet-PROJEKT' 74

Diez paneles, de 52 x 80 cm cada uno: la reproducción fotográfica en color de *La Botte d'asperges* (Manojo de espárragos) de Manet, con marco (tamaño real: 83 x 94 cm); en marcos negros y con cristal. Reproducción en color por Fotofachlabor Rolf Lillig, Colonia.
Expuesto por primera vez en una muestra individual, en la Galerie Paul Maenz de Colonia, 4-31 julio 1974.
Copia del artista.

La exposición *PROJEKT '74* pretendía recoger "aspectos del arte internacional de principios de los setenta". Estaba programada para el verano de 1974 por el Wallraf-Richartz-Museum de Colonia (en la actualidad, Wallraf-Richartz-Museum Ludwig), con motivo de su 150 aniversario, y se promovía con el eslogan "El arte siempre será arte". El Kunsthalle de Colonia (institución municipal, como el museo) y el Kunstverein local (institución privada subvencionada por el Ayuntamiento) se unieron al Wallraf-Richartz-Museum para presentar esta exposición.
Invitado a participar en la muestra, Haacke envió el proyecto de una nueva obra: "El cuadro de Manet *La Botte d'asperges* (Manojo de espárragos) (1880), colección Wallraf-Richartz-Museum, aparece colocado sobre un caballete de pintor, en una sala de PROJEKT '74, de unas dimensiones aproximadas de 6 x 8 m. En las paredes, unos paneles exponen la posición social y económica de todos los que han sido propietarios del cuadro en el transcurso de los años, así como el precio que cada uno de ellos pagó para adquirir la obra."

Evelyn Weiss, comisario de arte moderno del Wallraf-Richartz-Museum (en 1995, comisario y director adjunto del Museum Ludwig), y uno de los seis miembros del equipo organizador de PROJEKT '74, respondió que el proyecto "era uno de los mejores que se había presentado", pero que no podía realizarse en la exposición ni incluirse en el catálogo.
Esta decisión se había tomado mediante lo que se definió como "votación democrática" del equipo organizador; el resultado fue de tres a tres. Los votos a favor de la exhibición de la obra fueron de Evelyn Weiss; Manfred Schneckenburger, entonces director del Kunsthalle (organizador de Documenta en 1977 y 1987); y Wulf Herzongenrath, director del Kunstverein (actualmente director del Kunstverein de Bremen). Los votos en contra correspondían a Horst Keller, entonces director del Wallraf-Richartz-Museum; Albert Schug, director de la biblioteca del museo; y Dieter Ronte, secretario personal de Gert von der Osten, que a su vez era director de todos los museos municipales de Colonia y codirector del Wallraf-Richartz-Museum hasta su retiro en 1975 (actualmente, Ronte es director del Städisches Kunstmuseum de Bonn). A excepción del director del Kunstverein, que era una institución privada, todos los demás miembros del equipo estaban subordinados al profesor von der Osten.
Keller se oponía a incluir la lista de diecinueve cargos en consejos de administración de Hermann J. Abs. La obra ofrecía información sobre su posición económica y social porque, en su cargo de presidente del consejo, Abs representaba al Wallraf-Richartz-Kuratorium (Sociedad de Fomento del museo) cuando el museo adquirió el cuadro de Manet. En una carta al artista, Keller argumentó su postura. Tras explicar que el museo, aunque financiado por el Ayuntamiento y la administración estatal, dependía de donaciones privadas para las adquisiciones más importantes, continuó como sigue: "Asociar la multitud de cargos que este hombre ocupa en terrenos totalmente distintos de la vida con su compromiso tan idealista para con el arte implicaría ofrecer una valoración absolutamente inadecuada de su iniciativa espiritual... Por contra, un museo agradecido y una ciudad agradecida, cualquier persona dispuesta a sentir gratitud debería proteger tan extraordinarias iniciativas ante cualquier interpretación que pudiera arrojar la más leve sombra sobre ellas..."
Además, observó: "Un museo nada sabe del poder económico; pero en cambio, sí sabe algo del poder espiritual."
Keller y von der Osten nunca vieron ni mostraron ningún interés en ver la obra antes de rechazarla. Sin embargo, el 4 de julio, día de la inauguración para la prensa de PROJEKT '74, la obra se exponía en la Galerie Paul Maenz de Colonia, con una reproducción a todo color en lugar de la pintura original de Manet.
Daniel Buren había incorporado a su propia obra de PROJEKT'74 un facsímil a pequeña escala de Manet-PROJEKT'74, que Haacke le había facilitado por iniciativa del propio Buren. Además, agregó un cartel titulado "El arte siempre es política" aludiendo al eslogan oficial de la exposición, "El arte siempre será arte", con un extracto de "Limites Critiques", un artículo que Buren había escrito en 1970: "... El arte, sea como sea, es exclusivamente político. Hay que hacer un análisis de los límites formales y culturales (no de los otros) dentro de los cuales existe y lucha el arte. Esos límites son muchos y de distintas intensidades. Aunque la ideología dominante y los artistas asociados a ella intentan camuflarlos por todos los medios, y aunque todavía es muy pronto 'no se dan las condiciones' para quebrarlos, ha llegado el momento de desvelarlos."
La mañana antes de la inauguración, el profesor von der Osten cubrió la parte de la obra de Buren cedida por Haacke (incluyendo la reproducción en color del bodegón de Manet) con hojas dobles de papel blanco.
Varios artistas, entre ellos Antonio Díaz, Frank Gillette, Newton y Helen Harrison, clausuraron temporal o definitivamente sus obras en señal de protesta. Carl André, Robert Filliou y Sol LeWitt se habían retirado previamente de la exposición, al enterarse de que no se había admitido Manet-PROJEKT'74.
Cuando preparaba un artículo para *Art in America*, el profesor Carl R. Baldwin le escribió a Keller, preguntándole: "¿Tiene alguna razón para creer que al propio señor Abs le habría molestado la presentación objetiva de los hechos relativos a sus compromisos profesionales?" Y la respuesta de Keller fue: "Tengo que contestar a su pregunta con un sí categórico, tal como ya expliqué claramente en una carta a Hans Haacke."

Tras su retiro, y hasta su muerte en 1994, Hermann J. Abs estuvo asociado al Deutsche Bank y a la política cultural. Representó a un consorcio alemán en una subasta de Sotheby's Parke-Bernet en Londres, en la que pujó con éxito por un antiguo manuscrito alemán ilustrado, "Los Evangelios de Enrique el León", pagando por él 11,7 millones de dólares [32 millones de marcos alemanes]. Confirmó su reputación como "director secreto de la Consejería de Cultura" del consistorio de Francfort (título que le otorgó el director real de la consejería de cultura del Ayuntamiento), cuando Klaus Gallwitz, el director del Frankfurt Staedelsches Kunstinstitut, de financiación pública, fue forzado al retiro anticipado tras provocar la ira de Abs en 1992. Abs también se las ingenió para bloquear el nombramiento del candidato favorito para la vacante dirección del museo, un cargo de funcionario público, y logró que nombraran en su lugar a su propio protegido. En 1982, tras la implicación del Banco del Vaticano en el escándalo del Banco Ambrosiano de Milán, Abs fue designado por el Papa Juan Pablo II para dirigir el consejo asesor del Instituto de Obras Religiosas, a fin de sanear las finanzas del Vaticano. El nombramiento provocó enérgicas protestas por parte del Simon Wiesenthal Center de la Yeshiva University, de Los Ángeles, ya que el Deutsche Bank, bajo la dirección de Abs, había desempeñado un papel crucial en la "arianización" de la propiedad judía confiscada por los nazis. De hecho, Abs figuraba en una "lista de vigilancia" del gobierno de Estados Unidos y se le había prohibido la entrada en Estados Unidos.

Hans Haacke

1974

Lenders

Arlette Albert-Birot / Sandra Álvarez de Toledo / Ann and Jürgen Wilde Archives, Zülpich / Anni and Josef Albers Foundation, New Heaven / Annick and Anton Herbert Collection, Gent / Arte Telefónica Foundation, Madrid / Sharon Avery-Fahlström / Berinson Gallery, Berlin / Sergio Bessa / Beyeler Foundation, Bâle / Biblioteca Nacional de Catalunya, Barcelona / Bibliothèque historique de la Ville de Paris / Bibliothèque nationale de France, Paris / Jakob Bill / Blondeau & Assoc., Paris / Blu Gallery, Milan / Boetti Archives, Rome / J.M. Bonet / BOTEC, Geneva / Trisha Brown / Jean-Louis Bruguière / Pierre Brullé / Cabinet des Estampes de Genève / Angelo and Silvia Calmarini / Massimo Carrà / Cazeau-Béraudière Gallery, Paris / Cinémathèque de la danse, Paris / Clark Coolidge / Herman Daled / Daniel Malingue Gallery, Paris / Daros Collection, Zurich / David McKee Gallery, New York / Ginette Dufrêne / Estorick Collection of Modern Italian Art, London / Eric Fabre / Esther Ferrer / Fundació Antoni Tàpies Collection, Barcelona / Galerie de France, Paris / Galleria Nazionale d'Arte Moderna, Rome / Gego Foundation, Caracas / Groupe Lhoist Collection, Paris / Grupo Paramus, Madrid / Hans Haacke / Richard Hamilton / Hans and Sophie Taeuber-Arp Foundation, Rolandseck / Hauser & Wirth Zürich, London / Instituto Valenciano de Arte Moderno, IVAM, Valencia / Jacques Benador Gallery, Geneva / Jan Krugier, Ditesheim & Cie Gallery, Geneva / Jasper Johns Collection, Sharon / Jean Arp Foundation / Joan Miró Foundation, Barcelona / Georges Jolles / Marin Karmitz / Kewenig Gallery, Cologne / Uli Knecht / Kunsthaus Zürich / Kunstsammlung Basel / Kunstsammlung Nordrhein-Westfalen, Düsseldorf / Juan José Lahuerta / Larock-Granoff Gallery, Paris / Laurence Miller Gallery, New York / Robert Lehrman / Michael Levin / Libraire Les Autodidactes, Paris / Libraire Loliée, Paris / Librería Gulliver, Madrid / Florence Loeb / François Mairé / Manuel Barbié Gallery, Barcelona / Marc and Ursula Martin-Malburet / Massimo Carpi Collection. Futur-ism Associazione Culturale, Rome / Matthew Marks Gallery, New York / Fernando Millán / Ministerium für Wissenschaft, Weiterbildung, Forschung und Kultur, Mainz / Jean-Yves Mock / Moderna Museet, Stockholm / Hattula Moholy-Nagy / Philippe Morane / Musée Ceret, Paris / Musée d'art et d'histoire, Cabinet des dessins, Geneva / Musée d'art moderne de la Ville de Paris / Musée d'art moderne de Saint-Étienne / Musée d'art moderne de Villenueve d'Ascq Lille Métropole, Villenueve d'Ascq / Musée départemental de Rochechouart / Musée départemental Stéphane Mallarmé, Vulaines-sur-Seine / Musée des beaux-arts de Nantes / Musée Municipal de l'Évêché, Limoges / Musée national d'art moderne, Centre Georges Pompidou, Paris / Musée National Picasso, Paris / Musée Rodin, Paris / Museo Nacional Centro de Arte Reina Sofía, MNCARS, Madrid / Museo Patio Herreriano, Valladolid / Museu Abelló. Fundació Municipal d'Art Mollet del Vallés, Barcelona / Museum Folkwang, Essen / Museum Ludwig, Cologne / Natalie Seroussi Gallery, Paris / Yehuda Neiman / Neues Museum Weserburg Bremen / Paul Matisse Collection, New York / Micheline Phankim / Béatrice Picon-Vallin / Puni Archives, Zurich / Rafael Cansinos Assens Foundation, Madrid / Residencia de Estudiantes, Madrid / Anne and Marc Robelin / Robert Rauschenberg Collection, New York / Rogelio Buendía Foundation, Madrid / Guido Rossi / Thomas Schmidheiny / Sintra Museum of Modern Art, Lisbon / Prof. Dr. Reiner Speck / Sprengel Museum Hannover, Kurt und Ernst Schwitters Stiftung / Staatsgalerie Stuttgart, Stuttgart / Staatsgalerie Stuttgart. Dieter Roth Archive, Stuttgart / Stedelijk Museum, Amsterdam / Jean-Marie Straub & Danièle Huillet / Antoni Tàpies / Alain Tarica / Tate Gallery, London / The Mayor Gallery, London / Thyssen-Bornemisza Foundation, Madrid / François and Catherine Trèves / Van Abbemuseum Eindhoven / Jeff Wall / Yad Vashem, The Holocaust Martyr's and Heroe's Remembrance Authority, Jerusalem / Zara Collection, Paris / Rémy Zaugg

Acknowledgments

Daniel Abadie / Juan Vicente Aliaga / Valentina Anker / Katia Arfara / Arturo Schwartz Gallery / Jean-Paul Avice / Anne Baldassari / Marina Ballo-Charmet / Jacques Beauffet / Laure Beaumont-Maillet / Marie-Laure Bernadac / Madeleine Bernardin / Claude Berri / Bernard Blistène / Cini Boeri / Stefano Boeri / Julien Boitias / Enric Bou / Guy Brett / Mary-Puck Broodthaers / Günter Brus / Anne-Élisabeth Buxtorf / Marta Camps (University of Barcelona, Art Department) / Dominique Carré / Nicolas Cendo (Musée Cantini, Marseille) / Eric de Chassey / Hélène Chatelain / Émilie Chevrier / James Coleman / Octavi Comeron (University of Barcelona, Art Department) / Catherine Coquio / Cécile Coutin / Ellen Terry Craig and Marie-Joy Taylor / Véronique Dabin / Sylviane Dailleau / Dancer Martine / Brenda Danilowitz / Catherine David / Augusto de Campos / Sylviane De Decker-Heftler / Muriel Détrie / Corinne Diserens / Claudia Dohr / Christian Doumet / Martin Dreier (Collection Suisse du Théâtre, Bern) / Françoise Ducros / Jacques Dupin / Dominique Dupuis-Labbé / Berhard Echte (Robert-Walser-Archives, Zurich) / Gladys Fabre / Patrick Faigenbaum / Flavio Fergonzi / Carlos Flores Pazos / Ingrid Fontanet / Simone Forti / Sylvie Fresnault / Nathatlie Freyssard (Bibliothèque littéraire Jacques Doucet, Paris) / Elena Galtsova / Régis Gayraud / Generali Foundation / Maria Gilissen / Noëlle Giret / Catherine Goérès / Marion Graf / Nicole Guibert / Valérie Guillaume / Anne d'Harnoncourt / Rainer Hüben (Marguerite Arp Foundation, Locarno) / Étienne-Alain Hubert / Hélène Pinet / Tamara Ivancic / Hervé Joubeaux / Naum Kleiman / Hélène Klein / Sophie Krebs / Walburga Krupp / Agnès de La Beaumelle / Jeanne Lambert-Cabrejo (Médiathèque de l'École nationale supérieure des beaux-arts, Paris) / Claude Laugier / Alexandre Lavrentiev / Françoise Le Coz (Musée d'Orsay, Paris) / Franck Leibovici / Nathalie Leleu / Laure Léveillé (École normale supérieure, Paris) / Barbara Lindlar / Hans-Peter Litscher / Gunda Luyken (Berlinische Galerie, Berlin) / Rosa Maria Malet / Claudine Martin / Ángel Martínez / Tifenn Martinot-Lagarde / Rainer-Michael Mason / Josefina Matamoros / Jacqueline Matisse Monnier / Romaric de Meyer / Yvan Mignot / Teresa Muntaner / Musée Maillol / Museu de Vilanova i la Geltrú / Teresa Ocaña / Alfred Pacquement / Suzanne Pagé / Claudine Papillon / Arielle Pelenc / Elvire Perego / Carlos Pérez / Frans Peterse (Gemeentemuseum Den Haag) / Cathrin Pichler / Ponge Armande / Yvonne Rainer / Céline Rincé-Vaslin / Carol Rio / Inès Rottermund / Véra Roumiantseva / Inka Schube / Isabel Schulz / Natalia Shakalova (State Literature Museum, Moscow) / Werner Spies / Heinz Stahlhut (Puni Archives, Zurich) / Jeanne Sudour / Paul Sztulman, Jean-Marc Réol (École nationale d'arts, la Villa Arson, Nice) / Francine Tagliaferro / Claire Tenu / Jean Thibaudeau / Catherine Thieck / Christian Tomes (Gmurzynska Gallery) / Tetriakov Gallery / Jacques Tosquelles / Zelfira Tregulova / Christophe Tzara / Marco Valesi / Sr. Vallcorba / Miguel del Valle Inclán / Nicolas Villodre / Lara Vincy / Ornella Volta (Erik Satie Foundation Archives) / Jennifer Vorvach / Sr. Wagner (Centre for Brazilian Studies) / Immanuel Wallerstein / Claude Weil / Oliver Wick / Véronique Yersin / Servane Zanotti

FUNDACIÓN MUSEU
D'ART CONTEMPORANI
DE BARCELONA

Honorary President
S.M. La Reina Doña Sofía

President
Leopoldo Rodés Castañé*

First Vice-president
Javier Godó Muntañola,
Conde de Godó*

Second Vice-president
Lola Mitjans de Vilarasau*

Treasurer
Bruno Figueras*

Secretary
Joan-Jordi Bergós*

Trustees
Macià Alavedra i Moner*
Manuel Alorda Escalona
Plácido Arango Arias
Núria Basi More
José Felipe Bertrán de Caralt
Elena Calderón de Oya*
Josep M. Catà i Virgili*
Pedro de Esteben Ferrer
Josep Ferrer i Sala
Xavier M. Ferrero i Jordi
Santiago Fisas i Ayxelá
Ricard Fornesa i Ribó
Bonaventura Garriga i Brutau
Joan Gaspart i Solves
Liliana Godia Guardiola
Dinath de Grandi de Grijalbo
José M. Juncadella Salisachs*
Lady Jinty Latymer
Alfonso Líbano Daurella
Hans Meinke
Casimir Molins i Ribot
Ramon Negra Valls
Jorge de Pallejá Ricart
Alejandro Plasencia García
Marià Puig i Planas
Anna Ramon i Llopart
José Antonio Rumeu y de Delás*
M. Teresa Samaranch Salisachs
Jordi Soley i Mas
Josep Suñol Soler
Marta Uriach Torelló
Mercedes Vilá Recolons
Fernando Villalonga Campos
Victoria Ybarra de Oriol,
Baronesa de Güell
Juan Ybarra Mendaro

*** Members of the Executive Commission**

Corporate Trustees
ACCIONA
Aigües de Barcelona
Autopistas C.E.S.A.
BBVA
Cambra de Comerç, Indústria i
Navegació de Barcelona
Cementos Molins
Círculo de Lectores
Cobega
Codorníu
Danone
El País
F.E.C.S.A. E.N.H.E.R (grupo
ENDESA)
Freixenet
Fomento de Construcciones y
Contratas
Fundació Antoni Serra
Santamans
Fundació Banc de Sabadell
Fundació Catalana Occident
Fundació Miarnau
Fundació Puig
Gallina Blanca
Gas Natural SDG
Grupo Husa
Grupo Planeta
Grupo Torras
Grupo Zeta
"la Caixa"
Lafarge Asland
La Vanguardia
Nissan Motor Ibérica
Salvat Editores
SEAT
Uniland Cementera

SUPPORTERS

Honorary Members
Repsol YPF

Benefactores permanentes
Daniel Cordier
Juan March Delgado
Media Planning Group
Jorge Oteiza
Leopoldo Rodés Castañé
Fundación Bertrán
Sara Lee Corporation

Corporate Benefactors
Banco Urquijo
El Consorci de la Zona Franca
El Corte Inglés
Fundación Telefónica

Corporate Protectors
Fundación Cultural Banesto
Hotel Arts Barcelona
RACC Club

Corporate Contributors
Basi
Ernst & Young
Ferrater Campins Morales
Fundació Miguel Torres
Fundació Privada Damm
Gràfiques Pacífic
Grupo Esteve
JP Morgan Private Bank
KPMG
Obrascón Huarte Laín -OHL-
Recoletos Grupo de
Comunicación
Rodés & Sala, Abogados
Sono (Euphon Group)

Individual Protectors
M. Carmen Buqueras de Riera
Liliana Godia Guardiola
Lady Jinty Latymer
Enrique Ordóñez Las Heras

Individual Protectors
Elena Calderón de Oya
María Entrecanales Franco
Bruno Figueras Costa
Dinath de Grandi de Grijalbo
Fundación Herberto Gut
de Prosegur
José M. Juncadella Salisachs
Pere Portabella
Josep Suñol Soler

Individual Contributors
Fundación Cuatrecasas
Garrigues Advocats i Assessors
Tributaris
Equipo Singular
Eva de Villalonga
Ventura Garcés Bruses
Vigilancia y Sistemas
de Seguridad (VSS)

Contemporary Circle
Manuel Barbié
Instituto Dr. Javier de Benito
Jaime Beriestain
Manuel Curtichs Pérez-Villamil
Elisabeth de Nadal Clanchet
Jaime Malet
Jordi Prenafeta
Ernesto Ventós Omedes
Hubert de Wangen

El Taller
José Luis Blanco Ruiz
Cristina Castañer Sauras
Pilar Cortada Boada
Ana Díaz Suñer
María Entrecanales Franco
Fernando Escura Seres
Josep Gaspart i Bueno
Teresa Guardans de Waldburg
Pilar Líbano Daurella
Álvaro López Lamadrid
Juan Lladó Arburúa
Ignacio Malet Perdigó
Mercedes Mas de Xaxàs Faus
Sara Puig Alsina
Jordi Pujol Ferrusola
Alfonso Rodés Vilà
Francesc Surroca Cabeza
Tomas Tarruella Esteva

Director
Ainhoa Grandes Massa

Fundraising Department
Sandra Miranda Cirlot

Administration
Virginia García Suqué

Honorary Member

REPSOL YPF

MUSEU D'ART CONTEMPORANI
DE BARCELONA CONSORTIUM

HONORARY MEMBERS

President
Pasqual Maragall i Mira

First Vice-president
Joan Clos i Matheu

Second Vice-president
Leopoldo Rodés i Castané*

Members
Catalan Government
Caterina Mieras i Barceló
Gemma Sendra i Planas*
Assumpta Bailac i Puigdellívol*
Berta Sureda i Berná*
Claret Serrahima de Riba

City Council of Barcelona
Ferran Mascarell i Canalda*
Carles Martí i Jufresa*
Oriol Balaguer i Julià*
Sergi Aguilar

MACBA Foundation
Javier Godó, Comte de Godó
Lola Mitjans i Perelló*
José Antonio Rumeu y de Delàs
Marià Puig i Planas
Josep Maria Catà i Virgili
Jordi Soley Mas*

Official inspector
Pepita Casas Espitia*

Secretary in Chief
Anna Ramon i Llopart*

*** Membres de la Comissió Delegada**

SUPPORTING MEMBERS OF MACBA
Aon Gil y Carvajal
Marisa Díez de la Fuente
Carlos Durán
Luisa Ortínez

MUSEU D'ART CONTEMPORANI
DE BARCELONA

Director
Manuel J. Borja-Villel

Secretary to the Director
Núria Hernández

Advisory Committee
Lynne Cooke
María de Corral
Chris Dercon
Vicent Todolí

Chief Executive Officer
Anna Esteban

Financial Management Secretary
Arantxa Badosa

TEMPORARY EXHIBITIONS AND COLLECTION

Chief Curator
Bartomeu Marí

Collection Curator
Antònia M. Perelló

Head of Exhibition Production
Isabel Urpí

General Exhibition Coordinator
Anna Borrell

Exhibition Coordinators
Cristina Bonet
Teresa Grandas
Luz Gyalui
Rosario Peiró

Collection Assistant
Bénédicte Baqué

Exhibition Administration
Meritxell Colina
Ariadna Pons

Head of Register
Ariadna Robert

Register Coordinator
Aída Roger

Register Administration
Marta Badia

Head of Conservation and Restoration
Sílvia Noguer

Conservation Assistant
Xavier Rossell

Audiovisual Coordinator
Eudald Busquets

PUBLICATIONS

Head of Publications
Mela Dávila

Editorial Coordinator
Anna Jiménez Jorquera

Web Site Coordinator
Sònia López

Photographic Archives
Dolores Acebal

LIBRARY

Head of Library
Marta Vega

Library Administration
Iraïs Martí
Núria Roig

PUBLIC PROGRAMS

Head of Public Programs
Jorge Ribalta

Coordinators
Antònia M. Cerdà
Yolanda Nicolás
Myriam Rubio

MARKETING AND COMMUNICATION

Head of Marketing and Communication
Francesc Casadesús

Coordinator of Communication
Michelle Bianco Barazarte

Coordinator of Marketing
Gemma Romaguera

Coordinator of Graphics and Production
Elisabet Surís

PRESS AND PUBLIC RELATIONS

Head of Press and Public Relations
Nicola Wohlfarth

Administration
Mireia Collado
Victòria Cortés

FINANCIAL MANAGEMENT AND ADMINISTRATION

Head of Financial Management and Administration
Meritxell Company

Financial Management Assistant
David Salvat

Accounts Assistant
Montserrat Senra

Administrative Assistant
Mireia Calmell

Head of Human Resources
Carme Espinosa

Head of Computer Services and Telecommunications
Imma Losada

Computer Services and Telecommunication Assistant
Antoni Lucea

Administration
Alba Canal
Anna Coutado
Jordi Rodríguez

Receptionist
Erminda Rodríguez

ARCHITECTURE AND BUILDING CONSERVATION

Head of Architecture and Conservation
Isabel Bachs

Exhibition Architecture Coordinator
Adelina Casanovas

Maintenance Service Coordinator
José Luis Miguel

Maintenance Service Assistant
Alberto Parras

Security Coordinator
Alberto Santos

Patrons of MACBA

Tti
Técnicas de Transportes Internacionales, s.a.

Sponsors

hp invent
IBERIA
EPSON
LA VANGUARDIA
el Periódico
EL PAIS

With the support of

Microsoft Ibérica
Arlex
Hotel Axel
Jovi

This book is published in the occasion of *Art and Utopia. Limited Action*, which was presented in the Museu d'Art Contemporani de Barcelona (June 3 – September 12, 2004) in the context of the Fòrum Universal de les Cultures de Barcelona 2004.

EXHIBITION

Project Director
Manuel J. Borja-Villel

Curator
Jean-François Chevrier

Exhibition Coordinators
Rosario Peiró Carrasco
Élia Pijollet

Coordination Assistant
Susan Anderson

Graphic Material Coordination
Susan Anderson
Myriam Rubio

Interns
Patricia Quesada
Xavier Ruiz

Administration Assistant
Meritxell Colina

Register
Carme Ballíu
Elisabeth Carpenter
Xavier Mas
Ariadna Robert
Aída Roger
Sara Verdós

Register Assistant
Marta Badia

Conservation
Jordi Font
Silvia Noguer
Xavier Rossell

PUBLICATION

Concept
Jean-François Chevrier in collaboration with Élia Pijollet

Coordination
Anna Jiménez Jorquera
Élia Pijollet
Belén Roldán

Graphic Documentation
Dolores Acebal

Translations into English
Mary Ann Caws
John Tittensor
Marina Tsareva
Paul Hammond

Translations into Spanish
Núria Petit Fonserè
Oriol Izquierdo
Cristina Zelich
Alexander Kazachkov
Discobole

Design and Layout
Montse Sagarra

Digital Production
Carmen Galán
Oriol Rigat

Printing
Ingoprint S.A.

Distribution
ACTAR
Roca i Batlle, 2. 08023 Barcelona
Tel. +34 93 418 77 59
Fax +34 93 418 67 07
info@actar-mail.com
www.actar.es

Museu d'Art Contemporani de Barcelona
Plaça dels Àngels, 1. 08001 Barcelona
Tel. +34 93 412 08 10
Fax. +34 93 412 46 02
www.macba.es

© of this edition, 2005, Museu d'Art Contemporani de Barcelona and Actar. 1rst edition
© of the texts, their authors
© of the artists
Josef Albers, Carl Andre, Hans Arp, Antonin Artaud, Giacomo Balla, Alighiero Boetti, Constantin Brancusi, Georges Braque, Francesco Cangiullo, Carlo Carrà, Joseph Cornell, Giorgio de Chirico, Marcel Ducahmp, François Dufrêne, Max Ernst, Jean Fautrier, Lyonel Feininger, Julio González, Juan Gris, Hans Haacke, Raymond Hains, Richard Hamilton, Raoul Hausmann, Vassily Kandinsky, Paul Klee, Frantisek Kupka, Fernand Léger, Sol Lewitt, El Lissitzky, René Magritte, Man Ray (Emmanuel Radnitzky), Piero Manzoni, Filippo Tommaso Marinetti, Roberto Matta, Henri Michaux, László Moholy-Nagy, Bruce Nauman, Amédée Ozenfant, Francis Picabia, Lioubov Popova, Robert Rauschenberg, August Sander, Kurt Schwitters, Gino Severini, Sophie Taeuber-Arp, Joaquín Torres-García, Bart van der Leck, Wols (Alfred Otto Wolfgang Schulze), VEGAP, Barcelona / Robert Delaunay, Sonia Delaunay, L & M Services B.V. Amsterdam, VEGAP, Barcelona / Pablo Picasso, Succession Pablo Picasso, VEGAP / Tony Smith, The State of Tony Smith, VEGAP, Barcelona / Antoni Tàpies, Fundació Antoni Tàpies, VEGAP, Barcelona / Pierre Albert-Birot / Adolphe Appia / Umberto Boccioni / Marcel Broodthaers / Trisha Brown / Günter Brus / David Burljuk / Vladimir Burljuk / Julio Campal / Clark Coolidge / René Daniels / Guillermo de Torre / Walker Evans / Alexandra Exter / Morton Feldman / Esther Ferrer / Robert Filliou, Marianne Filliou / Naum Gabo / Gego / Edward Gordon Craig / Dan Graham / Philip Guston, The State of Philip Guston / Hannah Höch / Öyvind Fahlström, Sharon Avery-Fahlström / Ferdinand Hodler / Iliazd (Ilia Zdanevitch) / Josep Maria Junoy / Vassili Kamenski / Aleksei Krutxenykh / Helen Levitt / Vladimir Maïakovski / Kasimir Malevic / Vsevolod Meyerhold / Fernando Millán / Joan Miró, Successió Miró / Pablo Palazuelo / Ivan Puni / Diether Roth / Olga Rozanova / Nancy Spero / Wladislaw Strzeminski / Georges Vantongerloo / Jeff Wall / Rémy Zaugg, 2005

© of the photographs, Nic Aluf (p. 170) / Archives B. Picon-Vallin (p. 39-41) / Archivo Fotográfico Museo Nacional Centro de Arte Reina Sofía (p. 104) / Bibliothèque Nationale de France (p. 28-31, 60-61, 69) / Boris Becker, Colònia (p. 224, 223, 227) / Yves Bresson (p. 157) / Bruce C. Jones (p. 21) / Joachim Fliegner (p. 51) / Fondazione Marguerite Arp, Locarno (p. 220) / Gasull Fotografia (p. 23-25, 108, 113, 138-139, 141, 158, 204-205, 210, 229-231, 254, 257, 266, 281, 285, 288-289, 301, 328-323, 335, 338-341) / Jacqueline Hyde (p. 105, 126) / Walter Klein, Düsseldorf (p. 162) / Kurt Schwitters Archive at the Sprengel Museum Hannover. Michael Herling, Aline Gwose (p. 184-185) / Michael Korol, New York (p. 300) / Paolo Manusardi (p. 83) / Wolfgang Morell (p. 149, 169, 171, 173, 221-222) / Musée d'art et d'histoire (Cabinet des Dessins), Ville de Genève: [Maurice Aeschimann (p. 35), Bettina Jacot-Descombes (p. 34)] / Musée Municipal de l'Evêché Limoges. Photo Fréderic Magnoux (p. 73) / Musée Rodin: [Eugène Druet (p. 86), W. Isaiah Taber (p. 87)] / Museo Thyssen-Bornemizsa, Madrid (p. 144-145) / Paul Naurer (p. 302-303) / Tim Nightswander (p. 222, 225-226) / Oeffentliche Kunstsammlung Basel, Martin Bühler (p. 37) / Bacci Orazio (p. 124) / Photo Archiv Collection Speck, Colònia (p. 43) / Photo CNAC/MNAM Dist. RMN (p. 64-65, 77, 92, 94, 100, 103): [Christian Bahier (p. 247, 251), Béatrice Hatala (p. 101), Hervé Lewandowski (p. 99, 107, 253), Philippe Migeat (p. 76, 247-249, 251), Bertrand Prévost (p. 147)] / Christian Poite (p. 81) / Adam Rzepka (p. 55, 110) / Glenn Steigelman (p. 273, 275, 277) / Tate, London (p. 63, 119, 165) / The Bridgeman Art Library (p. 84, 133) / Dorothy Zeidman (p. 272, 276)

All rights reserved

ISBN: 84-95951-81-9
DL: B-8185-05

MACBA Museu d'Art Contemporani de Barcelona

ACTAR